D1131151

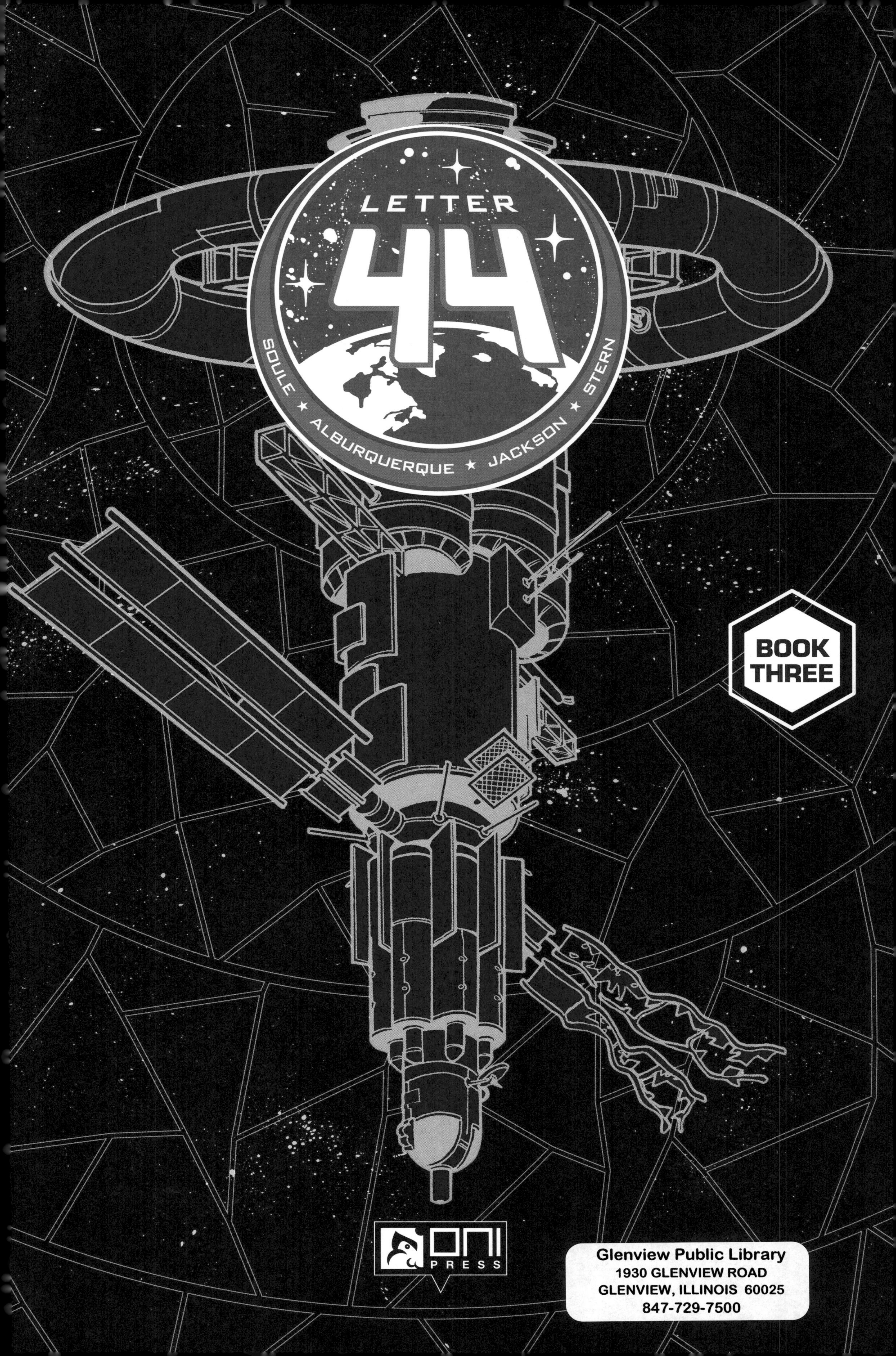
LETTER
44
SOULE ★ ALBURQUERQUE ★ JACKSON ★ STERN
BOOK THREE
ONI PRESS

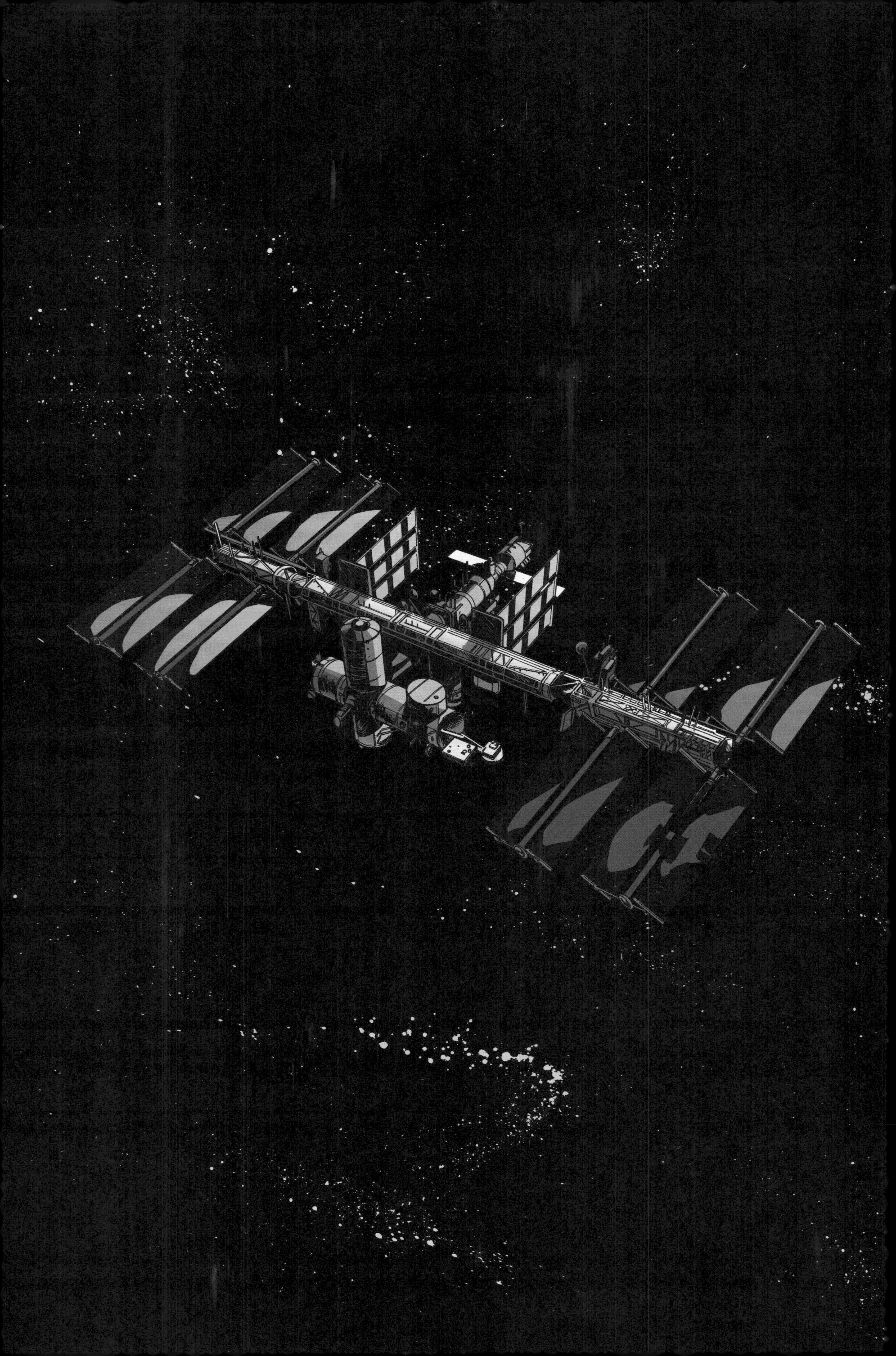

LETTER 44

SOULE ★ ALBURQUERQUE ★ JACKSON ★ STERN

BOOK THREE

WRITTEN BY
CHARLES SOULE

CHAPTERS 6-11 ILLUSTRATED BY
ALBERTO JIMÉNEZ ALBURQUERQUE

CHAPTER 1 ILLUSTRATED BY
JOËLLE JONES
CHAPTER 2 ILLUSTRATED BY
DREW MOSS
CHAPTER 3 ILLUSTRATED BY
RYAN KELLY
CHAPTER 4 ILLUSTRATED BY
ALISE GLUŠKOVA
CHAPTER 5 ILLUSTRATED BY
LANGDON FOSS

CHAPTERS 1-7, 9-11 COLORED BY
DAN JACKSON
CHAPTER 8 COLORED BY
SARAH STERN

CHAPTER 1 LETTERED BY
SHAWN DEPASQUALE
CHAPTERS 2-11 LETTERED BY
CRANK!

COVER ILLUSTRATED BY
ALBERTO JIMÉNEZ ALBURQUERQUE
AND COLORED BY
DAN JACKSON

DESIGNED BY
KATE Z. STONE, JASON STOREY, AND **TROY LOOK**

ORIGINAL SERIES EDITED BY
JILL BEATON AND ROBIN HERRERA

COLLECTION EDITED BY
ROBIN HERRERA

LETTER 44

PUBLISHED BY
ONI PRESS, INC.

Founder & Chief Financial Officer /// **Joe Nozemack**
Publisher /// **James Lucas Jones**
Editor in Chief /// **Sarah Gaydos**
V.P. of Creative & Business Development /// **Charlie Chu**
Director of Operations /// **Brad Rooks**
Director of Publicity /// **Melissa Meszaros**
Director of Sales /// **Margot Wood**
Marketing Design Manager /// **Sandy Tanaka**
Special Projects Manager /// **Amber O'Neill**
Director of Design and Production /// **Troy Look**
Senior Graphic Designer /// **Kate Z. Stone**
Graphic Designer /// **Sonja Synak**
Digital Prepress Lead /// **Angie Knowles**
Senior Editor /// **Robin Herrera**
Senior Editor /// **Ari Yarwood**
Associate Editor /// **Desiree Wilson**
Editorial Assistant /// **Kate Light**
Executive Assistant /// **Michelle Nguyen**
Logistics Coordinator /// **Jung Lee**

1319 SE Martin Luther King Jr. Blvd. Suite 240, Portland, OR 97214

onipress.com
facebook.com/onipress | twitter.com/onipress | onipress.tumblr.com

charlessoule.com | @charlessoule

ajaalbertojimenezalburquerque.blogspot.com

FIRST EDITION: July 2019
ISBN 978-1-62010-568-9

Library of Congress Control Number: 2018967455

10 9 8 7 6 5 4 3 2 1

FOREWORD BY GEORGE GUSTINES

I'VE LOVED COMIC BOOKS for nearly 40 years, starting with *Justice League of America* No. 200 (though my gateway drug was episodes of *Super Friends*). And, since 2002, it has been an absolute privilege to report about the comic book industry for *The New York Times*. Working for the paper is what led me to helping out—just a little—with a scene in *Letter 44* by Charles Soule and and Alberto Jiménez Alburquerque that is included in this collected edition.

I first encountered *Letter 44* when I wrote a piece for *The Times* recommending graphic novels for the 2014 holiday season. One of them was the first trade of *Letter 44*. The twin focus of the President of the United States dealing with things on Earth and the brave astronauts leaping into the unknown was immensely compelling and I became an immediate fan. I loved that for every big, mind-blowing moment, there were small, relatable ones that anchored readers firmly to the world being presented. At some point during writing that piece, I connected with Charles.

One of the best parts of covering comics for *The Times* has been meeting—usually by phone, sometimes face-to-face—the people who create them. It can be a challenge to toggle between being a fan (which I fully embrace) and being a journalist (which I strive to get better at every year), but it is infinitely easier when you're dealing with such an approachable person like Charles. On top of being talented, he is a super nice guy and genuine. I get a nerdy thrill every time I see him at a convention or a signing and I get to say hi.

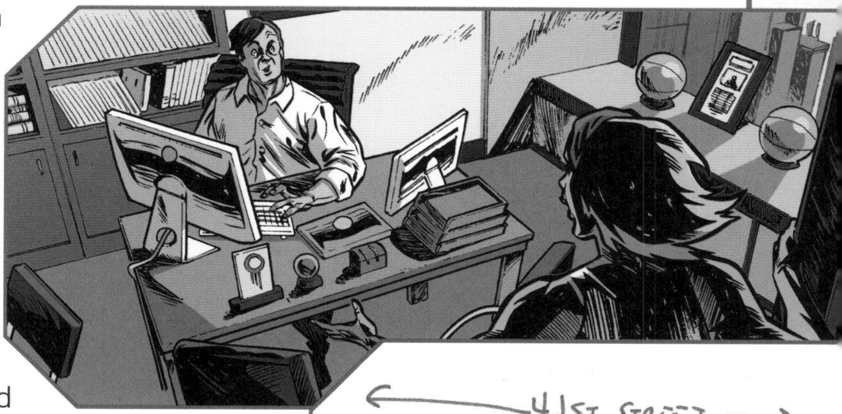

Charles told me early on that he was a fan of *The Times*—"a loyal subscriber to the weekend print section," he wrote me back in 2014. (Side note: I love his occasional tweets about *The Times* crossword puzzle.) So I should not have been surprised when he asked me, in January 2016, for help with a moment in issue No. 31 (Page 194 in this edition) that takes place in the newsroom.

He wrote: "I'm setting a *Letter 44* scene in the executive editor's office at the *Times*, and while I've seen some pictures of what it looks like, I can't tell what direction it faces in the city. Is that something you could answer off the top of your head? I just want to make sure whatever's shown outside the window is accurate."

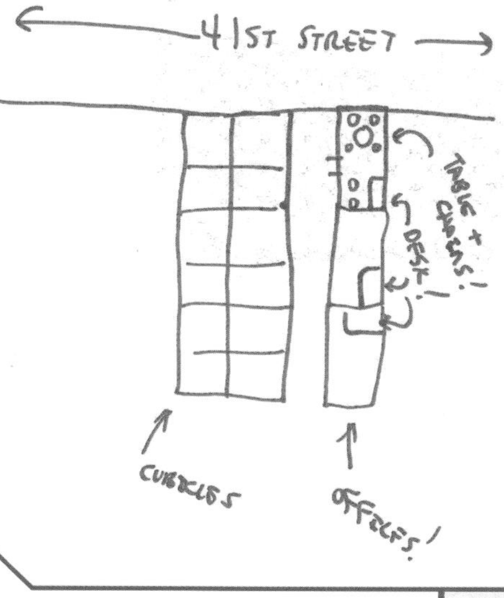
41ST STREET
CUBICLES
OFFICES!

I responded: "This is the most awesome question ever!"

And so we went back-and-forth—just a little—as I was being anal retentive ("The view isn't incredible." "If he were sitting at his desk, he'd be facing east!") and Charles was being sensible ("Fortunately, I get to use a little something those of us in the biz call 'the magic of comics.' So, I can (a) put him much higher in the building and (b) change it so that he has a clear view of downtown.").

In the end, what little assistance I provided (sketch, right) just put me more in awe of the effort that Charles and Alberto put into each issue, even for this one panel where no one would be the wiser with just about anything they showed. That's passion and dedication, folks!

There is another geeky moment in this collected edition that similarly thrilled me. The splash page of issue No. 34 opens with an unnamed writer at his desk mulling, oh, just the end of the world. I immediately recognized the writer as Charles (excellent work, Alberto!) and then nerded out over the original art displayed above his desk. When I read the issue, I reached out to Charles to identify the artwork, which were all pages from comics he had written. From left to right (Page 225 in this edition): Jesus Saiz drawing *Swamp Thing*, the very first page of *Letter 44* No. 1 (!), and a page from *Death of Wolverine* by Steve McNiven.

I've mentioned Charles and Alberto a couple of times, but I know that creating a comic book is a team effort. A newspaper article is similar: I'm lucky to have editors who read my words and make me better through their edits and questions. One of my goals in my coverage has been to be more inclusive of the whole creative team, not just the writer and artist, when I get to report on a comic book. In the case of *Letter 44*, I want to extend many thanks to Dan Jackson, Guy Major and Sarah Stern (colorists); Crank! and Shawn DePasquale (letterers); Jill Beaton and Robin Herrera (editors); and Troy Look, Kate Z. Stone and Jason Storey (designers) for the enjoyment the series has brought me.

Finally—and I hope this does not sound weird—I love that *Letter 44* has a definitive conclusion. I enjoy the eternal battles for truth and justice of superhero comics, but there is something darn satisfying about a complete story. *Letter 44* sits proudly on my virtual shelf of comic book perennials that have a beginning, middle and end.

Happy reading!

George Gustines

GEORGE GUSTINES

is a senior editor at *The New York Times*. He began writing about the comic book industry in 2002 and hopes to continue for many more years. He also wants to land a comic book story with his byline on the front page.

LETTER

44

CHAPTER I

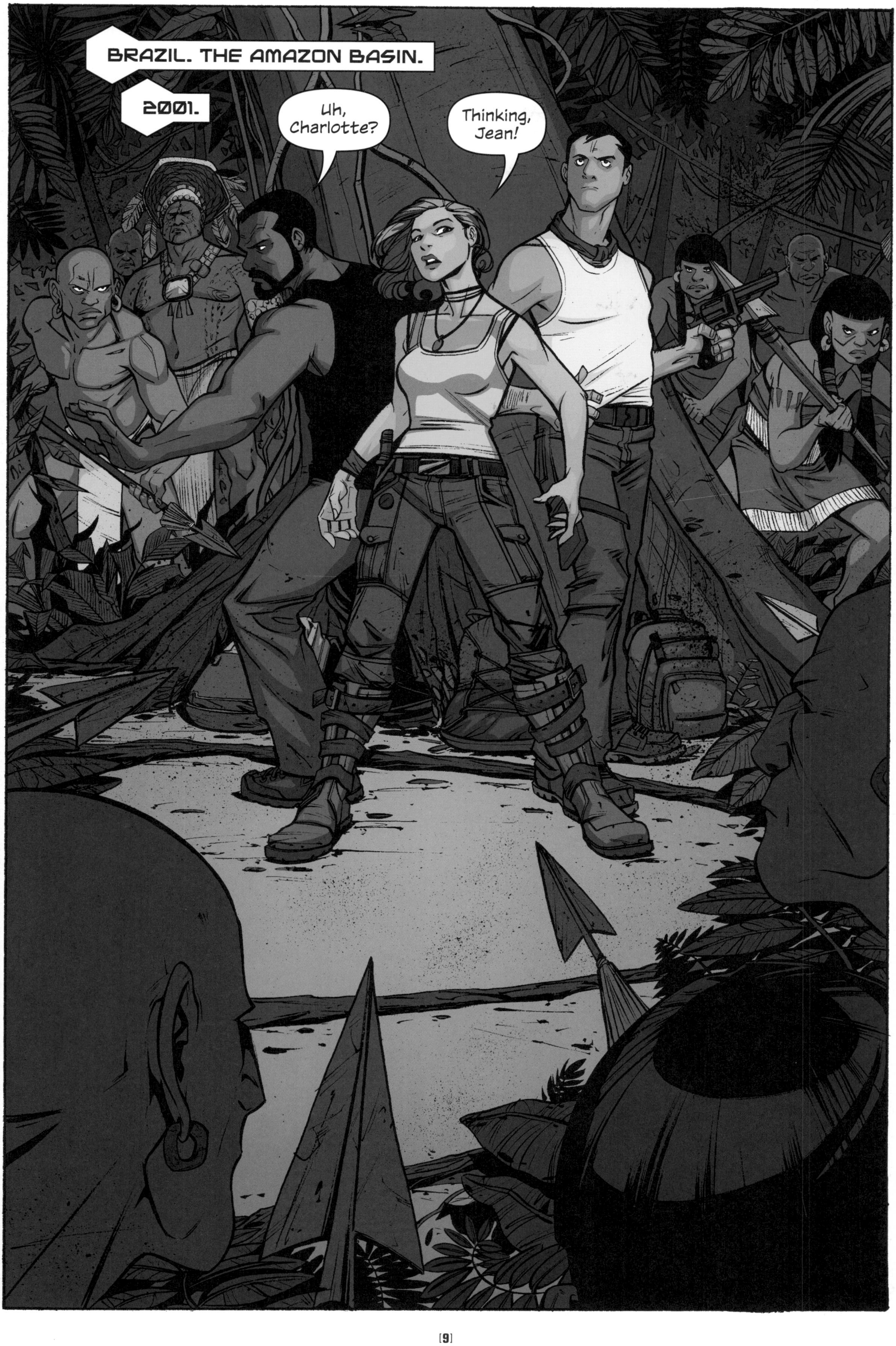

BRAZIL. THE AMAZON BASIN.
2001.
Uh, Charlotte?
Thinking, Jean!

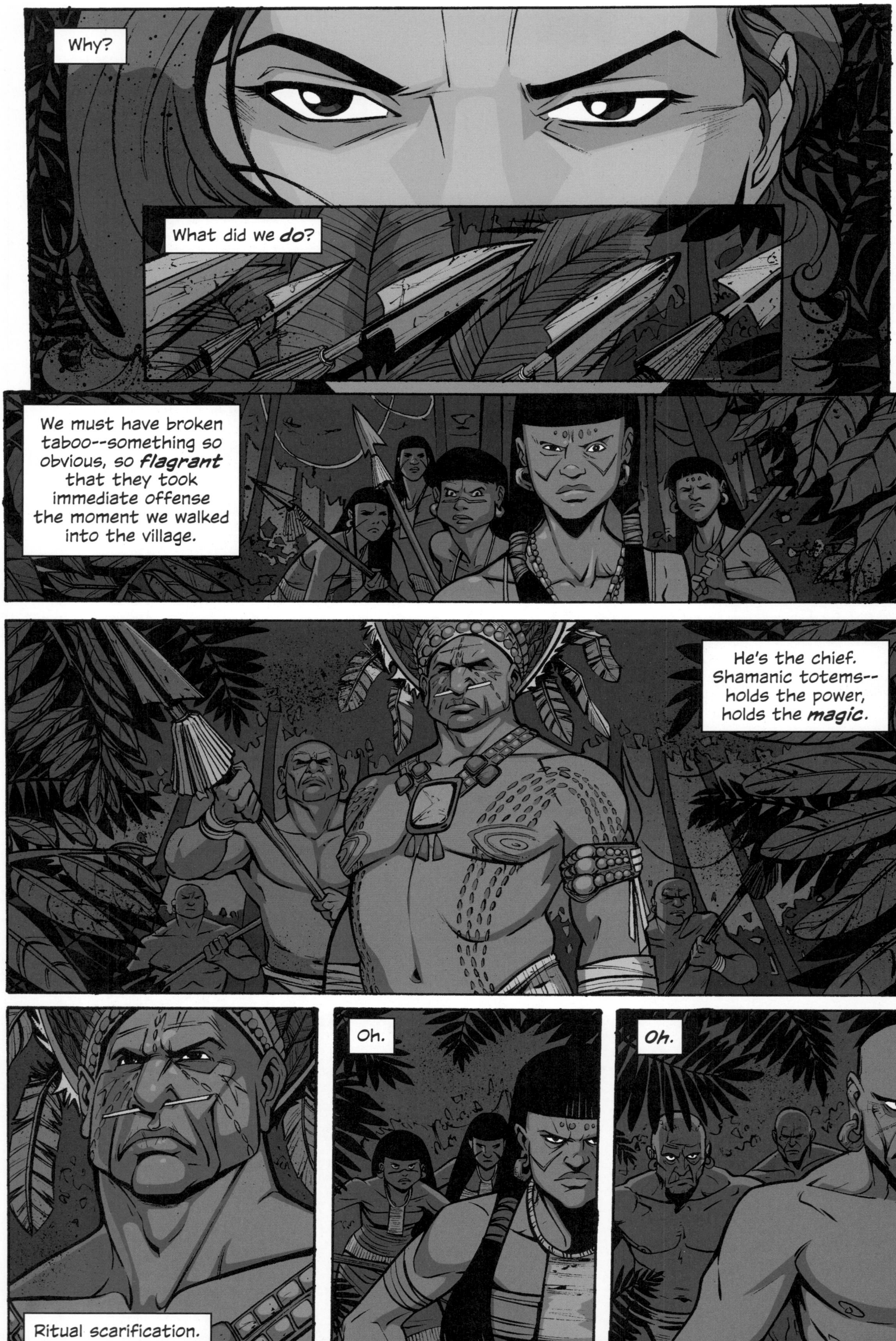
Why?
What did we *do*?
We must have broken taboo--something so obvious, so ***flagrant*** that they took immediate offense the moment we walked into the village.
He's the chief. Shamanic totems--holds the power, holds the ***magic***.
Ritual scarification.
Oh.
Oh.

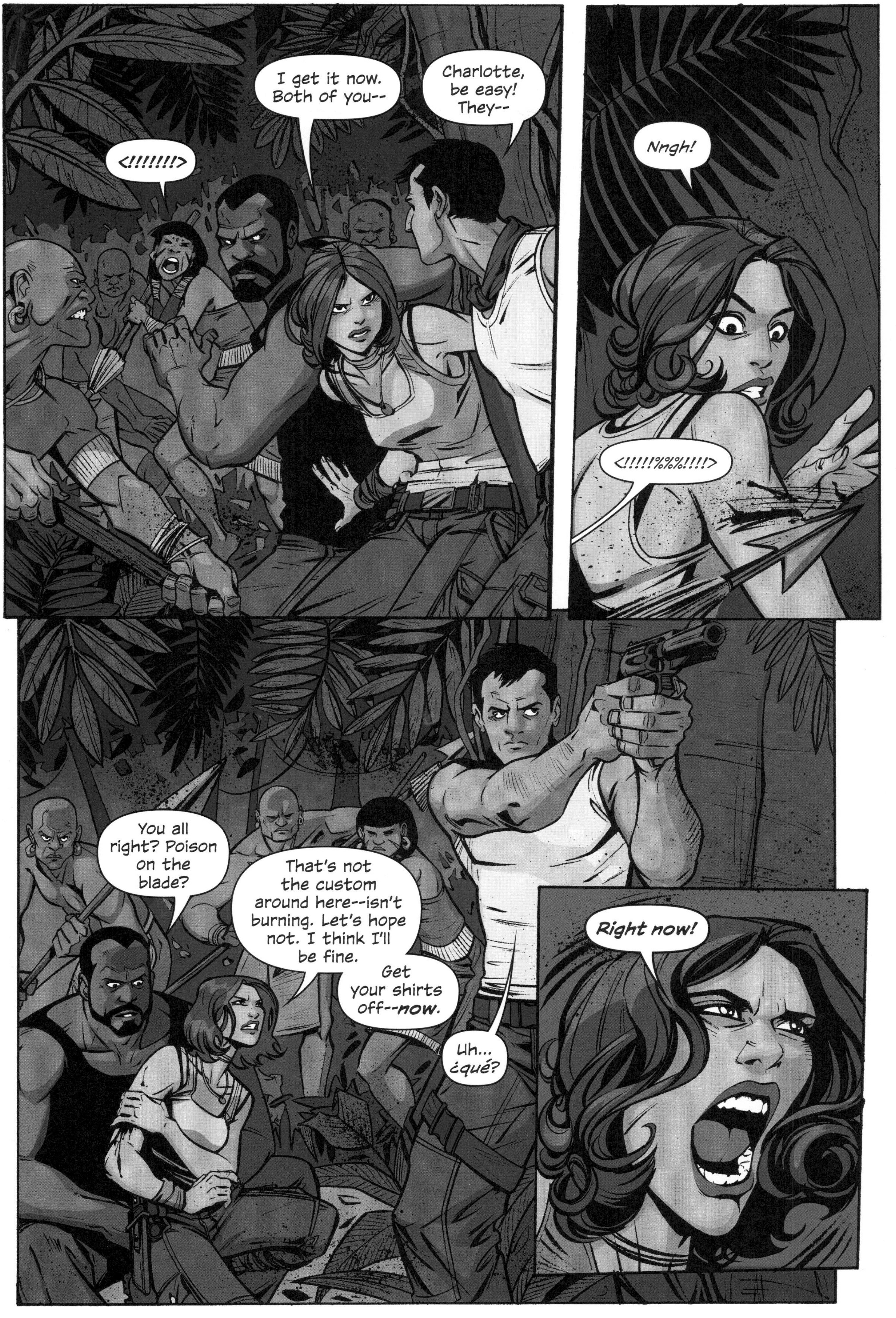
<!!!!!!!>
I get it now. Both of you--
Charlotte, be easy! They--
Nngh!
<!!!!!%%!!!!>
You all right? Poison on the blade?
That's not the custom around here--isn't burning. Let's hope not. I think I'll be fine.
Get your shirts off--*now*.
Uh... ¿qué?
Right now!

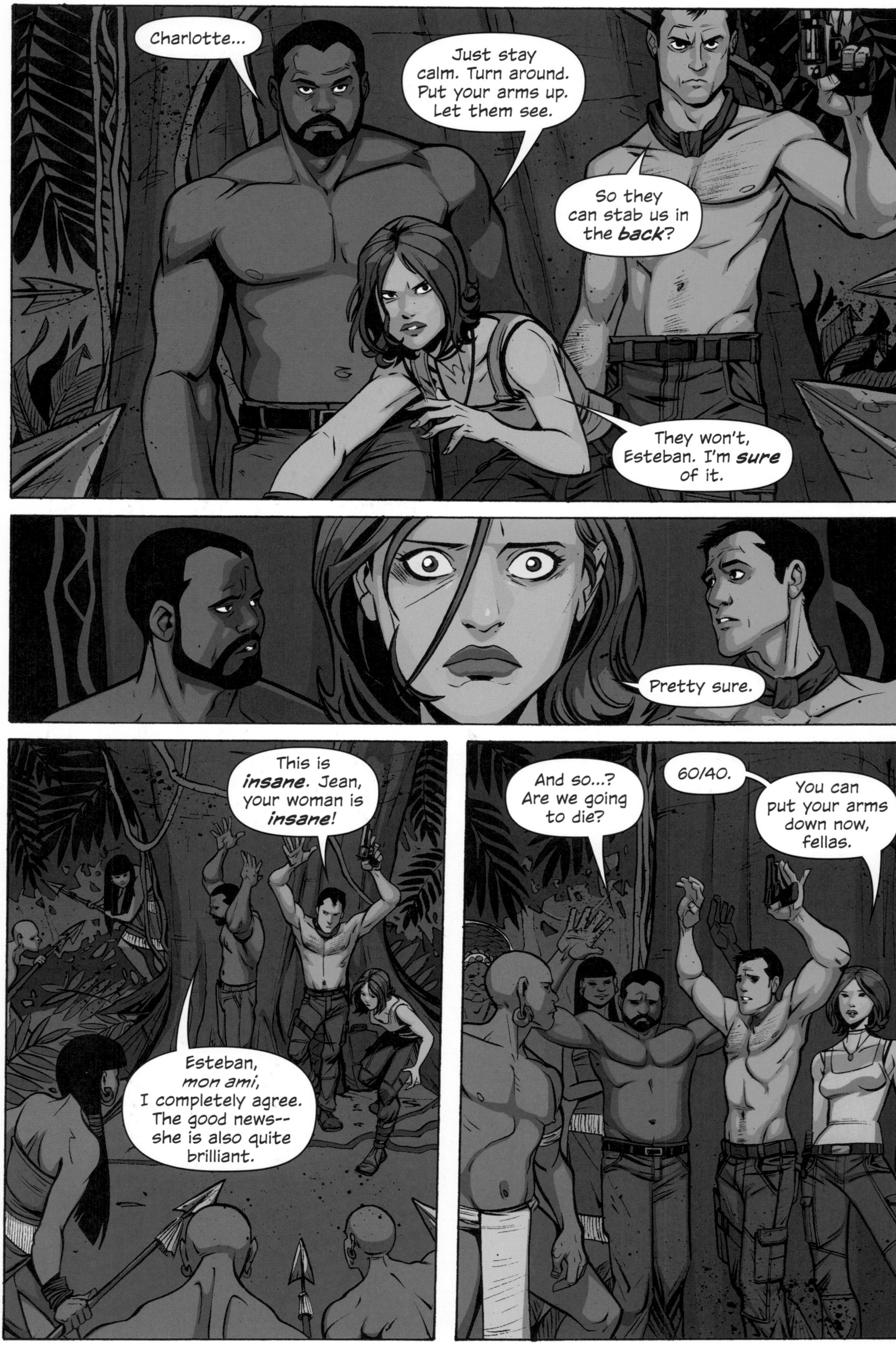
Charlotte...
Just stay calm. Turn around. Put your arms up. Let them see.
So they can stab us in the *back*?
They won't, Esteban. I'm *sure* of it.
Pretty sure.
This is *insane*. Jean, your woman is *insane*!
Esteban, *mon ami*, I completely agree. The good news-- she is also quite brilliant.
And so...? Are we going to die?
60/40.
You can put your arms down now, fellas.

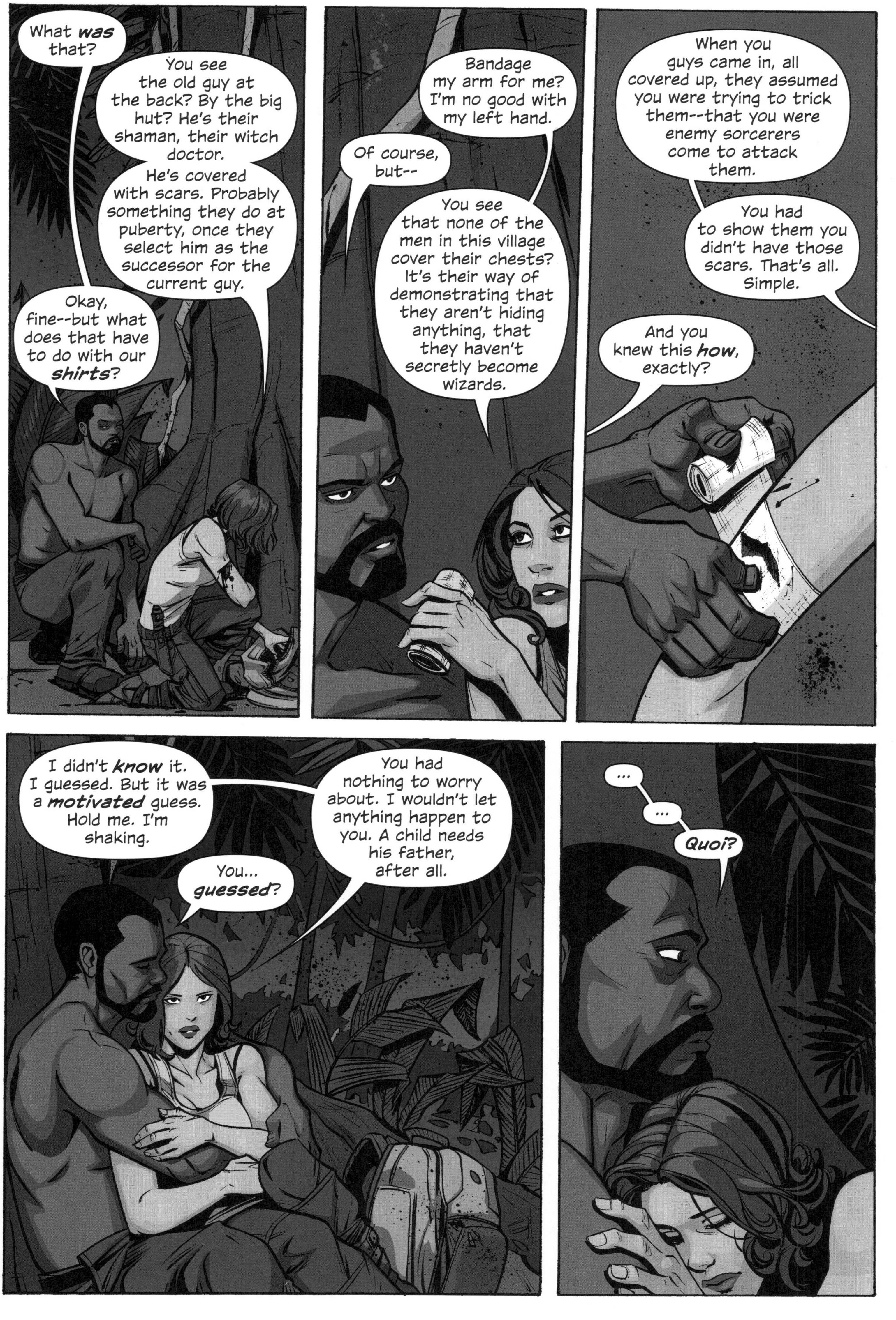
What *was* that?
You see the old guy at the back? By the big hut? He's their shaman, their witch doctor.
He's covered with scars. Probably something they do at puberty, once they select him as the successor for the current guy.
Okay, fine--but what does that have to do with our *shirts*?
Bandage my arm for me? I'm no good with my left hand.
Of course, but--
You see that none of the men in this village cover their chests? It's their way of demonstrating that they aren't hiding anything, that they haven't secretly become wizards.
When you guys came in, all covered up, they assumed you were trying to trick them--that you were enemy sorcerers come to attack them.
You had to show them you didn't have those scars. That's all. Simple.
And you knew this *how*, exactly?
I didn't *know* it. I guessed. But it was a *motivated* guess. Hold me. I'm shaking.
You... *guessed*?
You had nothing to worry about. I wouldn't let anything happen to you. A child needs his father, after all.
...
...
Quoi?

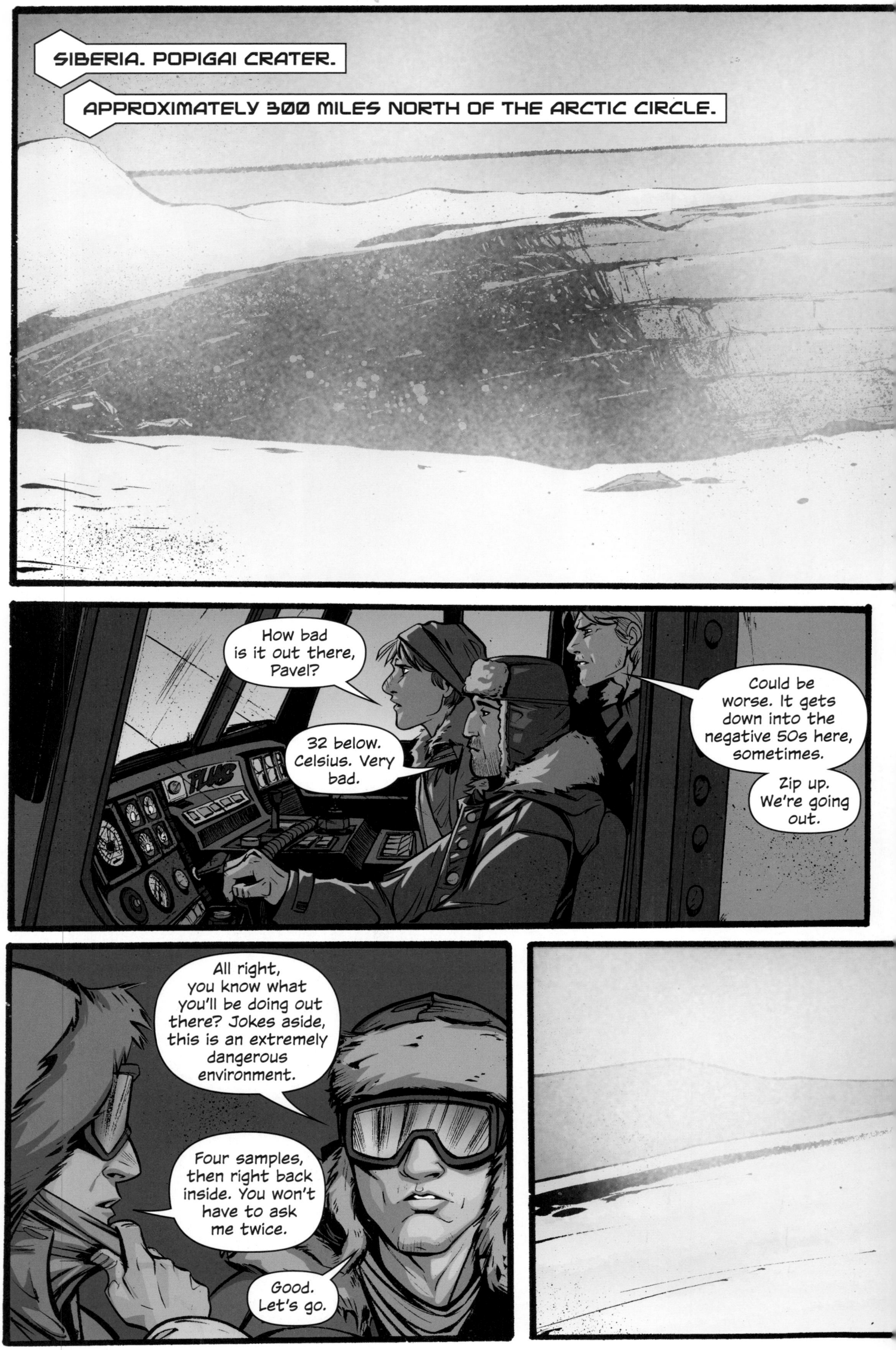
SIBERIA. POPIGAI CRATER.
APPROXIMATELY 300 MILES NORTH OF THE ARCTIC CIRCLE.
How bad is it out there, Pavel?
32 below. Celsius. Very bad.
Could be worse. It gets down into the negative 50s here, sometimes.
Zip up. We're going out.
All right, you know what you'll be doing out there? Jokes aside, this is an extremely dangerous environment.
Four samples, then right back inside. You won't have to ask me twice.
Good. Let's go.

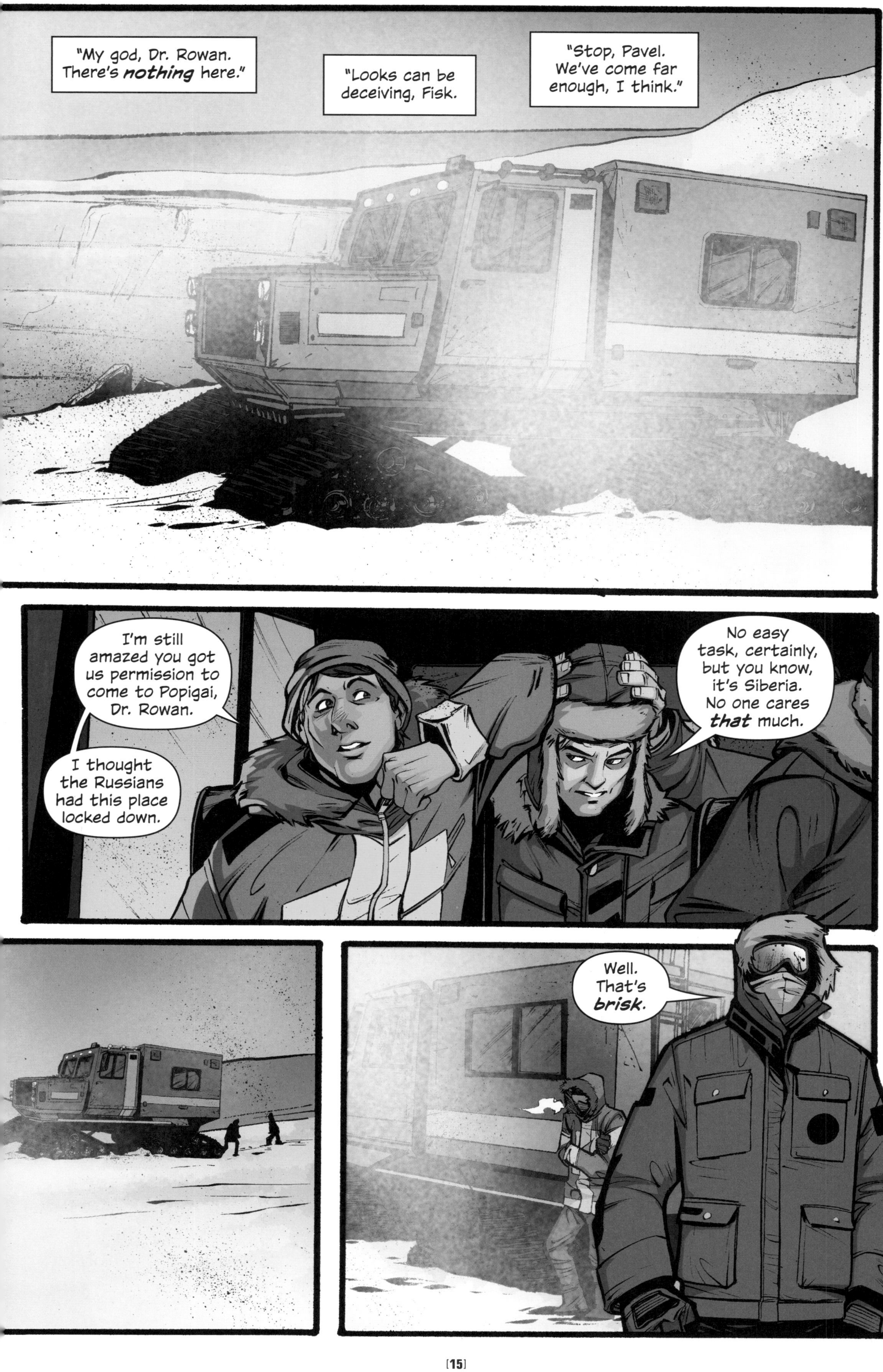
"My god, Dr. Rowan. There's ***nothing*** here."
"Looks can be deceiving, Fisk.
"Stop, Pavel. We've come far enough, I think."
I'm still amazed you got us permission to come to Popigai, Dr. Rowan.
I thought the Russians had this place locked down.
No easy task, certainly, but you know, it's Siberia. No one cares ***that*** much.
Well. That's ***brisk***.

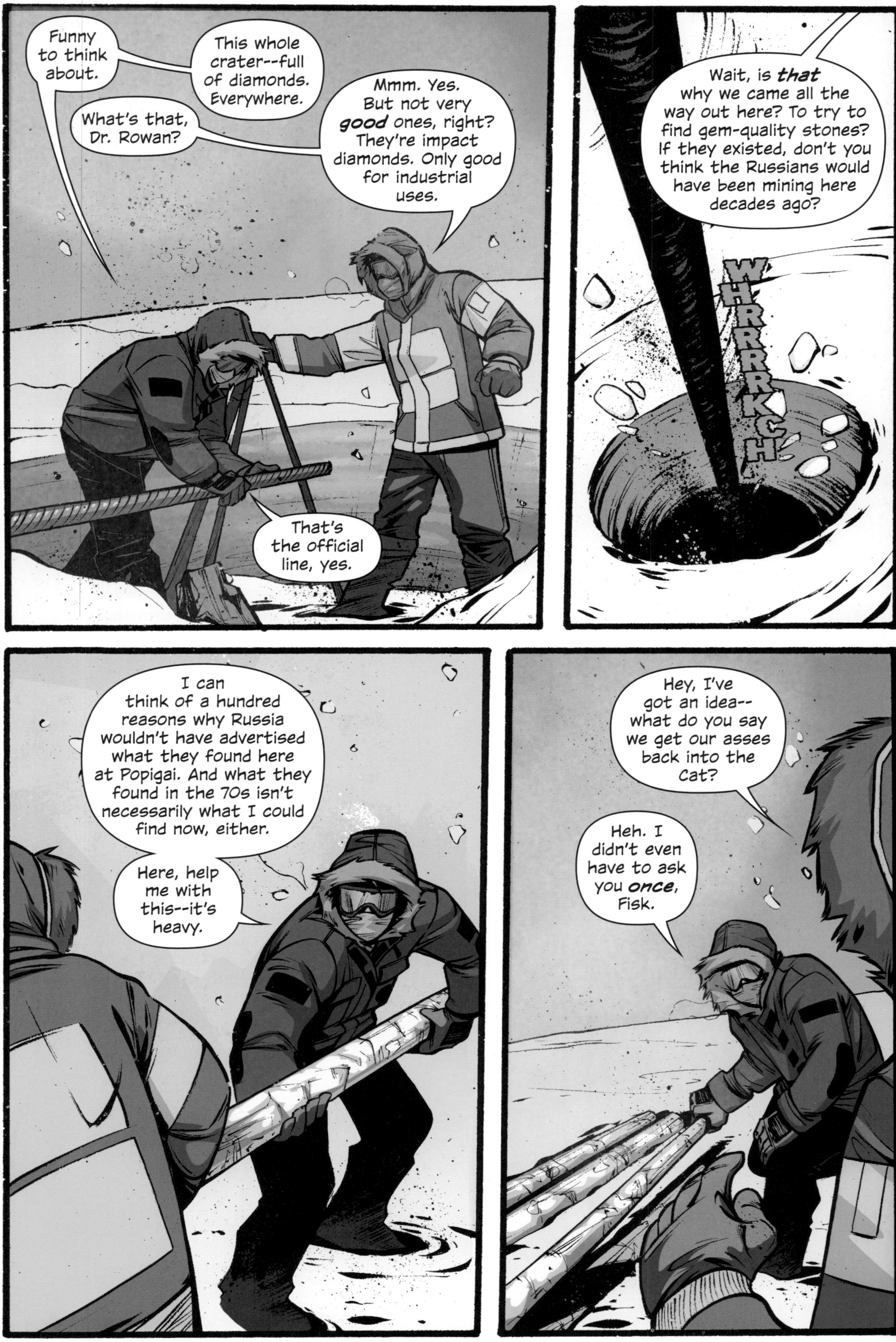
Funny to think about.
This whole crater--full of diamonds. Everywhere.
What's that, Dr. Rowan?
Mmm. Yes. But not very *good* ones, right? They're impact diamonds. Only good for industrial uses.
That's the official line, yes.
Wait, is *that* why we came all the way out here? To try to find gem-quality stones? If they existed, don't you think the Russians would have been mining here decades ago?
WHRRRKCH
I can think of a hundred reasons why Russia wouldn't have advertised what they found here at Popigai. And what they found in the 70s isn't necessarily what I could find now, either.
Here, help me with this--it's heavy.
Hey, I've got an idea--what do you say we get our asses back into the Cat?
Heh. I didn't even have to ask you *once*, Fisk.

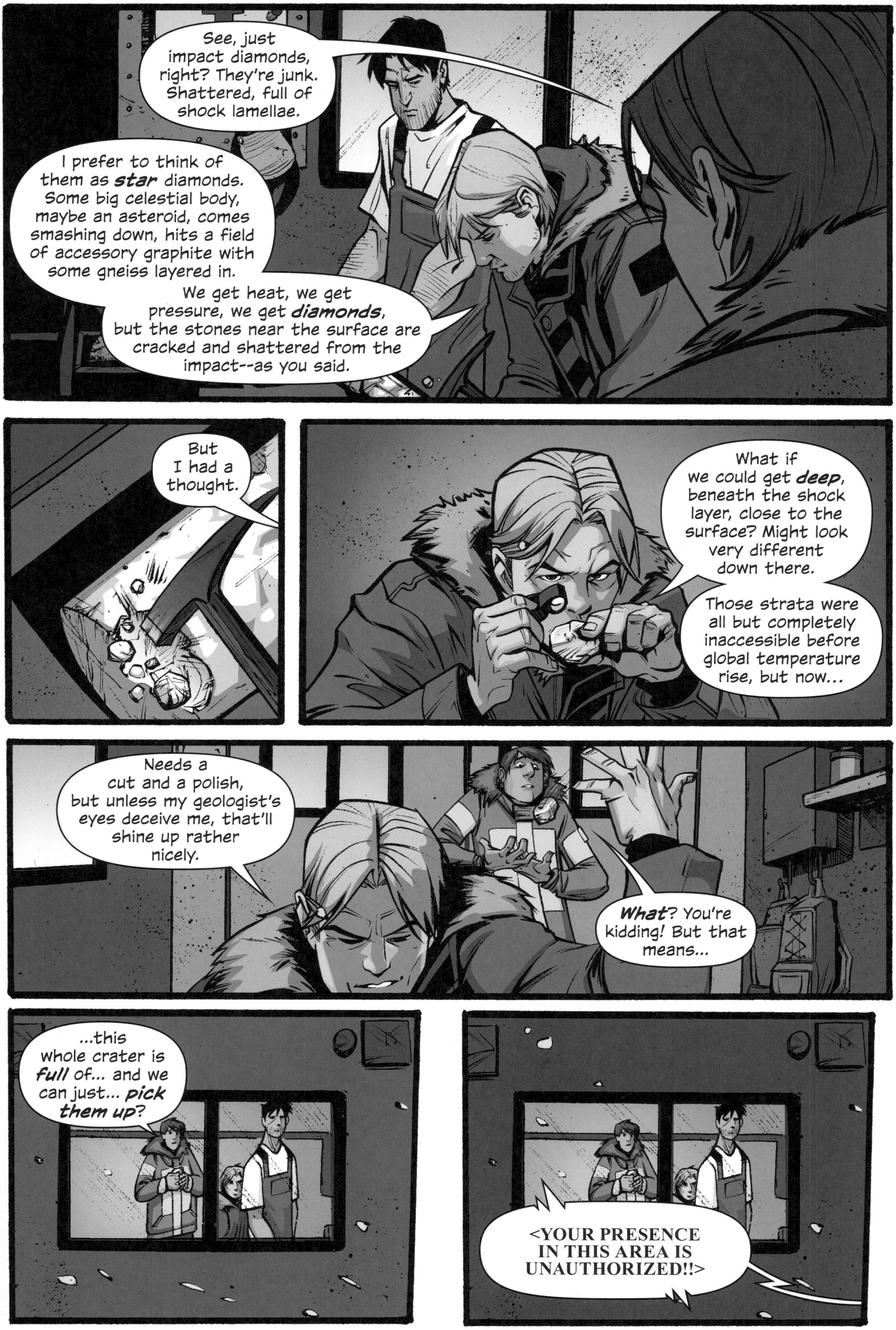
See, just impact diamonds, right? They're junk. Shattered, full of shock lamellae.
I prefer to think of them as **star** diamonds. Some big celestial body, maybe an asteroid, comes smashing down, hits a field of accessory graphite with some gneiss layered in.
We get heat, we get pressure, we get **diamonds**, but the stones near the surface are cracked and shattered from the impact--as you said.
But I had a thought.
What if we could get **deep**, beneath the shock layer, close to the surface? Might look very different down there.
Those strata were all but completely inaccessible before global temperature rise, but now...
Needs a cut and a polish, but unless my geologist's eyes deceive me, that'll shine up rather nicely.
What? You're kidding! But that means...
...this whole crater is **full** of... and we can just... **pick them up**?
<YOUR PRESENCE IN THIS AREA IS UNAUTHORIZED!!>

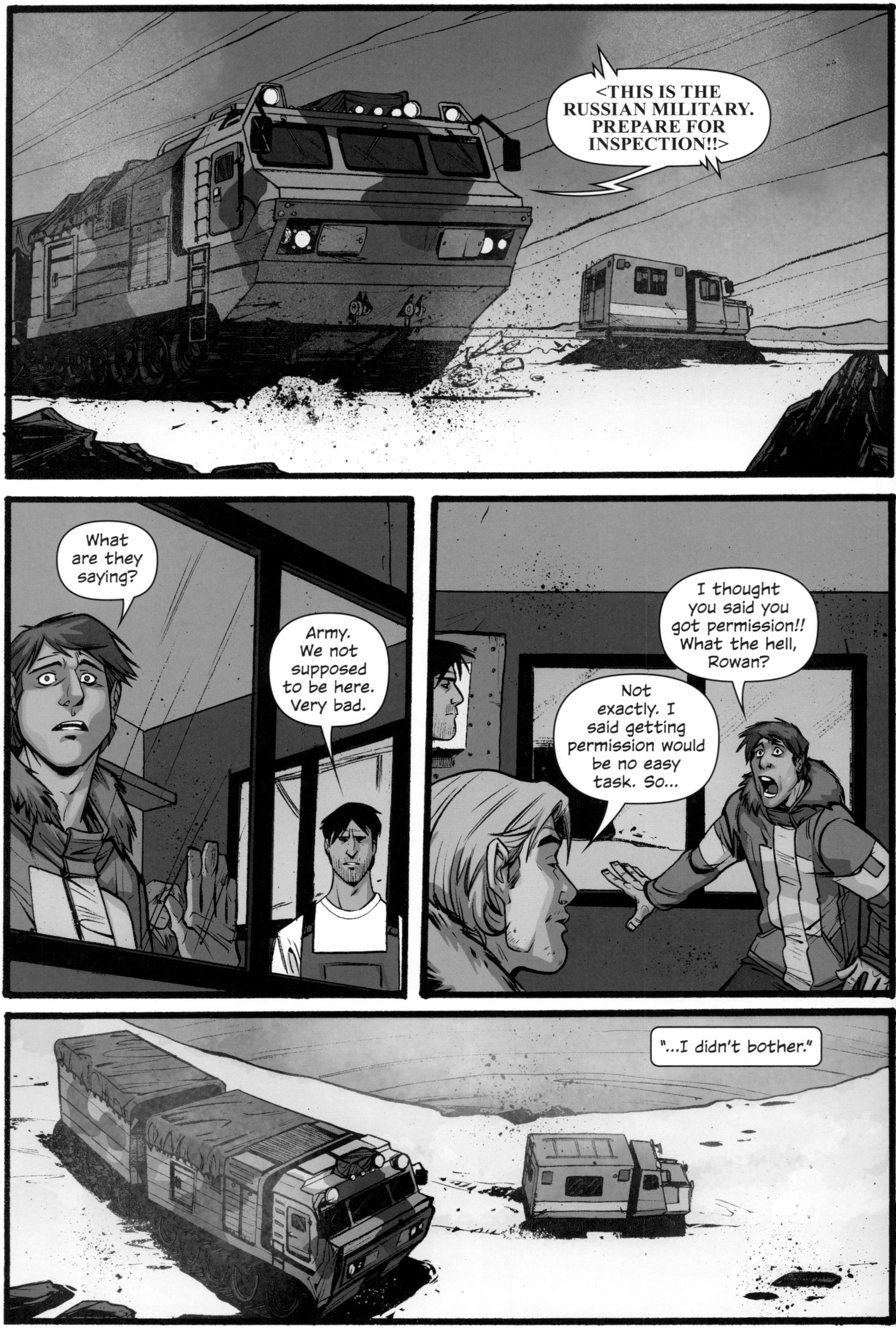
<THIS IS THE RUSSIAN MILITARY. PREPARE FOR INSPECTION!!>
What are they saying?
Army. We not supposed to be here. Very bad.
I thought you said you got permission!! What the hell, Rowan?
Not exactly. I said getting permission would be no easy task. So...
"...I didn't bother."

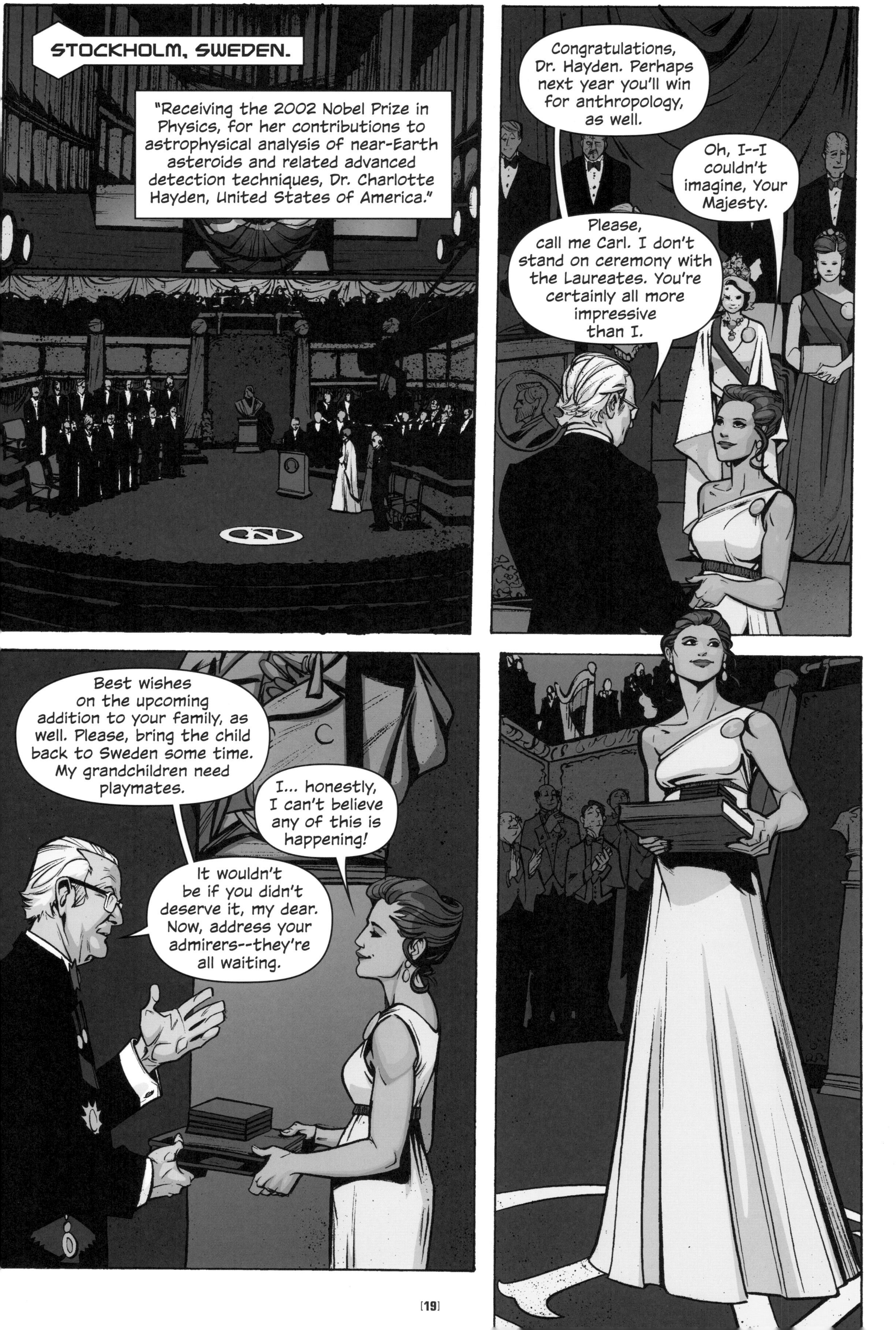
STOCKHOLM, SWEDEN.
"Receiving the 2002 Nobel Prize in Physics, for her contributions to astrophysical analysis of near-Earth asteroids and related advanced detection techniques, Dr. Charlotte Hayden, United States of America."
Congratulations, Dr. Hayden. Perhaps next year you'll win for anthropology, as well.
Oh, I--I couldn't imagine, Your Majesty.
Please, call me Carl. I don't stand on ceremony with the Laureates. You're certainly all more impressive than I.
Best wishes on the upcoming addition to your family, as well. Please, bring the child back to Sweden some time. My grandchildren need playmates.
I... honestly, I can't believe any of this is happening!
It wouldn't be if you didn't deserve it, my dear. Now, address your admirers--they're all waiting.

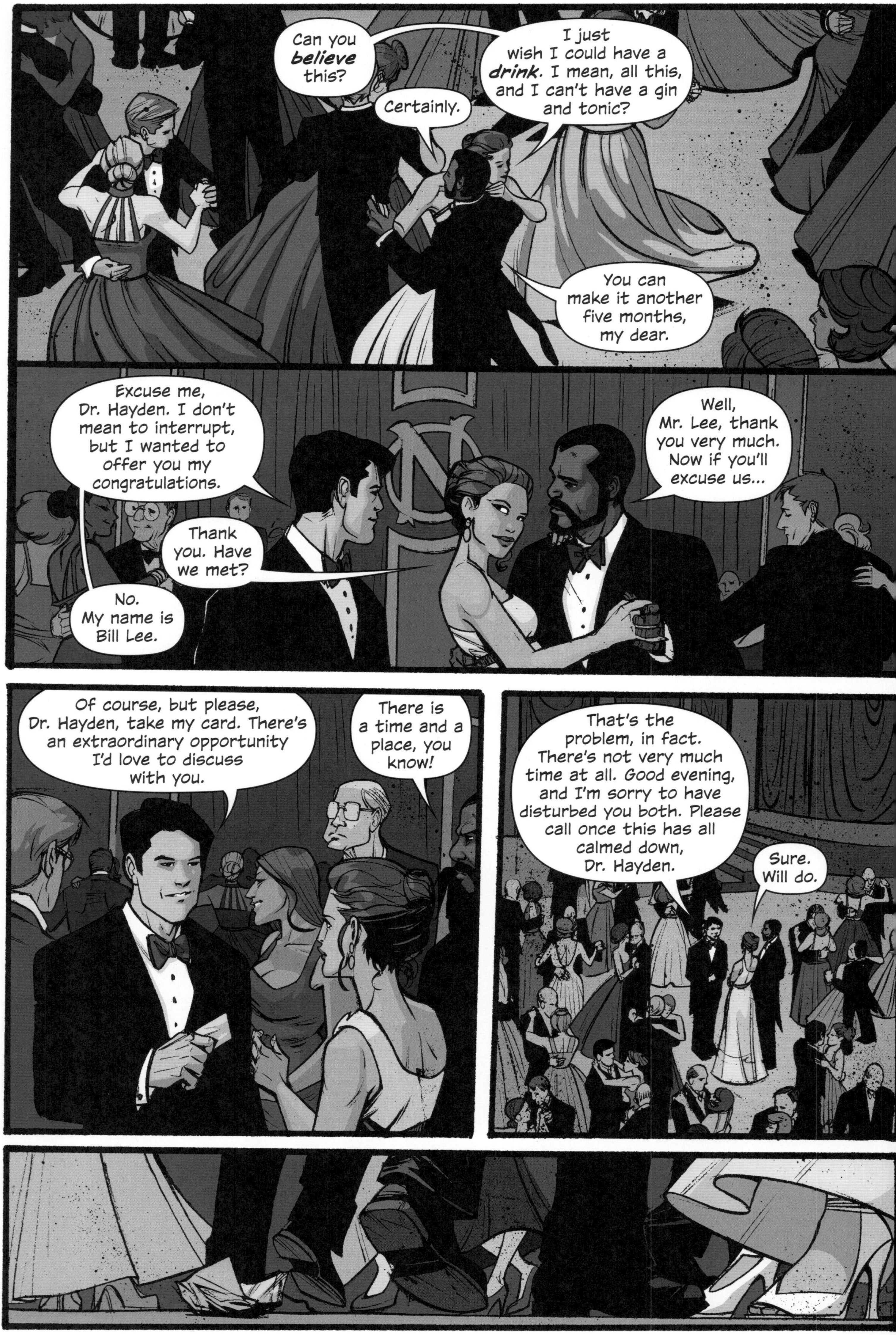
Can you *believe* this?
Certainly.
I just wish I could have a *drink*. I mean, all this, and I can't have a gin and tonic?
You can make it another five months, my dear.
Excuse me, Dr. Hayden. I don't mean to interrupt, but I wanted to offer you my congratulations.
Thank you. Have we met?
No. My name is Bill Lee.
Well, Mr. Lee, thank you very much. Now if you'll excuse us...
Of course, but please, Dr. Hayden, take my card. There's an extraordinary opportunity I'd love to discuss with you.
There is a time and a place, you know!
That's the problem, in fact. There's not very much time at all. Good evening, and I'm sorry to have disturbed you both. Please call once this has all calmed down, Dr. Hayden.
Sure. Will do.

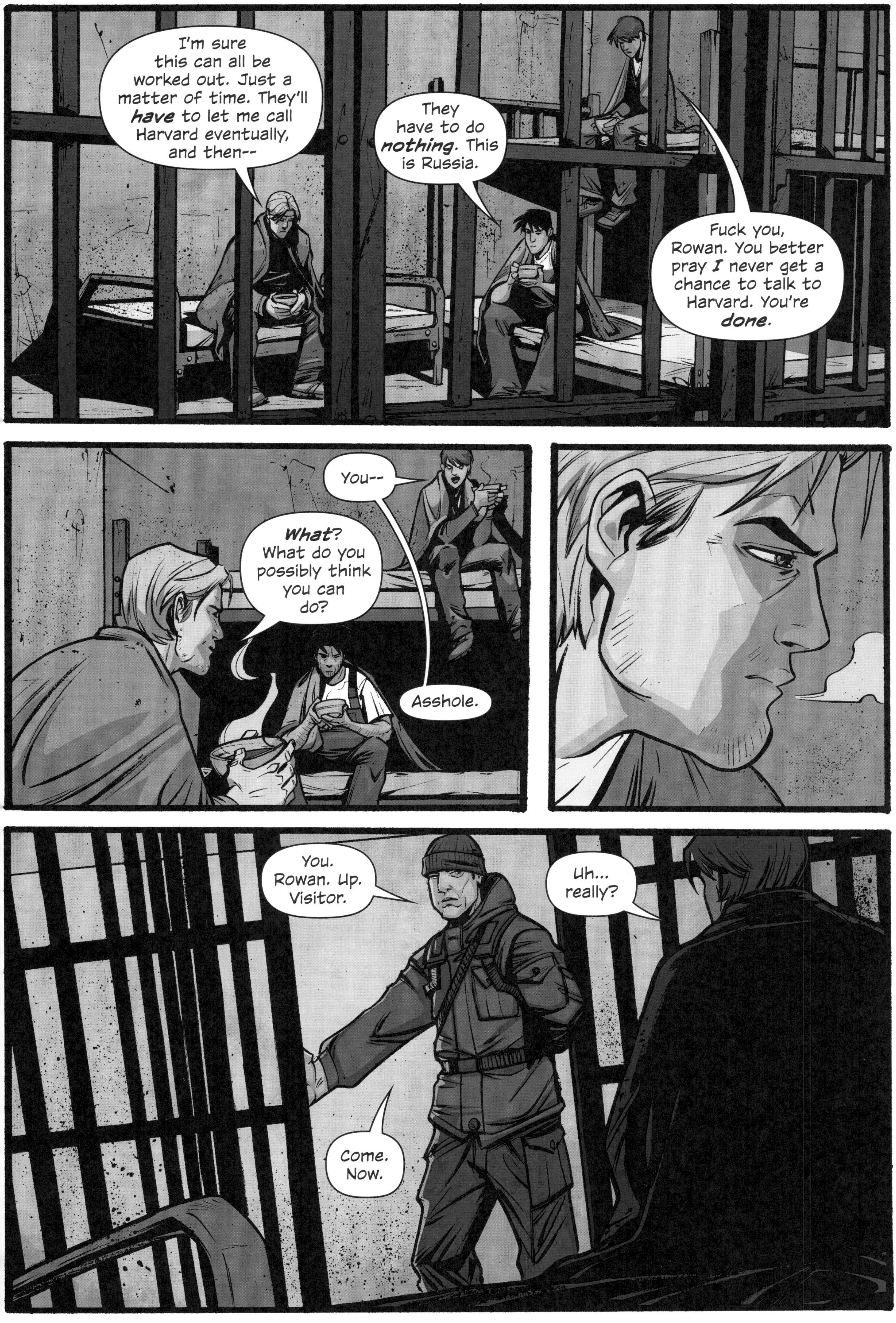
I'm sure this can all be worked out. Just a matter of time. They'll *have* to let me call Harvard eventually, and then--
They have to do *nothing*. This is Russia.
Fuck you, Rowan. You better pray *I* never get a chance to talk to Harvard. You're *done*.
You--
What? What do you possibly think you can do?
Asshole.
You. Rowan. Up. Visitor.
Uh... really?
Come. Now.

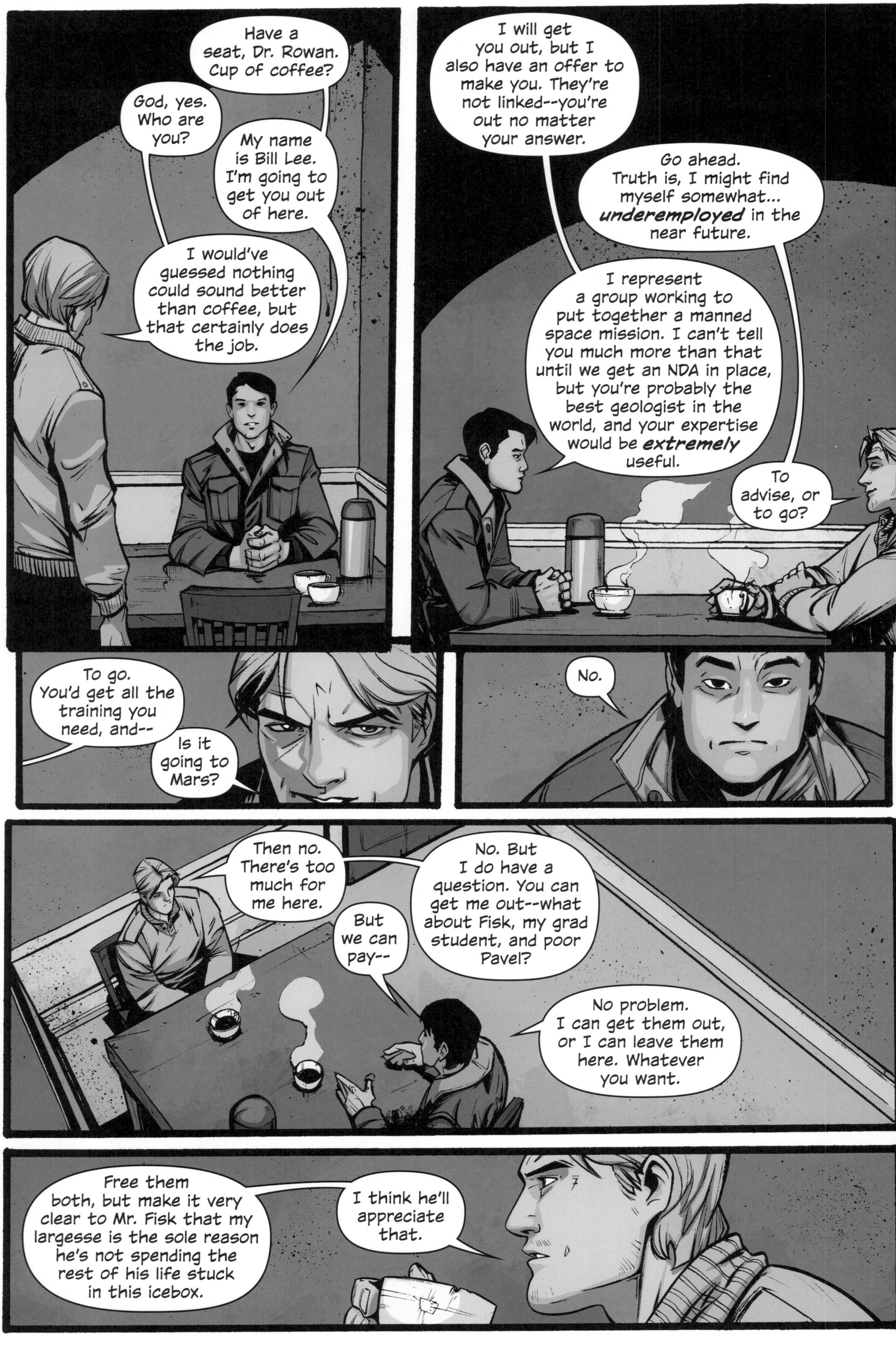
Have a seat, Dr. Rowan. Cup of coffee?
God, yes. Who are you?
My name is Bill Lee. I'm going to get you out of here.
I would've guessed nothing could sound better than coffee, but that certainly does the job.
I will get you out, but I also have an offer to make you. They're not linked--you're out no matter your answer.
Go ahead. Truth is, I might find myself somewhat... *underemployed* in the near future.
I represent a group working to put together a manned space mission. I can't tell you much more than that until we get an NDA in place, but you're probably the best geologist in the world, and your expertise would be *extremely* useful.
To advise, or to go?
To go. You'd get all the training you need, and--
Is it going to Mars?
No.
Then no. There's too much for me here.
But we can pay--
No. But I do have a question. You can get me out--what about Fisk, my grad student, and poor Pavel?
No problem. I can get them out, or I can leave them here. Whatever you want.
Free them both, but make it very clear to Mr. Fisk that my largesse is the sole reason he's not spending the rest of his life stuck in this icebox.
I think he'll appreciate that.

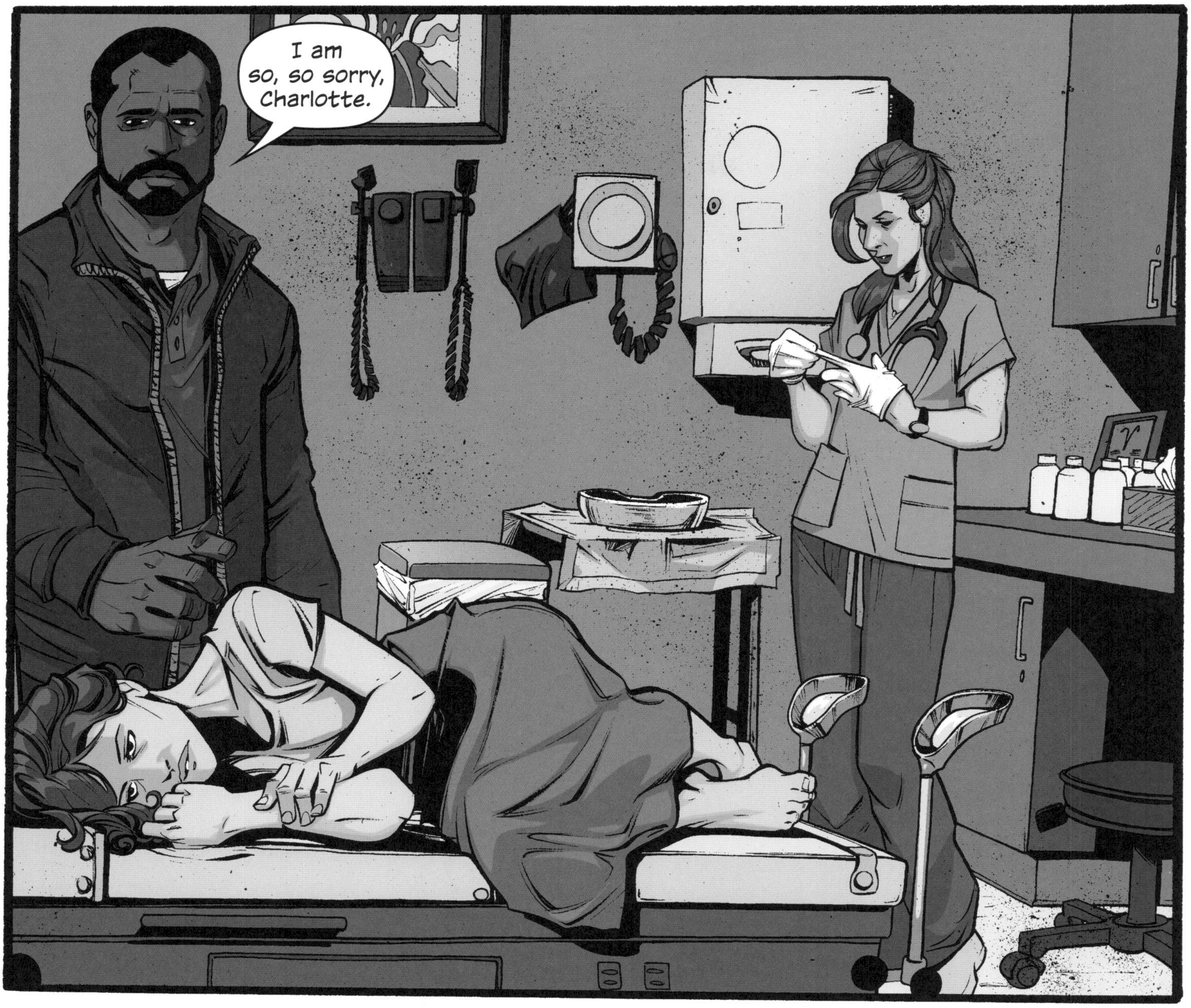
I am so, so sorry, Charlotte.

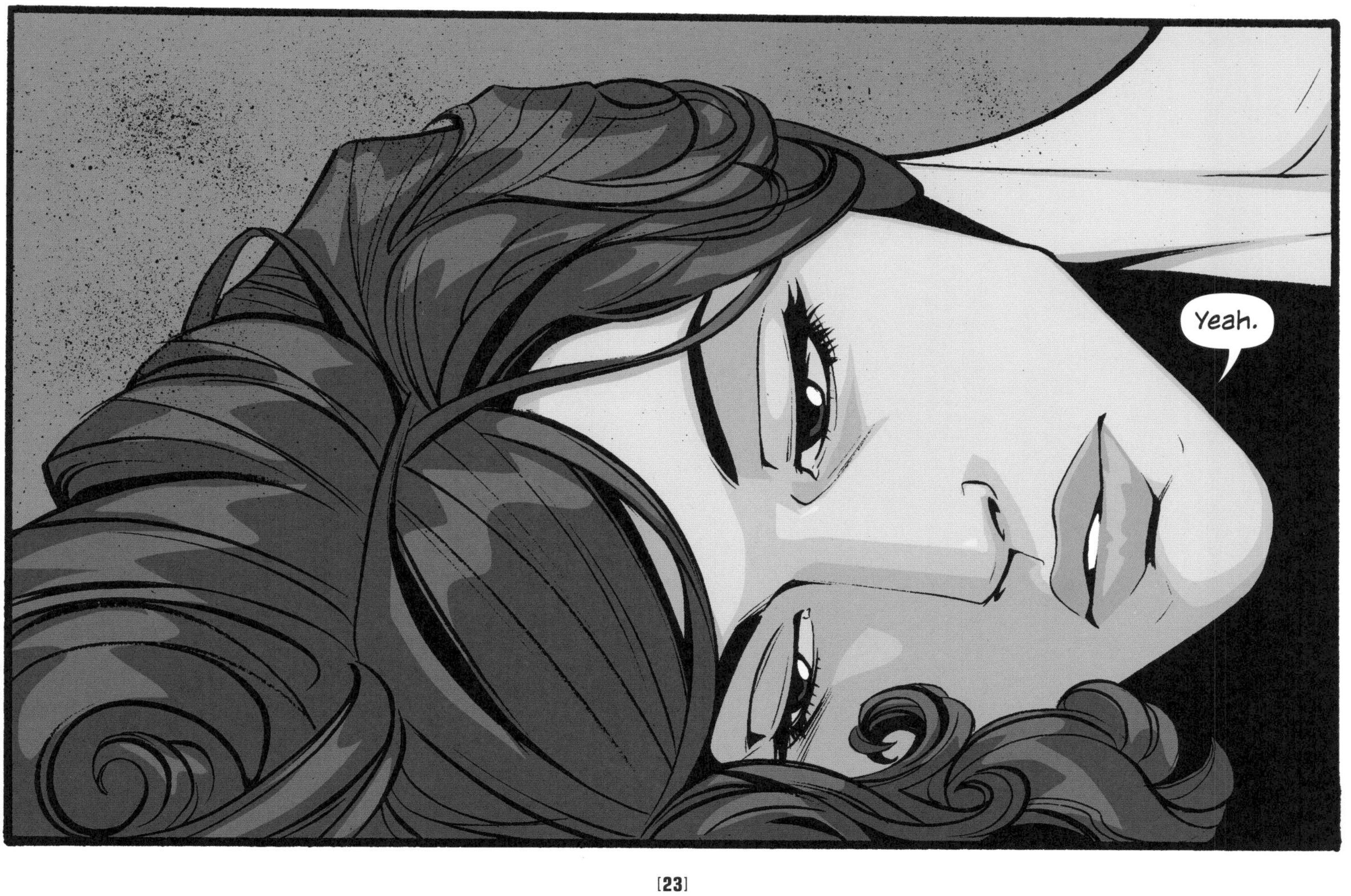
Yeah.

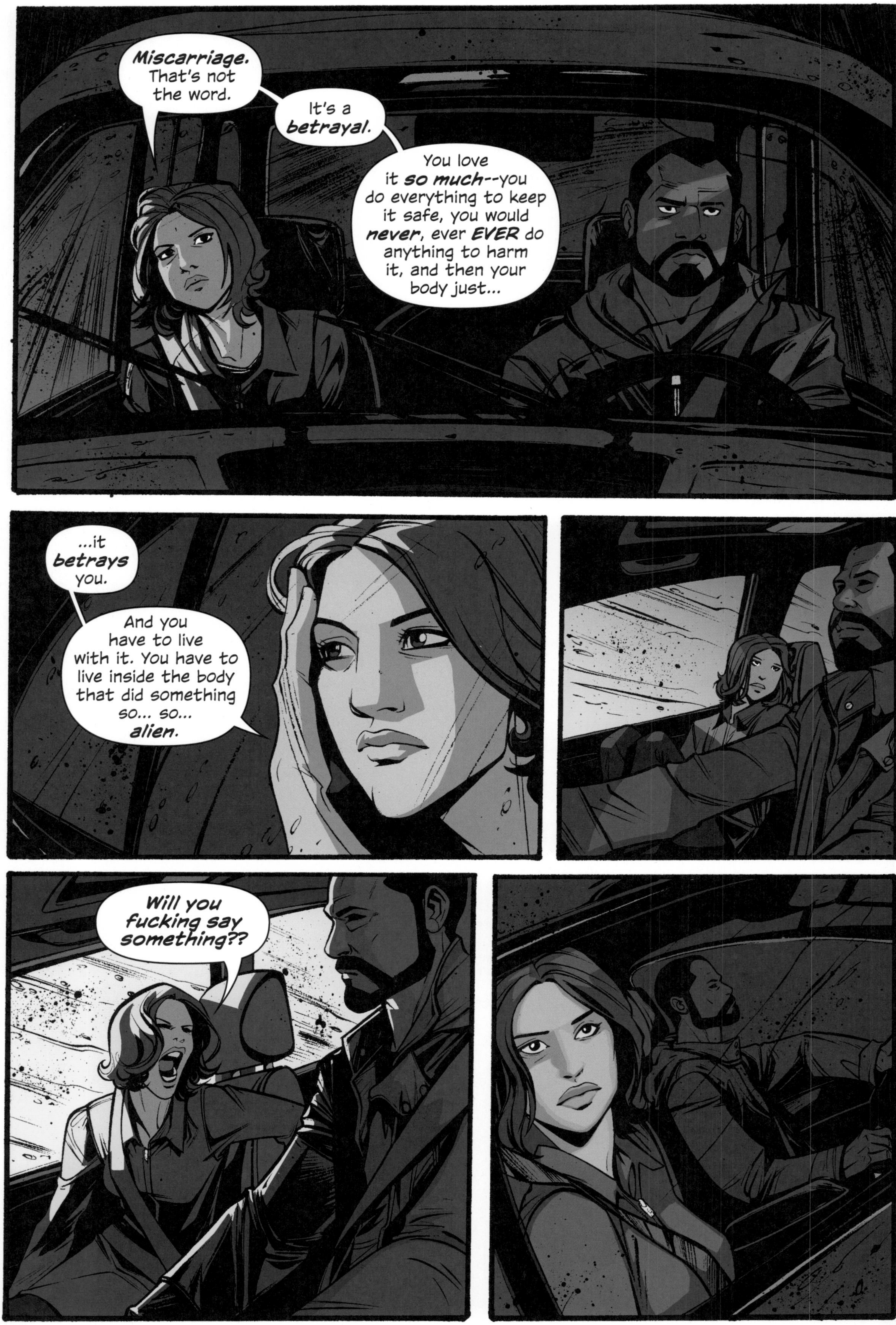

Miscarriage. That's not the word.
It's a ***betrayal.***
You love it ***so much***--you do everything to keep it safe, you would ***never***, ever ***EVER*** do anything to harm it, and then your body just...
...it ***betrays*** you.
And you have to live with it. You have to live inside the body that did something so... so... ***alien***.
Will you fucking say something??

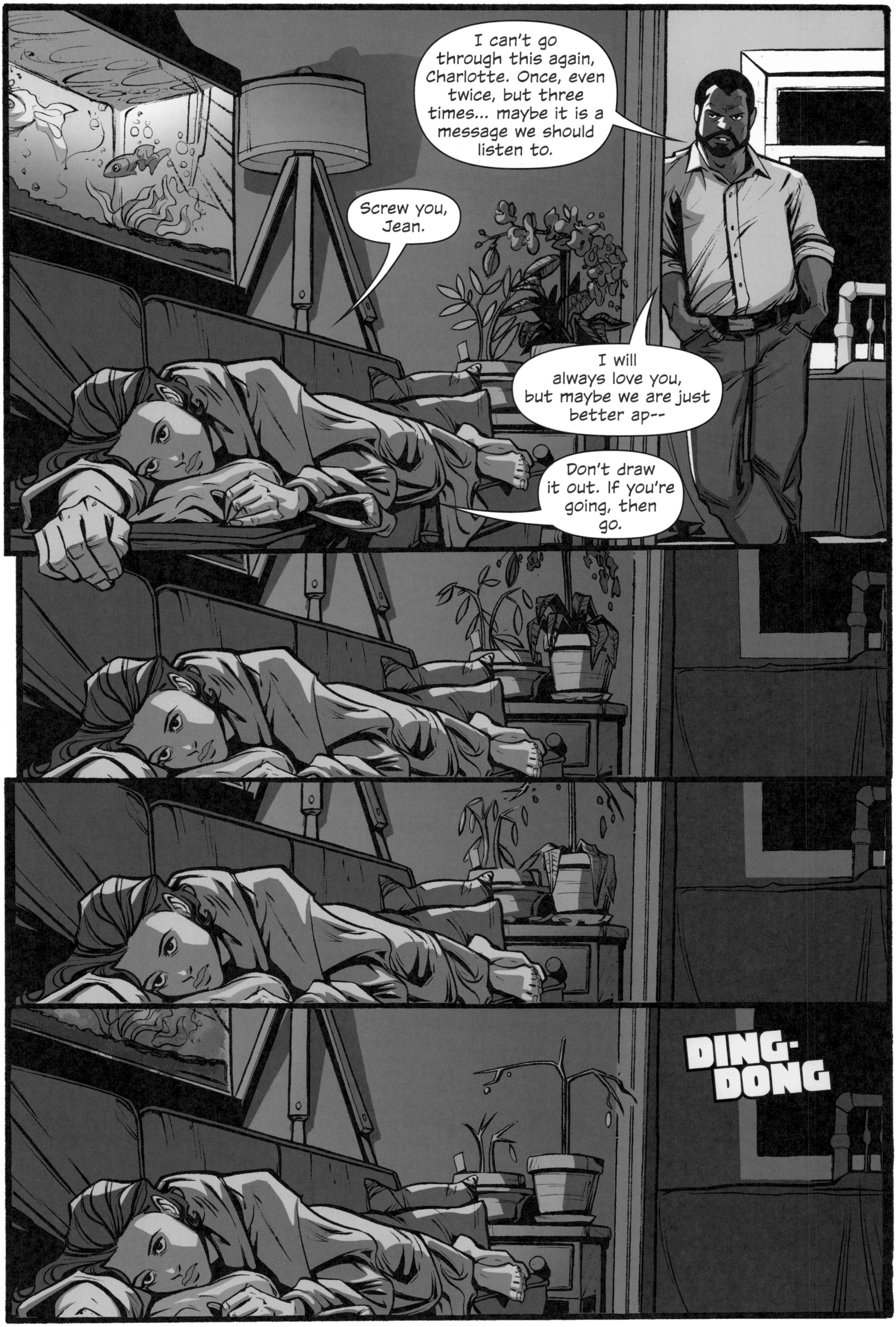
I can't go through this again, Charlotte. Once, even twice, but three times... maybe it is a message we should listen to.
Screw you, Jean.
I will always love you, but maybe we are just better ap--
Don't draw it out. If you're going, then go.
DING-DONG

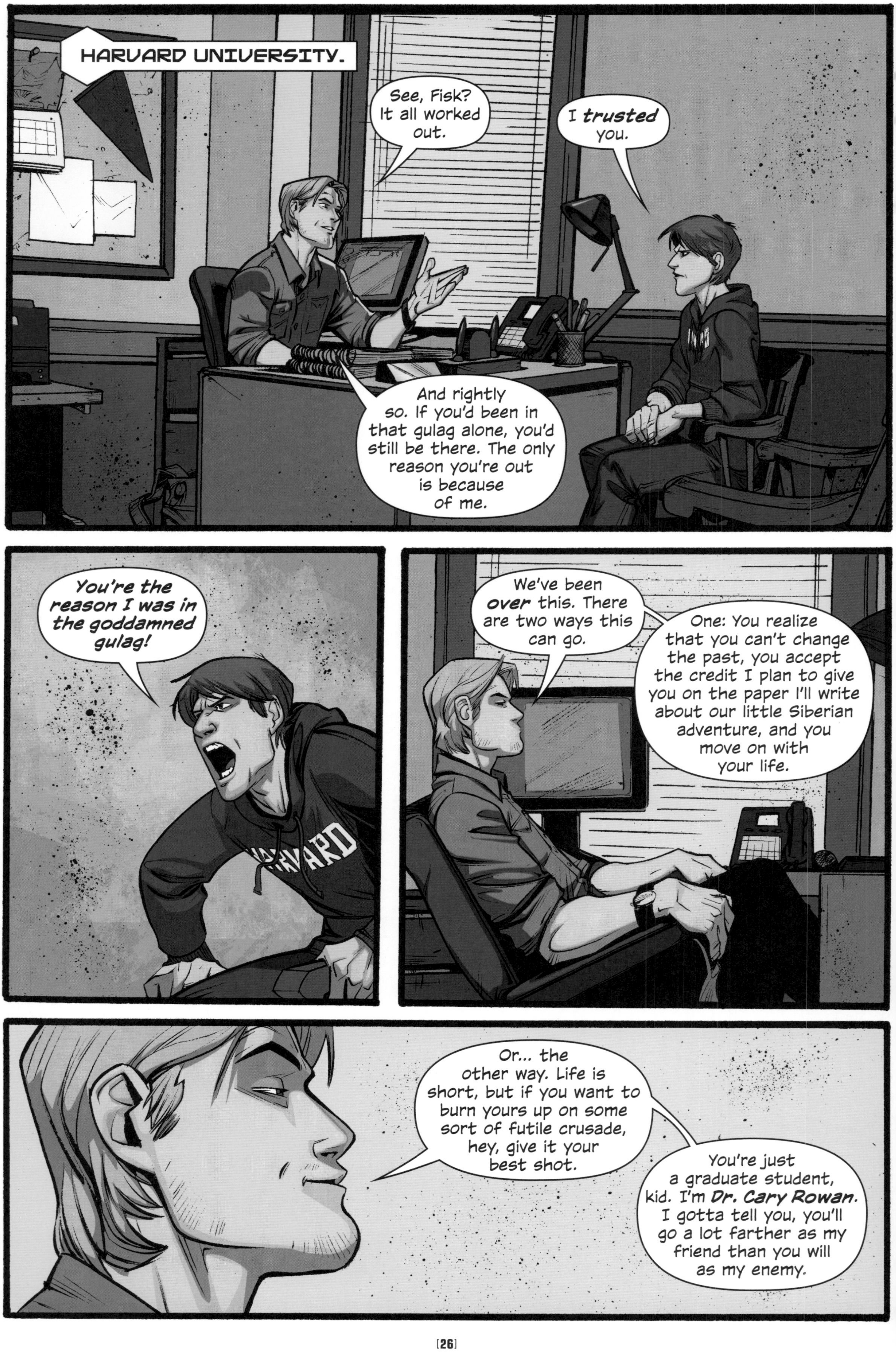
HARVARD UNIVERSITY.
See, Fisk? It all worked out.
I *trusted* you.
And rightly so. If you'd been in that gulag alone, you'd still be there. The only reason you're out is because of me.
You're the reason I was in the goddamned gulag!
We've been *over* this. There are two ways this can go.
One: You realize that you can't change the past, you accept the credit I plan to give you on the paper I'll write about our little Siberian adventure, and you move on with your life.
Or... the other way. Life is short, but if you want to burn yours up on some sort of futile crusade, hey, give it your best shot.
You're just a graduate student, kid. I'm *Dr. Cary Rowan.* I gotta tell you, you'll go a lot farther as my friend than you will as my enemy.

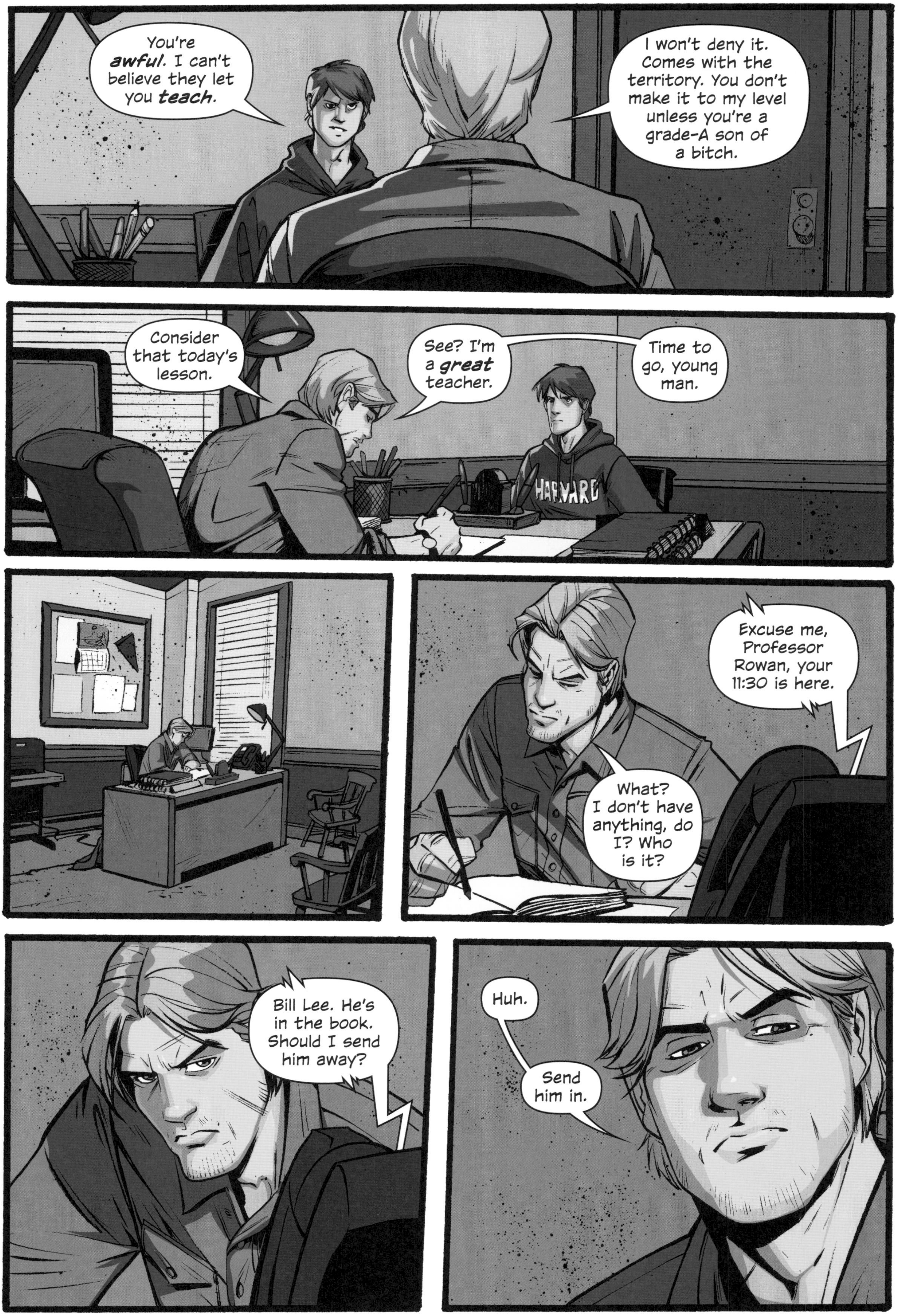
You're *awful*. I can't believe they let you *teach*.
I won't deny it. Comes with the territory. You don't make it to my level unless you're a grade-A son of a bitch.
Consider that today's lesson.
See? I'm a *great* teacher.
Time to go, young man.
HARVARD
Excuse me, Professor Rowan, your 11:30 is here.
What? I don't have anything, do I? Who is it?
Bill Lee. He's in the book. Should I send him away?
Huh.
Send him in.

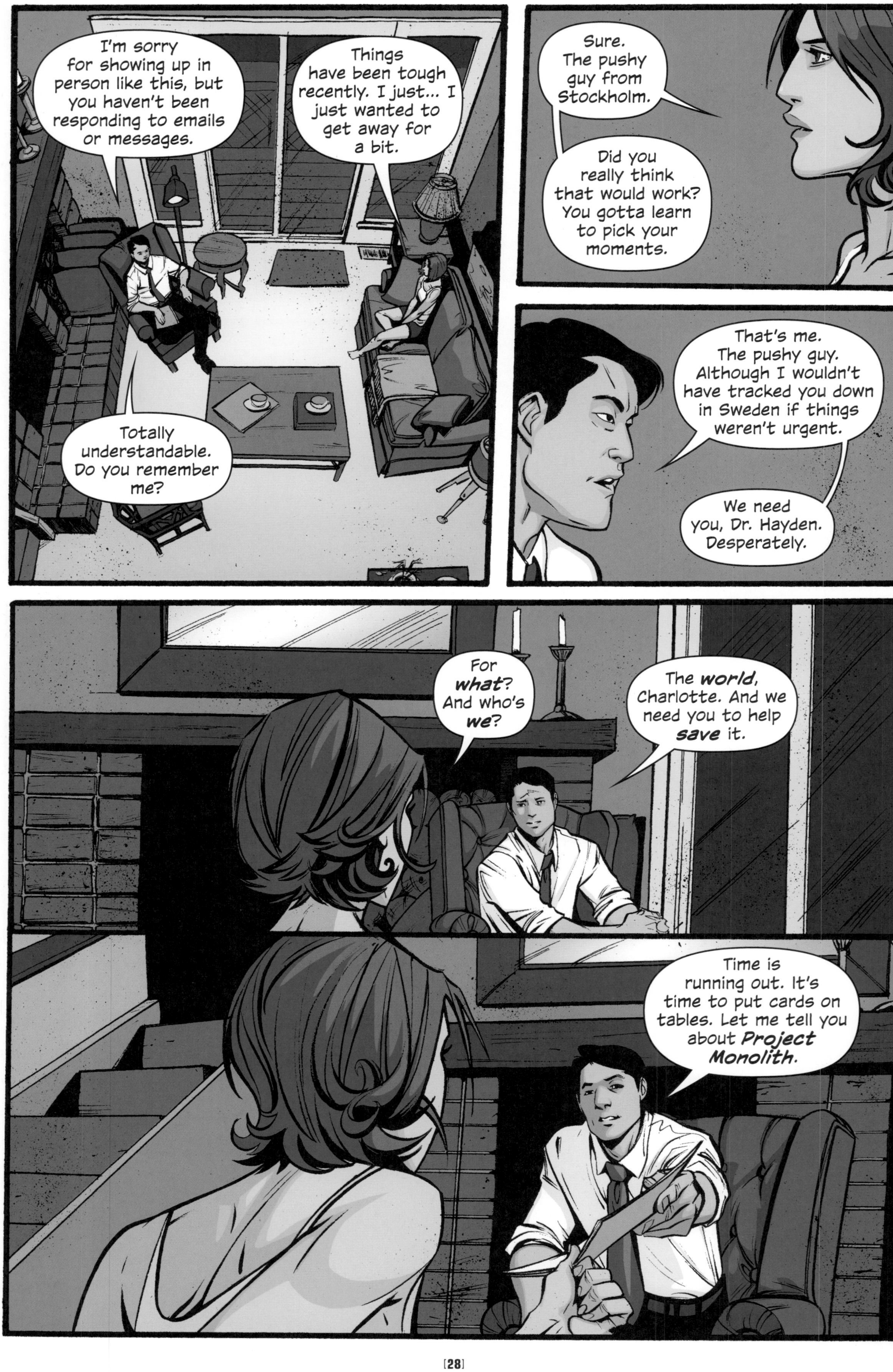
I'm sorry for showing up in person like this, but you haven't been responding to emails or messages.
Things have been tough recently. I just... I just wanted to get away for a bit.
Totally understandable. Do you remember me?
Sure. The pushy guy from Stockholm.
Did you really think that would work? You gotta learn to pick your moments.
That's me. The pushy guy. Although I wouldn't have tracked you down in Sweden if things weren't urgent.
We need you, Dr. Hayden. Desperately.
For *what*? And who's *we*?
The *world*, Charlotte. And we need you to help *save* it.
Time is running out. It's time to put cards on tables. Let me tell you about *Project Monolith*.

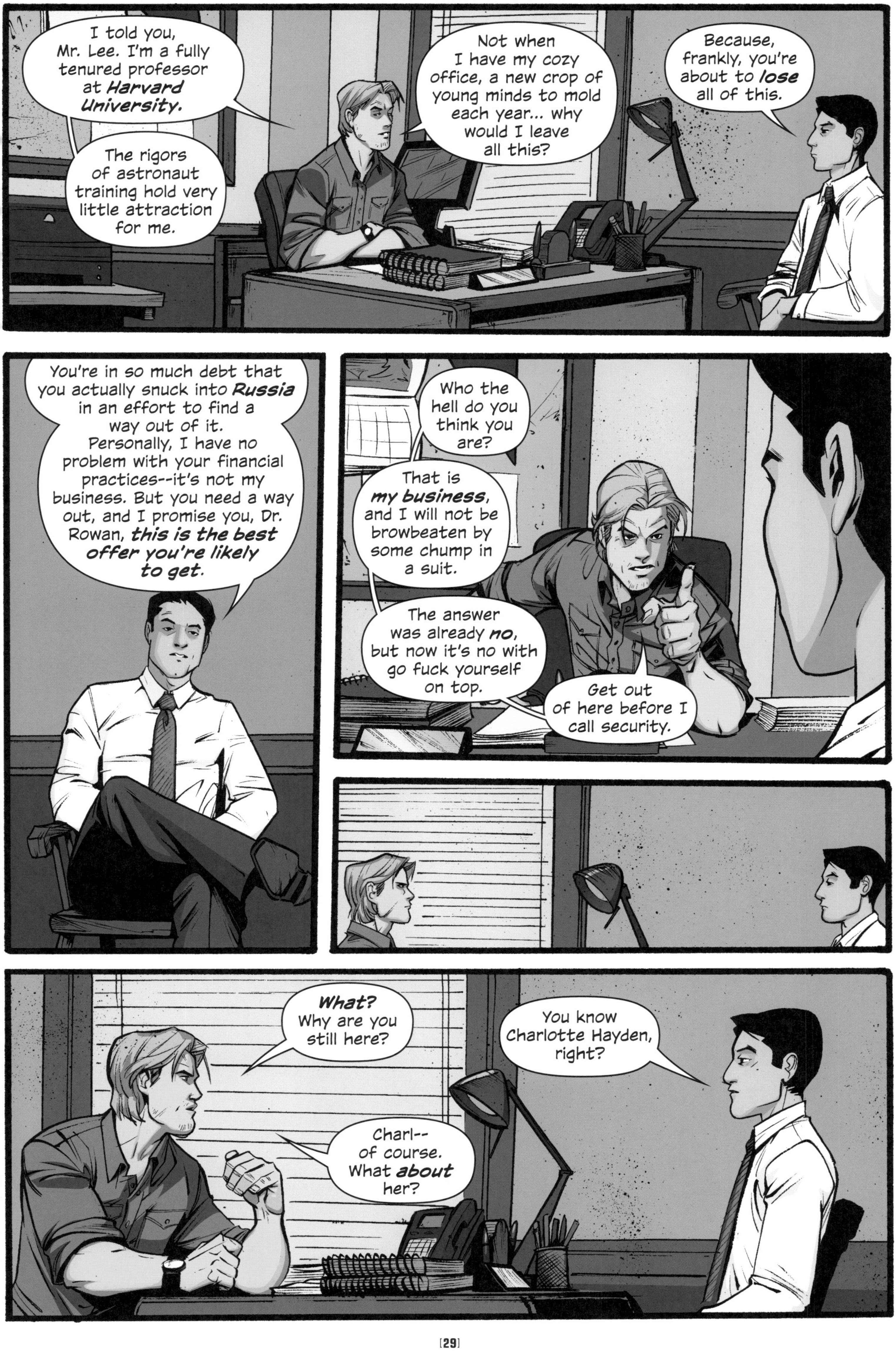

I told you, Mr. Lee. I'm a fully tenured professor at *Harvard University.*
The rigors of astronaut training hold very little attraction for me.
Not when I have my cozy office, a new crop of young minds to mold each year... why would I leave all this?
Because, frankly, you're about to *lose* all of this.
You're in so much debt that you actually snuck into *Russia* in an effort to find a way out of it. Personally, I have no problem with your financial practices--it's not my business. But you need a way out, and I promise you, Dr. Rowan, *this is the best offer you're likely to get*.
Who the hell do you think you are?
That is *my business*, and I will not be browbeaten by some chump in a suit.
The answer was already *no*, but now it's no with go fuck yourself on top.
Get out of here before I call security.
What? Why are you still here?
You know Charlotte Hayden, right?
Charl-- of course. What *about* her?

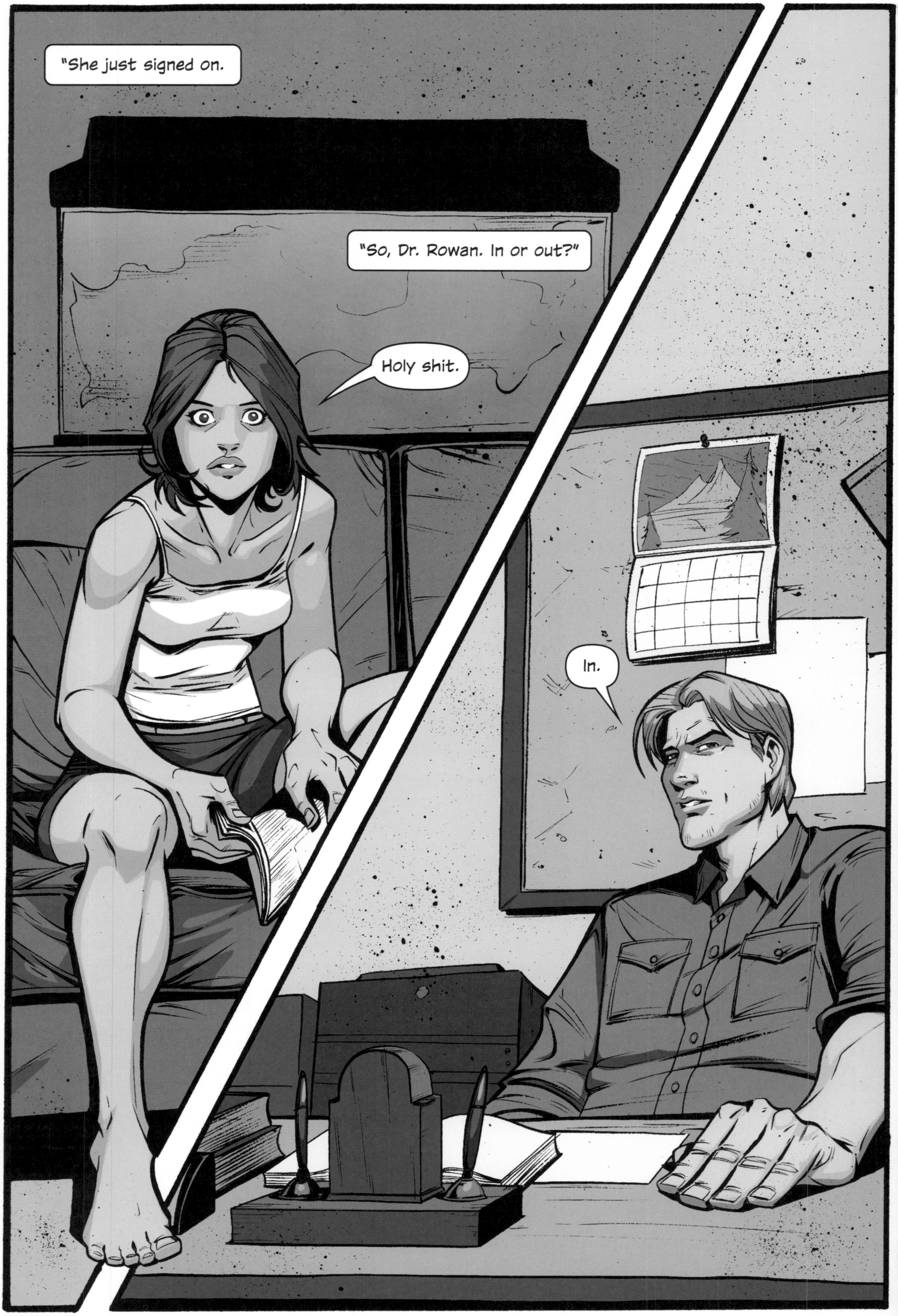
"She just signed on.
"So, Dr. Rowan. In or out?"
Holy shit.
In.

LETTER 44

CHAPTER II

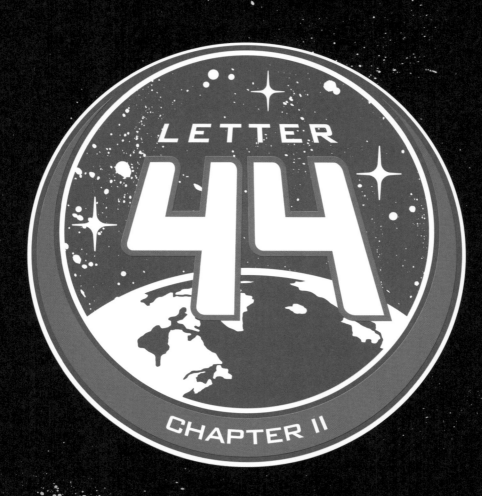

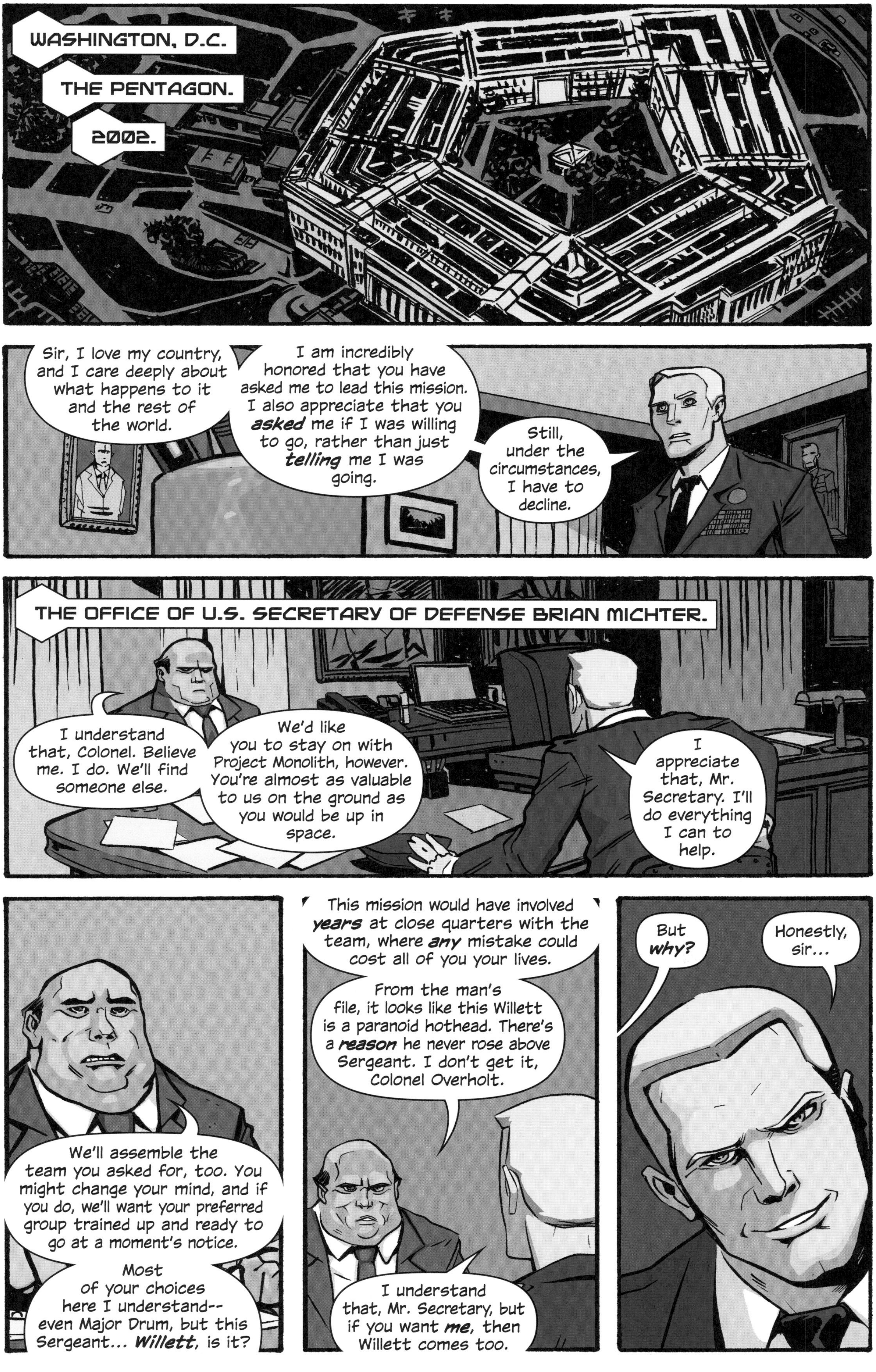
WASHINGTON, D.C.
THE PENTAGON.
2002.
Sir, I love my country, and I care deeply about what happens to it and the rest of the world.
I am incredibly honored that you have asked me to lead this mission. I also appreciate that you *asked* me if I was willing to go, rather than just *telling* me I was going.
Still, under the circumstances, I have to decline.
THE OFFICE OF U.S. SECRETARY OF DEFENSE BRIAN MICHTER.
I understand that, Colonel. Believe me. I do. We'll find someone else.
We'd like you to stay on with Project Monolith, however. You're almost as valuable to us on the ground as you would be up in space.
I appreciate that, Mr. Secretary. I'll do everything I can to help.
We'll assemble the team you asked for, too. You might change your mind, and if you do, we'll want your preferred group trained up and ready to go at a moment's notice.
Most of your choices here I understand-- even Major Drum, but this Sergeant... *Willett*, is it?
This mission would have involved *years* at close quarters with the team, where *any* mistake could cost all of you your lives.
From the man's file, it looks like this Willett is a paranoid hothead. There's a *reason* he never rose above Sergeant. I don't get it, Colonel Overholt.
I understand that, Mr. Secretary, but if you want *me*, then Willett comes too.
But *why?*
Honestly, sir...

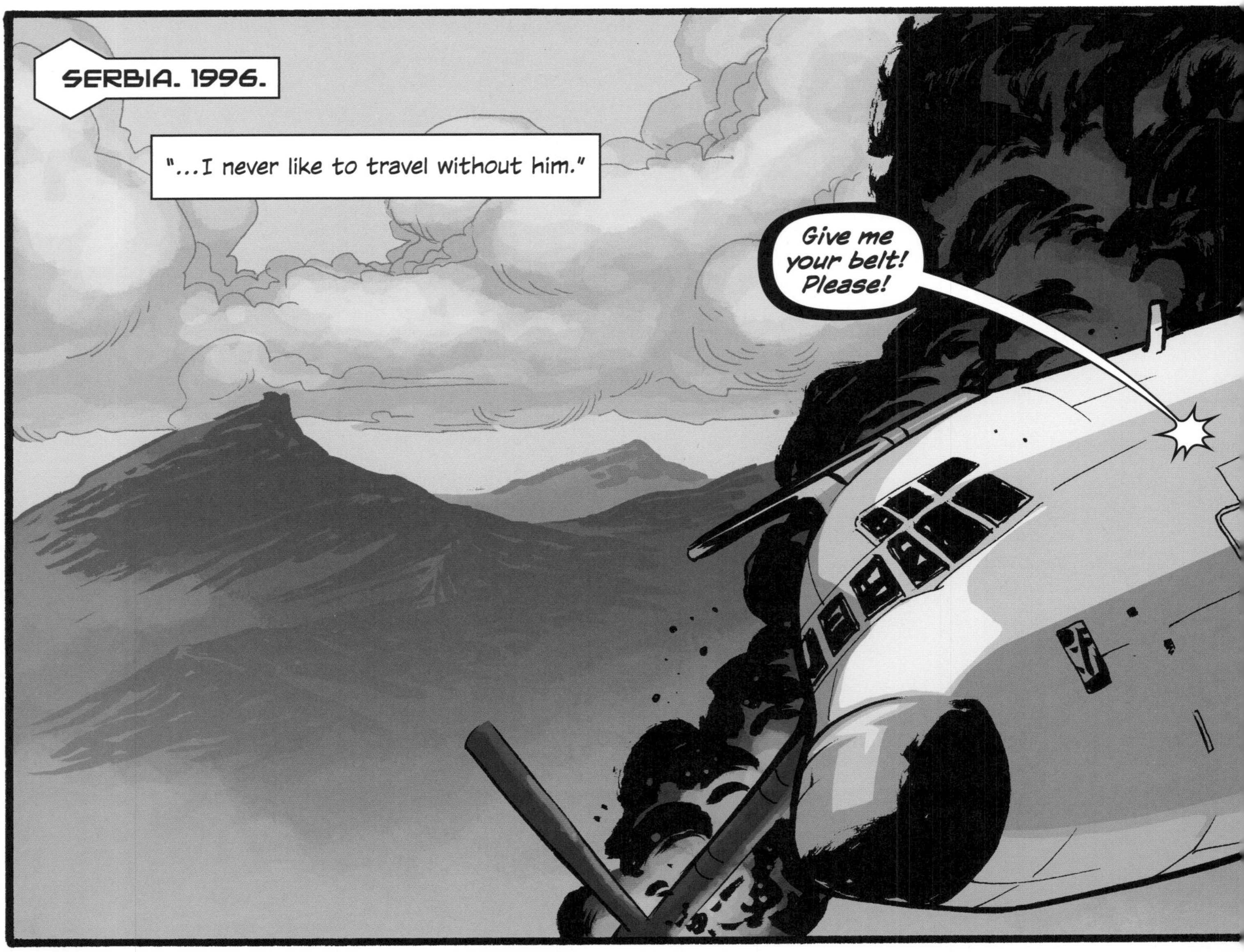
SERBIA. 1996.
"...I never like to travel without him."
Give me your belt! Please!

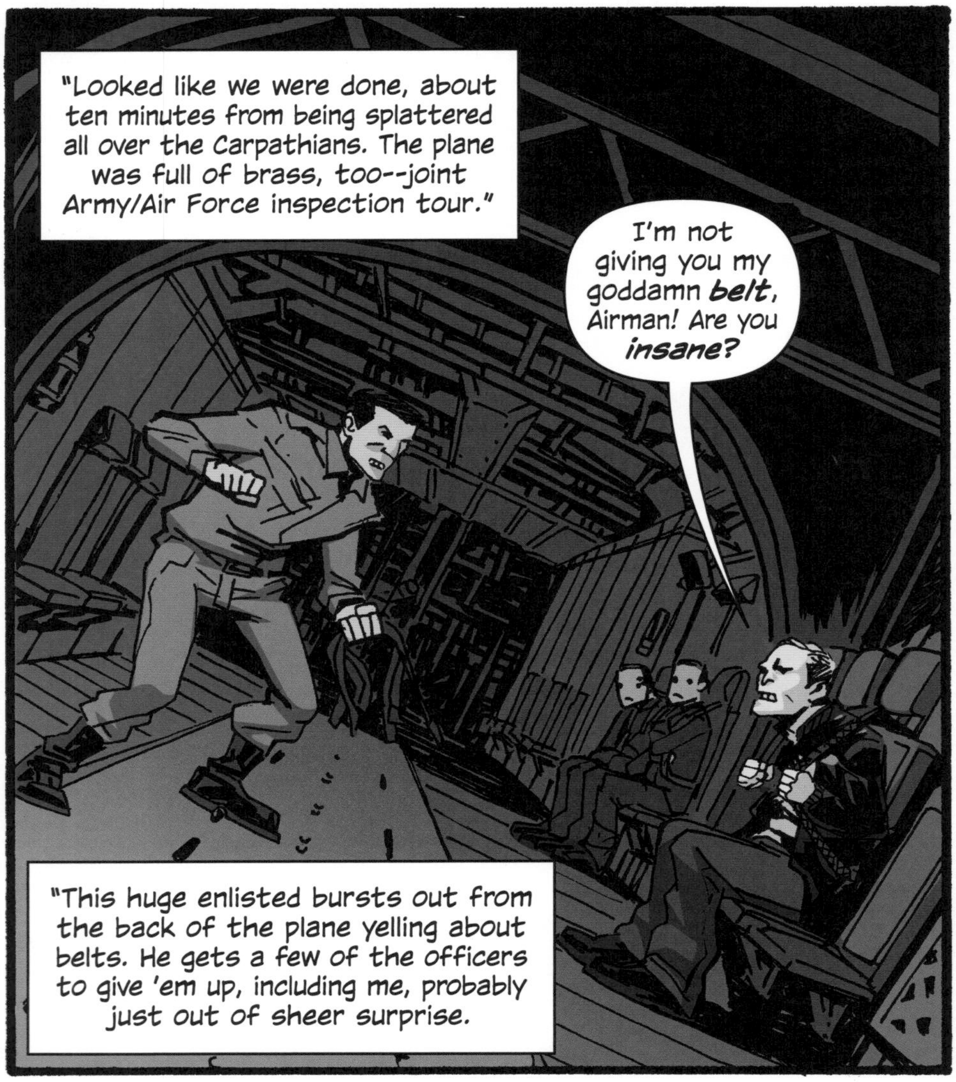
"Looked like we were done, about ten minutes from being splattered all over the Carpathians. The plane was full of brass, too--joint Army/Air Force inspection tour."
I'm not giving you my goddamn *belt*, Airman! Are you *insane?*
"This huge enlisted bursts out from the back of the plane yelling about belts. He gets a few of the officers to give 'em up, including me, probably just out of sheer surprise.

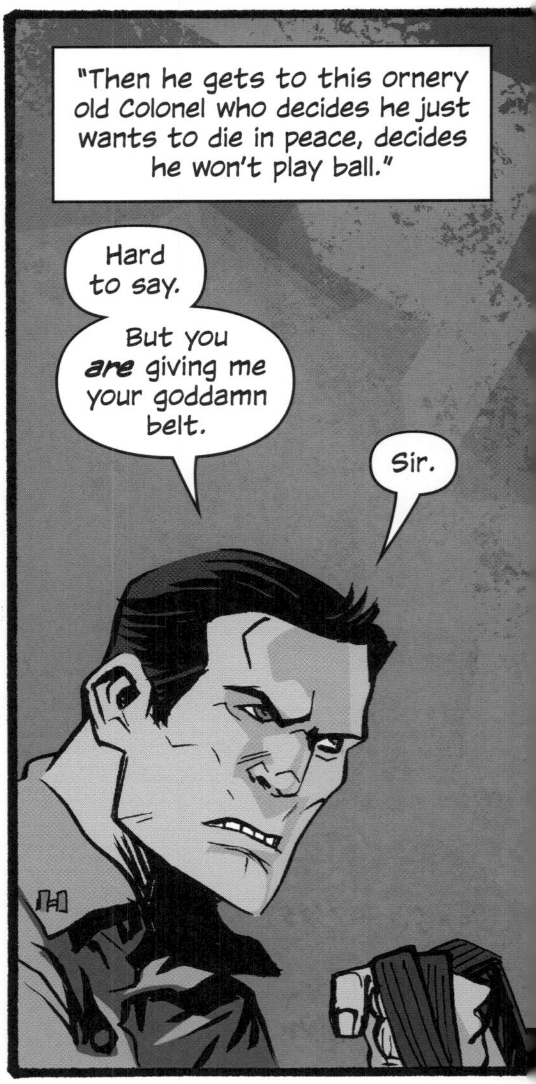
"Then he gets to this ornery old Colonel who decides he just wants to die in peace, decides he won't play ball."
Hard to say.
But you *are* giving me your goddamn belt.
Sir.

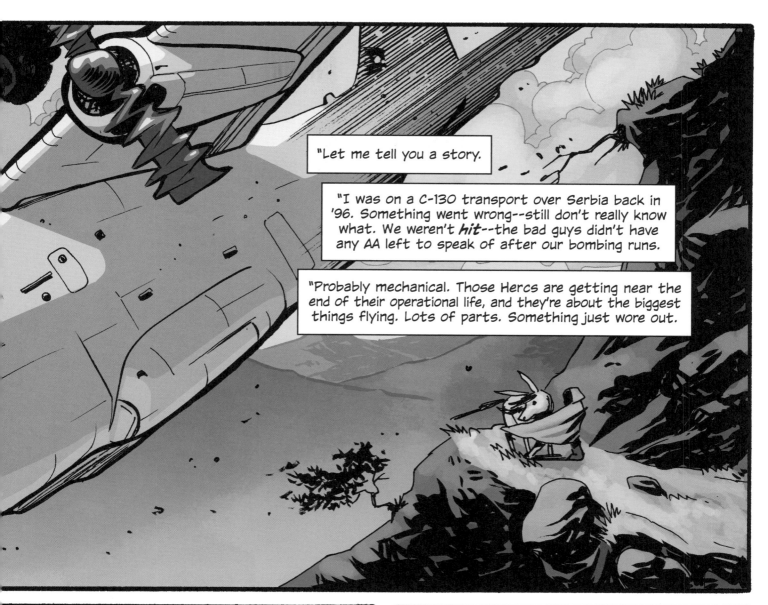

"Let me tell you a story.

"I was on a C-130 transport over Serbia back in '96. Something went wrong--still don't really know what. We weren't *hit*--the bad guys didn't have any AA left to speak of after our bombing runs.

"Probably mechanical. Those Hercs are getting near the end of their operational life, and they're about the biggest things flying. Lots of parts. Something just wore out.

"Willett didn't really stand for that."

Get your hands off me!

Sorry, sir.

"A few minutes later, we leveled out.

"Never did find out what he did with the belts, but whatever it was, it worked."

But I did say please.

"That was the *first* time Willett saved my life.

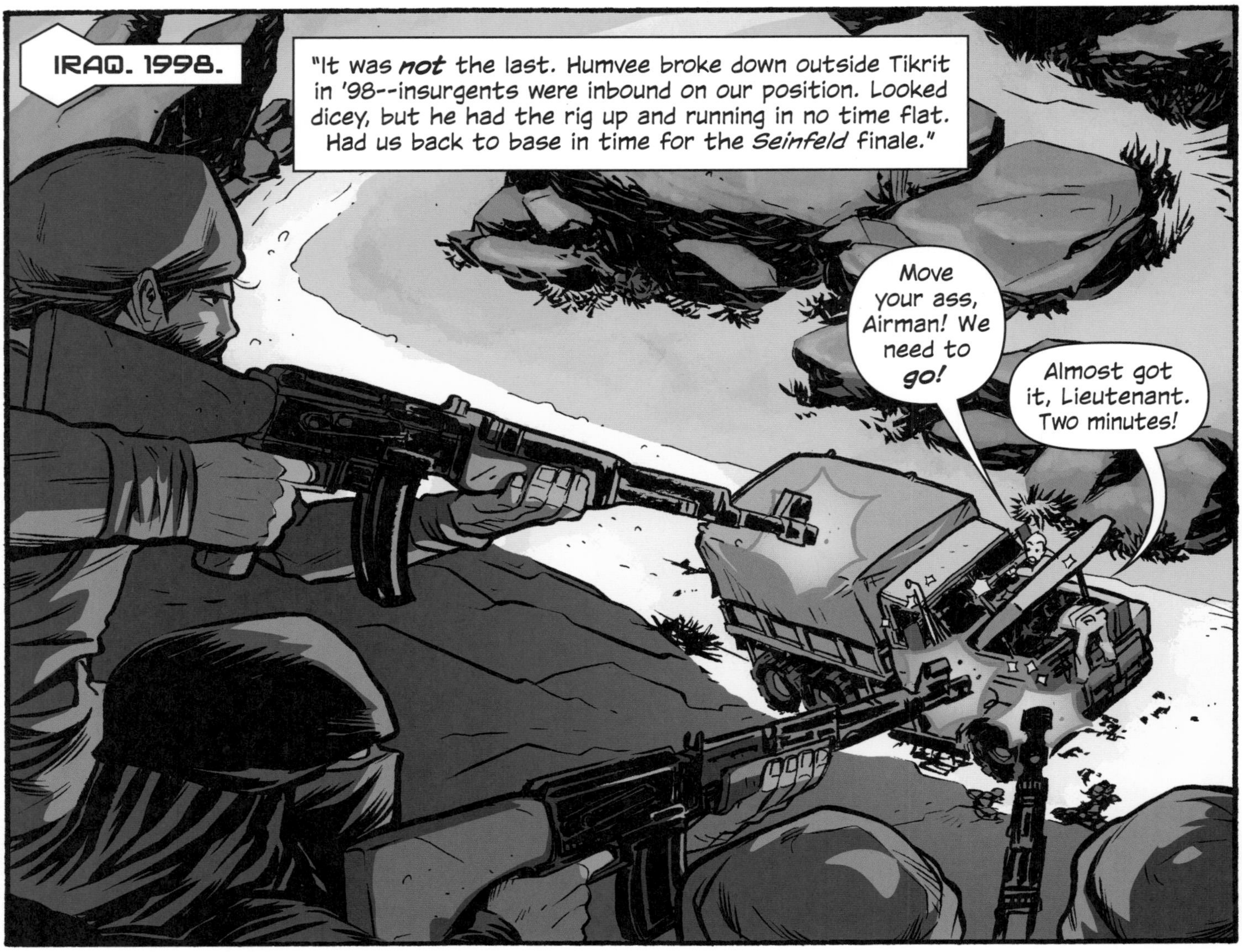
IRAQ. 1998.
"It was *not* the last. Humvee broke down outside Tikrit in '98--insurgents were inbound on our position. Looked dicey, but he had the rig up and running in no time flat. Had us back to base in time for the *Seinfeld* finale."
Move your ass, Airman! We need to *go!*
Almost got it, Lieutenant. Two minutes!

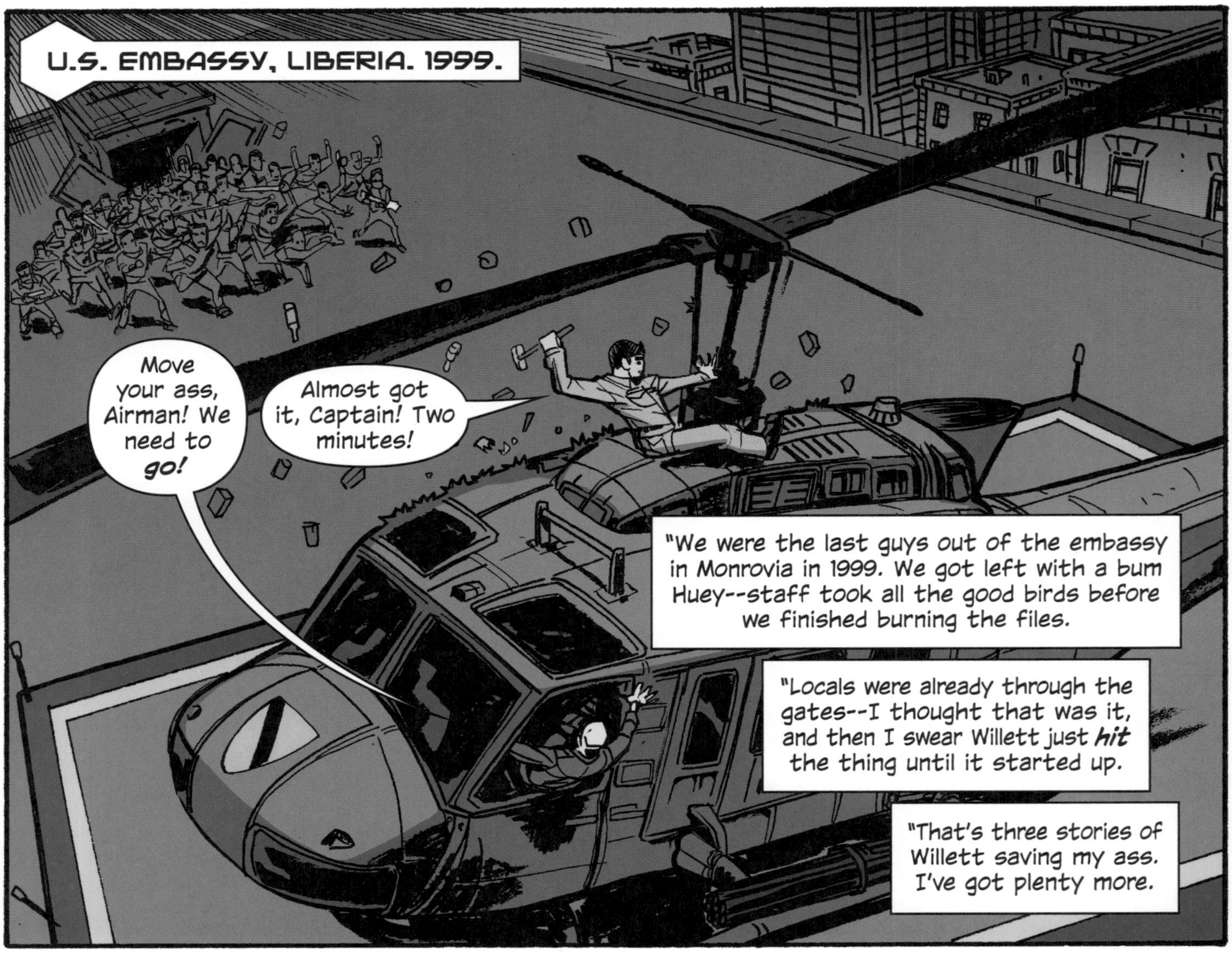
U.S. EMBASSY, LIBERIA. 1999.
Move your ass, Airman! We need to *go!*
Almost got it, Captain! Two minutes!
"We were the last guys out of the embassy in Monrovia in 1999. We got left with a bum Huey--staff took all the good birds before we finished burning the files.
"Locals were already through the gates--I thought that was it, and then I swear Willett just *hit* the thing until it started up.
"That's three stories of Willett saving my ass. I've got plenty more.

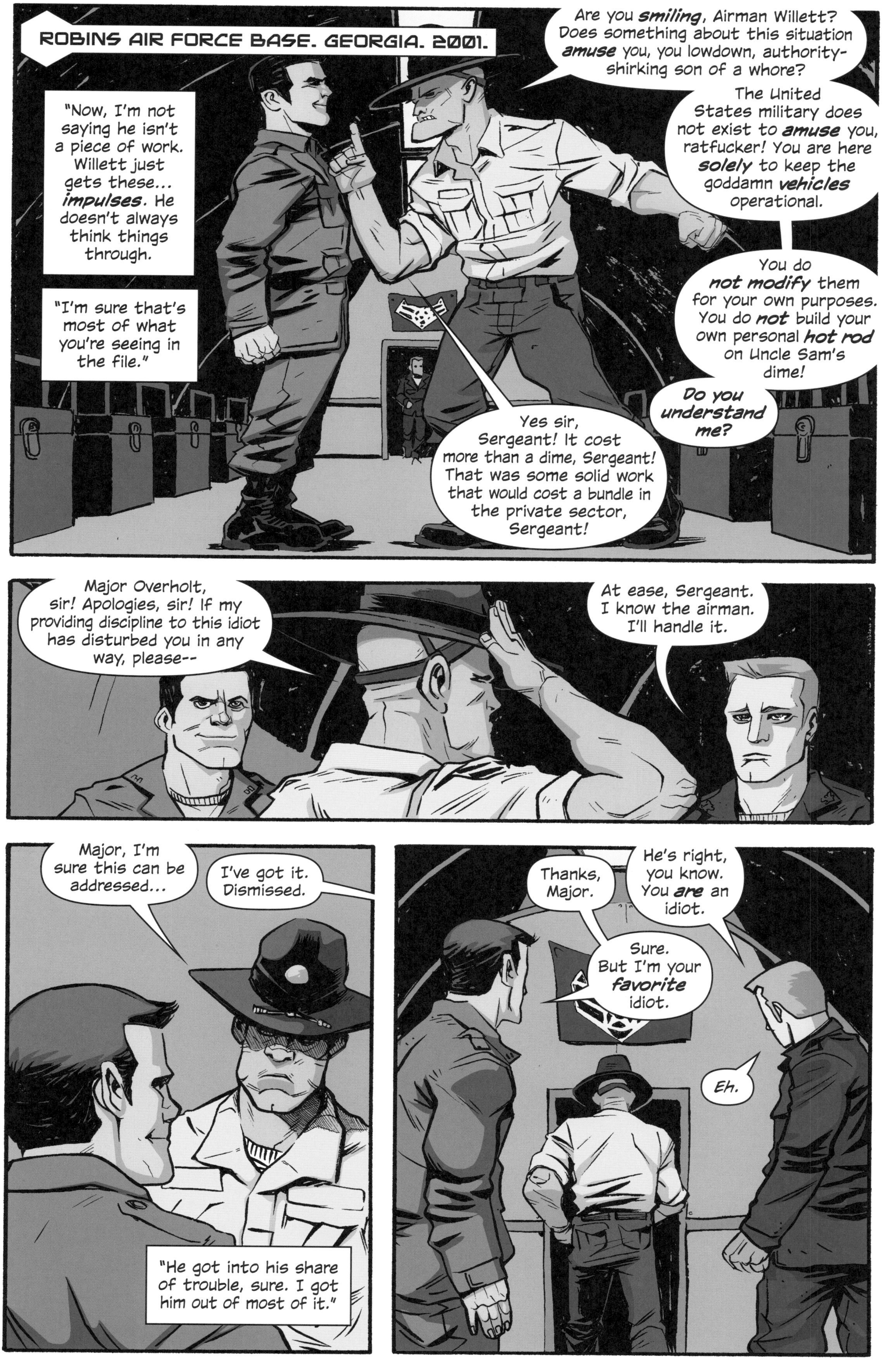

ROBINS AIR FORCE BASE. GEORGIA. 2001.
"Now, I'm not saying he isn't a piece of work. Willett just gets these... impulses. He doesn't always think things through.
"I'm sure that's most of what you're seeing in the file."
Are you smiling, Airman Willett? Does something about this situation amuse you, you lowdown, authority-shirking son of a whore?
The United States military does not exist to amuse you, ratfucker! You are here solely to keep the goddamn vehicles operational.
You do not modify them for your own purposes. You do not build your own personal hot rod on Uncle Sam's dime!
Do you understand me?
Yes sir, Sergeant! It cost more than a dime, Sergeant! That was some solid work that would cost a bundle in the private sector, Sergeant!
Major Overholt, sir! Apologies, sir! If my providing discipline to this idiot has disturbed you in any way, please--
At ease, Sergeant. I know the airman. I'll handle it.
Major, I'm sure this can be addressed...
I've got it. Dismissed.
"He got into his share of trouble, sure. I got him out of most of it."
Thanks, Major.
He's right, you know. You are an idiot.
Sure. But I'm your favorite idiot.
Eh.

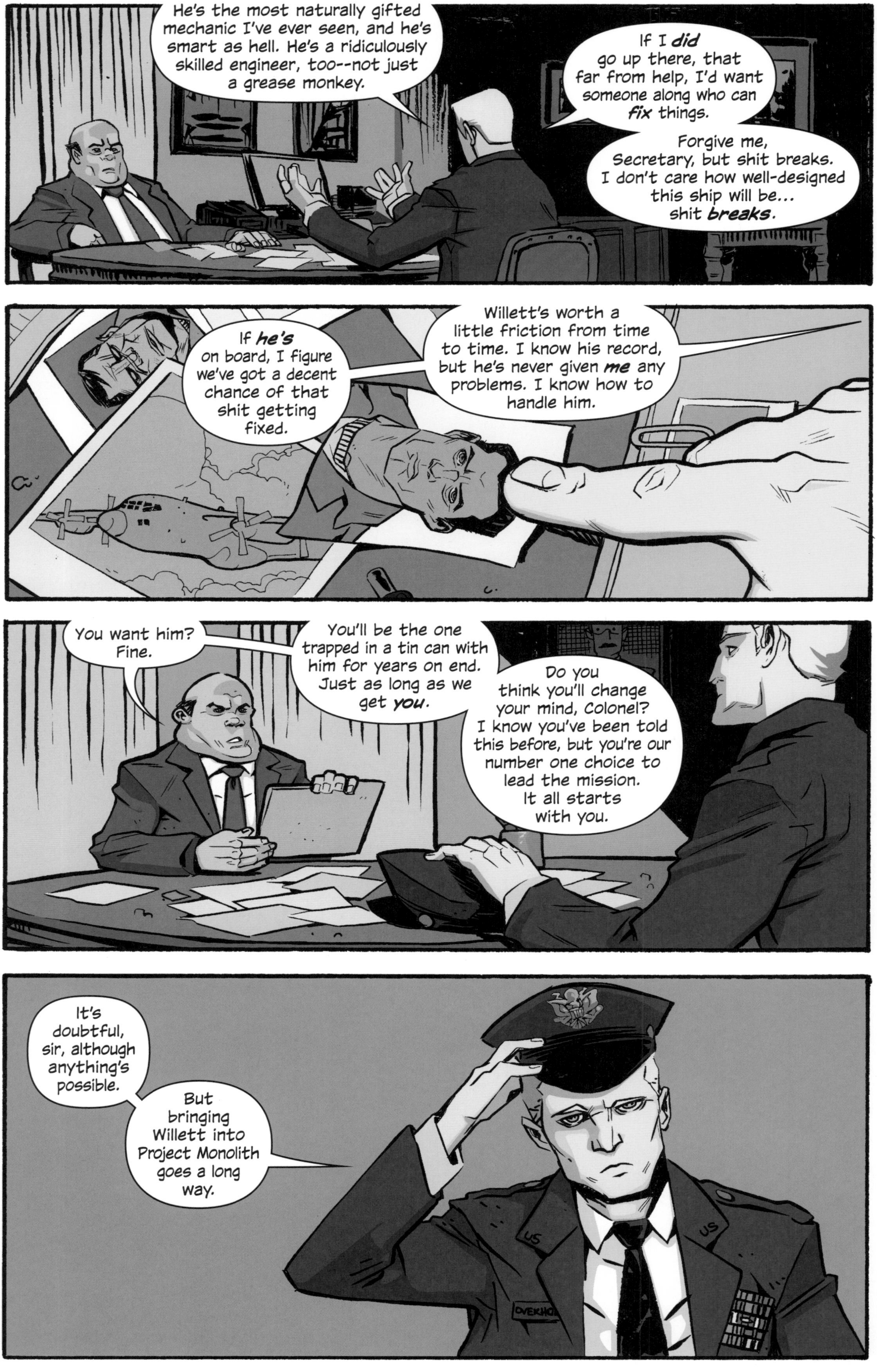
He's the most naturally gifted mechanic I've ever seen, and he's smart as hell. He's a ridiculously skilled engineer, too--not just a grease monkey.
If I *did* go up there, that far from help, I'd want someone along who can *fix* things.
Forgive me, Secretary, but shit breaks. I don't care how well-designed this ship will be... shit *breaks*.
If *he's* on board, I figure we've got a decent chance of that shit getting fixed.
Willett's worth a little friction from time to time. I know his record, but he's never given *me* any problems. I know how to handle him.
You want him? Fine.
You'll be the one trapped in a tin can with him for years on end. Just as long as we get *you*.
Do you think you'll change your mind, Colonel? I know you've been told this before, but you're our number one choice to lead the mission. It all starts with you.
It's doubtful, sir, although anything's possible.
But bringing Willett into Project Monolith goes a long way.

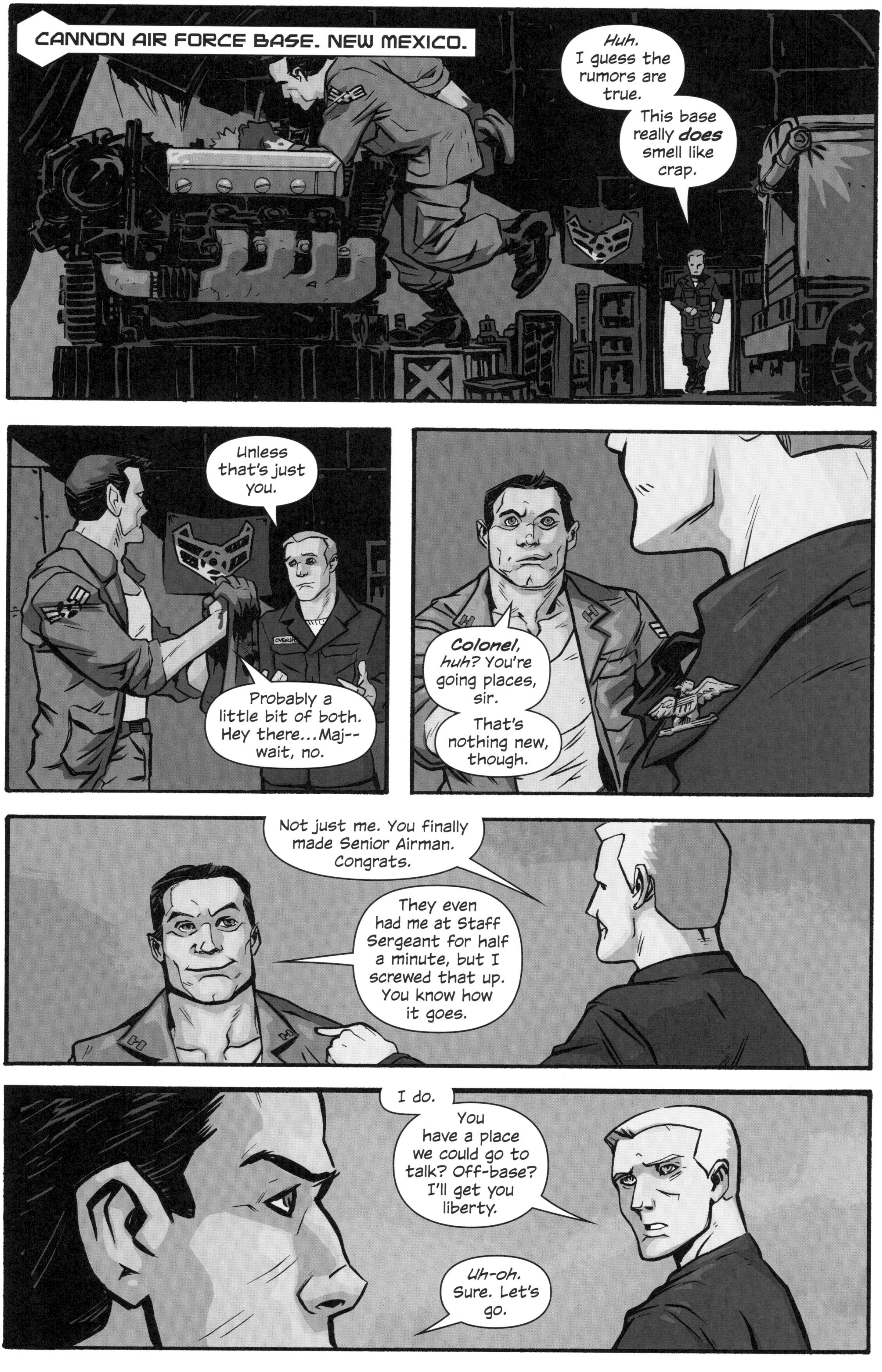
CANNON AIR FORCE BASE. NEW MEXICO.
Huh. I guess the rumors are true.
This base really does smell like crap.
Unless that's just you.
Probably a little bit of both. Hey there...Maj--wait, no.
Colonel, huh? You're going places, sir.
That's nothing new, though.
Not just me. You finally made Senior Airman. Congrats.
They even had me at Staff Sergeant for half a minute, but I screwed that up. You know how it goes.
I do.
You have a place we could go to talk? Off-base? I'll get you liberty.
Uh-oh. Sure. Let's go.

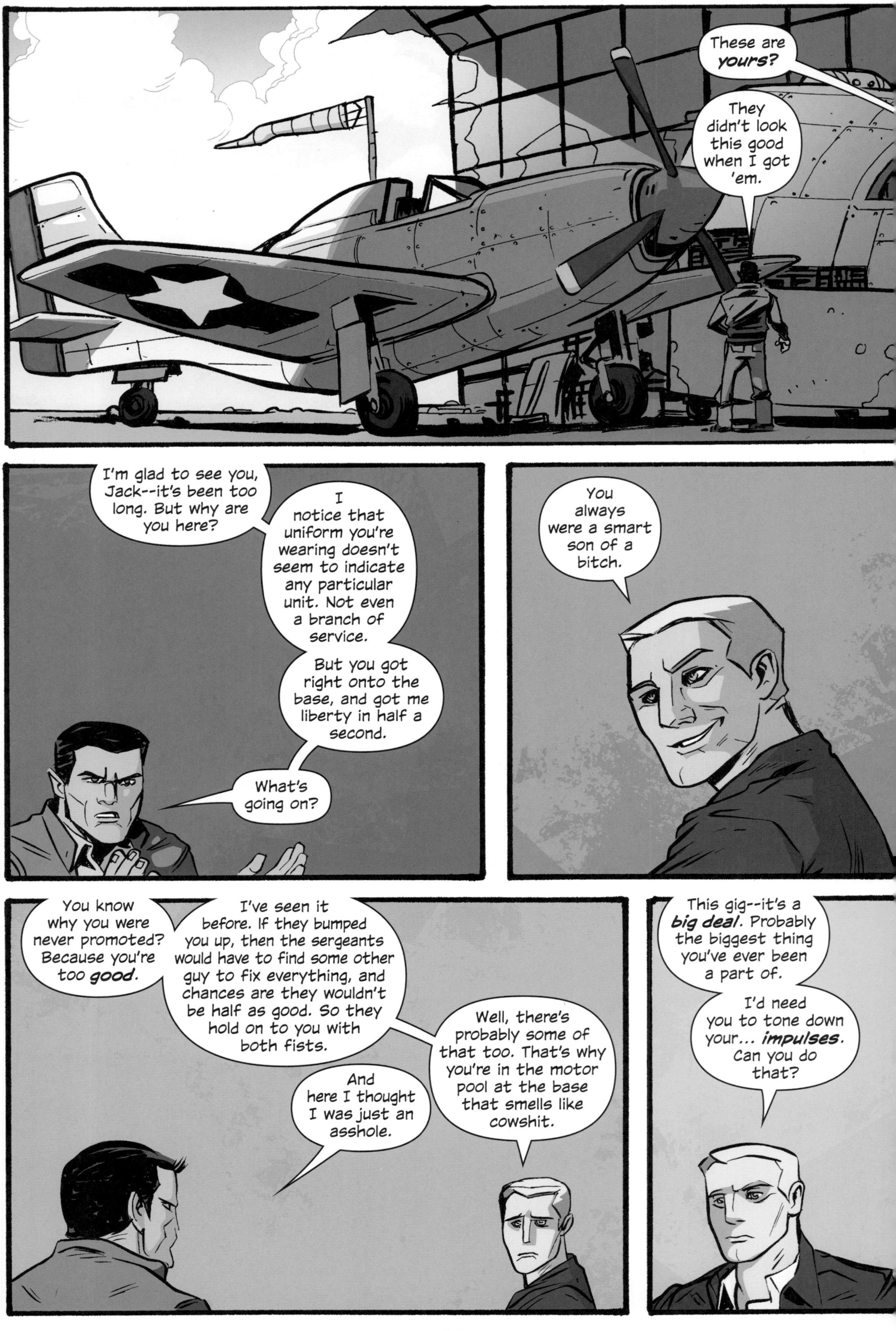
These are *yours?*
They didn't look this good when I got 'em.
I'm glad to see you, Jack--it's been too long. But why are you here?
I notice that uniform you're wearing doesn't seem to indicate any particular unit. Not even a branch of service.
But you got right onto the base, and got me liberty in half a second.
What's going on?
You always were a smart son of a bitch.
You know why you were never promoted? Because you're too *good*.
I've seen it before. If they bumped you up, then the sergeants would have to find some other guy to fix everything, and chances are they wouldn't be half as good. So they hold on to you with both fists.
And here I thought I was just an asshole.
Well, there's probably some of that too. That's why you're in the motor pool at the base that smells like cowshit.
This gig--it's a *big deal*. Probably the biggest thing you've ever been a part of.
I'd need you to tone down your... *impulses*. Can you do that?

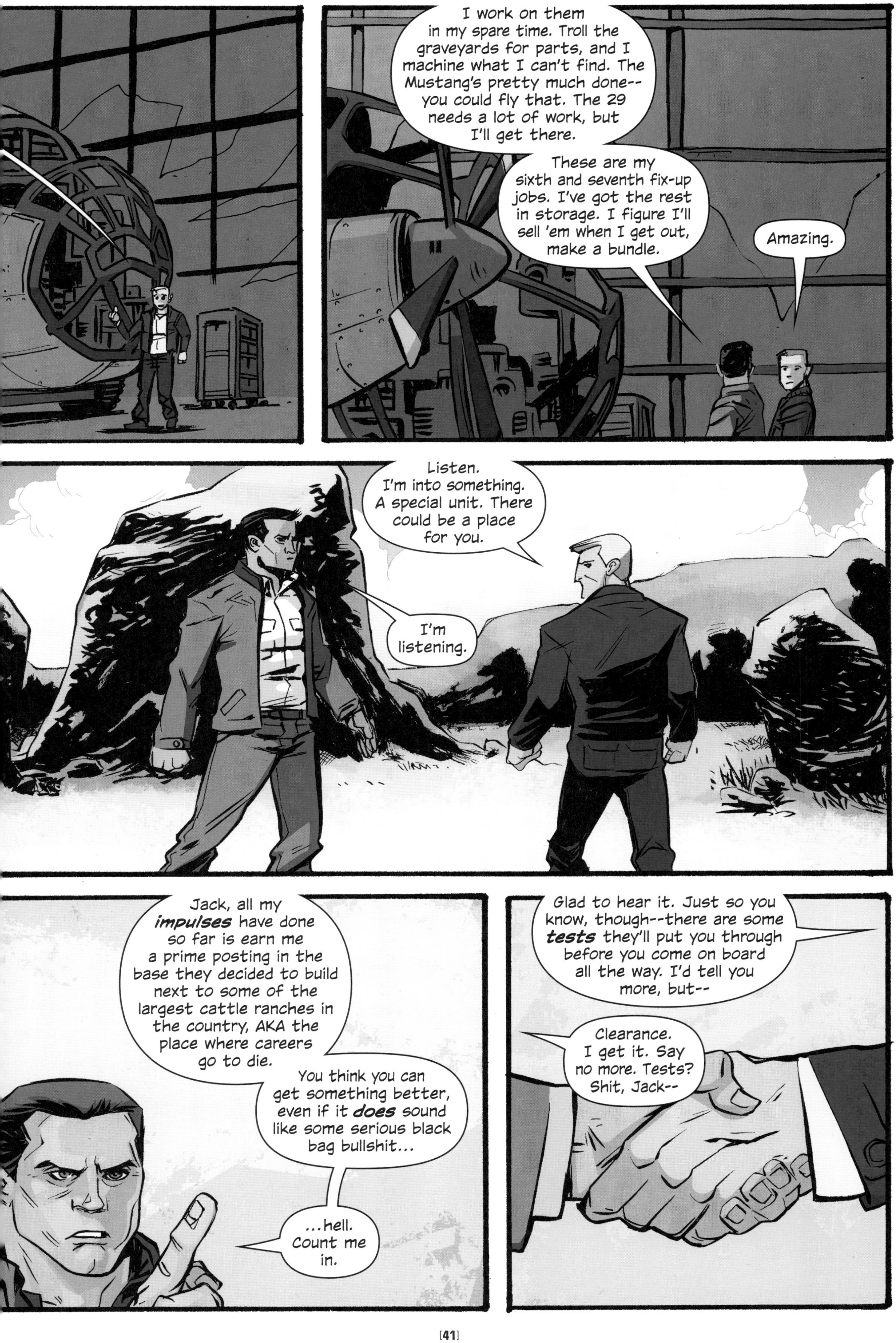

I work on them in my spare time. Troll the graveyards for parts, and I machine what I can't find. The Mustang's pretty much done-- you could fly that. The 29 needs a lot of work, but I'll get there.
These are my sixth and seventh fix-up jobs. I've got the rest in storage. I figure I'll sell 'em when I get out, make a bundle.
Amazing.
Listen. I'm into something. A special unit. There could be a place for you.
I'm listening.
Jack, all my *impulses* have done so far is earn me a prime posting in the base they decided to build next to some of the largest cattle ranches in the country, AKA the place where careers go to die.
You think you can get something better, even if it *does* sound like some serious black bag bullshit...
...hell. Count me in.
Glad to hear it. Just so you know, though--there are some *tests* they'll put you through before you come on board all the way. I'd tell you more, but--
Clearance. I get it. Say no more. Tests? Shit, Jack--

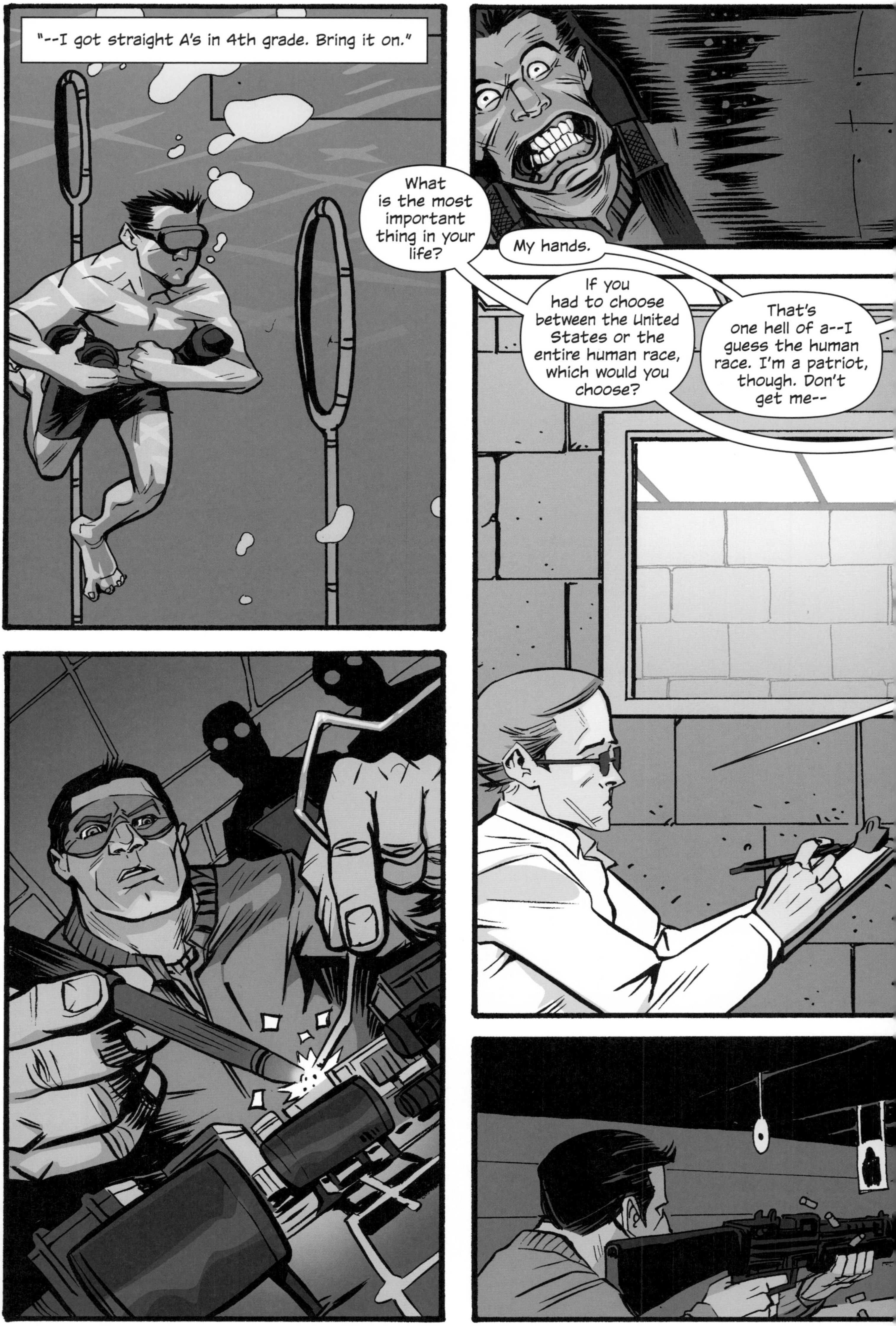
"--I got straight A's in 4th grade. Bring it on."
What is the most important thing in your life?
My hands.
If you had to choose between the United States or the entire human race, which would you choose?
That's one hell of a--I guess the human race. I'm a patriot, though. Don't get me--

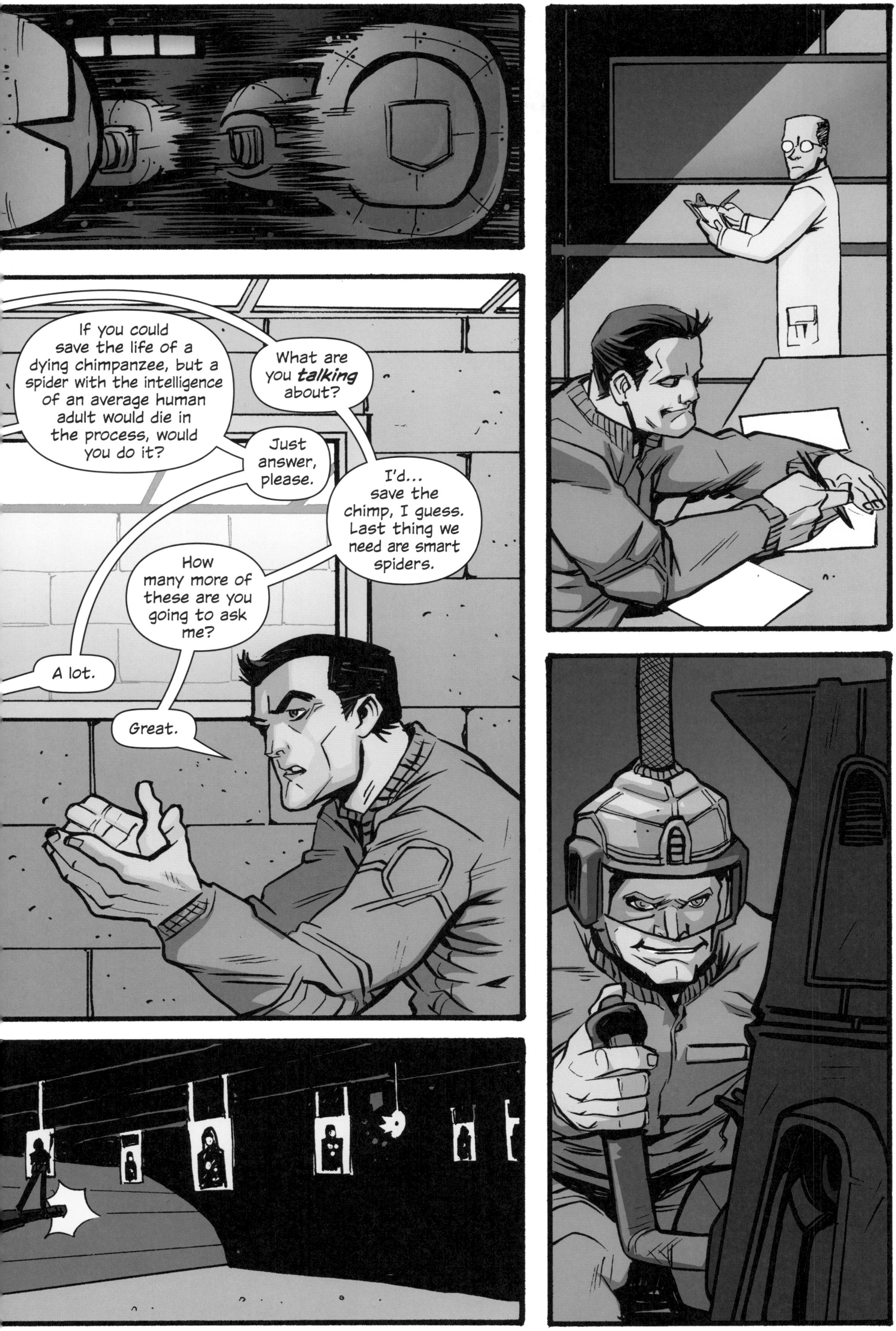
If you could save the life of a dying chimpanzee, but a spider with the intelligence of an average human adult would die in the process, would you do it?
What are you *talking* about?
Just answer, please.
I'd... save the chimp, I guess. Last thing we need are smart spiders.
How many more of these are you going to ask me?
A lot.
Great.

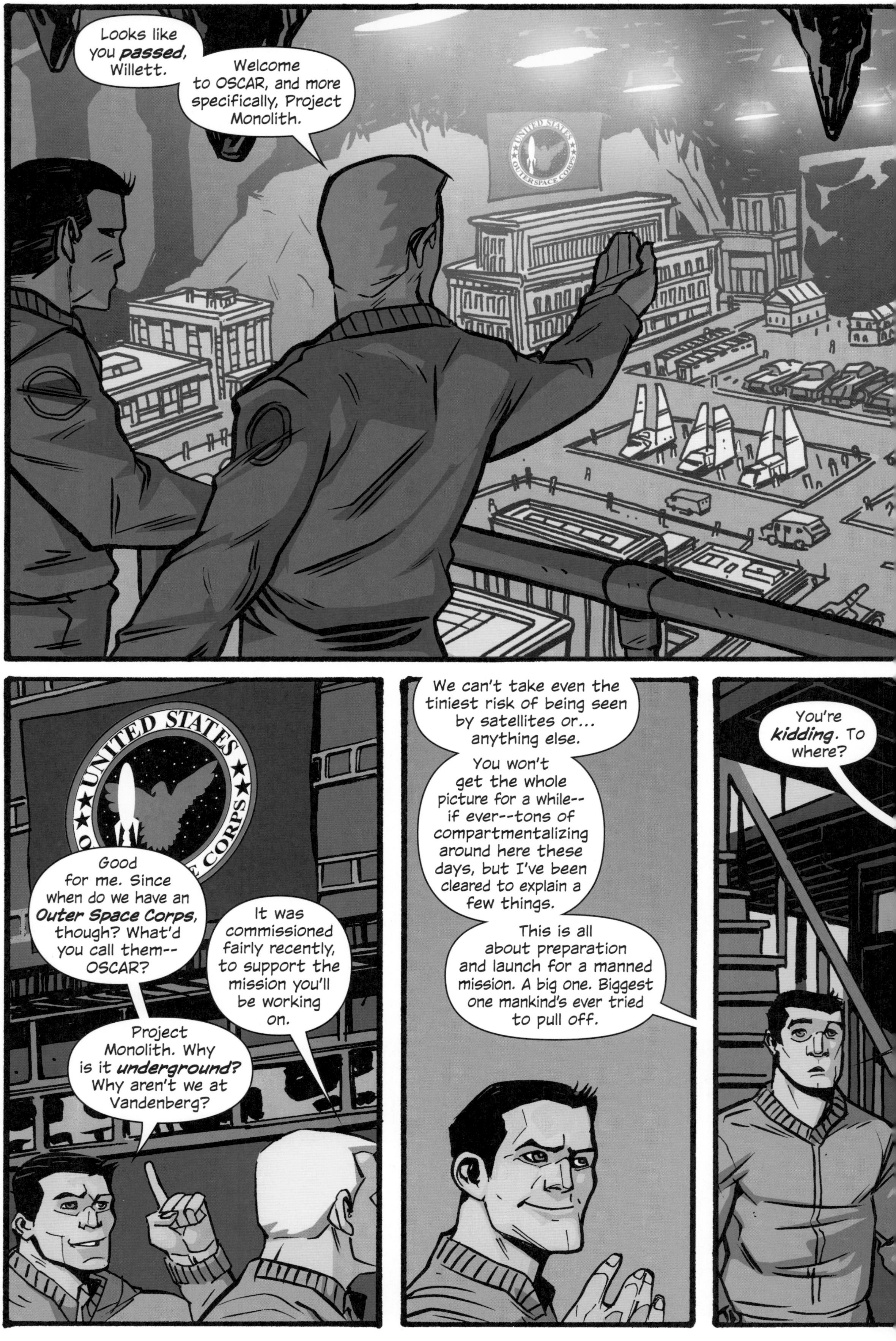

Looks like you *passed*, Willett.
Welcome to OSCAR, and more specifically, Project Monolith.
UNITED STATES OUTERSPACE CORPS
Good for me. Since when do we have an *Outer Space Corps*, though? What'd you call them--OSCAR?
It was commissioned fairly recently, to support the mission you'll be working on.
Project Monolith. Why is it *underground?* Why aren't we at Vandenberg?
We can't take even the tiniest risk of being seen by satellites or... anything else.
You won't get the whole picture for a while--if ever--tons of compartmentalizing around here these days, but I've been cleared to explain a few things.
This is all about preparation and launch for a manned mission. A big one. Biggest one mankind's ever tried to pull off.
You're *kidding*. To where?

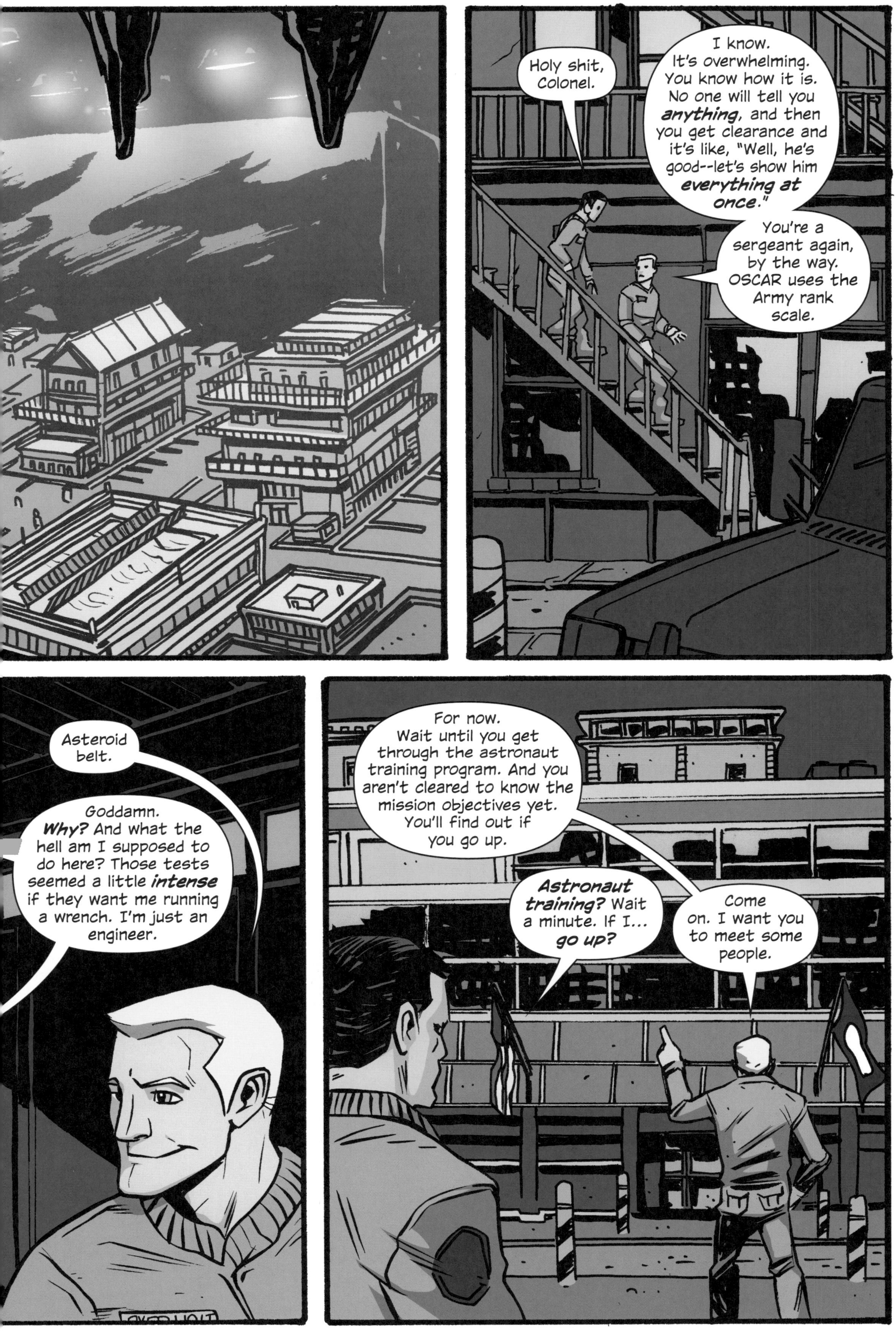
Holy shit, Colonel.
I know. It's overwhelming. You know how it is. No one will tell you **anything**, and then you get clearance and it's like, "Well, he's good--let's show him **everything at once**."
You're a sergeant again, by the way. OSCAR uses the Army rank scale.
Asteroid belt.
Goddamn. **Why?** And what the hell am I supposed to do here? Those tests seemed a little **intense** if they want me running a wrench. I'm just an engineer.
For now. Wait until you get through the astronaut training program. And you aren't cleared to know the mission objectives yet. You'll find out if you go up.
Astronaut training? Wait a minute. If I... **go up?**
Come on. I want you to meet some people.

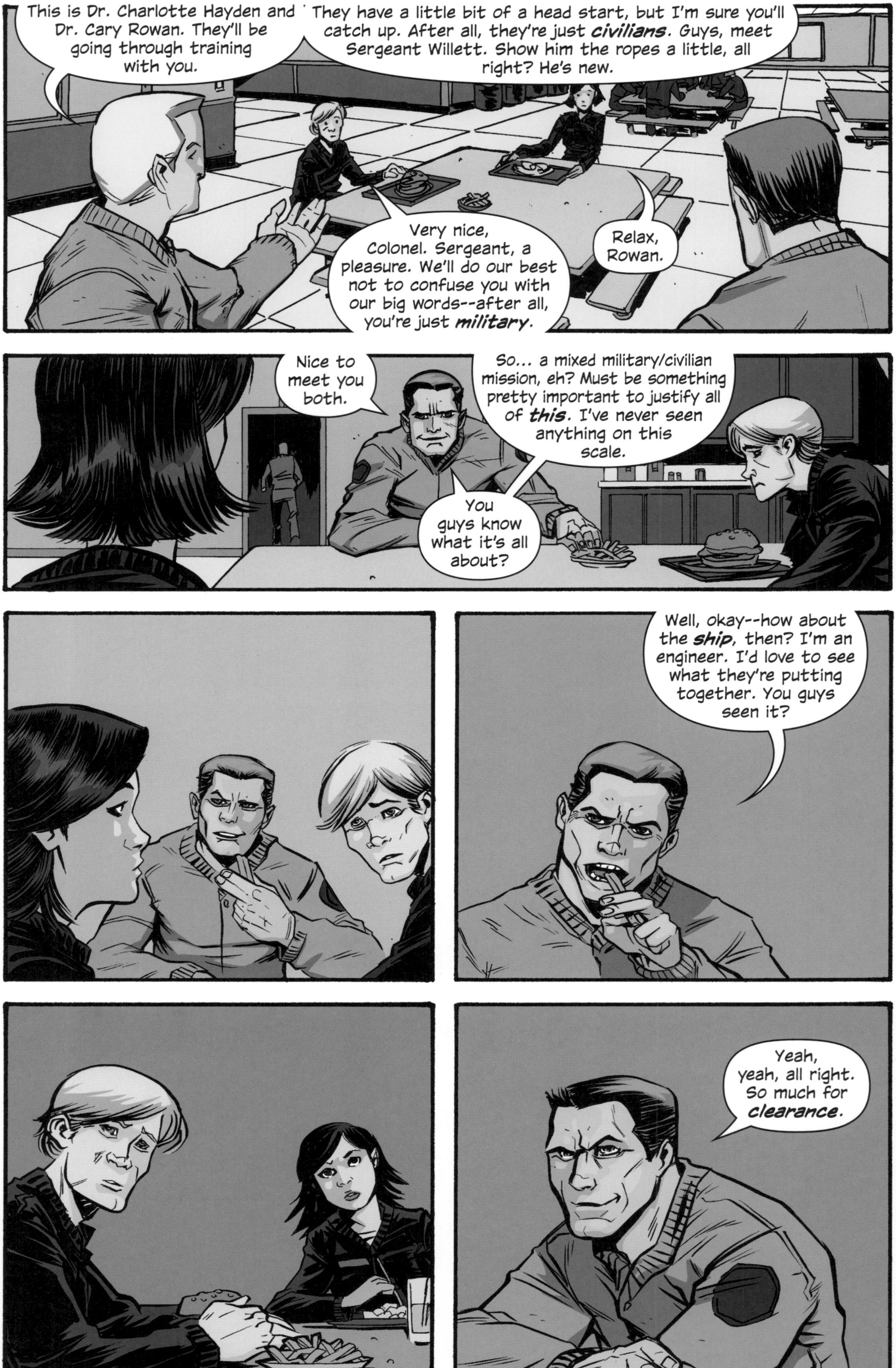
This is Dr. Charlotte Hayden and Dr. Cary Rowan. They'll be going through training with you.
They have a little bit of a head start, but I'm sure you'll catch up. After all, they're just *civilians*. Guys, meet Sergeant Willett. Show him the ropes a little, all right? He's new.
Very nice, Colonel. Sergeant, a pleasure. We'll do our best not to confuse you with our big words--after all, you're just *military*.
Relax, Rowan.
Nice to meet you both.
So... a mixed military/civilian mission, eh? Must be something pretty important to justify all of *this*. I've never seen anything on this scale.
You guys know what it's all about?
Well, okay--how about the *ship*, then? I'm an engineer. I'd love to see what they're putting together. You guys seen it?
Yeah, yeah, all right. So much for *clearance*.

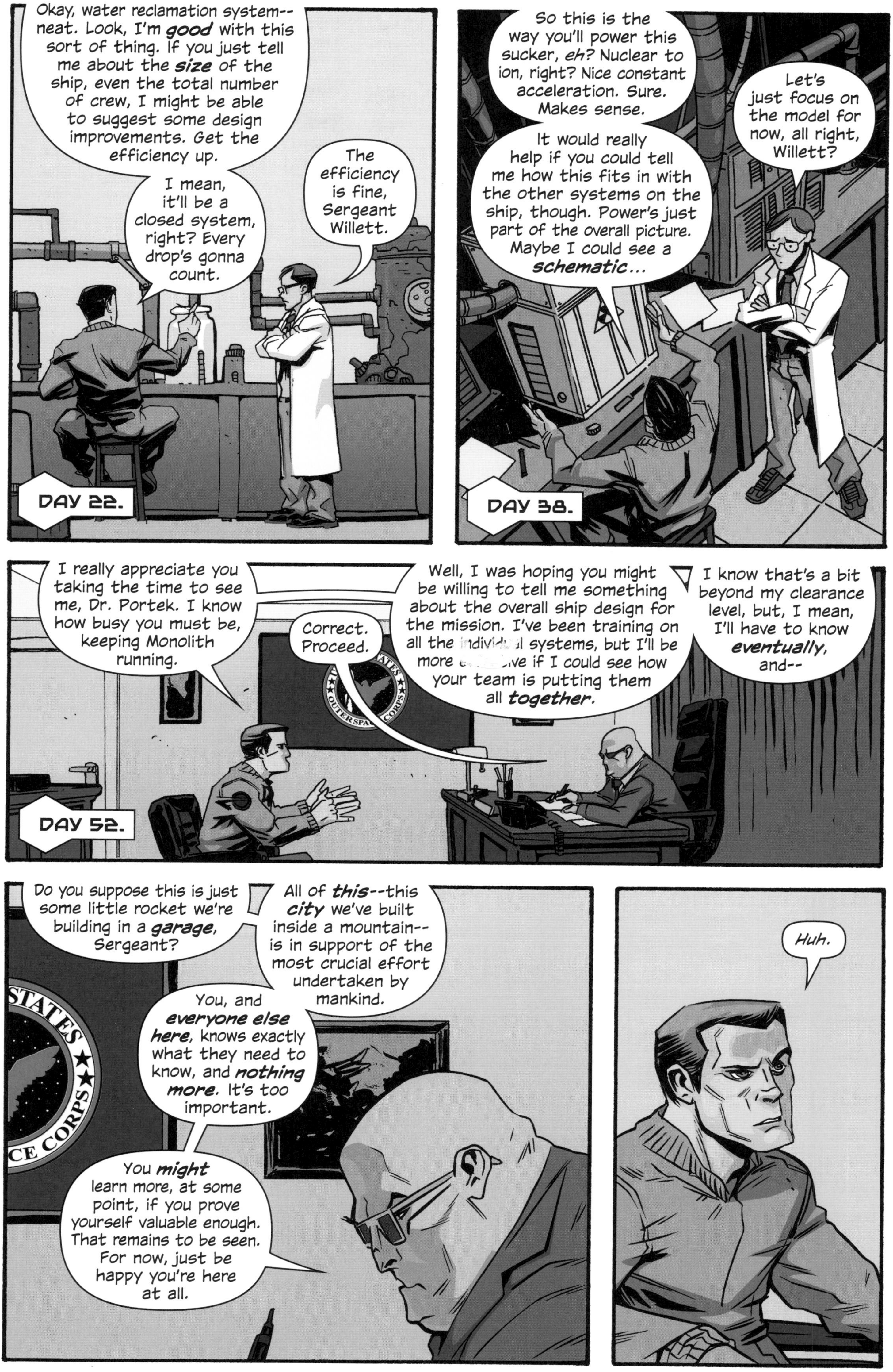
Okay, water reclamation system--neat. Look, I'm **good** with this sort of thing. If you just tell me about the **size** of the ship, even the total number of crew, I might be able to suggest some design improvements. Get the efficiency up.
I mean, it'll be a closed system, right? Every drop's gonna count.
The efficiency is fine, Sergeant Willett.
DAY 22.
So this is the way you'll power this sucker, *eh*? Nuclear to ion, right? Nice constant acceleration. Sure. Makes sense.
It would really help if you could tell me how this fits in with the other systems on the ship, though. Power's just part of the overall picture. Maybe I could see a **schematic...**
Let's just focus on the model for now, all right, Willett?
DAY 38.
I really appreciate you taking the time to see me, Dr. Portek. I know how busy you must be, keeping Monolith running.
Correct. Proceed.
Well, I was hoping you might be willing to tell me something about the overall ship design for the mission. I've been training on all the individual systems, but I'll be more e...ive if I could see how your team is putting them all **together**.
I know that's a bit beyond my clearance level, but, I mean, I'll have to know **eventually**, and--
DAY 52.
Do you suppose this is just some little rocket we're building in a **garage**, Sergeant?
All of **this**--this **city** we've built inside a mountain--is in support of the most crucial effort undertaken by mankind.
You, and **everyone else here**, knows exactly what they need to know, and **nothing more**. It's too important.
You **might** learn more, at some point, if you prove yourself valuable enough. That remains to be seen. For now, just be happy you're here at all.
Huh.

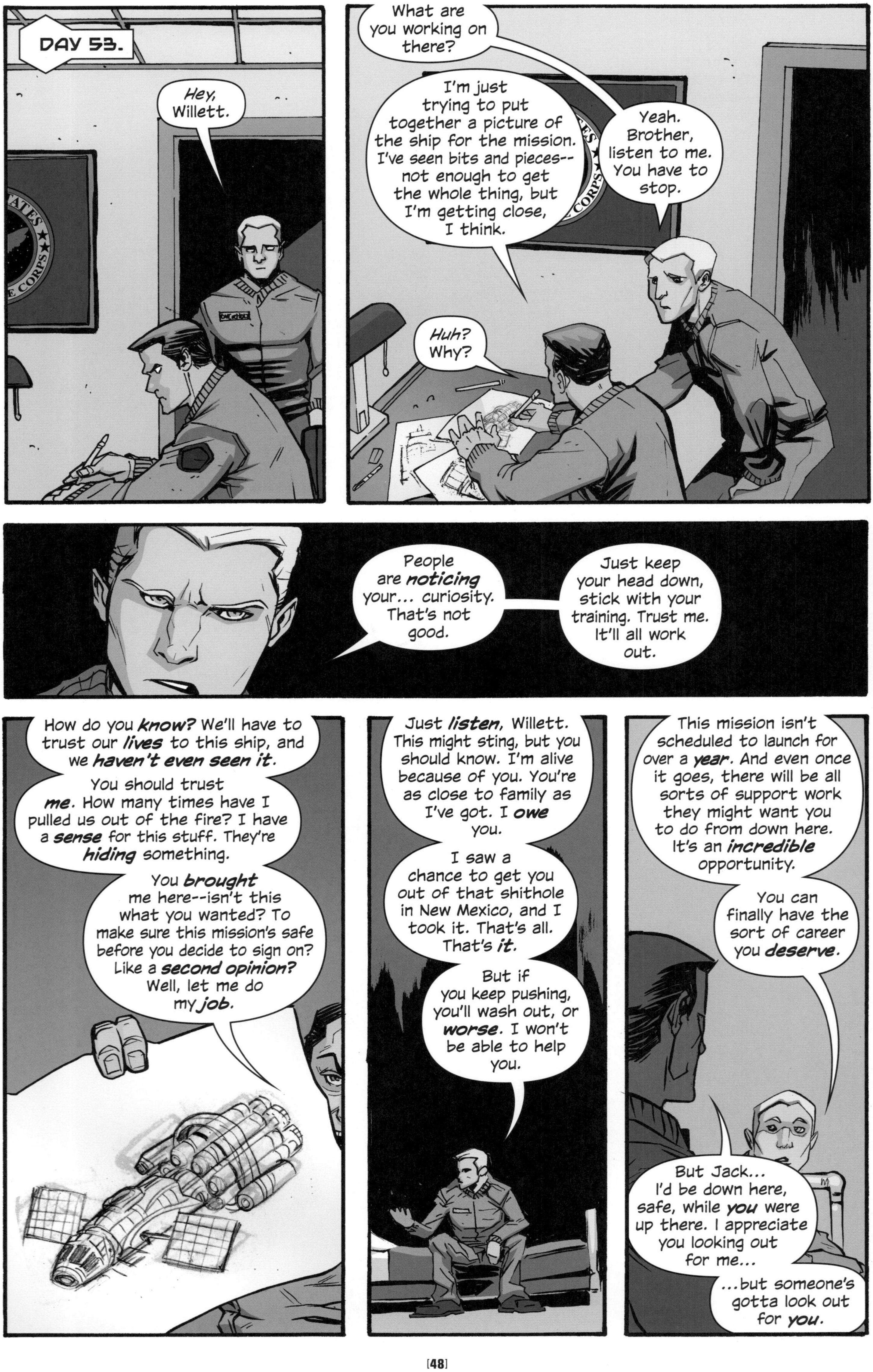
DAY 53.
Hey, Willett.
What are you working on there?
I'm just trying to put together a picture of the ship for the mission. I've seen bits and pieces--not enough to get the whole thing, but I'm getting close, I think.
Yeah. Brother, listen to me. You have to stop.
Huh? Why?
People are noticing your... curiosity. That's not good.
Just keep your head down, stick with your training. Trust me. It'll all work out.
How do you know? We'll have to trust our lives to this ship, and we haven't even seen it.
You should trust me. How many times have I pulled us out of the fire? I have a sense for this stuff. They're hiding something.
You brought me here--isn't this what you wanted? To make sure this mission's safe before you decide to sign on? Like a second opinion? Well, let me do my job.
Just listen, Willett. This might sting, but you should know. I'm alive because of you. You're as close to family as I've got. I owe you.
I saw a chance to get you out of that shithole in New Mexico, and I took it. That's all. That's it.
But if you keep pushing, you'll wash out, or worse. I won't be able to help you.
This mission isn't scheduled to launch for over a year. And even once it goes, there will be all sorts of support work they might want you to do from down here. It's an incredible opportunity.
You can finally have the sort of career you deserve.
But Jack... I'd be down here, safe, while you were up there. I appreciate you looking out for me...
...but someone's gotta look out for you.

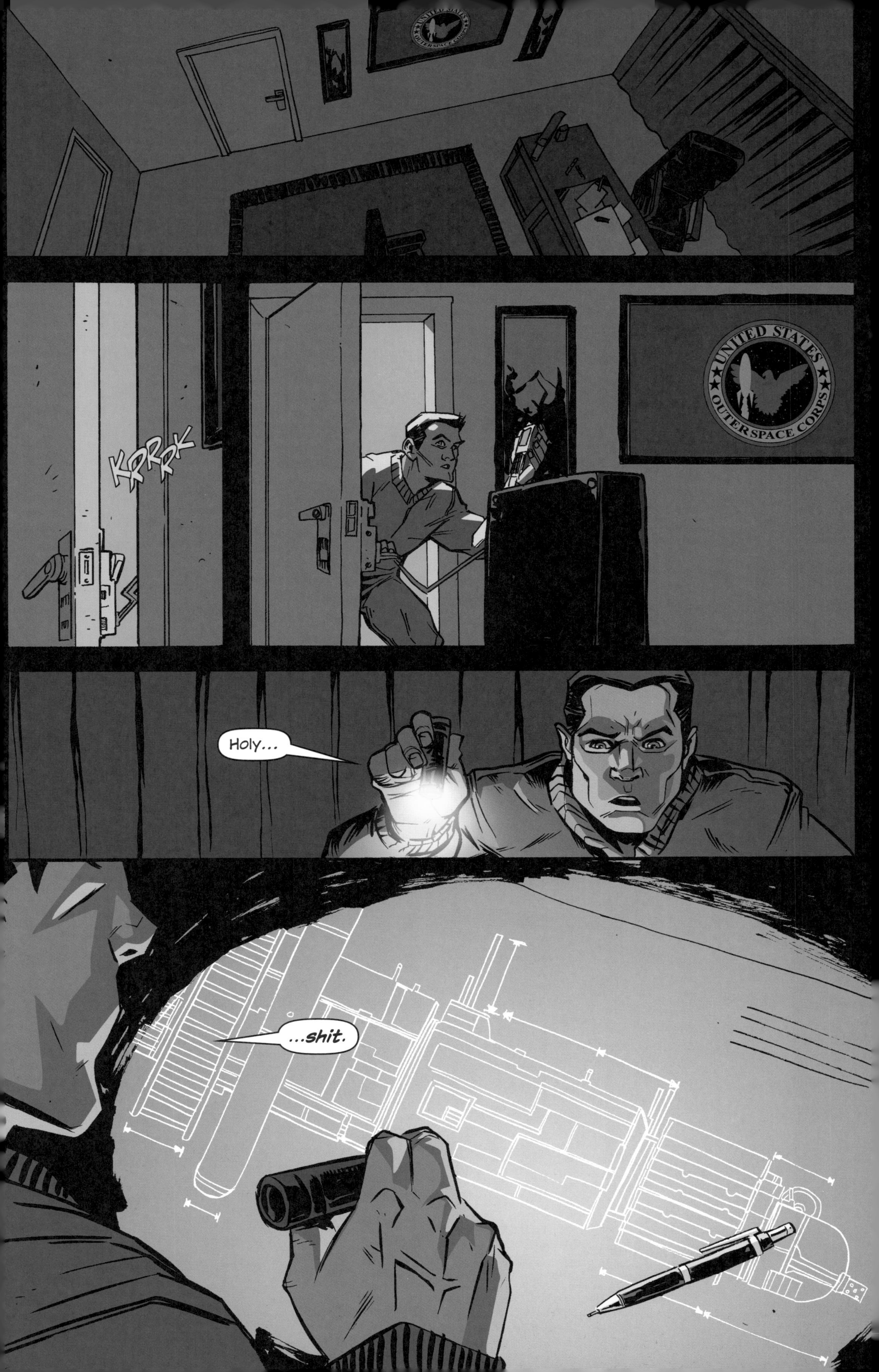
UNITED STATES OUTERSPACE CORPS
KRRRK
Holy...
...shit.

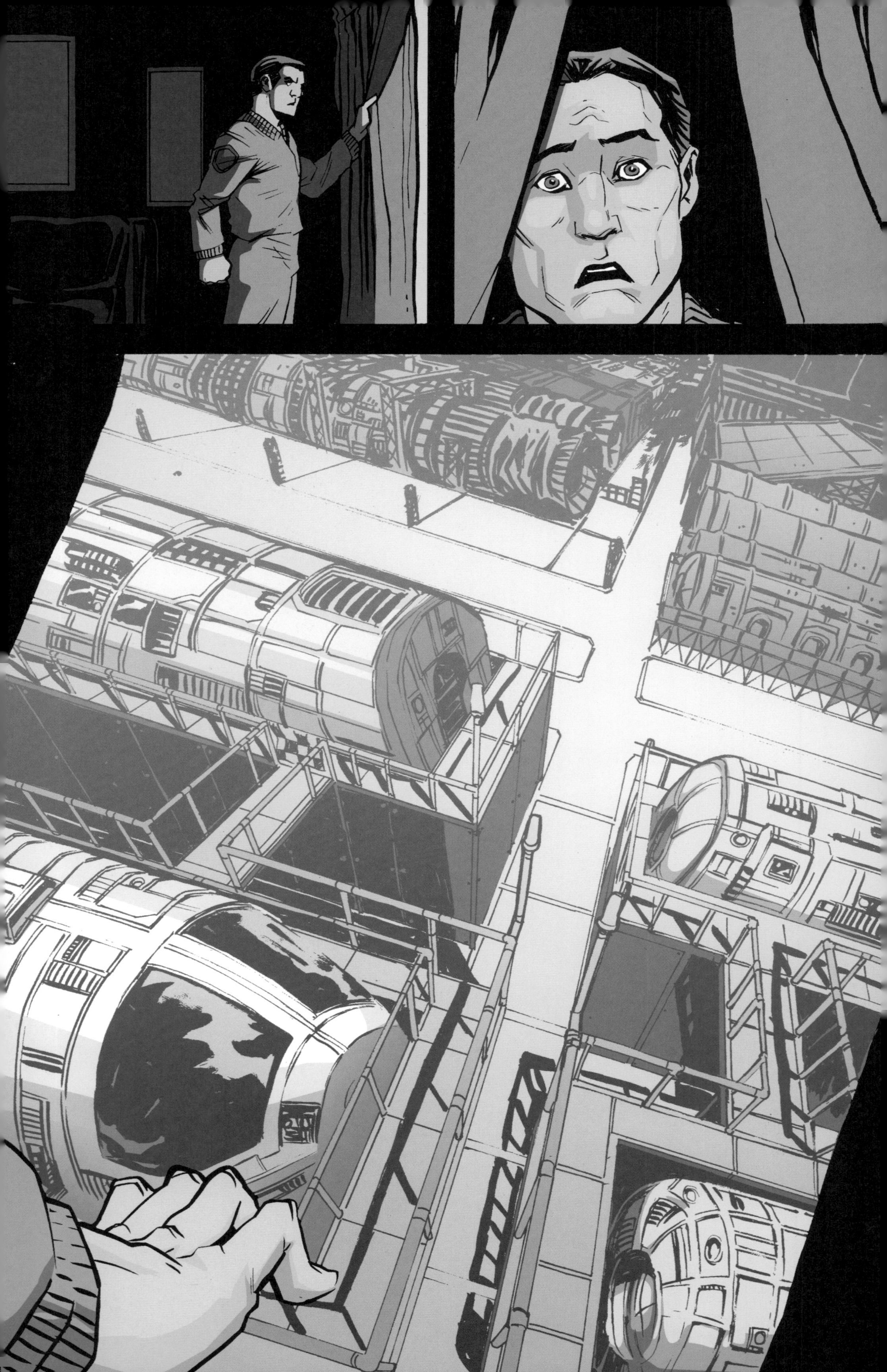

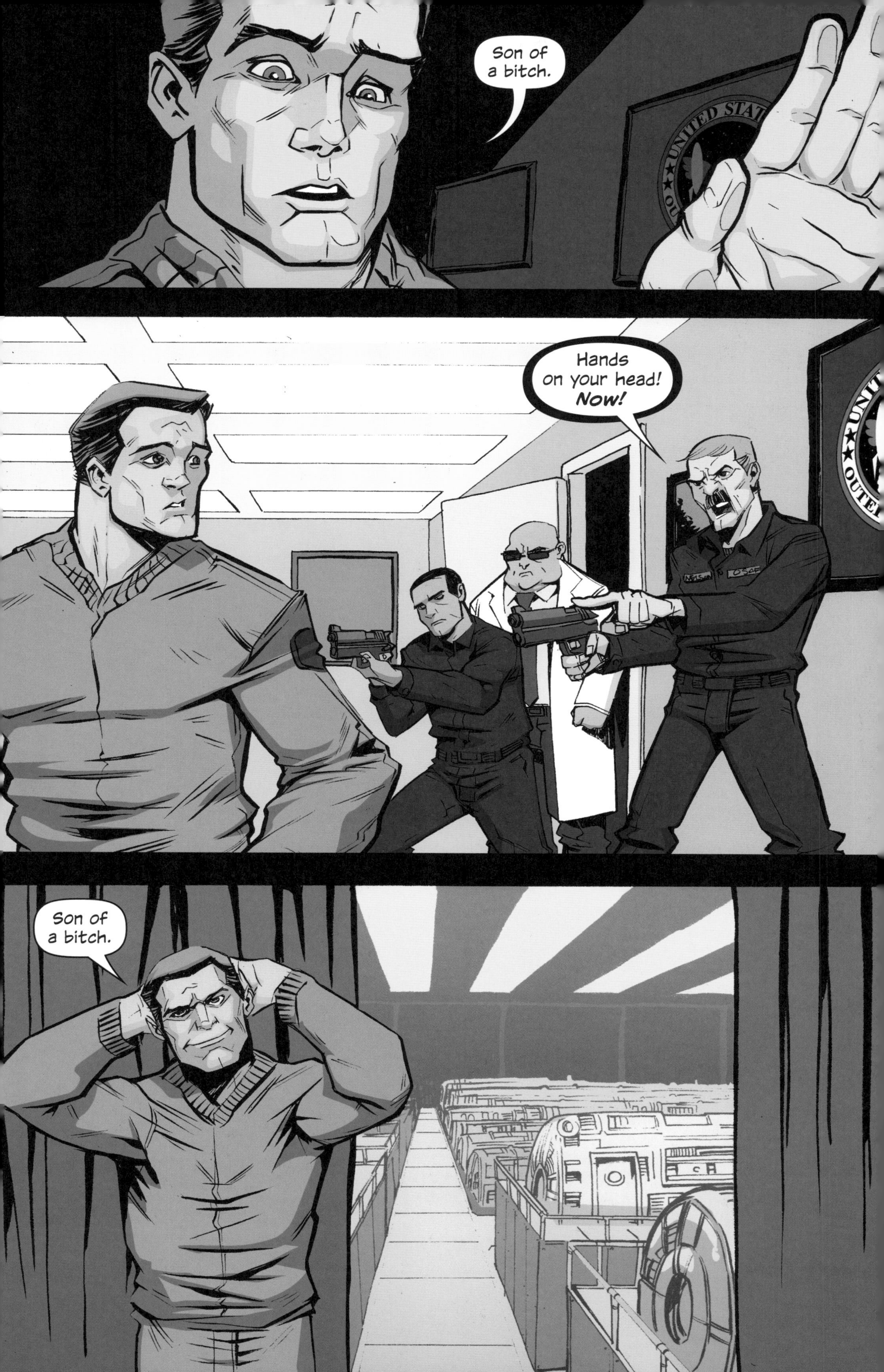
Son of a bitch.
Hands on your head! **Now!**
Son of a bitch.

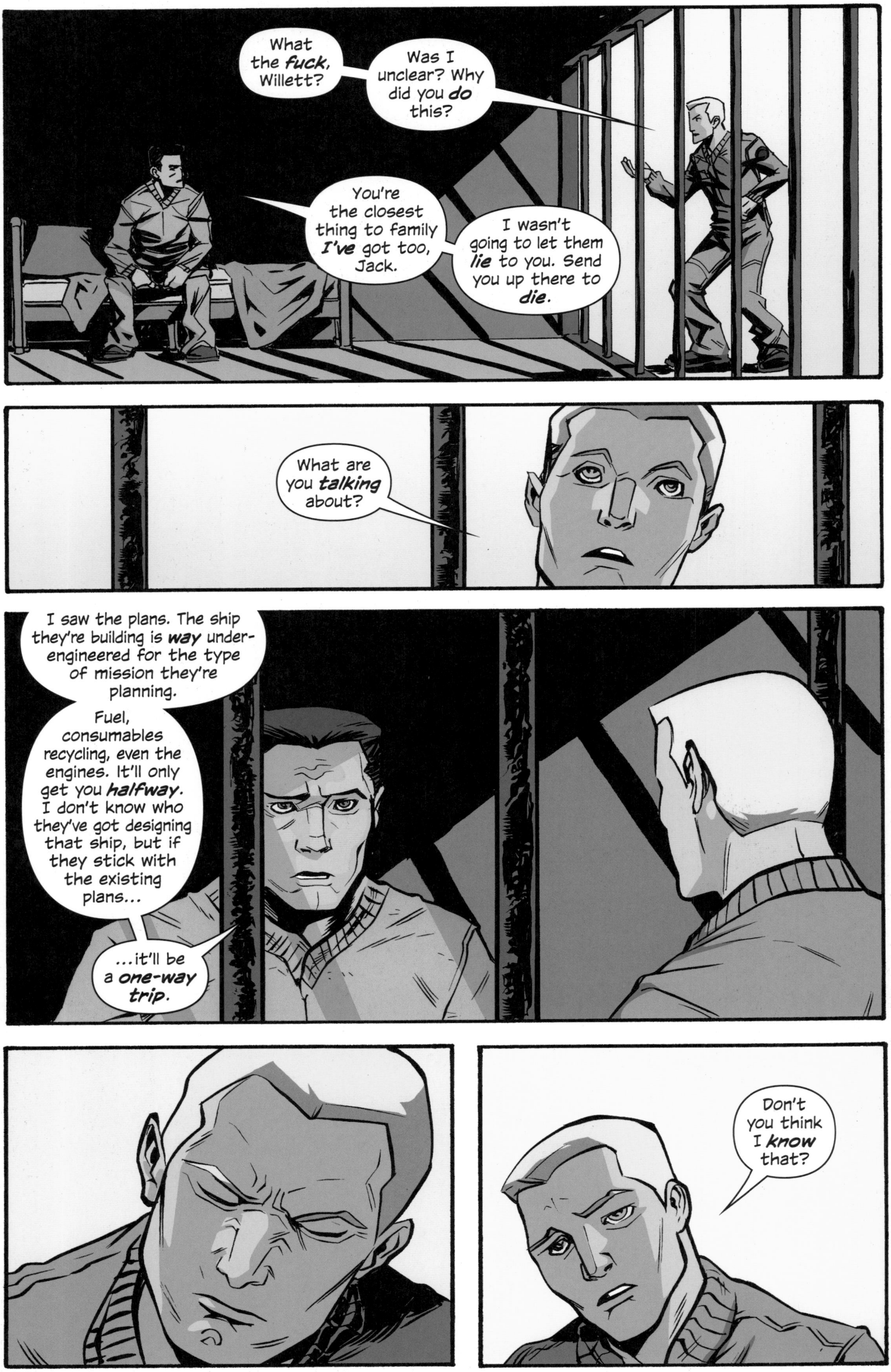
What the *fuck*, Willett?
Was I unclear? Why did you *do* this?
You're the closest thing to family *I've* got too, Jack.
I wasn't going to let them *lie* to you. Send you up there to *die*.
What are you *talking* about?
I saw the plans. The ship they're building is *way* under-engineered for the type of mission they're planning.
Fuel, consumables recycling, even the engines. It'll only get you *halfway*. I don't know who they've got designing that ship, but if they stick with the existing plans...
...it'll be a *one-way trip*.
Don't you think I *know* that?

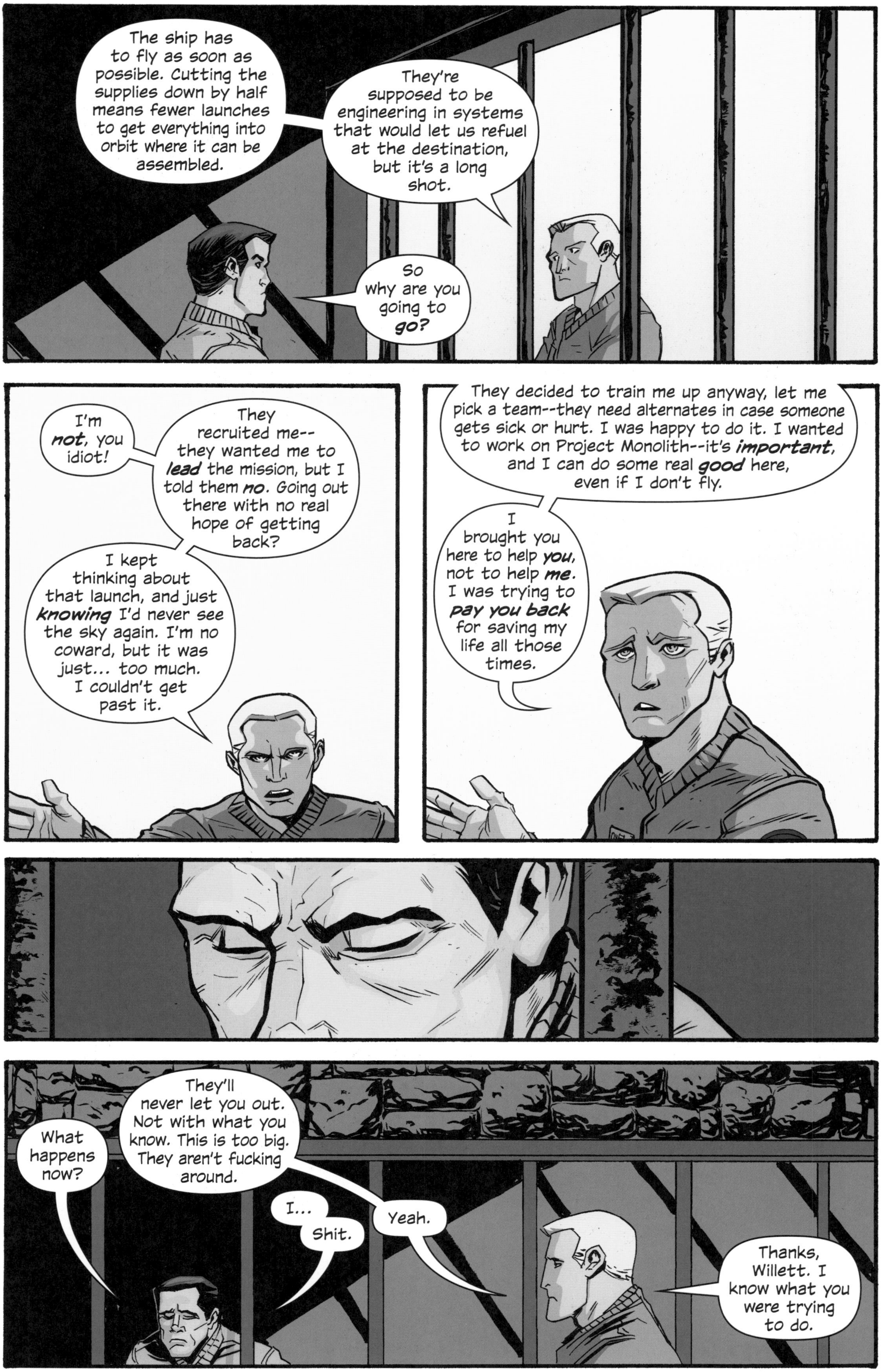
The ship has to fly as soon as possible. Cutting the supplies down by half means fewer launches to get everything into orbit where it can be assembled.
They're supposed to be engineering in systems that would let us refuel at the destination, but it's a long shot.
So why are you going to *go?*
I'm *not*, you idiot!
They recruited me--they wanted me to *lead* the mission, but I told them *no*. Going out there with no real hope of getting back?
I kept thinking about that launch, and just *knowing* I'd never see the sky again. I'm no coward, but it was just... too much. I couldn't get past it.
They decided to train me up anyway, let me pick a team--they need alternates in case someone gets sick or hurt. I was happy to do it. I wanted to work on Project Monolith--it's *important*, and I can do some real *good* here, even if I don't fly.
I brought you here to help *you*, not to help *me*. I was trying to *pay you back* for saving my life all those times.
What happens now?
They'll never let you out. Not with what you know. This is too big. They aren't fucking around.
I... Shit.
Yeah.
Thanks, Willett. I know what you were trying to do.

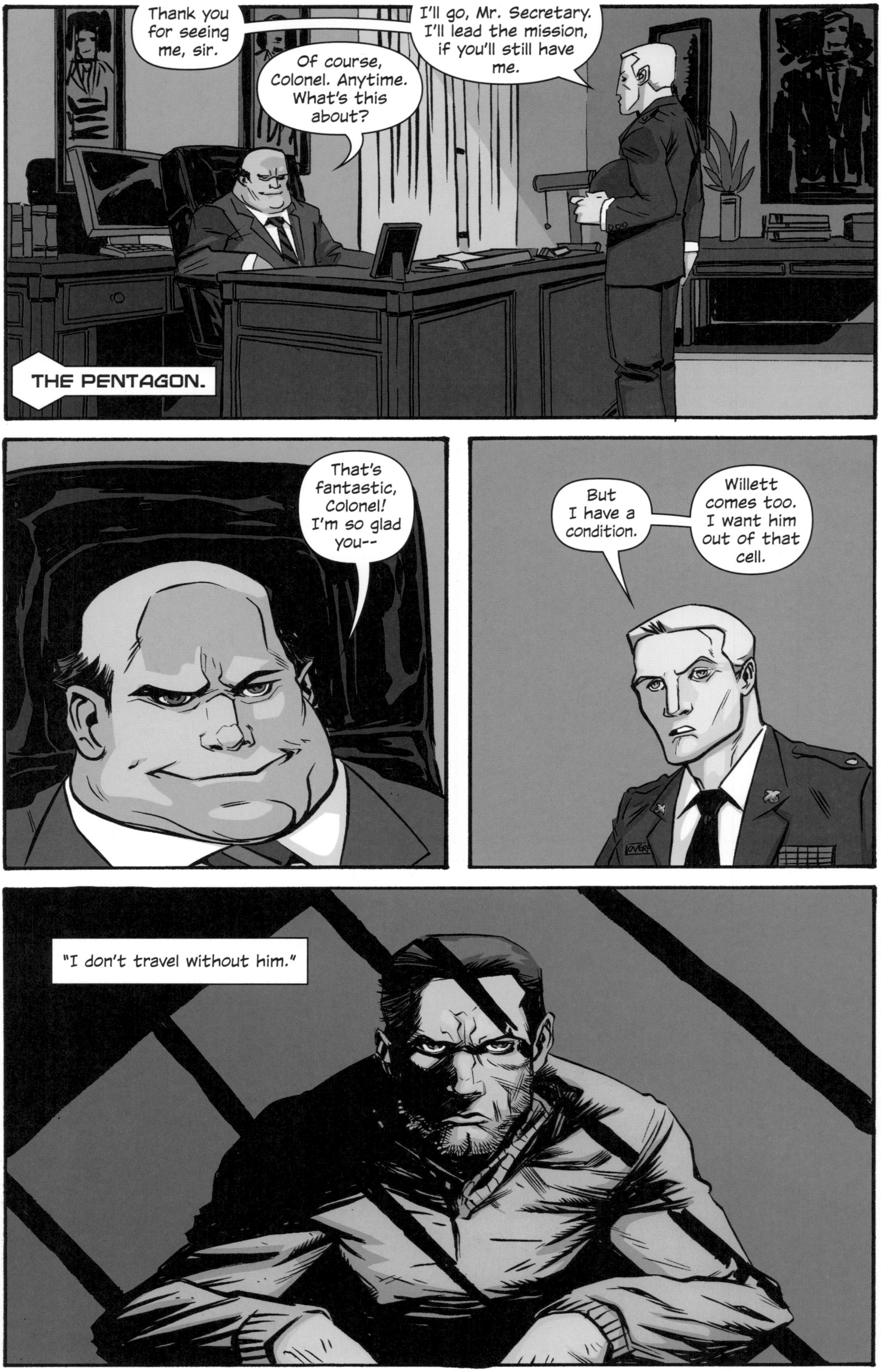
Thank you for seeing me, sir.
Of course, Colonel. Anytime. What's this about?
I'll go, Mr. Secretary. I'll lead the mission, if you'll still have me.
THE PENTAGON.
That's fantastic, Colonel! I'm so glad you--
But I have a condition.
Willett comes too. I want him out of that cell.
"I don't travel without him."

LETTER 44

CHAPTER III

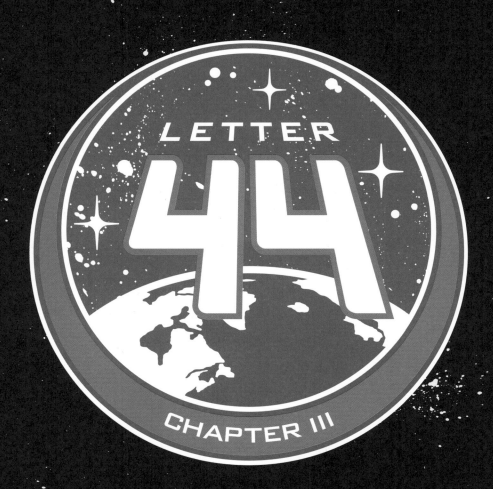

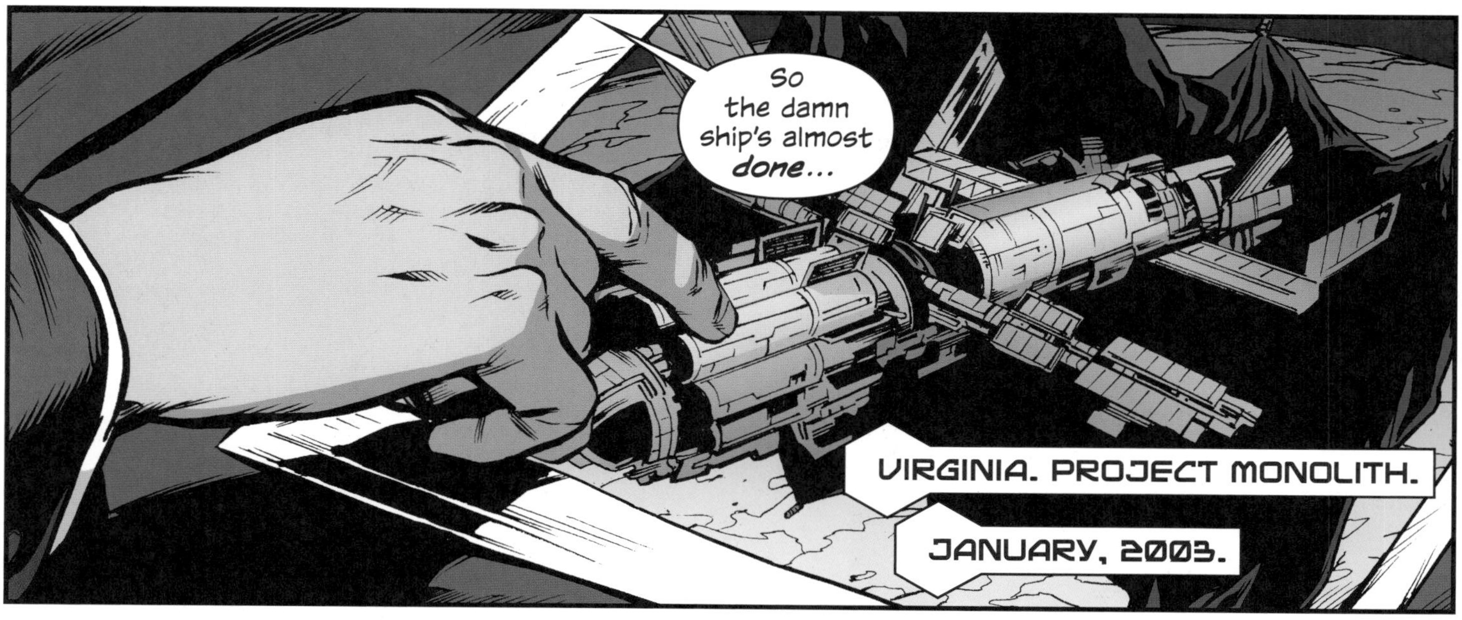
So the damn ship's almost *done*...
VIRGINIA. PROJECT MONOLITH.
JANUARY, 2003.

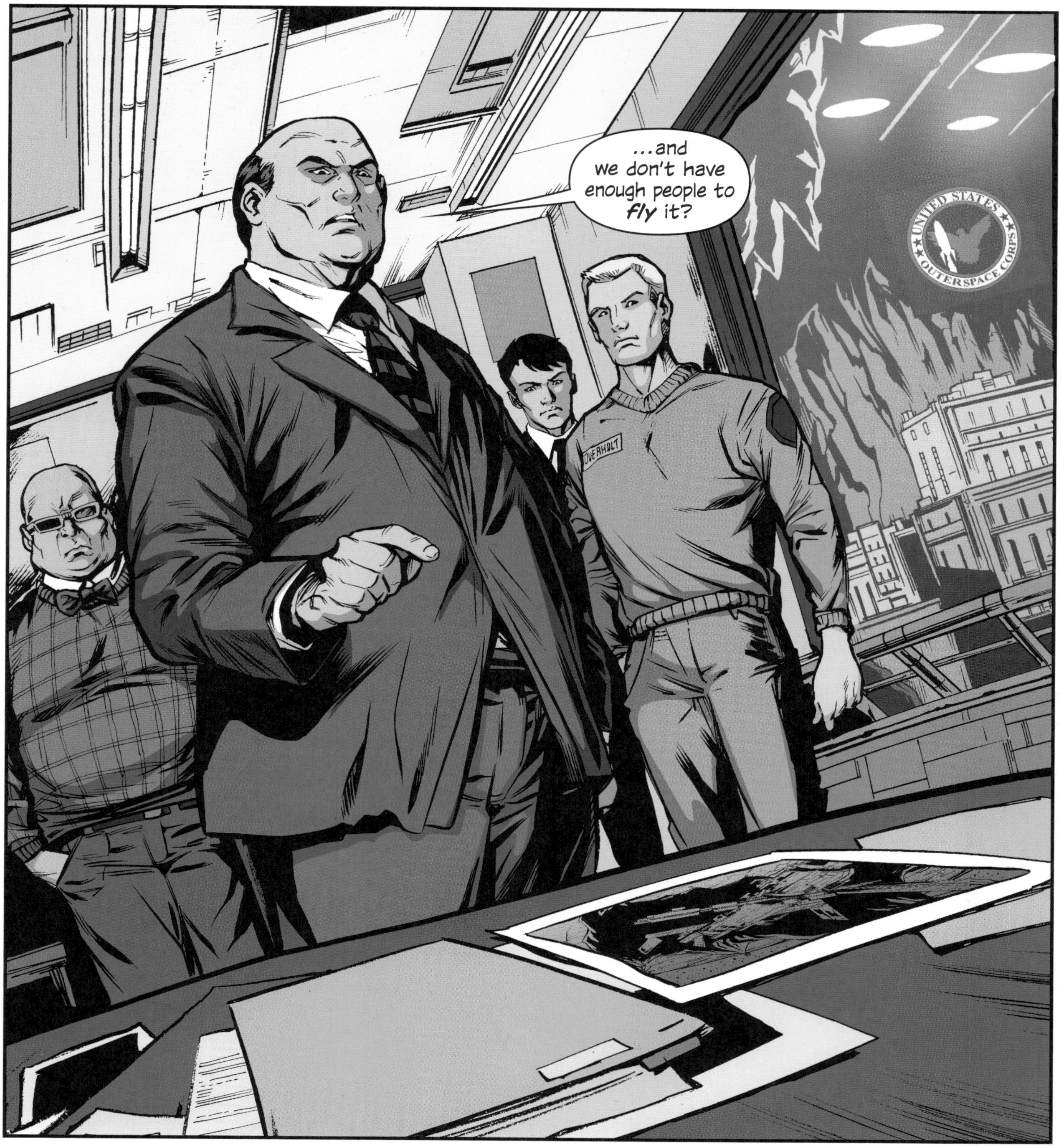
...and we don't have enough people to *fly* it?
OVERHOLT
UNITED STATES OUTERSPACE CORPS

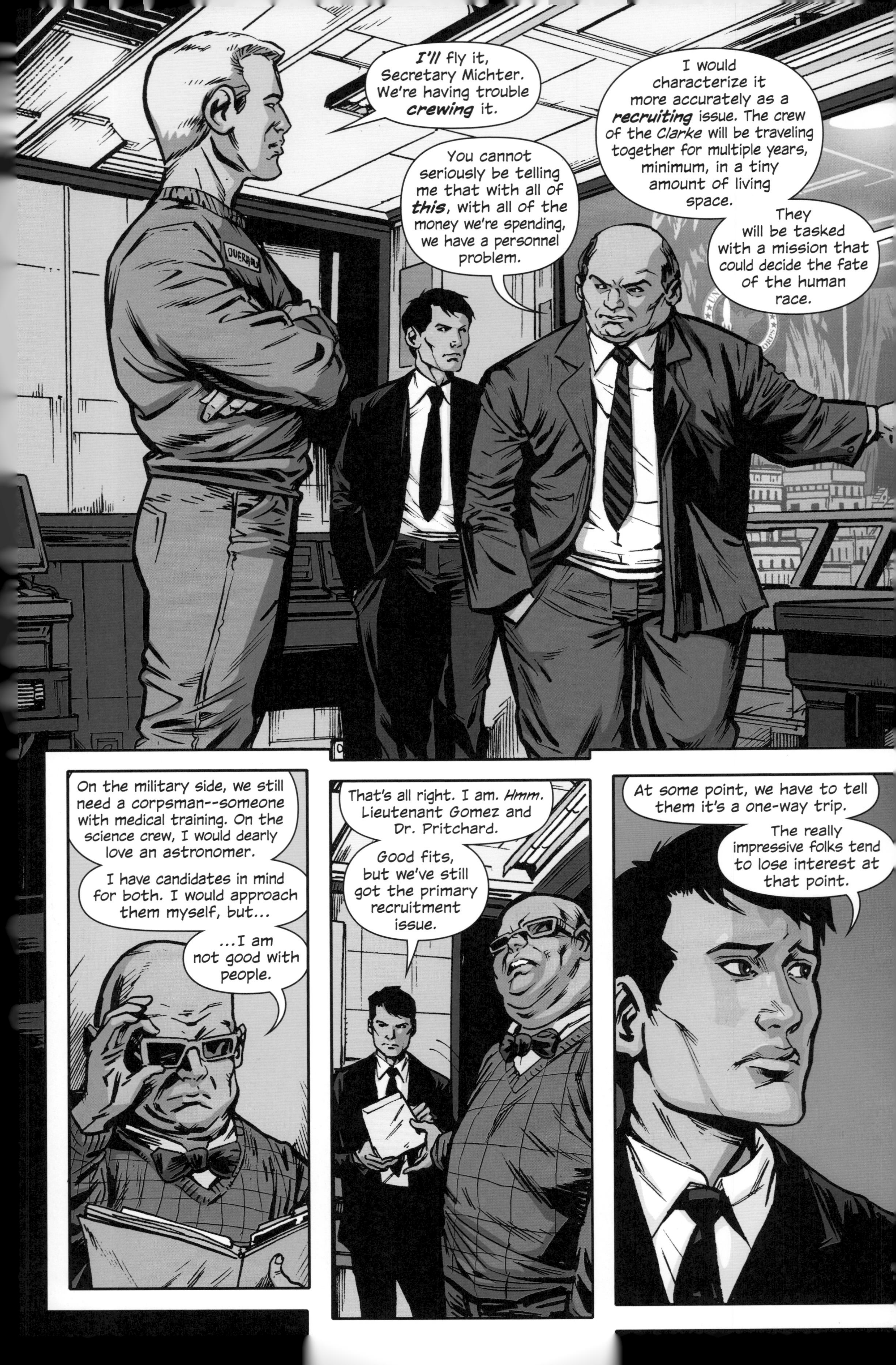

I'll fly it, Secretary Michter. We're having trouble *crewing* it.
You cannot seriously be telling me that with all of *this*, with all of the money we're spending, we have a personnel problem.
I would characterize it more accurately as a *recruiting* issue. The crew of the *Clarke* will be traveling together for multiple years, minimum, in a tiny amount of living space.
They will be tasked with a mission that could decide the fate of the human race.
On the military side, we still need a corpsman--someone with medical training. On the science crew, I would dearly love an astronomer.
I have candidates in mind for both. I would approach them myself, but...
...I am not good with people.
That's all right. I am. *Hmm.* Lieutenant Gomez and Dr. Pritchard.
Good fits, but we've still got the primary recruitment issue.
At some point, we have to tell them it's a one-way trip.
The really impressive folks tend to lose interest at that point.

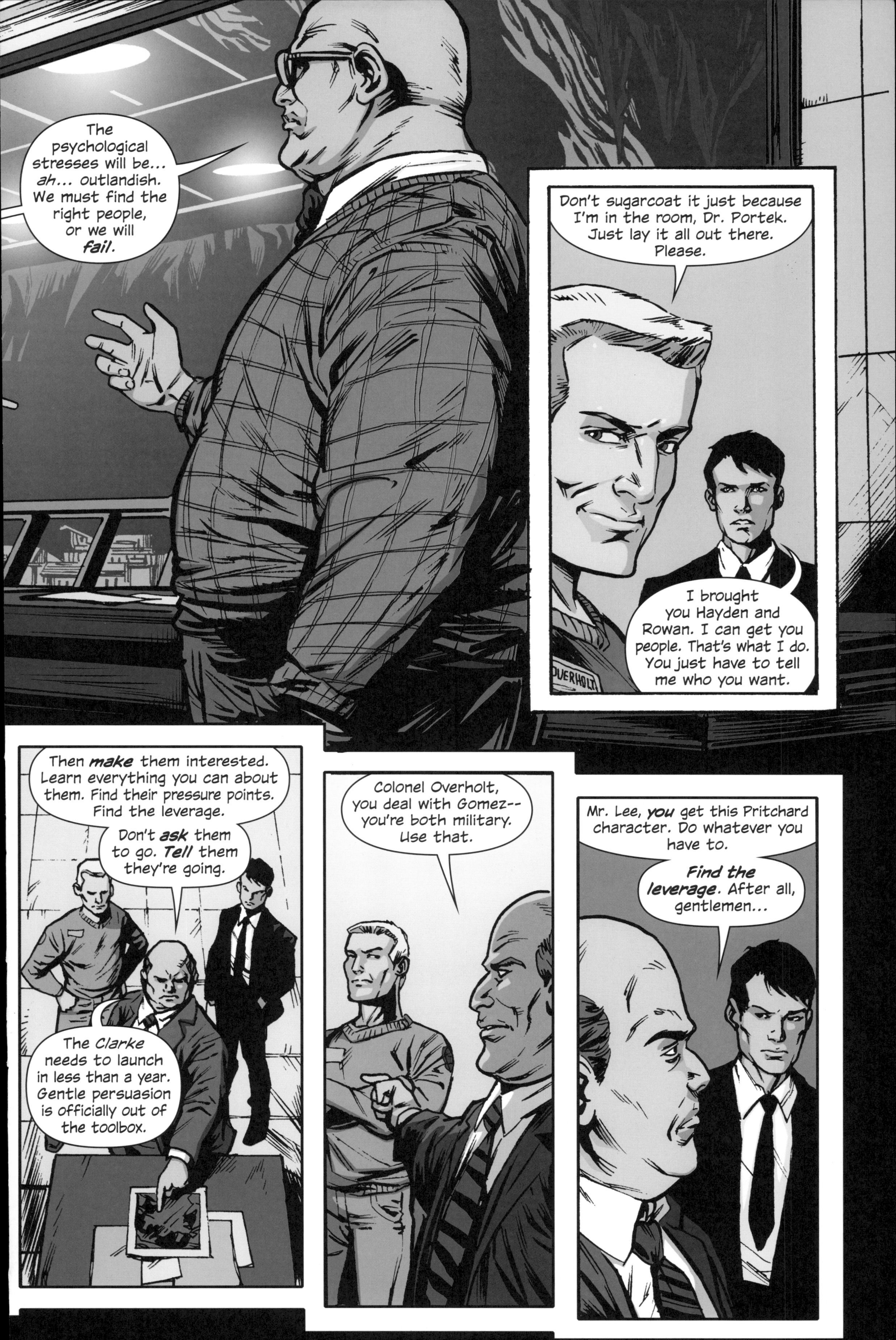

The psychological stresses will be... *ah...* outlandish. We must find the right people, or we will ***fail***.
Don't sugarcoat it just because I'm in the room, Dr. Portek. Just lay it all out there. Please.
I brought you Hayden and Rowan. I can get you people. That's what I do. You just have to tell me who you want.
OVERHOLT
Then ***make*** them interested. Learn everything you can about them. Find their pressure points. Find the leverage.
Don't ***ask*** them to go. ***Tell*** them they're going.
The *Clarke* needs to launch in less than a year. Gentle persuasion is officially out of the toolbox.
Colonel Overholt, you deal with Gomez-- you're both military. Use that.
Mr. Lee, ***you*** get this Pritchard character. Do whatever you have to.
Find the leverage. After all, gentlemen...

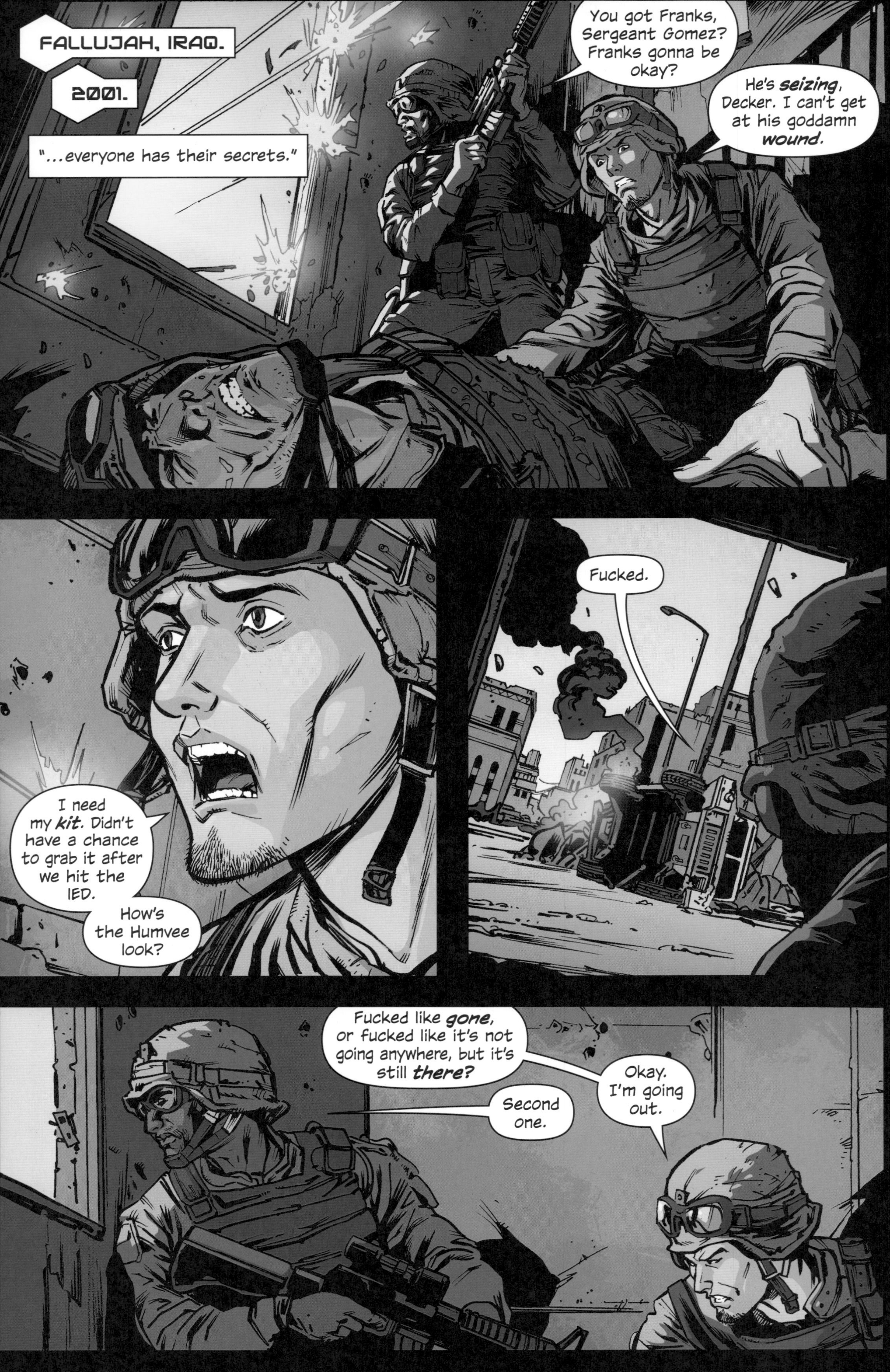
FALLUJAH, IRAQ.
2001.
"...everyone has their secrets."
You got Franks, Sergeant Gomez? Franks gonna be okay?
He's *seizing*, Decker. I can't get at his goddamn *wound*.
I need my *kit*. Didn't have a chance to grab it after we hit the IED.
How's the Humvee look?
Fucked.
Fucked like *gone*, or fucked like it's not going anywhere, but it's still *there?*
Second one.
Okay. I'm going out.

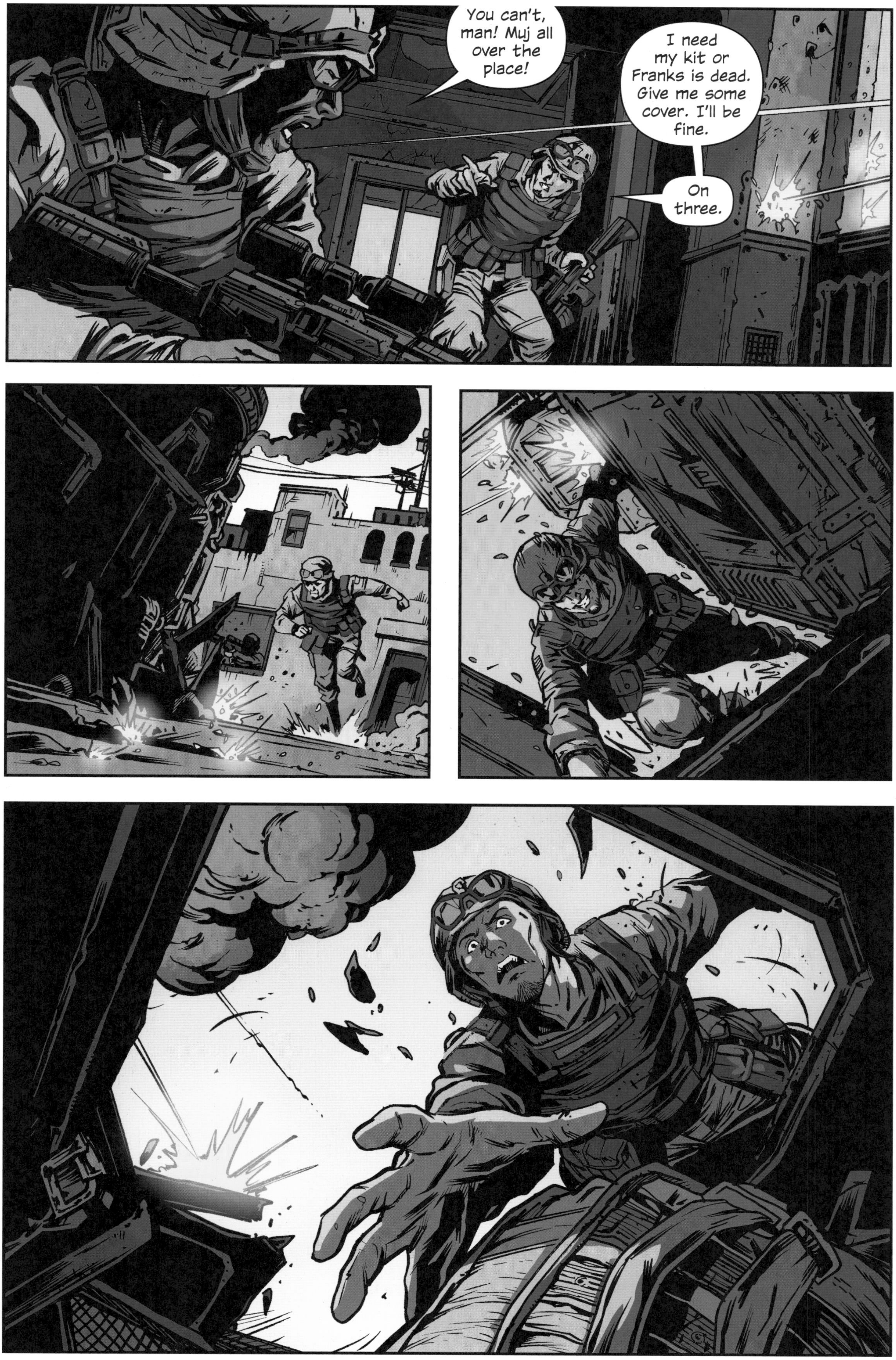
You can't, man! Muj all over the place!
I need my kit or Franks is dead. Give me some cover. I'll be fine.
On three.

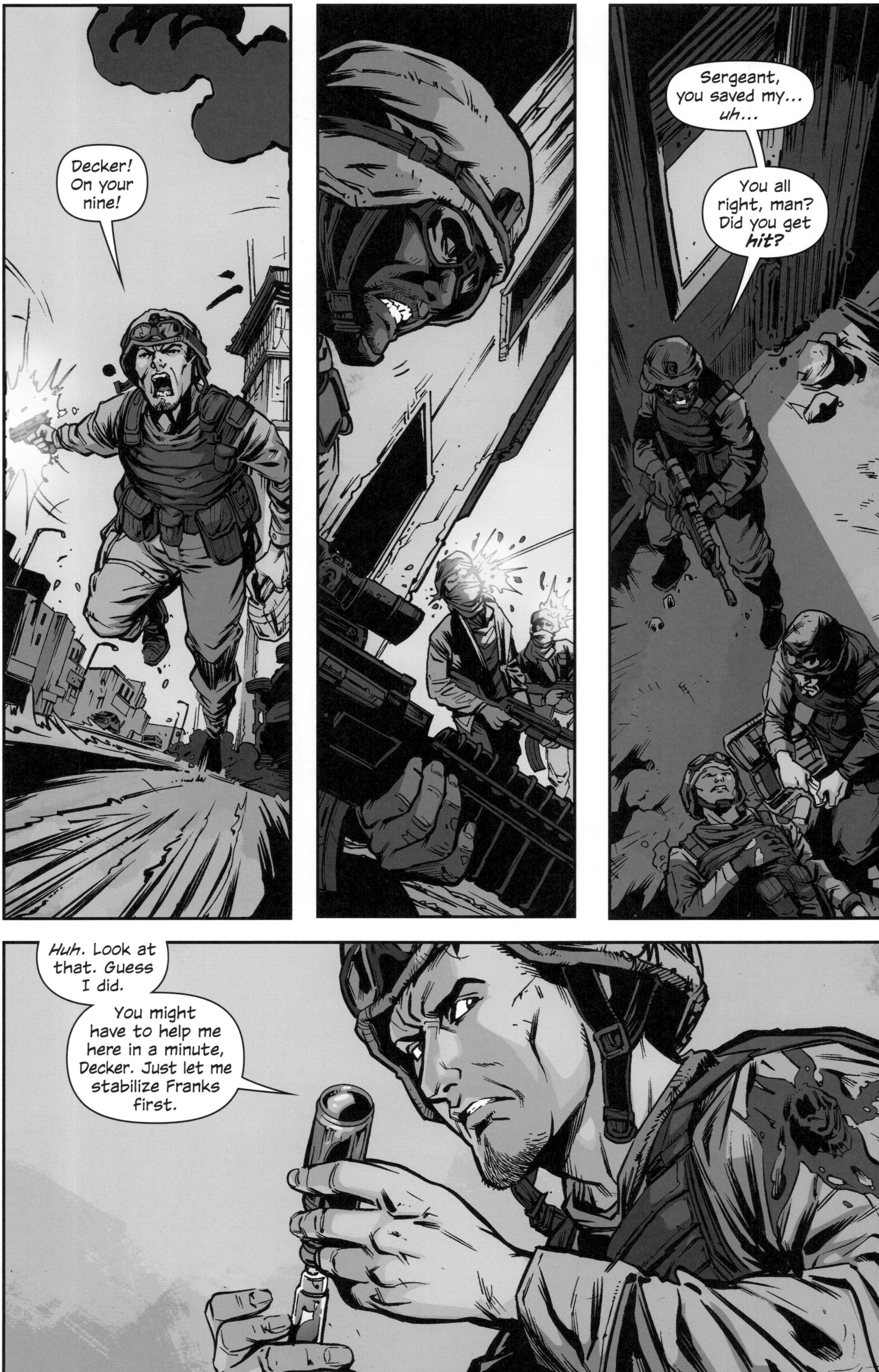
Decker! On your nine!
Sergeant, you saved my... *uh*...
You all right, man? Did you get ***hit?***
Huh. Look at that. Guess I did.
You might have to help me here in a minute, Decker. Just let me stabilize Franks first.

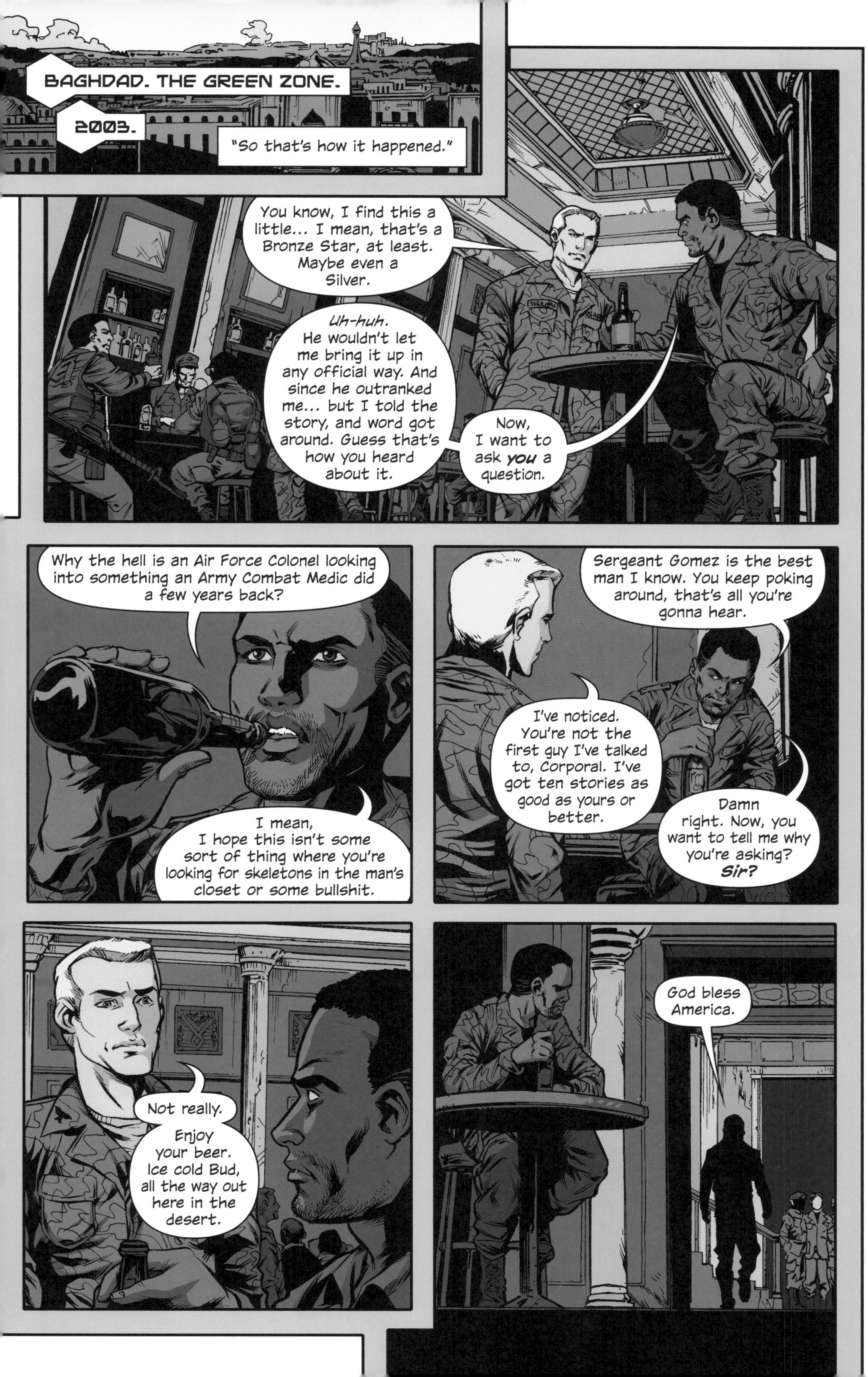
BAGHDAD. THE GREEN ZONE.
2003.
"So that's how it happened."
You know, I find this a little... I mean, that's a Bronze Star, at least. Maybe even a Silver.
Uh-huh. He wouldn't let me bring it up in any official way. And since he outranked me... but I told the story, and word got around. Guess that's how you heard about it.
Now, I want to ask ***you*** a question.
Why the hell is an Air Force Colonel looking into something an Army Combat Medic did a few years back?
I mean, I hope this isn't some sort of thing where you're looking for skeletons in the man's closet or some bullshit.
Sergeant Gomez is the best man I know. You keep poking around, that's all you're gonna hear.
I've noticed. You're not the first guy I've talked to, Corporal. I've got ten stories as good as yours or better.
Damn right. Now, you want to tell me why you're asking? ***Sir?***
Not really.
Enjoy your beer. Ice cold Bud, all the way out here in the desert.
God bless America.

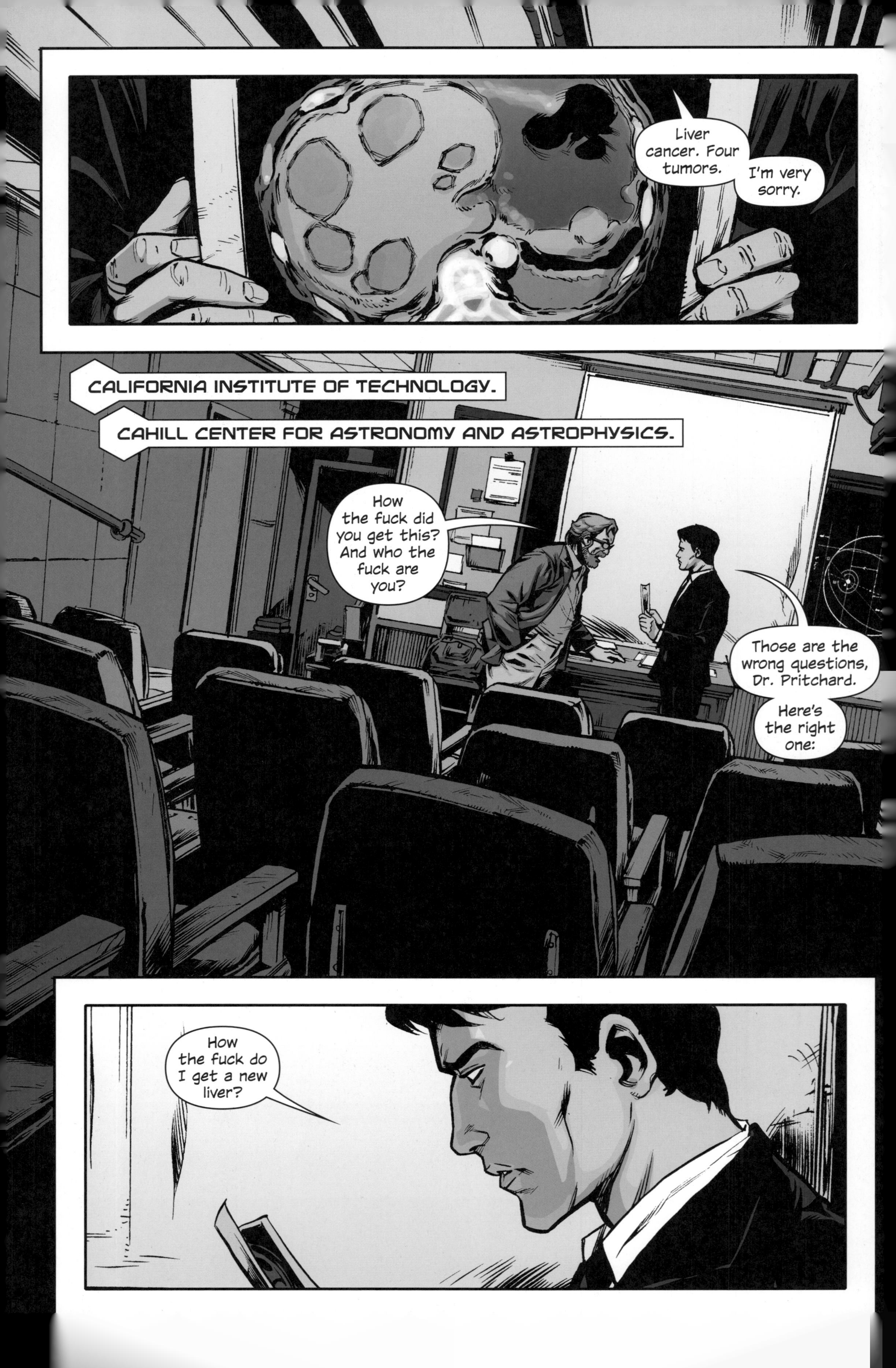
Liver cancer. Four tumors.
I'm very sorry.
CALIFORNIA INSTITUTE OF TECHNOLOGY.
CAHILL CENTER FOR ASTRONOMY AND ASTROPHYSICS.
How the fuck did you get this? And who the fuck are you?
Those are the wrong questions, Dr. Pritchard.
Here's the right one:
How the fuck do I get a new liver?

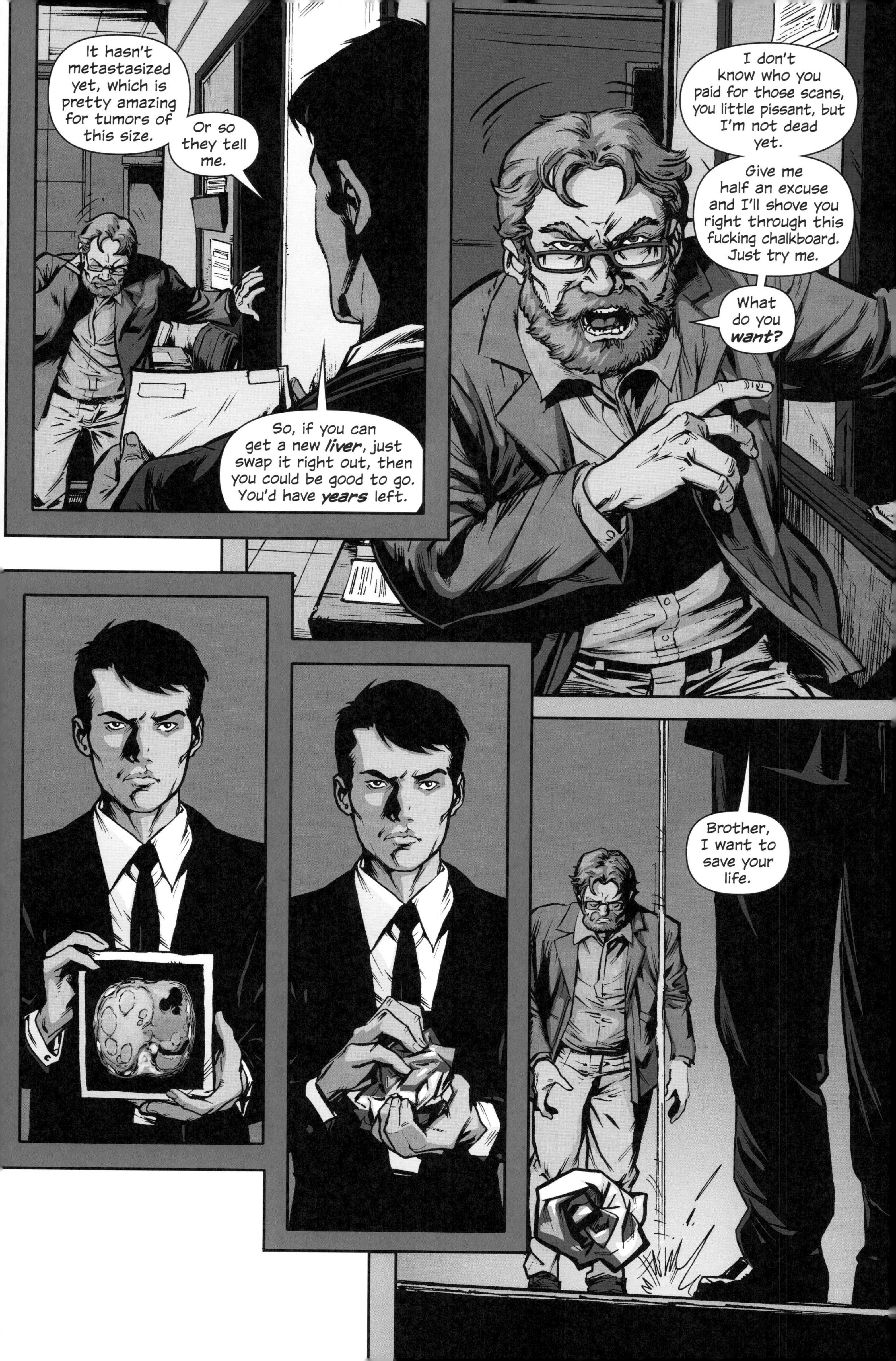
It hasn't metastasized yet, which is pretty amazing for tumors of this size.
Or so they tell me.
So, if you can get a new *liver*, just swap it right out, then you could be good to go. You'd have *years* left.
I don't know who you paid for those scans, you little pissant, but I'm not dead yet.
Give me half an excuse and I'll shove you right through this fucking chalkboard. Just try me.
What do you *want?*
Brother, I want to save your life.

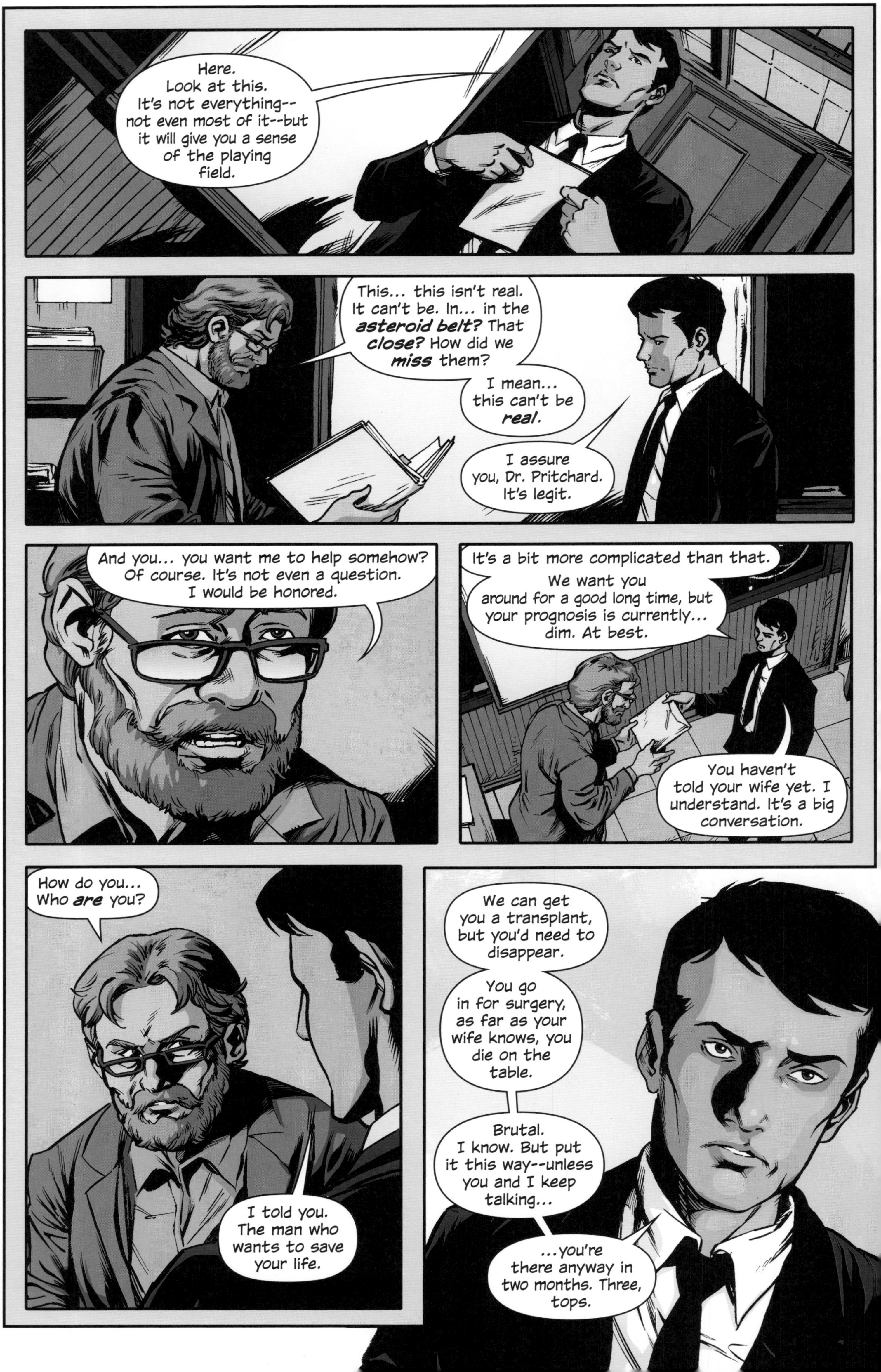
Here. Look at this. It's not everything--not even most of it--but it will give you a sense of the playing field.
This... this isn't real. It can't be. In... in the ***asteroid belt?*** That ***close?*** How did we ***miss*** them?
I mean... this can't be ***real***.
I assure you, Dr. Pritchard. It's legit.
And you... you want me to help somehow? Of course. It's not even a question. I would be honored.
It's a bit more complicated than that.
We want you around for a good long time, but your prognosis is currently... dim. At best.
You haven't told your wife yet. I understand. It's a big conversation.
How do you... Who ***are*** you?
I told you. The man who wants to save your life.
We can get you a transplant, but you'd need to disappear.
You go in for surgery, as far as your wife knows, you die on the table.
Brutal. I know. But put it this way--unless you and I keep talking...
...you're there anyway in two months. Three, tops.

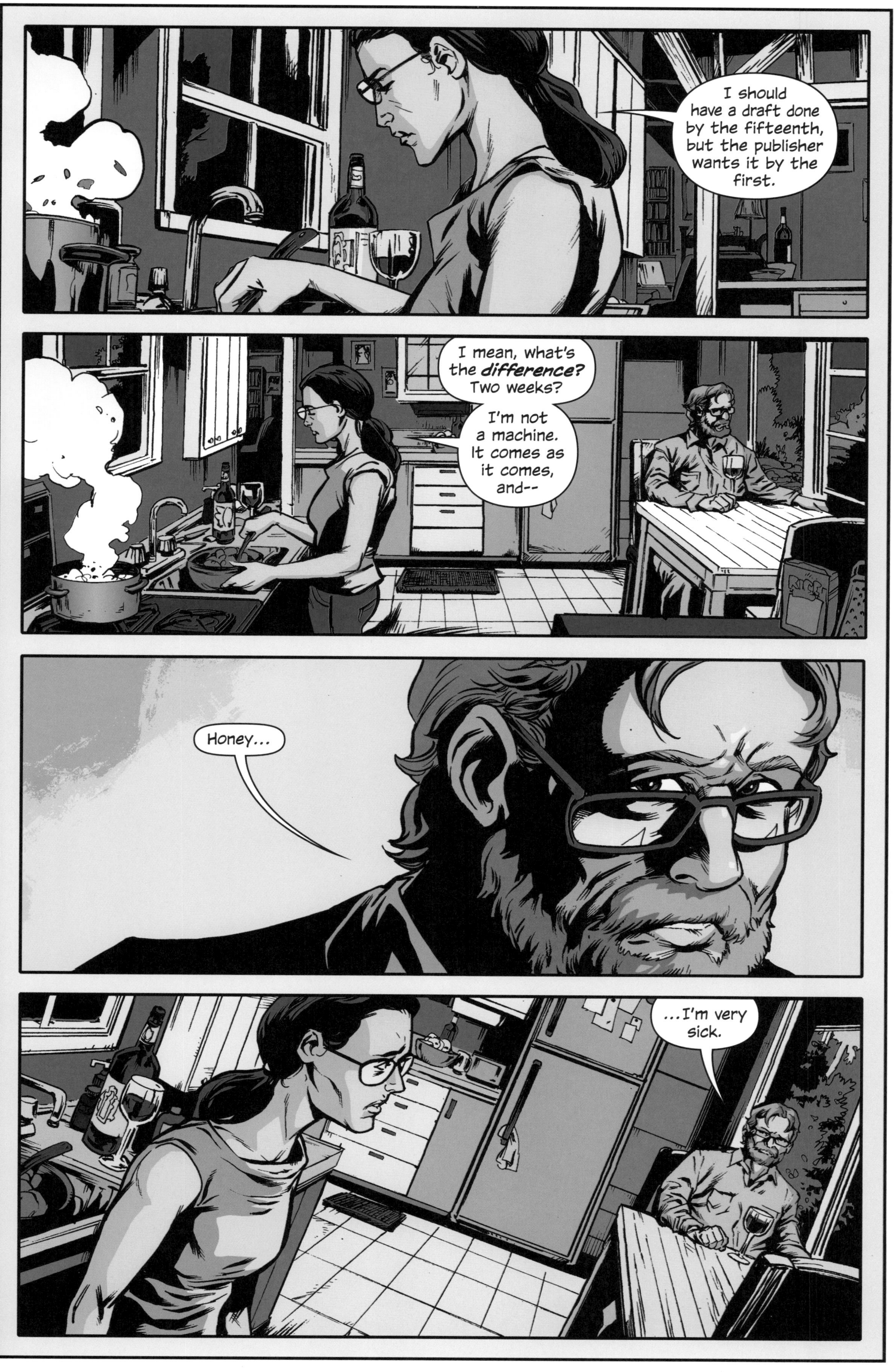
I should have a draft done by the fifteenth, but the publisher wants it by the first.
I mean, what's the *difference?* Two weeks?
I'm not a machine. It comes as it comes, and--
Honey...
...I'm very sick.

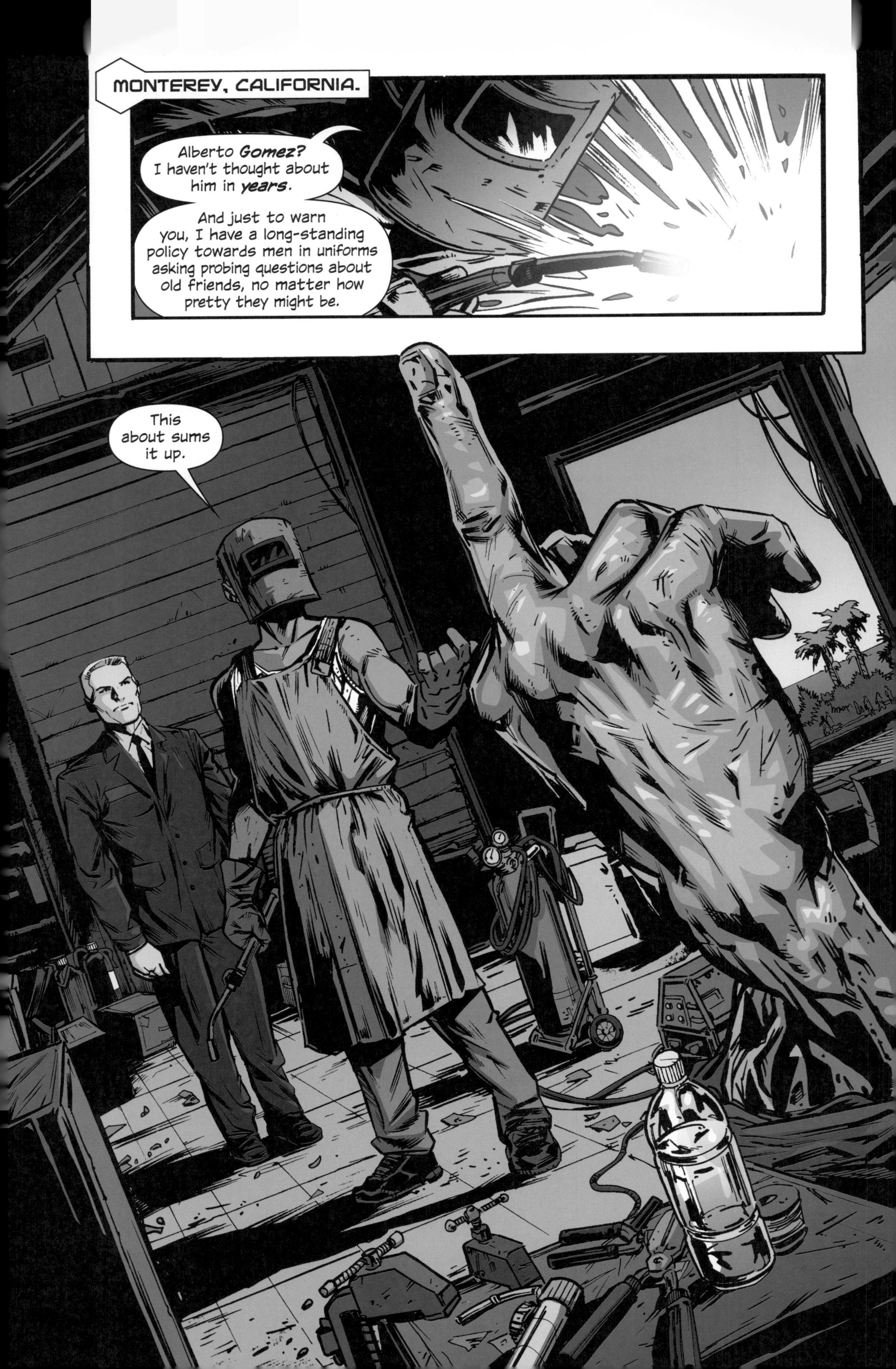

MONTEREY, CALIFORNIA.
Alberto Gomez? I haven't thought about him in years.
And just to warn you, I have a long-standing policy towards men in uniforms asking probing questions about old friends, no matter how pretty they might be.
This about sums it up.

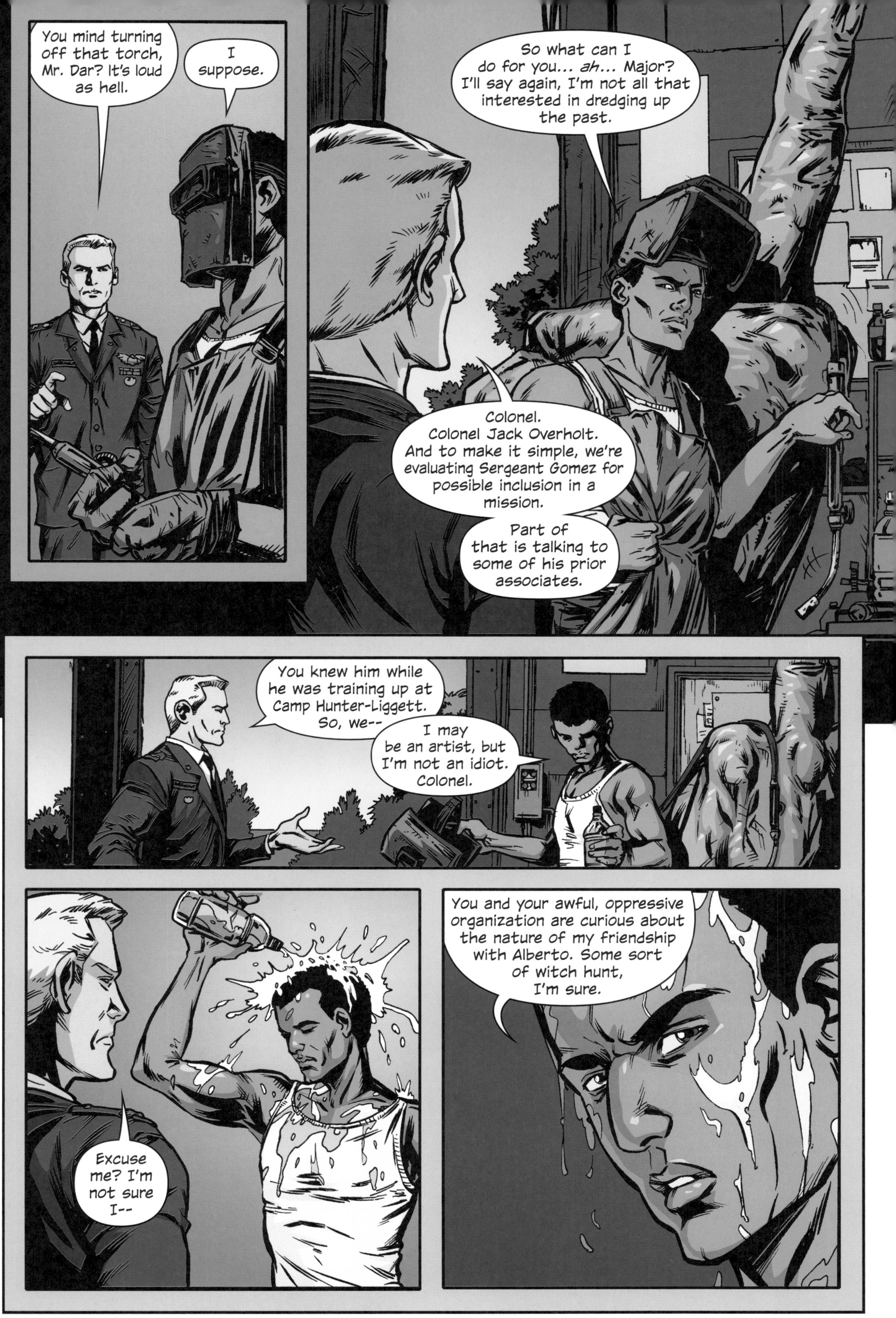
You mind turning off that torch, Mr. Dar? It's loud as hell.
I suppose.
So what can I do for you... *ah*... Major? I'll say again, I'm not all that interested in dredging up the past.
Colonel. Colonel Jack Overholt. And to make it simple, we're evaluating Sergeant Gomez for possible inclusion in a mission.
Part of that is talking to some of his prior associates.
You knew him while he was training up at Camp Hunter-Liggett. So, we--
I may be an artist, but I'm not an idiot. Colonel.
Excuse me? I'm not sure I--
You and your awful, oppressive organization are curious about the nature of my friendship with Alberto. Some sort of witch hunt, I'm sure.

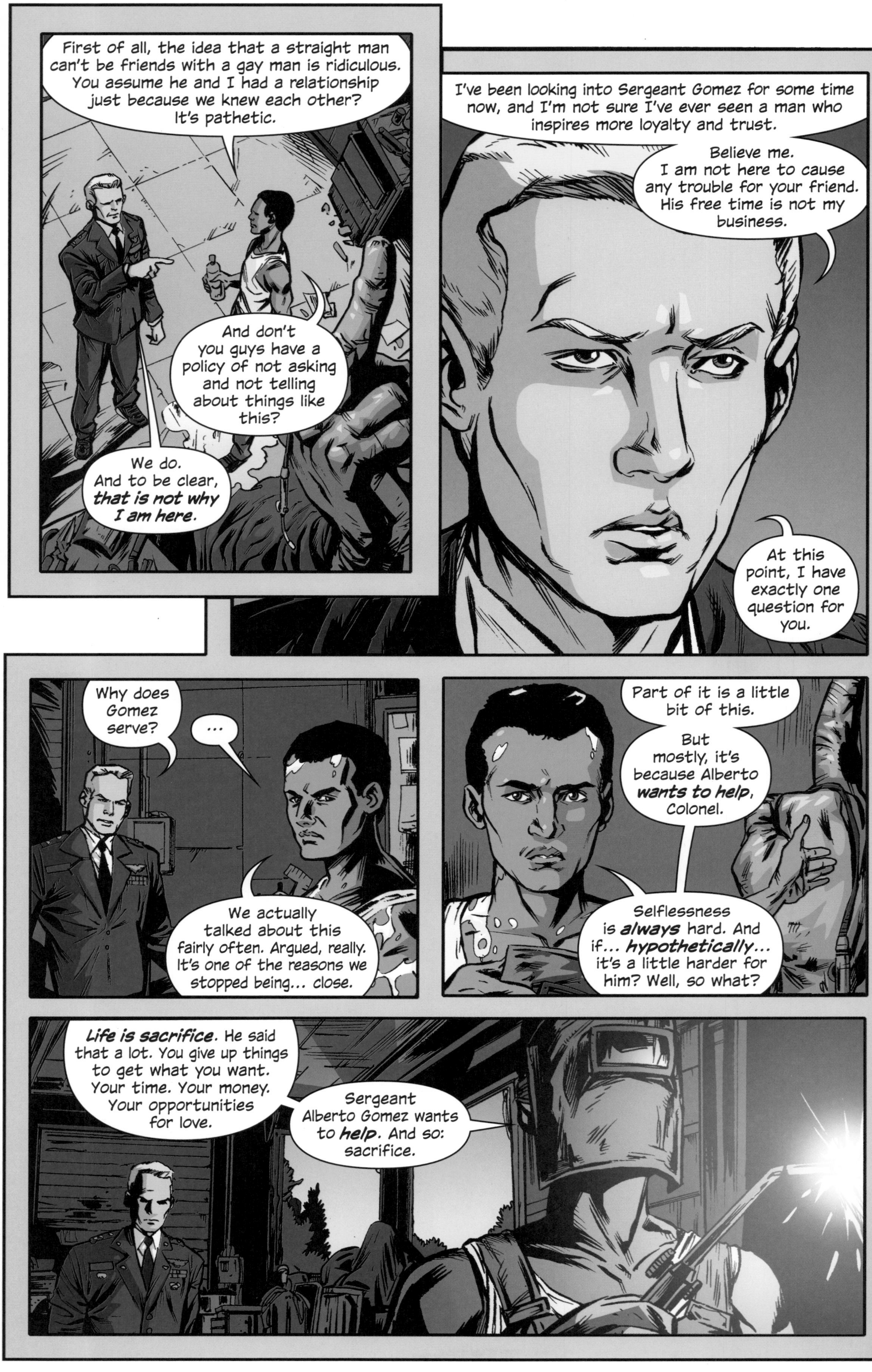
First of all, the idea that a straight man can't be friends with a gay man is ridiculous. You assume he and I had a relationship just because we knew each other? It's pathetic.
And don't you guys have a policy of not asking and not telling about things like this?
We do. And to be clear, *that is not why I am here*.
I've been looking into Sergeant Gomez for some time now, and I'm not sure I've ever seen a man who inspires more loyalty and trust.
Believe me. I am not here to cause any trouble for your friend. His free time is not my business.
At this point, I have exactly one question for you.
Why does Gomez serve?
...
We actually talked about this fairly often. Argued, really. It's one of the reasons we stopped being... close.
Part of it is a little bit of this.
But mostly, it's because Alberto *wants to help*, Colonel.
Selflessness is *always* hard. And if... *hypothetically*... it's a little harder for him? Well, so what?
Life is sacrifice. He said that a lot. You give up things to get what you want. Your time. Your money. Your opportunities for love.
Sergeant Alberto Gomez wants to *help*. And so: sacrifice.

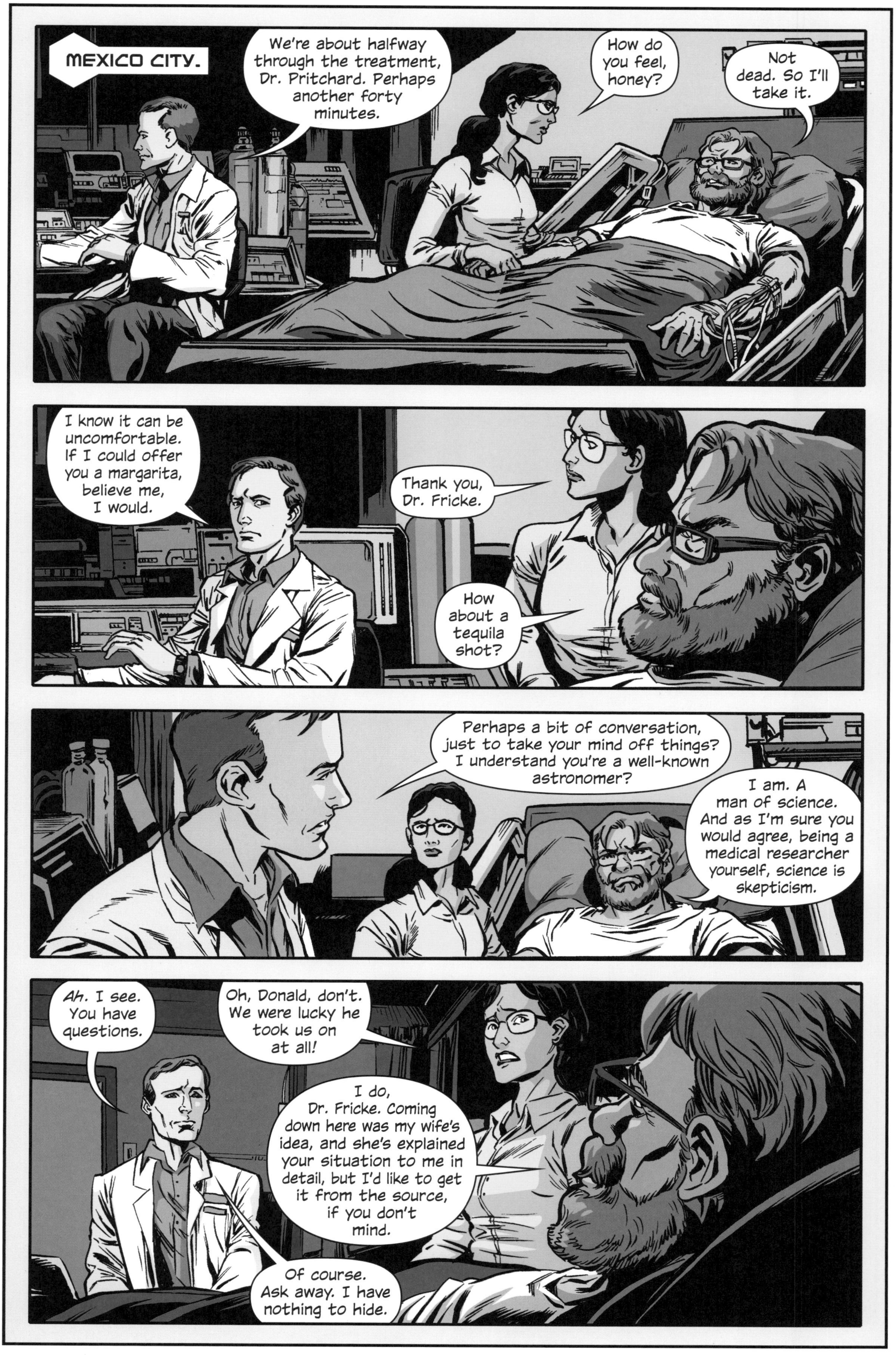
MEXICO CITY.
We're about halfway through the treatment, Dr. Pritchard. Perhaps another forty minutes.
How do you feel, honey?
Not dead. So I'll take it.
I know it can be uncomfortable. If I could offer you a margarita, believe me, I would.
Thank you, Dr. Fricke.
How about a tequila shot?
Perhaps a bit of conversation, just to take your mind off things? I understand you're a well-known astronomer?
I am. A man of science. And as I'm sure you would agree, being a medical researcher yourself, science is skepticism.
Ah. I see. You have questions.
Oh, Donald, don't. We were lucky he took us on at all!
I do, Dr. Fricke. Coming down here was my wife's idea, and she's explained your situation to me in detail, but I'd like to get it from the source, if you don't mind.
Of course. Ask away. I have nothing to hide.

What are you giving me?

A proprietary combination of natural and synthetic chemicals I have formulated over many years that can attack and eliminate many of the more aggressive forms of cancer.

In other words... anything from a ground up Snickers bar to a giraffe. *Everything* is a combination of natural and synthetic chemicals, at this point.

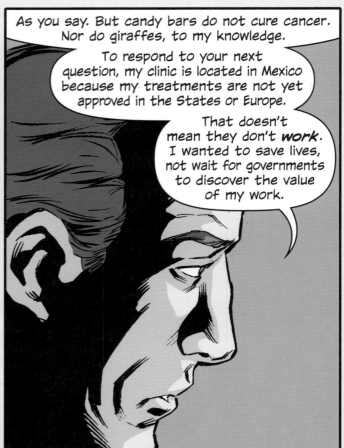

As you say. But candy bars do not cure cancer. Nor do giraffes, to my knowledge.

To respond to your next question, my clinic is located in Mexico because my treatments are not yet approved in the States or Europe.

That doesn't mean they don't **work**. I wanted to save lives, not wait for governments to discover the value of my work.

So, answers for you, now an answer for me.

You are trying to save your life. What will you do with it once we have cured you? Tell me of **your** work. What do you have left to achieve?

... Everything, really.

Oh, please, Donald. You're one of the most respected men in your field in the **world**.

Maybe so, Dorothy, but that's due to a career based on incremental insights into other people's big discoveries. Refinements.

Certainly, I deserve my position. But in all the galaxy, in all that immensity, what have I discovered?

The endless heavens, and not one thing with my name on it.

That's what I'd do.

Find something new.

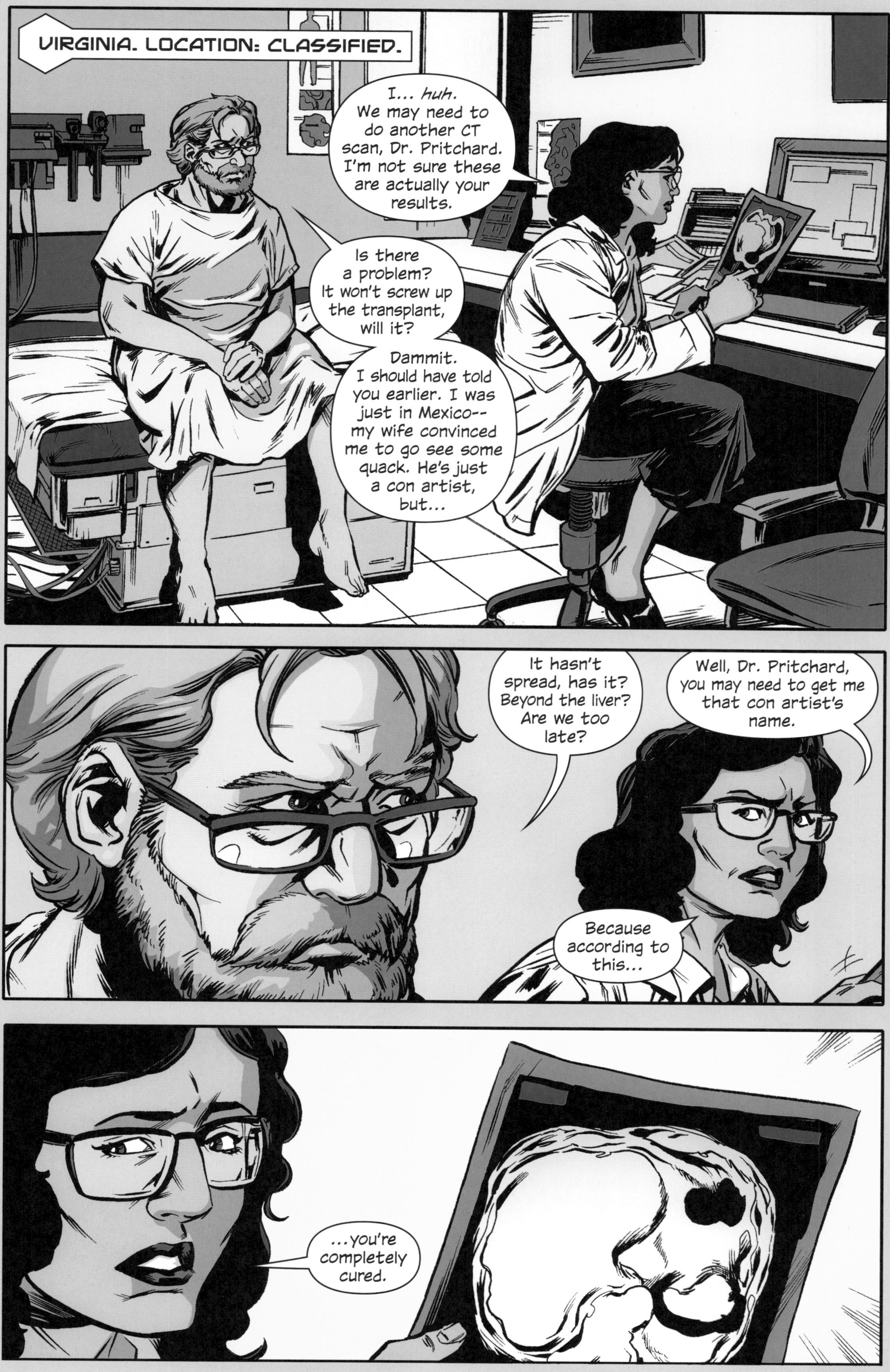
VIRGINIA. LOCATION: CLASSIFIED.
I... *huh.* We may need to do another CT scan, Dr. Pritchard. I'm not sure these are actually your results.
Is there a problem? It won't screw up the transplant, will it?
Dammit. I should have told you earlier. I was just in Mexico-- my wife convinced me to go see some quack. He's just a con artist, but...
It hasn't spread, has it? Beyond the liver? Are we too late?
Well, Dr. Pritchard, you may need to get me that con artist's name.
Because according to this...
...you're completely cured.

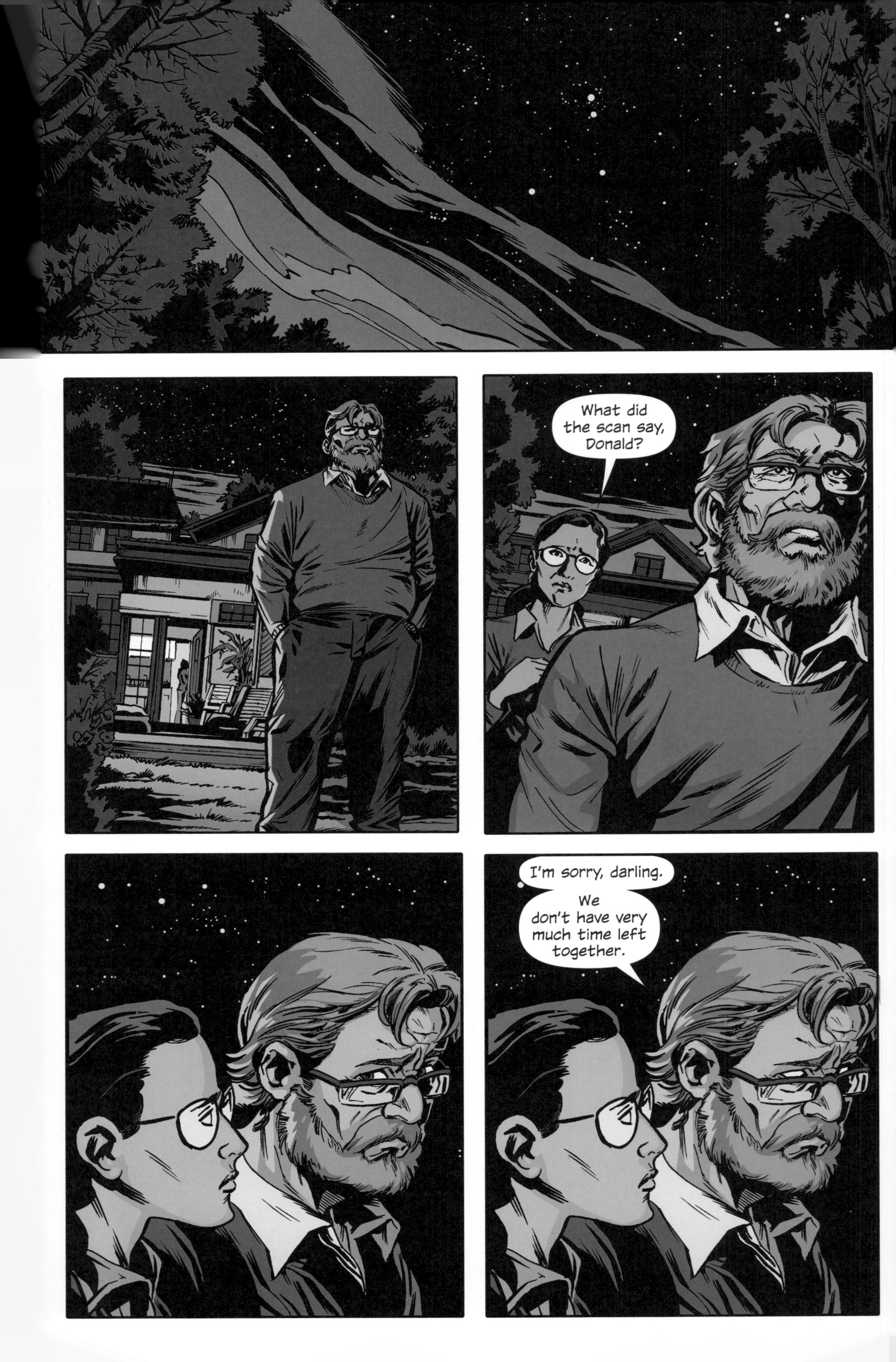
What did the scan say, Donald?
I'm sorry, darling.
We don't have very much time left together.

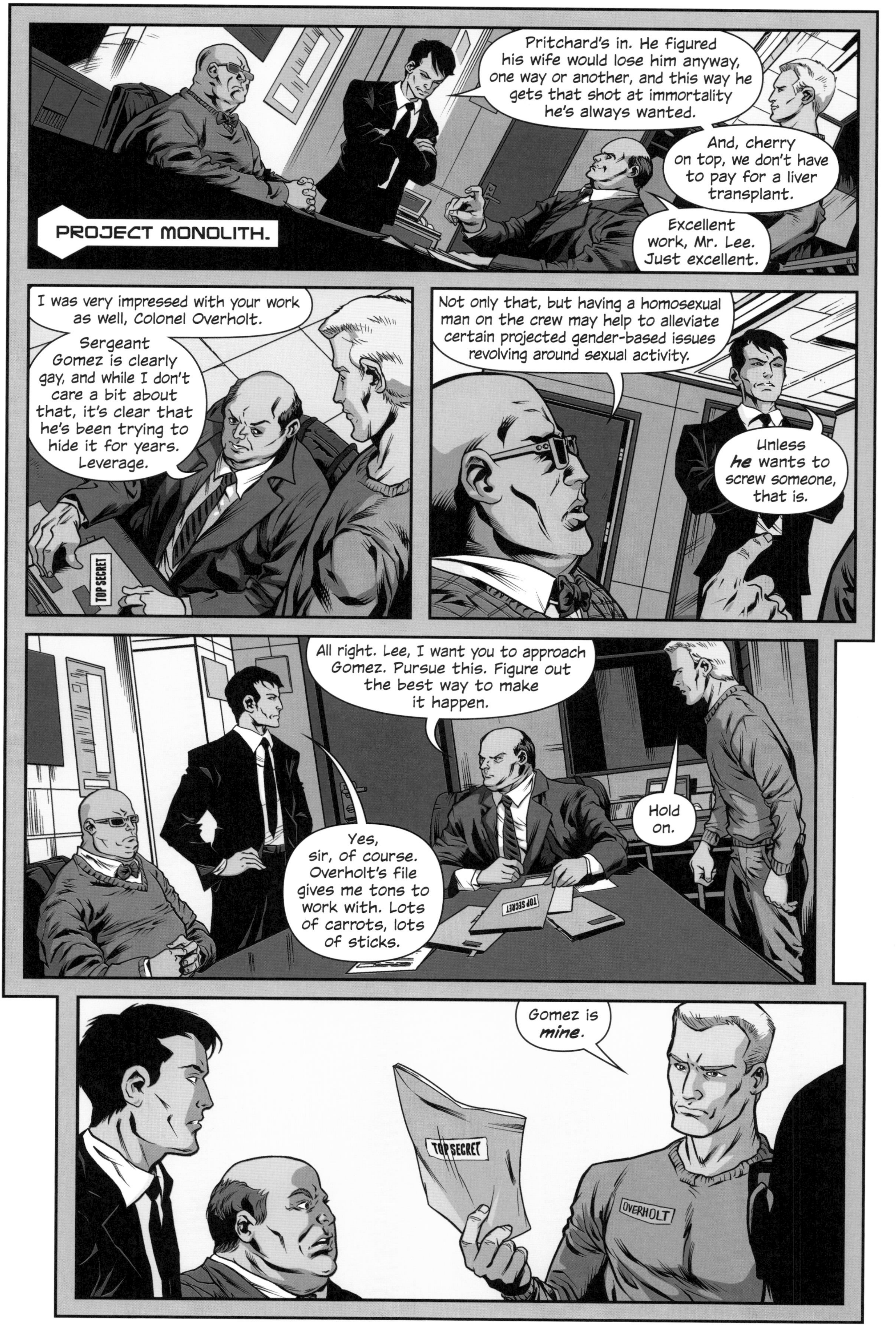
Pritchard's in. He figured his wife would lose him anyway, one way or another, and this way he gets that shot at immortality he's always wanted.
And, cherry on top, we don't have to pay for a liver transplant.
PROJECT MONOLITH.
Excellent work, Mr. Lee. Just excellent.
I was very impressed with your work as well, Colonel Overholt.
Sergeant Gomez is clearly gay, and while I don't care a bit about that, it's clear that he's been trying to hide it for years. Leverage.
TOP SECRET
Not only that, but having a homosexual man on the crew may help to alleviate certain projected gender-based issues revolving around sexual activity.
Unless *he* wants to screw someone, that is.
All right. Lee, I want you to approach Gomez. Pursue this. Figure out the best way to make it happen.
Hold on.
Yes, sir, of course. Overholt's file gives me tons to work with. Lots of carrots, lots of sticks.
TOP SECRET
Gomez is *mine*.
TOP SECRET
OVERHOLT

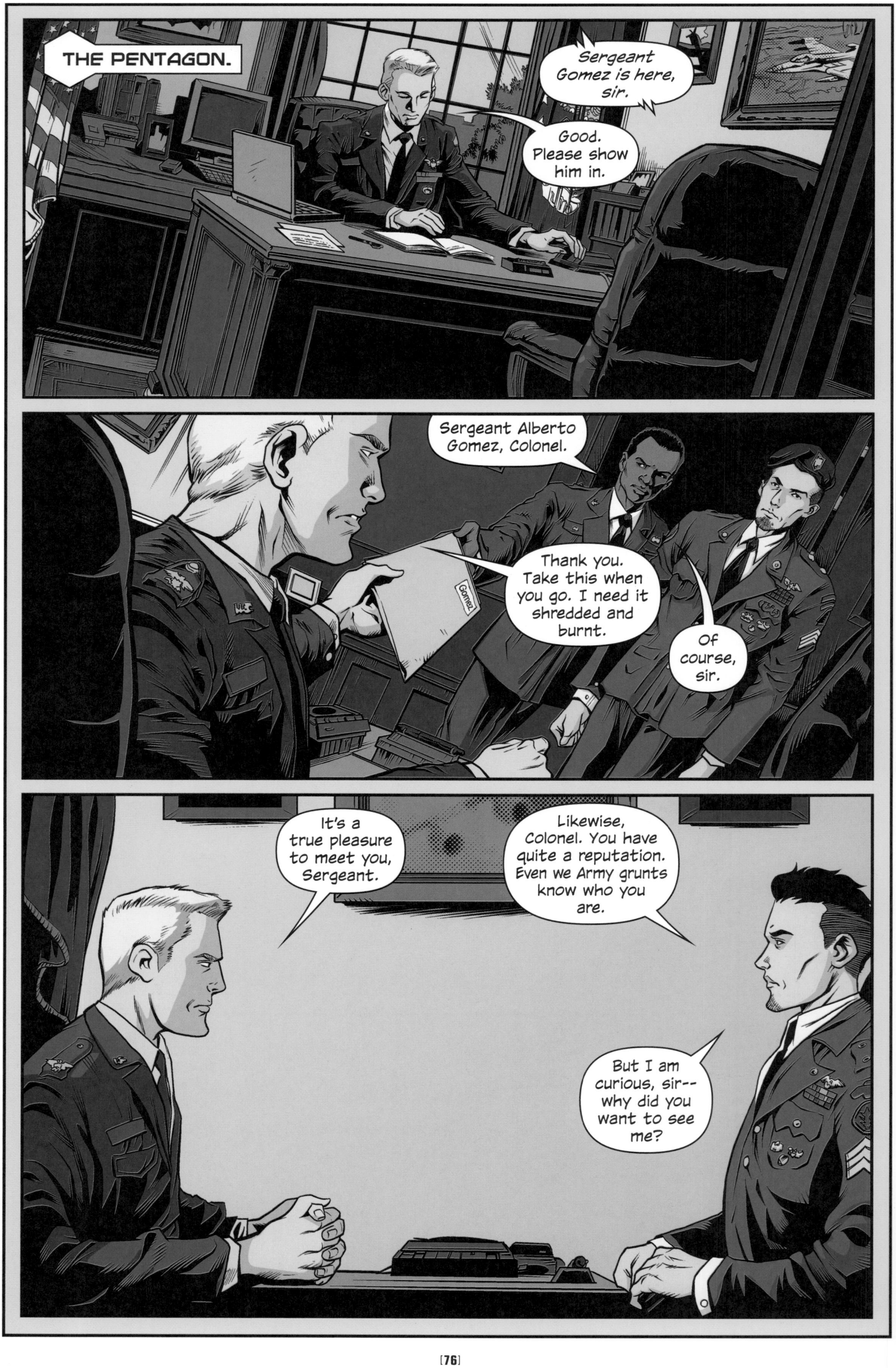
THE PENTAGON.
Sergeant Gomez is here, sir.
Good. Please show him in.
Sergeant Alberto Gomez, Colonel.
Thank you. Take this when you go. I need it shredded and burnt.
Gomez
Of course, sir.
It's a true pleasure to meet you, Sergeant.
Likewise, Colonel. You have quite a reputation. Even we Army grunts know who you are.
But I am curious, sir--why did you want to see me?

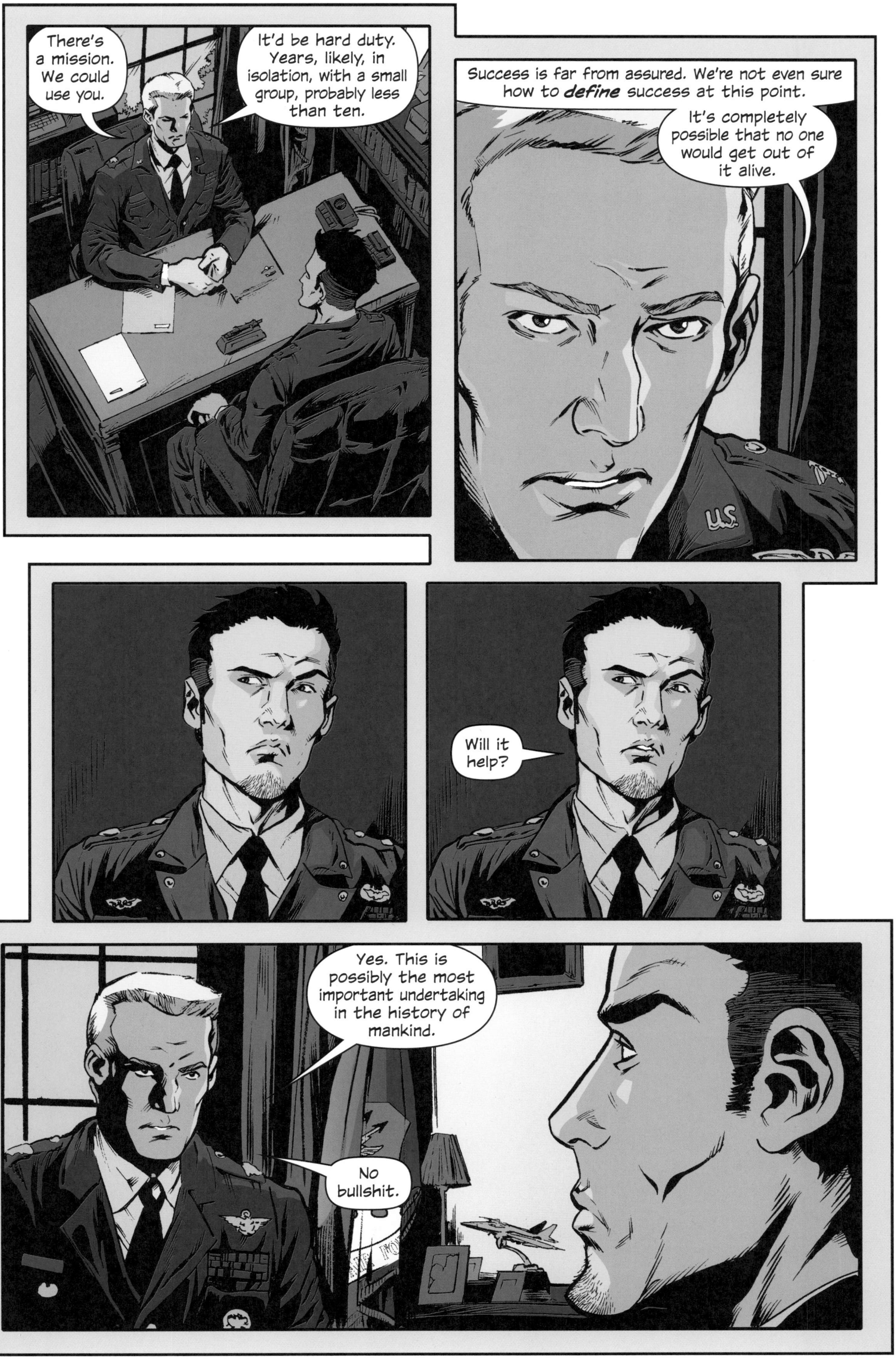
There's a mission. We could use you.
It'd be hard duty. Years, likely, in isolation, with a small group, probably less than ten.
Success is far from assured. We're not even sure how to *define* success at this point.
It's completely possible that no one would get out of it alive.
Will it help?
Yes. This is possibly the most important undertaking in the history of mankind.
No bullshit.
U.S.

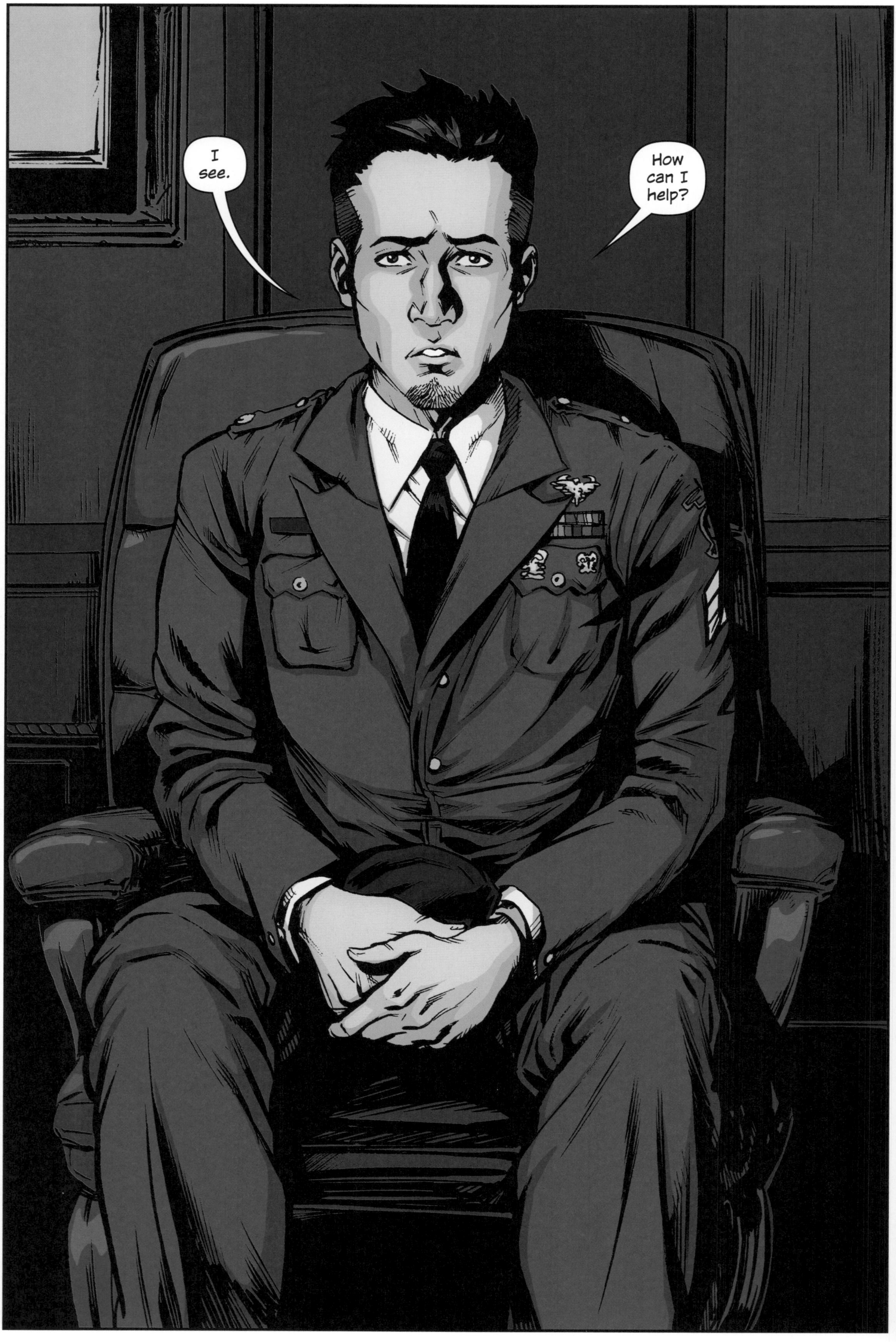
I see.
How can I help?

LETTER 44

CHAPTER IV

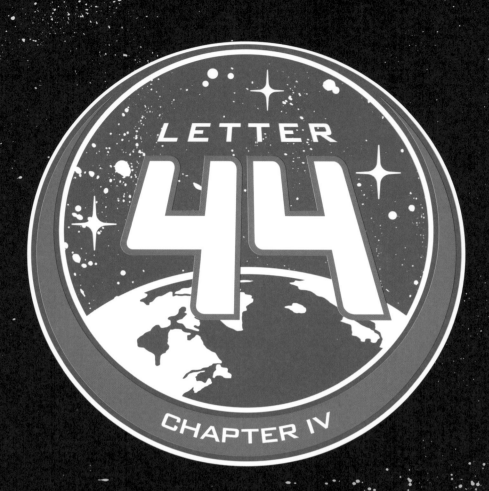

THE CLARKE.

JANUARY 2003.

WATER POTABLE

You know, Charlotte, this whole thing will probably go terribly wrong at some point or another.

It's inevitable-- the mission's too complex, the ship has too many parts, and worst of all, there are *human beings involved.*

Seems a little defeatist, doesn't it, Rowan?

They tried sending probes, and it didn't work. Humans have to be part of this.

No, you miss my point. We're the problem, but we're also the solution.

People are *flexible.*

When something negative happens, we can *adapt.*

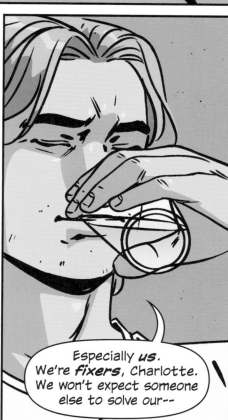

Especially *us.* We're *fixers,* Charlotte. We won't expect someone else to solve our--

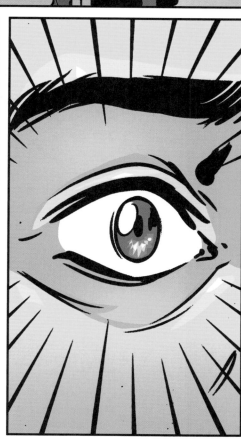

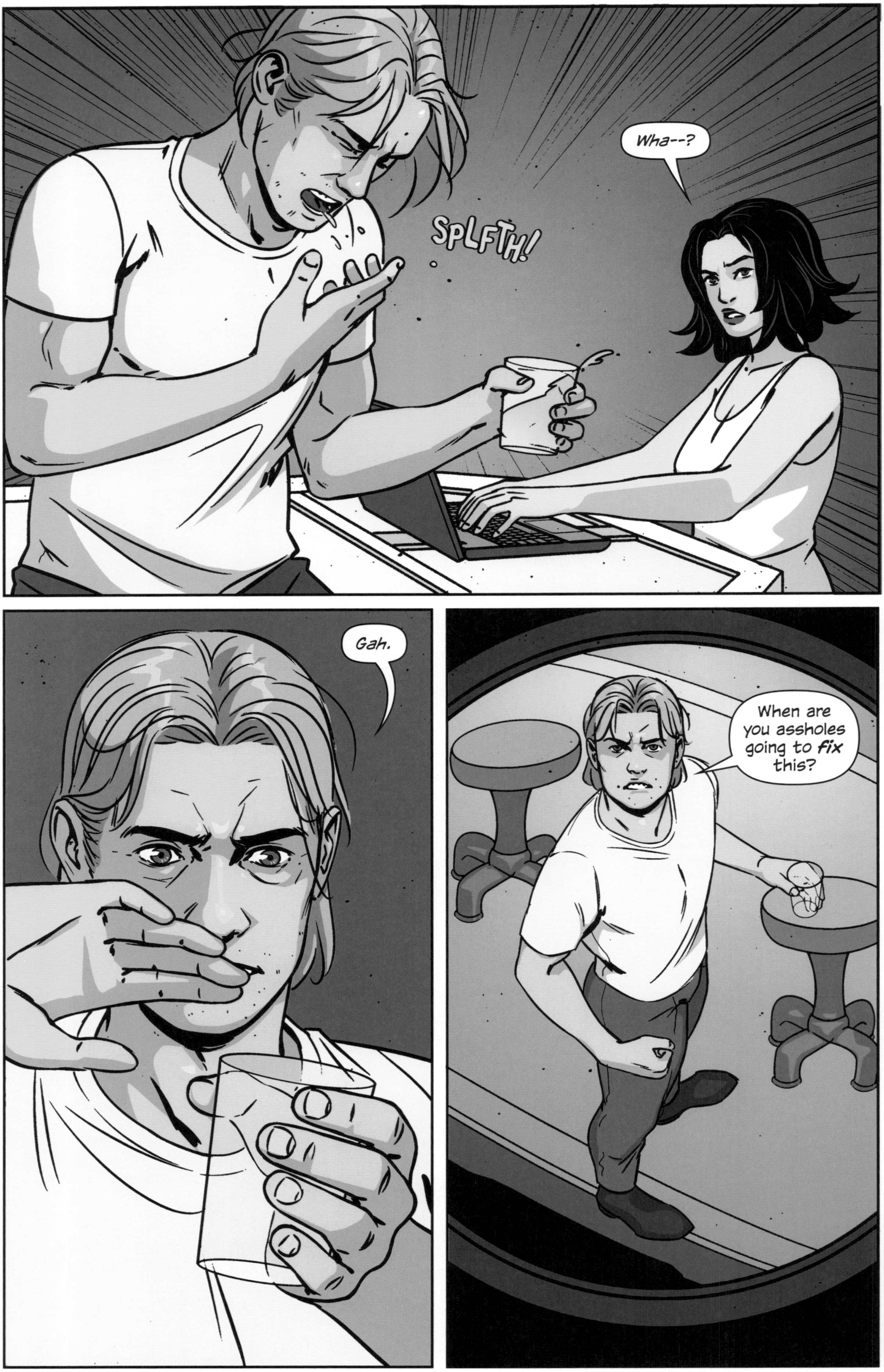
Wha--?
SPLFTH!
Gah.
When are you assholes going to ***fix*** this?

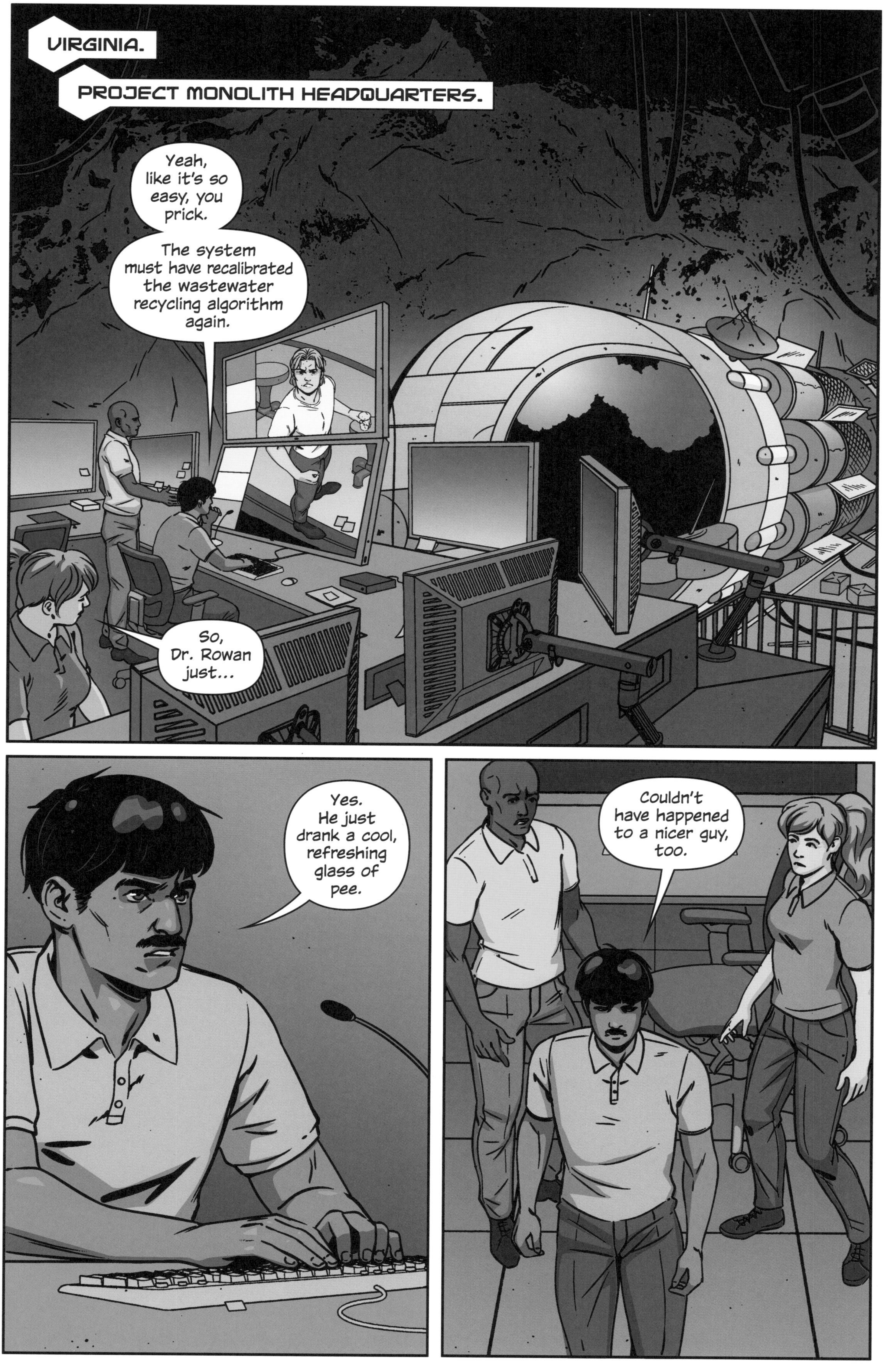
VIRGINIA.
PROJECT MONOLITH HEADQUARTERS.
Yeah, like it's so easy, you prick.
The system must have recalibrated the wastewater recycling algorithm again.
So, Dr. Rowan just...
Yes. He just drank a cool, refreshing glass of pee.
Couldn't have happened to a nicer guy, too.

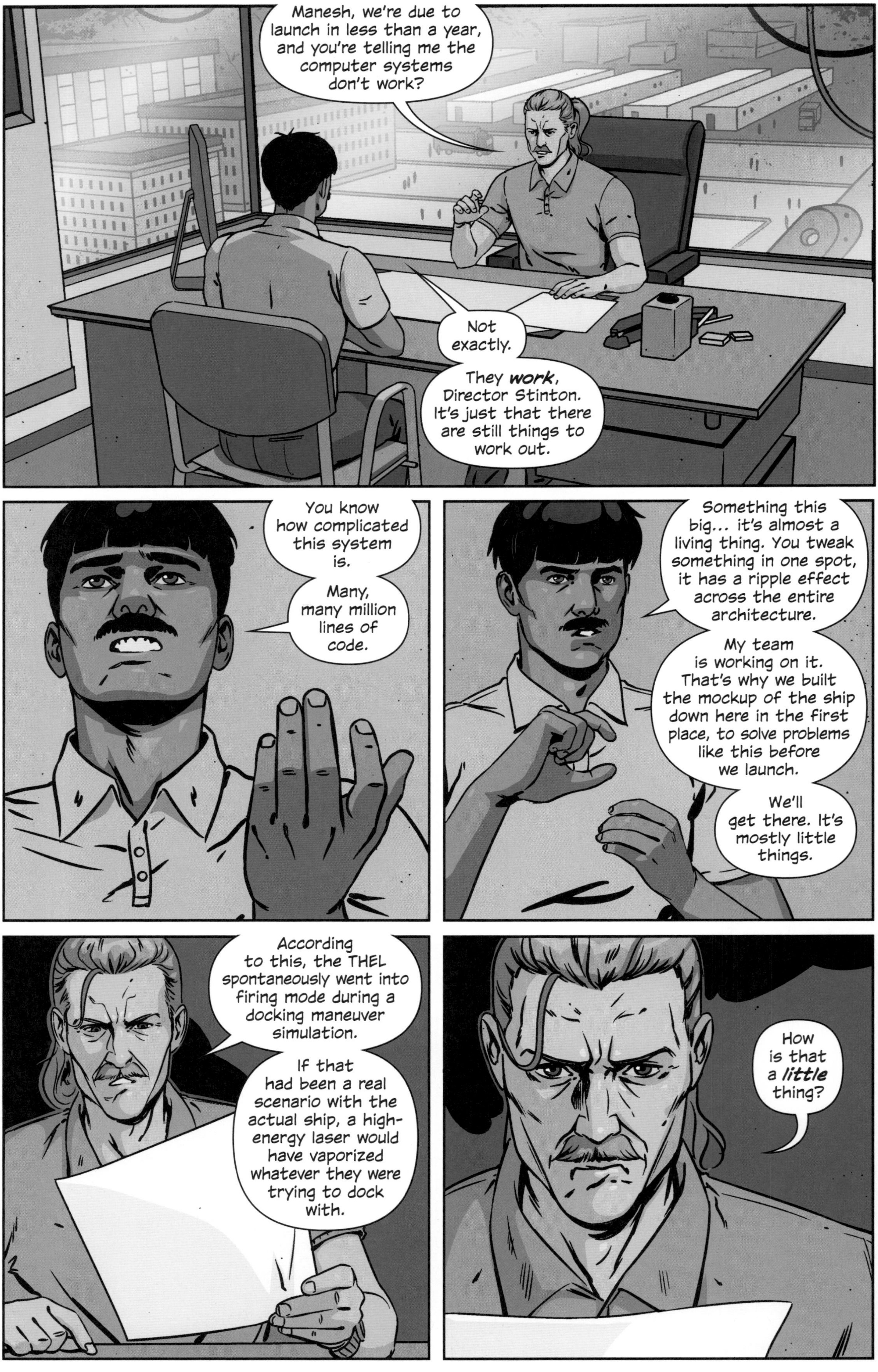

Manesh, we're due to launch in less than a year, and you're telling me the computer systems don't work?
Not exactly.
They *work*, Director Stinton. It's just that there are still things to work out.
You know how complicated this system is.
Many, many million lines of code.
Something this big... it's almost a living thing. You tweak something in one spot, it has a ripple effect across the entire architecture.
My team is working on it. That's why we built the mockup of the ship down here in the first place, to solve problems like this before we launch.
We'll get there. It's mostly little things.
According to this, the THEL spontaneously went into firing mode during a docking maneuver simulation.
If that had been a real scenario with the actual ship, a high-energy laser would have vaporized whatever they were trying to dock with.
How is that a *little* thing?

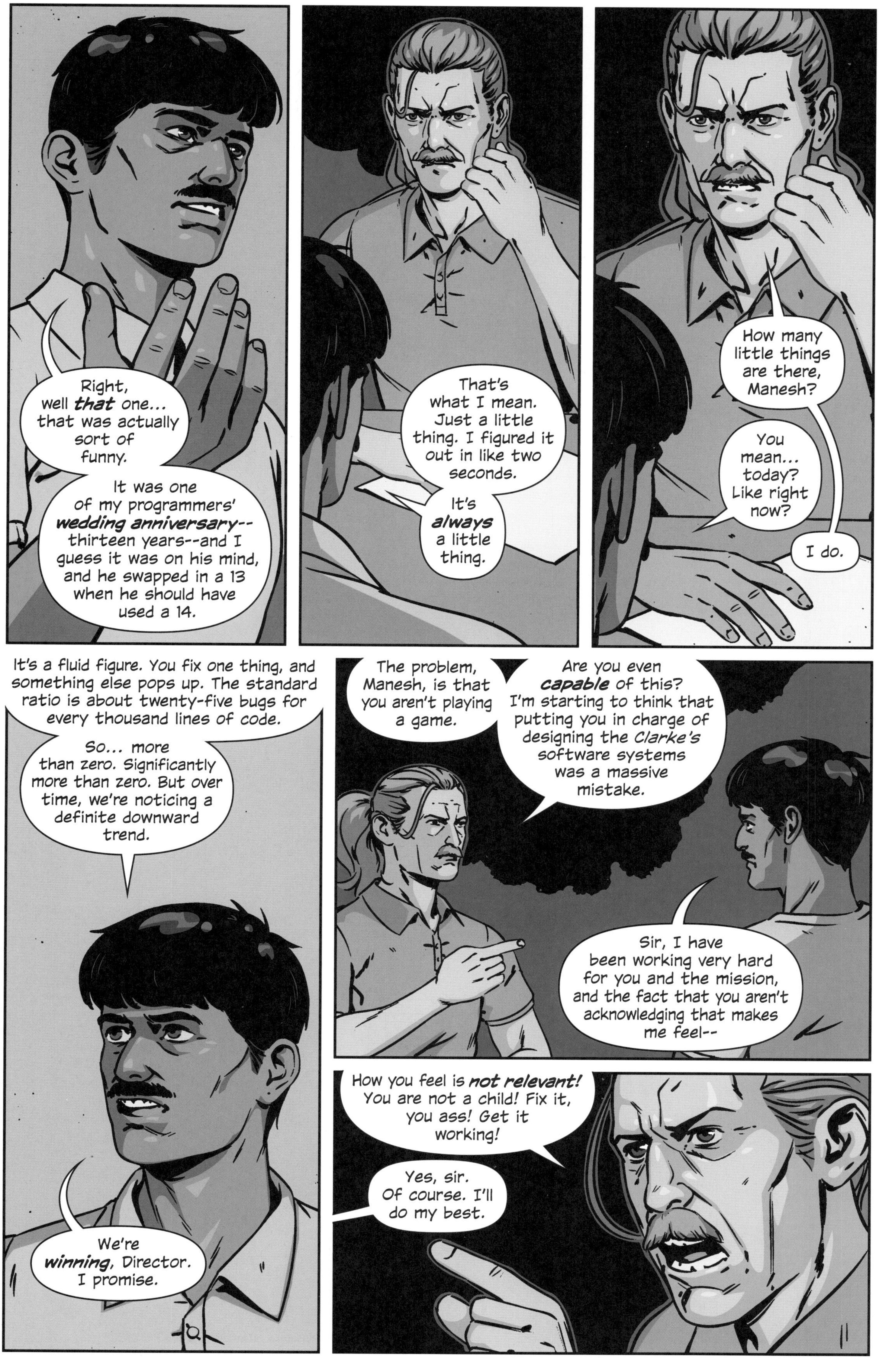

Right, well that one... that was actually sort of funny.
It was one of my programmers' wedding anniversary--thirteen years--and I guess it was on his mind, and he swapped in a 13 when he should have used a 14.
That's what I mean. Just a little thing. I figured it out in like two seconds.
It's always a little thing.
How many little things are there, Manesh?
You mean... today? Like right now?
I do.
It's a fluid figure. You fix one thing, and something else pops up. The standard ratio is about twenty-five bugs for every thousand lines of code.
So... more than zero. Significantly more than zero. But over time, we're noticing a definite downward trend.
We're winning, Director. I promise.
The problem, Manesh, is that you aren't playing a game.
Are you even capable of this? I'm starting to think that putting you in charge of designing the Clarke's software systems was a massive mistake.
Sir, I have been working very hard for you and the mission, and the fact that you aren't acknowledging that makes me feel--
How you feel is not relevant! You are not a child! Fix it, you ass! Get it working!
Yes, sir. Of course. I'll do my best.

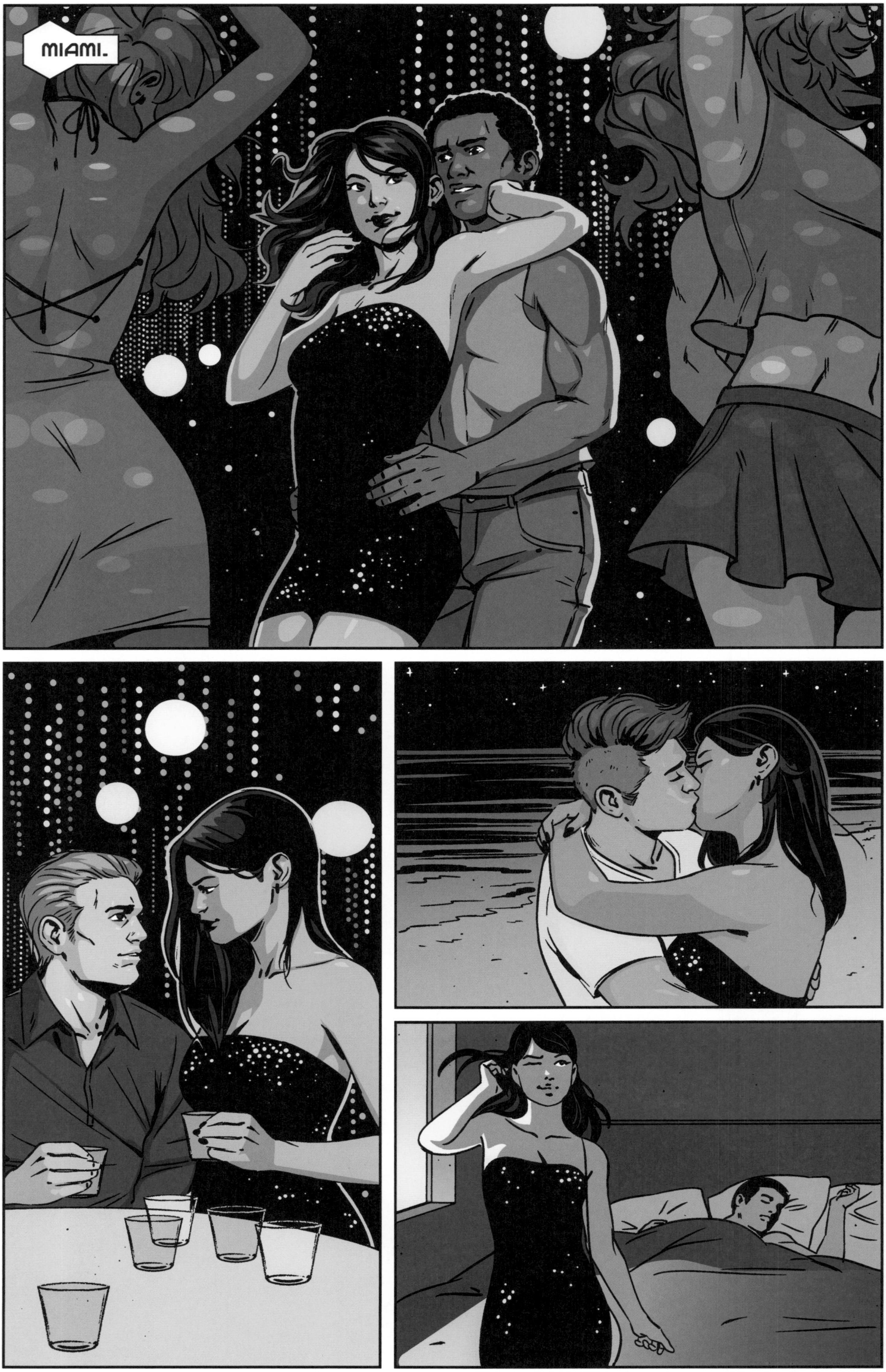
MIAMI.

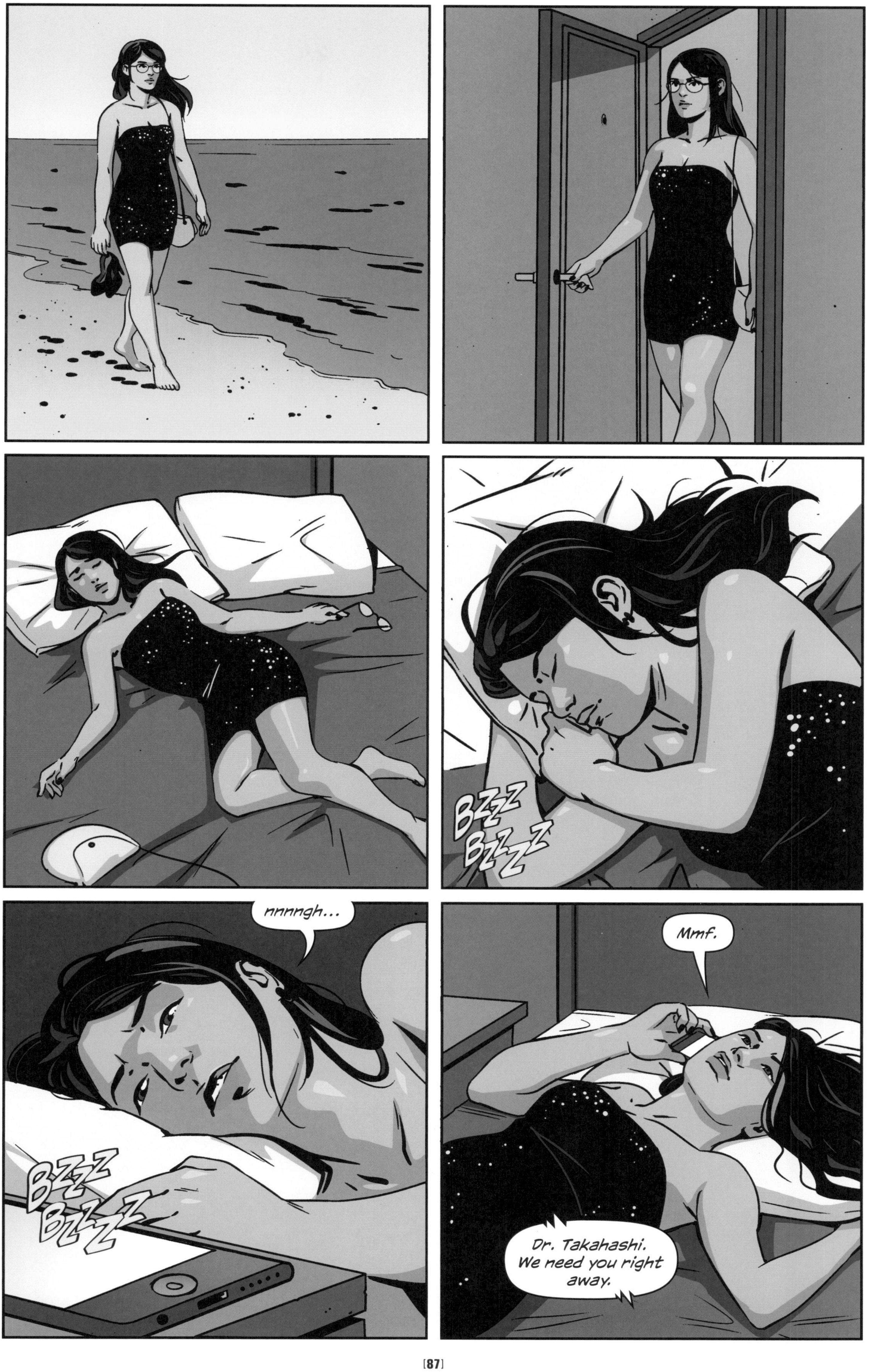
BZZZ
BZZZZ
nnnngh...
BZZZ
BZZZZ
Mmf.
Dr. Takahashi. We need you right away.

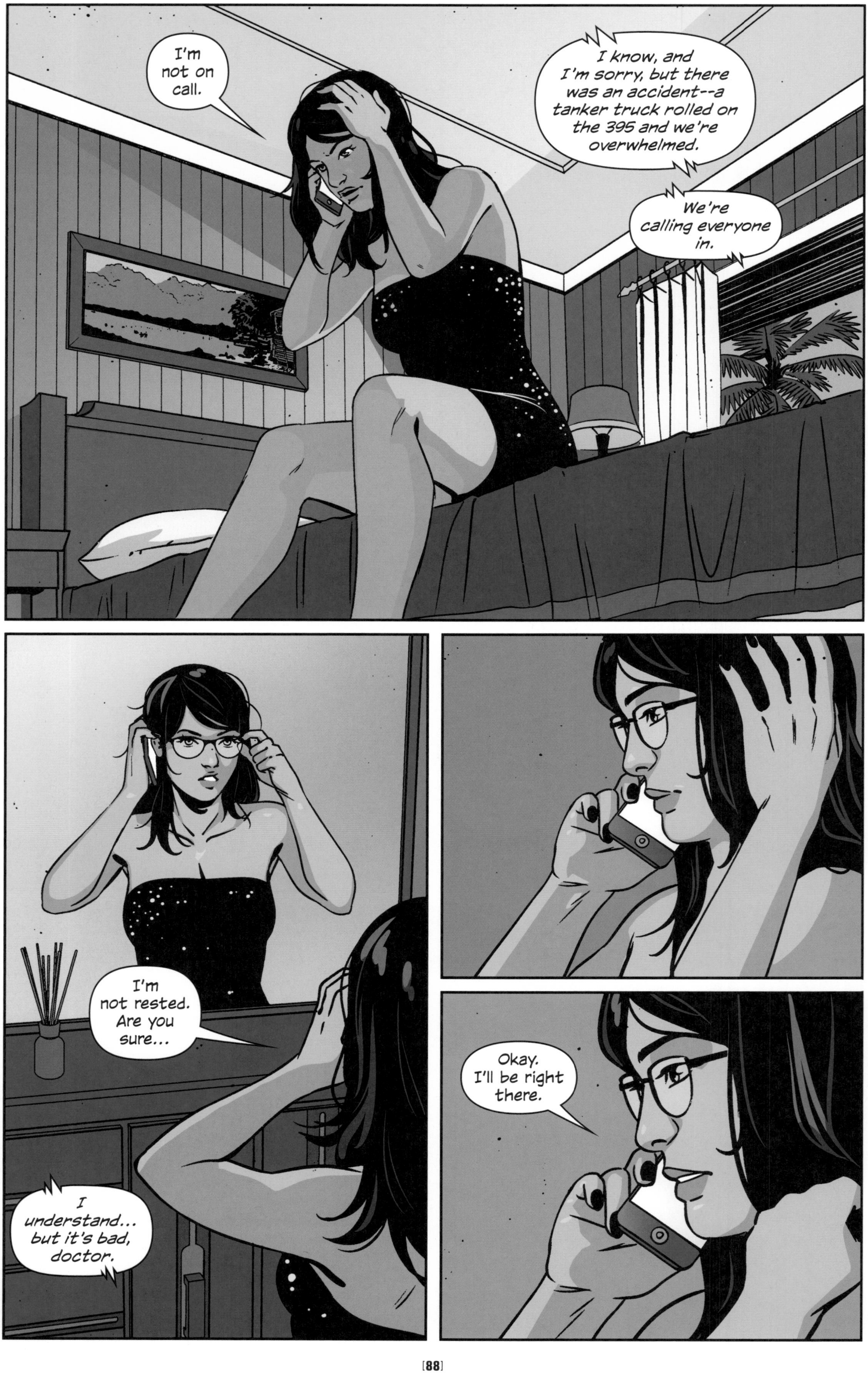
I'm not on call.
I know, and I'm sorry, but there was an accident--a tanker truck rolled on the 395 and we're overwhelmed.
We're calling everyone in.
I'm not rested. Are you sure...
I understand... but it's bad, doctor.
Okay. I'll be right there.

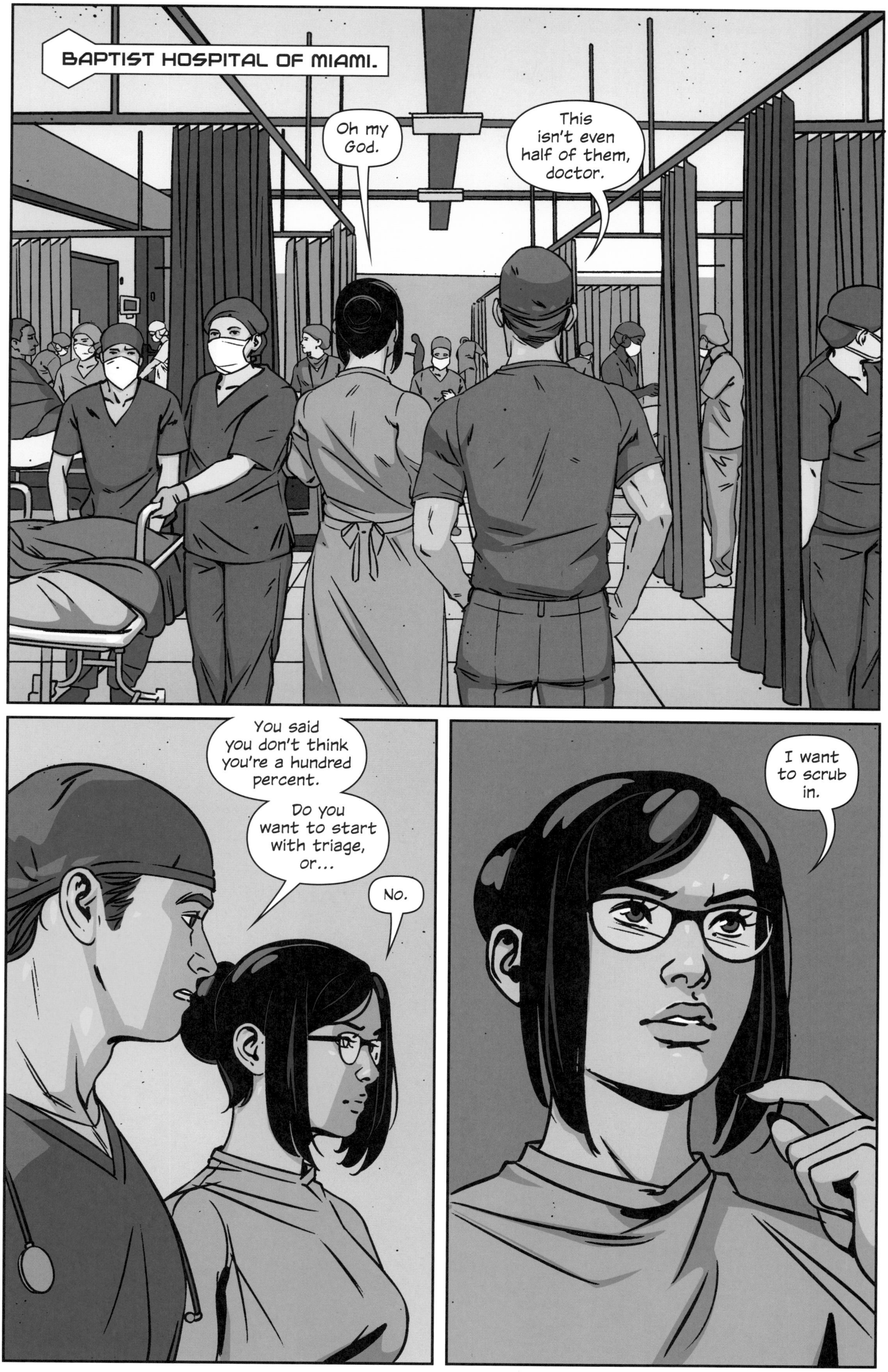
BAPTIST HOSPITAL OF MIAMI.
Oh my God.
This isn't even half of them, doctor.
You said you don't think you're a hundred percent.
Do you want to start with triage, or...
No.
I want to scrub in.

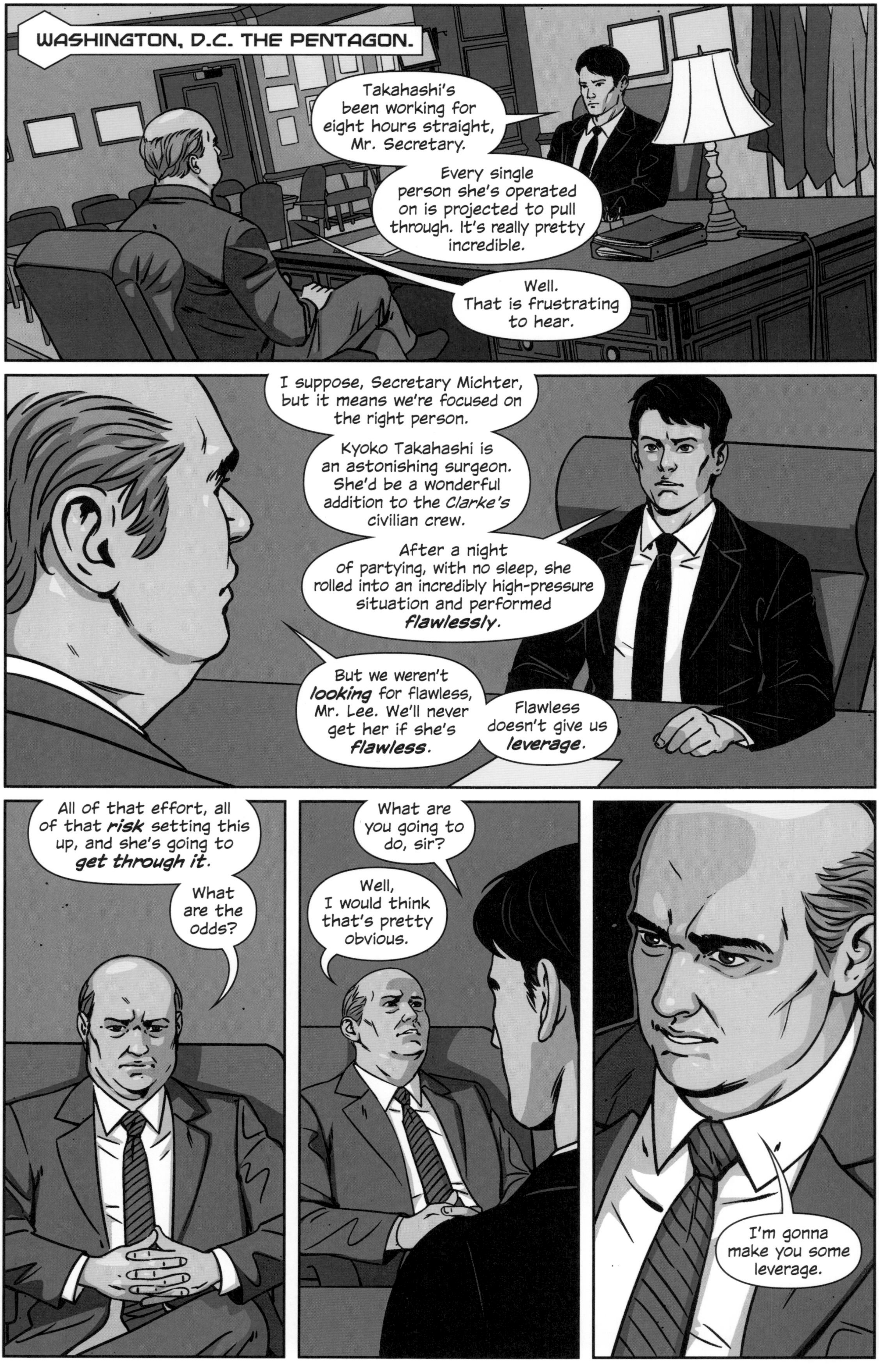
WASHINGTON, D.C. THE PENTAGON.
Takahashi's been working for eight hours straight, Mr. Secretary.
Every single person she's operated on is projected to pull through. It's really pretty incredible.
Well. That is frustrating to hear.
I suppose, Secretary Michter, but it means we're focused on the right person.
Kyoko Takahashi is an astonishing surgeon. She'd be a wonderful addition to the *Clarke's* civilian crew.
After a night of partying, with no sleep, she rolled into an incredibly high-pressure situation and performed ***flawlessly***.
But we weren't ***looking*** for flawless, Mr. Lee. We'll never get her if she's ***flawless***.
Flawless doesn't give us ***leverage***.
All of that effort, all of that ***risk*** setting this up, and she's going to ***get through it***.
What are the odds?
What are you going to do, sir?
Well, I would think that's pretty obvious.
I'm gonna make you some leverage.

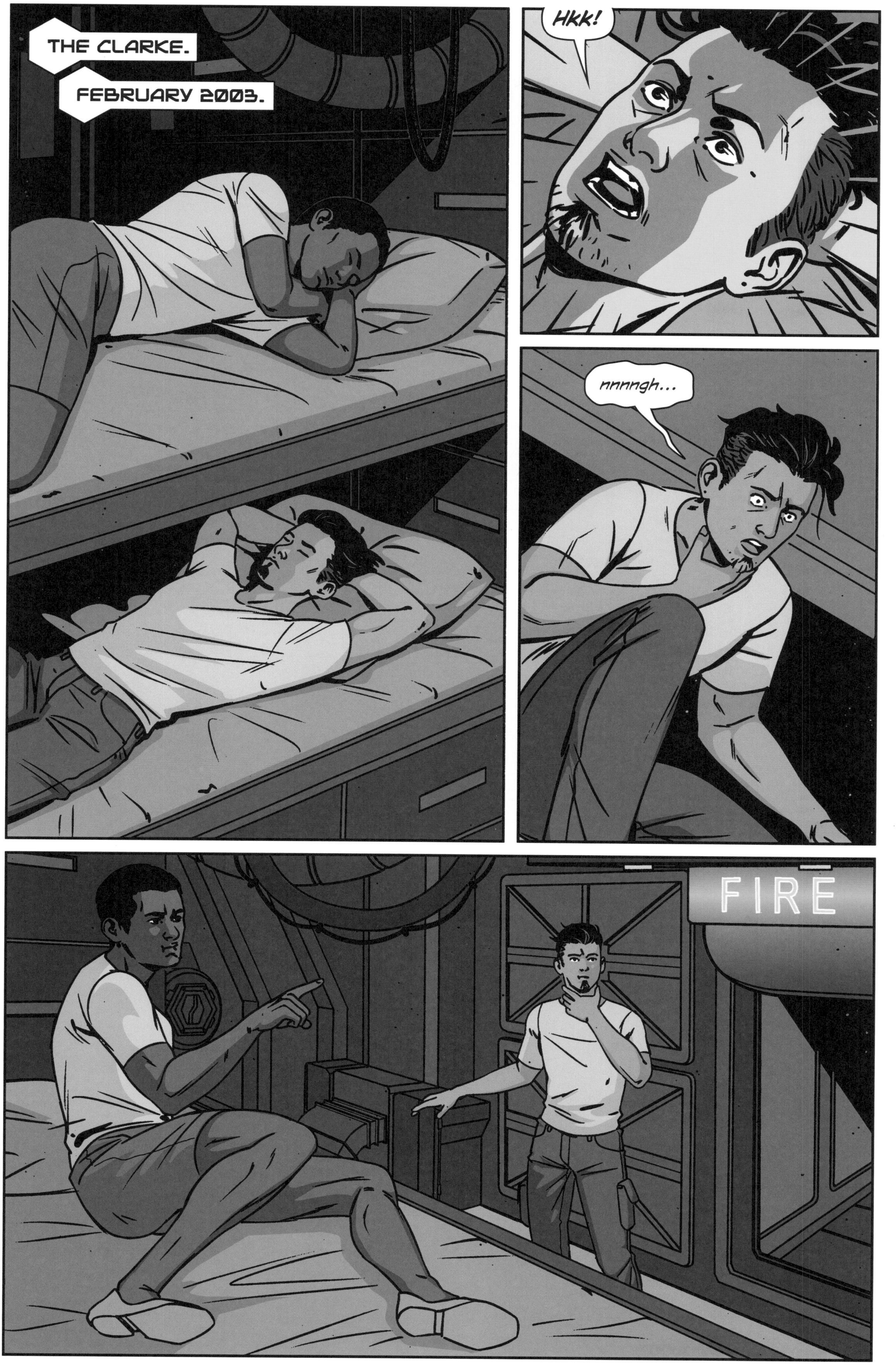
THE CLARKE.
FEBRUARY 2003.
Hkk!
nnnngh...
FIRE

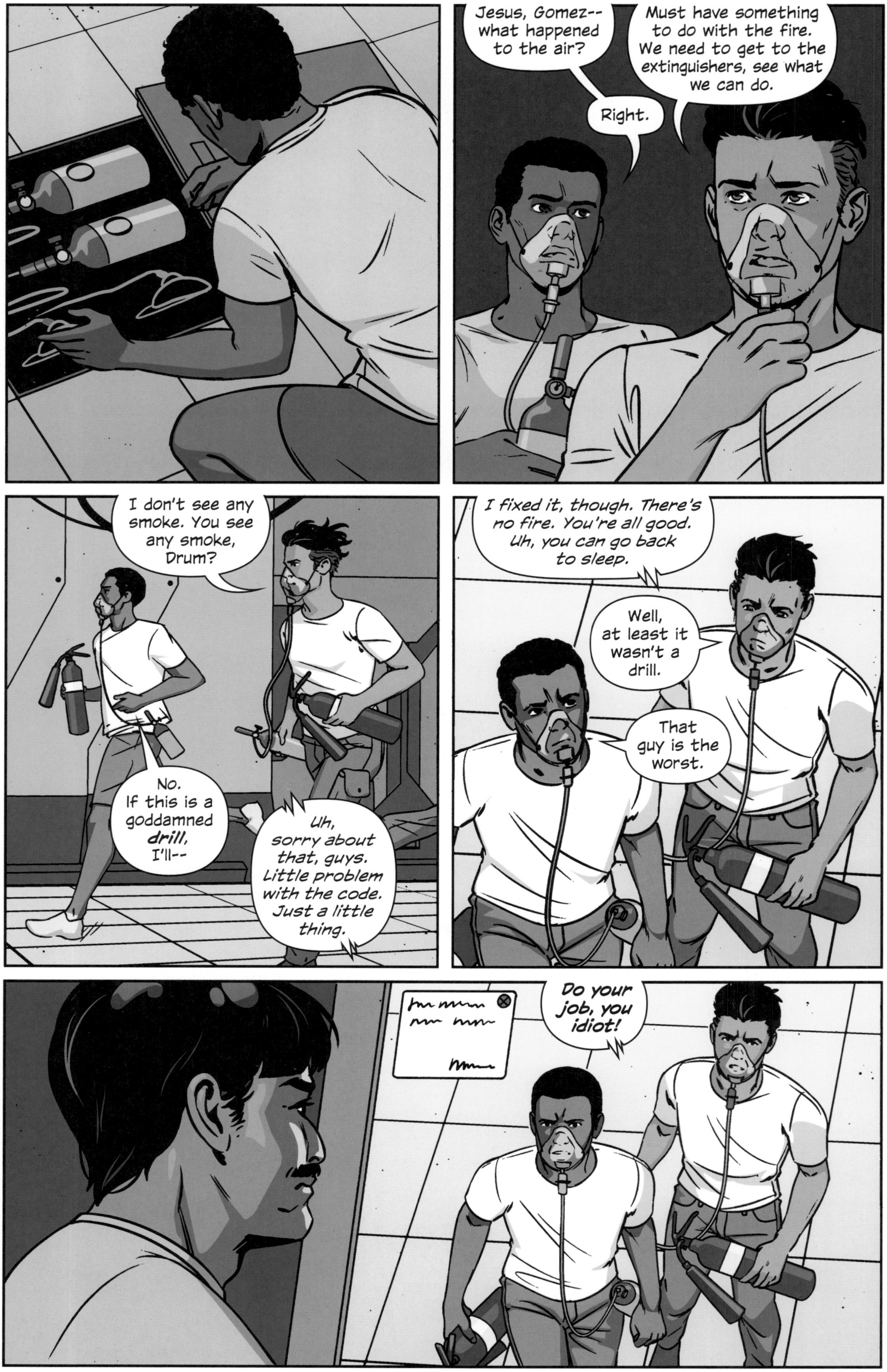
Jesus, Gomez--
what happened
to the air?
Must have something
to do with the fire.
We need to get to the
extinguishers, see what
we can do.
Right.
I don't see any
smoke. You see
any smoke,
Drum?
No.
If this is a
goddamned
drill,
I'll--
Uh,
sorry about
that, guys.
Little problem
with the code.
Just a little
thing.
I fixed it, though. There's
no fire. You're all good.
Uh, you can go back
to sleep.
Well,
at least it
wasn't a
drill.
That
guy is the
worst.
Do your
job, you
idiot!

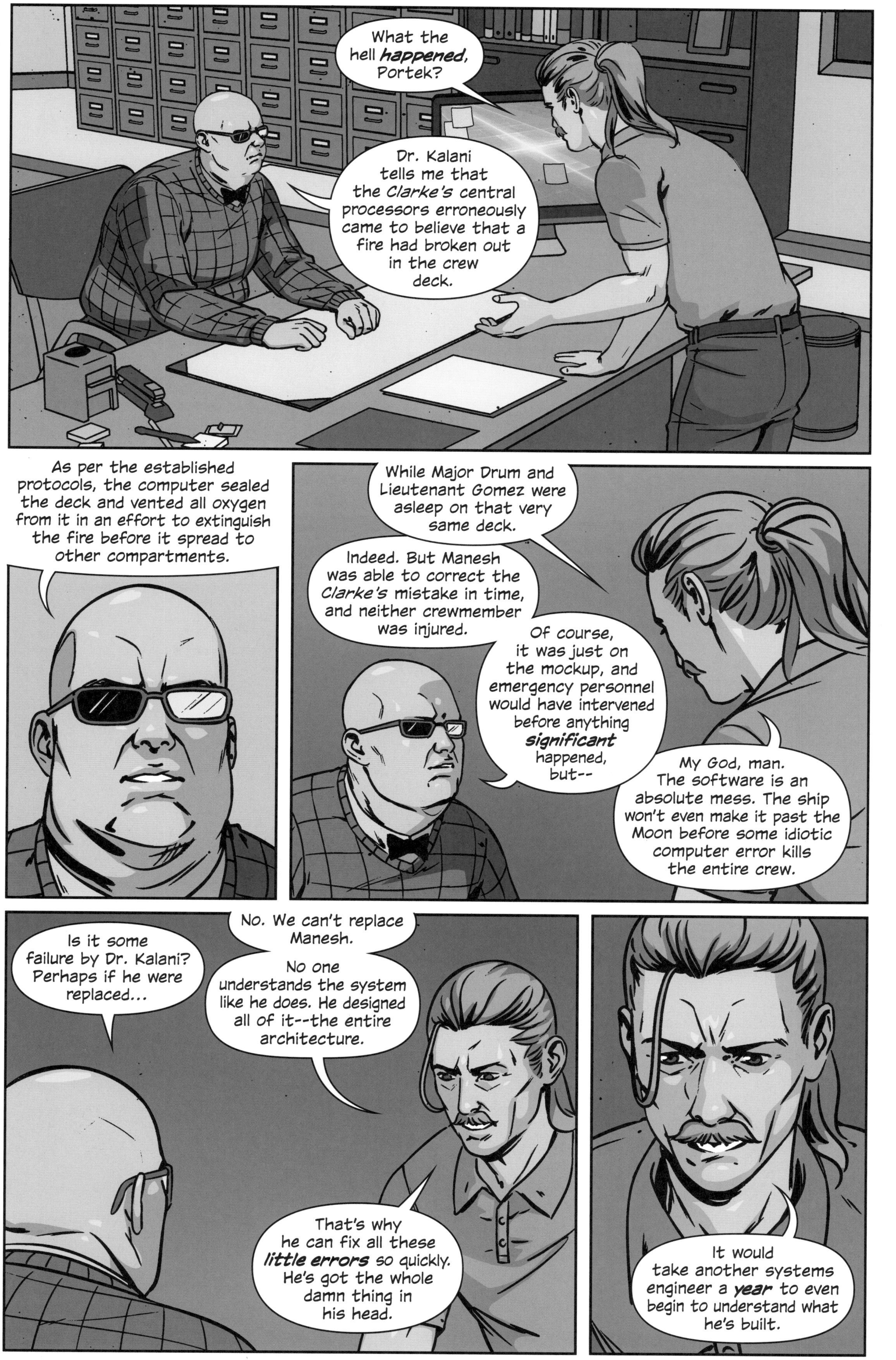
What the hell *happened*, Portek?
Dr. Kalani tells me that the *Clarke's* central processors erroneously came to believe that a fire had broken out in the crew deck.
As per the established protocols, the computer sealed the deck and vented all oxygen from it in an effort to extinguish the fire before it spread to other compartments.
While Major Drum and Lieutenant Gomez were asleep on that very same deck.
Indeed. But Manesh was able to correct the *Clarke's* mistake in time, and neither crewmember was injured.
Of course, it was just on the mockup, and emergency personnel would have intervened before anything ***significant*** happened, but--
My God, man. The software is an absolute mess. The ship won't even make it past the Moon before some idiotic computer error kills the entire crew.
Is it some failure by Dr. Kalani? Perhaps if he were replaced...
No. We can't replace Manesh.
No one understands the system like he does. He designed all of it--the entire architecture.
That's why he can fix all these ***little errors*** so quickly. He's got the whole damn thing in his head.
It would take another systems engineer a ***year*** to even begin to understand what he's built.

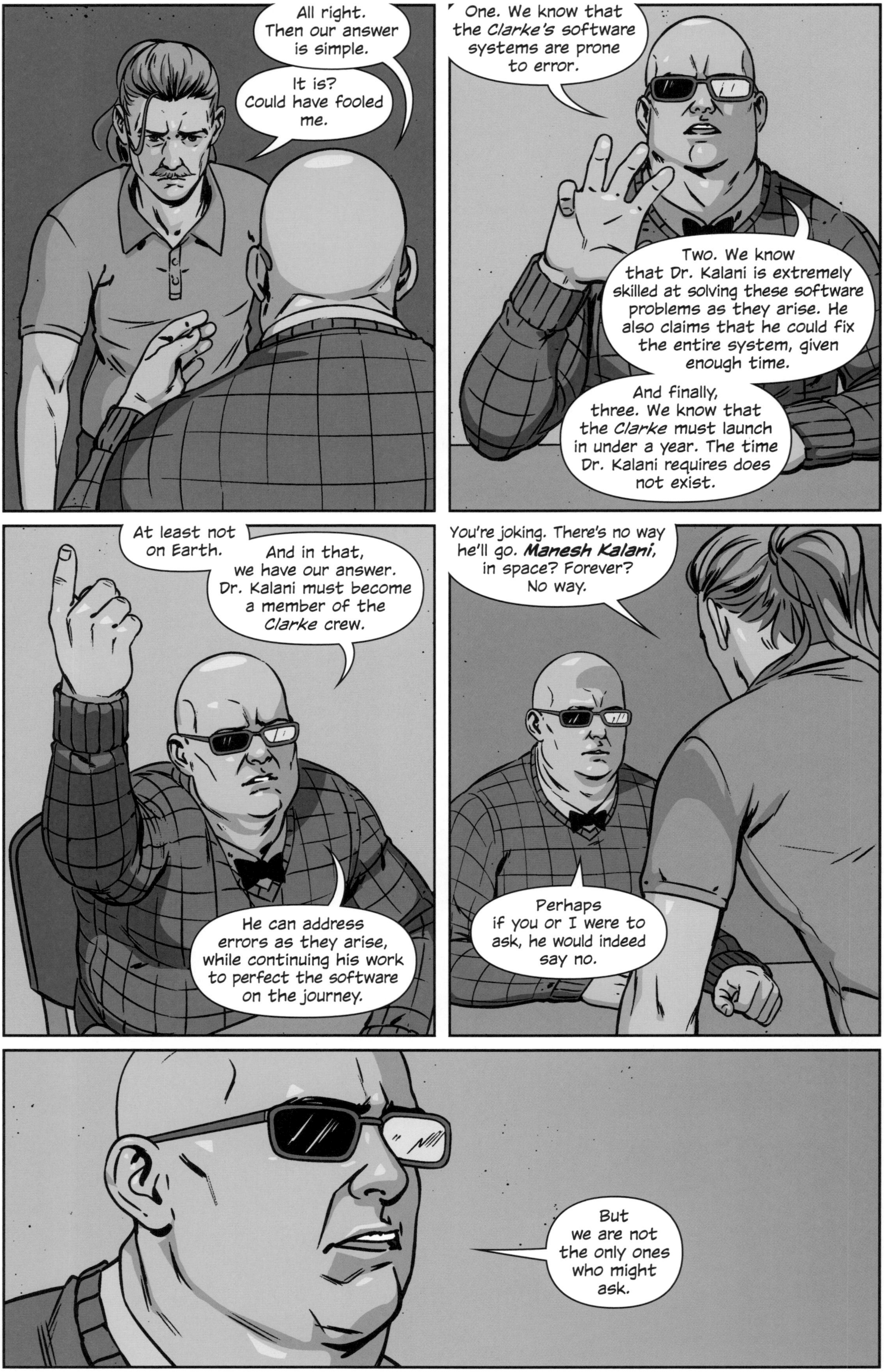
All right. Then our answer is simple.
It is? Could have fooled me.
One. We know that the *Clarke's* software systems are prone to error.
Two. We know that Dr. Kalani is extremely skilled at solving these software problems as they arise. He also claims that he could fix the entire system, given enough time.
And finally, three. We know that the *Clarke* must launch in under a year. The time Dr. Kalani requires does not exist.
At least not on Earth.
And in that, we have our answer. Dr. Kalani must become a member of the *Clarke* crew.
He can address errors as they arise, while continuing his work to perfect the software on the journey.
You're joking. There's no way he'll go. ***Manesh Kalani***, in space? Forever? No way.
Perhaps if you or I were to ask, he would indeed say no.
But we are not the only ones who might ask.

No, this is impossible. This woman was fine. I fixed her.

How the hell is she dead?

I'm so sorry, Kyoko.

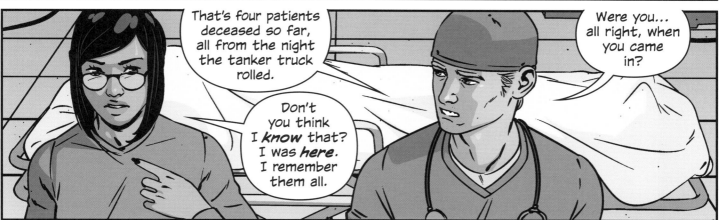

That's four patients deceased so far, all from the night the tanker truck rolled.

Don't you think I *know* that? I was *here*. I remember them all.

Were you... all right, when you came in?

What does *that* mean?

We spoke to the dispatcher, and--

We? Who the hell is *we*?

The administrative board. The dispatcher said you were exhausted. Didn't want to come in.

She *begged* me to pull a shift. I wasn't on call, and I came in anyway. To *help*. What are you saying, John?

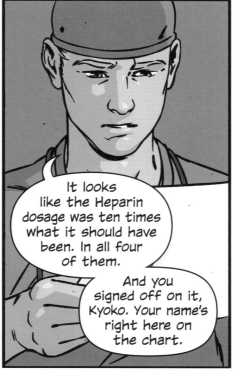

It looks like the Heparin dosage was ten times what it should have been. In all four of them.

And you signed off on it, Kyoko. Your name's right here on the chart.

Fuck. I... fuck.

[95]

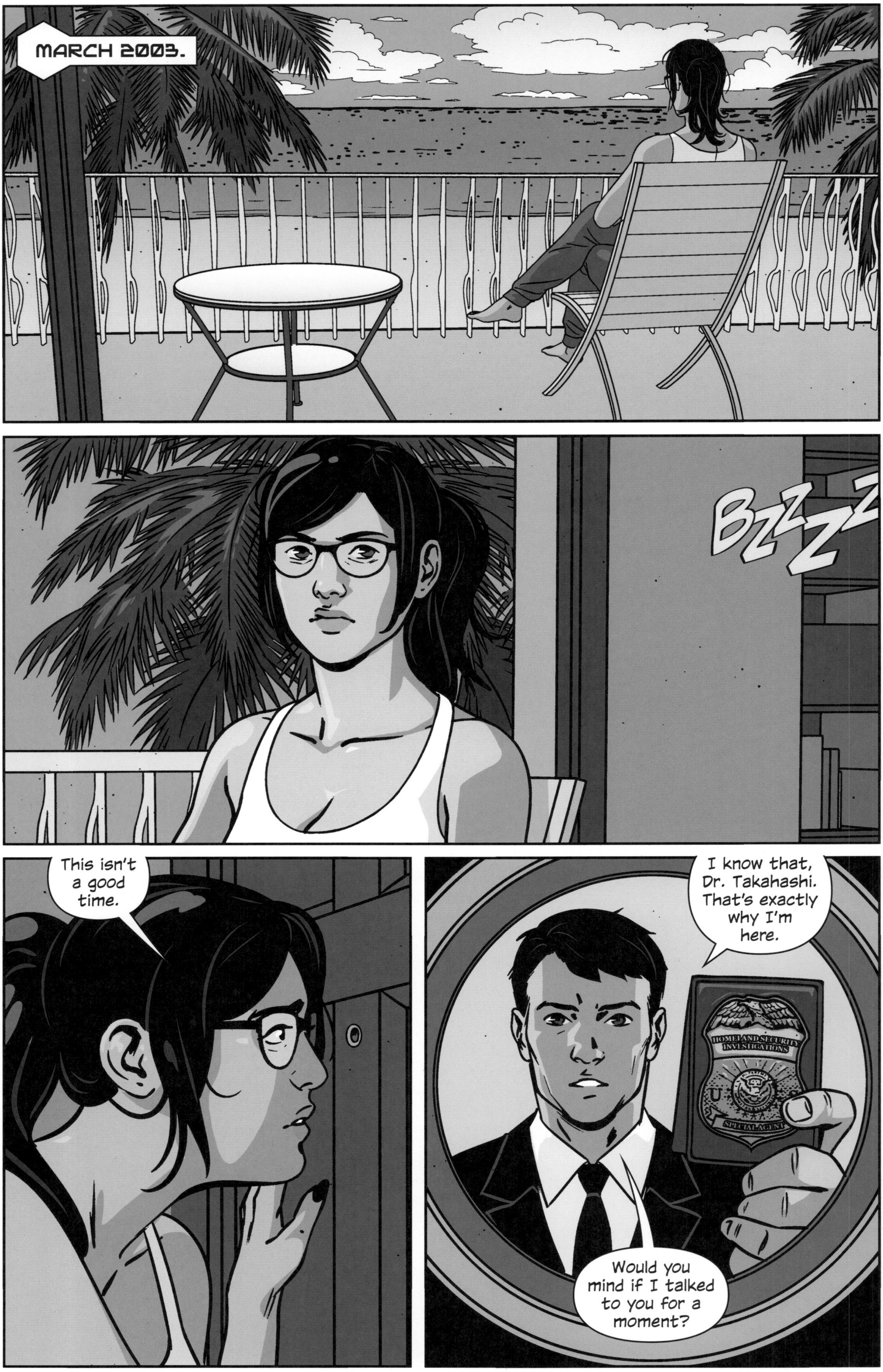
MARCH 2003.
BZZZZ
This isn't a good time.
I know that, Dr. Takahashi. That's exactly why I'm here.
Would you mind if I talked to you for a moment?

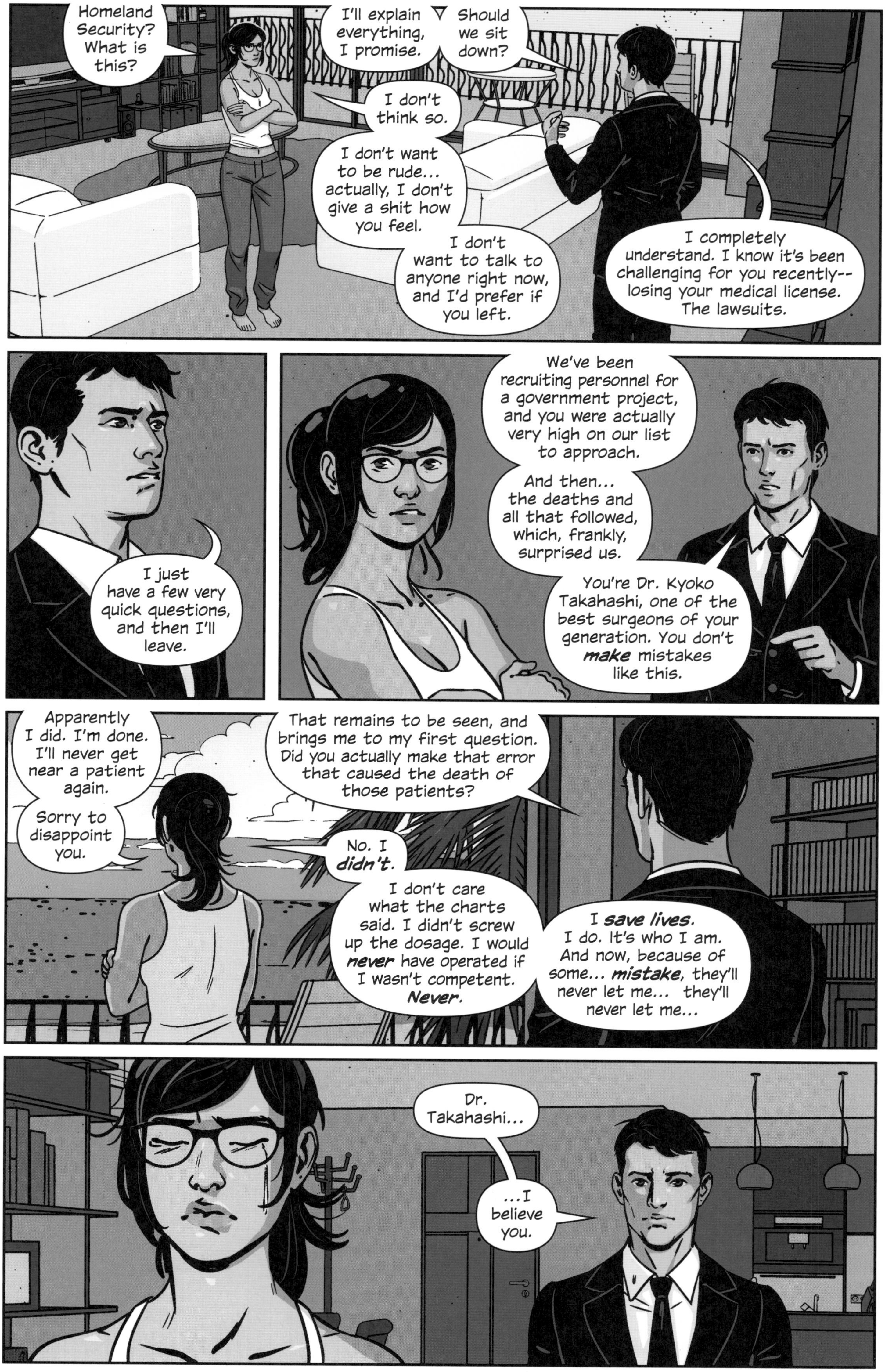
Homeland Security? What is this?
I'll explain everything, I promise.
Should we sit down?
I don't think so.
I don't want to be rude... actually, I don't give a shit how you feel.
I don't want to talk to anyone right now, and I'd prefer if you left.
I completely understand. I know it's been challenging for you recently-- losing your medical license. The lawsuits.
I just have a few very quick questions, and then I'll leave.
We've been recruiting personnel for a government project, and you were actually very high on our list to approach.
And then... the deaths and all that followed, which, frankly, surprised us.
You're Dr. Kyoko Takahashi, one of the best surgeons of your generation. You don't *make* mistakes like this.
Apparently I did. I'm done. I'll never get near a patient again.
Sorry to disappoint you.
That remains to be seen, and brings me to my first question. Did you actually make that error that caused the death of those patients?
No. I *didn't*.
I don't care what the charts said. I didn't screw up the dosage. I would *never* have operated if I wasn't competent. *Never*.
I *save lives*. I do. It's who I am. And now, because of some... *mistake*, they'll never let me... they'll never let me...
Dr. Takahashi...
...I believe you.

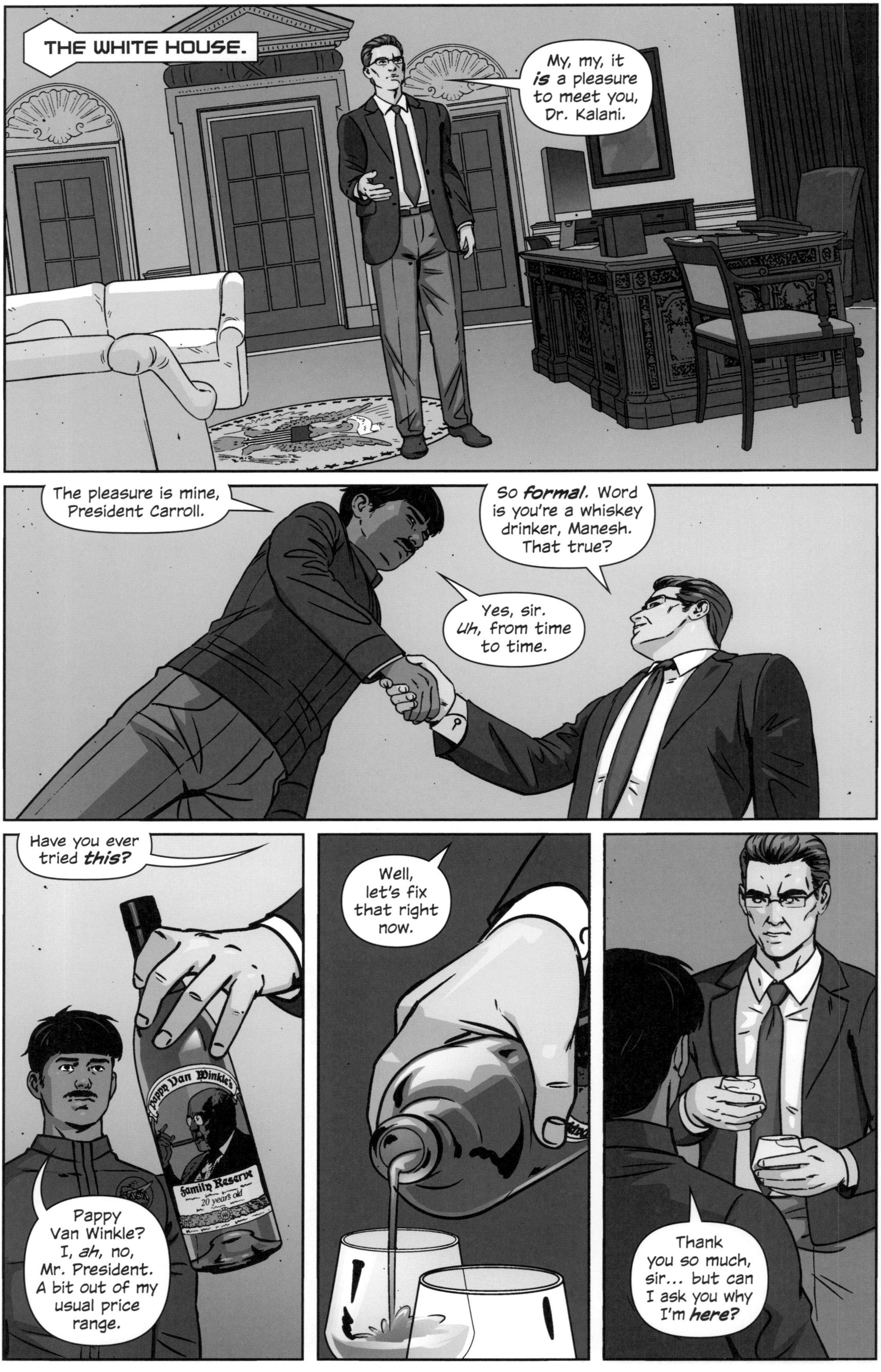
THE WHITE HOUSE.
My, my, it *is* a pleasure to meet you, Dr. Kalani.
The pleasure is mine, President Carroll.
So *formal.* Word is you're a whiskey drinker, Manesh. That true?
Yes, sir. *Uh,* from time to time.
Have you ever tried *this?*
Pappy Van Winkle's
Family Reserve
20 years old
Pappy Van Winkle? I, *ah,* no, Mr. President. A bit out of my usual price range.
Well, let's fix that right now.
Thank you so much, sir... but can I ask you why I'm *here?*

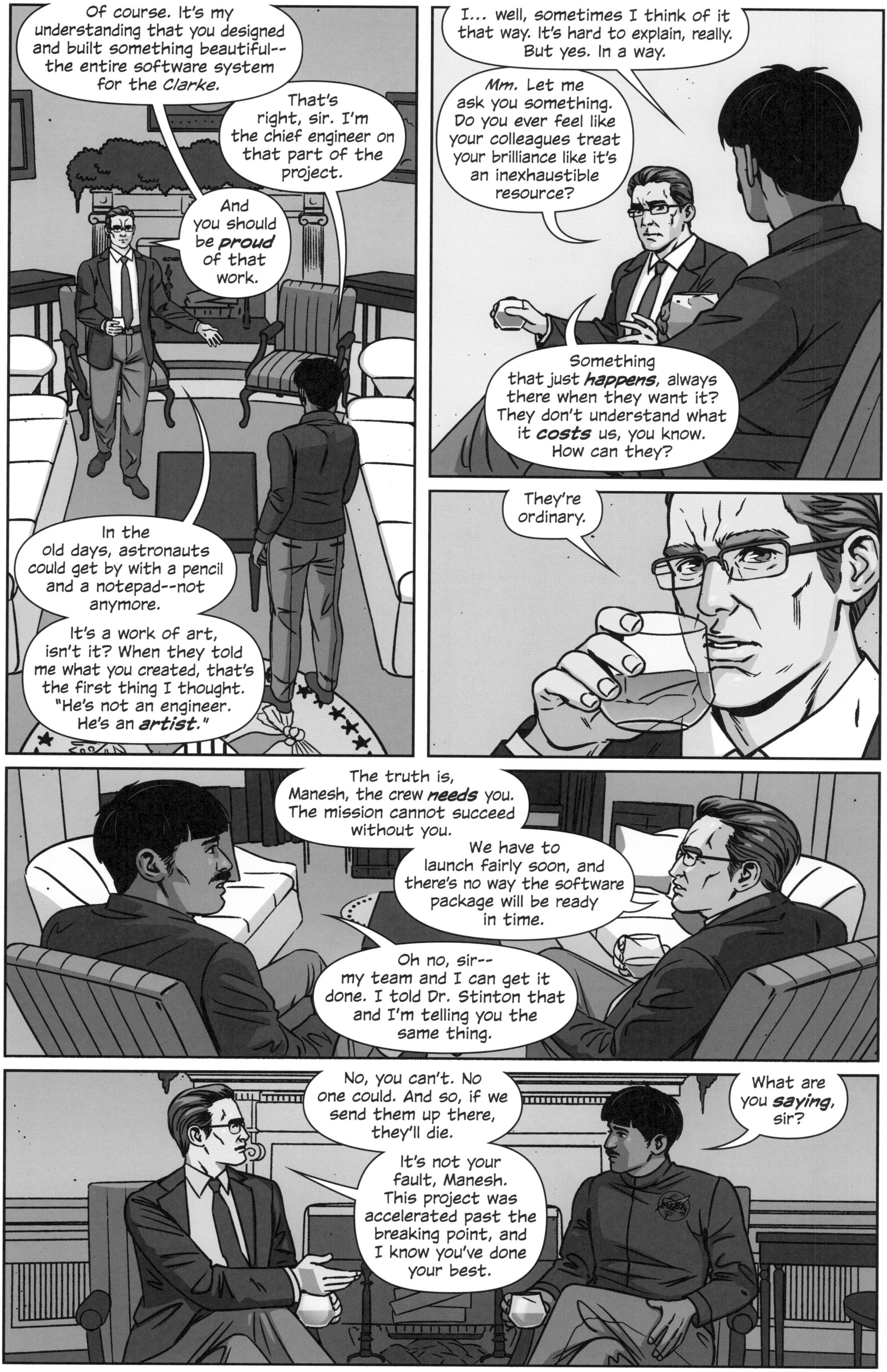
Of course. It's my understanding that you designed and built something beautiful--the entire software system for the *Clarke*.
That's right, sir. I'm the chief engineer on that part of the project.
And you should be ***proud*** of that work.
In the old days, astronauts could get by with a pencil and a notepad--not anymore.
It's a work of art, isn't it? When they told me what you created, that's the first thing I thought. "He's not an engineer. He's an ***artist***."
I... well, sometimes I think of it that way. It's hard to explain, really. But yes. In a way.
Mm. Let me ask you something. Do you ever feel like your colleagues treat your brilliance like it's an inexhaustible resource?
Something that just ***happens***, always there when they want it? They don't understand what it ***costs*** us, you know. How can they?
They're ordinary.
The truth is, Manesh, the crew ***needs*** you. The mission cannot succeed without you.
We have to launch fairly soon, and there's no way the software package will be ready in time.
Oh no, sir--my team and I can get it done. I told Dr. Stinton that and I'm telling you the same thing.
No, you can't. No one could. And so, if we send them up there, they'll die.
It's not your fault, Manesh. This project was accelerated past the breaking point, and I know you've done your best.
What are you ***saying***, sir?

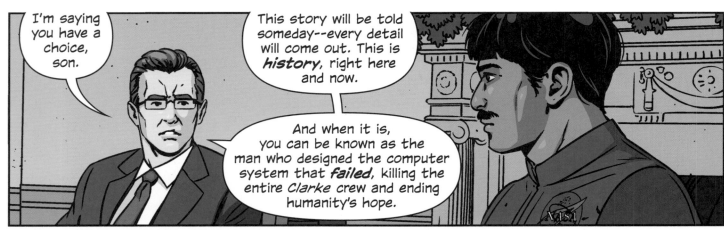

I'm saying you have a choice, son.

This story will be told someday--every detail will come out. This is *history*, right here and now.

And when it is, you can be known as the man who designed the computer system that *failed*, killing the entire *Clarke* crew and ending humanity's hope.

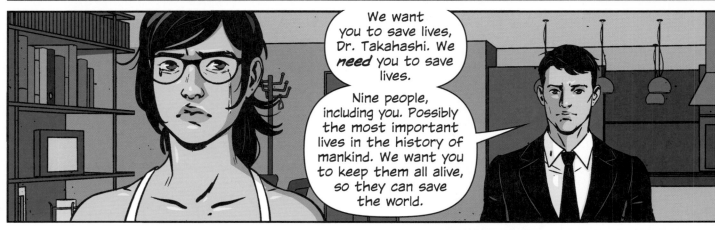

We want you to save lives, Dr. Takahashi. We *need* you to save lives.

Nine people, including you. Possibly the most important lives in the history of mankind. We want you to keep them all alive, so they can save the world.

Or... you can be the man who created the perfect, beautiful systems that made the whole thing possible.

But they have to be finished to make them perfect, and I want you to ask yourself if *anyone* else in the world can actually do that. Who else can *see* it like you do?

As far as we're concerned, nothing has changed. We want you as much as we ever did.

So, now, before I say anything else... my second question. Do you still want me to leave?

Who else has the *art*?

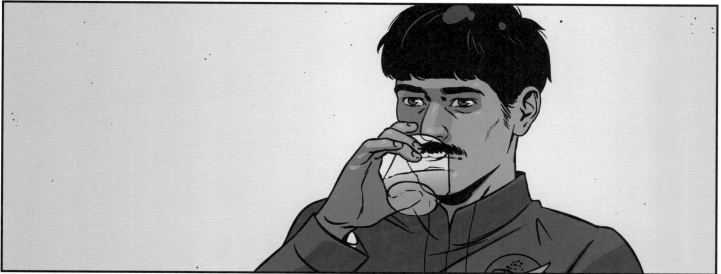

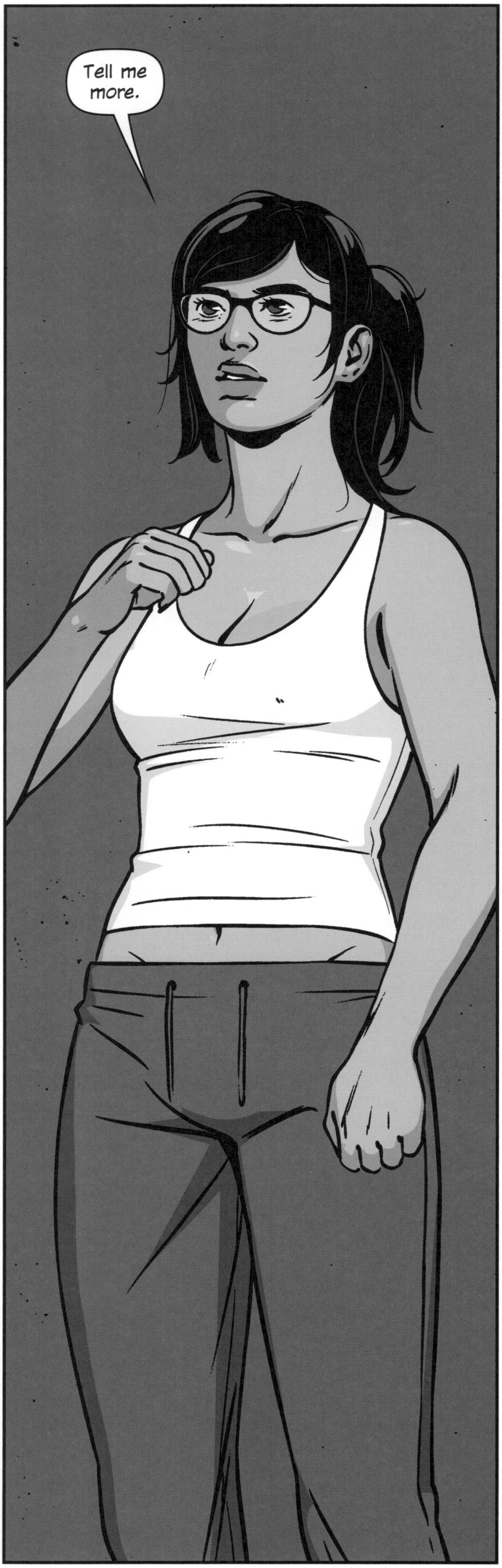
Tell me more.

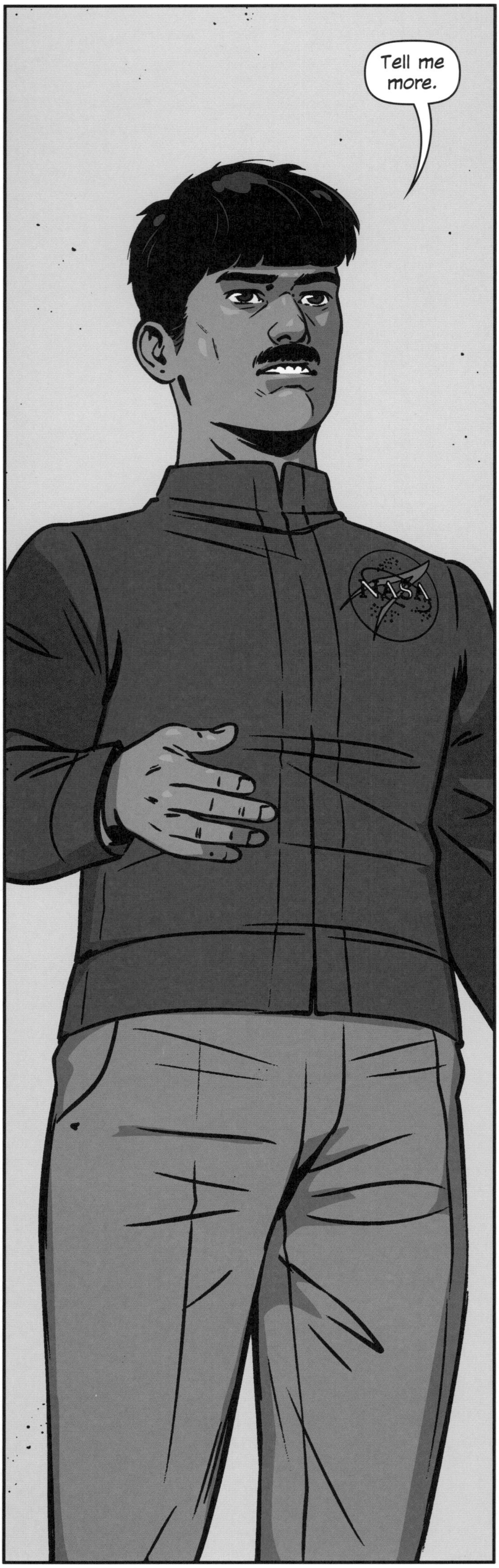
Tell me more.
NASA

LETTER 44

CHAPTER V

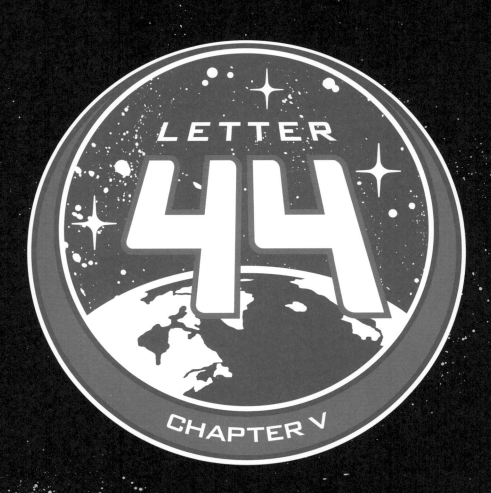

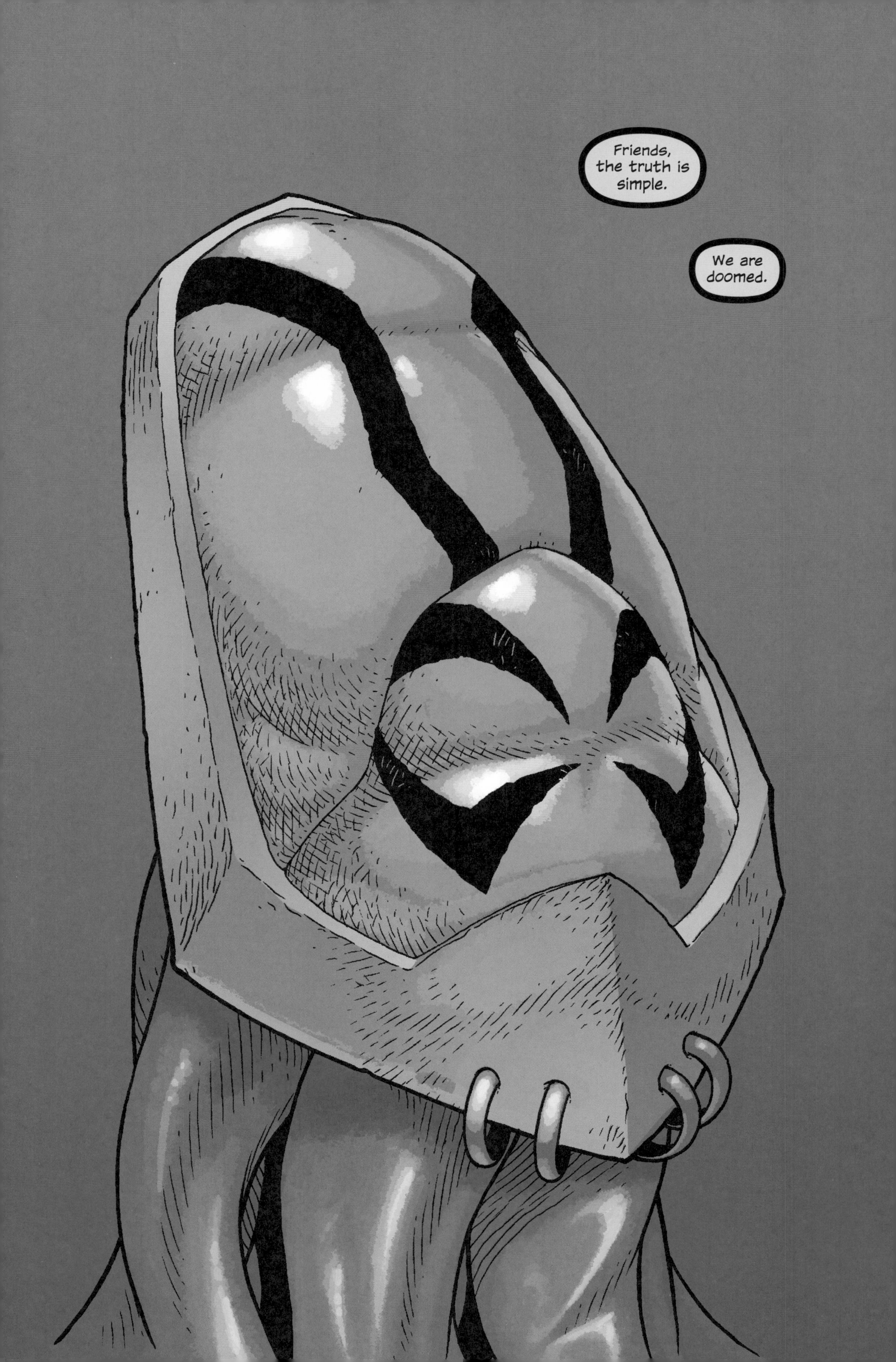
Friends, the truth is simple.
We are doomed.

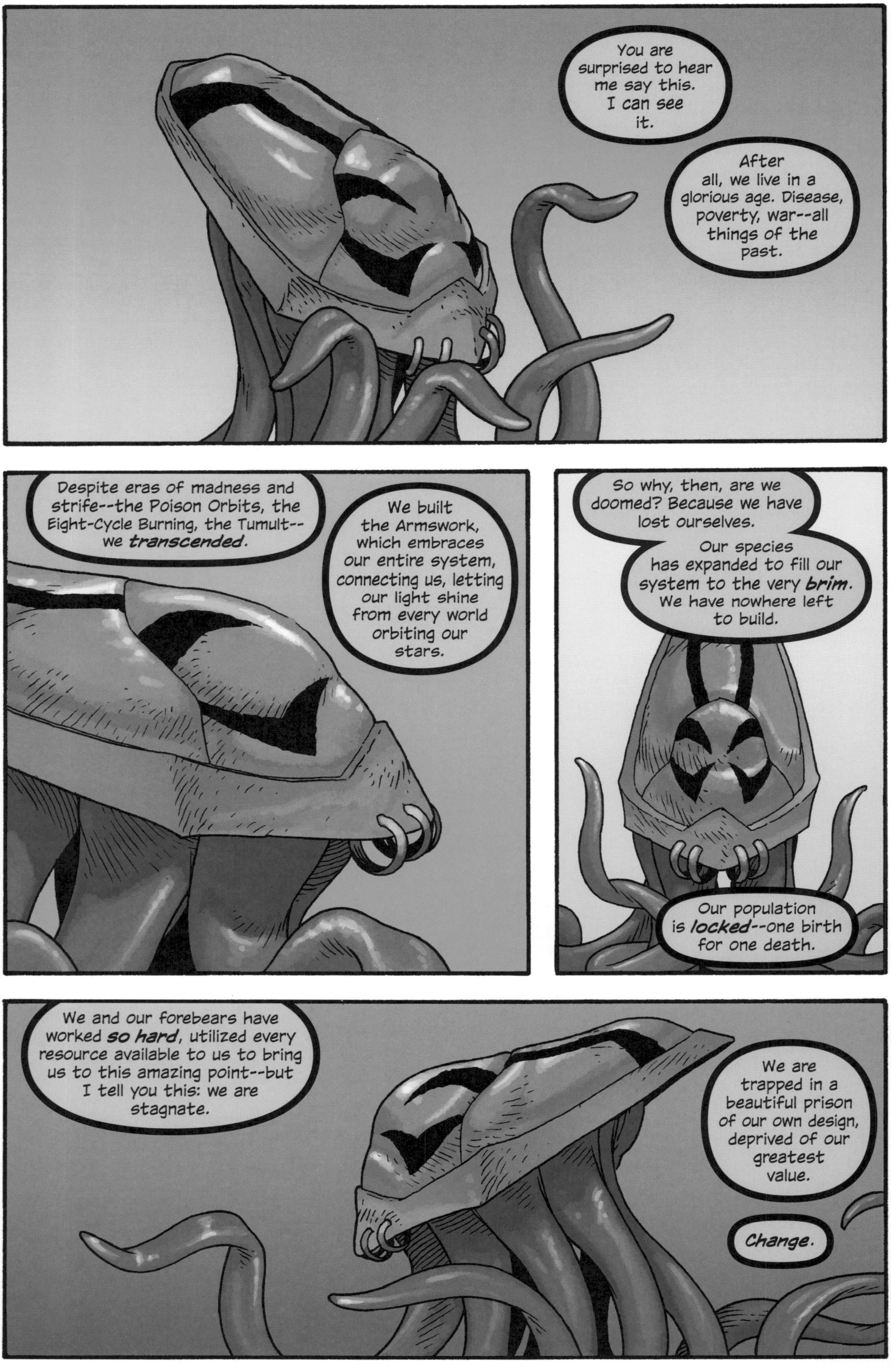
You are surprised to hear me say this. I can see it.
After all, we live in a glorious age. Disease, poverty, war--all things of the past.
Despite eras of madness and strife--the Poison Orbits, the Eight-Cycle Burning, the Tumult--we *transcended*.
We built the Armswork, which embraces our entire system, connecting us, letting our light shine from every world orbiting our stars.
So why, then, are we doomed? Because we have lost ourselves.
Our species has expanded to fill our system to the very *brim*. We have nowhere left to build.
Our population is *locked*--one birth for one death.
We and our forebears have worked *so hard*, utilized every resource available to us to bring us to this amazing point--but I tell you this: we are stagnate.
We are trapped in a beautiful prison of our own design, deprived of our greatest value.
Change.

You elected me to our species' highest office so I could address whatever problems may arise in our present.

The truth is, there are none, or so few as to be meaningless.

And so, I spend most of my time considering our *future*.

What will *we* leave behind? What will we give our buds, as they bloom from our sacred arms?

Will we give them only what we have? Or will we reach for more?

Will we stretch beyond the bounds of this system, so our descendants might bring our light to the great darkness beyond?

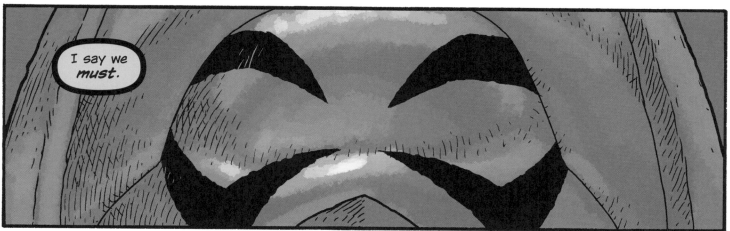

I say we *must*.

We must give *opportunity* to future generations. It is our *duty*. Our *destiny*.

What we have built together is magnificent--but on a *galactic* scale, when weighed against the possibilities of the future...

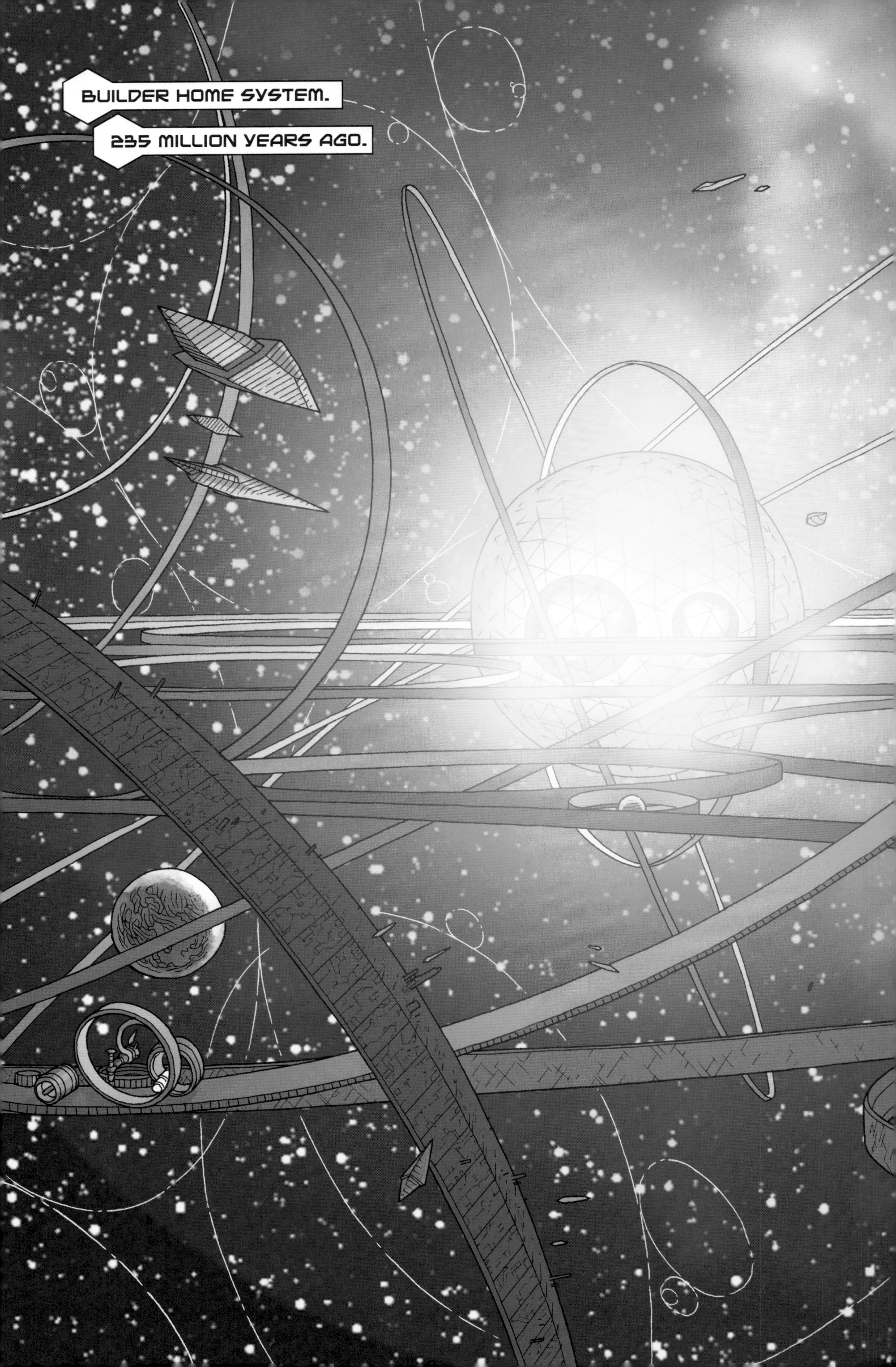
BUILDER HOME SYSTEM.
235 MILLION YEARS AGO.

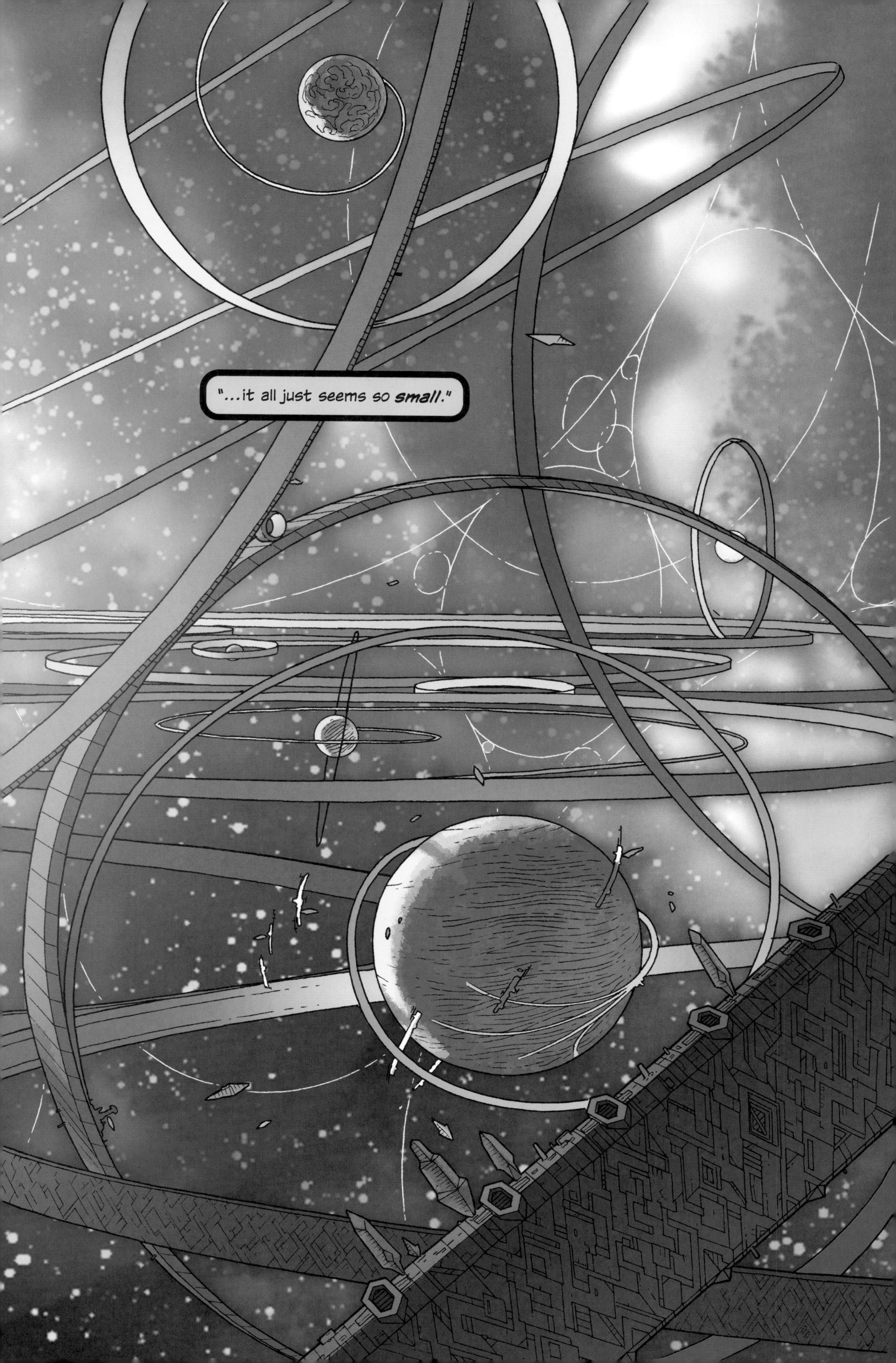
"...it all just seems so *small*."

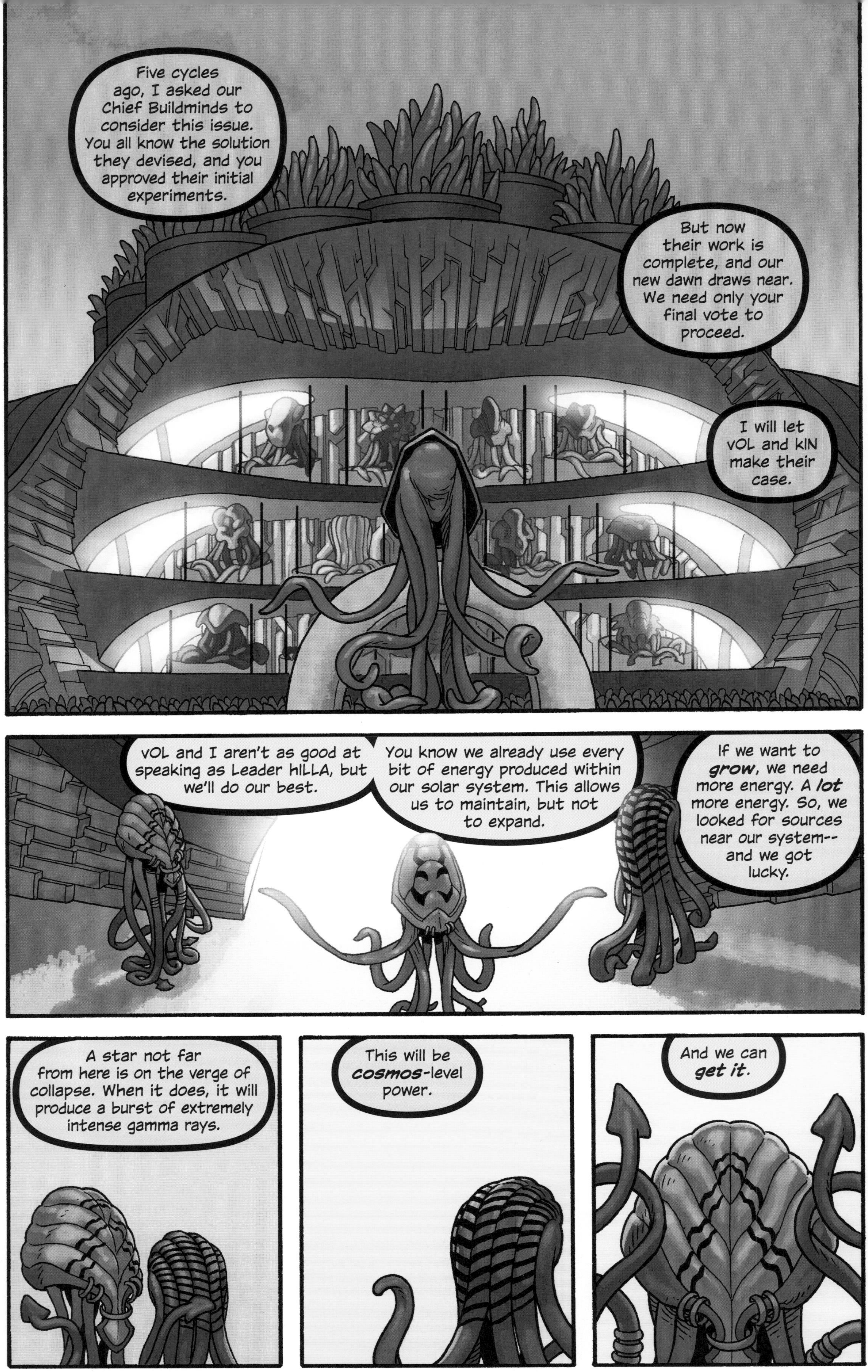
Five cycles ago, I asked our Chief Buildminds to consider this issue. You all know the solution they devised, and you approved their initial experiments.
But now their work is complete, and our new dawn draws near. We need only your final vote to proceed.
I will let vOL and kIN make their case.
vOL and I aren't as good at speaking as Leader hILLA, but we'll do our best.
You know we already use every bit of energy produced within our solar system. This allows us to maintain, but not to expand.
If we want to *grow*, we need more energy. A *lot* more energy. So, we looked for sources near our system--and we got lucky.
A star not far from here is on the verge of collapse. When it does, it will produce a burst of extremely intense gamma rays.
This will be *cosmos*-level power.
And we can *get it*.

This is an incredible opportunity-- and it won't come again.

Stars don't collapse every day. They don't usually produce gamma bursts, and the fact that this one is within gate range is unbelievable.

My friends, you are empowered to decide on behalf of your communities--in this room sits the will of our species.

I implore you--allow VOL and KIN to proceed with their plan. Give our children the *unknown*.

For if we don't, then we will give them only what we have ourselves. We will never spread our light beyond this system.

We must always grow. We must always change. That is our most sacred value. Without it... we are doomed.

The time is now.

Decide.

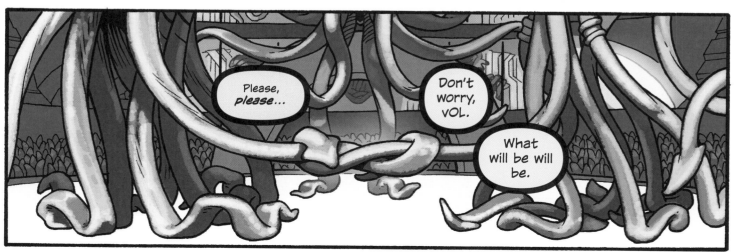

Please, *please*...

Don't worry, VOL.

What will be will be.

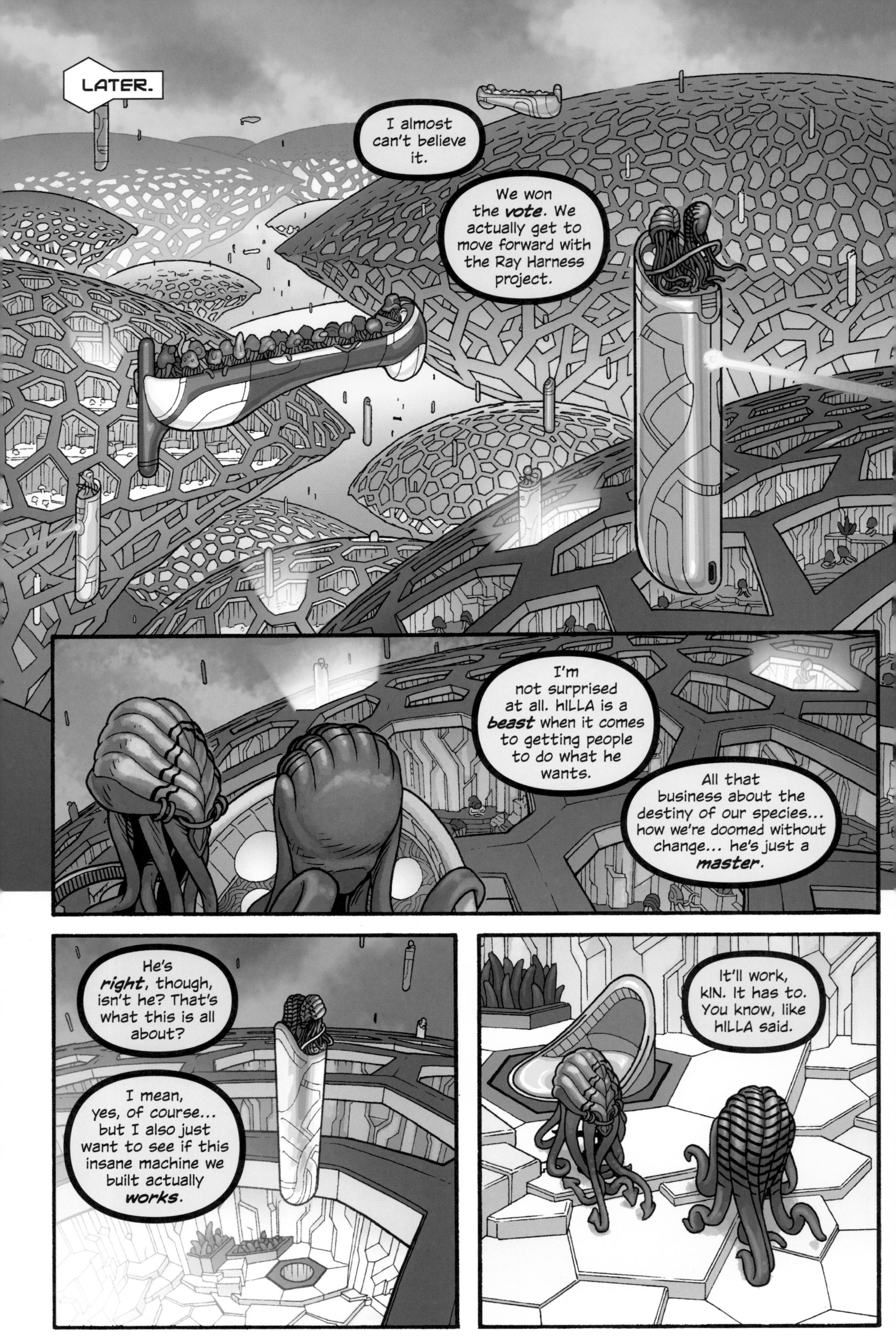
LATER.
I almost can't believe it.
We won the vote. We actually get to move forward with the Ray Harness project.
I'm not surprised at all. hILLA is a beast when it comes to getting people to do what he wants.
All that business about the destiny of our species... how we're doomed without change... he's just a master.
He's right, though, isn't he? That's what this is all about?
I mean, yes, of course... but I also just want to see if this insane machine we built actually works.
It'll work, kIN. It has to. You know, like hILLA said.

For the *children*.

Did the Council... did they agree?

Yes. A unanimous vote. They're going to let us activate the Ray Harness.

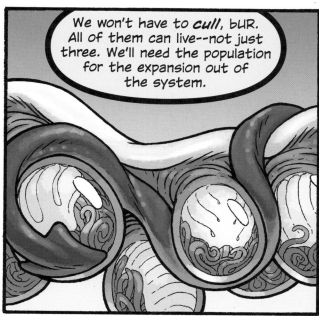

We won't have to *cull*, bUR. All of them can live--not just three. We'll need the population for the expansion out of the system.

None, I suppose.

All right, loves.

Let's go make some joy.

I... can't believe it. You've saved us. You've *saved us all*.

I'd say we should celebrate, if I weren't *already* gravid.

What difference does *that* make?

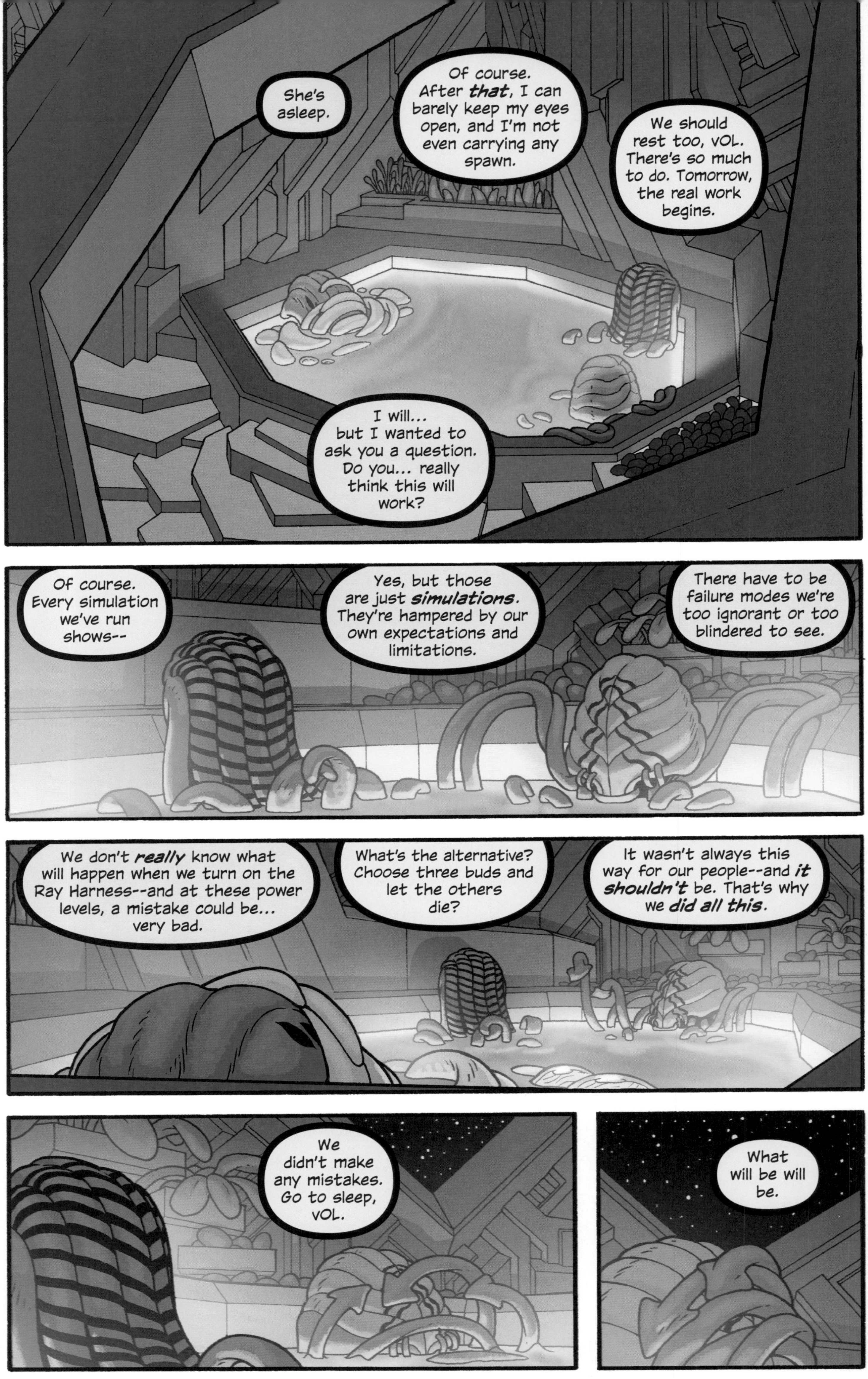
She's asleep.
Of course. After *that*, I can barely keep my eyes open, and I'm not even carrying any spawn.
We should rest too, vOL. There's so much to do. Tomorrow, the real work begins.
I will... but I wanted to ask you a question. Do you... really think this will work?
Of course. Every simulation we've run shows--
Yes, but those are just *simulations*. They're hampered by our own expectations and limitations.
There have to be failure modes we're too ignorant or too blindered to see.
We don't *really* know what will happen when we turn on the Ray Harness--and at these power levels, a mistake could be... very bad.
What's the alternative? Choose three buds and let the others die?
It wasn't always this way for our people--and *it shouldn't* be. That's why we *did all this*.
We didn't make any mistakes. Go to sleep, vOL.
What will be will be.

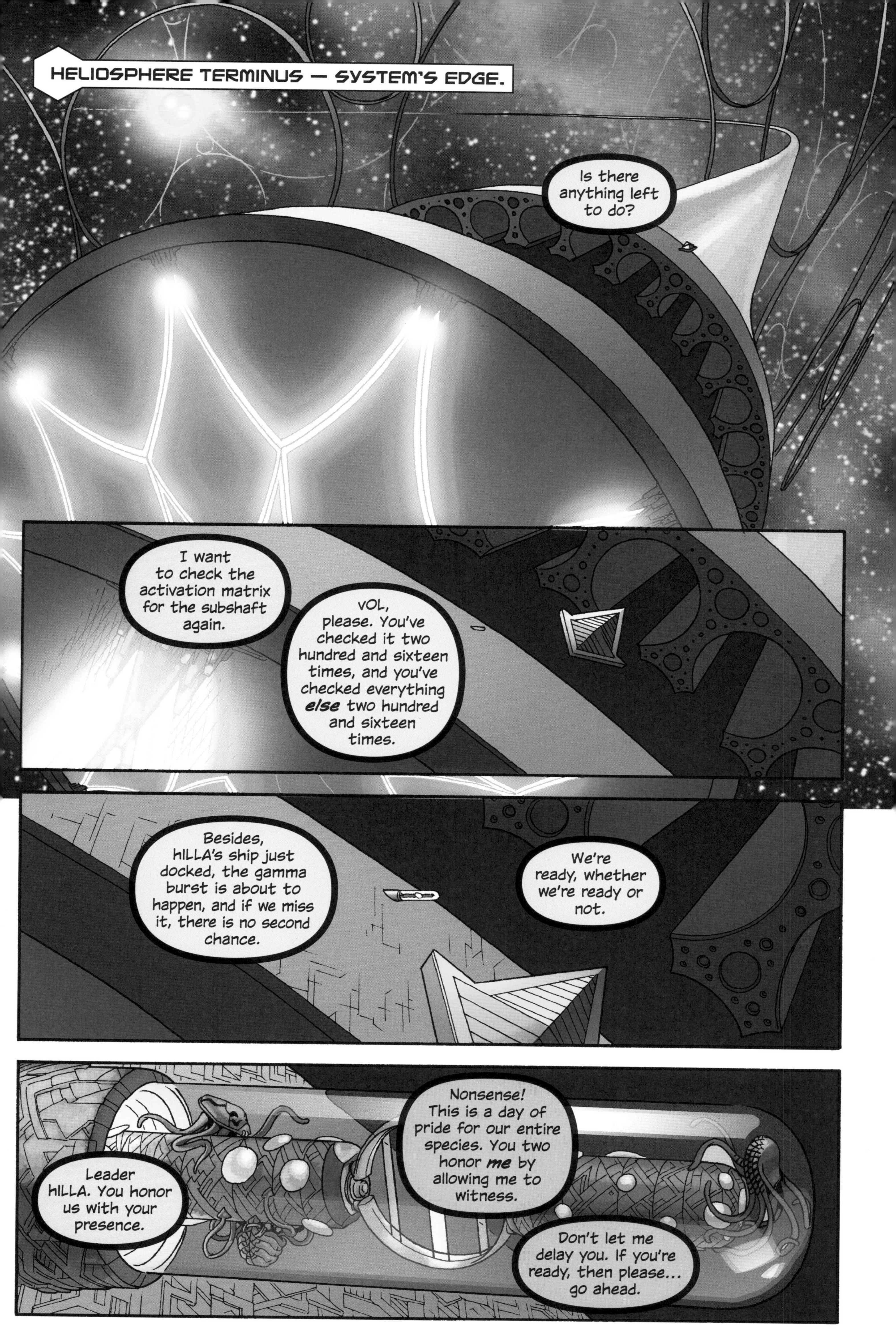
HELIOSPHERE TERMINUS — SYSTEM'S EDGE.
Is there anything left to do?
I want to check the activation matrix for the subshaft again.
VOL, please. You've checked it two hundred and sixteen times, and you've checked everything *else* two hundred and sixteen times.
Besides, hILLA's ship just docked, the gamma burst is about to happen, and if we miss it, there is no second chance.
We're ready, whether we're ready or not.
Leader hILLA. You honor us with your presence.
Nonsense! This is a day of pride for our entire species. You two honor *me* by allowing me to witness.
Don't let me delay you. If you're ready, then please... go ahead.

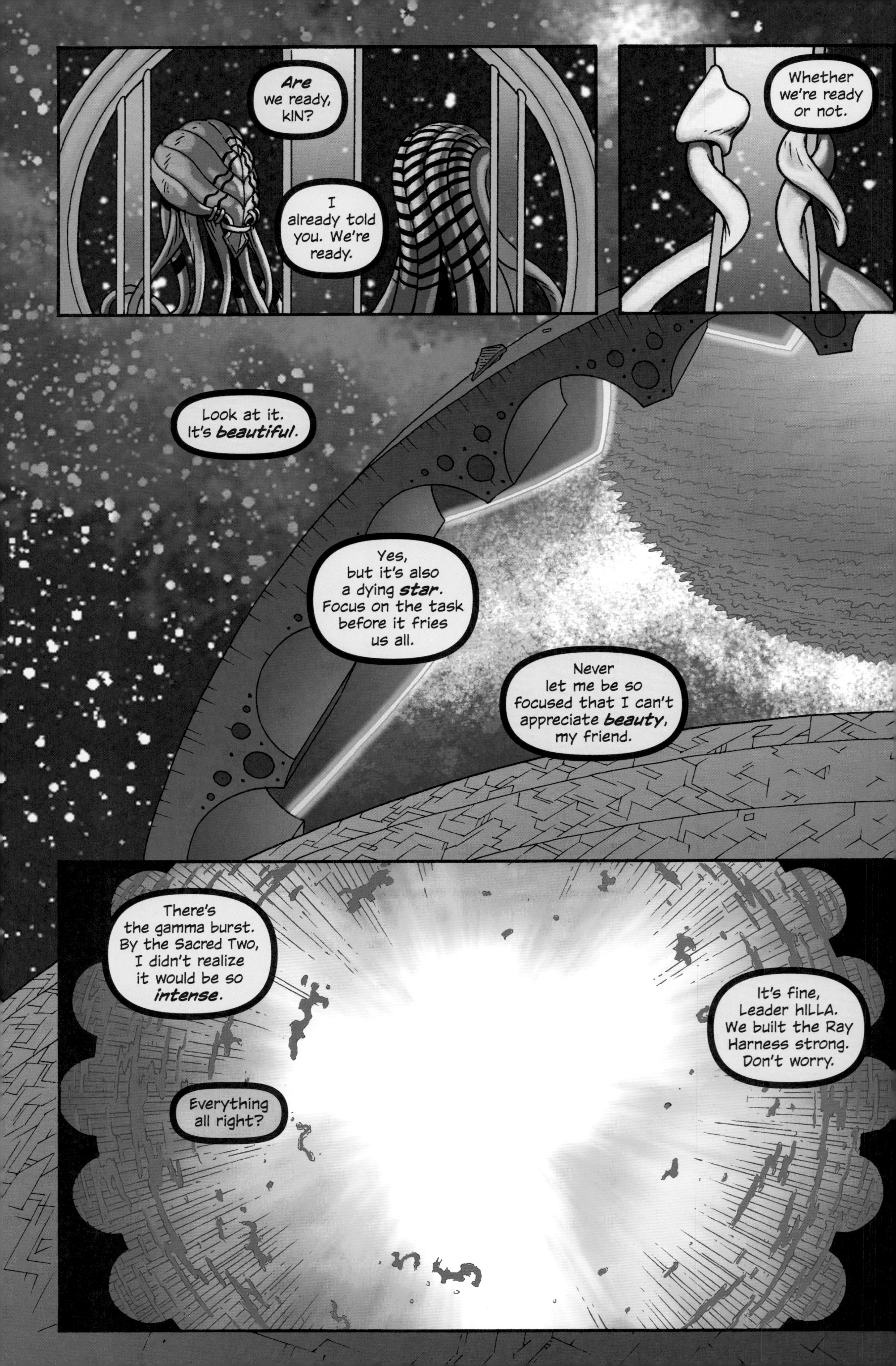

Are we ready, kIN?
I already told you. We're ready.
Whether we're ready or not.
Look at it. It's beautiful.
Yes, but it's also a dying star. Focus on the task before it fries us all.
Never let me be so focused that I can't appreciate beauty, my friend.
There's the gamma burst. By the Sacred Two, I didn't realize it would be so intense.
Everything all right?
It's fine, Leader hILLA. We built the Ray Harness strong. Don't worry.

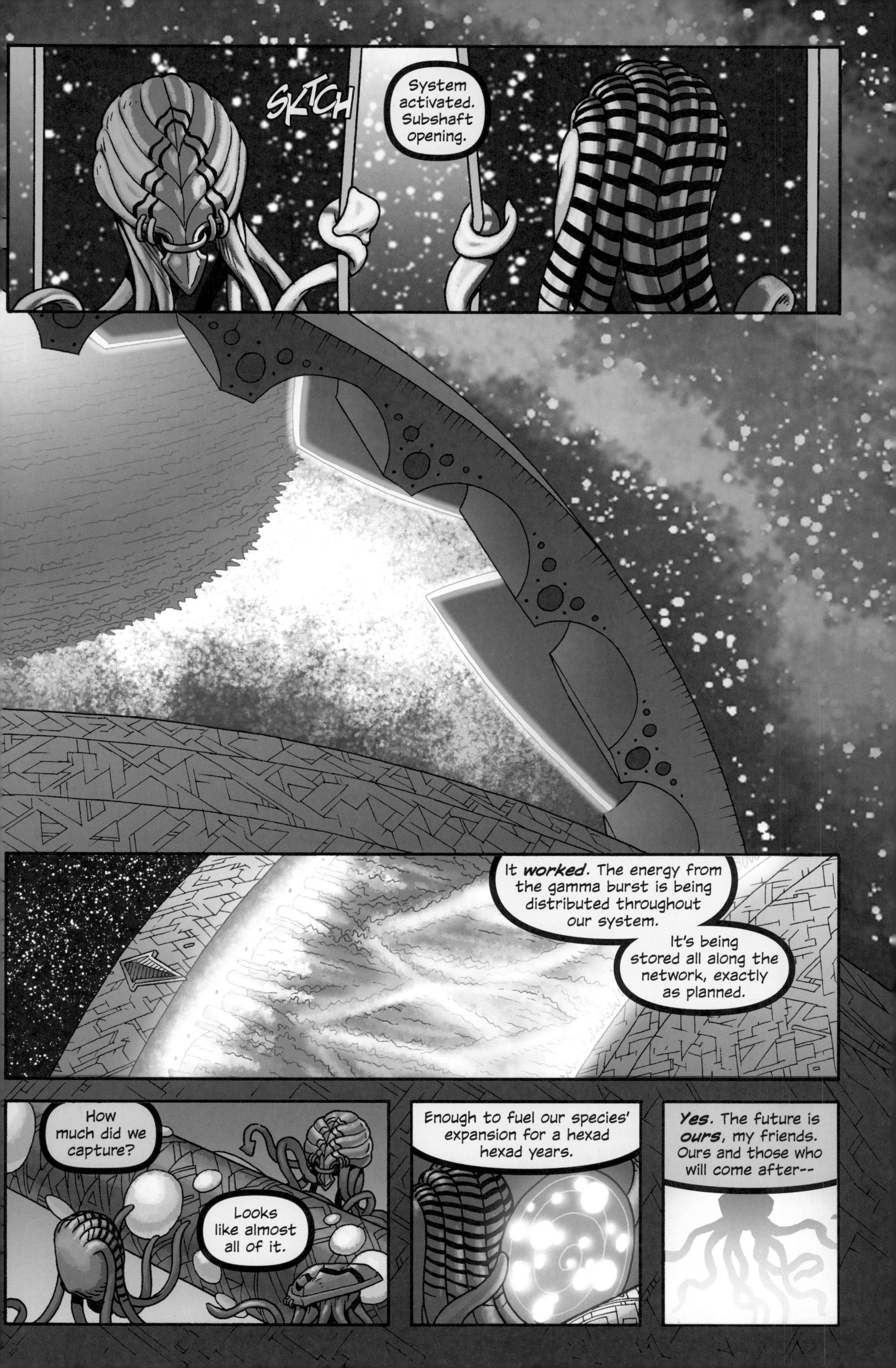
SKTCH
System activated. Subshaft opening.
It *worked*. The energy from the gamma burst is being distributed throughout our system.
It's being stored all along the network, exactly as planned.
How much did we capture?
Looks like almost all of it.
Enough to fuel our species' expansion for a hexad hexad years.
Yes. The future is *ours*, my friends. Ours and those who will come after--

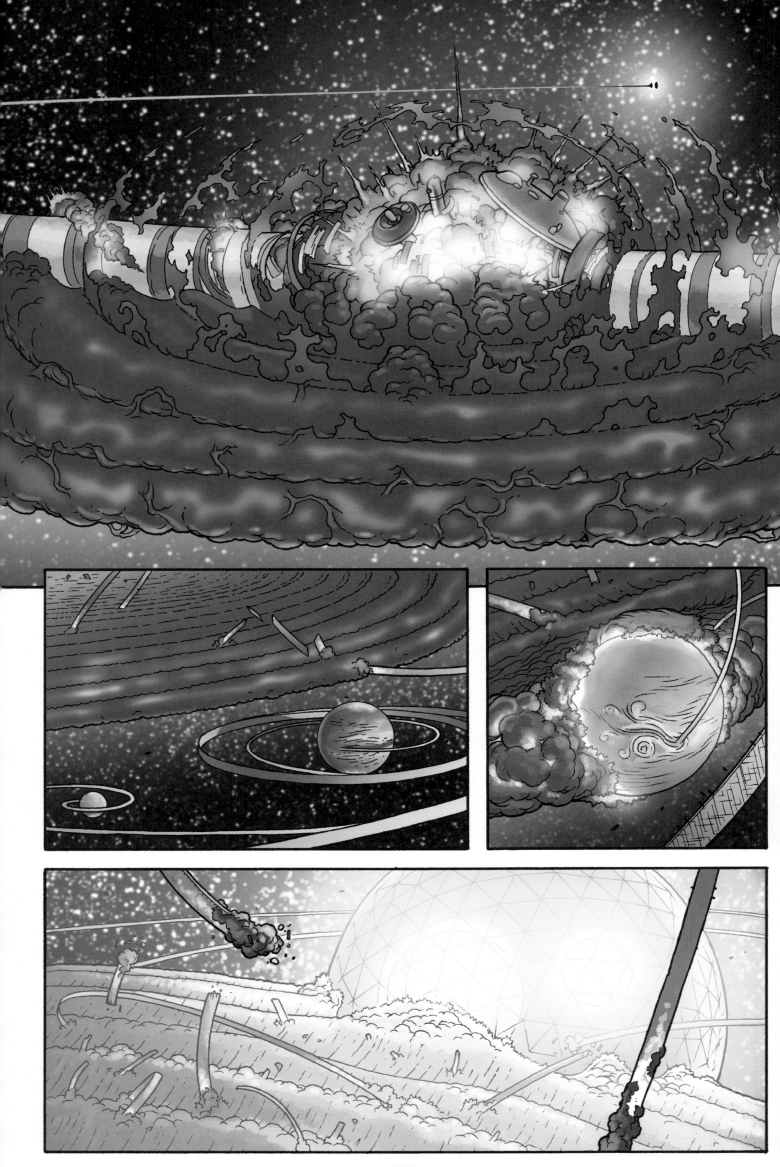

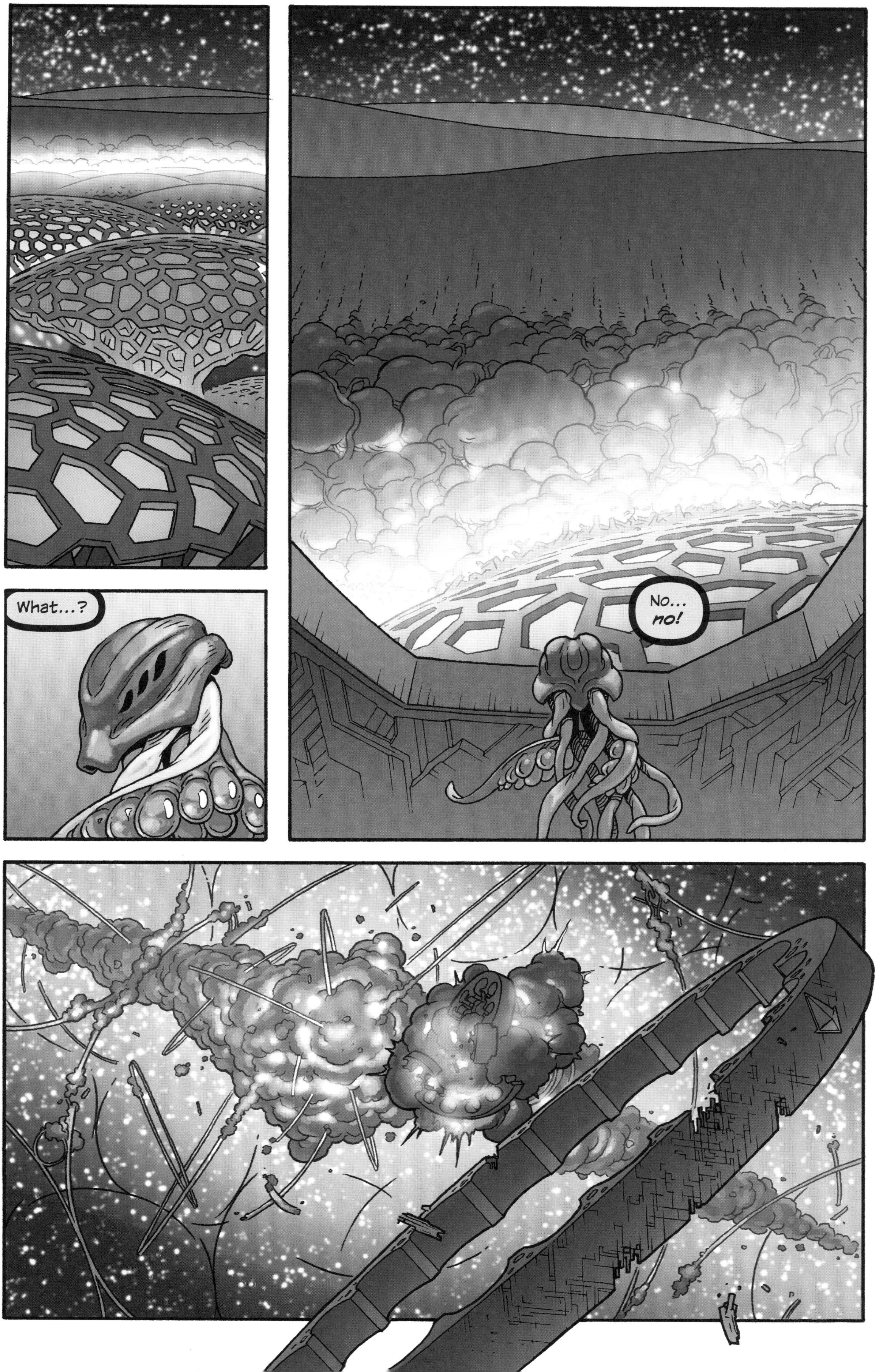
What...?
No... no!

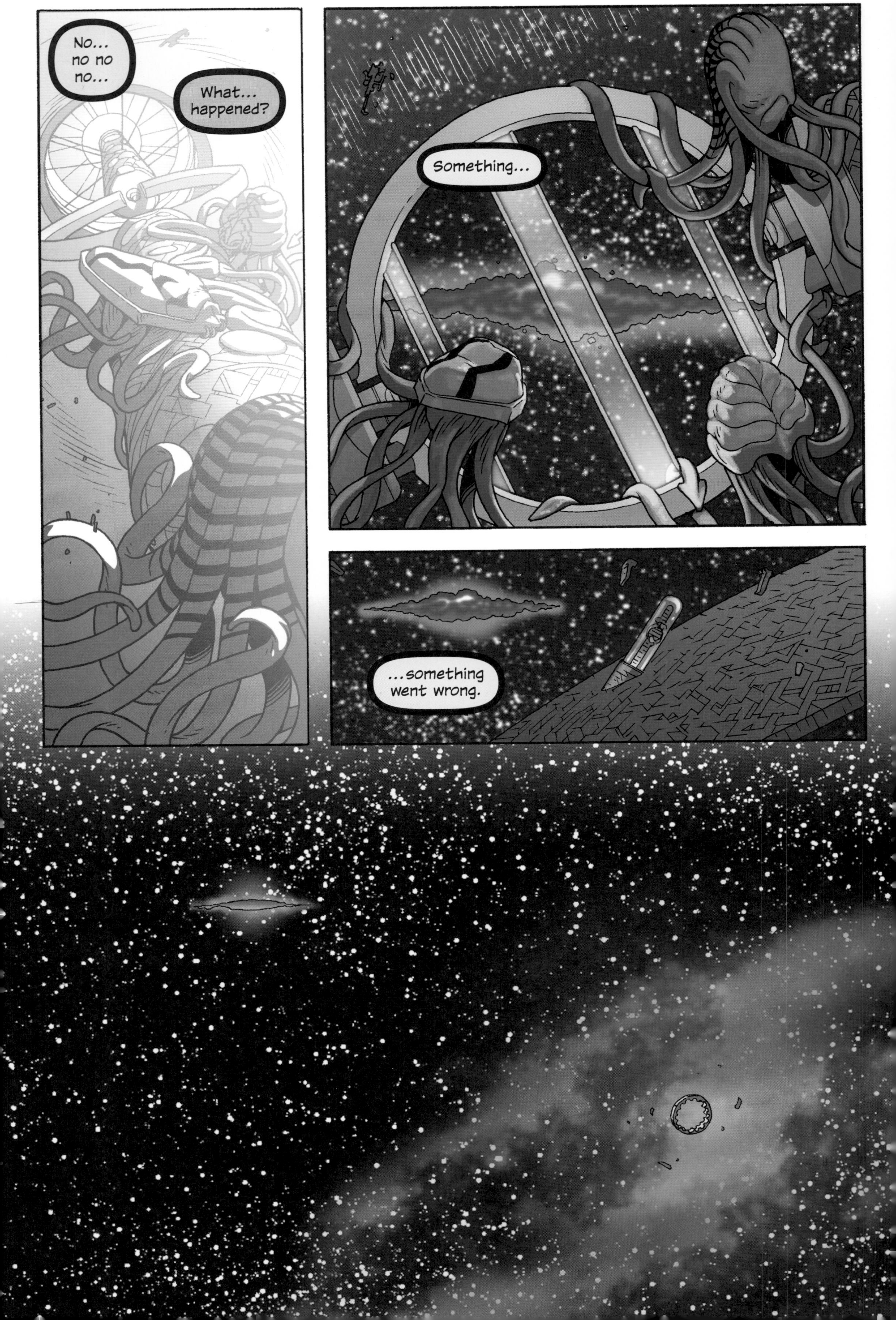
No... no no no...
What... happened?
Something...
...something went wrong.

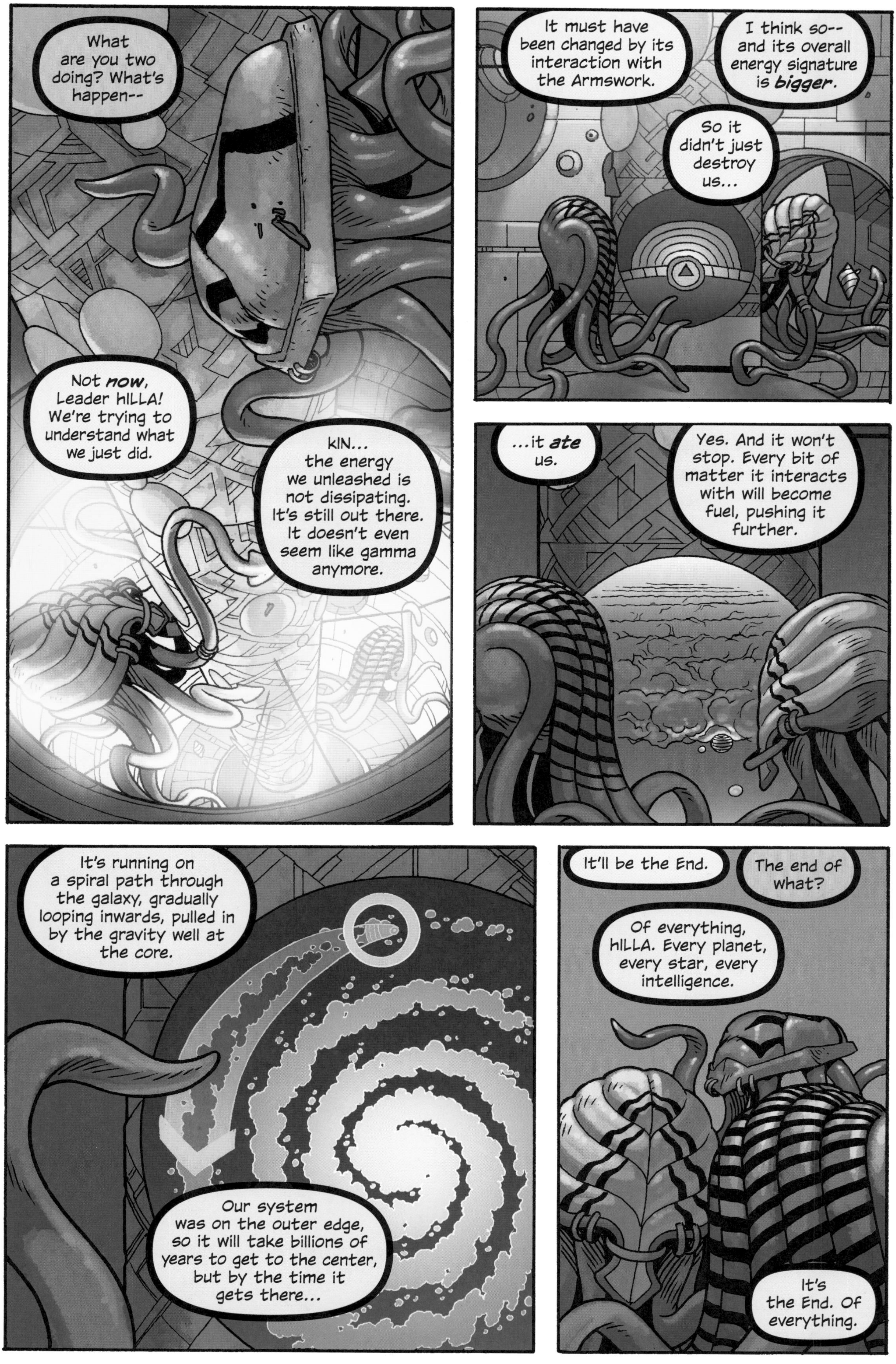
What are you two doing? What's happen--
Not *now*, Leader hILLA! We're trying to understand what we just did.
kIN... the energy we unleashed is not dissipating. It's still out there. It doesn't even seem like gamma anymore.
It must have been changed by its interaction with the Armswork.
I think so-- and its overall energy signature is ***bigger***.
So it didn't just destroy us...
...it ***ate*** us.
Yes. And it won't stop. Every bit of matter it interacts with will become fuel, pushing it further.
It's running on a spiral path through the galaxy, gradually looping inwards, pulled in by the gravity well at the core.
Our system was on the outer edge, so it will take billions of years to get to the center, but by the time it gets there...
It'll be the End.
The end of what?
Of everything, hILLA. Every planet, every star, every intelligence.
It's the End. Of everything.

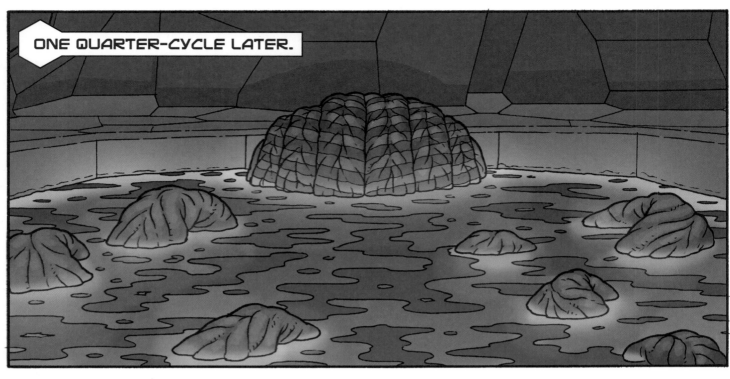

ONE QUARTER-CYCLE LATER.

THIRD-CYCLE.

HALF-CYCLE.

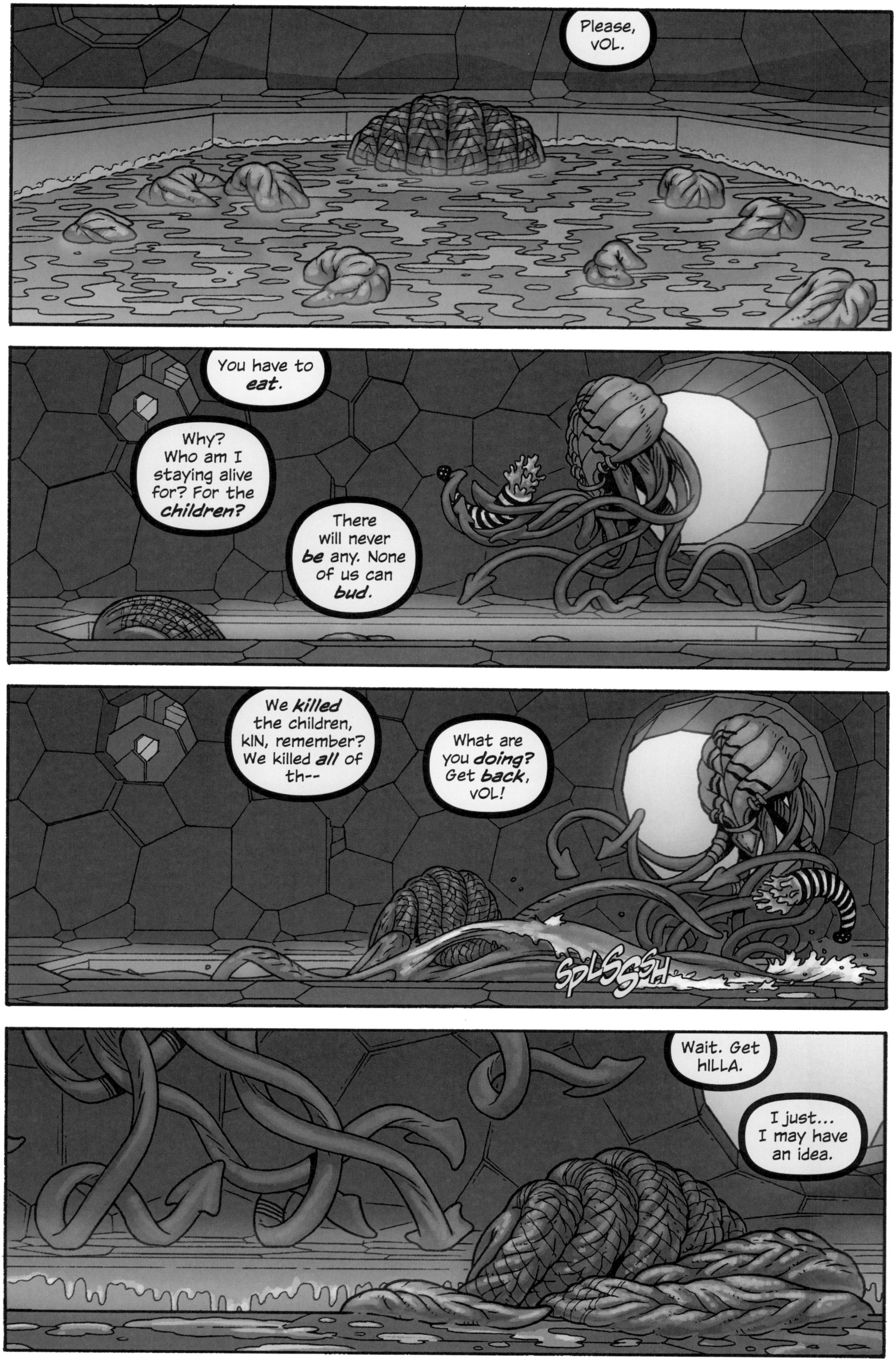
Please, VOL.
You have to *eat*.
Why? Who am I staying alive for? For the *children?*
There will never *be* any. None of us can *bud*.
We *killed* the children, KIN, remember? We killed *all* of th--
What are you *doing?* Get *back*, VOL!
SPLSSSH
Wait. Get HILLA.
I just... I may have an idea.

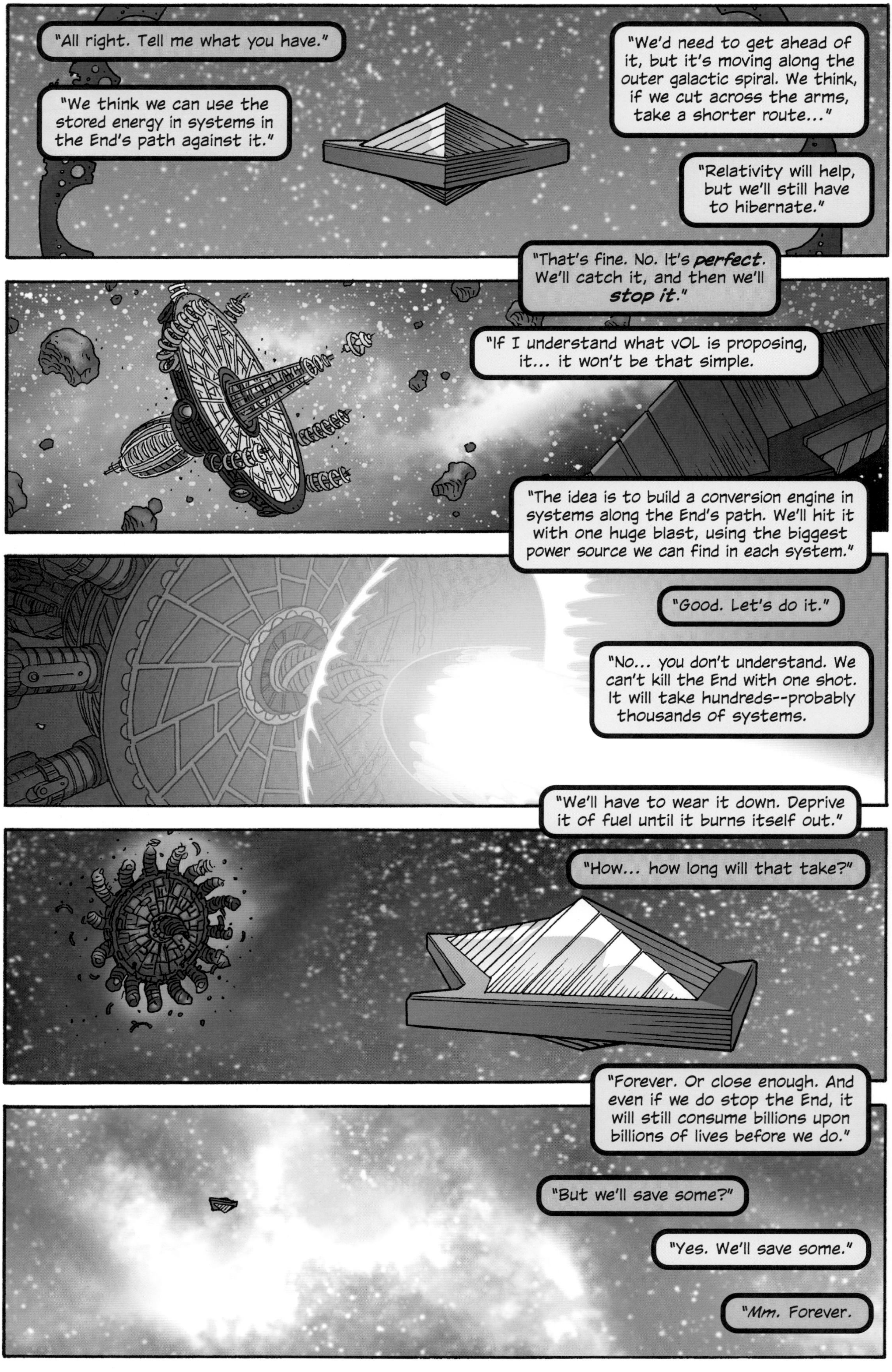
"All right. Tell me what you have."
"We think we can use the stored energy in systems in the End's path against it."
"We'd need to get ahead of it, but it's moving along the outer galactic spiral. We think, if we cut across the arms, take a shorter route..."
"Relativity will help, but we'll still have to hibernate."
"That's fine. No. It's *perfect*. We'll catch it, and then we'll ***stop it***."
"If I understand what vOL is proposing, it... it won't be that simple.
"The idea is to build a conversion engine in systems along the End's path. We'll hit it with one huge blast, using the biggest power source we can find in each system."
"Good. Let's do it."
"No... you don't understand. We can't kill the End with one shot. It will take hundreds--probably thousands of systems.
"We'll have to wear it down. Deprive it of fuel until it burns itself out."
"How... how long will that take?"
"Forever. Or close enough. And even if we do stop the End, it will still consume billions upon billions of lives before we do."
"But we'll save some?"
"Yes. We'll save some."
"*Mm*. Forever.

"Then we should probably hurry."

AFTER AEONS.

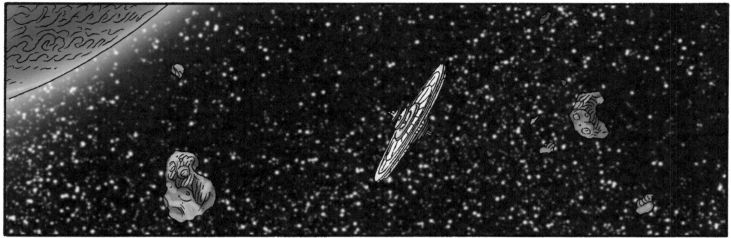

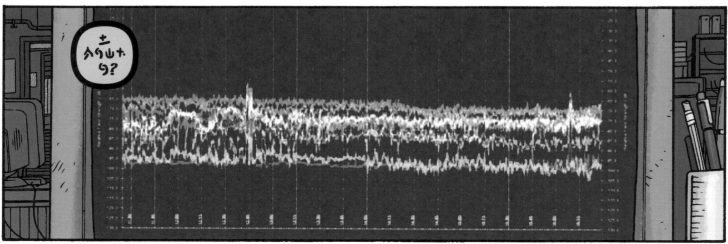

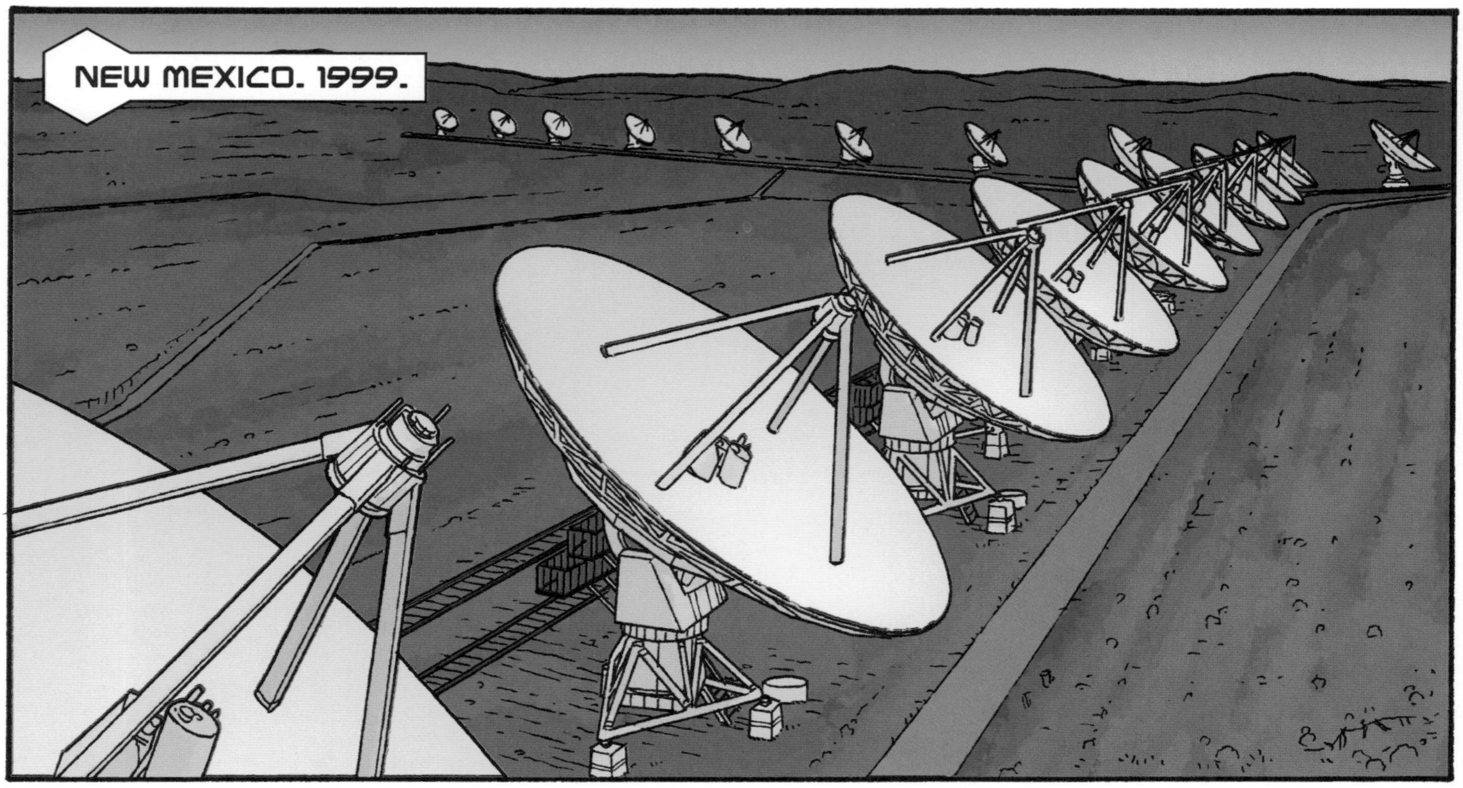
NEW MEXICO. 1999.

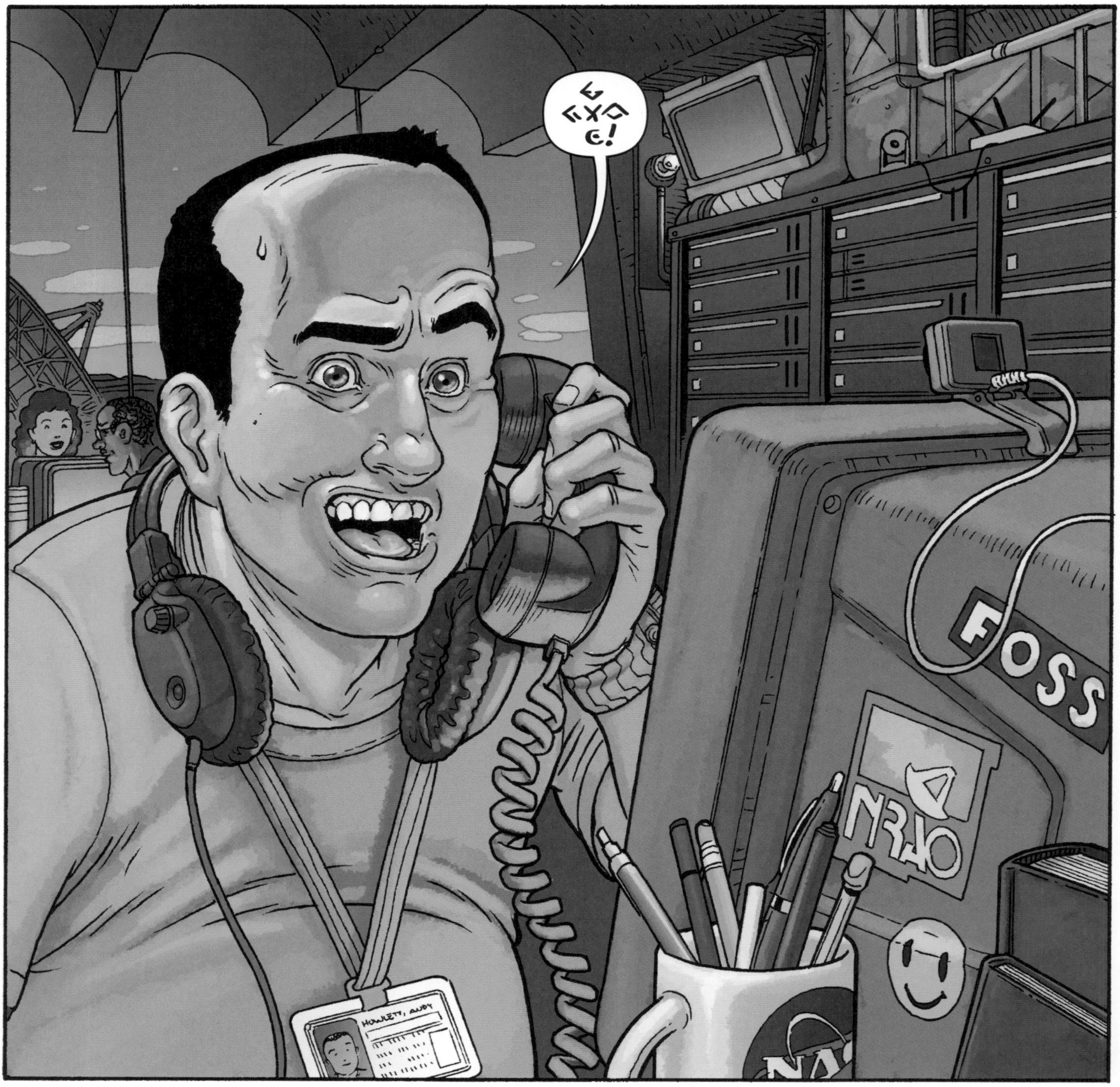
FOSS
HOWLETT, ANDY

LETTER
44

CHAPTER VI

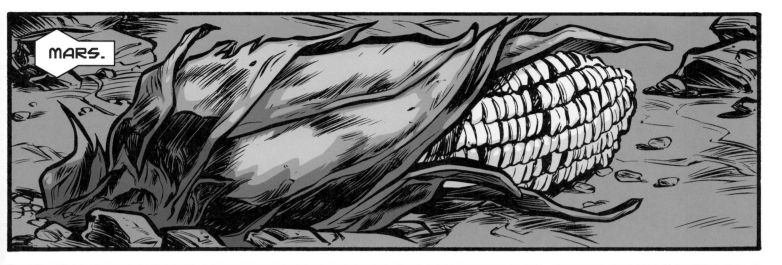

MARS.

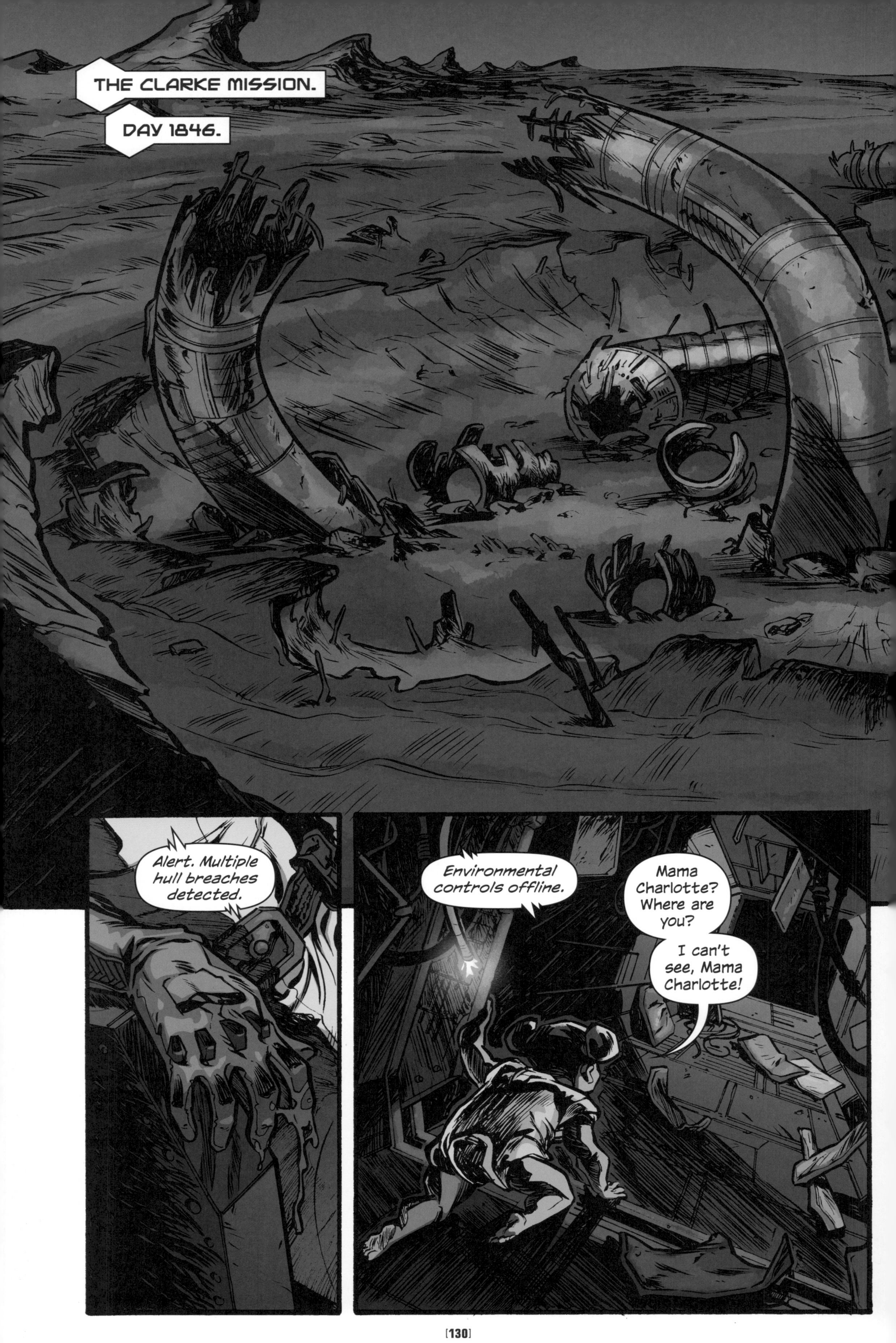

THE CLARKE MISSION.
DAY 1846.
Alert. Multiple hull breaches detected.
Environmental controls offline.
Mama Charlotte? Where are you?
I can't see, Mama Charlotte!

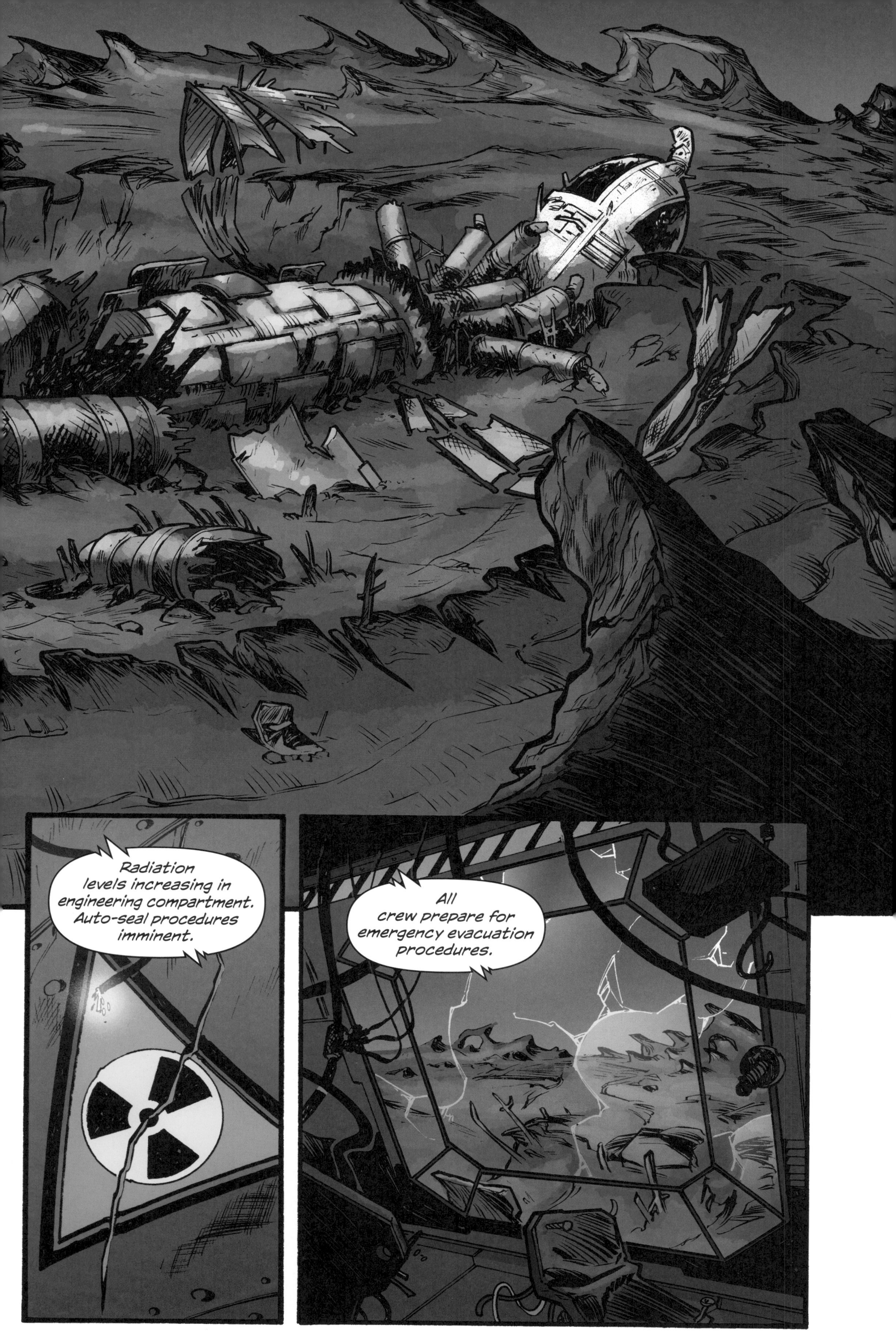
Radiation levels increasing in engineering compartment. Auto-seal procedures imminent.
All crew prepare for emergency evacuation procedures.

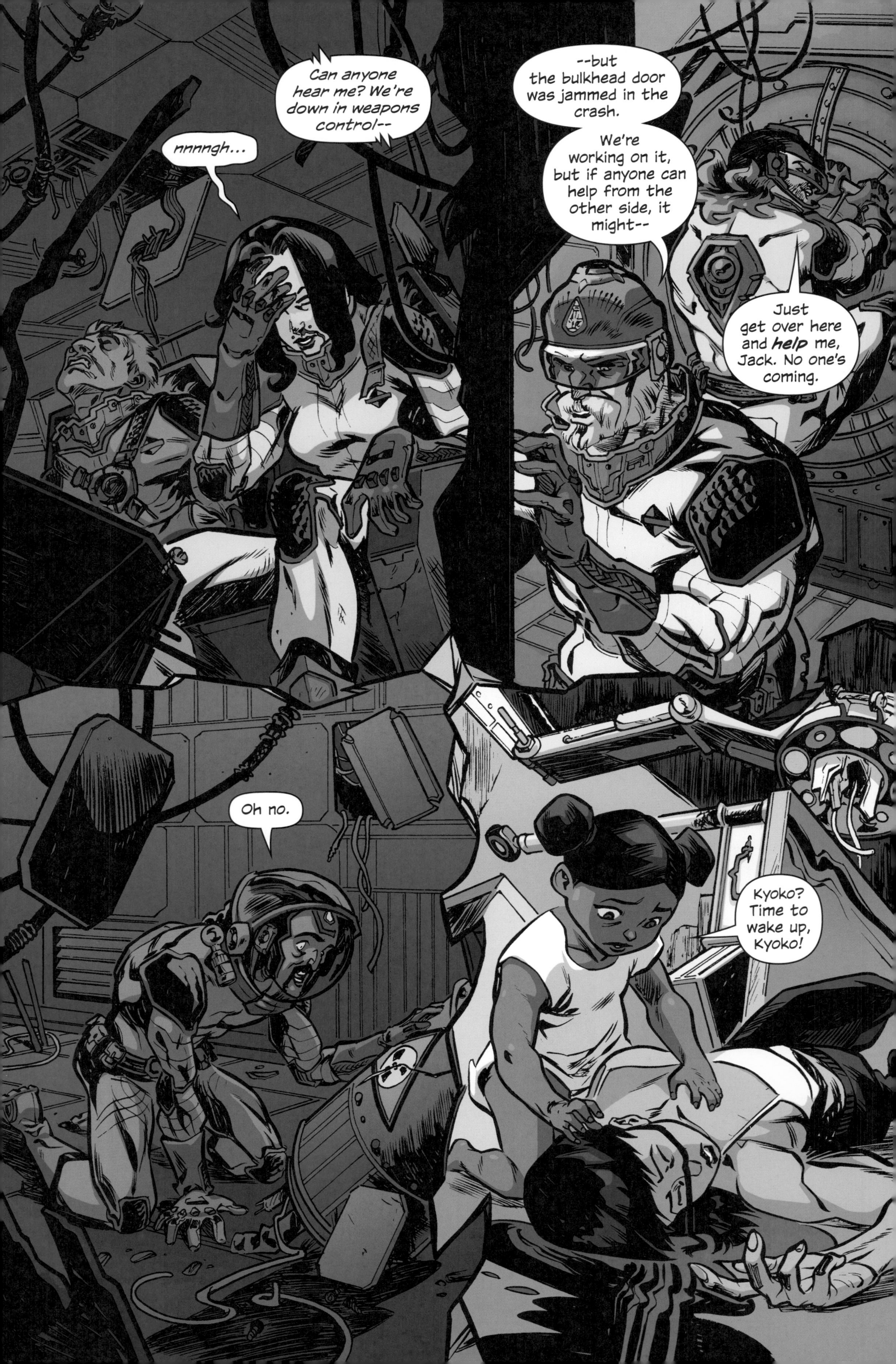
Can anyone hear me? We're down in weapons control--
nnnngh...
--but the bulkhead door was jammed in the crash.
We're working on it, but if anyone can help from the other side, it might--
Just get over here and ***help*** me, Jack. No one's coming.
Oh no.
Kyoko? Time to wake up, Kyoko!

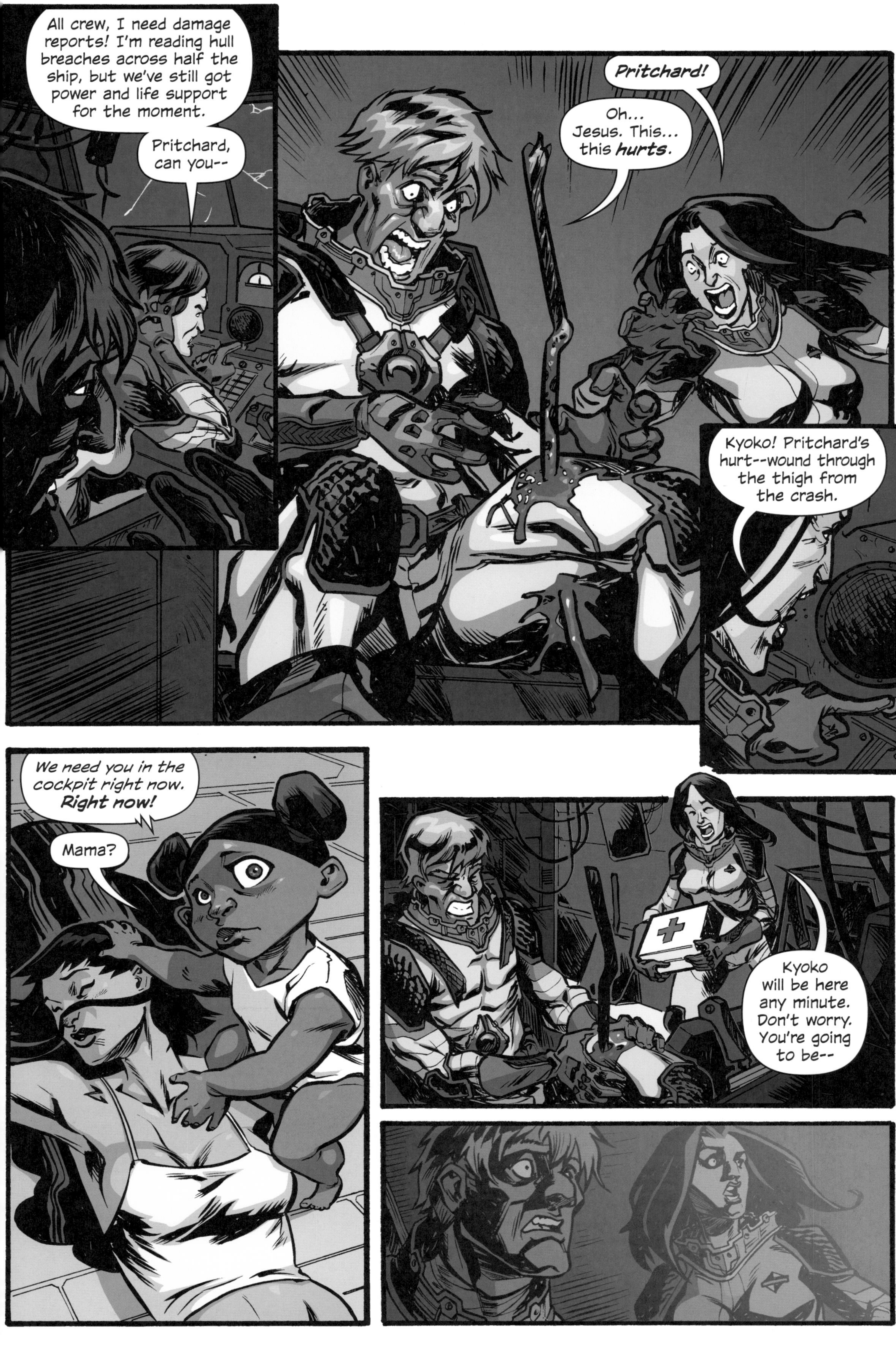
All crew, I need damage reports! I'm reading hull breaches across half the ship, but we've still got power and life support for the moment.
Pritchard, can you--
Pritchard!
Oh... Jesus. This... this hurts.
Kyoko! Pritchard's hurt--wound through the thigh from the crash.
We need you in the cockpit right now. Right now!
Mama?
Kyoko will be here any minute. Don't worry. You're going to be--

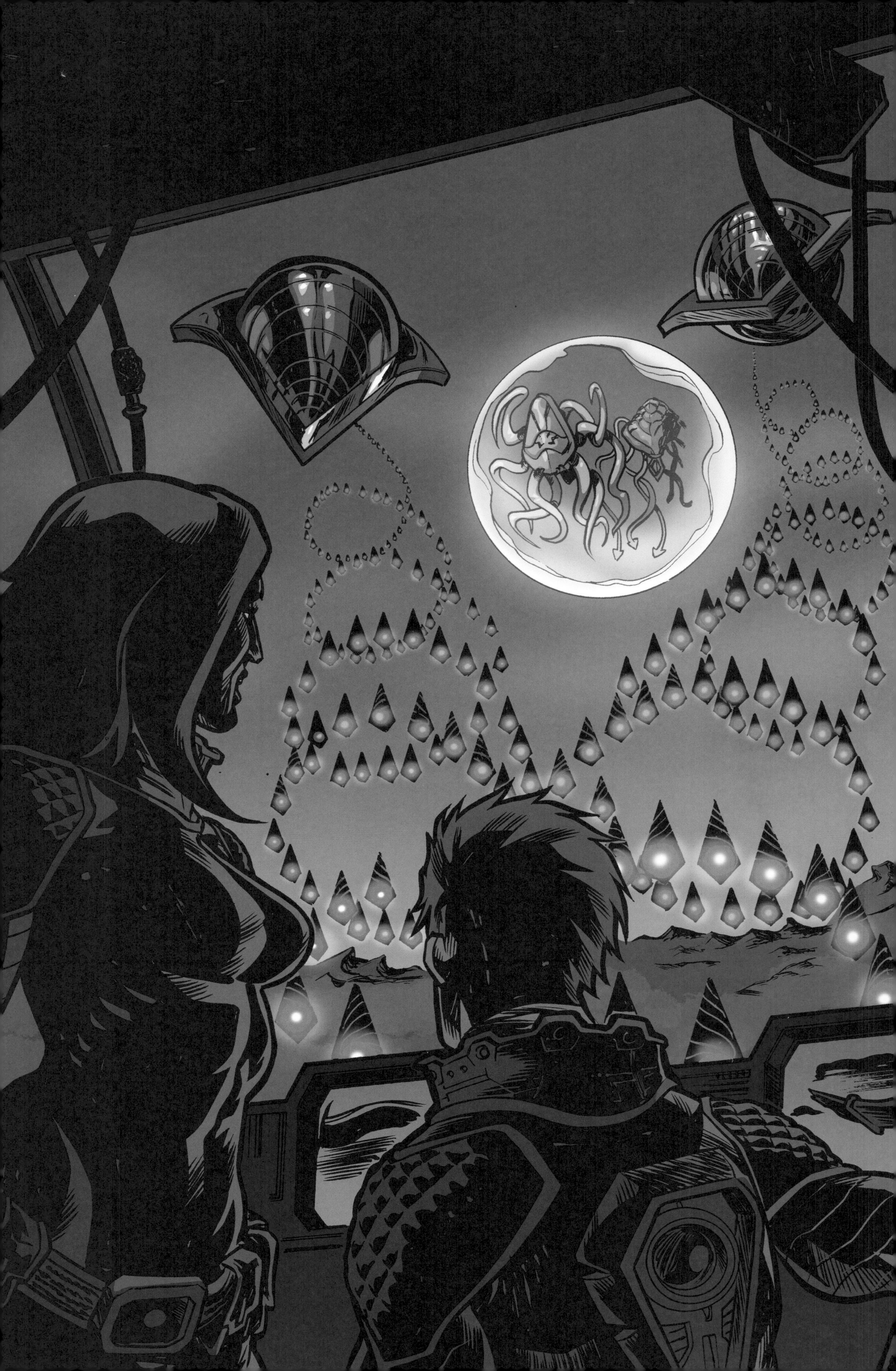

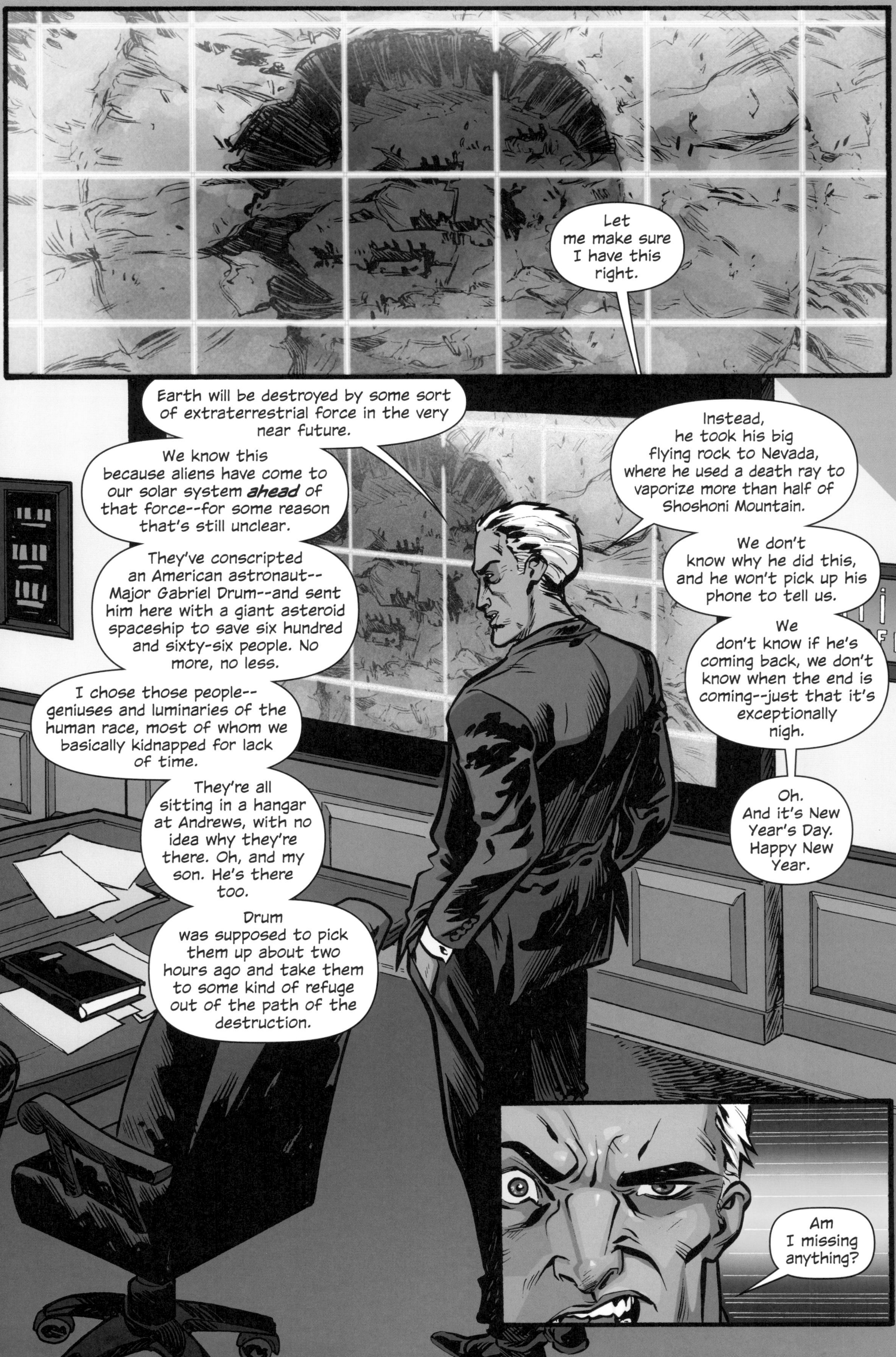
Let me make sure I have this right.
Earth will be destroyed by some sort of extraterrestrial force in the very near future.
We know this because aliens have come to our solar system *ahead* of that force--for some reason that's still unclear.
They've conscripted an American astronaut--Major Gabriel Drum--and sent him here with a giant asteroid spaceship to save six hundred and sixty-six people. No more, no less.
I chose those people--geniuses and luminaries of the human race, most of whom we basically kidnapped for lack of time.
They're all sitting in a hangar at Andrews, with no idea why they're there. Oh, and my son. He's there too.
Drum was supposed to pick them up about two hours ago and take them to some kind of refuge out of the path of the destruction.
Instead, he took his big flying rock to Nevada, where he used a death ray to vaporize more than half of Shoshoni Mountain.
We don't know why he did this, and he won't pick up his phone to tell us.
We don't know if he's coming back, we don't know when the end is coming--just that it's exceptionally nigh.
Oh. And it's New Year's Day. Happy New Year.
Am I missing anything?

The mountain's contents, Mr. President. Shoshoni Mountain was the site of a decommissioned continuance of government bunker.

A refuge where U.S. leadership could ride out a nuclear war.

Huh. Zoom in for me, AJ.

Decommissioned.

Then who the hell are *they*?

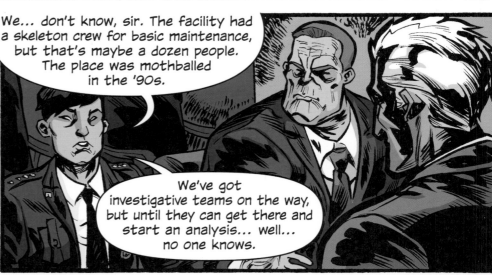

We... don't know, sir. The facility had a skeleton crew for basic maintenance, but that's maybe a dozen people. The place was mothballed in the '90s.

We've got investigative teams on the way, but until they can get there and start an analysis... well... no one knows.

Does it seem likely that Major Drum blew up a mountain at random--

--and the one he picked just *happened* to be hiding a nuclear bunker that's supposed to be empty but was in fact full?

Ah... no, Mr. President. That does not seem likely.

I agree. So, it's incorrect to say that *no one* knows what was going on in there.

Drum knows.

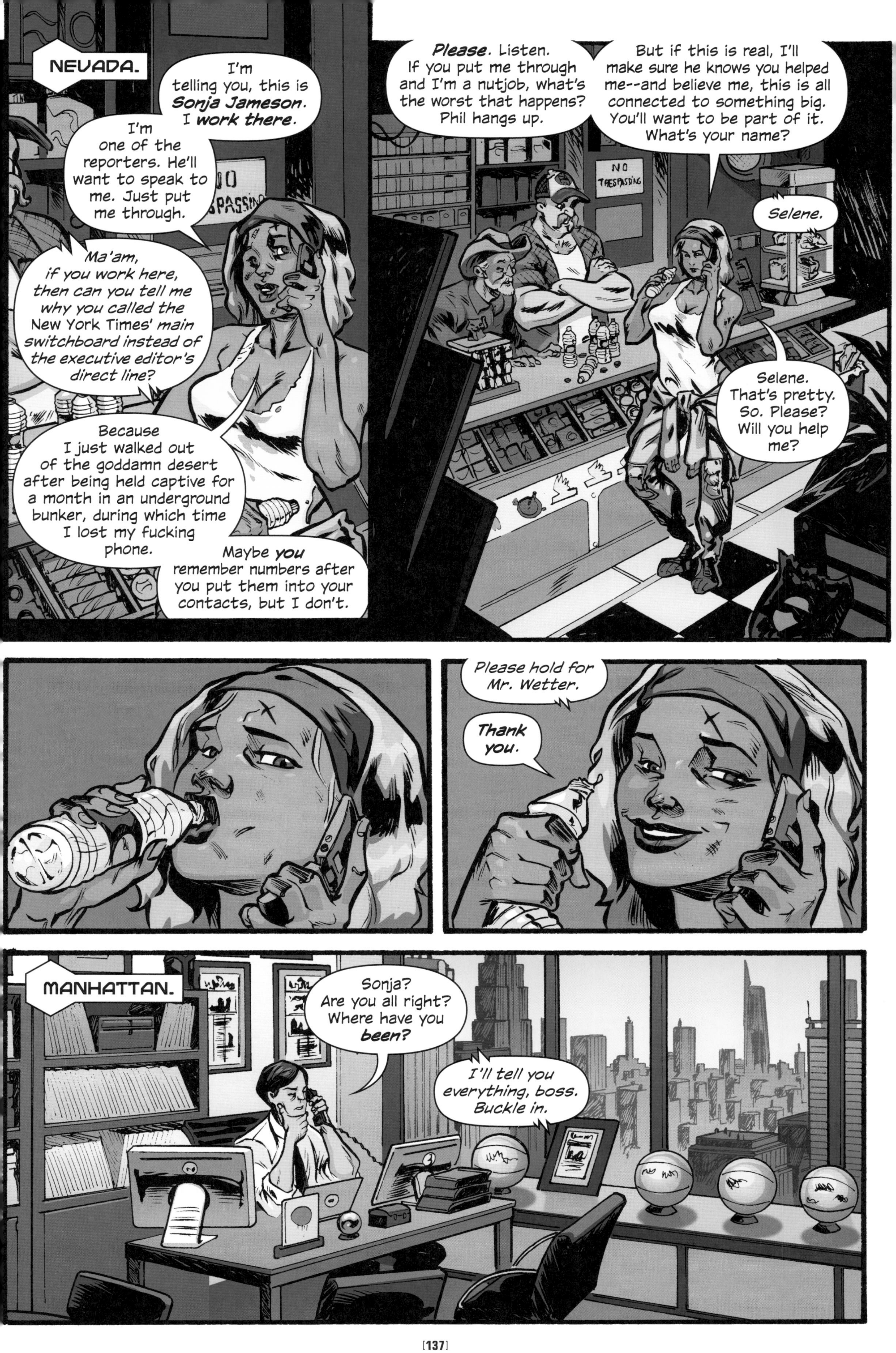
NEVADA.
I'm telling you, this is Sonja Jameson. I work there.
I'm one of the reporters. He'll want to speak to me. Just put me through.
Ma'am, if you work here, then can you tell me why you called the New York Times' main switchboard instead of the executive editor's direct line?
Because I just walked out of the goddamn desert after being held captive for a month in an underground bunker, during which time I lost my fucking phone.
Maybe you remember numbers after you put them into your contacts, but I don't.
Please. Listen. If you put me through and I'm a nutjob, what's the worst that happens? Phil hangs up.
But if this is real, I'll make sure he knows you helped me--and believe me, this is all connected to something big. You'll want to be part of it. What's your name?
NO TRESPASSING
Selene.
Selene. That's pretty. So. Please? Will you help me?
Please hold for Mr. Wetter.
Thank you.
MANHATTAN.
Sonja? Are you all right? Where have you been?
I'll tell you everything, boss. Buckle in.

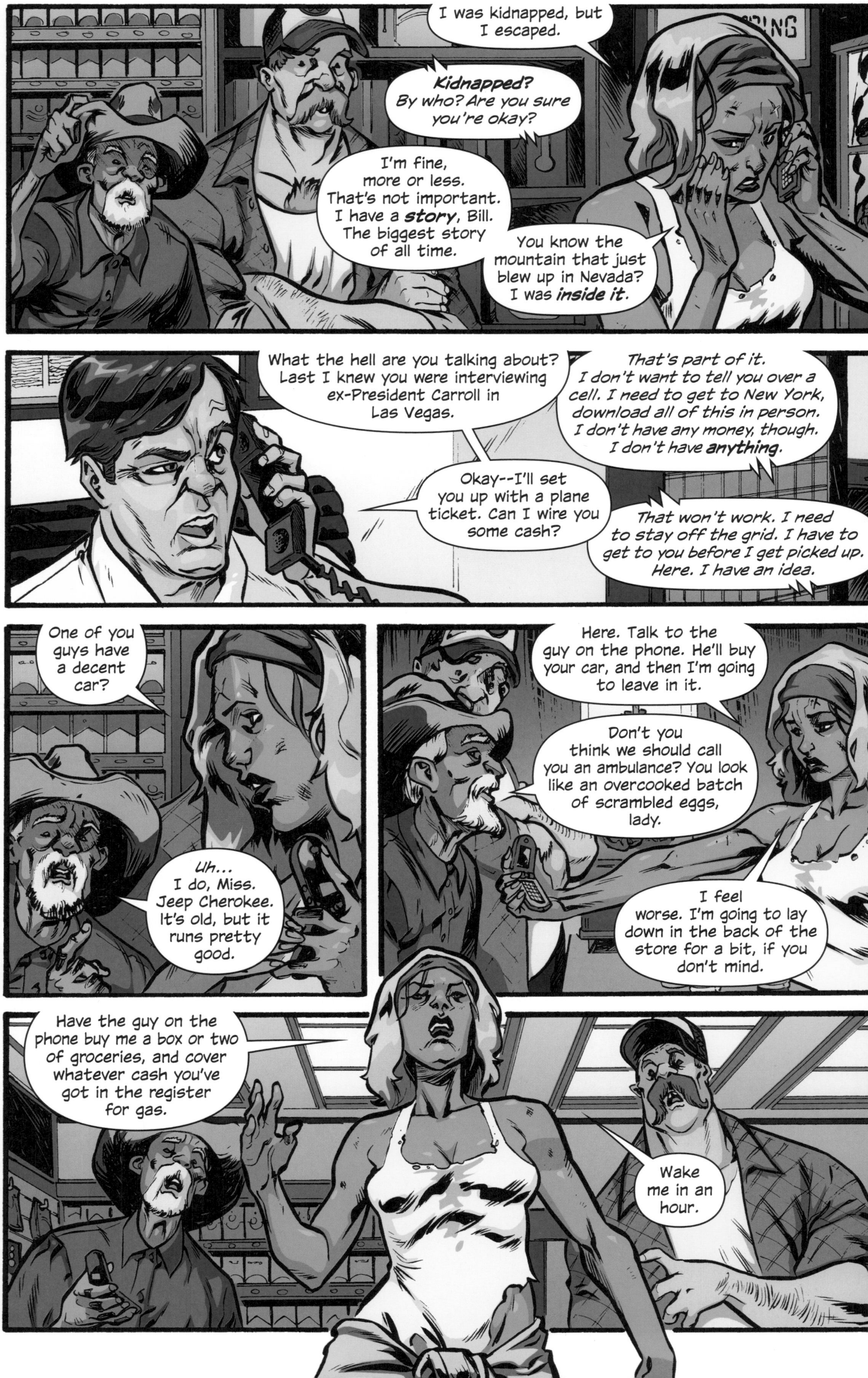
I was kidnapped, but I escaped.
Kidnapped? By who? Are you sure you're okay?
I'm fine, more or less. That's not important. I have a story, Bill. The biggest story of all time.
You know the mountain that just blew up in Nevada? I was inside it.
What the hell are you talking about? Last I knew you were interviewing ex-President Carroll in Las Vegas.
That's part of it. I don't want to tell you over a cell. I need to get to New York, download all of this in person. I don't have any money, though. I don't have anything.
Okay--I'll set you up with a plane ticket. Can I wire you some cash?
That won't work. I need to stay off the grid. I have to get to you before I get picked up. Here. I have an idea.
One of you guys have a decent car?
Uh... I do, Miss. Jeep Cherokee. It's old, but it runs pretty good.
Here. Talk to the guy on the phone. He'll buy your car, and then I'm going to leave in it.
Don't you think we should call you an ambulance? You look like an overcooked batch of scrambled eggs, lady.
I feel worse. I'm going to lay down in the back of the store for a bit, if you don't mind.
Have the guy on the phone buy me a box or two of groceries, and cover whatever cash you've got in the register for gas.
Wake me in an hour.

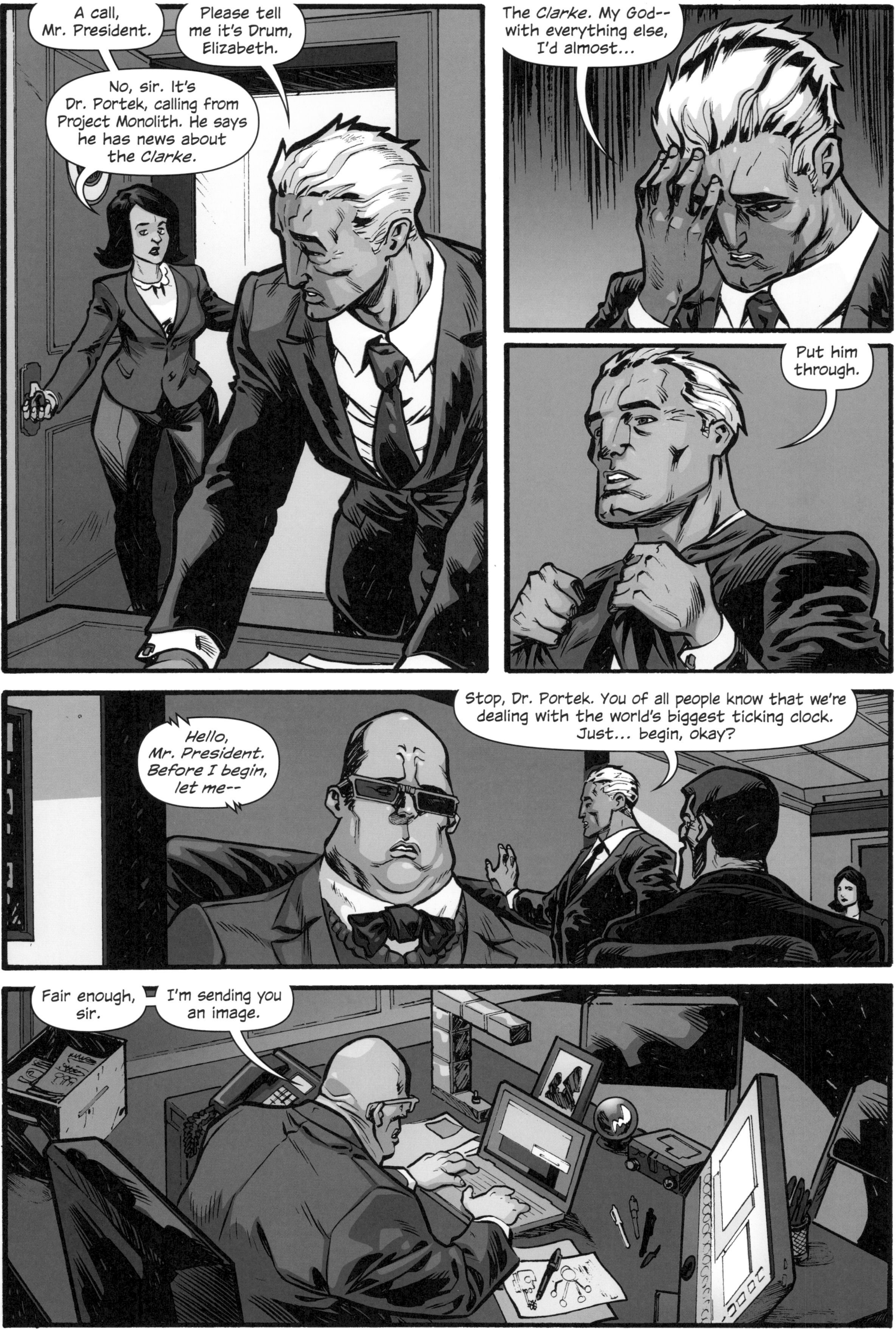
A call, Mr. President.
Please tell me it's Drum, Elizabeth.
No, sir. It's Dr. Portek, calling from Project Monolith. He says he has news about the *Clarke*.
The *Clarke*. My God-- with everything else, I'd almost...
Put him through.
Hello, Mr. President. Before I begin, let me--
Stop, Dr. Portek. You of all people know that we're dealing with the world's biggest ticking clock. Just... begin, okay?
Fair enough, sir.
I'm sending you an image.

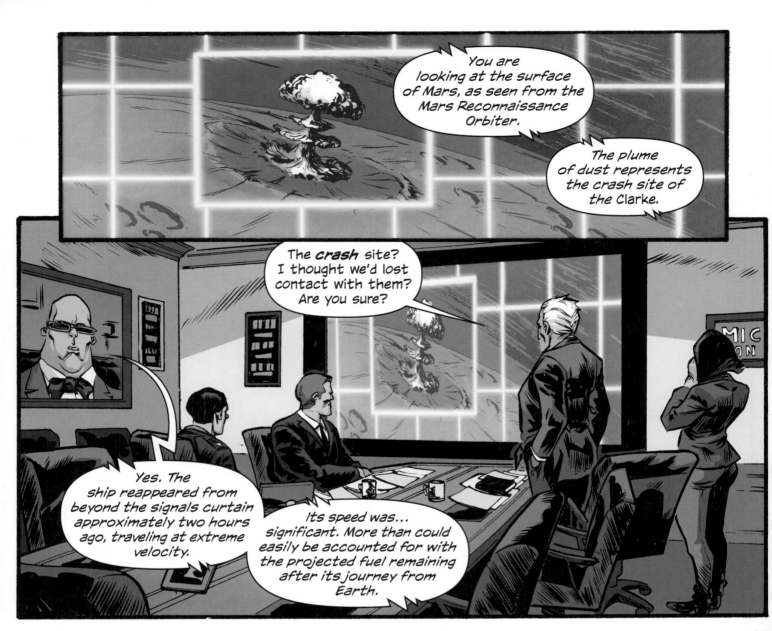

You are looking at the surface of Mars, as seen from the Mars Reconnaissance Orbiter.

The plume of dust represents the crash site of the Clarke.

The **crash** site? I thought we'd lost contact with them? Are you sure?

Yes. The ship reappeared from beyond the signals curtain approximately two hours ago, traveling at extreme velocity.

Its speed was... significant. More than could easily be accounted for with the projected fuel remaining after its journey from Earth.

Was anyone alive aboard? Did they send a message?

The Clarke executed a change of vector shortly after its re-emergence, angling itself towards Mars.

It then completed a braking burn to shed velocity after it entered the Martian atmosphere. Neither maneuver could have been executed absent human intervention.

So they were alive.

Were is the operative word, sir. They impacted the surface at high speed. And even if they survived, they aren't equipped for a long-term stay on the planet.

If they aren't dead now... it's just a matter of time. I'm sorry.

And do we know **why**? Do we know **anything**?

Little more than I've told you, sir. We'll keep watching the crash site for activity.

I know we were hoping the Clarke crew could somehow work with the aliens to save this planet, or at least learn more about what's coming.

As that hope now seems... ah, **slim**... I thought you should be informed.

Yes, of course. Thank you for telling me. Please let me know if you learn anything else.

This, whatever happened at that bunker... it's all connected.

I'm sure of it.

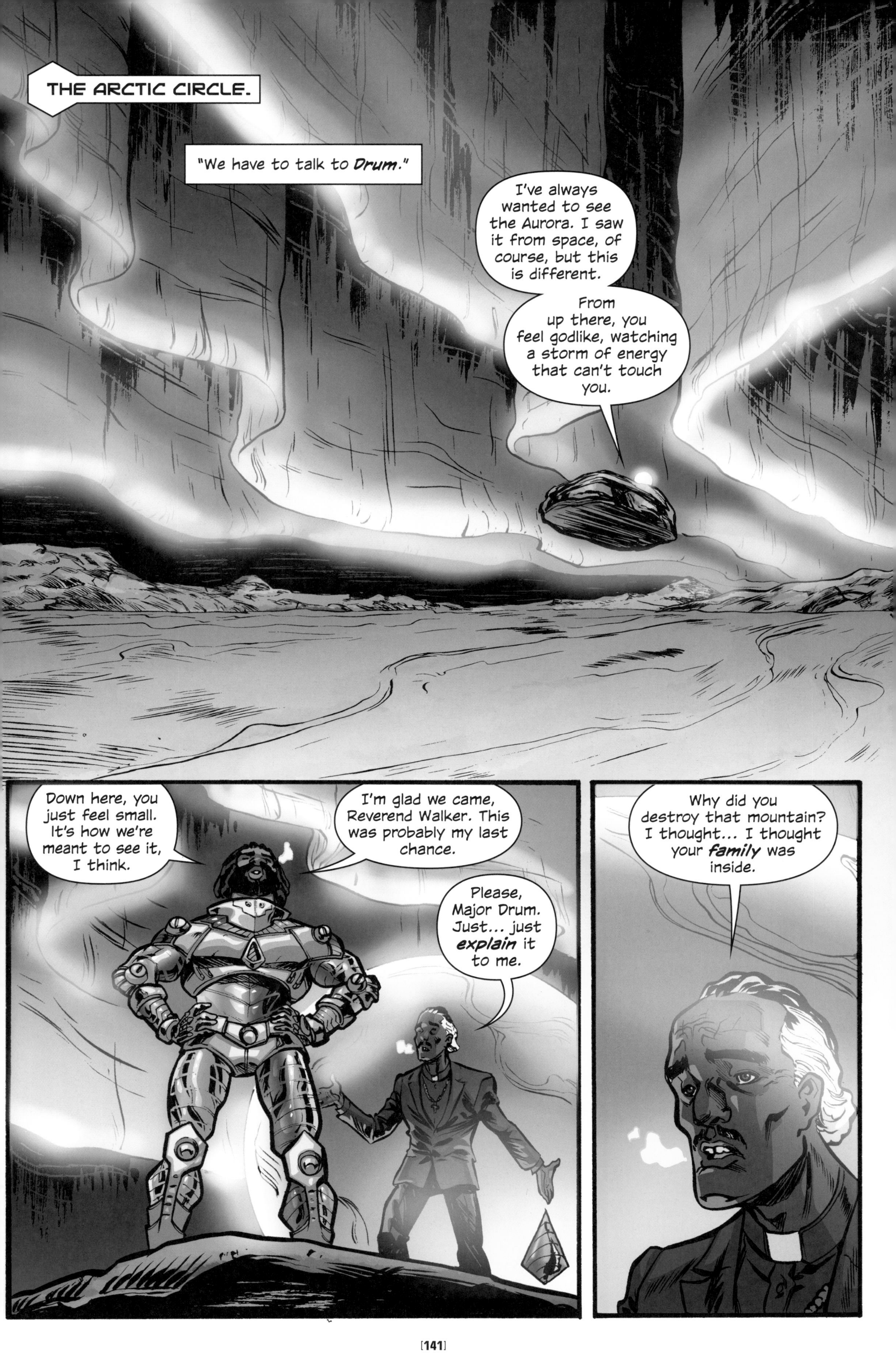
THE ARCTIC CIRCLE.
"We have to talk to *Drum*."
I've always wanted to see the Aurora. I saw it from space, of course, but this is different.
From up there, you feel godlike, watching a storm of energy that can't touch you.
Down here, you just feel small. It's how we're meant to see it, I think.
I'm glad we came, Reverend Walker. This was probably my last chance.
Please, Major Drum. Just... just *explain* it to me.
Why did you destroy that mountain? I thought... I thought your *family* was inside.

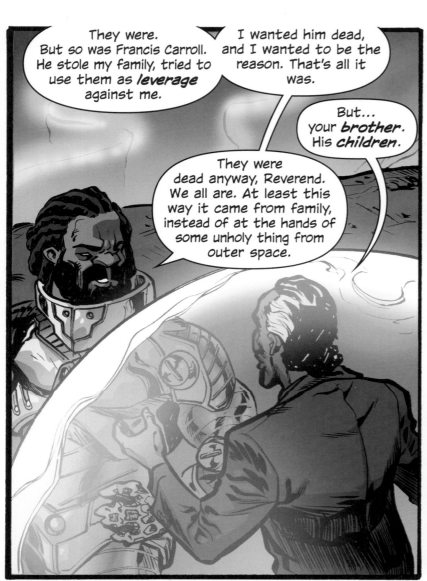

They were. But so was Francis Carroll. He stole my family, tried to use them as *leverage* against me.

I wanted him dead, and I wanted to be the reason. That's all it was.

But... your *brother*. His *children*.

They were dead anyway, Reverend. We all are. At least this way it came from family, instead of at the hands of some unholy thing from outer space.

I think I've seen enough here.

Is there anywhere you'd like to go in the world? Something you'd like to see?

None of it will be around for very long.

TWEE TWEE

The satellite phone the President gave me... it's him. It has to be.

Don't you think you should tell him the truth? Doesn't he deserve to know?

Doesn't *everyone* deserve to know?

I... suppose you're right.

Mr. President, I--

Thank God I finally got you, Major Drum. I have news about your colleagues on the Clarke.

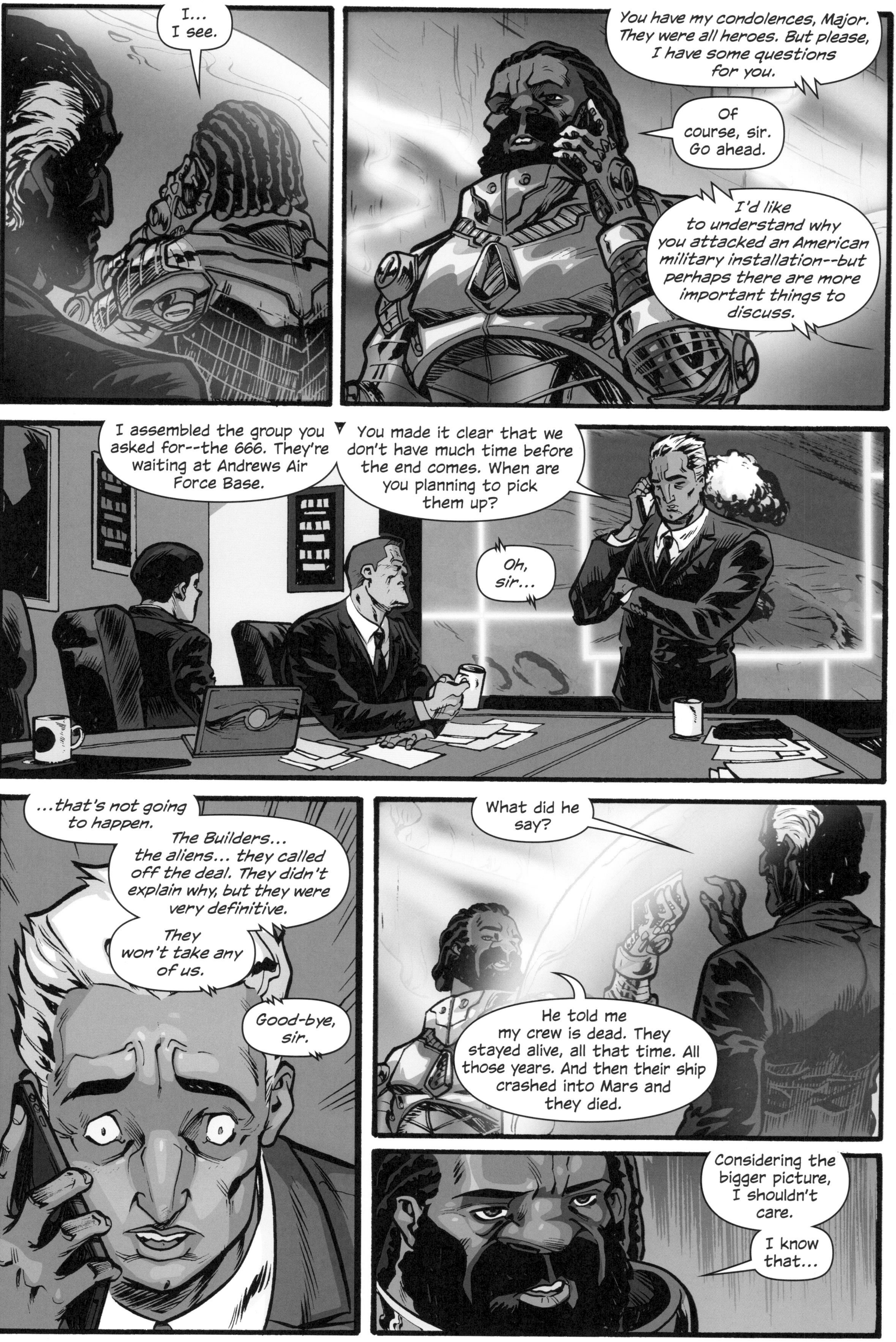
I... I see.
You have my condolences, Major. They were all heroes. But please, I have some questions for you.
Of course, sir. Go ahead.
I'd like to understand why you attacked an American military installation--but perhaps there are more important things to discuss.
I assembled the group you asked for--the 666. They're waiting at Andrews Air Force Base.
You made it clear that we don't have much time before the end comes. When are you planning to pick them up?
Oh, sir...
...that's not going to happen.
The Builders... the aliens... they called off the deal. They didn't explain why, but they were very definitive.
They won't take any of us.
Good-bye, sir.
What did he say?
He told me my crew is dead. They stayed alive, all that time. All those years. And then their ship crashed into Mars and they died.
Considering the bigger picture, I shouldn't care.
I know that...

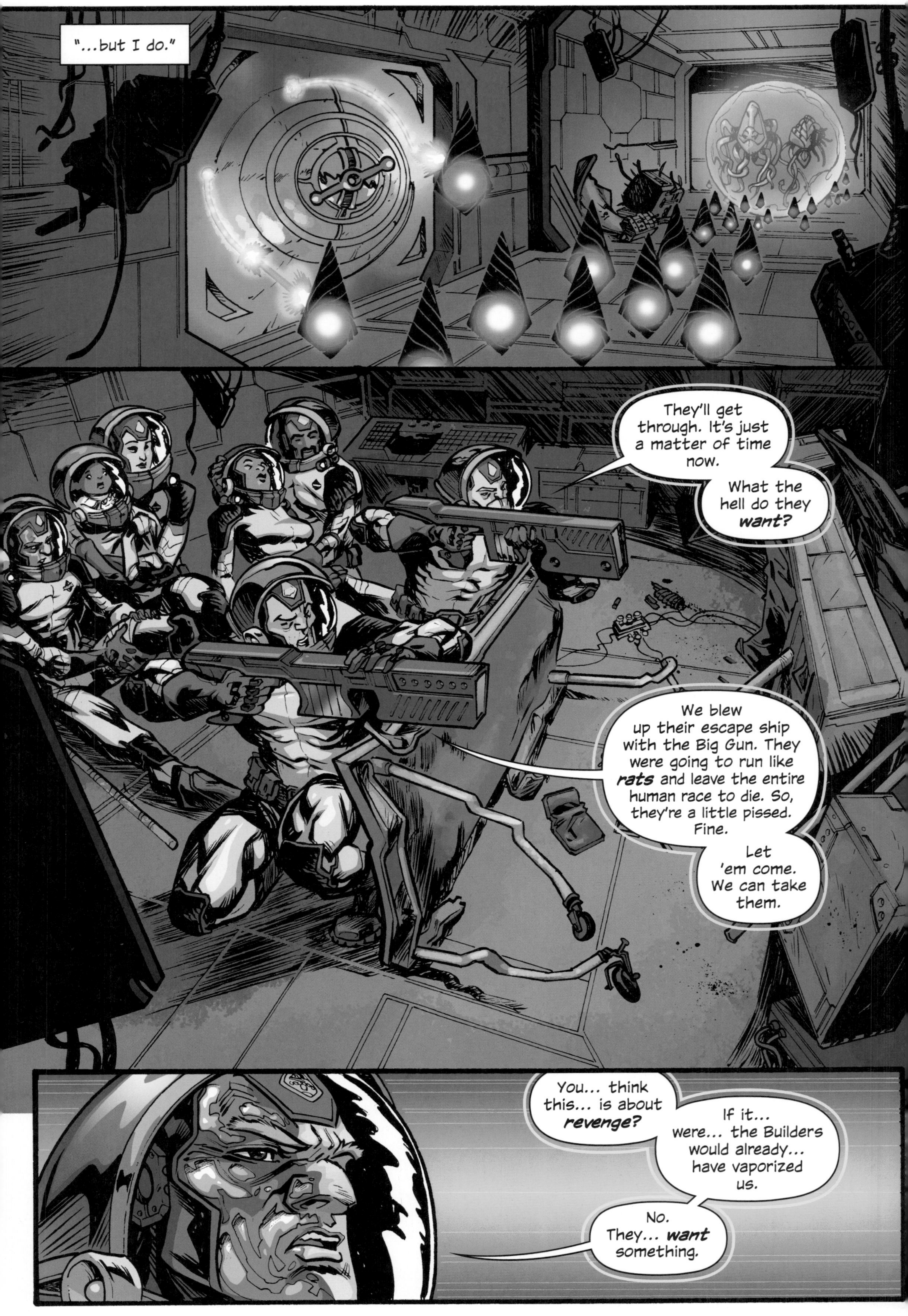
"...but I do."
They'll get through. It's just a matter of time now.
What the hell do they *want?*
We blew up their escape ship with the Big Gun. They were going to run like *rats* and leave the entire human race to die. So, they're a little pissed. Fine.
Let 'em come. We can take them.
You... think this... is about *revenge?*
If it... were... the Builders would already... have vaporized us.
No. They... *want* something.

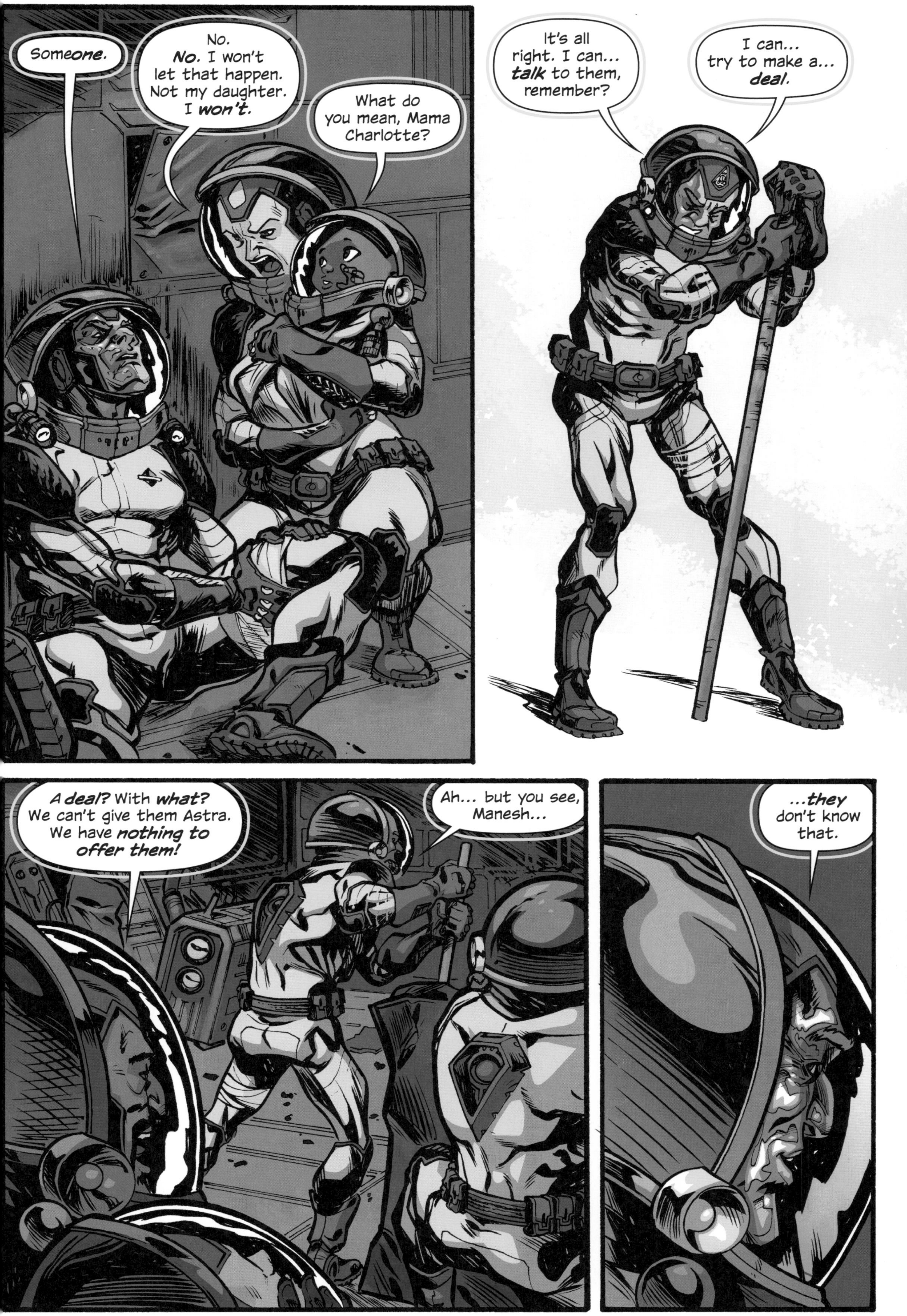
Someone.
No. No. I won't let that happen. Not my daughter. I won't.
What do you mean, Mama Charlotte?
It's all right. I can... talk to them, remember?
I can... try to make a... deal.
A deal? With what? We can't give them Astra. We have nothing to offer them!
Ah... but you see, Manesh...
...they don't know that.

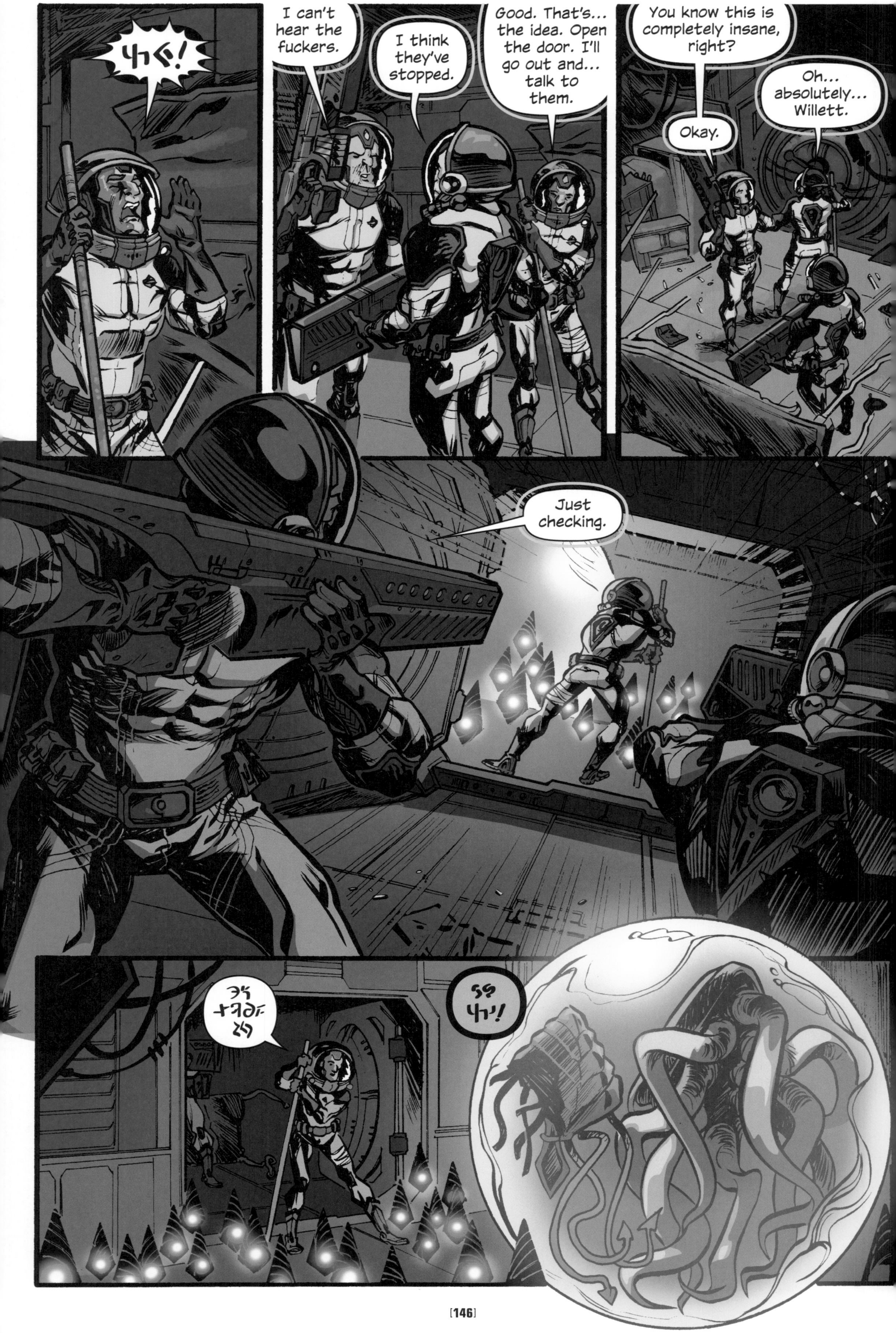
I can't hear the fuckers.
I think they've stopped.
Good. That's... the idea. Open the door. I'll go out and... talk to them.
You know this is completely insane, right?
Okay.
Oh... absolutely... Willett.
Just checking.

We're talking. They're angry--very angry--but we're talking.

I think--

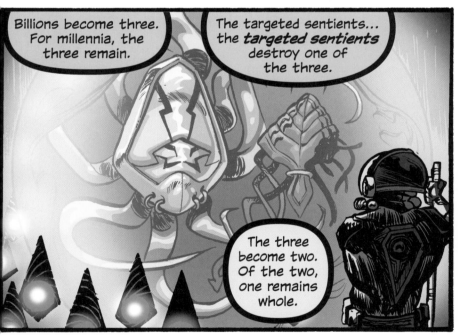

Billions become three. For millennia, the three remain.

The targeted sentients... the *targeted sentients* destroy one of the three.

The three become two. Of the two, one remains whole.

Oh shit.

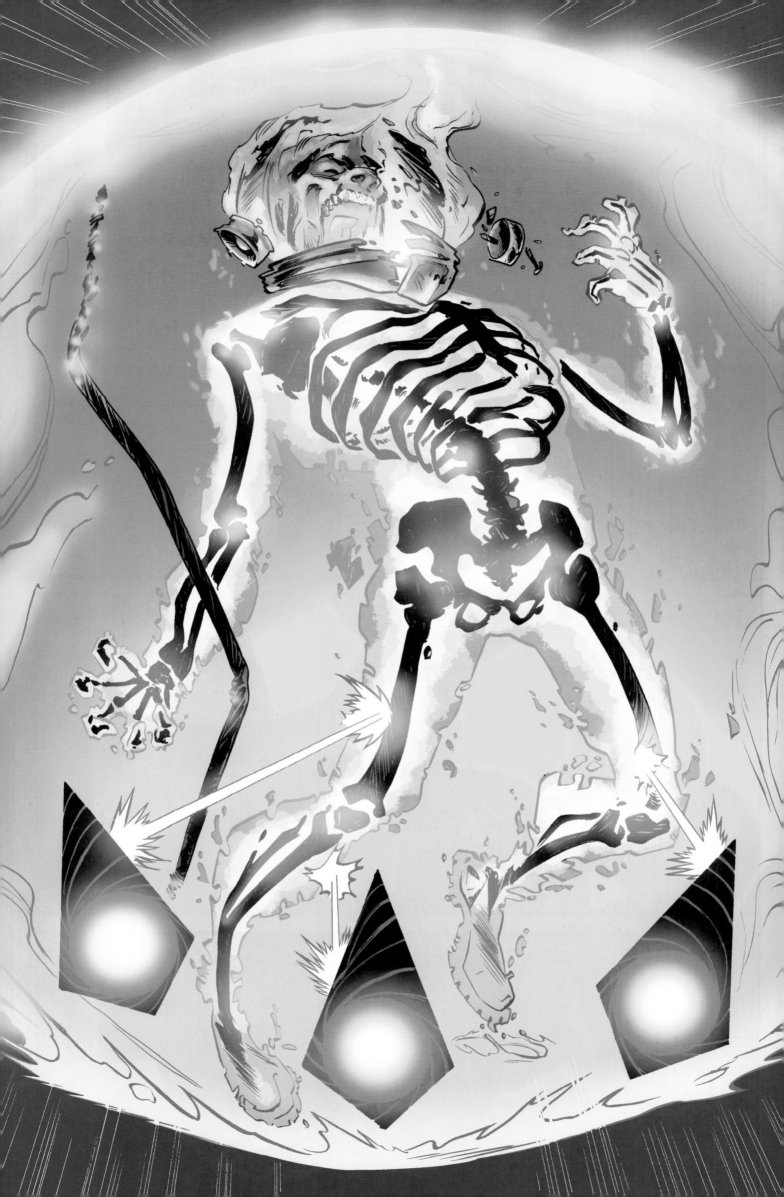

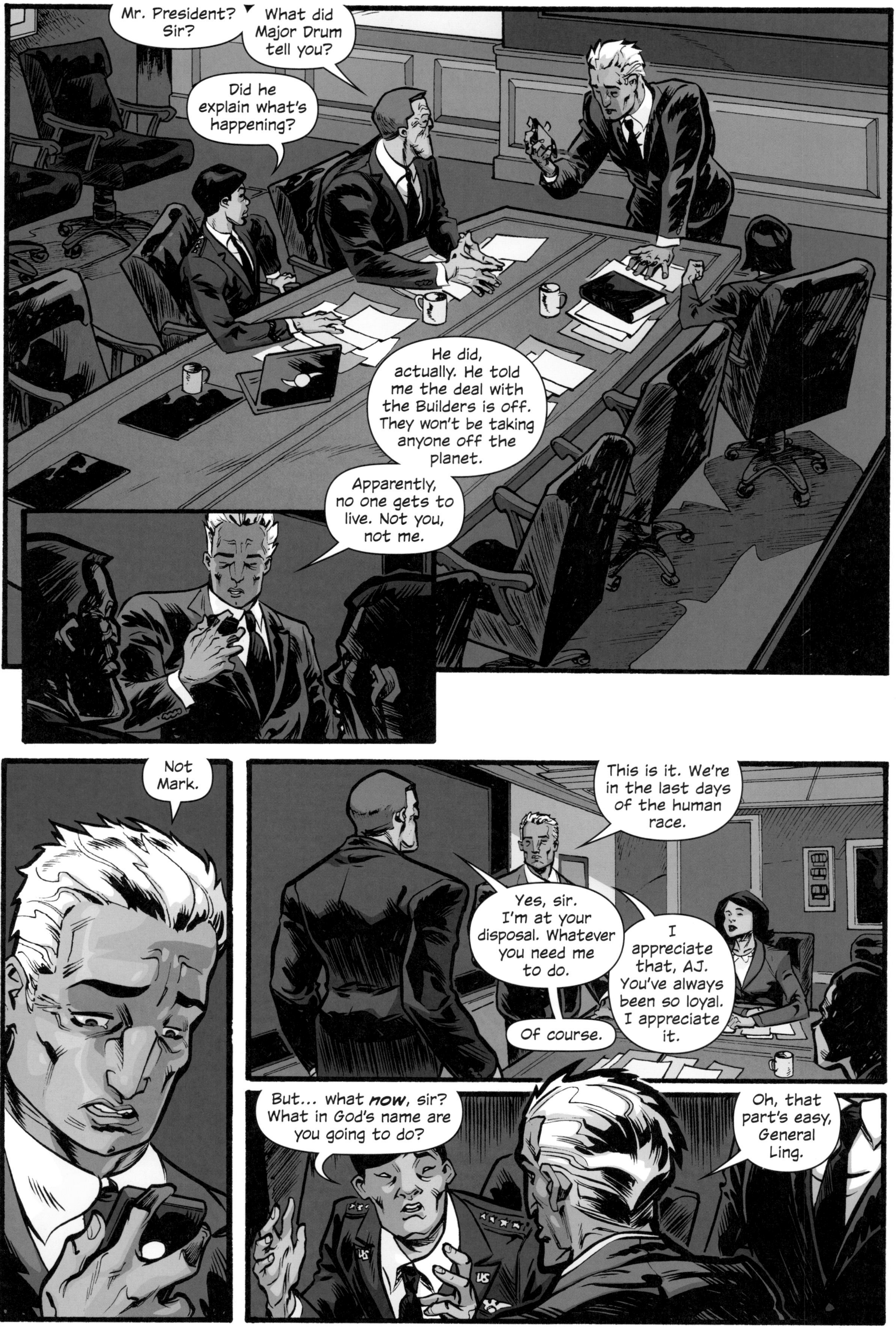
Mr. President? Sir?
What did Major Drum tell you?
Did he explain what's happening?
He did, actually. He told me the deal with the Builders is off. They won't be taking anyone off the planet.
Apparently, no one gets to live. Not you, not me.
Not Mark.
This is it. We're in the last days of the human race.
Yes, sir. I'm at your disposal. Whatever you need me to do.
I appreciate that, AJ. You've always been so loyal. I appreciate it.
Of course.
But... what ***now***, sir? What in God's name are you going to do?
Oh, that part's easy, General Ling.

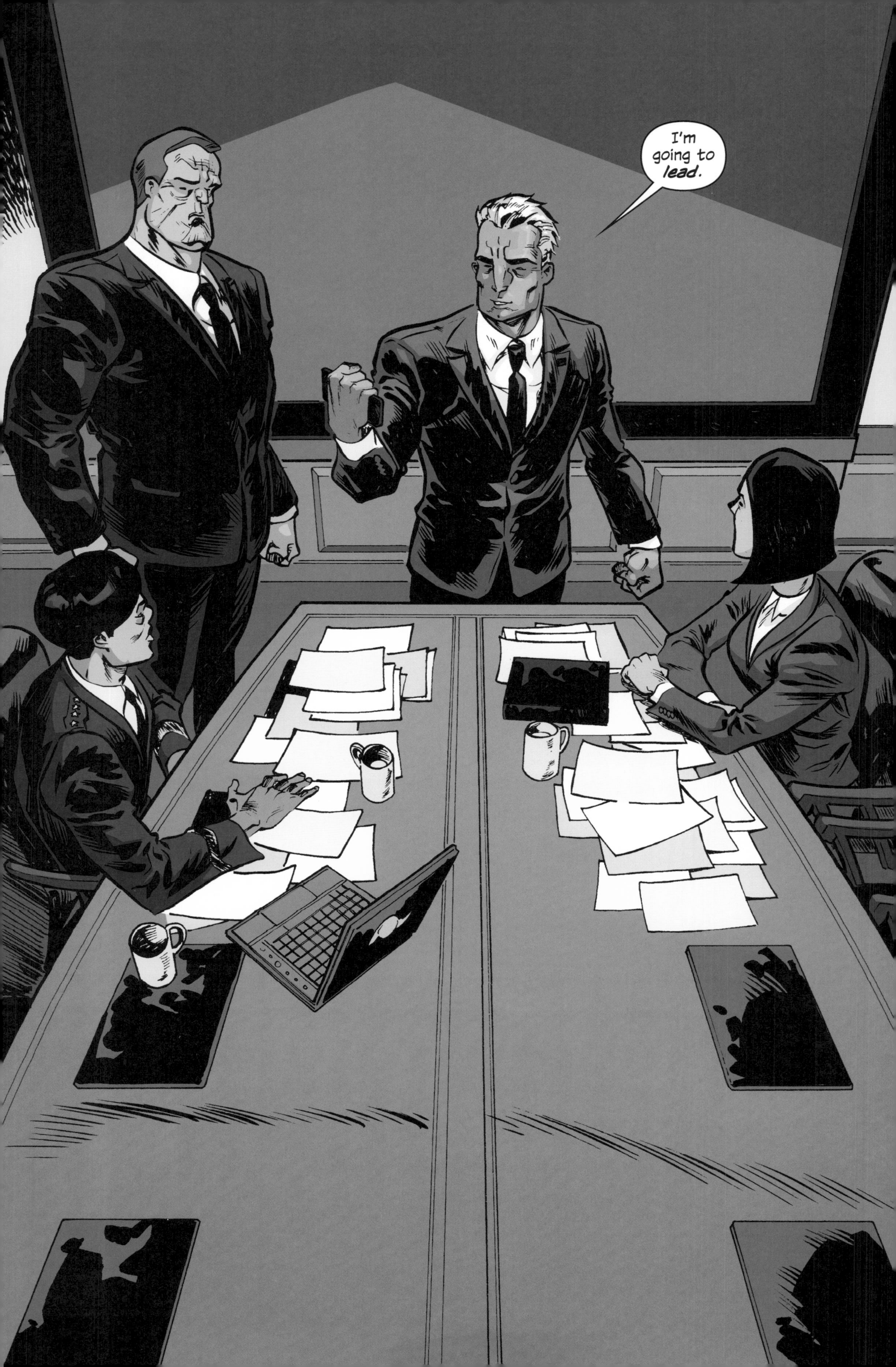
I'm going to *lead*.

LETTER 44

CHAPTER VII

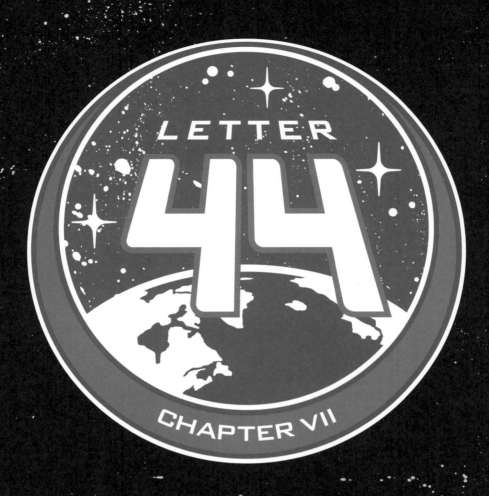

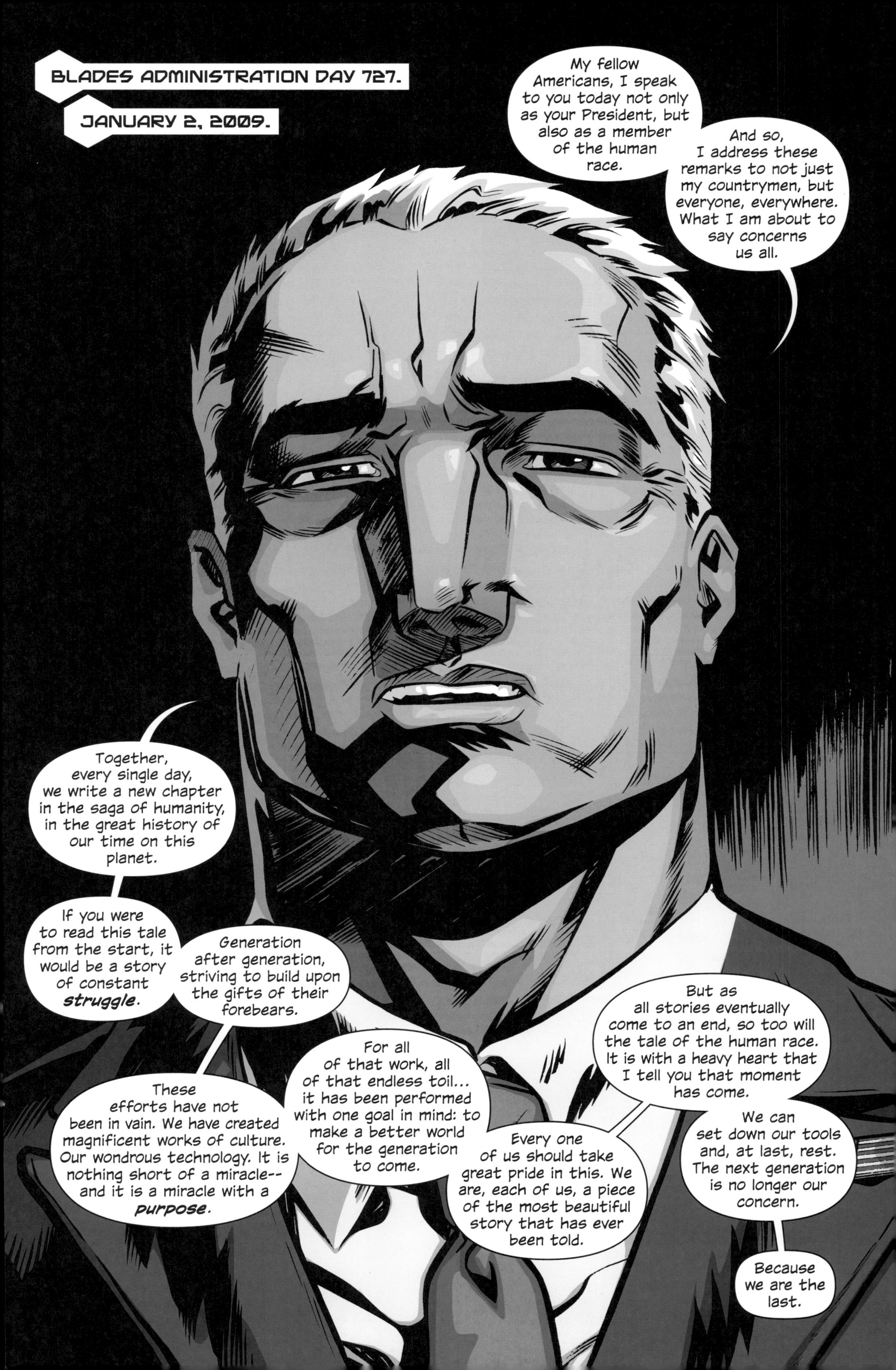
BLADES ADMINISTRATION DAY 727.
JANUARY 2, 2009.
My fellow Americans, I speak to you today not only as your President, but also as a member of the human race.
And so, I address these remarks to not just my countrymen, but everyone, everywhere. What I am about to say concerns us all.
Together, every single day, we write a new chapter in the saga of humanity, in the great history of our time on this planet.
If you were to read this tale from the start, it would be a story of constant ***struggle***.
Generation after generation, striving to build upon the gifts of their forebears.
These efforts have not been in vain. We have created magnificent works of culture. Our wondrous technology. It is nothing short of a miracle-- and it is a miracle with a ***purpose***.
For all of that work, all of that endless toil... it has been performed with one goal in mind: to make a better world for the generation to come.
Every one of us should take great pride in this. We are, each of us, a piece of the most beautiful story that has ever been told.
But as all stories eventually come to an end, so too will the tale of the human race. It is with a heavy heart that I tell you that moment has come.
We can set down our tools and, at last, rest. The next generation is no longer our concern.
Because we are the last.

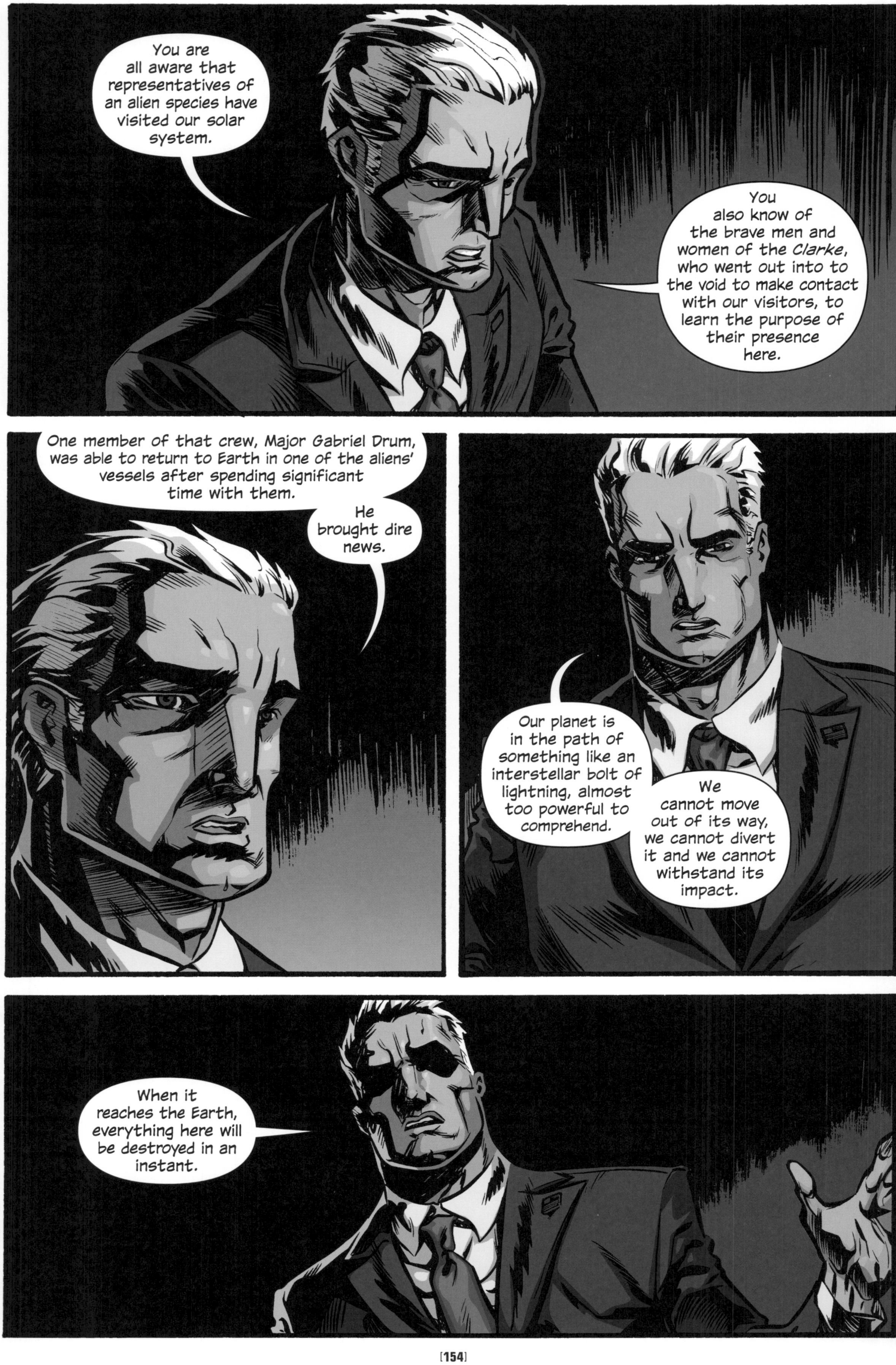

You are all aware that representatives of an alien species have visited our solar system.
You also know of the brave men and women of the *Clarke*, who went out into to the void to make contact with our visitors, to learn the purpose of their presence here.
One member of that crew, Major Gabriel Drum, was able to return to Earth in one of the aliens' vessels after spending significant time with them.
He brought dire news.
Our planet is in the path of something like an interstellar bolt of lightning, almost too powerful to comprehend.
We cannot move out of its way, we cannot divert it and we cannot withstand its impact.
When it reaches the Earth, everything here will be destroyed in an instant.

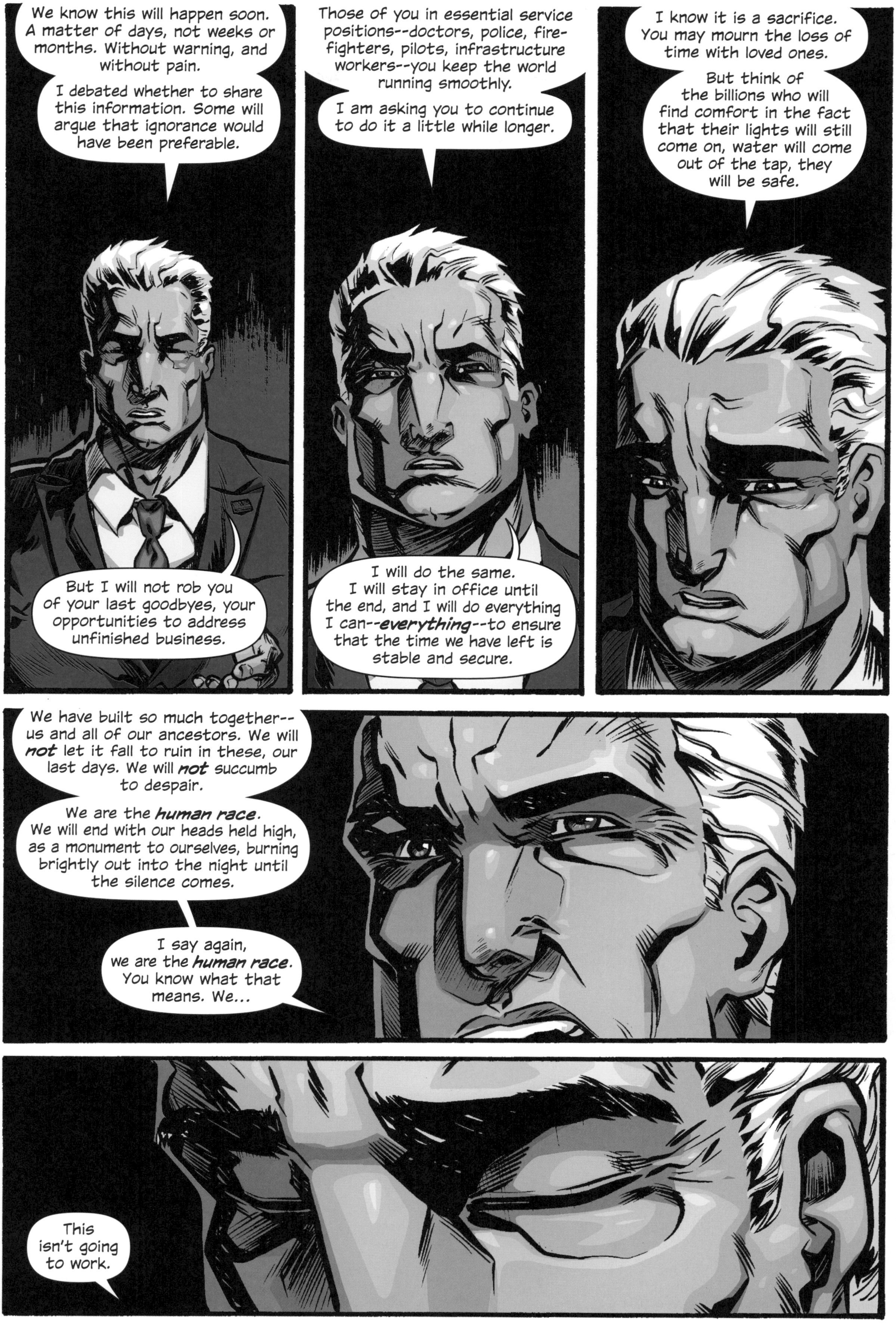
We know this will happen soon. A matter of days, not weeks or months. Without warning, and without pain.
I debated whether to share this information. Some will argue that ignorance would have been preferable.
But I will not rob you of your last goodbyes, your opportunities to address unfinished business.
Those of you in essential service positions--doctors, police, fire-fighters, pilots, infrastructure workers--you keep the world running smoothly.
I am asking you to continue to do it a little while longer.
I will do the same. I will stay in office until the end, and I will do everything I can--*everything*--to ensure that the time we have left is stable and secure.
I know it is a sacrifice. You may mourn the loss of time with loved ones.
But think of the billions who will find comfort in the fact that their lights will still come on, water will come out of the tap, they will be safe.
We have built so much together--us and all of our ancestors. We will *not* let it fall to ruin in these, our last days. We will *not* succumb to despair.
We are the *human race*. We will end with our heads held high, as a monument to ourselves, burning brightly out into the night until the silence comes.
I say again, we are the *human race*. You know what that means. We...
This isn't going to work.

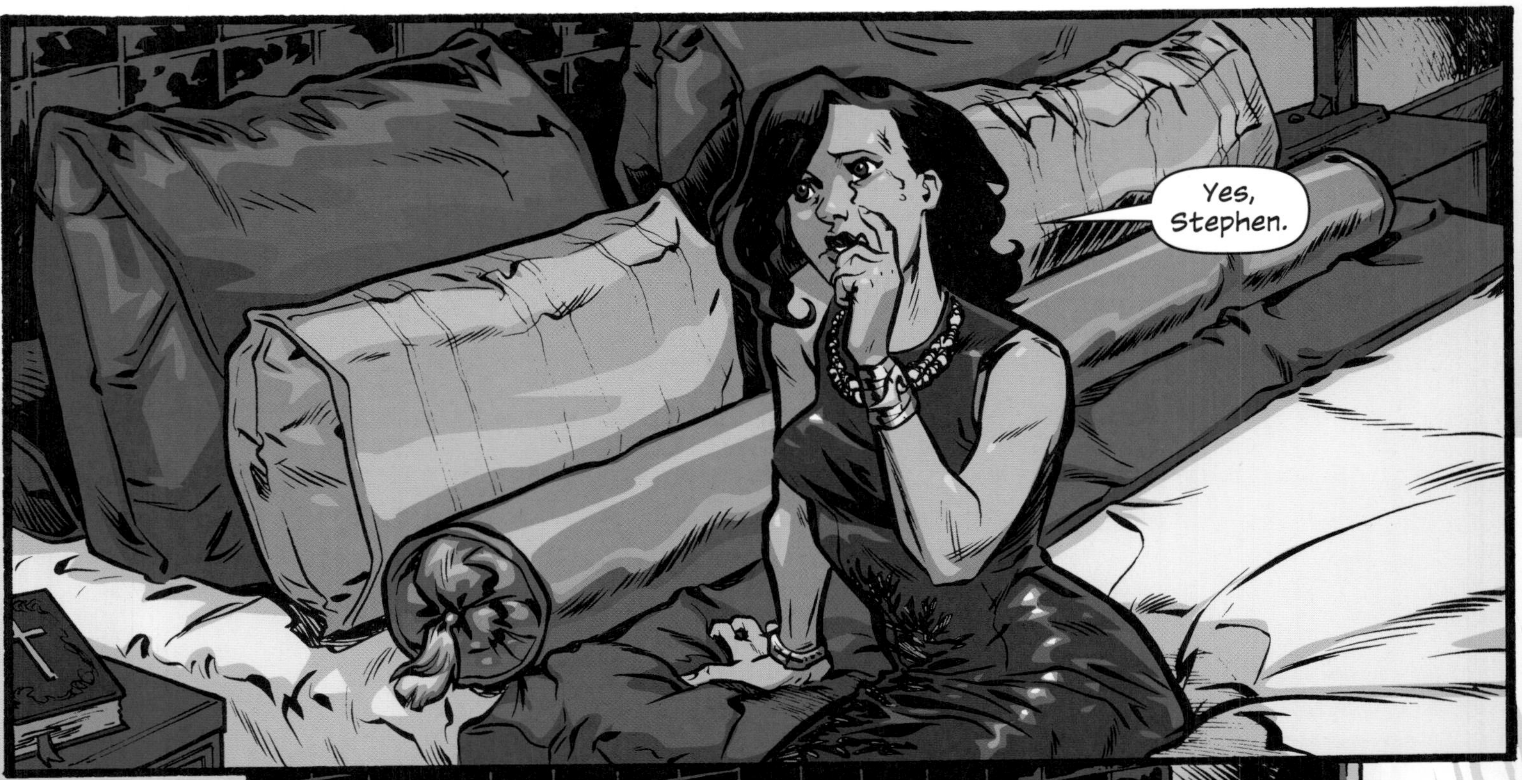
Yes, Stephen.
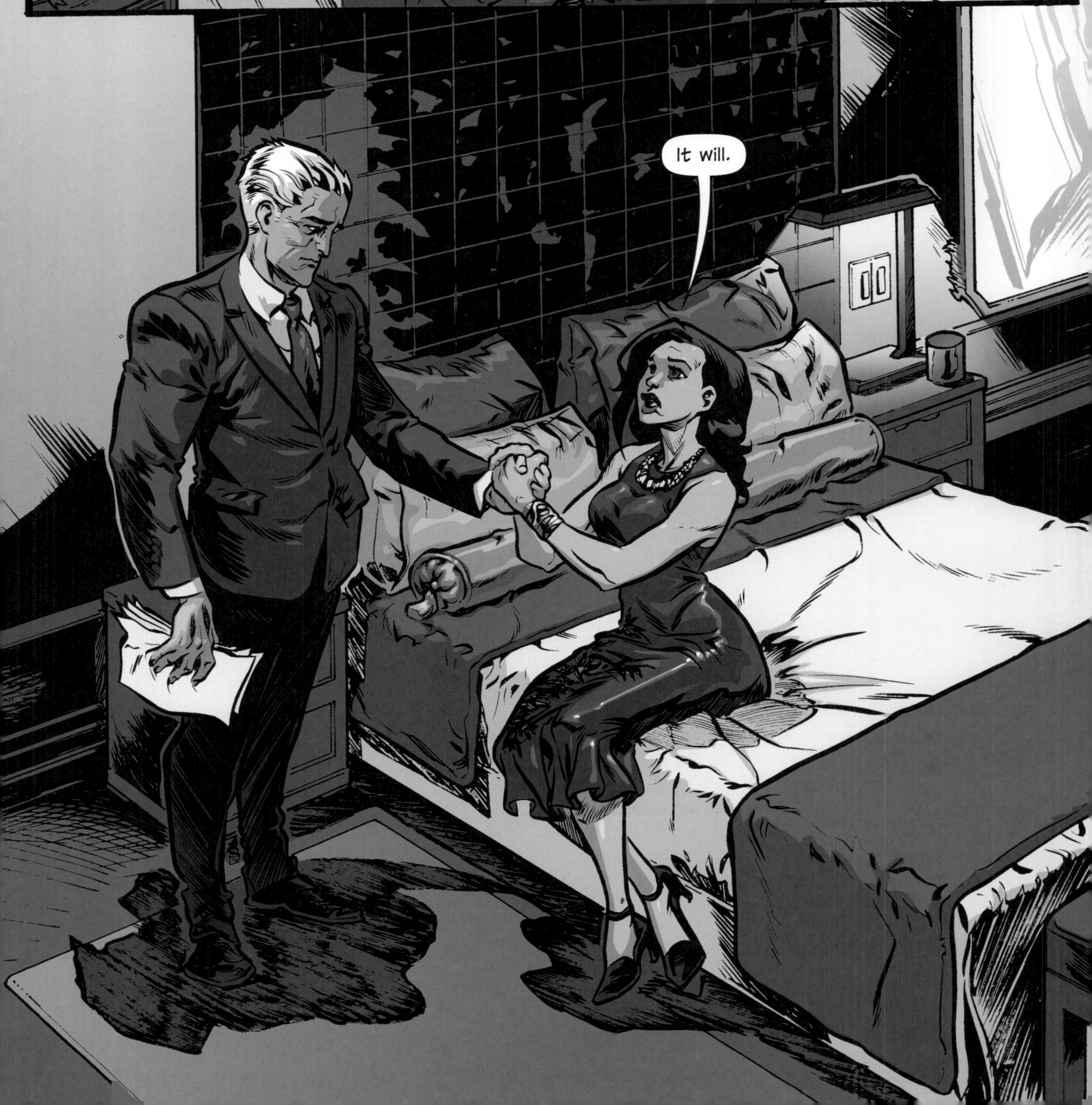
It will.

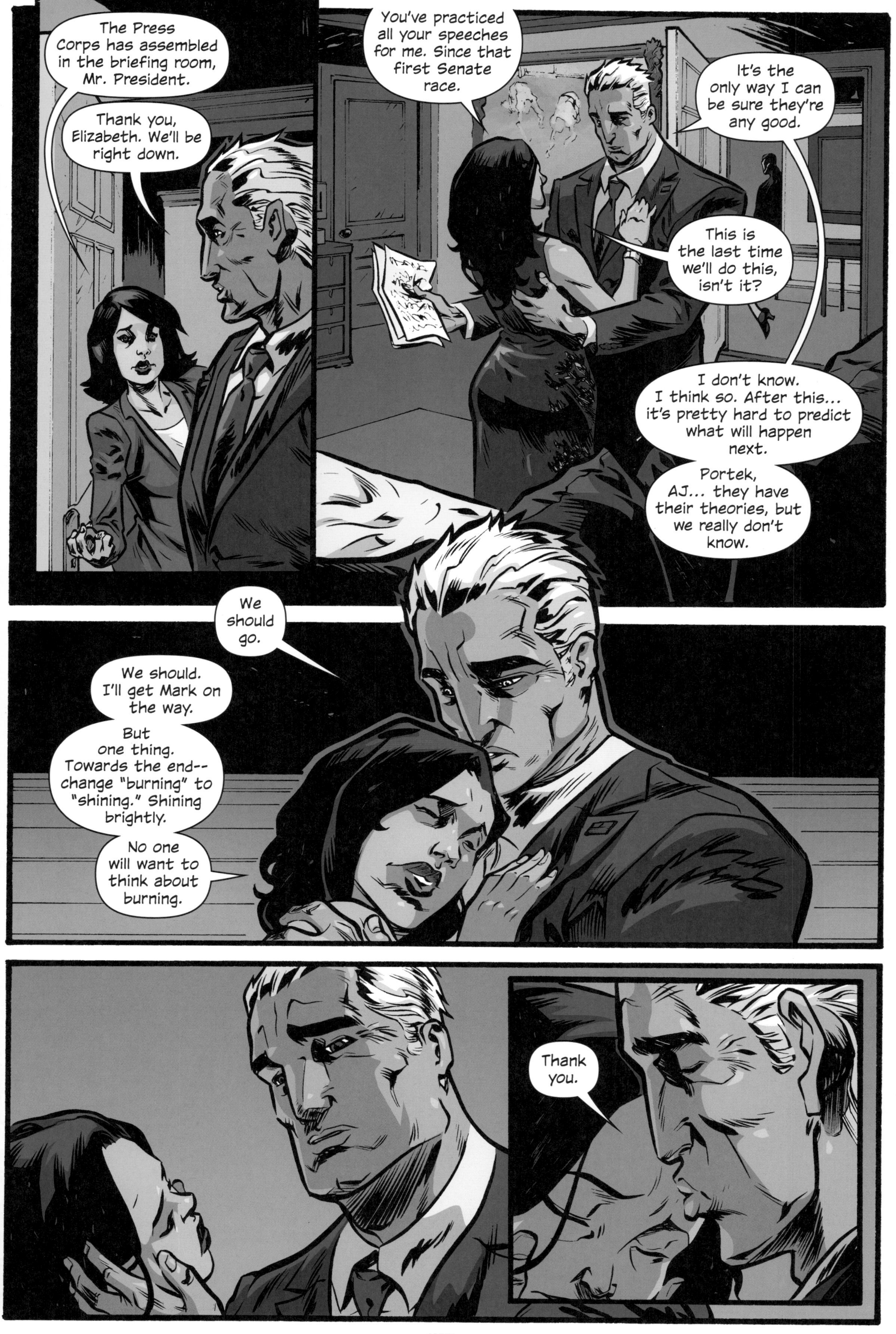
The Press Corps has assembled in the briefing room, Mr. President.
Thank you, Elizabeth. We'll be right down.
You've practiced all your speeches for me. Since that first Senate race.
It's the only way I can be sure they're any good.
This is the last time we'll do this, isn't it?
I don't know. I think so. After this... it's pretty hard to predict what will happen next.
Portek, AJ... they have their theories, but we really don't know.
We should go.
We should. I'll get Mark on the way.
But one thing. Towards the end-- change "burning" to "shining." Shining brightly.
No one will want to think about burning.
Thank you.

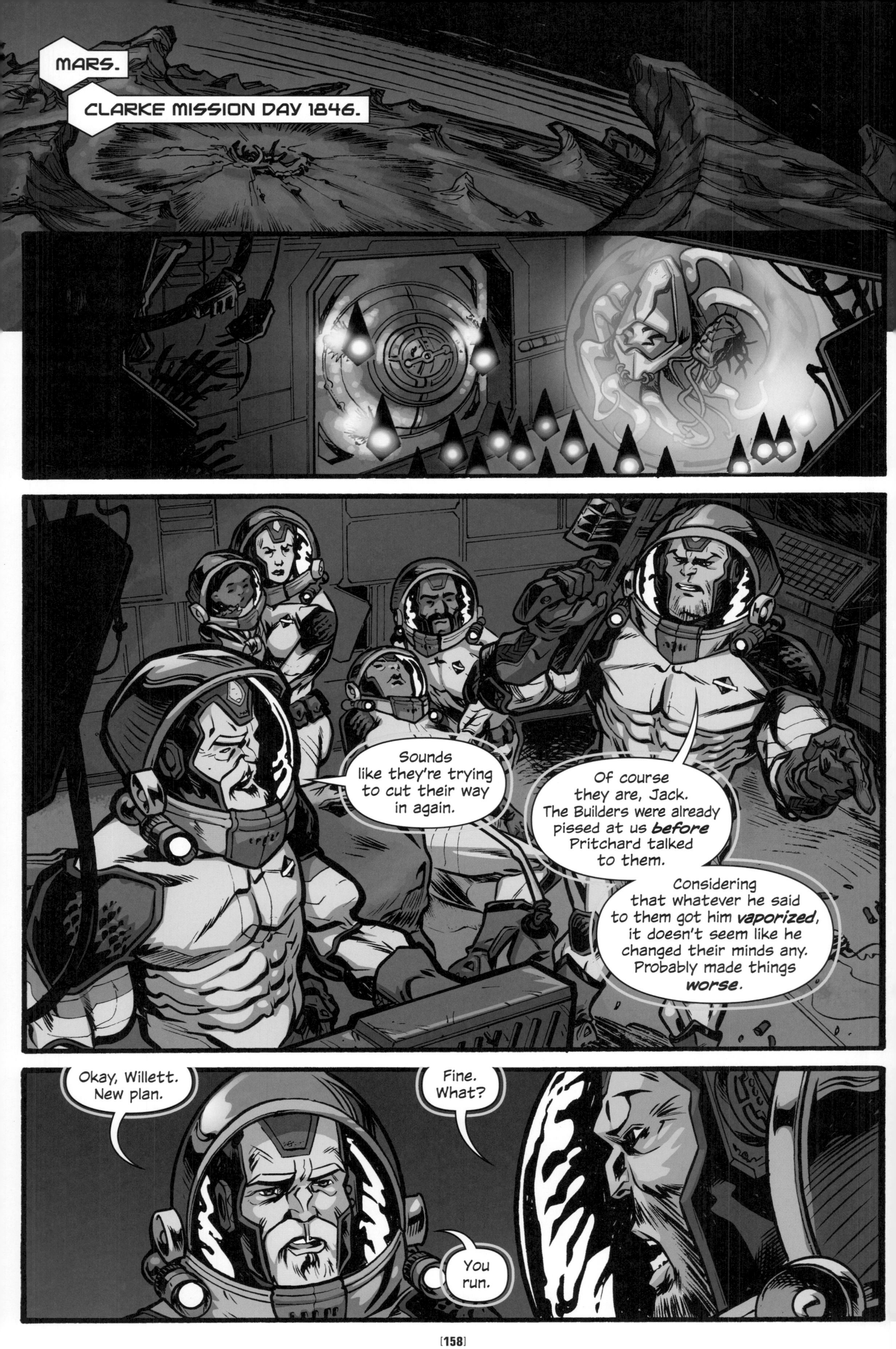
MARS.
CLARKE MISSION DAY 1846.
Sounds like they're trying to cut their way in again.
Of course they are, Jack. The Builders were already pissed at us *before* Pritchard talked to them.
Considering that whatever he said to them got him *vaporized*, it doesn't seem like he changed their minds any. Probably made things *worse*.
Okay, Willett. New plan.
Fine. What?
You run.

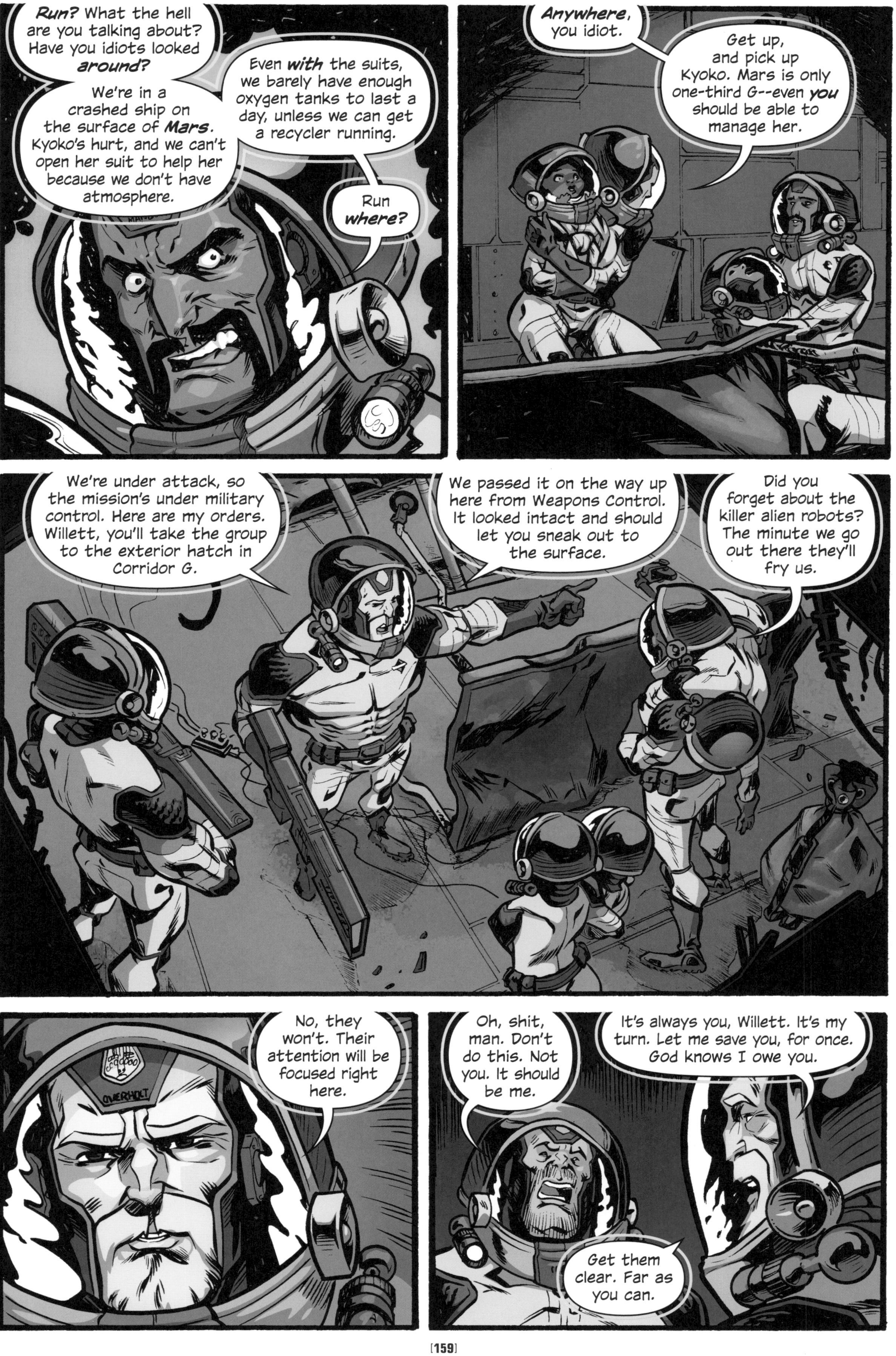
Run? What the hell are you talking about? Have you idiots looked *around?*
We're in a crashed ship on the surface of *Mars*. Kyoko's hurt, and we can't open her suit to help her because we don't have atmosphere.
Even *with* the suits, we barely have enough oxygen tanks to last a day, unless we can get a recycler running.
Run *where?*
Anywhere, you idiot.
Get up, and pick up Kyoko. Mars is only one-third G--even *you* should be able to manage her.
We're under attack, so the mission's under military control. Here are my orders. Willett, you'll take the group to the exterior hatch in Corridor G.
We passed it on the way up here from Weapons Control. It looked intact and should let you sneak out to the surface.
Did you forget about the killer alien robots? The minute we go out there they'll fry us.
OVERHOLT
No, they won't. Their attention will be focused right here.
Oh, shit, man. Don't do this. Not you. It should be me.
It's always you, Willett. It's my turn. Let me save you, for once. God knows I owe you.
Get them clear. Far as you can.

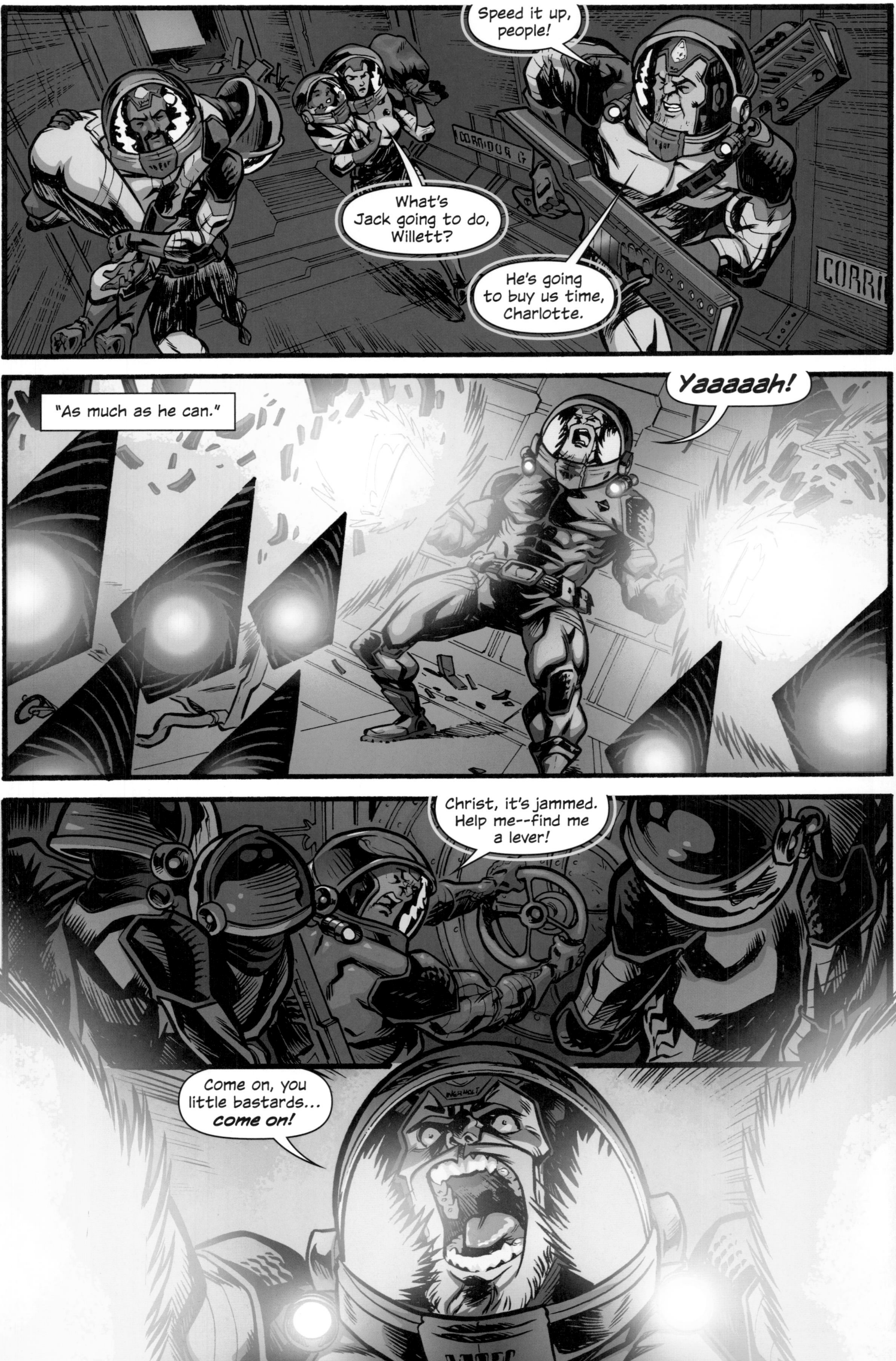
Speed it up, people!
What's Jack going to do, Willett?
He's going to buy us time, Charlotte.
CORRI
"As much as he can."
Yaaaaah!
Christ, it's jammed. Help me--find me a lever!
Come on, you little bastards... come on!

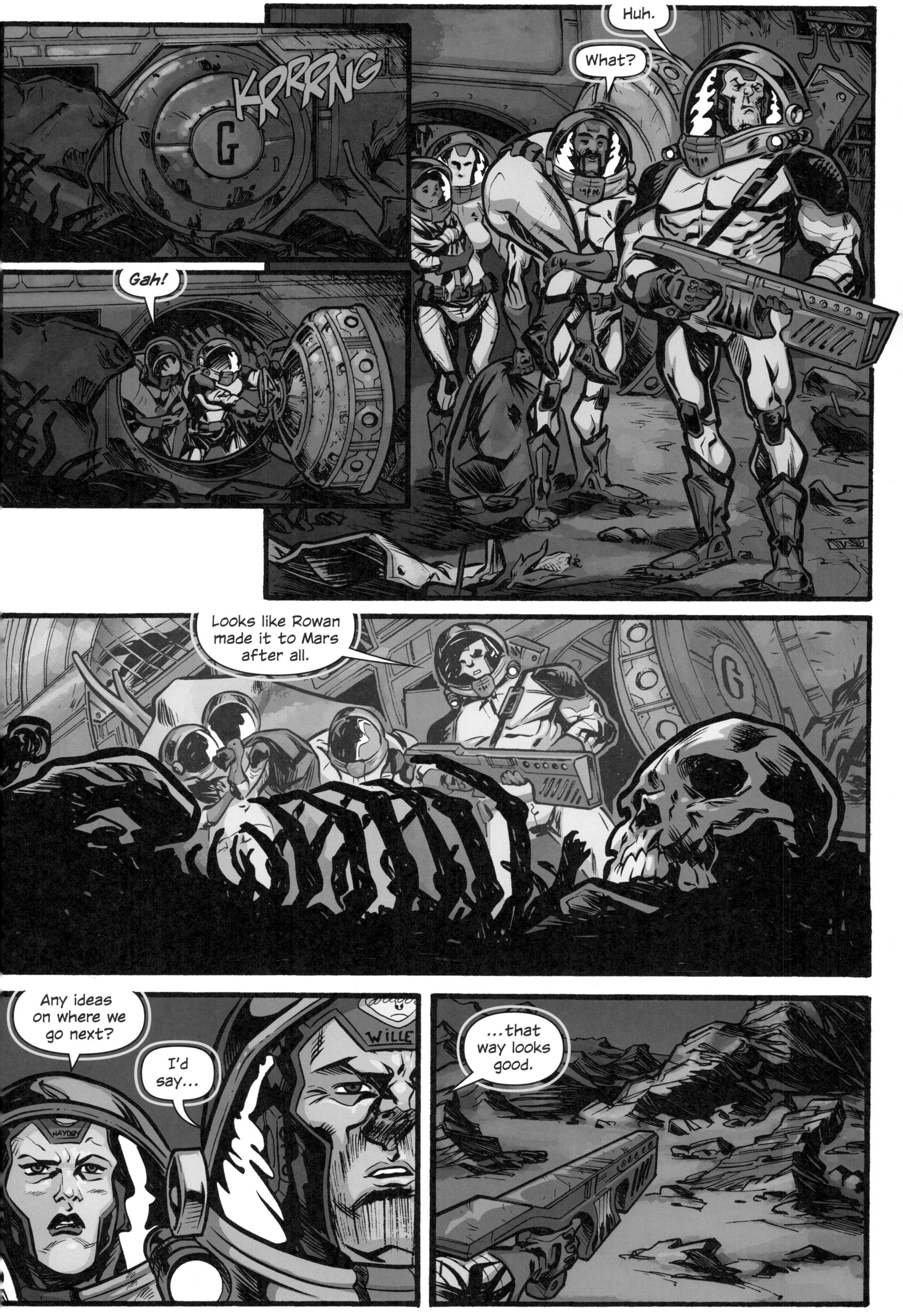
KRRRNG
Gah!
Huh.
What?
Looks like Rowan made it to Mars after all.
Any ideas on where we go next?
I'd say...
...that way looks good.

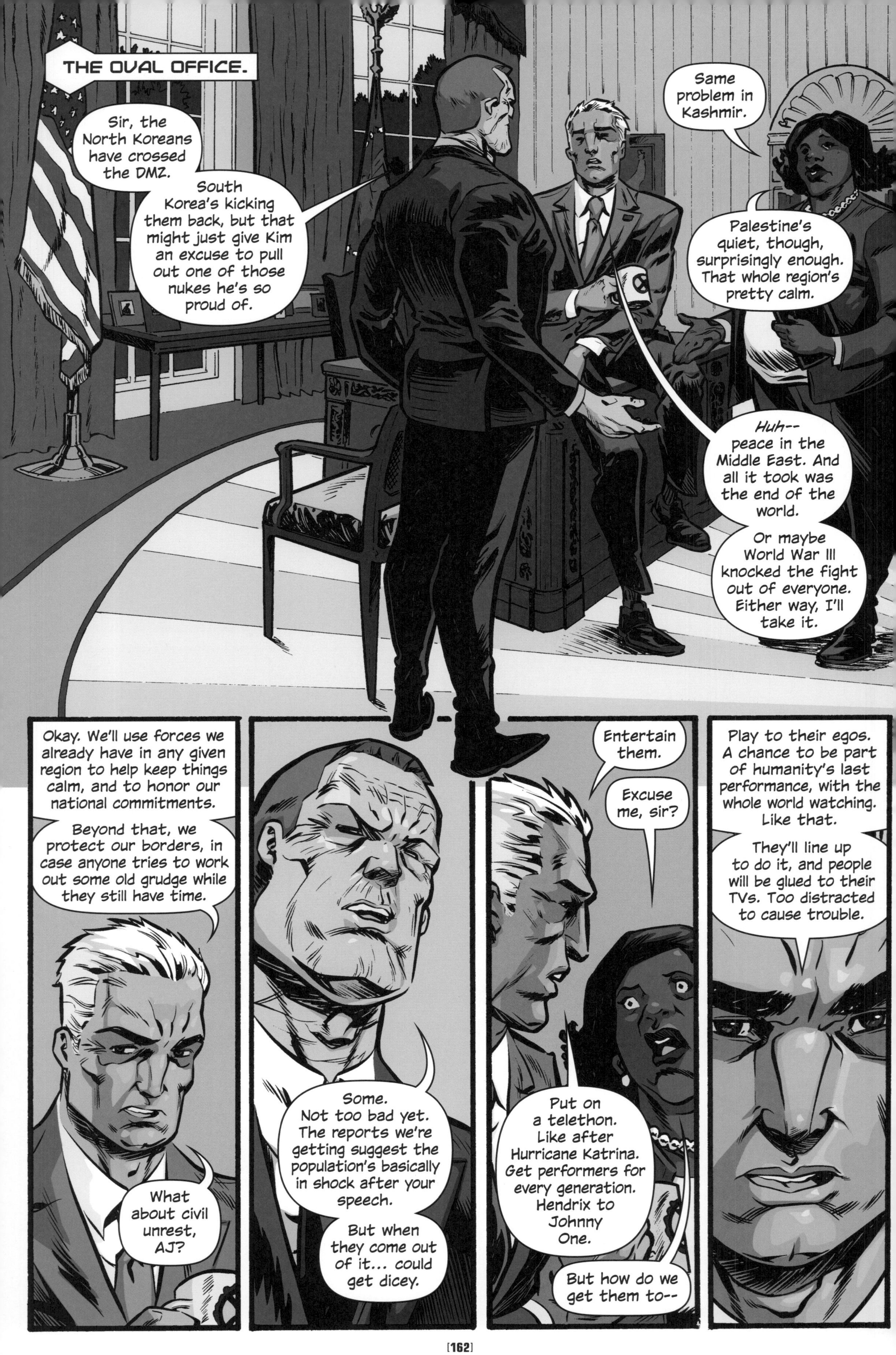

THE OVAL OFFICE.
Sir, the North Koreans have crossed the DMZ.
South Korea's kicking them back, but that might just give Kim an excuse to pull out one of those nukes he's so proud of.
Same problem in Kashmir.
Palestine's quiet, though, surprisingly enough. That whole region's pretty calm.
Huh-- peace in the Middle East. And all it took was the end of the world.
Or maybe World War III knocked the fight out of everyone. Either way, I'll take it.
Okay. We'll use forces we already have in any given region to help keep things calm, and to honor our national commitments.
Beyond that, we protect our borders, in case anyone tries to work out some old grudge while they still have time.
What about civil unrest, AJ?
Some. Not too bad yet. The reports we're getting suggest the population's basically in shock after your speech.
But when they come out of it... could get dicey.
Entertain them.
Excuse me, sir?
Put on a telethon. Like after Hurricane Katrina. Get performers for every generation. Hendrix to Johnny One.
But how do we get them to--
Play to their egos. A chance to be part of humanity's last performance, with the whole world watching. Like that.
They'll line up to do it, and people will be glued to their TVs. Too distracted to cause trouble.

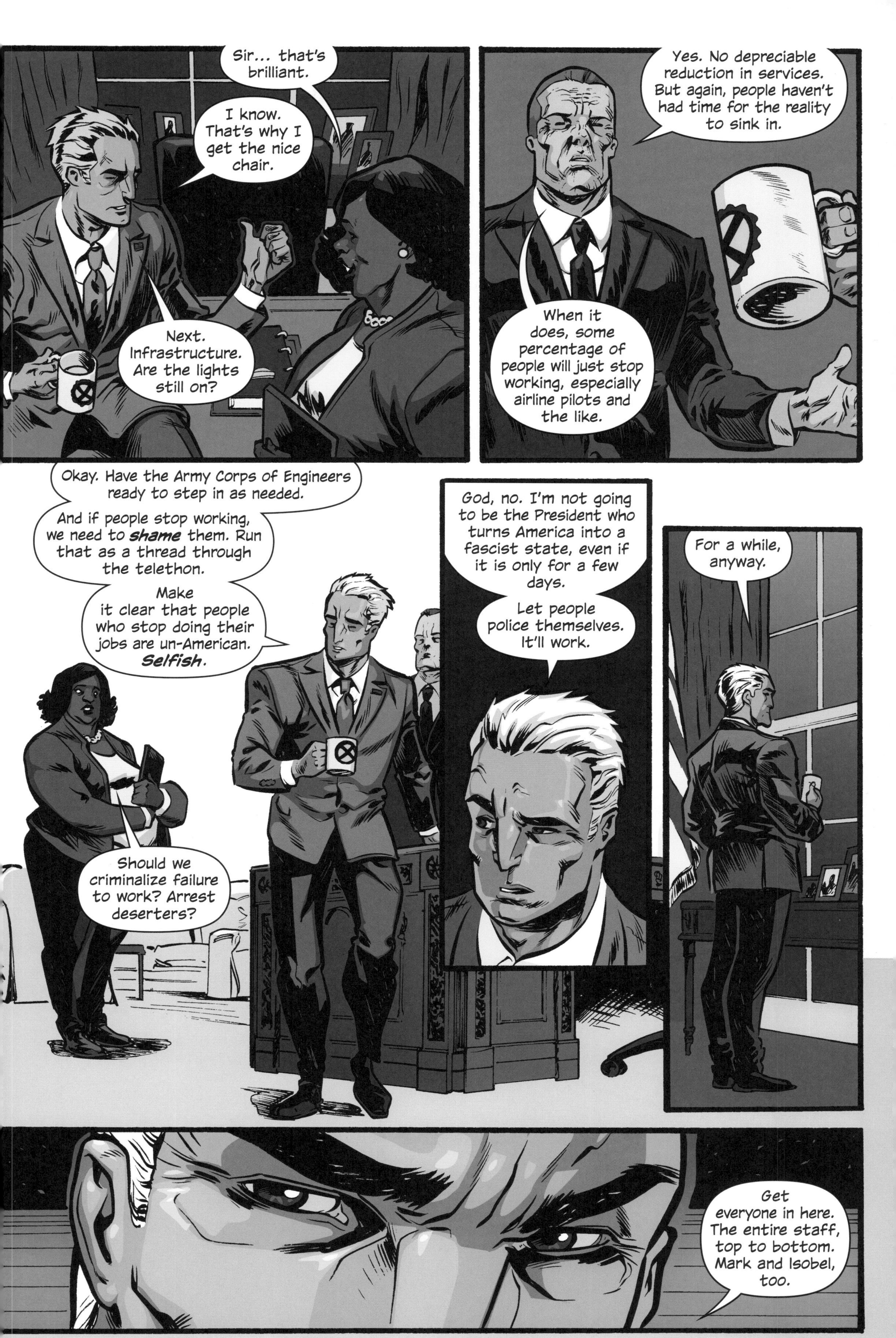

Sir... that's brilliant.
I know. That's why I get the nice chair.
Next. Infrastructure. Are the lights still on?
Yes. No depreciable reduction in services. But again, people haven't had time for the reality to sink in.
When it does, some percentage of people will just stop working, especially airline pilots and the like.
Okay. Have the Army Corps of Engineers ready to step in as needed.
And if people stop working, we need to *shame* them. Run that as a thread through the telethon.
Make it clear that people who stop doing their jobs are un-American. ***Selfish***.
Should we criminalize failure to work? Arrest deserters?
God, no. I'm not going to be the President who turns America into a fascist state, even if it is only for a few days.
Let people police themselves. It'll work.
For a while, anyway.
Get everyone in here. The entire staff, top to bottom. Mark and Isobel, too.

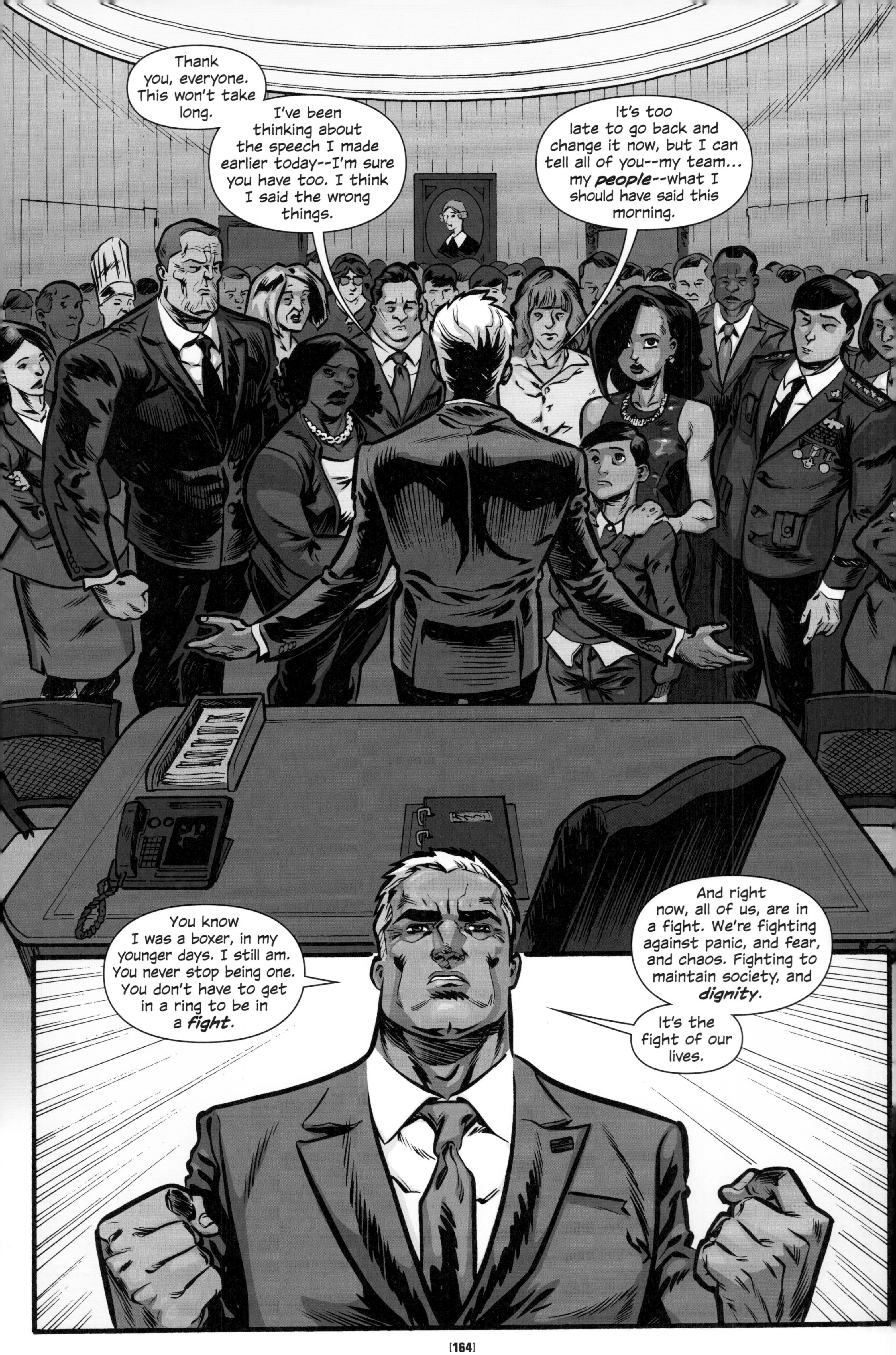
Thank you, everyone. This won't take long.
I've been thinking about the speech I made earlier today--I'm sure you have too. I think I said the wrong things.
It's too late to go back and change it now, but I can tell all of you--my team... my *people*--what I should have said this morning.
You know I was a boxer, in my younger days. I still am. You never stop being one. You don't have to get in a ring to be in a *fight*.
And right now, all of us, are in a fight. We're fighting against panic, and fear, and chaos. Fighting to maintain society, and *dignity*.
It's the fight of our lives.

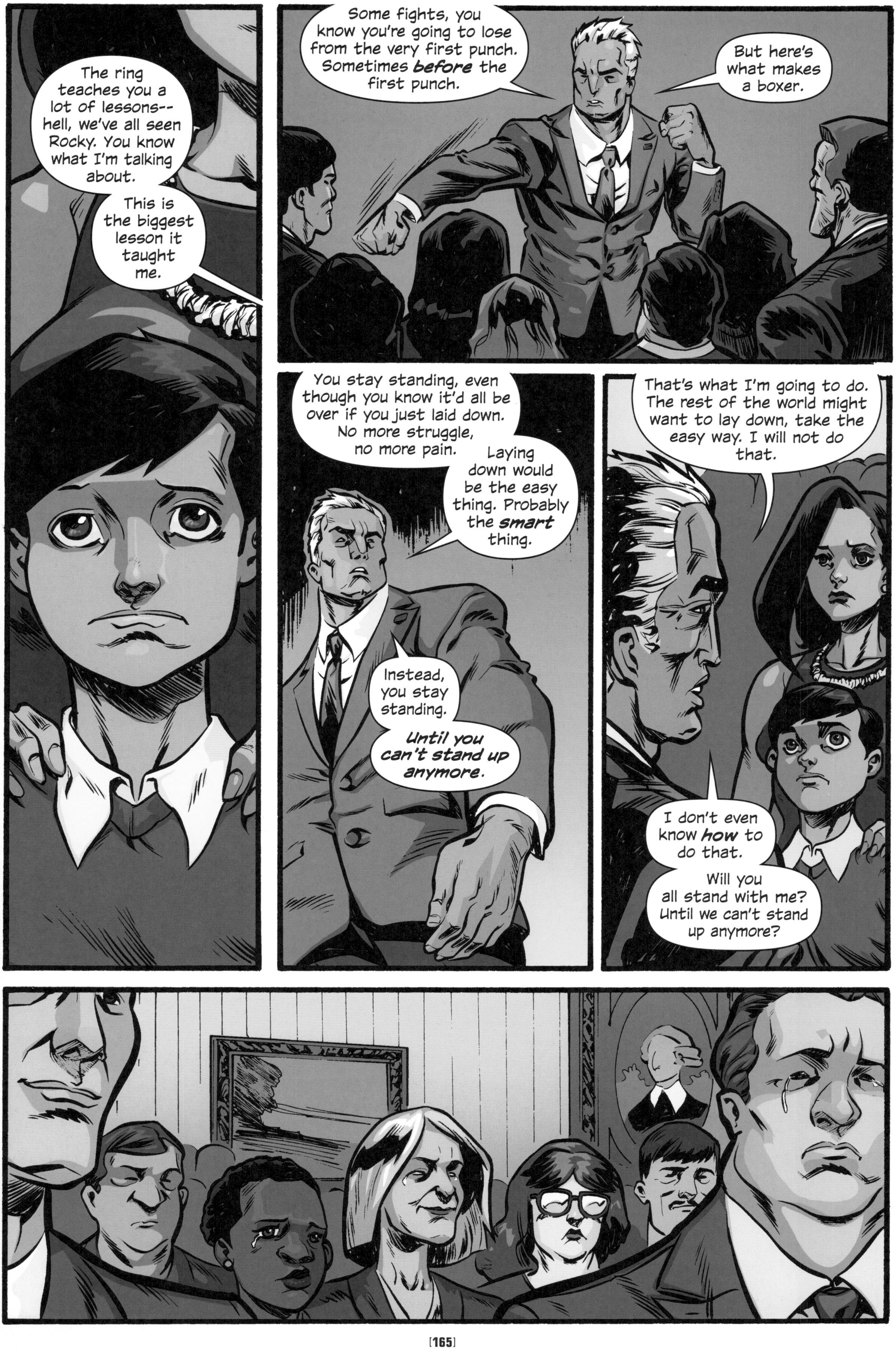
The ring teaches you a lot of lessons-- hell, we've all seen Rocky. You know what I'm talking about.
This is the biggest lesson it taught me.
Some fights, you know you're going to lose from the very first punch. Sometimes *before* the first punch.
But here's what makes a boxer.
You stay standing, even though you know it'd all be over if you just laid down. No more struggle, no more pain.
Laying down would be the easy thing. Probably the *smart* thing.
Instead, you stay standing.
Until you can't stand up anymore.
That's what I'm going to do. The rest of the world might want to lay down, take the easy way. I will not do that.
I don't even know *how* to do that.
Will you all stand with me? Until we can't stand up anymore?

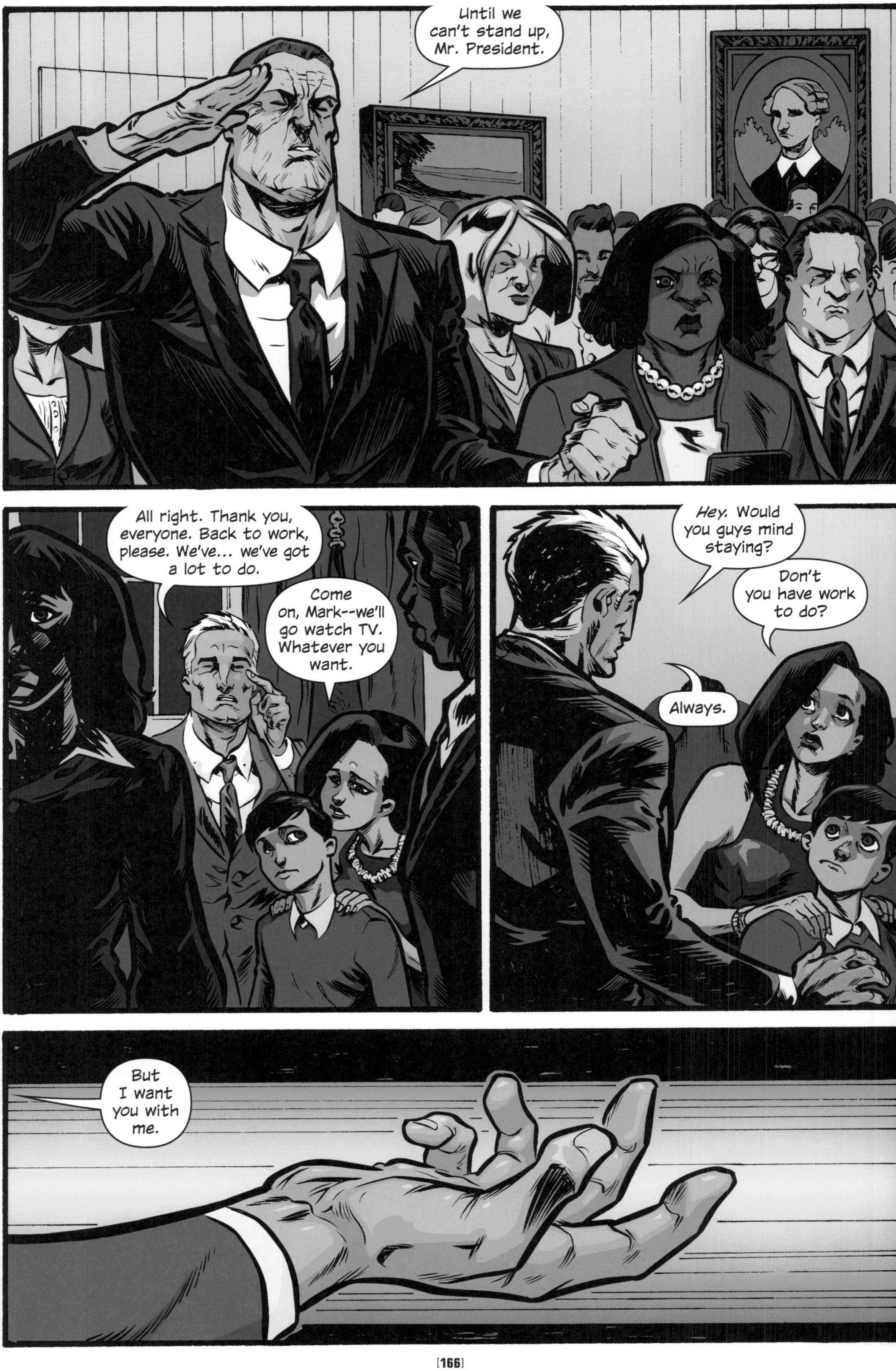

Until we can't stand up, Mr. President.
All right. Thank you, everyone. Back to work, please. We've... we've got a lot to do.
Come on, Mark--we'll go watch TV. Whatever you want.
Hey. Would you guys mind staying?
Don't you have work to do?
Always.
But I want you with me.

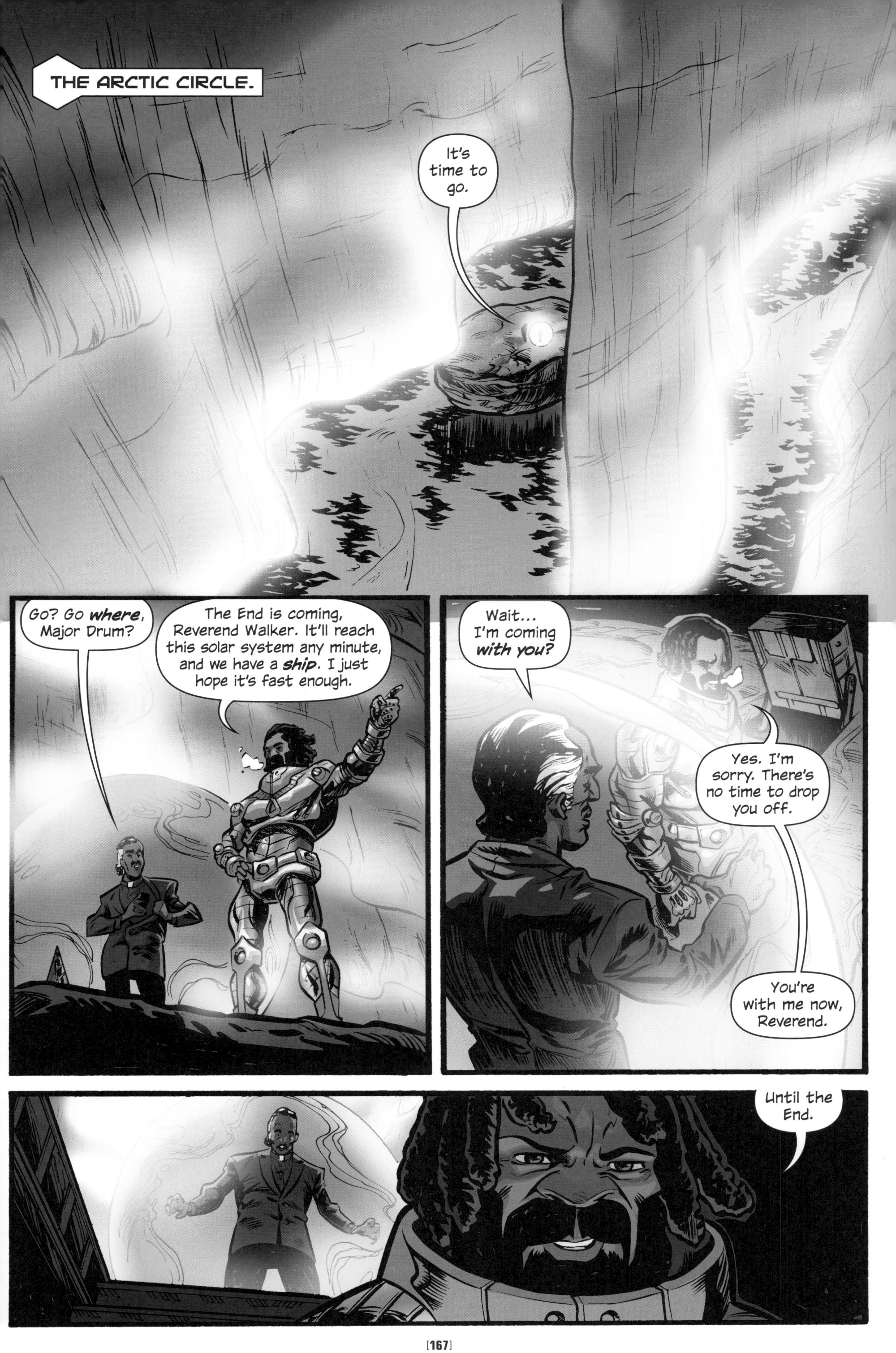
THE ARCTIC CIRCLE.
It's time to go.
Go? Go *where*, Major Drum?
The End is coming, Reverend Walker. It'll reach this solar system any minute, and we have a *ship*. I just hope it's fast enough.
Wait... I'm coming *with you?*
Yes. I'm sorry. There's no time to drop you off.
You're with me now, Reverend.
Until the End.

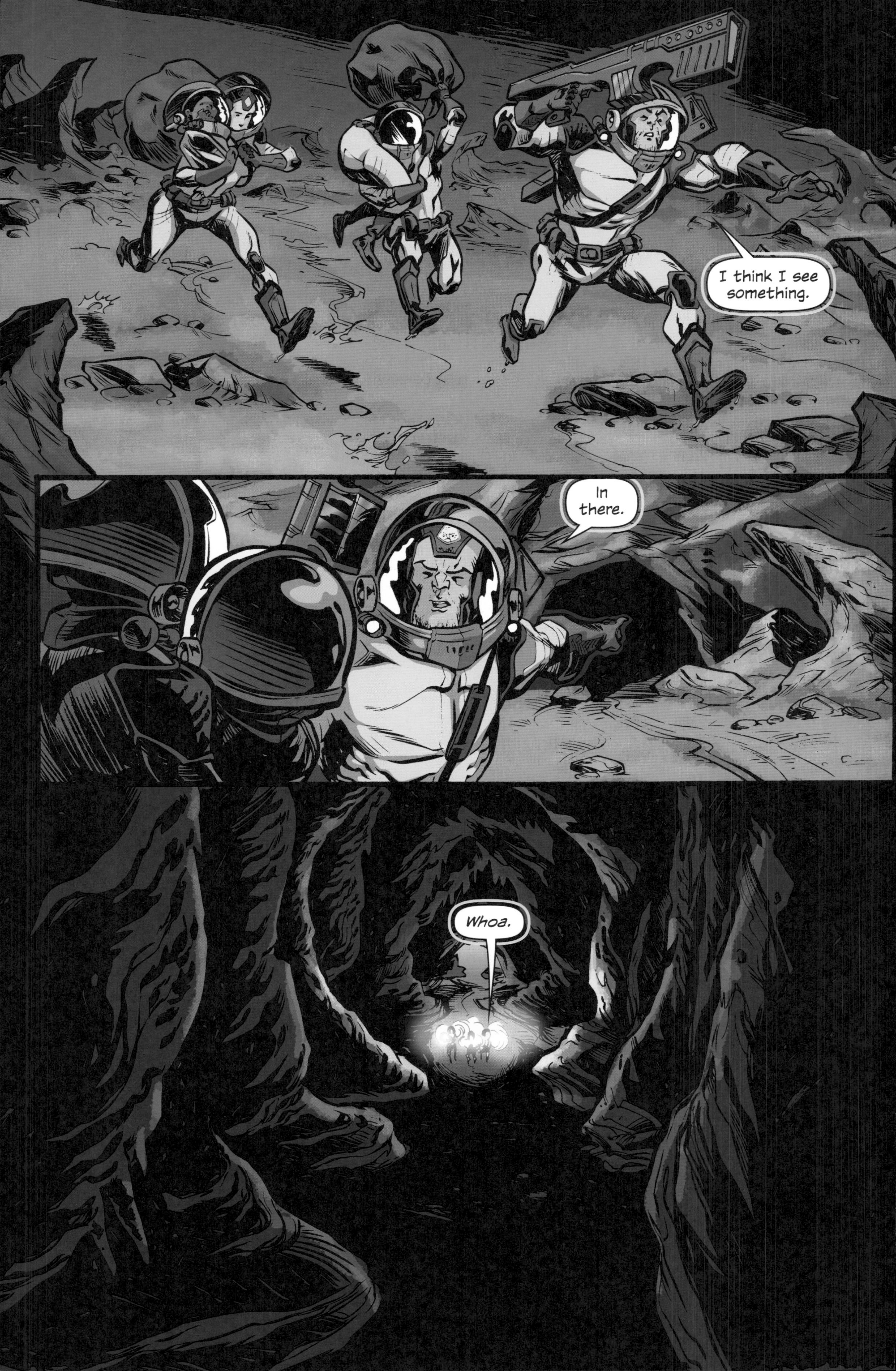
I think I see something.
In there.
Whoa.

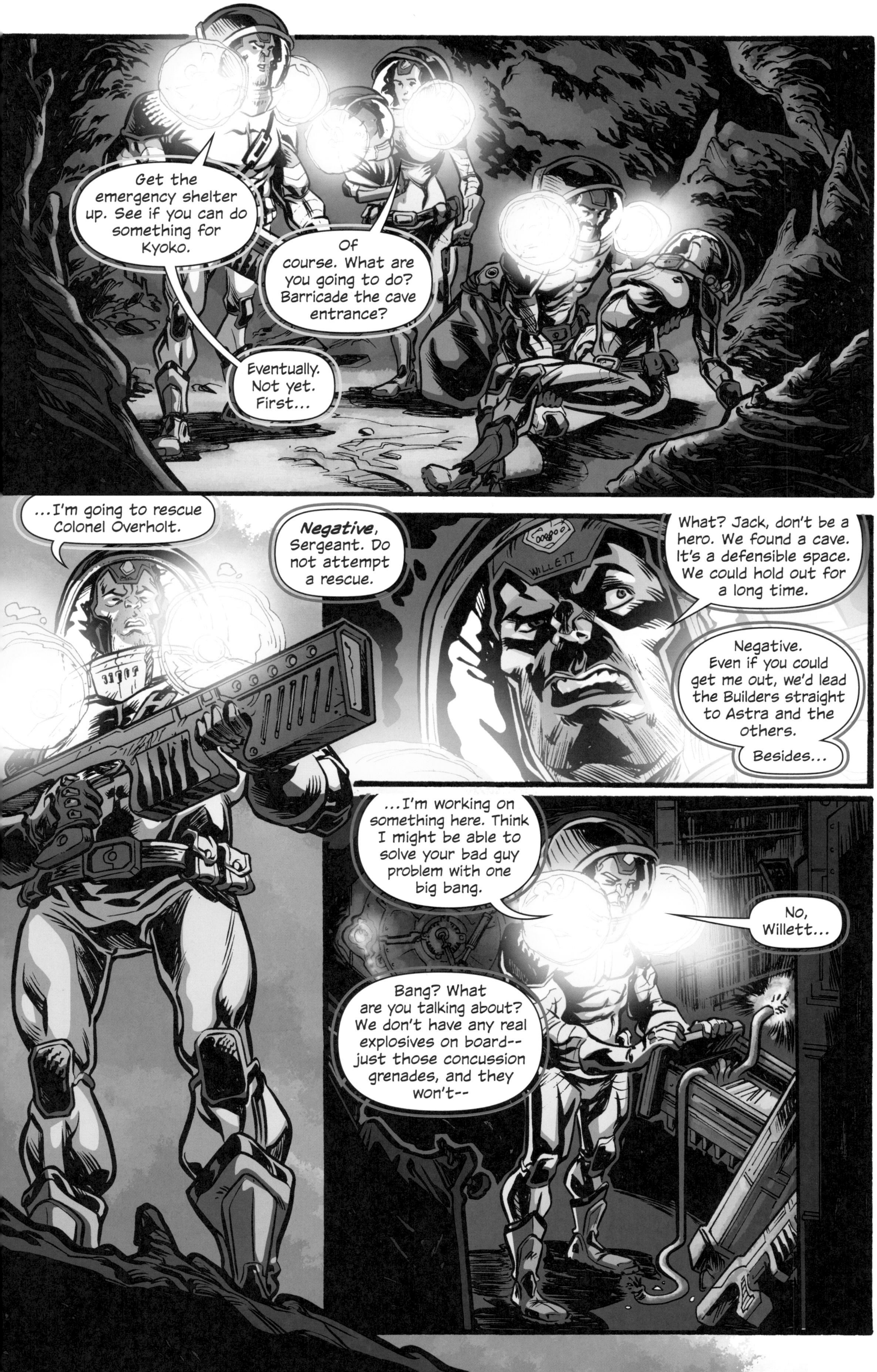

Get the emergency shelter up. See if you can do something for Kyoko.
Of course. What are you going to do? Barricade the cave entrance?
Eventually. Not yet. First...
...I'm going to rescue Colonel Overholt.
Negative, Sergeant. Do not attempt a rescue.
WILLETT
What? Jack, don't be a hero. We found a cave. It's a defensible space. We could hold out for a long time.
Negative. Even if you could get me out, we'd lead the Builders straight to Astra and the others.
Besides...
...I'm working on something here. Think I might be able to solve your bad guy problem with one big bang.
No, Willett...
Bang? What are you talking about? We don't have any real explosives on board--just those concussion grenades, and they won't--

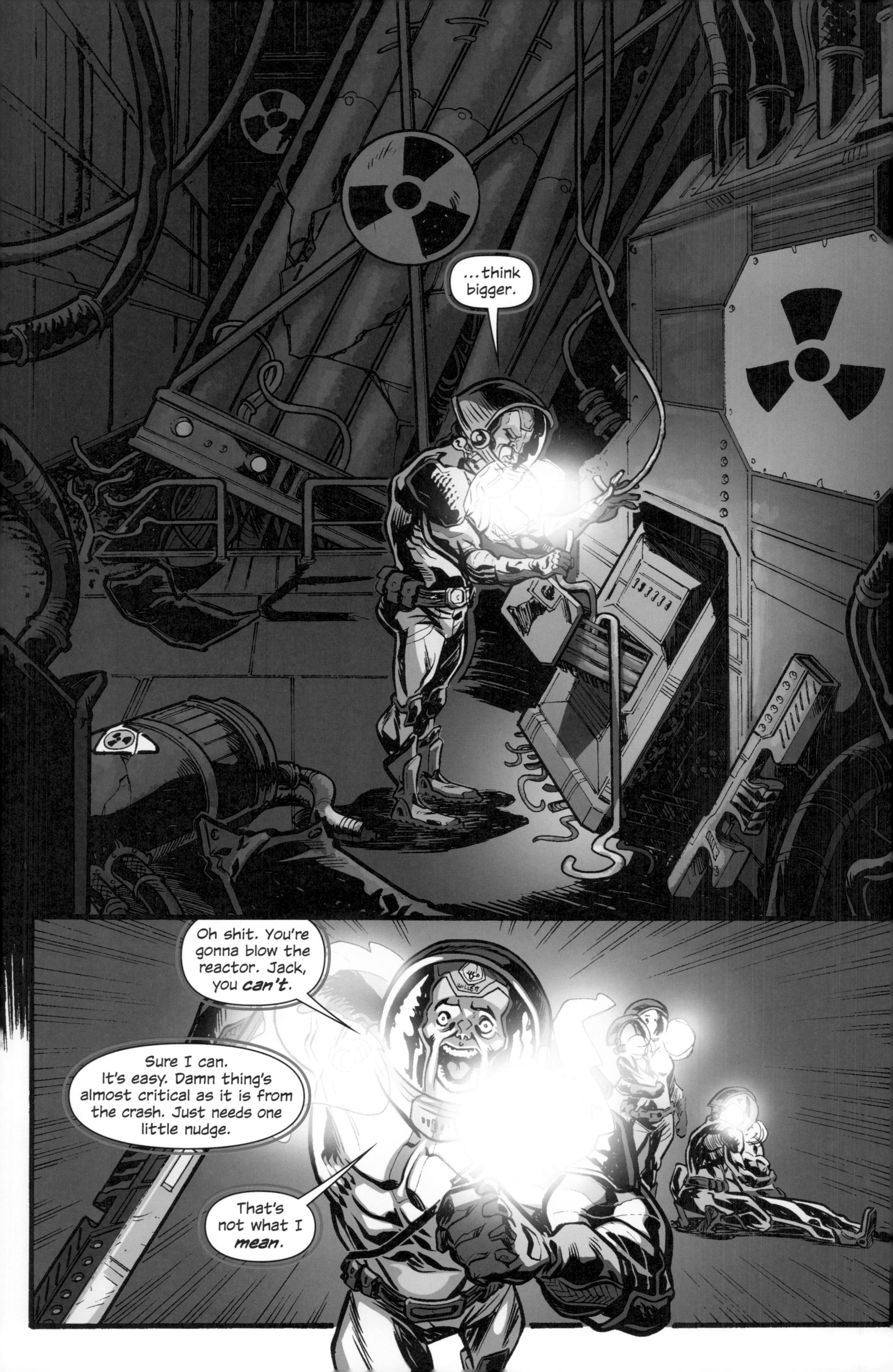
...think bigger.
Oh shit. You're gonna blow the reactor. Jack, you *can't*.
Sure I can. It's easy. Damn thing's almost critical as it is from the crash. Just needs one little nudge.
That's not what I *mean*.

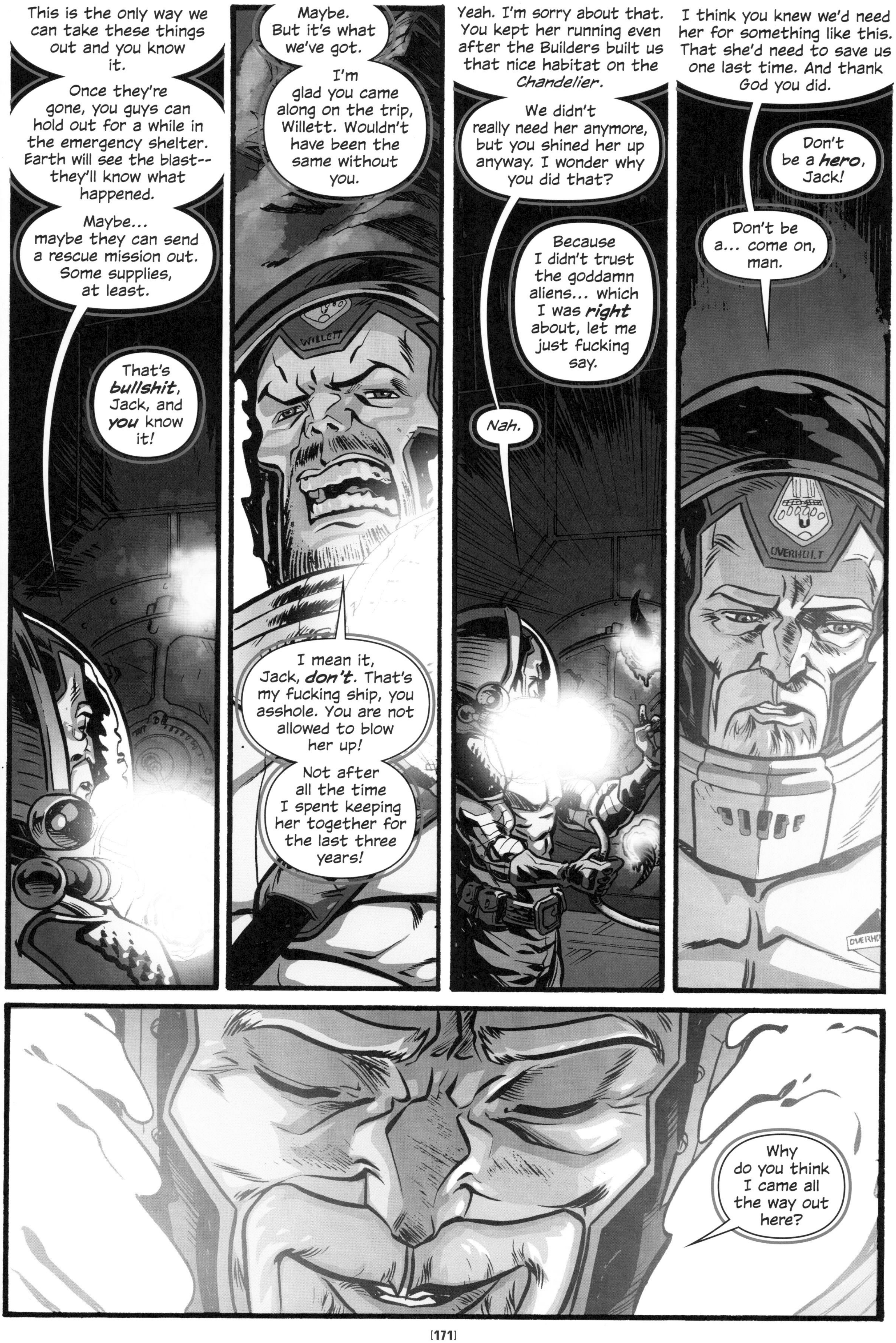
This is the only way we can take these things out and you know it.
Once they're gone, you guys can hold out for a while in the emergency shelter. Earth will see the blast-- they'll know what happened.
Maybe... maybe they can send a rescue mission out. Some supplies, at least.
That's **bullshit**, Jack, and **you** know it!
Maybe. But it's what we've got.
I'm glad you came along on the trip, Willett. Wouldn't have been the same without you.
WILLETT
I mean it, Jack, **don't**. That's my fucking ship, you asshole. You are not allowed to blow her up!
Not after all the time I spent keeping her together for the last three years!
Yeah. I'm sorry about that. You kept her running even after the Builders built us that nice habitat on the *Chandelier*.
We didn't really need her anymore, but you shined her up anyway. I wonder why you did that?
Because I didn't trust the goddamn aliens... which I was **right** about, let me just fucking say.
Nah.
I think you knew we'd need her for something like this. That she'd need to save us one last time. And thank God you did.
Don't be a **hero**, Jack!
Don't be a... come on, man.
OVERHOLT
Why do you think I came all the way out here?

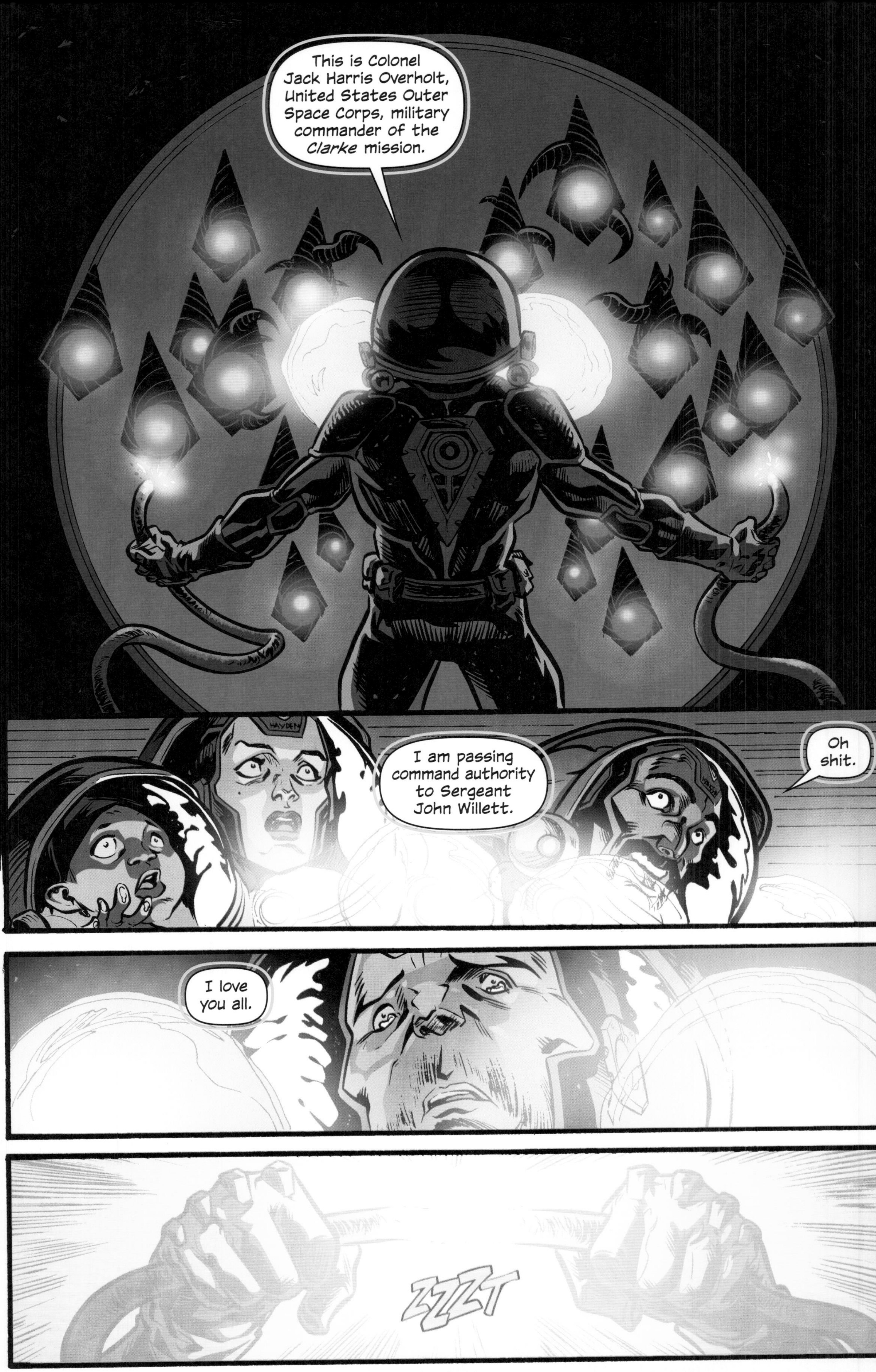
This is Colonel Jack Harris Overholt, United States Outer Space Corps, military commander of the *Clarke* mission.
I am passing command authority to Sergeant John Willett.
Oh shit.
I love you all.
ZZZT

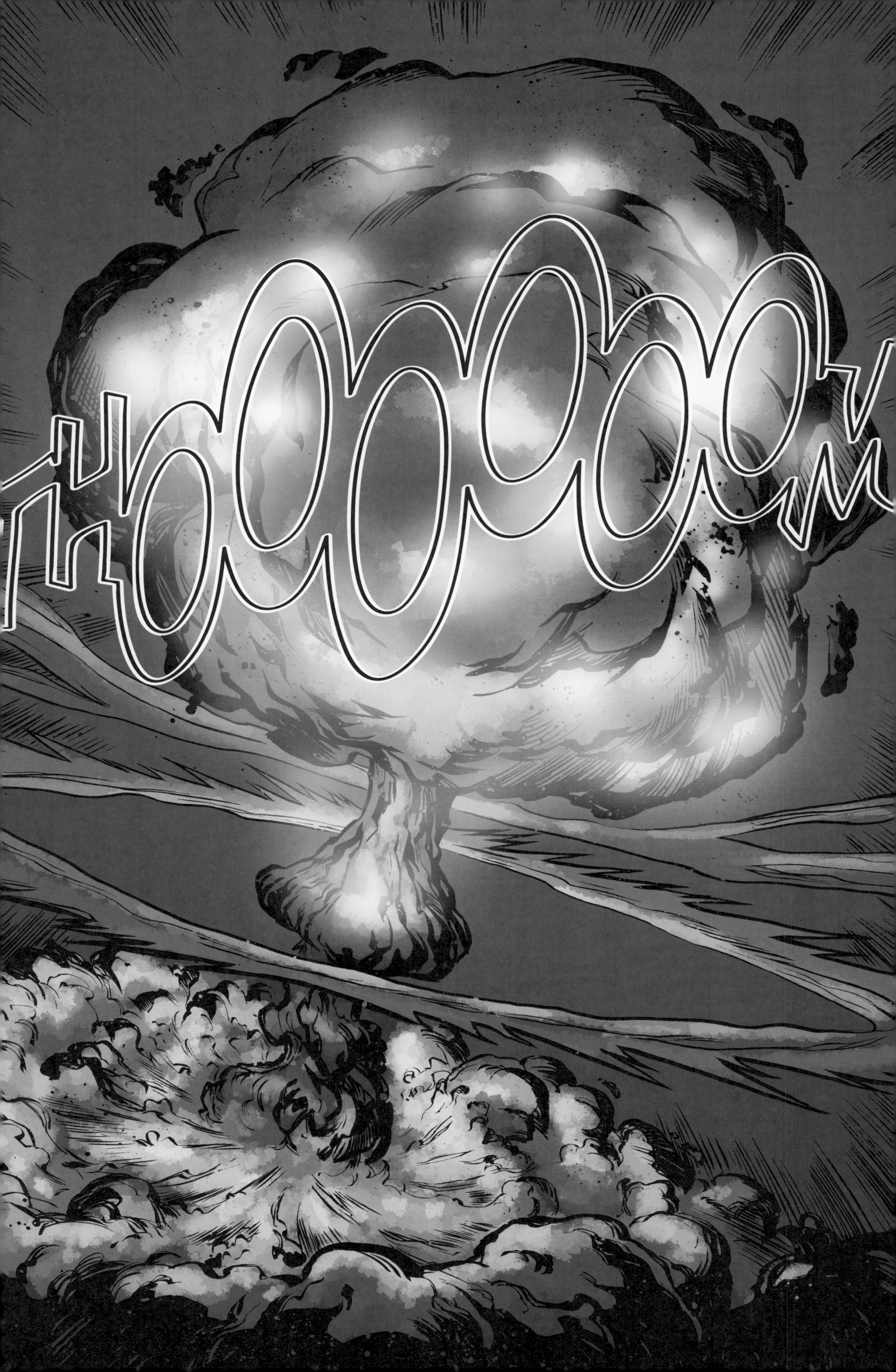
THOOOOOOM

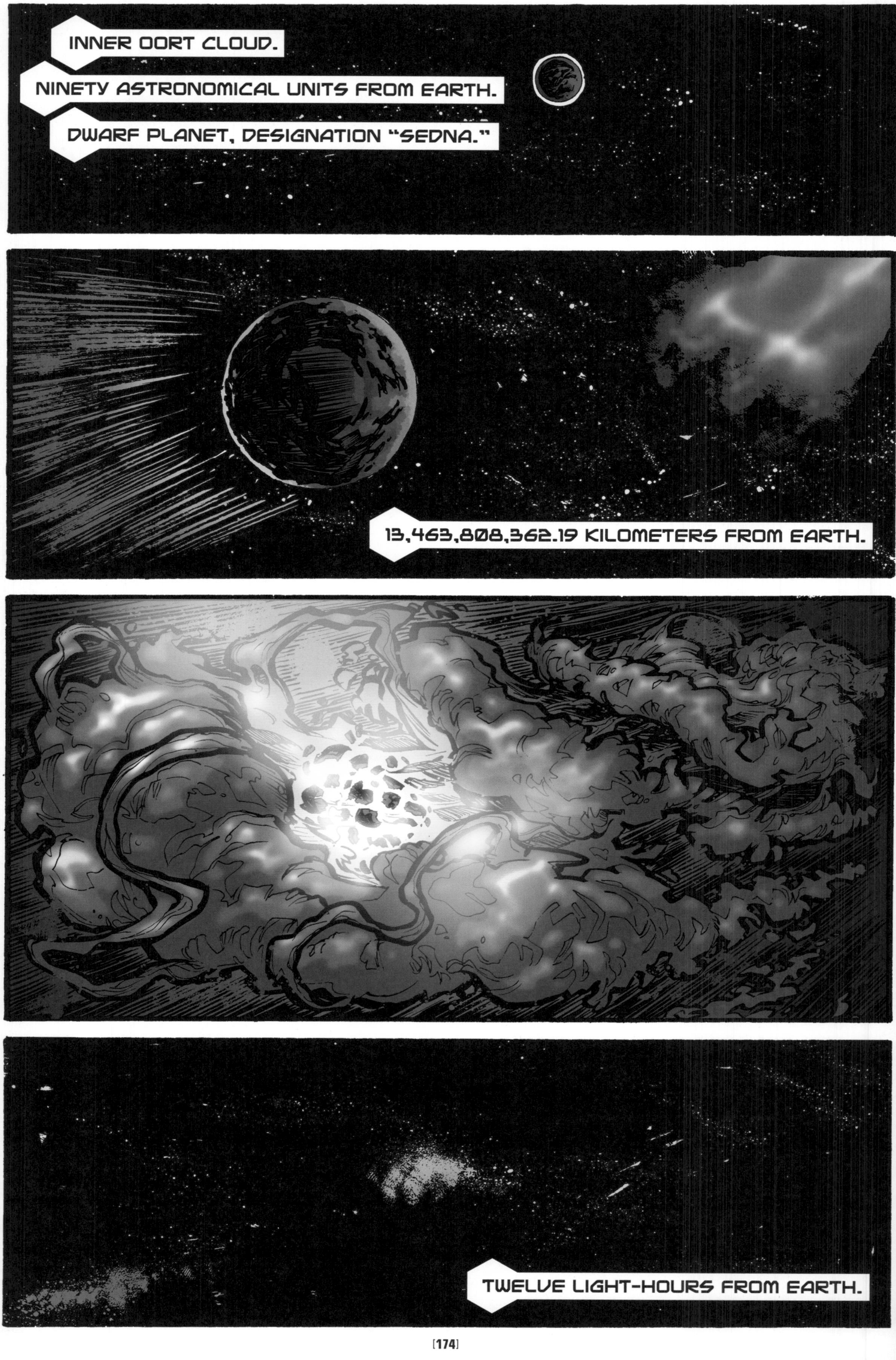
INNER OORT CLOUD.
NINETY ASTRONOMICAL UNITS FROM EARTH.
DWARF PLANET, DESIGNATION "SEDNA."
13,463,808,362.19 KILOMETERS FROM EARTH.
TWELVE LIGHT-HOURS FROM EARTH.

LETTER
44

CHAPTER VIII

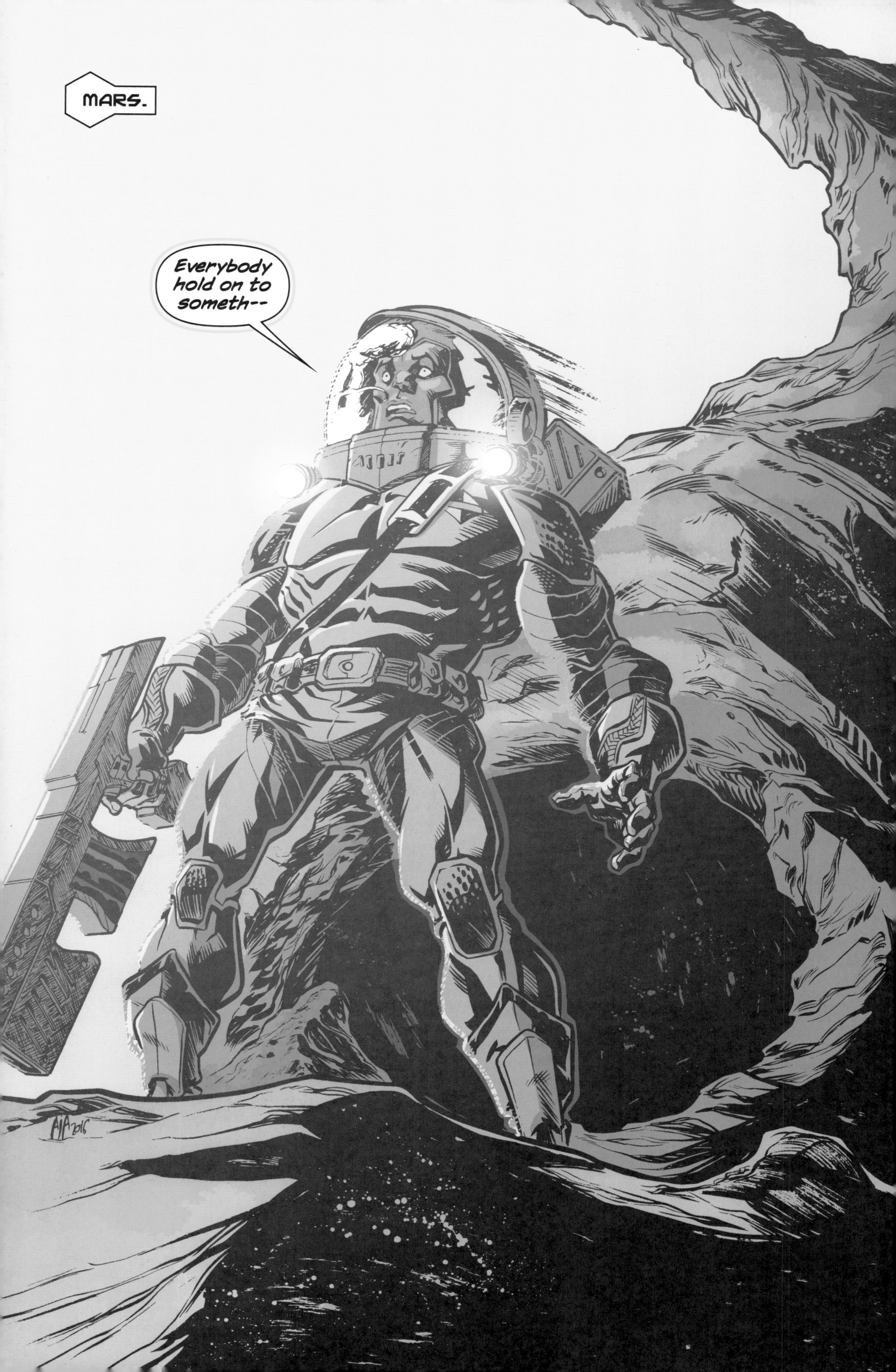
MARS.
Everybody hold on to someth--
AJA 2016

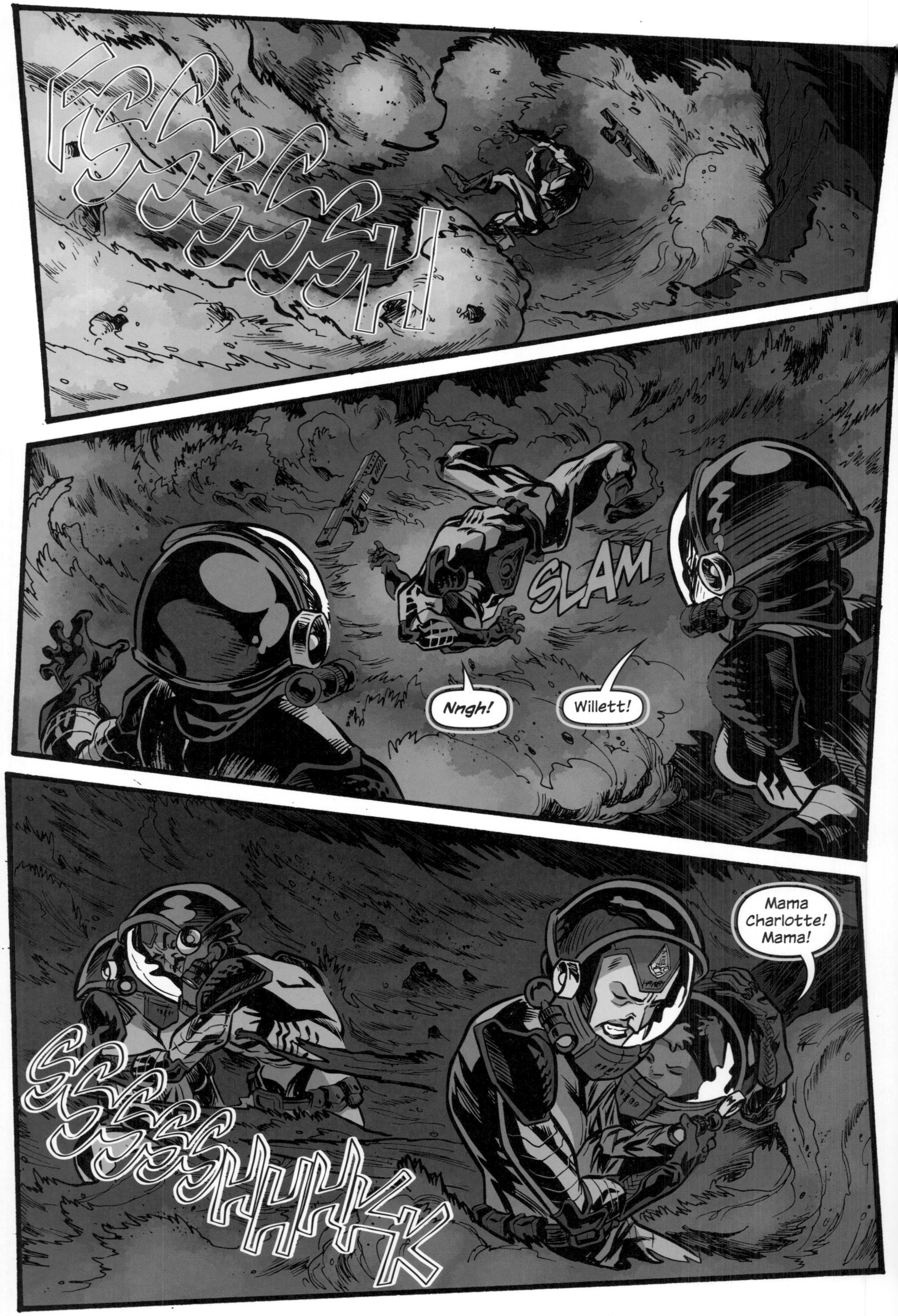
SLAM
Nngh!
Willett!
Mama Charlotte! Mama!

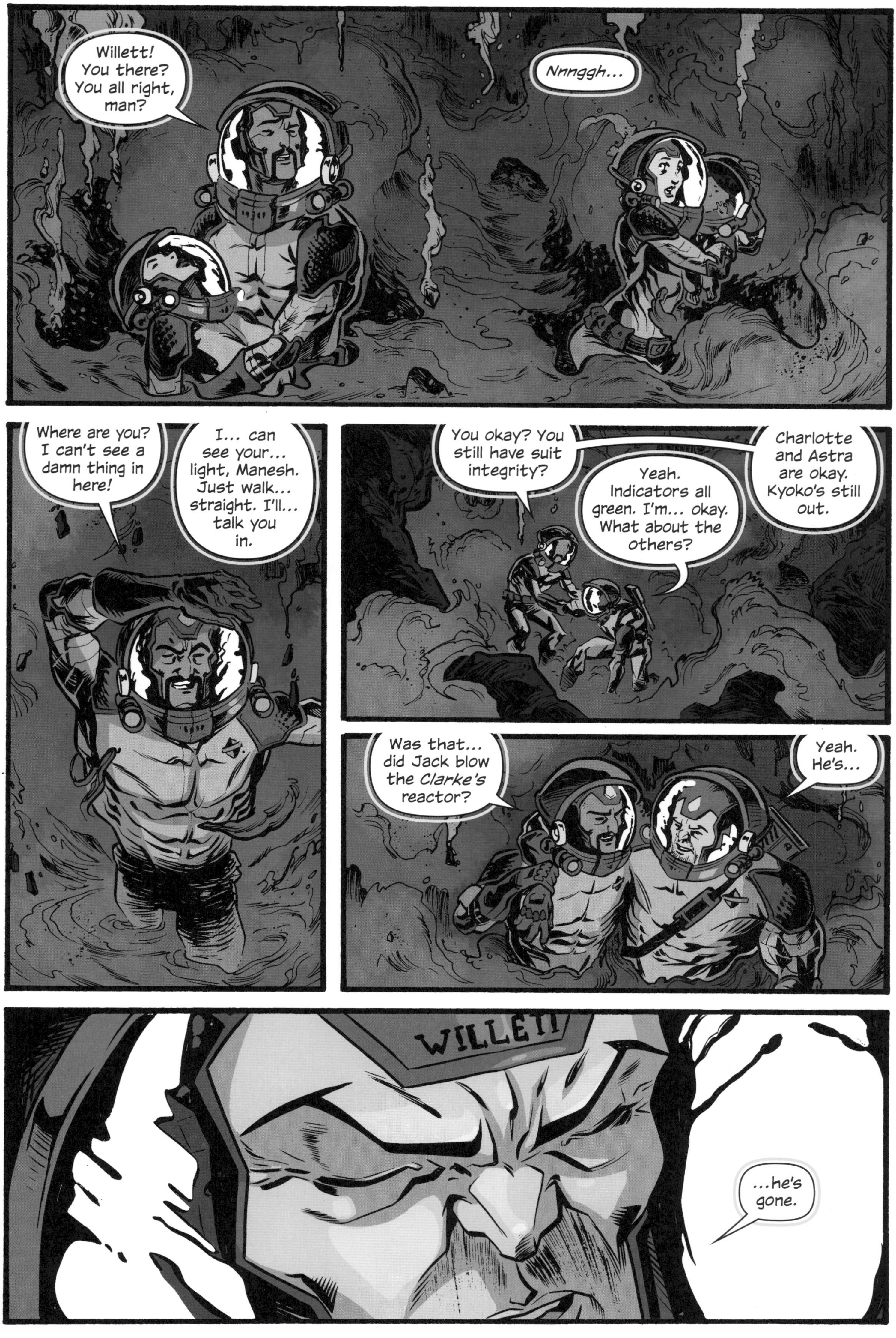
Willett! You there? You all right, man?
Nnngh...
Where are you? I can't see a damn thing in here!
I... can see your... light, Manesh. Just walk... straight. I'll... talk you in.
You okay? You still have suit integrity?
Yeah. Indicators all green. I'm... okay. What about the others?
Charlotte and Astra are okay. Kyoko's still out.
Was that... did Jack blow the *Clarke's* reactor?
Yeah. He's...
WILLETT
...he's gone.

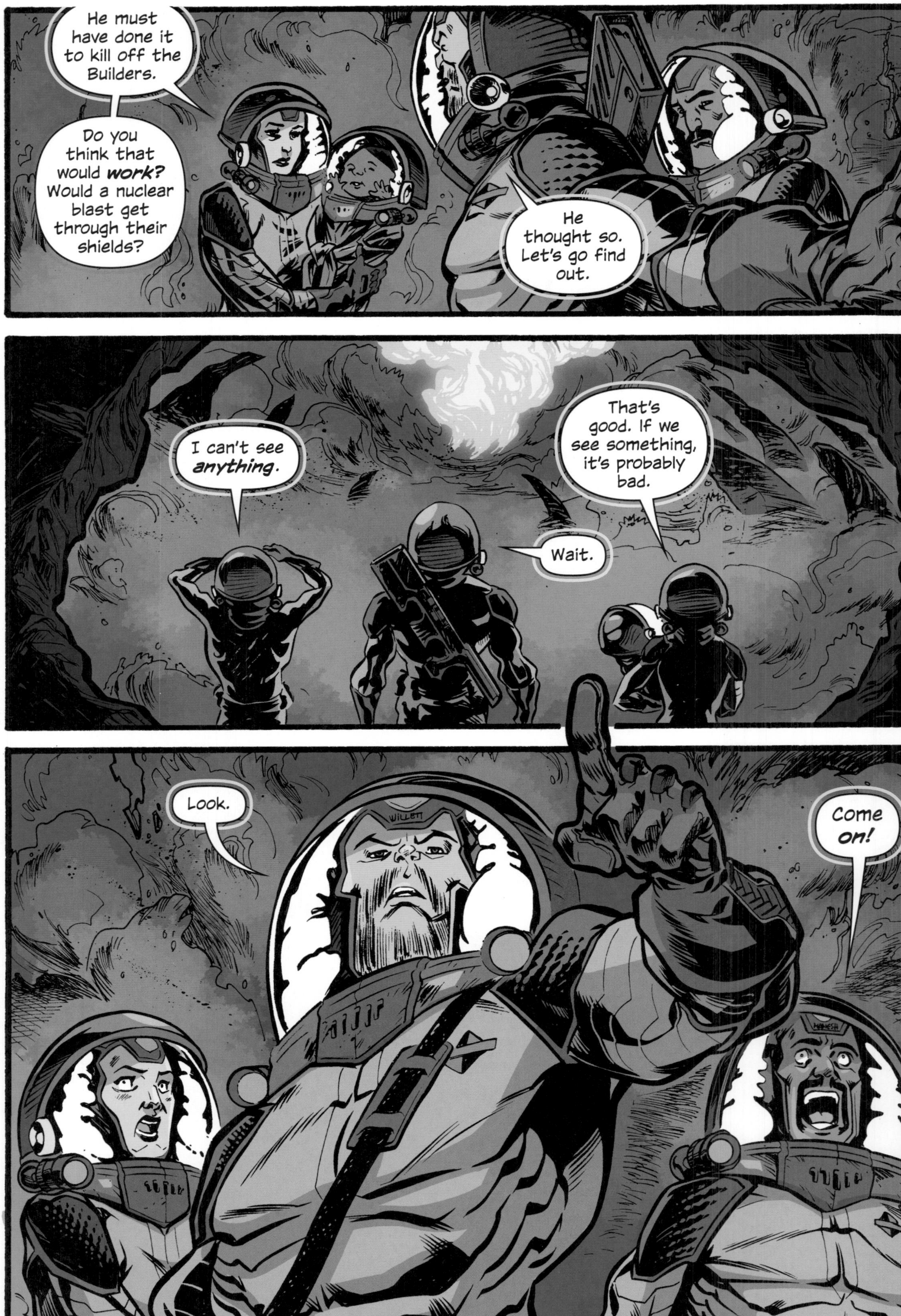
He must have done it to kill off the Builders.
Do you think that would **work?** Would a nuclear blast get through their shields?
He thought so. Let's go find out.
I can't see *anything*.
That's good. If we see something, it's probably bad.
Wait.
Look.
Come *on!*

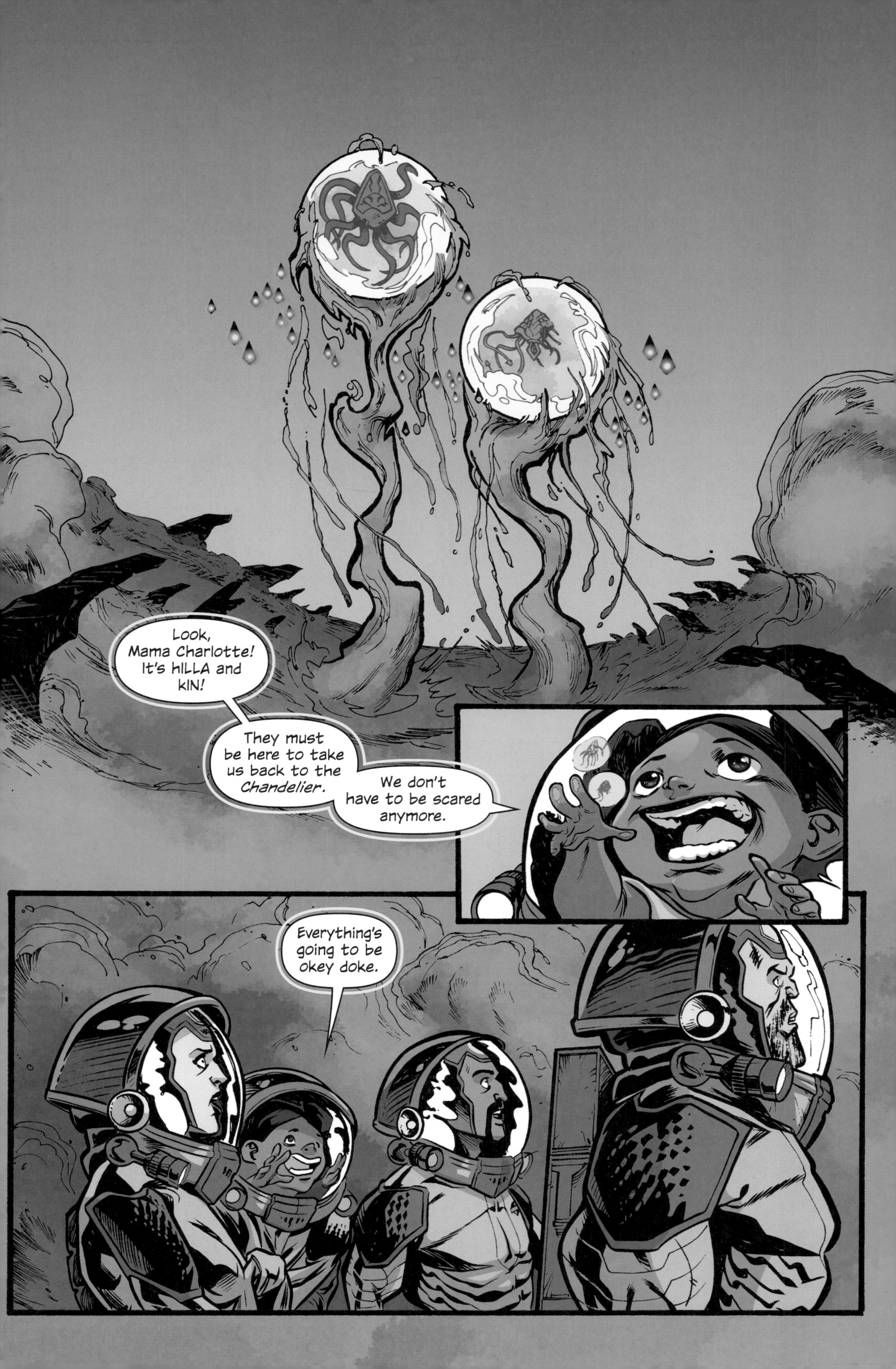
Look, Mama Charlotte! It's HILLA and KIN!
They must be here to take us back to the *Chandelier*.
We don't have to be scared anymore.
Everything's going to be okey doke.

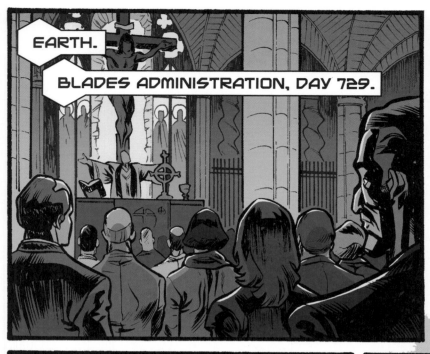

EARTH.

BLADES ADMINISTRATION, DAY 729.

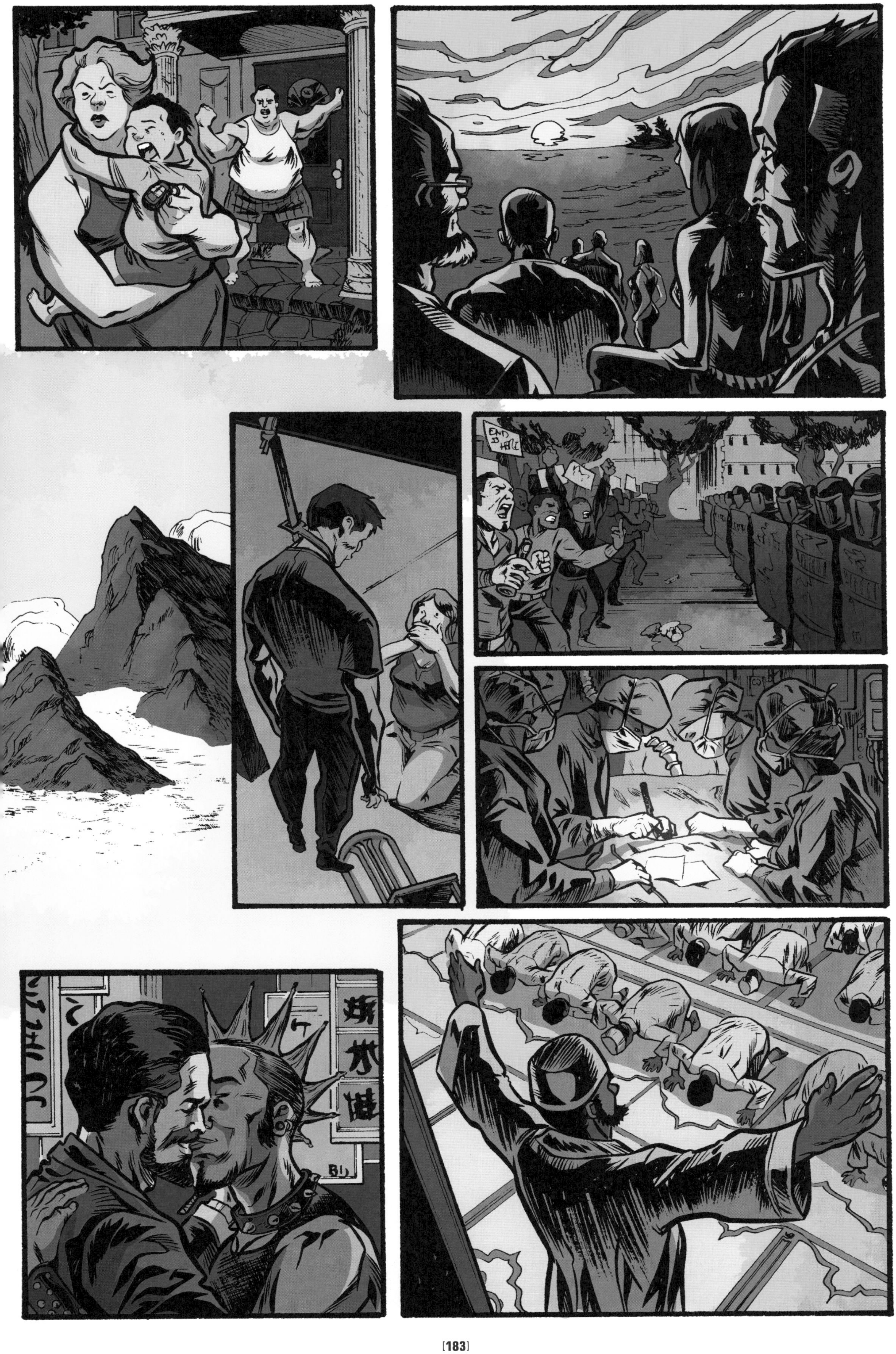
END

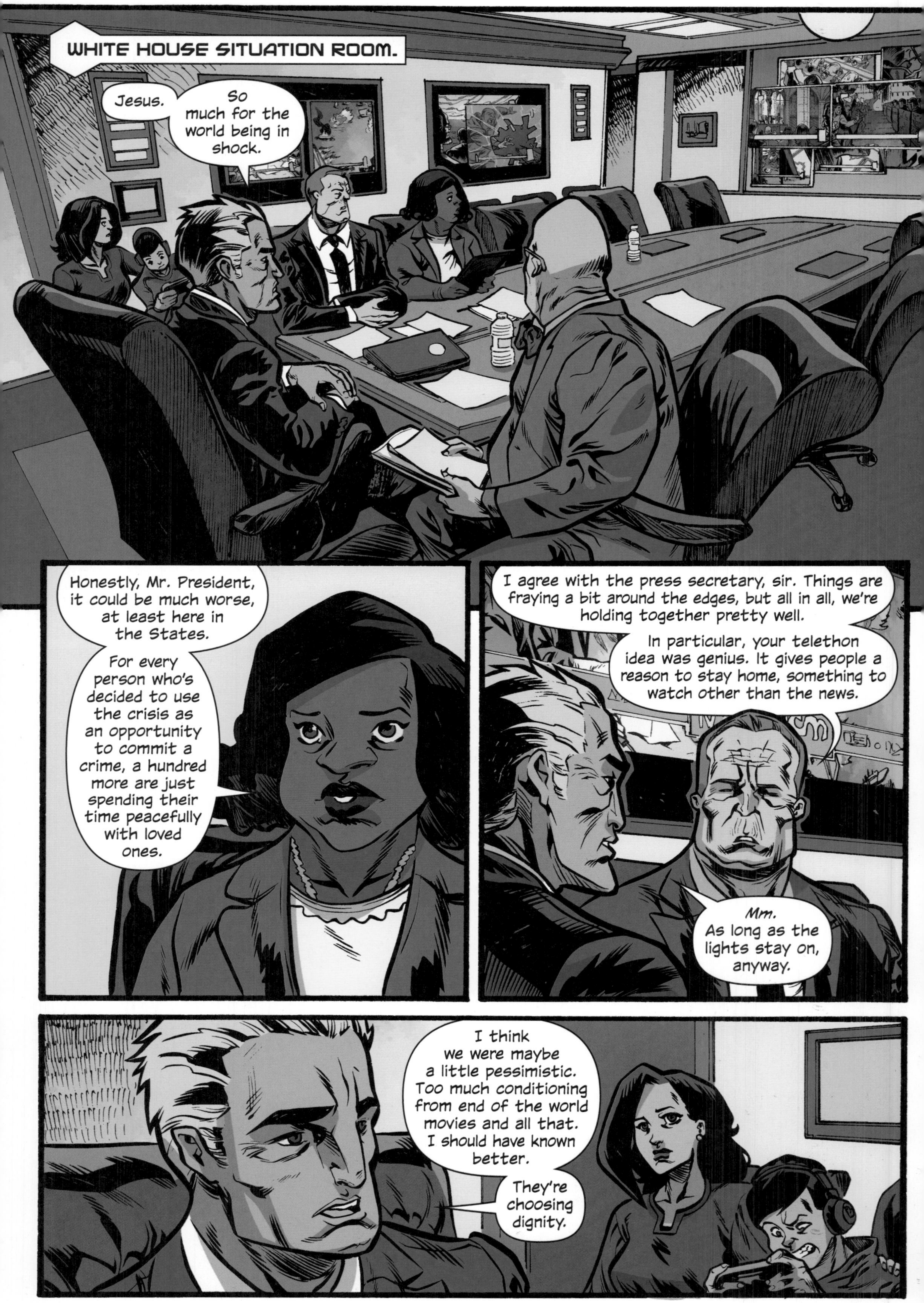

WHITE HOUSE SITUATION ROOM.
Jesus.
So much for the world being in shock.
Honestly, Mr. President, it could be much worse, at least here in the States.
For every person who's decided to use the crisis as an opportunity to commit a crime, a hundred more are just spending their time peacefully with loved ones.
I agree with the press secretary, sir. Things are fraying a bit around the edges, but all in all, we're holding together pretty well.
In particular, your telethon idea was genius. It gives people a reason to stay home, something to watch other than the news.
Mm. As long as the lights stay on, anyway.
I think we were maybe a little pessimistic. Too much conditioning from end of the world movies and all that. I should have known better.
They're choosing dignity.

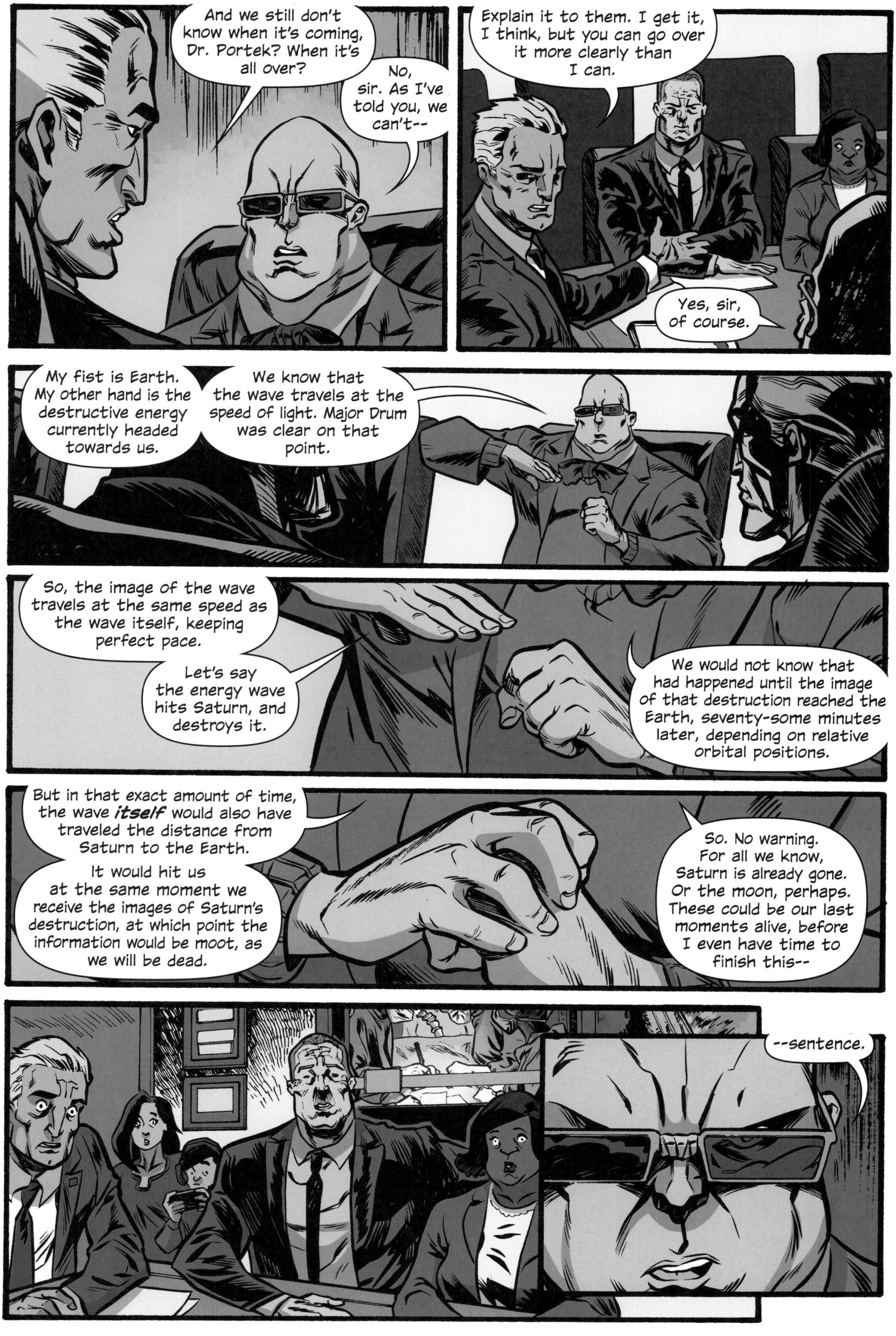
And we still don't know when it's coming, Dr. Portek? When it's all over?
No, sir. As I've told you, we can't--
Explain it to them. I get it, I think, but you can go over it more clearly than I can.
Yes, sir, of course.
My fist is Earth. My other hand is the destructive energy currently headed towards us.
We know that the wave travels at the speed of light. Major Drum was clear on that point.
So, the image of the wave travels at the same speed as the wave itself, keeping perfect pace.
Let's say the energy wave hits Saturn, and destroys it.
We would not know that had happened until the image of that destruction reached the Earth, seventy-some minutes later, depending on relative orbital positions.
But in that exact amount of time, the wave *itself* would also have traveled the distance from Saturn to the Earth.
It would hit us at the same moment we receive the images of Saturn's destruction, at which point the information would be moot, as we will be dead.
So. No warning. For all we know, Saturn is already gone. Or the moon, perhaps. These could be our last moments alive, before I even have time to finish this--
--sentence.

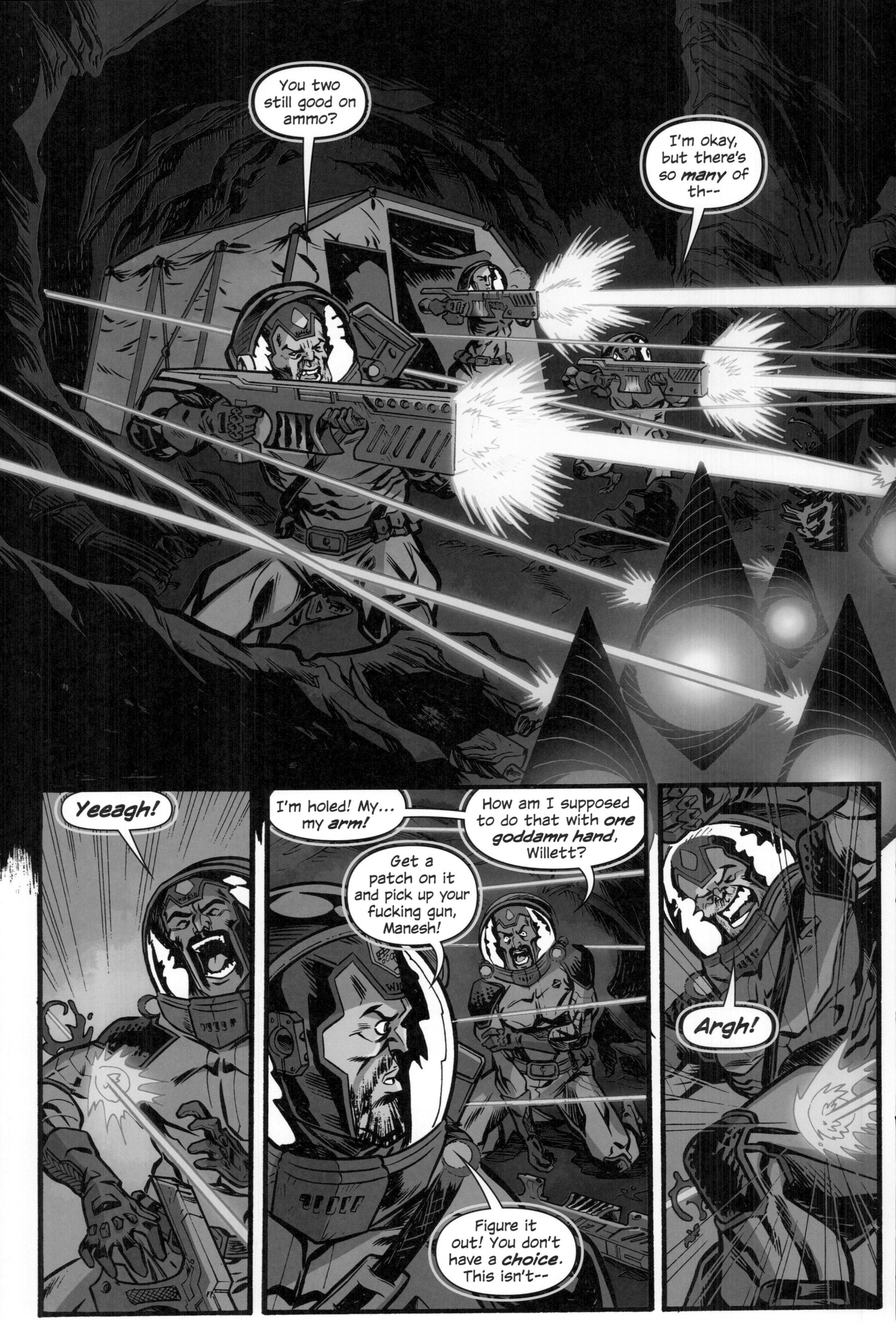
You two still good on ammo?
I'm okay, but there's so *many* of th--
Yeeagh!
I'm holed! My... my *arm!*
Get a patch on it and pick up your fucking gun, Manesh!
How am I supposed to do that with *one goddamn hand*, Willett?
Figure it out! You don't have a *choice*. This isn't--
Argh!

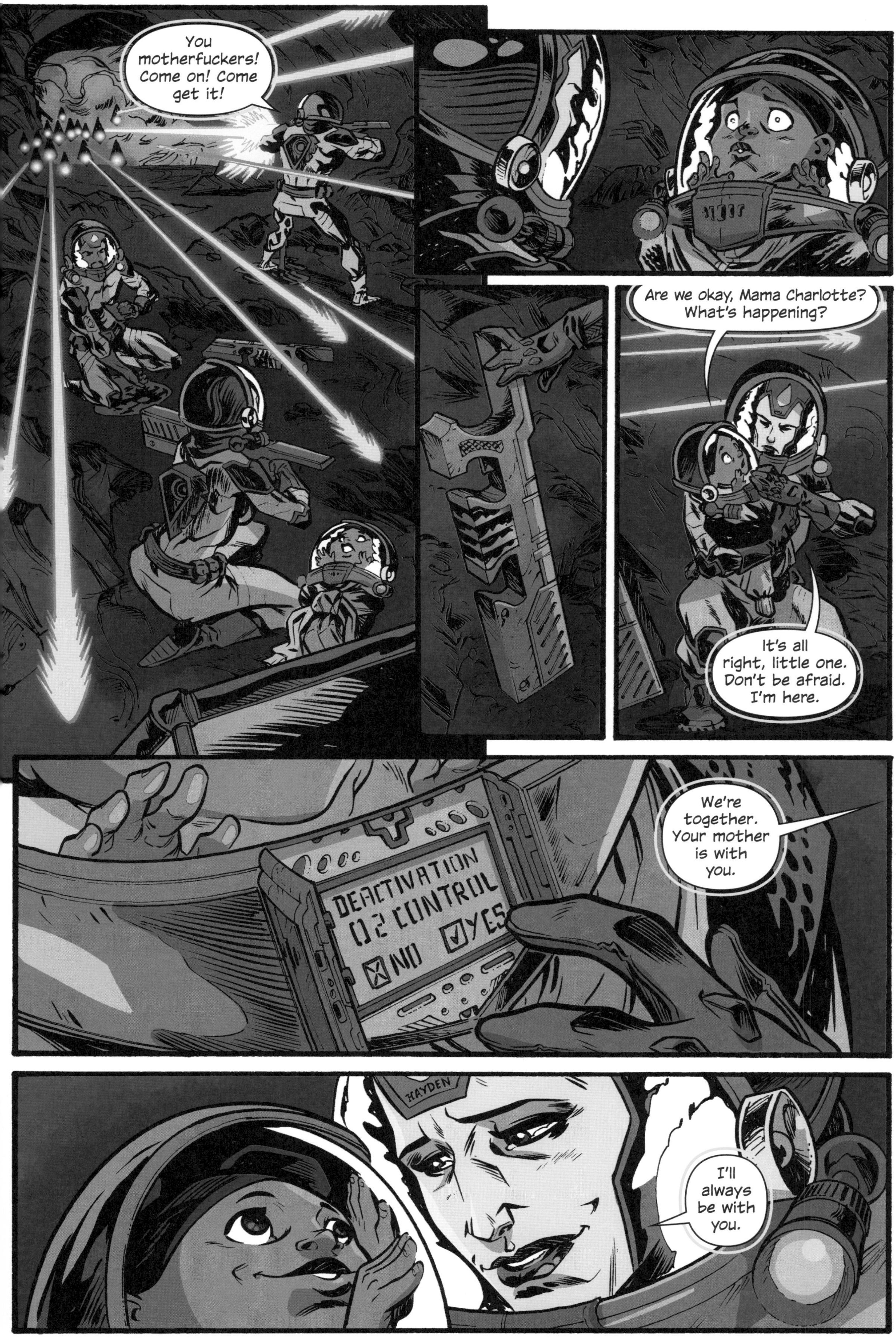

You motherfuckers! Come on! Come get it!
Are we okay, Mama Charlotte? What's happening?
It's all right, little one. Don't be afraid. I'm here.
DEACTIVATION
O2 CONTROL
NO
YES
We're together. Your mother is with you.
HAYDEN
I'll always be with you.

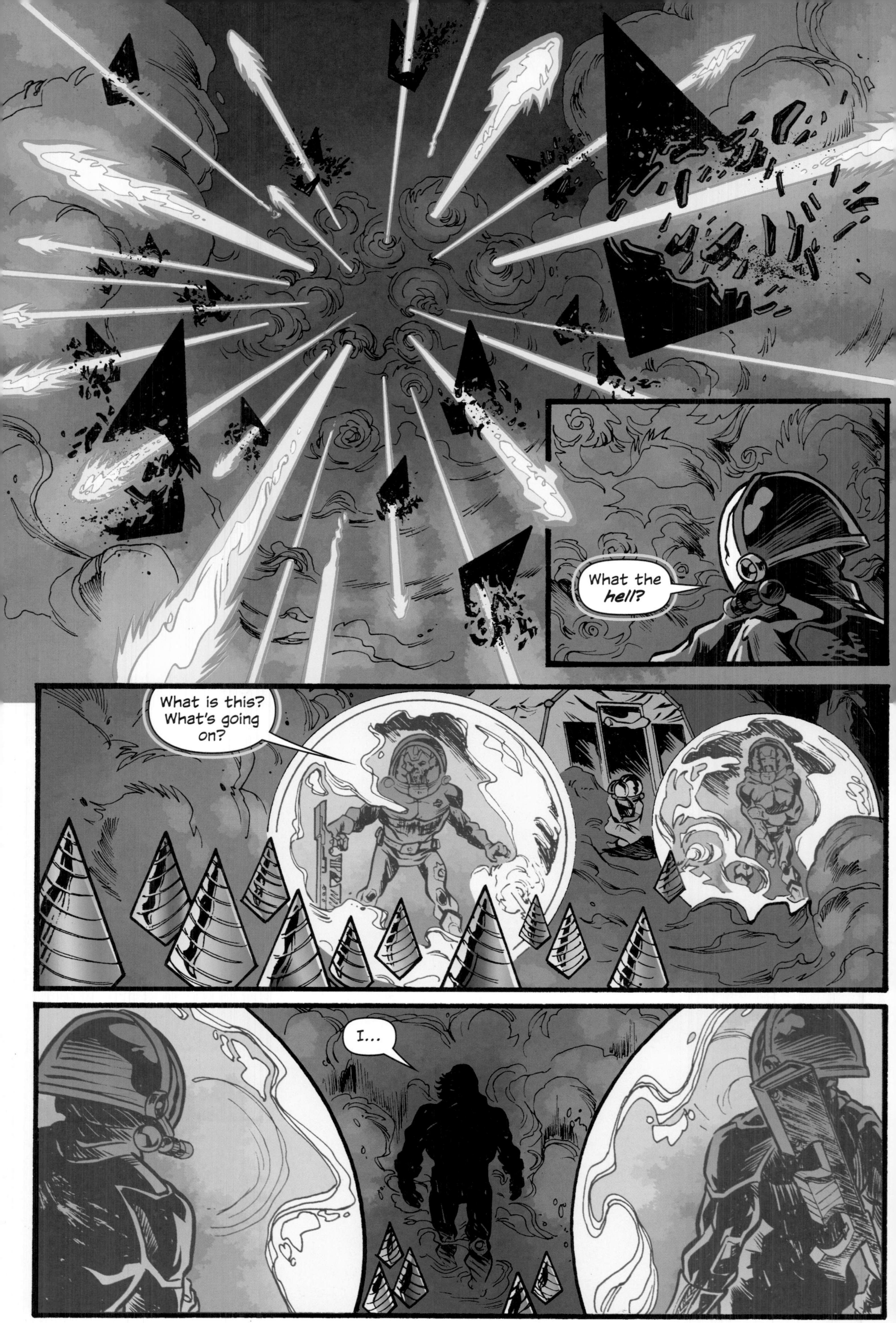
What the *hell?*
What is this? What's going on?
I...

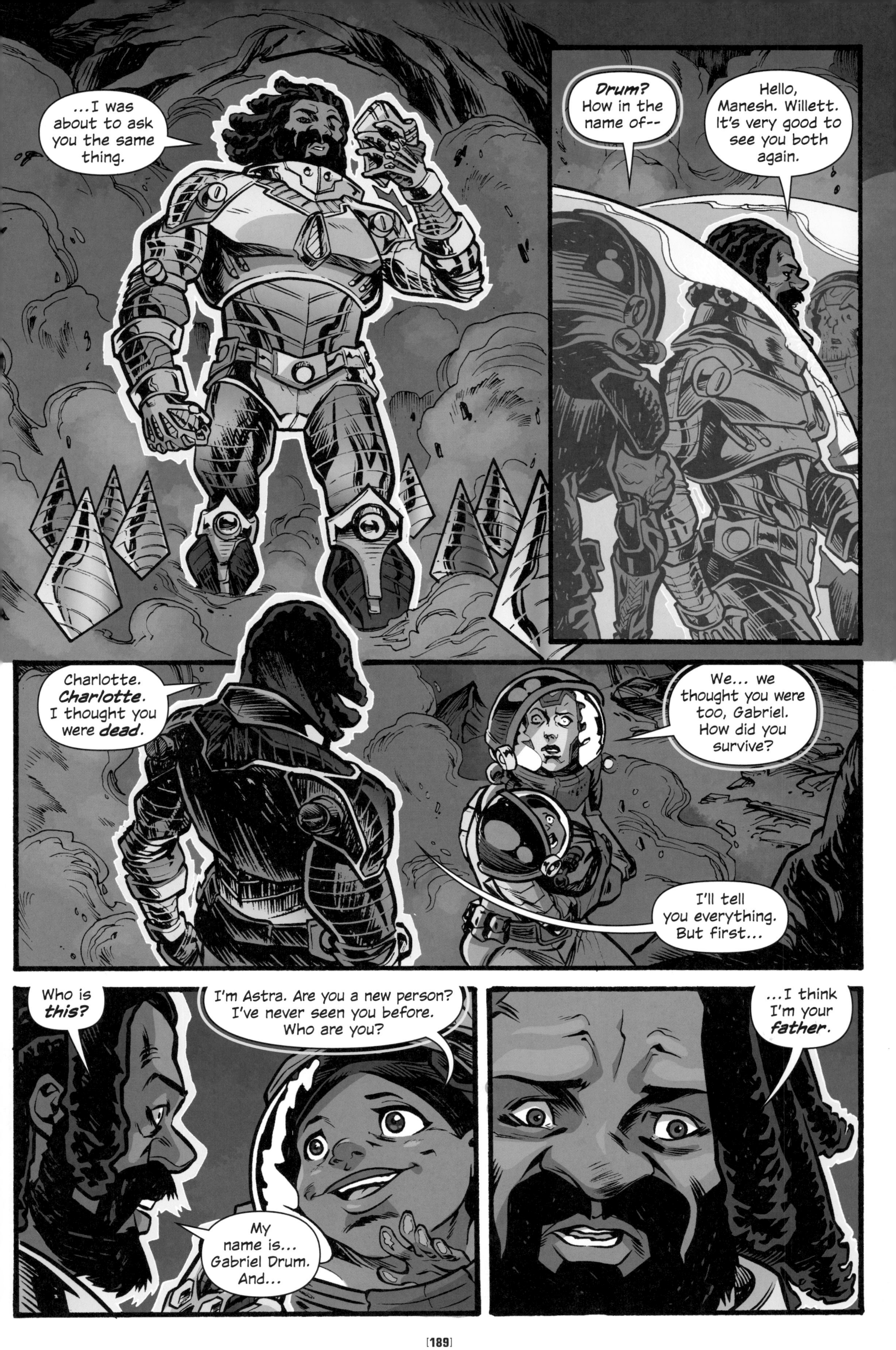

...I was about to ask you the same thing.
Drum? How in the name of--
Hello, Manesh. Willett. It's very good to see you both again.
Charlotte. Charlotte. I thought you were dead.
We... we thought you were too, Gabriel. How did you survive?
I'll tell you everything. But first...
Who is this?
I'm Astra. Are you a new person? I've never seen you before. Who are you?
My name is... Gabriel Drum. And...
...I think I'm your father.

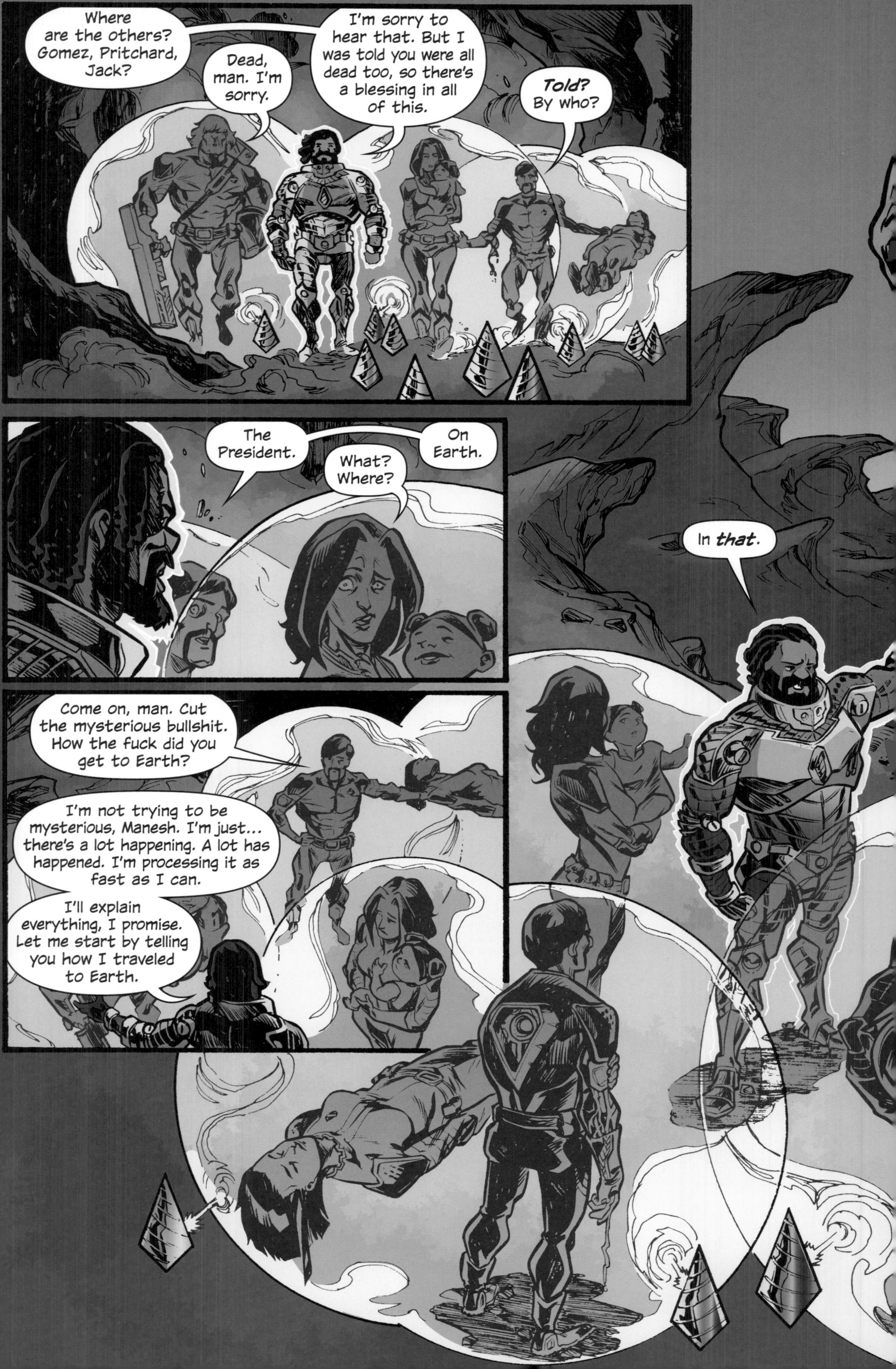
Where are the others? Gomez, Pritchard, Jack?
Dead, man. I'm sorry.
I'm sorry to hear that. But I was told you were all dead too, so there's a blessing in all of this.
Told? By who?
The President.
On Earth.
What? Where?
In *that*.
Come on, man. Cut the mysterious bullshit. How the fuck did you get to Earth?
I'm not trying to be mysterious, Manesh. I'm just... there's a lot happening. A lot has happened. I'm processing it as fast as I can.
I'll explain everything, I promise. Let me start by telling you how I traveled to Earth.

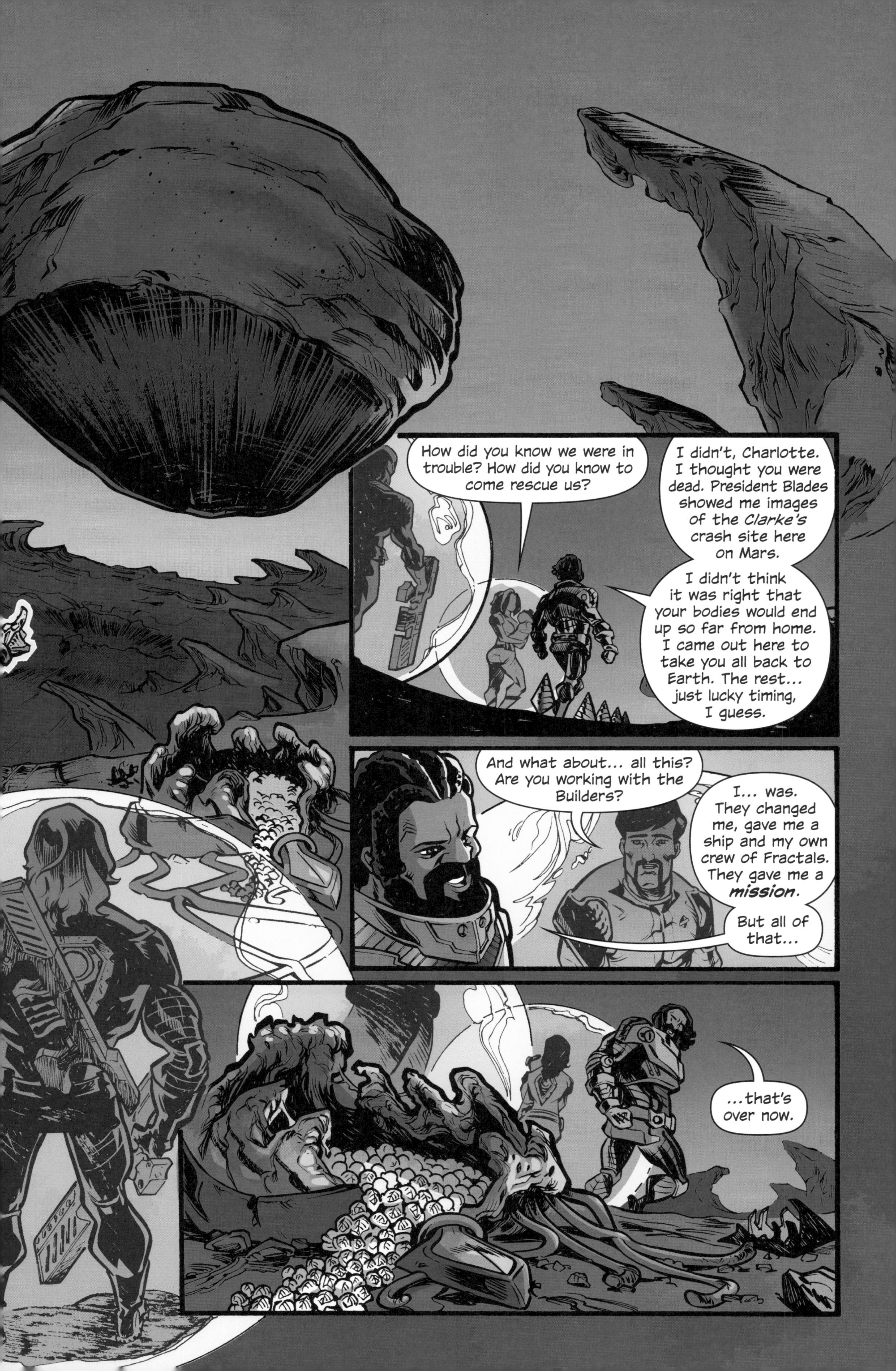
How did you know we were in trouble? How did you know to come rescue us?
I didn't, Charlotte. I thought you were dead. President Blades showed me images of the *Clarke's* crash site here on Mars.
I didn't think it was right that your bodies would end up so far from home. I came out here to take you all back to Earth. The rest... just lucky timing, I guess.
And what about... all this? Are you working with the Builders?
I... was. They changed me, gave me a ship and my own crew of Fractals. They gave me a ***mission***.
But all of that...
...that's over now.

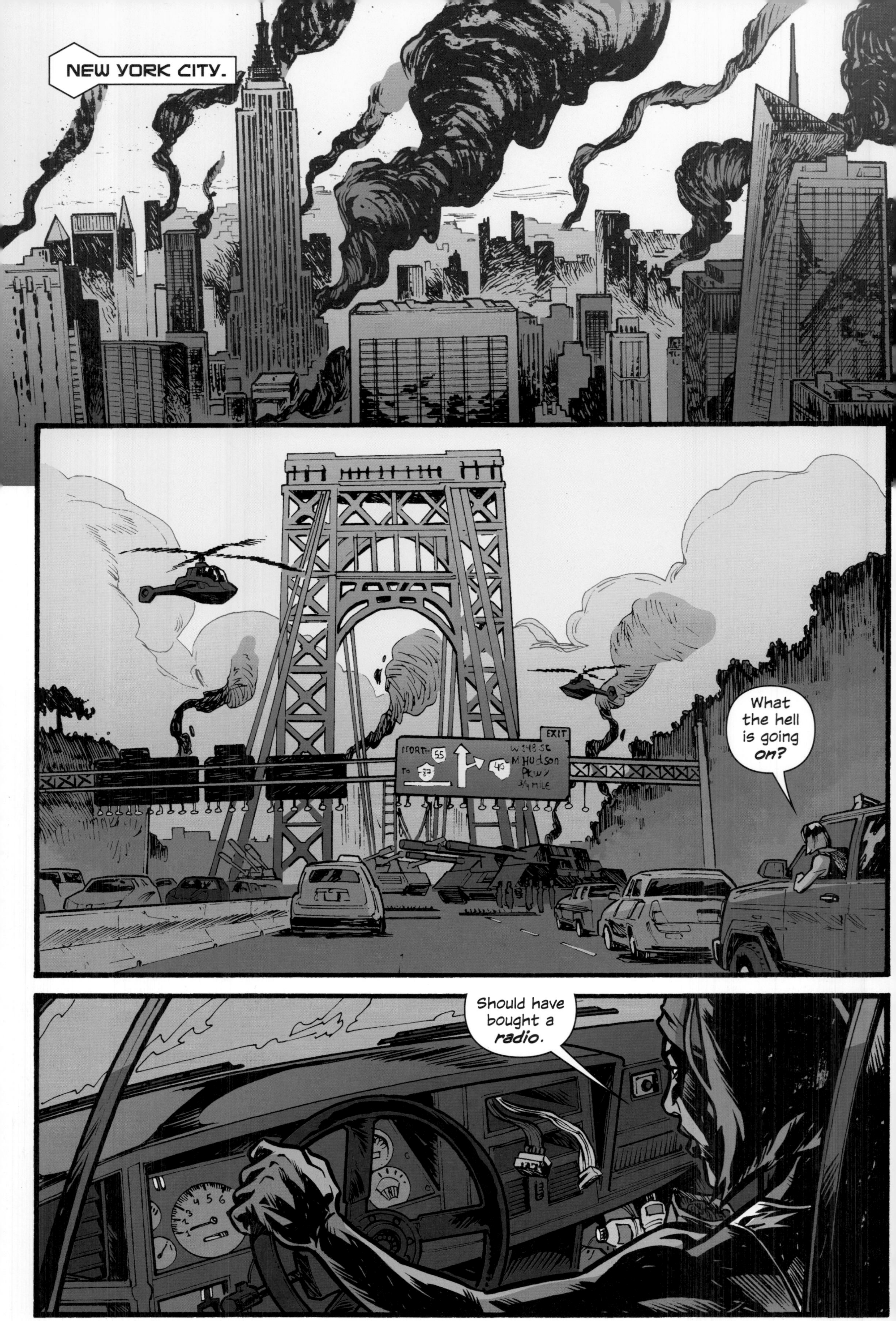
NEW YORK CITY.
EXIT
What the hell is going *on?*
Should have bought a *radio*.

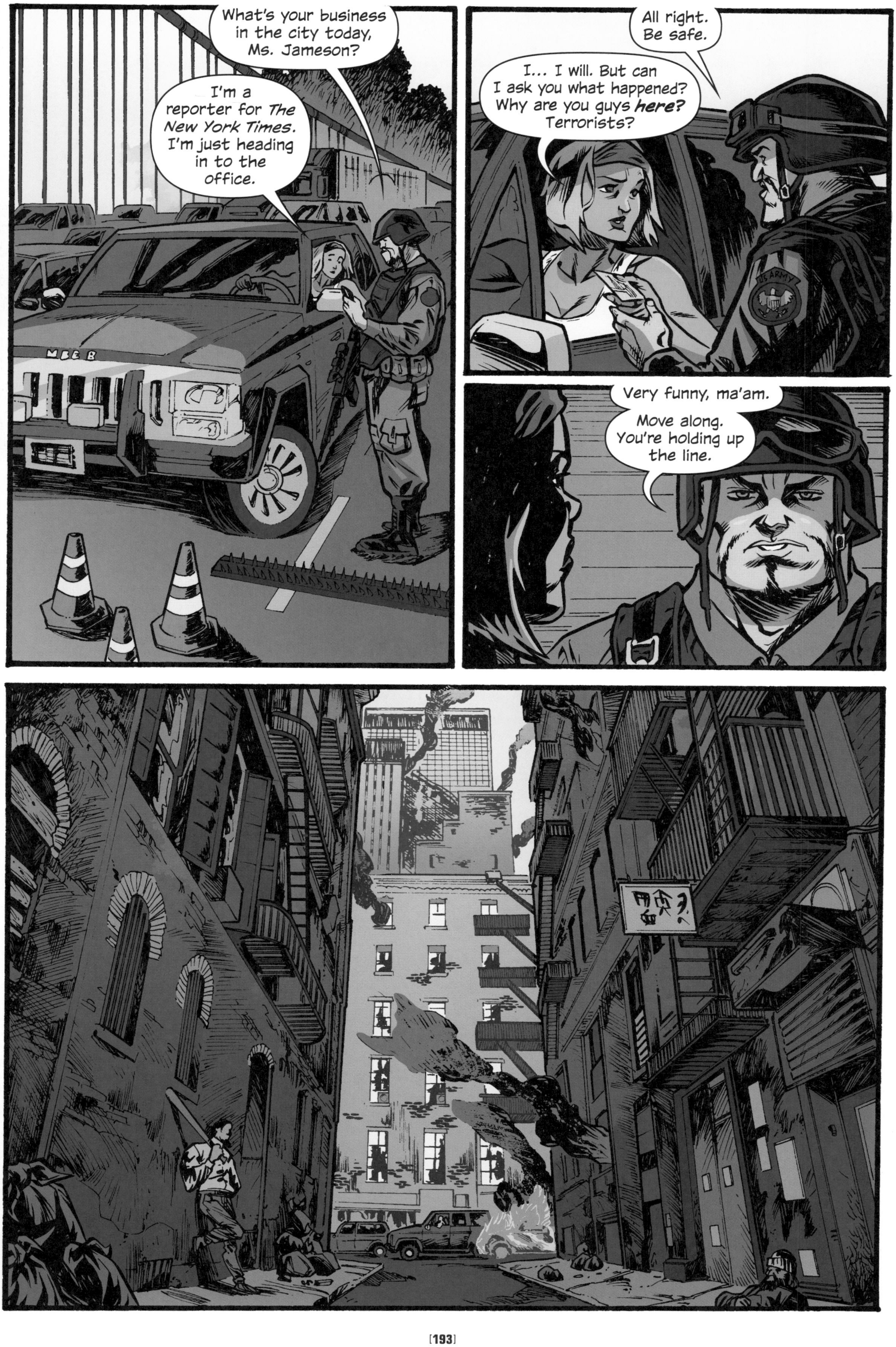

What's your business in the city today, Ms. Jameson?
I'm a reporter for *The New York Times*. I'm just heading in to the office.
All right. Be safe.
I... I will. But can I ask you what happened? Why are you guys ***here?*** Terrorists?
Very funny, ma'am.
Move along. You're holding up the line.
US ARMY

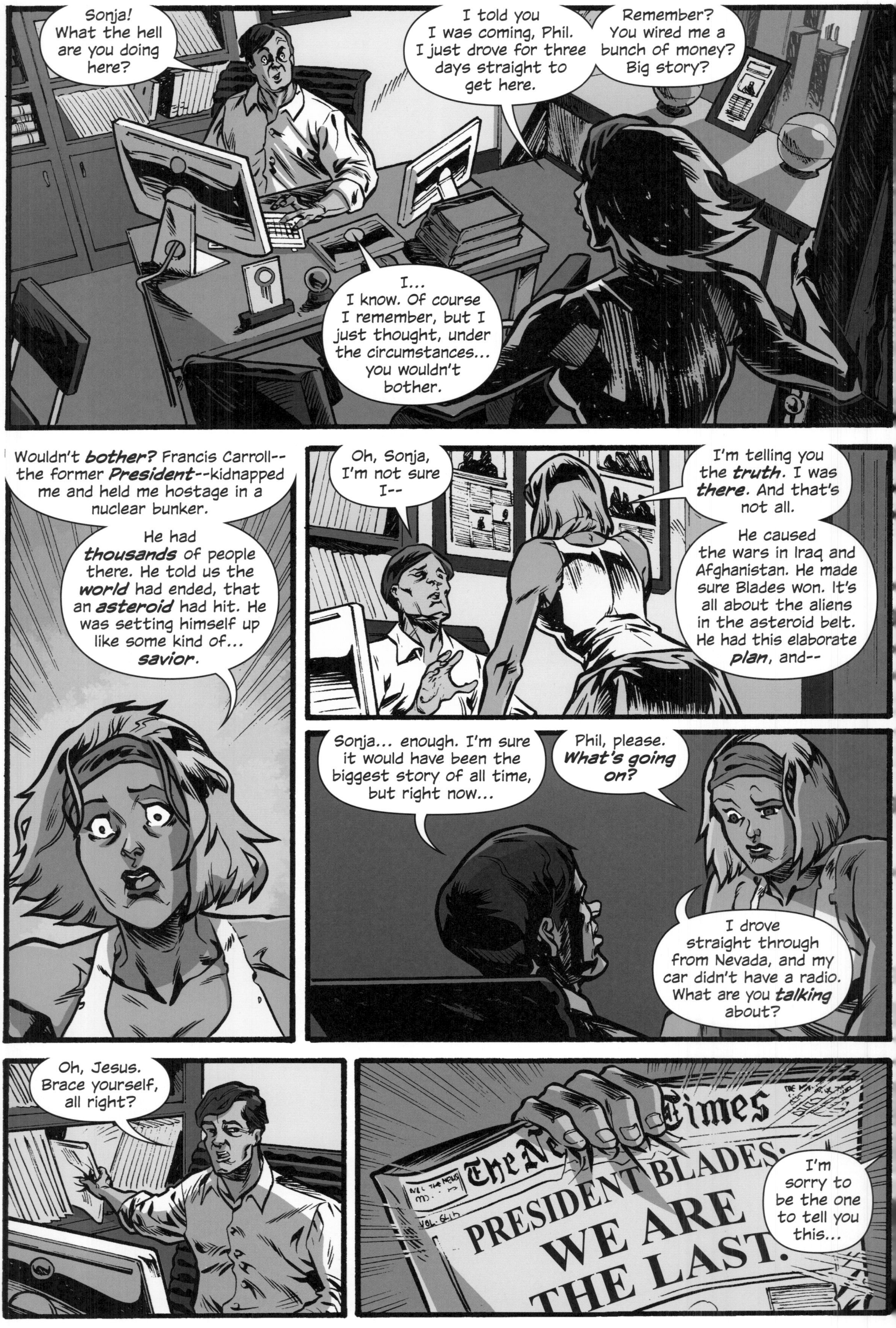
Sonja! What the hell are you doing here?
I told you I was coming, Phil. I just drove for three days straight to get here.
Remember? You wired me a bunch of money? Big story?
I... I know. Of course I remember, but I just thought, under the circumstances... you wouldn't bother.
Wouldn't *bother?* Francis Carroll--the former *President*--kidnapped me and held me hostage in a nuclear bunker.
He had *thousands* of people there. He told us the *world* had ended, that an *asteroid* had hit. He was setting himself up like some kind of... *savior*.
Oh, Sonja, I'm not sure I--
I'm telling you the *truth*. I was *there*. And that's not all.
He caused the wars in Iraq and Afghanistan. He made sure Blades won. It's all about the aliens in the asteroid belt. He had this elaborate *plan*, and--
Sonja... enough. I'm sure it would have been the biggest story of all time, but right now...
Phil, please. *What's going on?*
I drove straight through from Nevada, and my car didn't have a radio. What are you *talking* about?
Oh, Jesus. Brace yourself, all right?
Times
PRESIDENT BLADES:
WE ARE THE LAST.
I'm sorry to be the one to tell you this...

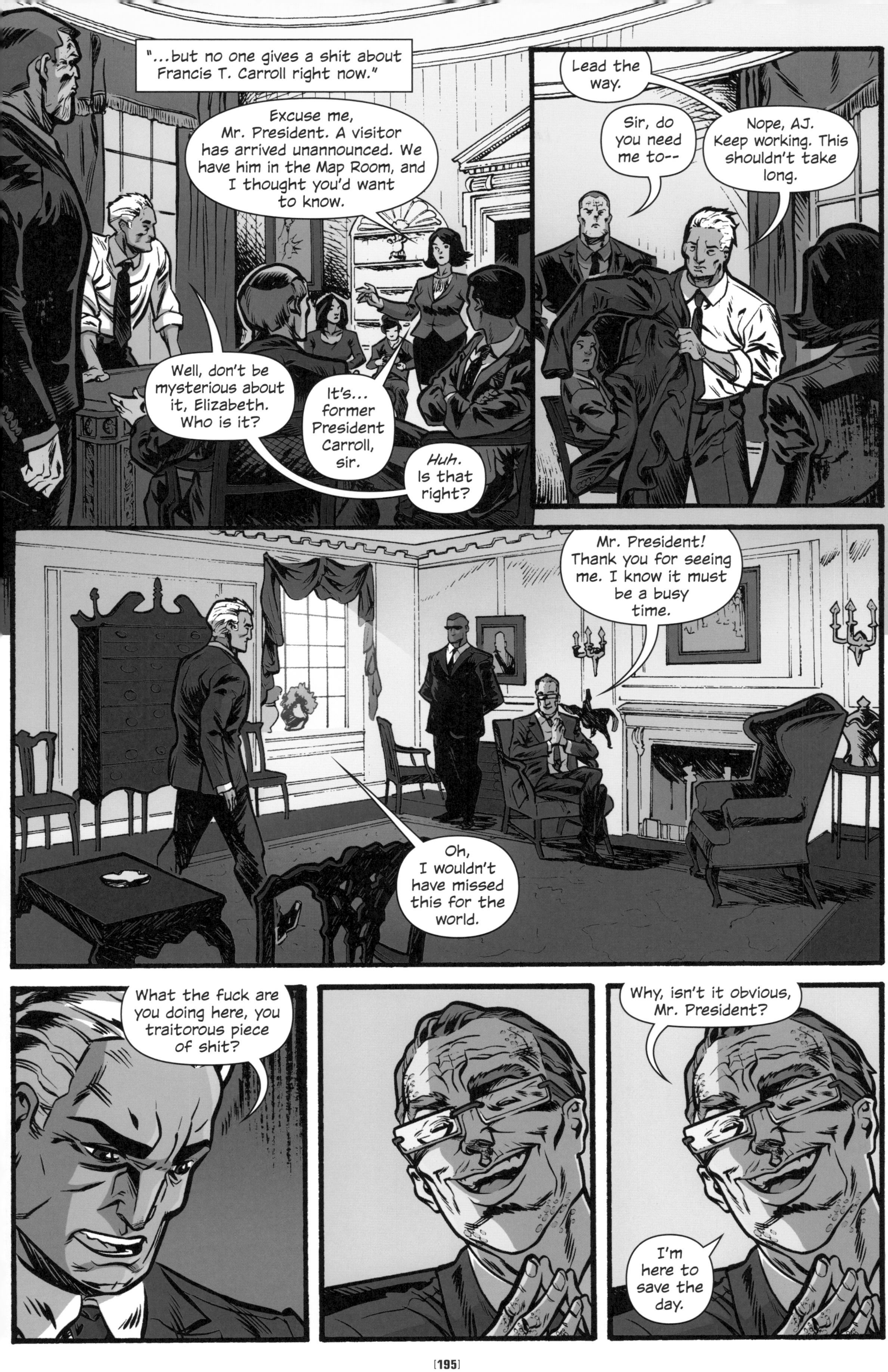
"...but no one gives a shit about Francis T. Carroll right now."
Excuse me, Mr. President. A visitor has arrived unannounced. We have him in the Map Room, and I thought you'd want to know.
Well, don't be mysterious about it, Elizabeth. Who is it?
It's... former President Carroll, sir.
Huh. Is that right?
Lead the way.
Sir, do you need me to--
Nope, AJ. Keep working. This shouldn't take long.
Mr. President! Thank you for seeing me. I know it must be a busy time.
Oh, I wouldn't have missed this for the world.
What the fuck are you doing here, you traitorous piece of shit?
Why, isn't it obvious, Mr. President?
I'm here to save the day.

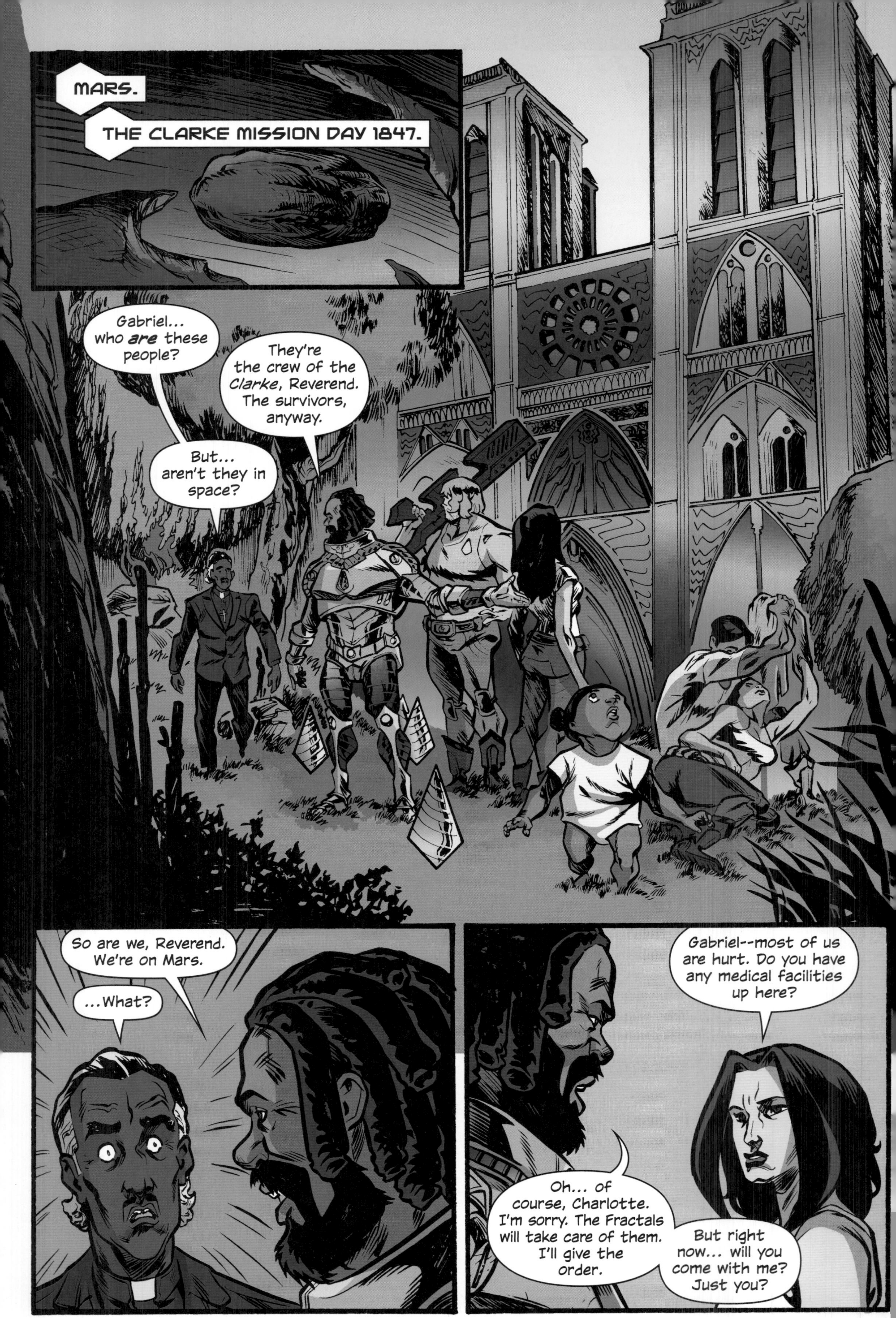
MARS.
THE CLARKE MISSION DAY 1847.
Gabriel... who *are* these people?
They're the crew of the *Clarke*, Reverend. The survivors, anyway.
But... aren't they in space?
So are we, Reverend. We're on Mars.
...What?
Gabriel--most of us are hurt. Do you have any medical facilities up here?
Oh... of course, Charlotte. I'm sorry. The Fractals will take care of them. I'll give the order.
But right now... will you come with me? Just you?

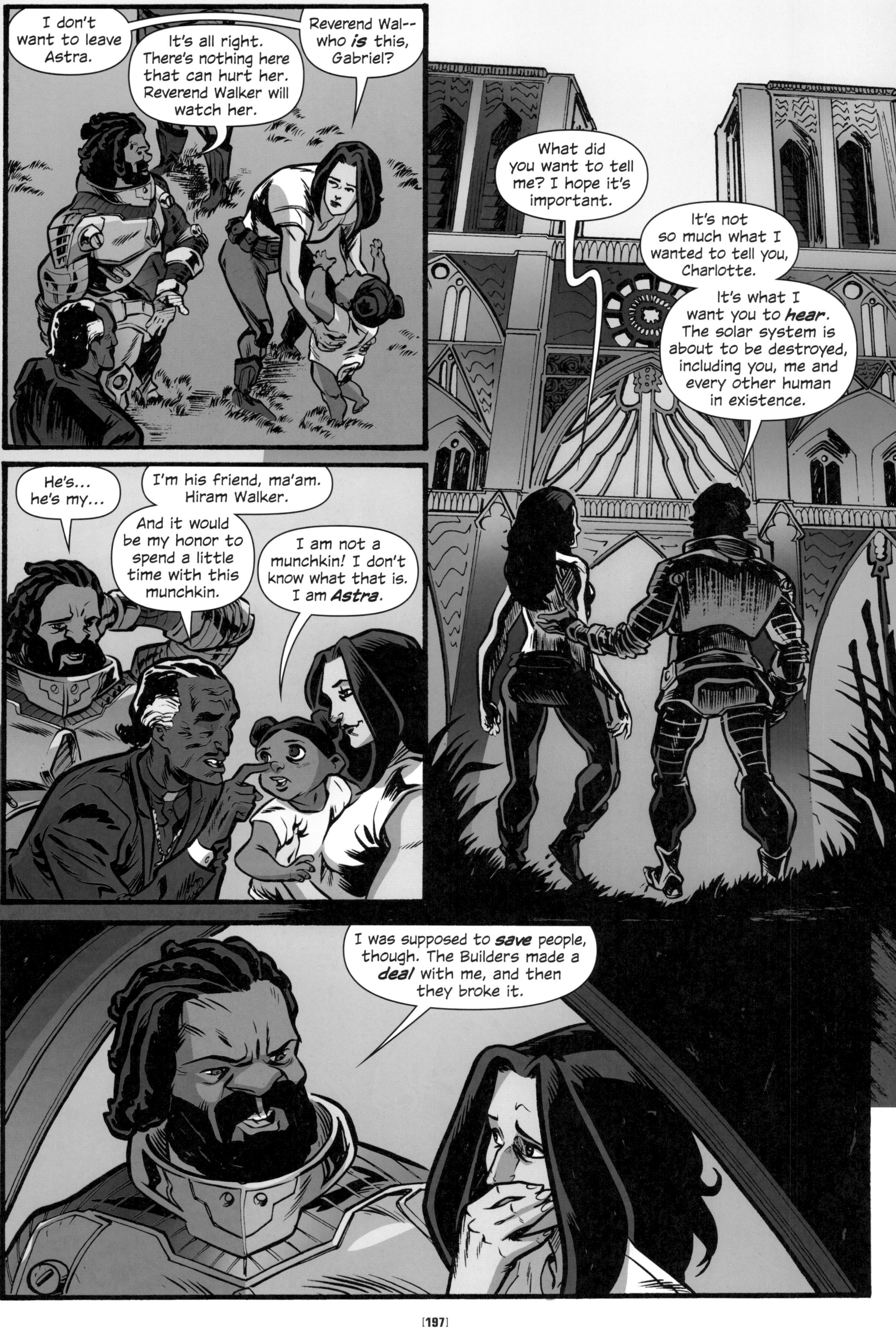
I don't want to leave Astra.
It's all right. There's nothing here that can hurt her. Reverend Walker will watch her.
Reverend Wal-- who *is* this, Gabriel?
What did you want to tell me? I hope it's important.
It's not so much what I wanted to tell you, Charlotte.
It's what I want you to *hear*. The solar system is about to be destroyed, including you, me and every other human in existence.
He's... he's my...
I'm his friend, ma'am. Hiram Walker.
And it would be my honor to spend a little time with this munchkin.
I am not a munchkin! I don't know what that is. I am *Astra*.
I was supposed to *save* people, though. The Builders made a *deal* with me, and then they broke it.

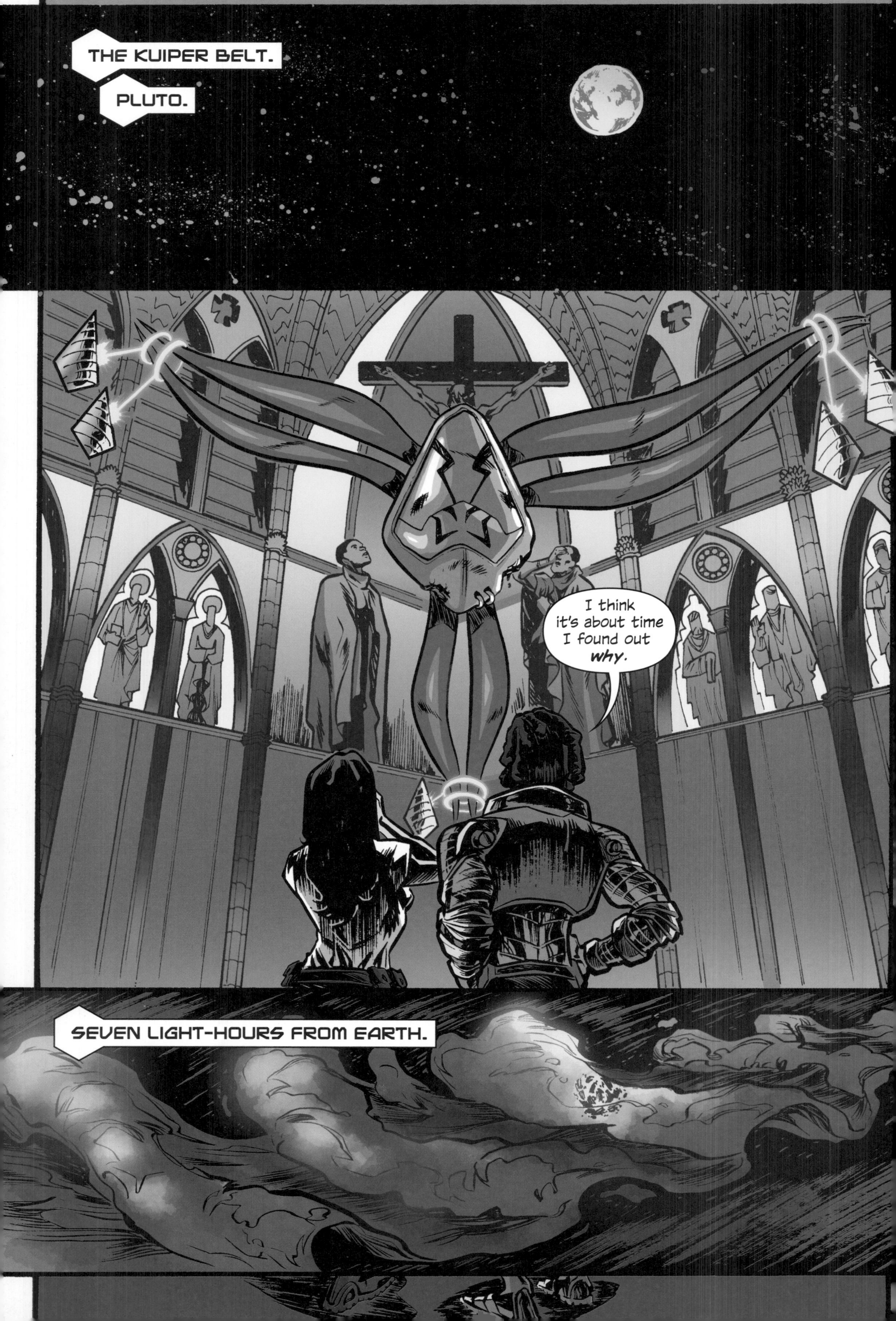
THE KUIPER BELT.
PLUTO.
I think it's about time I found out *why*.
SEVEN LIGHT-HOURS FROM EARTH.

LETTER 44

CHAPTER IX

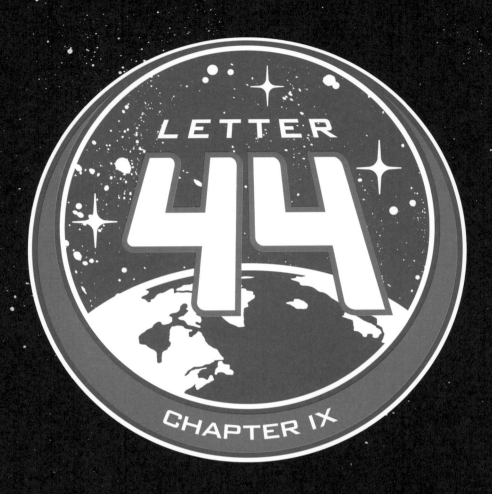

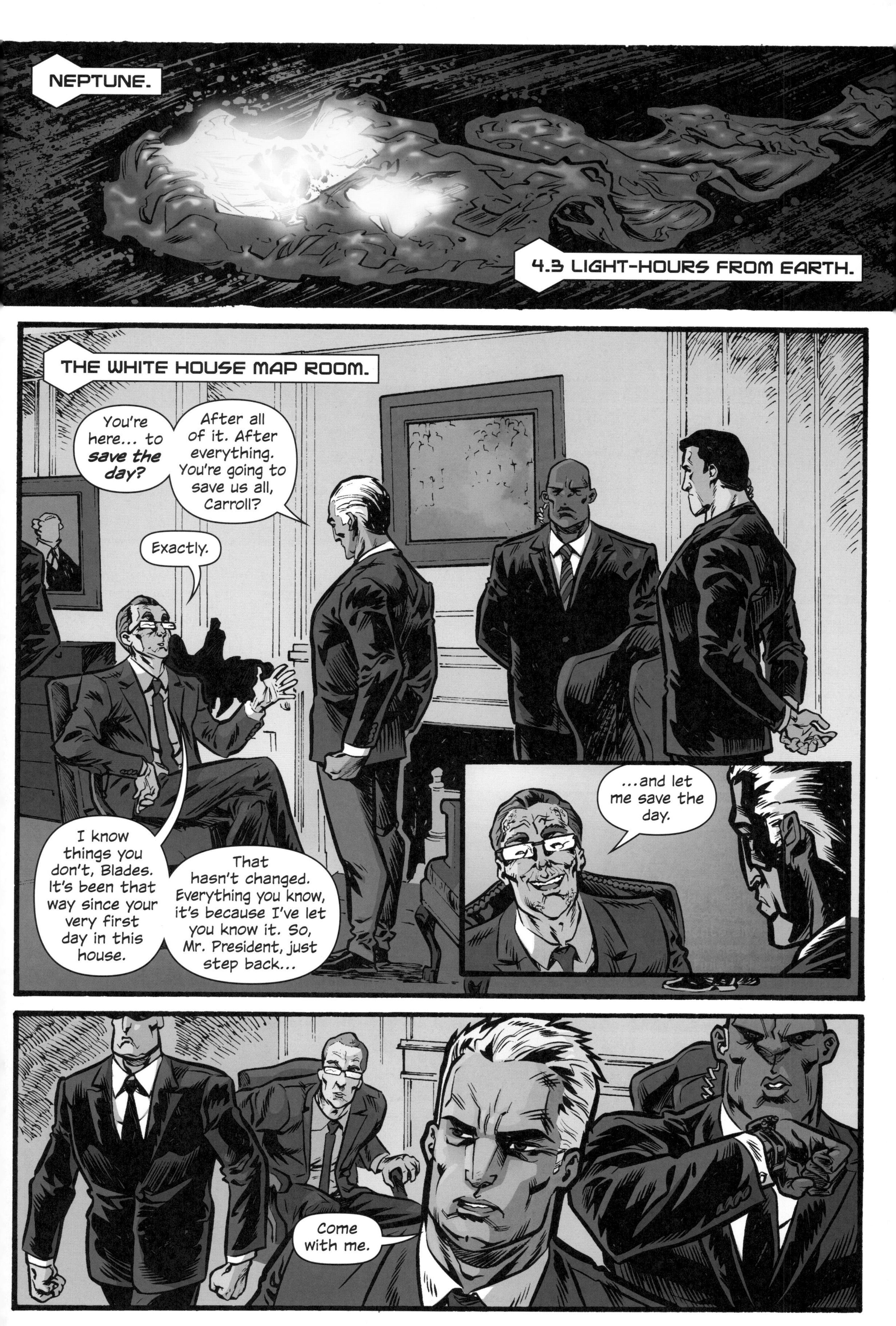
NEPTUNE.
4.3 LIGHT-HOURS FROM EARTH.
THE WHITE HOUSE MAP ROOM.
You're here... to *save the day?*
After all of it. After everything. You're going to save us all, Carroll?
Exactly.
I know things you don't, Blades. It's been that way since your very first day in this house.
That hasn't changed. Everything you know, it's because I've let you know it. So, Mr. President, just step back...
...and let me save the day.
Come with me.

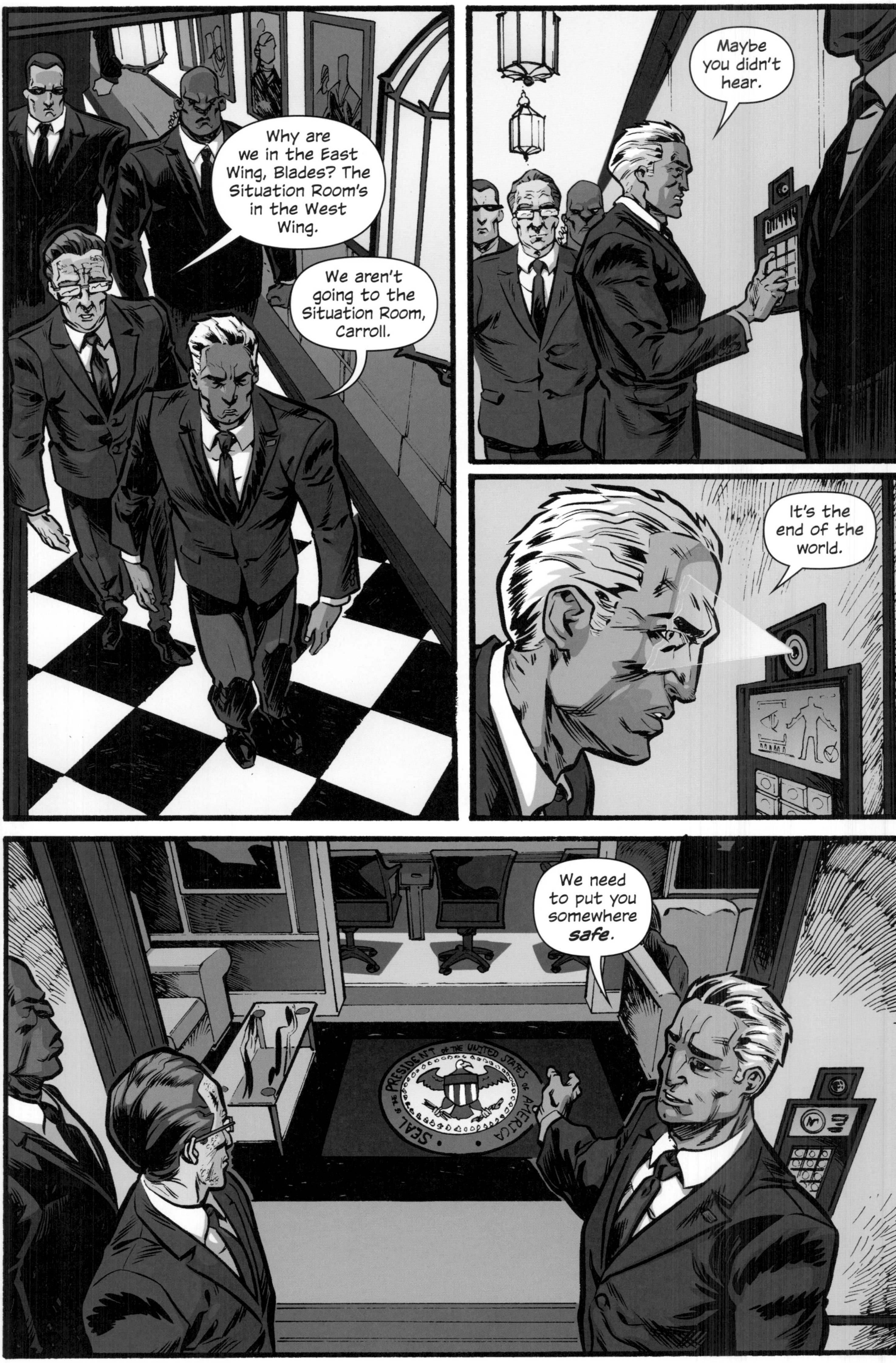
Why are we in the East Wing, Blades? The Situation Room's in the West Wing.
We aren't going to the Situation Room, Carroll.
Maybe you didn't hear.
It's the end of the world.
We need to put you somewhere *safe*.
SEAL OF THE PRESIDENT OF THE UNITED STATES OF AMERICA

The PEOC. Makes sense. This is probably the safest spot on the Eastern Seaboard.

Good place to ride things out.

You'll want to call Dr. Portek so he and I can start to coordinate the defense plan.

Yeah. Defense plan.

There is no defense plan, Carroll, and there is no saving the day. Not for you, and not for me. I think you know that, too.

It's all over.

Your sidearm, please, Jim.

Sir? My...

You heard me. Give it to me.

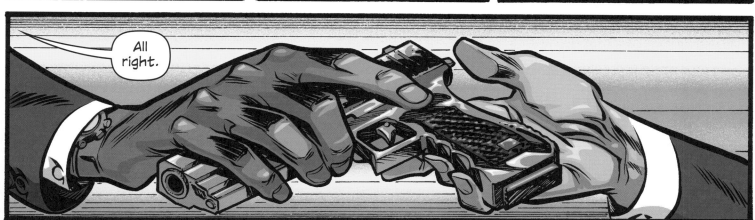

All right.

Blades... *Stephen*... what are you *doing*?

Call it... an *experiment*. Francis.

These men are sworn to protect me, as the sitting President of the United States.

But, they are also sworn to protect *you*, as the former President. Without hesitation. So, in a situation like this...

...I wonder what they'd do?

If I pulled the trigger right now, knowing that you started World War III *against your own country*, among many other sins and treasons large and small.

Don't... don't do it!

I just wanted to save the world! Everything I did... I was trying to save the *world*!

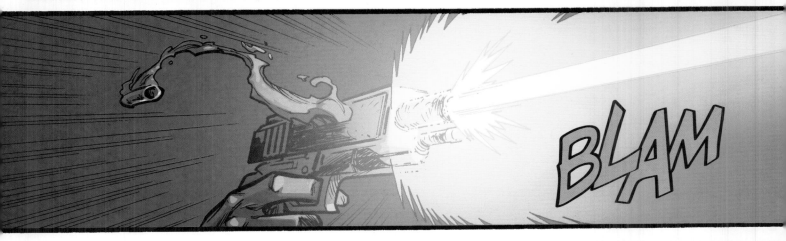

BLAM

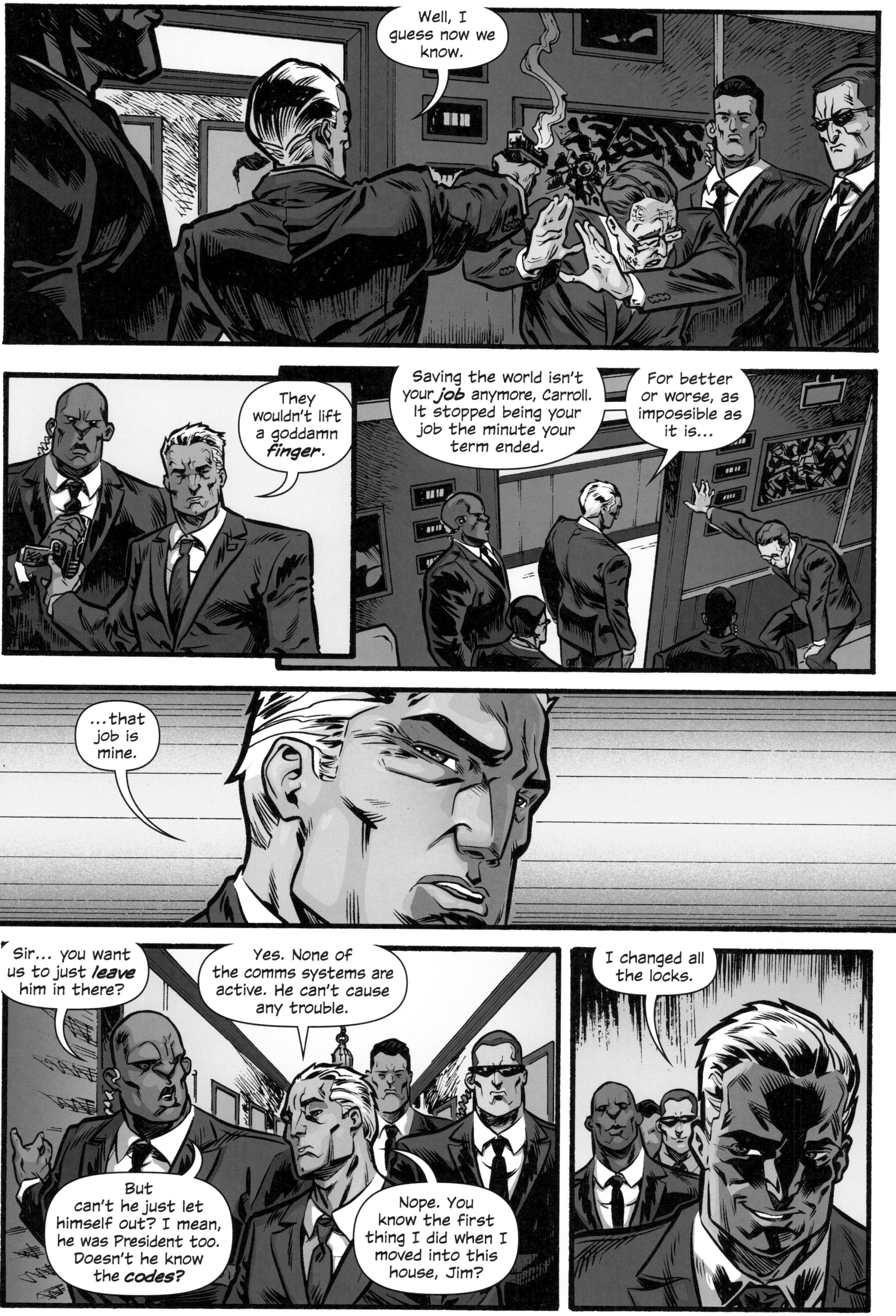
Well, I guess now we know.
They wouldn't lift a goddamn *finger*.
Saving the world isn't your *job* anymore, Carroll. It stopped being your job the minute your term ended.
For better or worse, as impossible as it is...
...that job is mine.
Sir... you want us to just *leave* him in there?
Yes. None of the comms systems are active. He can't cause any trouble.
But can't he just let himself out? I mean, he was President too. Doesn't he know the *codes?*
Nope. You know the first thing I did when I moved into this house, Jim?
I changed all the locks.

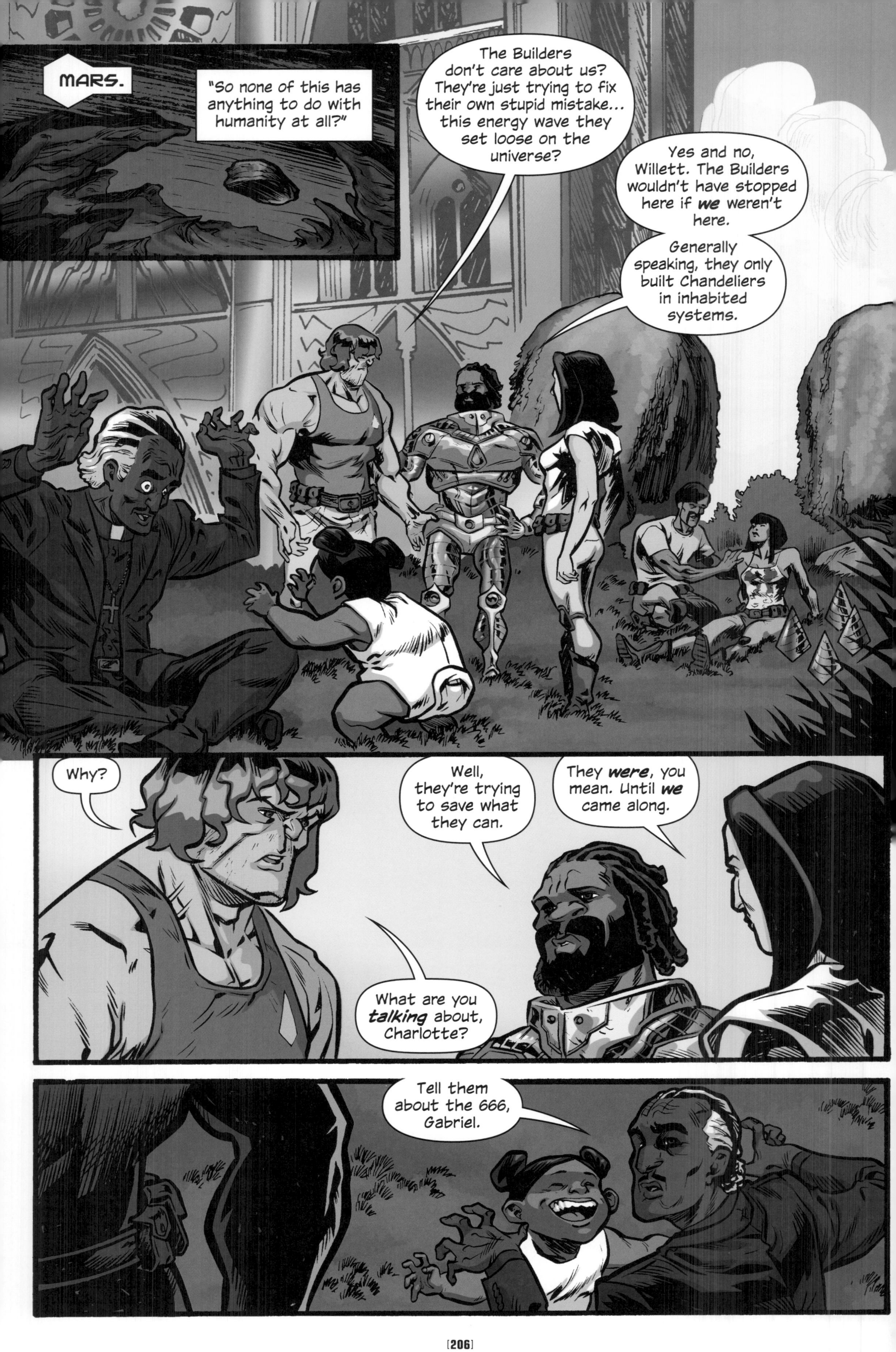
MARS.
"So none of this has anything to do with humanity at all?"
The Builders don't care about us? They're just trying to fix their own stupid mistake... this energy wave they set loose on the universe?
Yes and no, Willett. The Builders wouldn't have stopped here if *we* weren't here.
Generally speaking, they only built Chandeliers in inhabited systems.
Why?
Well, they're trying to save what they can.
They *were*, you mean. Until *we* came along.
What are you *talking* about, Charlotte?
Tell them about the 666, Gabriel.

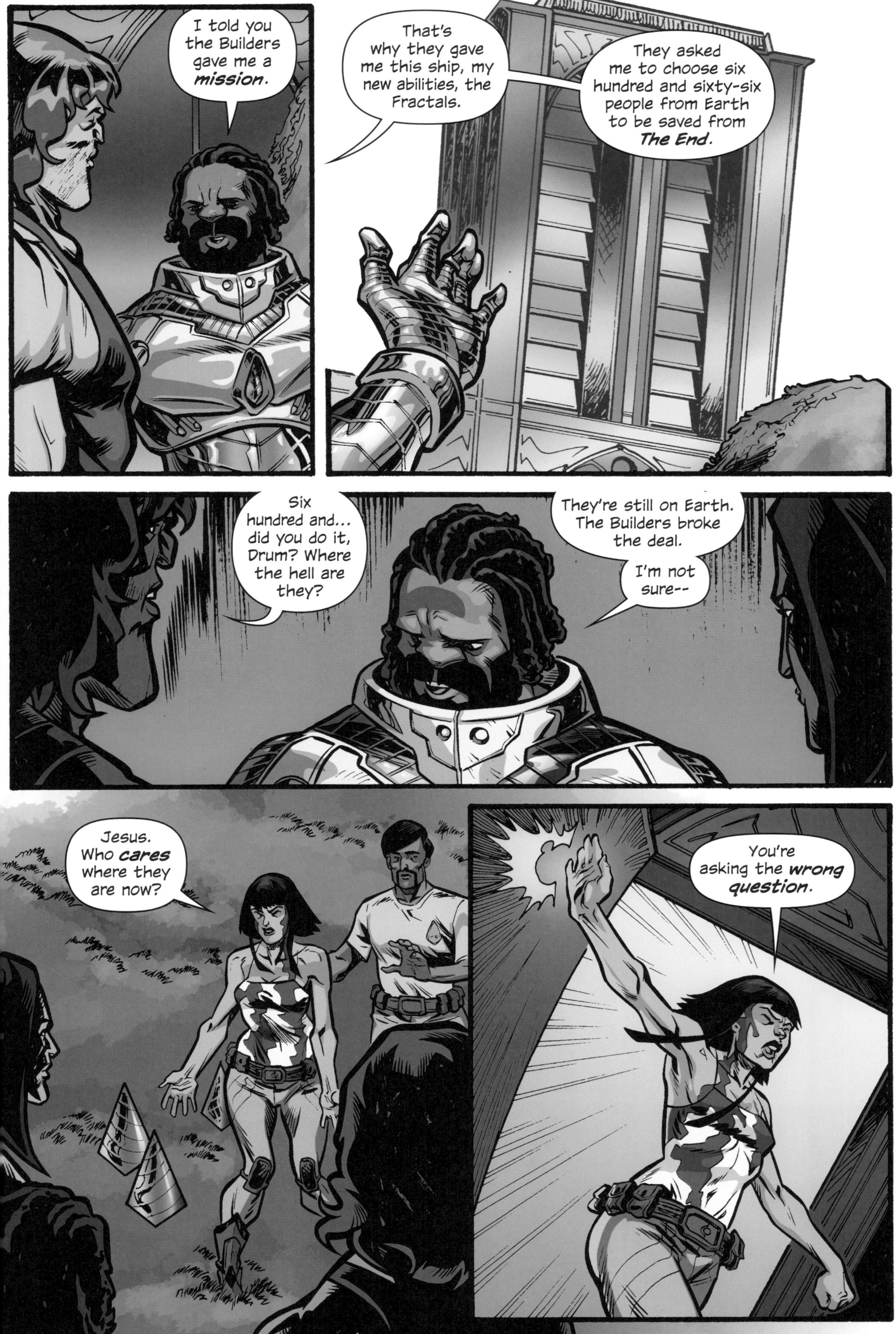
I told you the Builders gave me a ***mission***.
That's why they gave me this ship, my new abilities, the Fractals.
They asked me to choose six hundred and sixty-six people from Earth to be saved from ***The End***.
Six hundred and... did you do it, Drum? Where the hell are they?
They're still on Earth. The Builders broke the deal.
I'm not sure--
Jesus. Who ***cares*** where they are now?
You're asking the ***wrong question***.

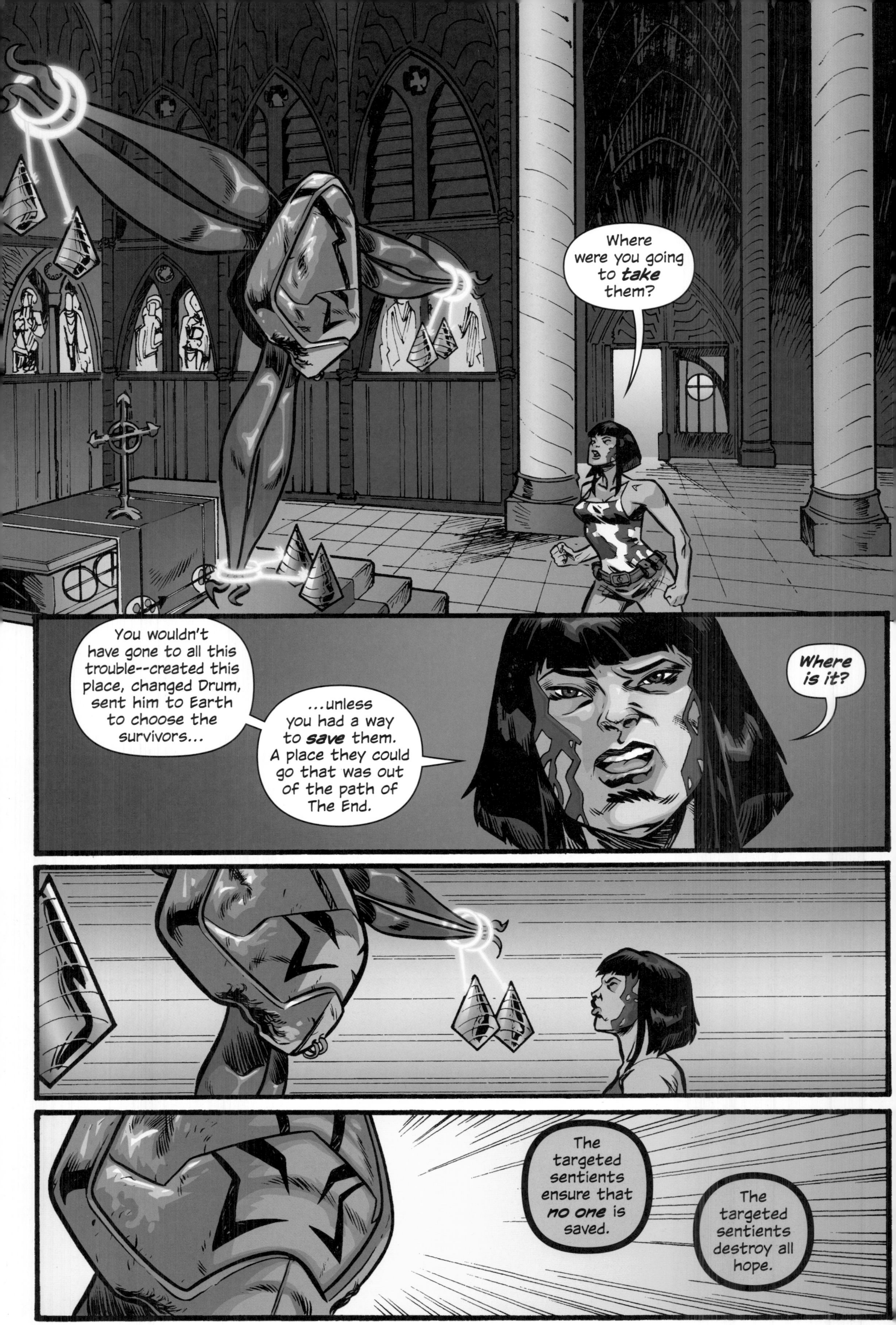
Where were you going to *take* them?
You wouldn't have gone to all this trouble--created this place, changed Drum, sent him to Earth to choose the survivors...
...unless you had a way to *save* them. A place they could go that was out of the path of The End.
Where is it?
The targeted sentients ensure that *no one* is saved.
The targeted sentients destroy all hope.

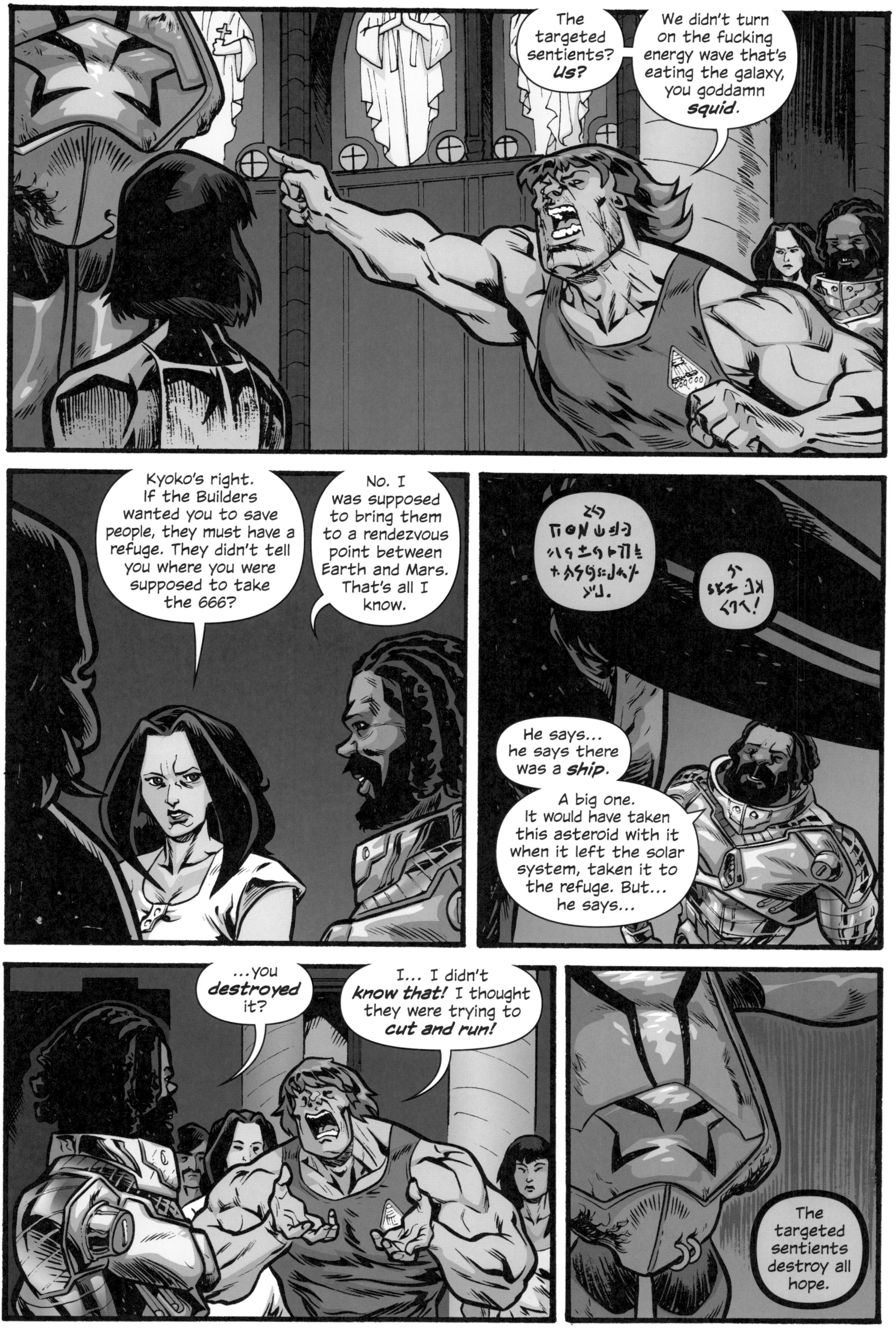
The targeted sentients? *Us?*
We didn't turn on the fucking energy wave that's eating the galaxy, you goddamn ***squid***.
Kyoko's right. If the Builders wanted you to save people, they must have a refuge. They didn't tell you where you were supposed to take the 666?
No. I was supposed to bring them to a rendezvous point between Earth and Mars. That's all I know.
He says... he says there was a ***ship***.
A big one. It would have taken this asteroid with it when it left the solar system, taken it to the refuge. But... he says...
...you ***destroyed*** it?
I... I didn't ***know that!*** I thought they were trying to ***cut and run!***
The targeted sentients destroy all hope.

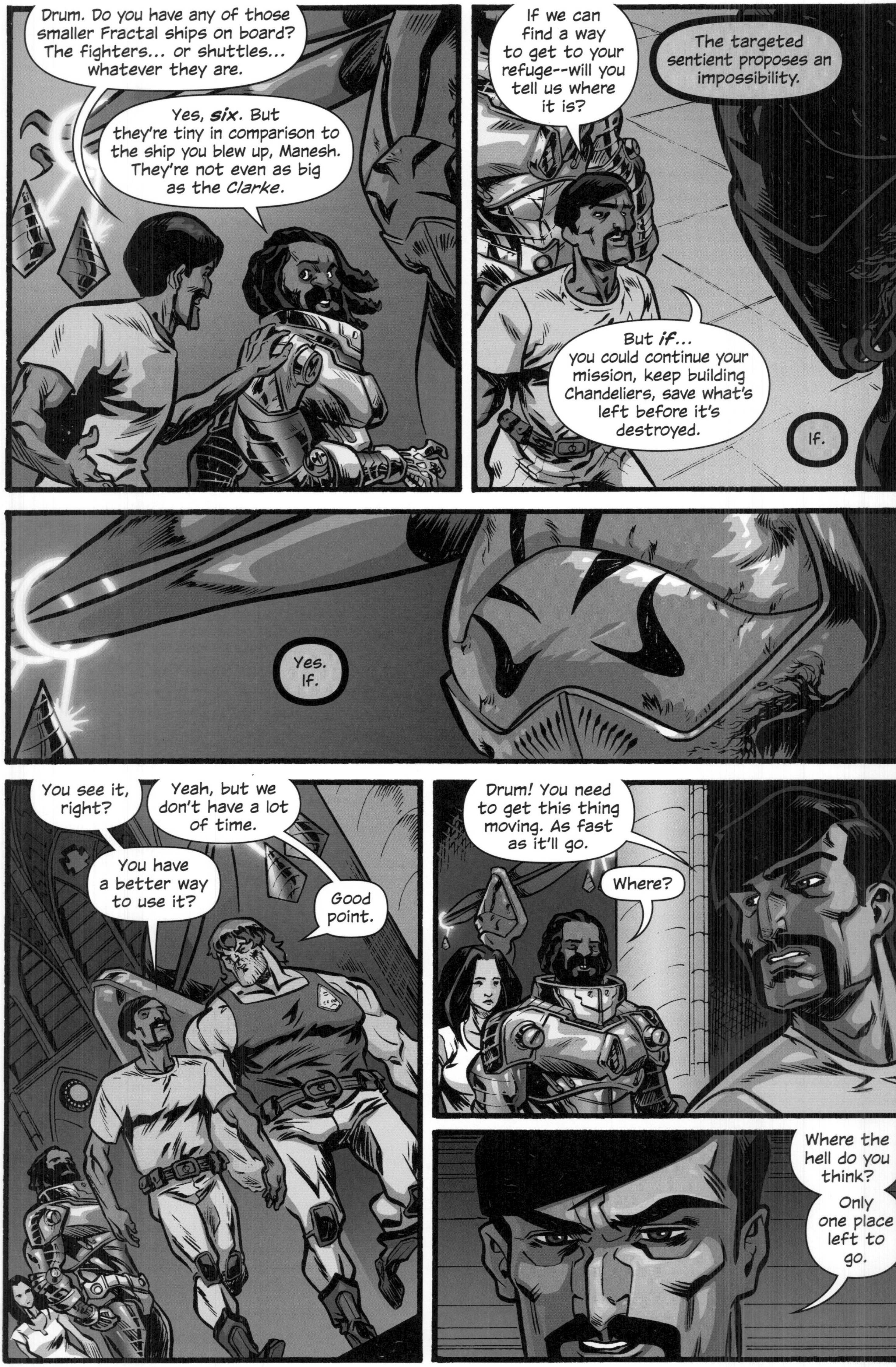

Drum. Do you have any of those smaller Fractal ships on board? The fighters... or shuttles... whatever they are.
Yes, *six*. But they're tiny in comparison to the ship you blew up, Manesh. They're not even as big as the *Clarke*.
If we can find a way to get to your refuge--will you tell us where it is?
The targeted sentient proposes an impossibility.
But *if*... you could continue your mission, keep building Chandeliers, save what's left before it's destroyed.
If.
Yes. If.
You see it, right?
Yeah, but we don't have a lot of time.
You have a better way to use it?
Good point.
Drum! You need to get this thing moving. As fast as it'll go.
Where?
Where the hell do you think?
Only one place left to go.

URANUS.

2.75 LIGHT-HOURS FROM EARTH.

We have a call from Reverend Hiram Walker for you, sir. Well, more of a message, really. We're experiencing significant lag on the line--almost four minutes.

Reverend Walker? He's with *Drum*. Aren't they in the Arctic, Elizabeth? Why are we getting lag?

They aren't in the Arctic, Mr. President. They're... well...

I'll just let him tell you.

Hello, Mr. President. I'm with the surviving crew of the Clarke, on Major Drum's asteroid.

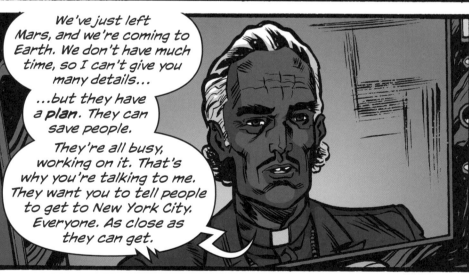

We've just left Mars, and we're coming to Earth. We don't have much time, so I can't give you many details...

...but they have a *plan*. They can save people.

They're all busy, working on it. That's why you're talking to me. They want you to tell people to get to New York City. Everyone. As close as they can get.

Reverend-- I need to know. This plan.

Will it save *everyone*?

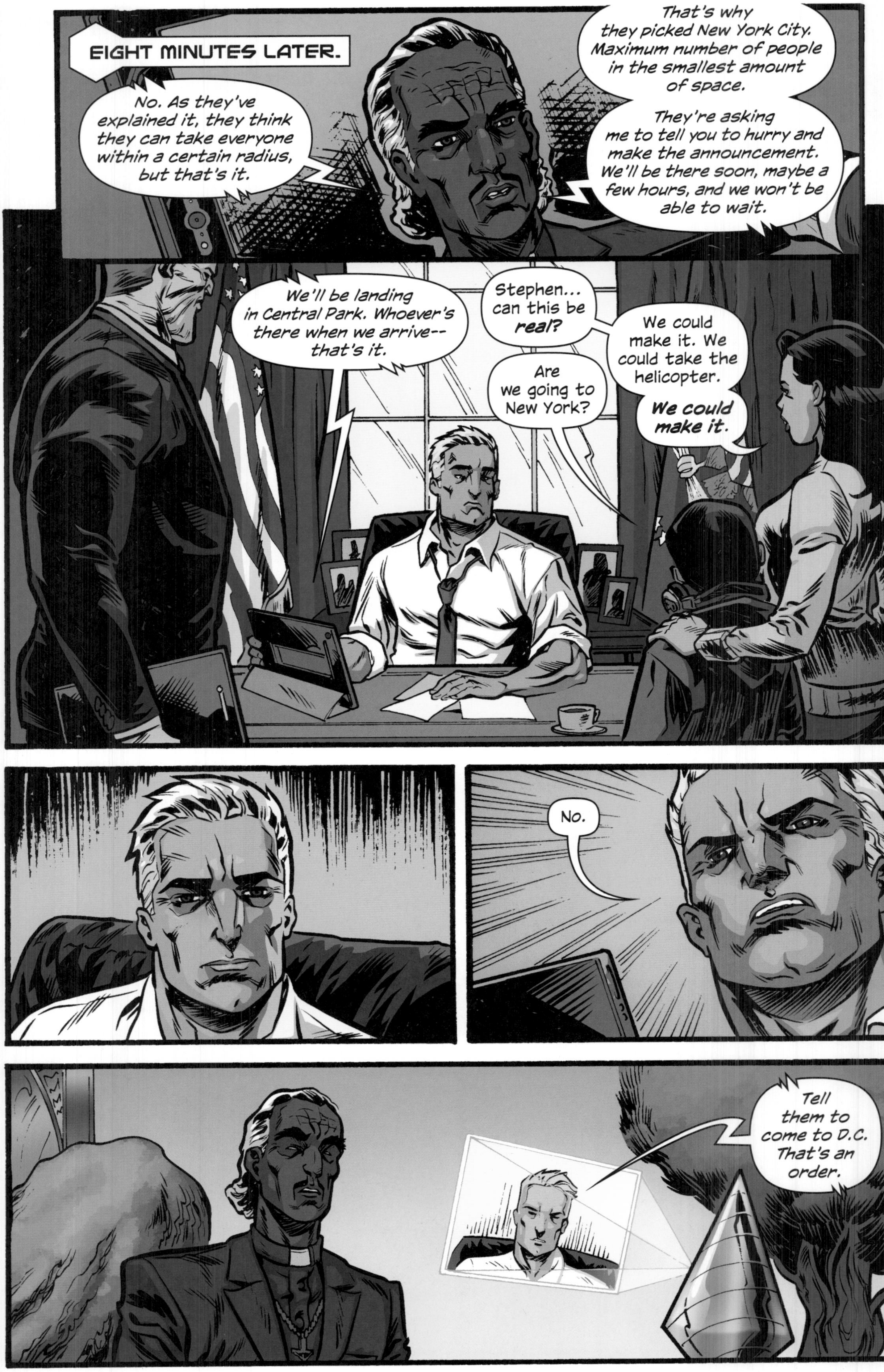
EIGHT MINUTES LATER.
No. As they've explained it, they think they can take everyone within a certain radius, but that's it.
That's why they picked New York City. Maximum number of people in the smallest amount of space.
They're asking me to tell you to hurry and make the announcement. We'll be there soon, maybe a few hours, and we won't be able to wait.
We'll be landing in Central Park. Whoever's there when we arrive-- that's it.
Stephen... can this be *real?*
Are we going to New York?
We could make it. We could take the helicopter.
We could make it.
No.
Tell them to come to D.C. That's an order.

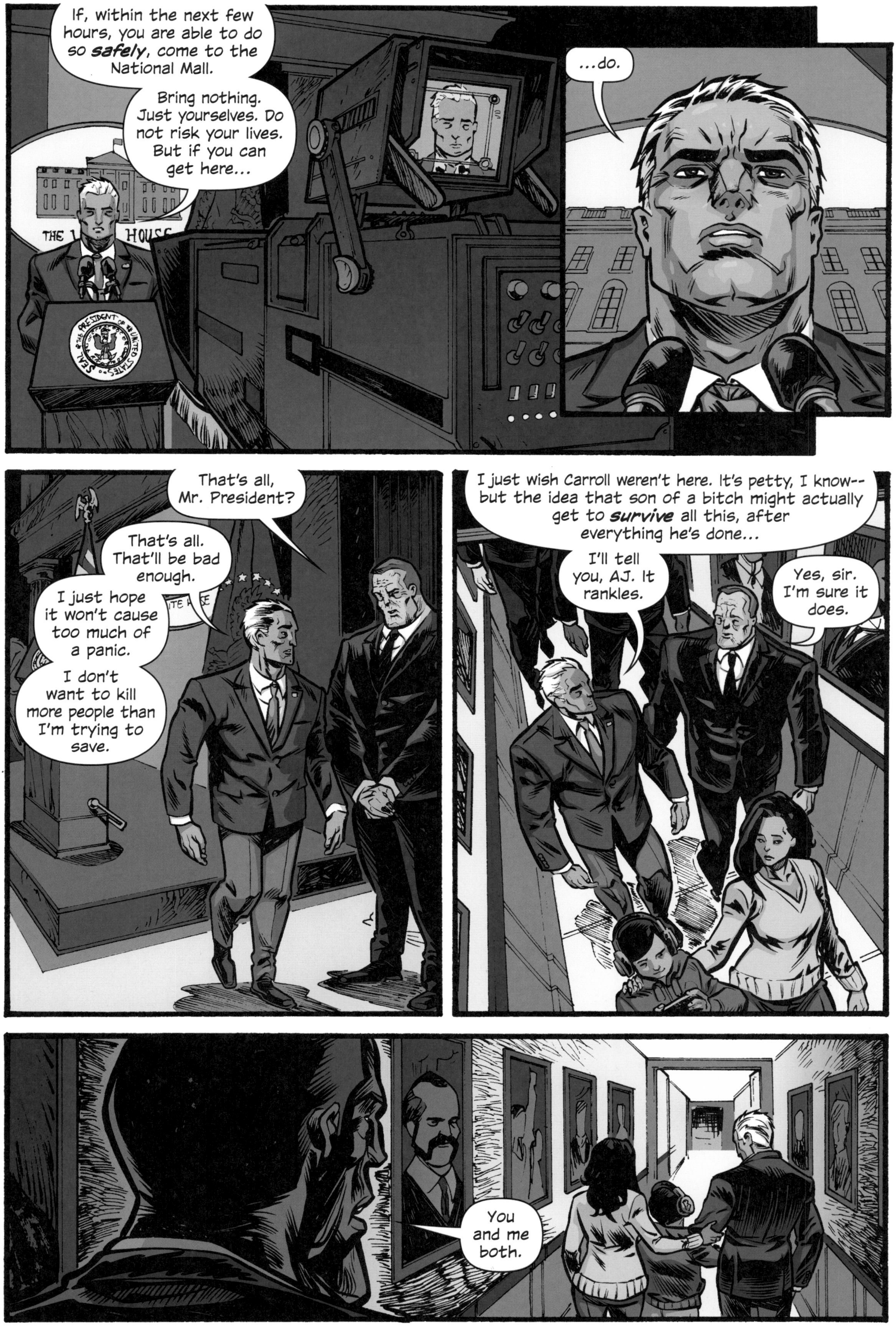
If, within the next few hours, you are able to do so *safely*, come to the National Mall.
Bring nothing. Just yourselves. Do not risk your lives. But if you can get here...
THE HOUSE
THE PRESIDENT OF THE UNITED STATES
...do.
That's all, Mr. President?
That's all. That'll be bad enough.
I just hope it won't cause too much of a panic.
I don't want to kill more people than I'm trying to save.
I just wish Carroll weren't here. It's petty, I know--but the idea that son of a bitch might actually get to *survive* all this, after everything he's done...
I'll tell you, AJ. It rankles.
Yes, sir. I'm sure it does.
You and me both.

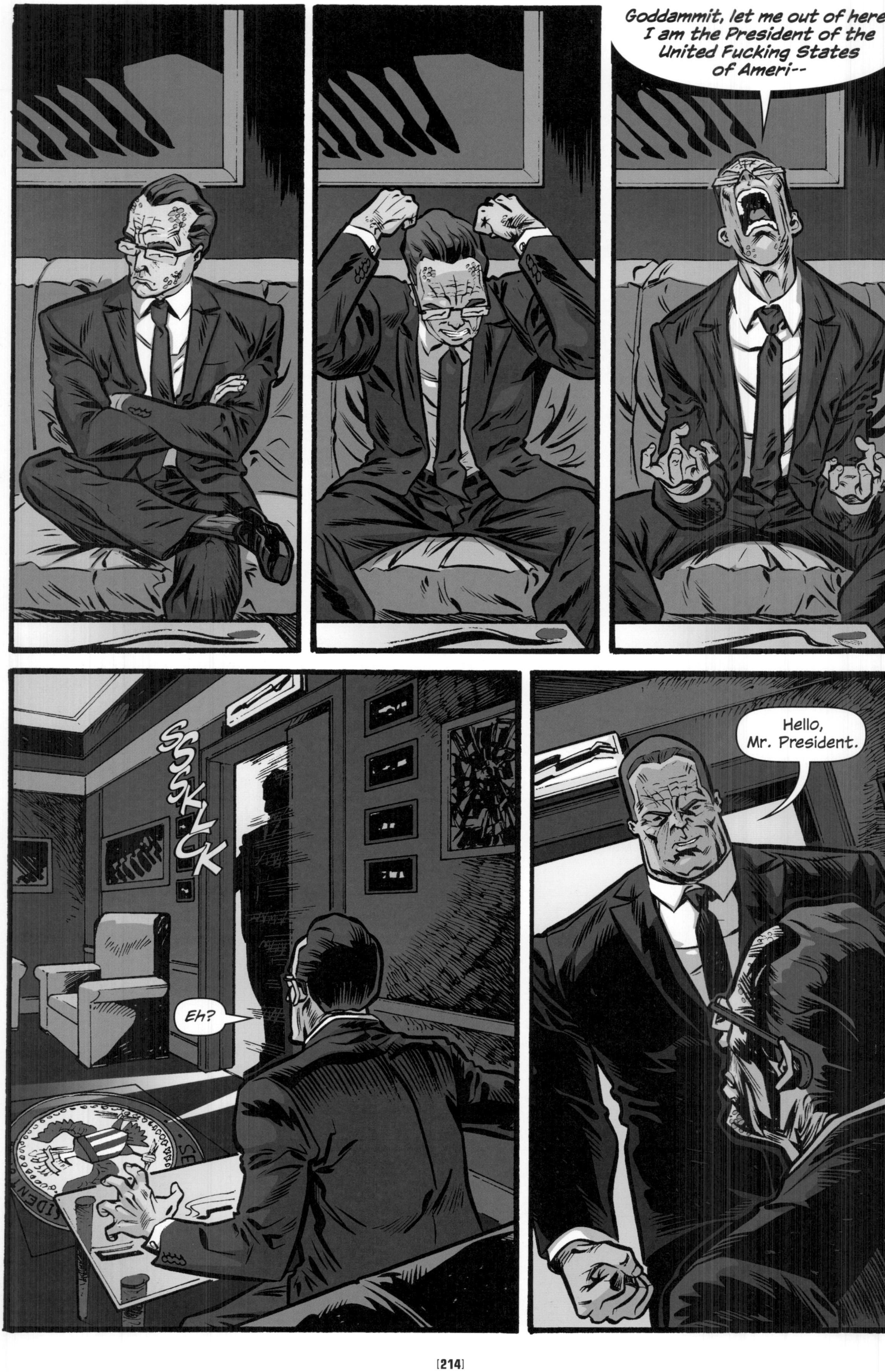
Goddammit, let me out of here! I am the President of the United Fucking States of Ameri--
SSSKLCK
Eh?
Hello, Mr. President.

I don't understand why you think this will work, Manesh.

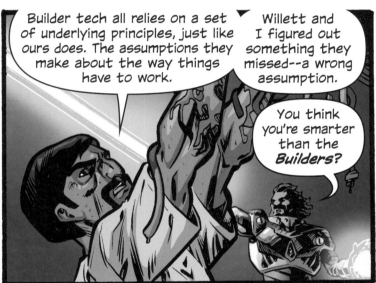

Builder tech all relies on a set of underlying principles, just like ours does. The assumptions they make about the way things have to work.

Willett and I figured out something they missed--a wrong assumption.

You think you're smarter than the Builders?

We're not just *saying* it, Drum.

SPLTCH

We *know* it.

This will work. I mean...

SATURN.

45 LIGHT-MINUTES FROM EARTH.

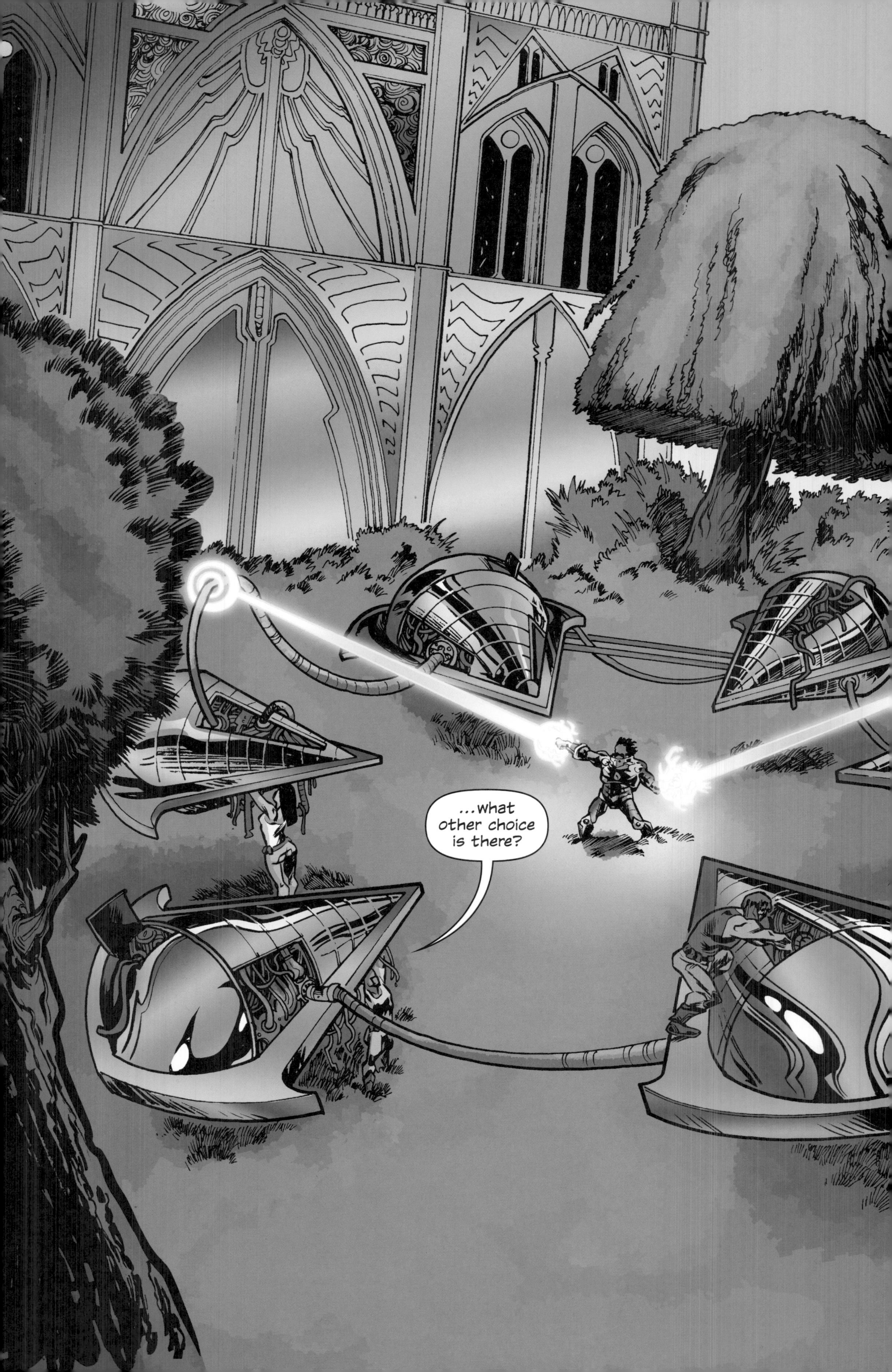
...what other choice is there?

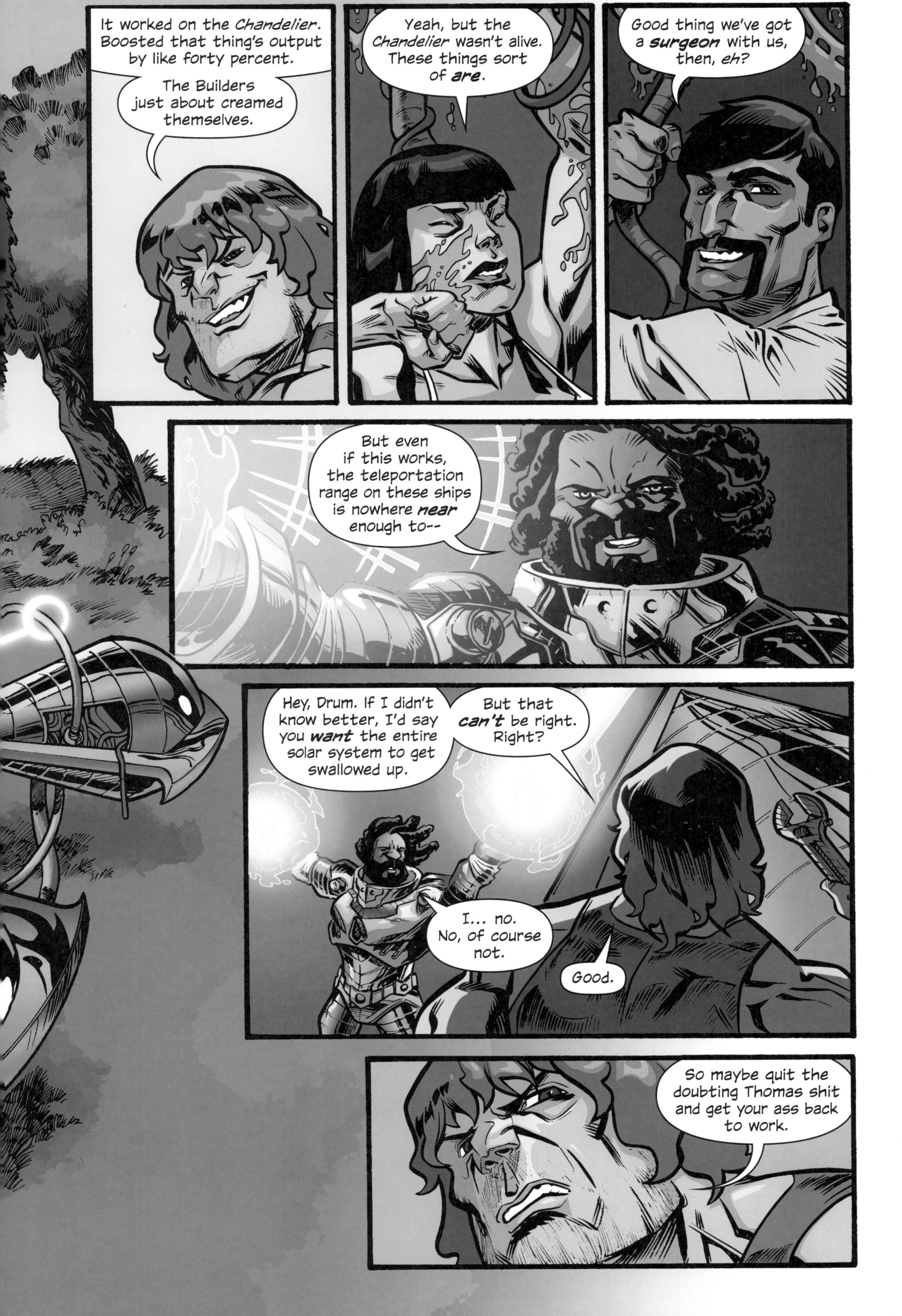

It worked on the *Chandelier*. Boosted that thing's output by like forty percent.
The Builders just about creamed themselves.
Yeah, but the *Chandelier* wasn't alive. These things sort of ***are***.
Good thing we've got a ***surgeon*** with us, then, *eh?*
But even if this works, the teleportation range on these ships is nowhere ***near*** enough to--
Hey, Drum. If I didn't know better, I'd say you ***want*** the entire solar system to get swallowed up.
But that ***can't*** be right. Right?
I... no. No, of course not.
Good.
So maybe quit the doubting Thomas shit and get your ass back to work.

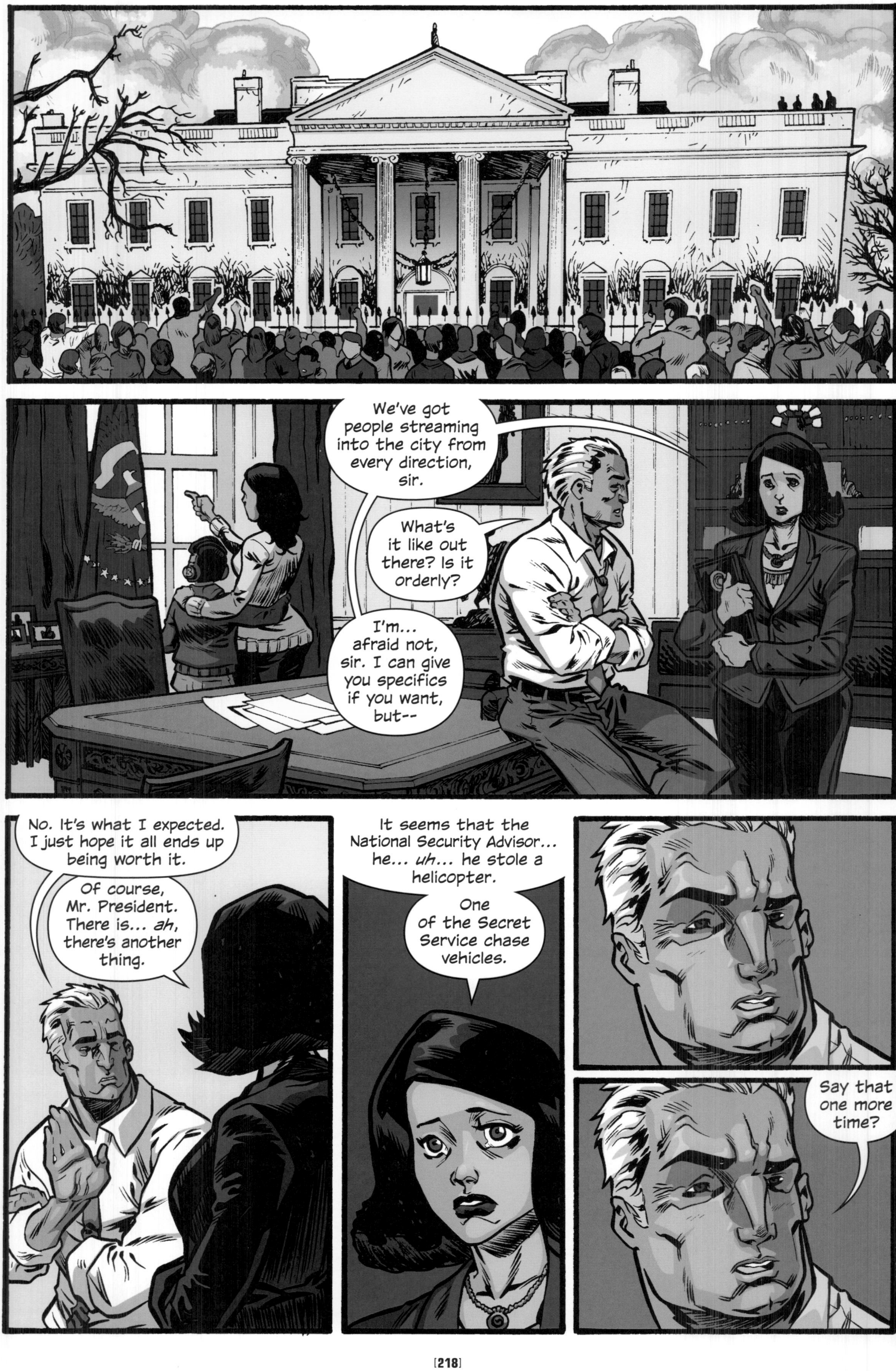
We've got people streaming into the city from every direction, sir.
What's it like out there? Is it orderly?
I'm... afraid not, sir. I can give you specifics if you want, but--
No. It's what I expected. I just hope it all ends up being worth it.
Of course, Mr. President. There is... *ah*, there's another thing.
It seems that the National Security Advisor... he... *uh*... he stole a helicopter.
One of the Secret Service chase vehicles.
Say that one more time?

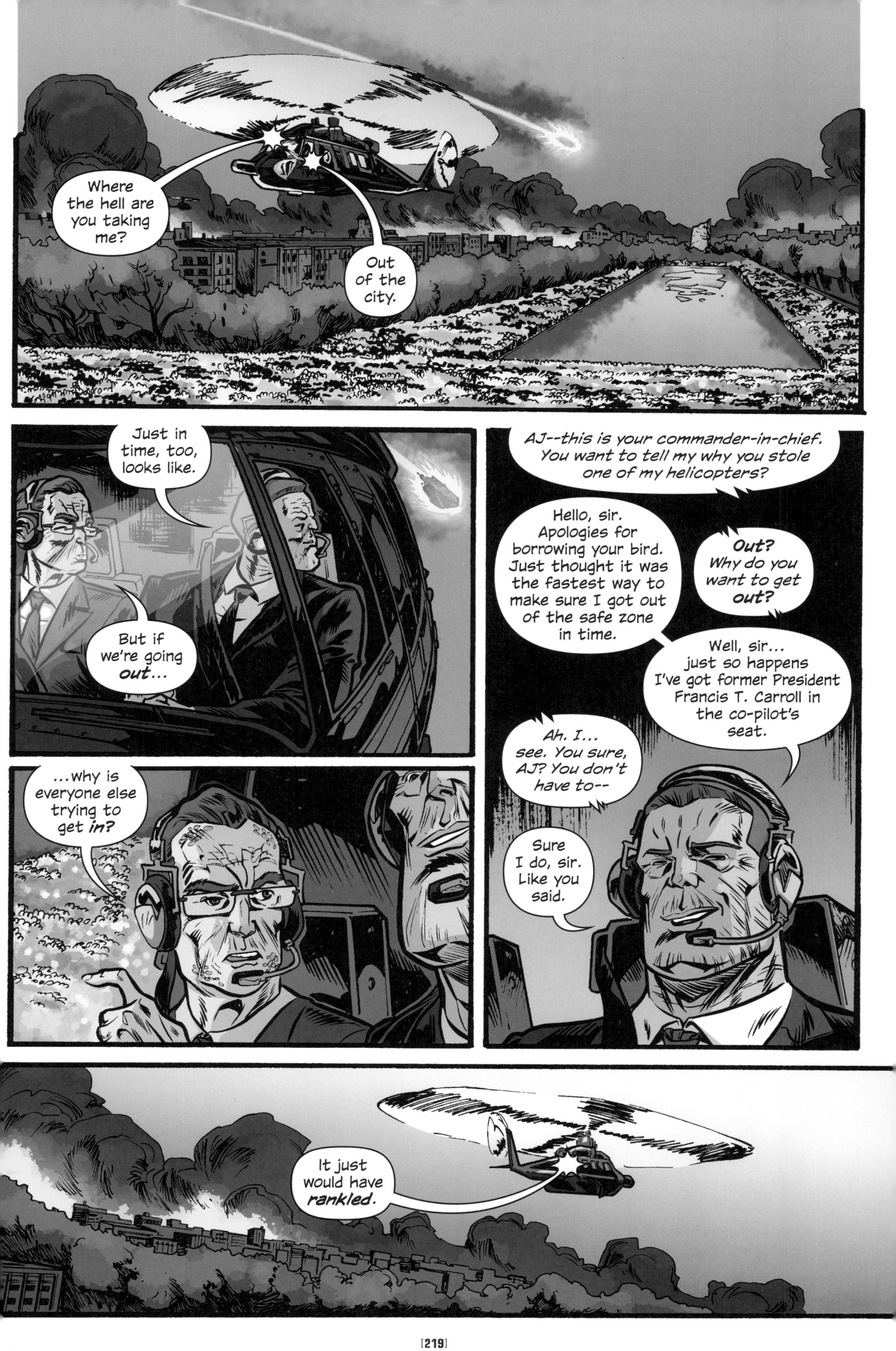
Where the hell are you taking me?
Out of the city.
Just in time, too, looks like.
But if we're going *out*...
...why is everyone else trying to get *in?*
AJ--this is your commander-in-chief. You want to tell my why you stole one of my helicopters?
Hello, sir. Apologies for borrowing your bird. Just thought it was the fastest way to make sure I got out of the safe zone in time.
Out? Why do you want to get *out?*
Well, sir... just so happens I've got former President Francis T. Carroll in the co-pilot's seat.
Ah. I... see. You sure, AJ? You don't have to--
Sure I do, sir. Like you said.
It just would have *rankled*.

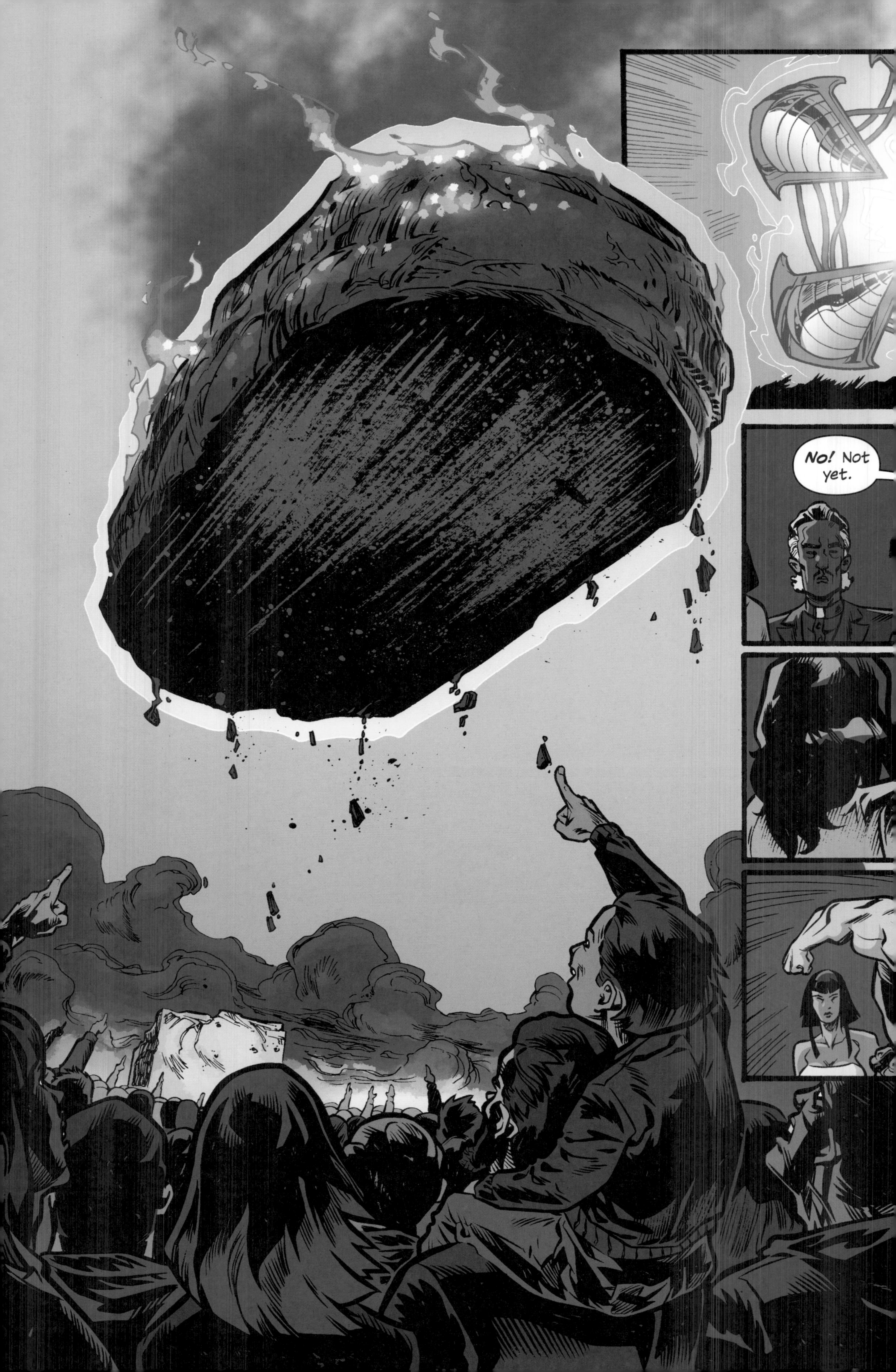
No! Not yet.

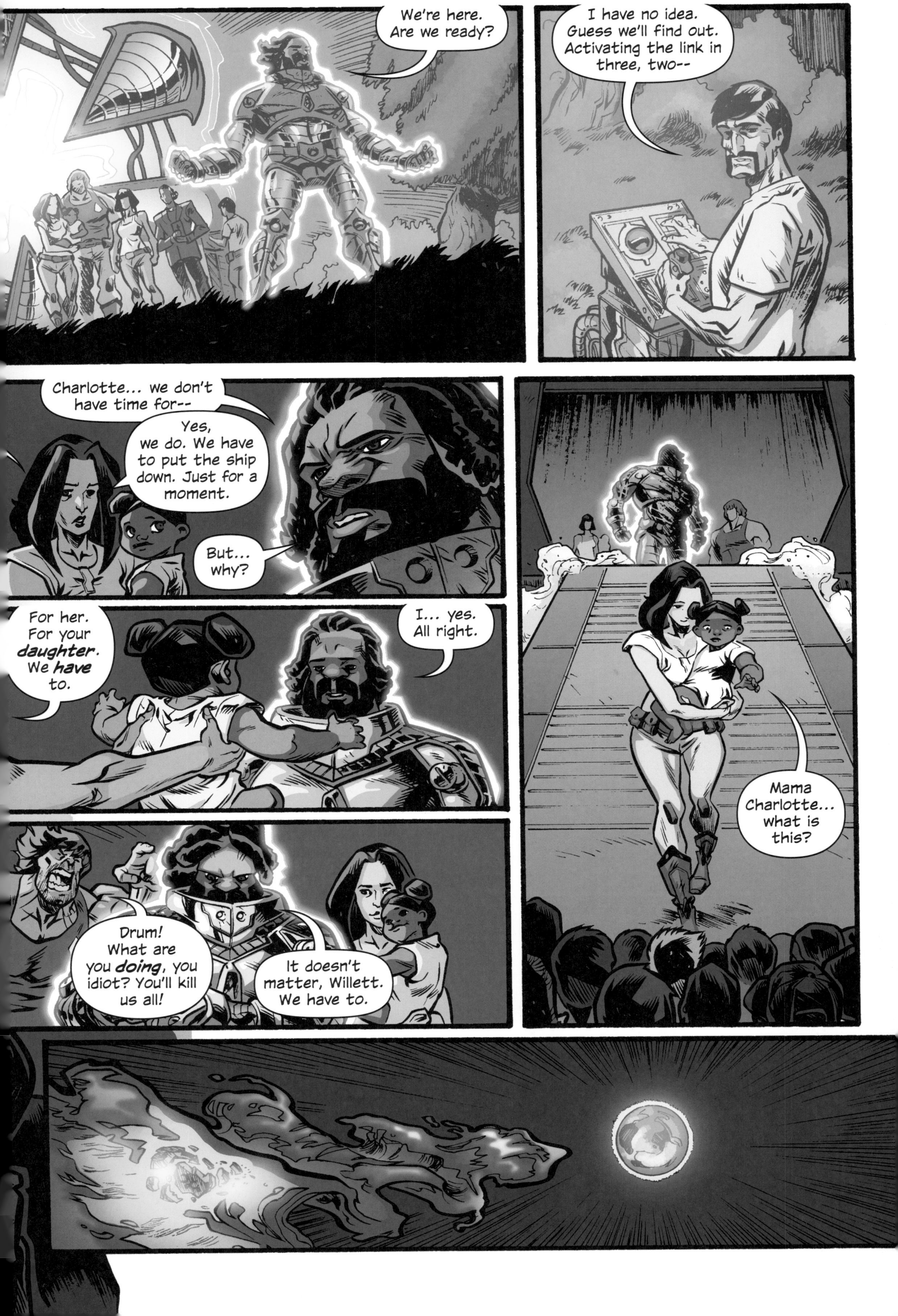
We're here.
Are we ready?
I have no idea.
Guess we'll find out.
Activating the link in three, two--
Charlotte... we don't have time for--
Yes, we do. We have to put the ship down. Just for a moment.
But... why?
For her. For your *daughter*. We *have* to.
I... yes. All right.
Drum! What are you *doing*, you idiot? You'll kill us all!
It doesn't matter, Willett. We have to.
Mama Charlotte... what is this?

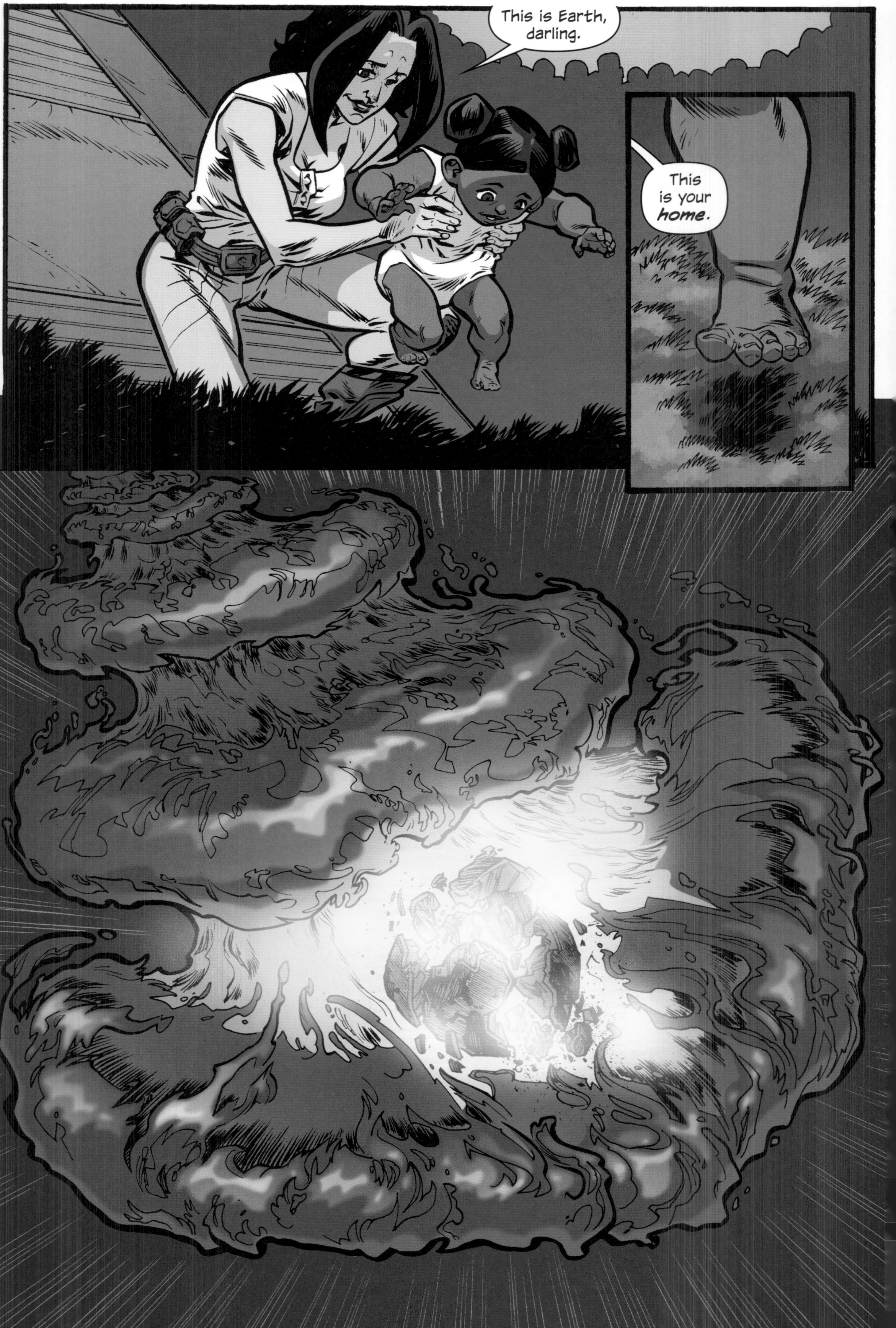
This is Earth, darling.
This is your *home*.

LETTER 44

CHAPTER X

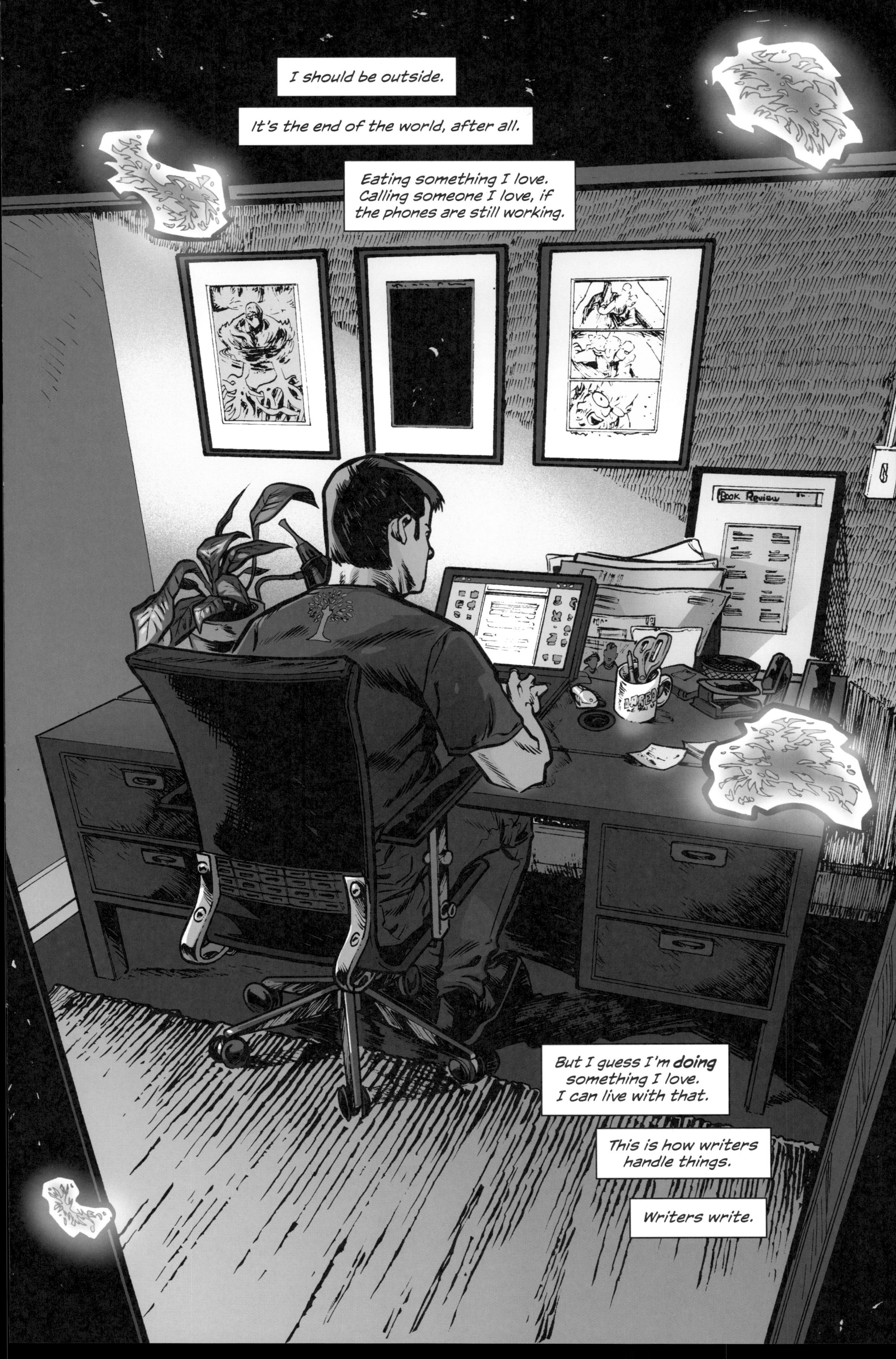
I should be outside.
It's the end of the world, after all.
Eating something I love. Calling someone I love, if the phones are still working.
BOOK Review
But I guess I'm **doing** something I love. I can live with that.
This is how writers handle things.
Writers write.

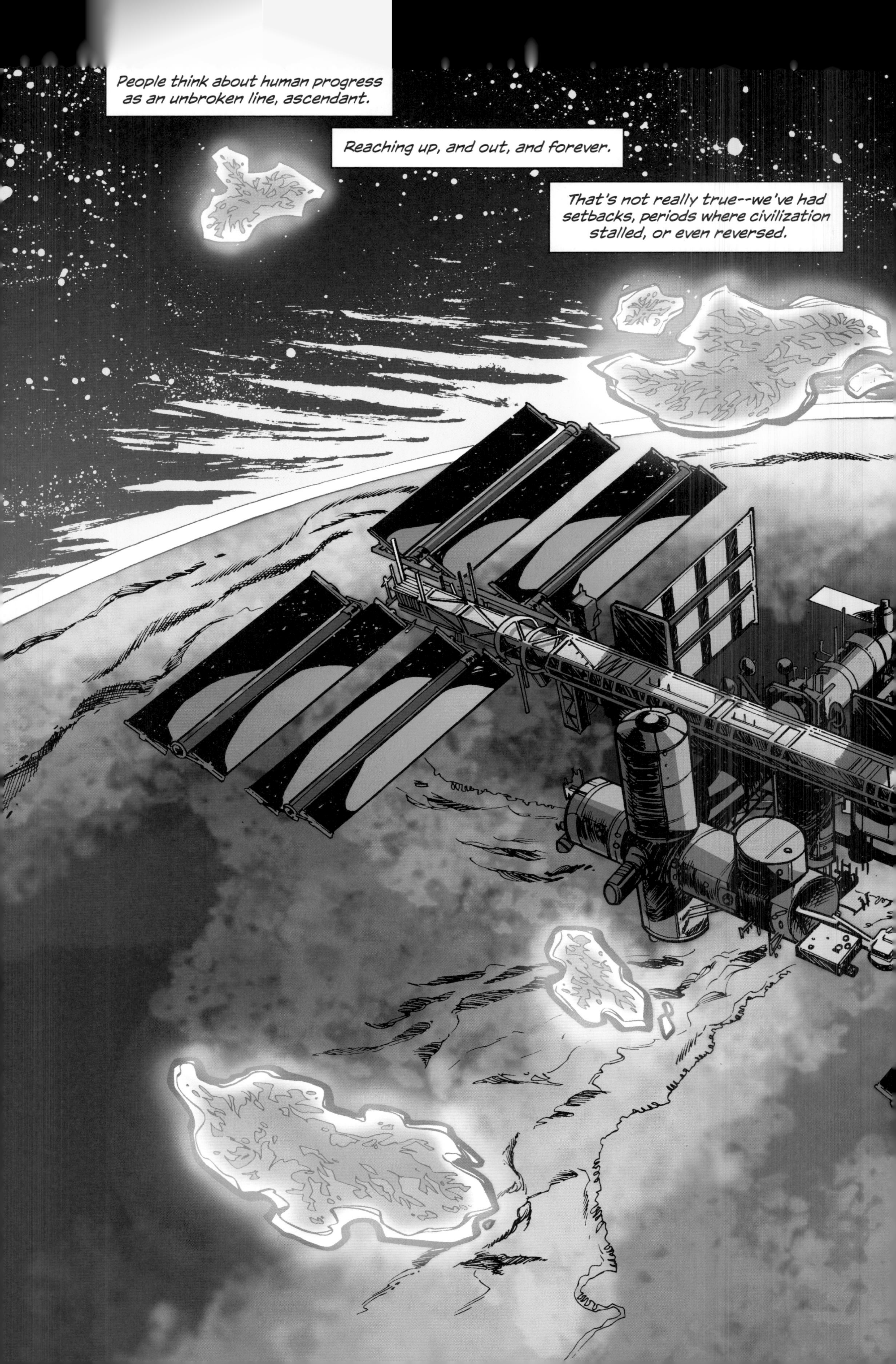
People think about human progress as an unbroken line, ascendant.
Reaching up, and out, and forever.
That's not really true--we've had setbacks, periods where civilization stalled, or even reversed.

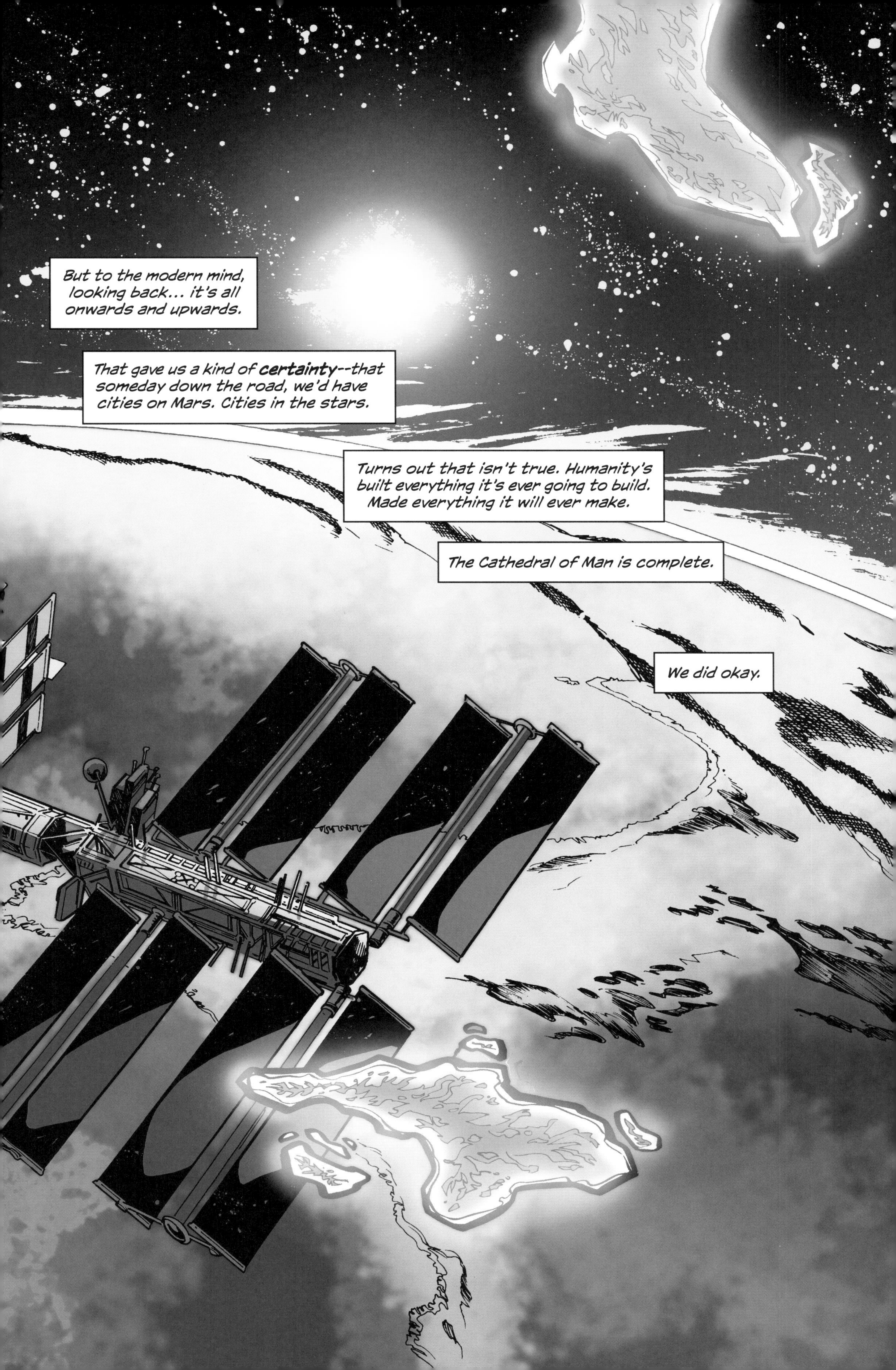
But to the modern mind, looking back... it's all onwards and upwards.
That gave us a kind of **certainty**--that someday down the road, we'd have cities on Mars. Cities in the stars.
Turns out that isn't true. Humanity's built everything it's ever going to build. Made everything it will ever make.
The Cathedral of Man is complete.
We did okay.

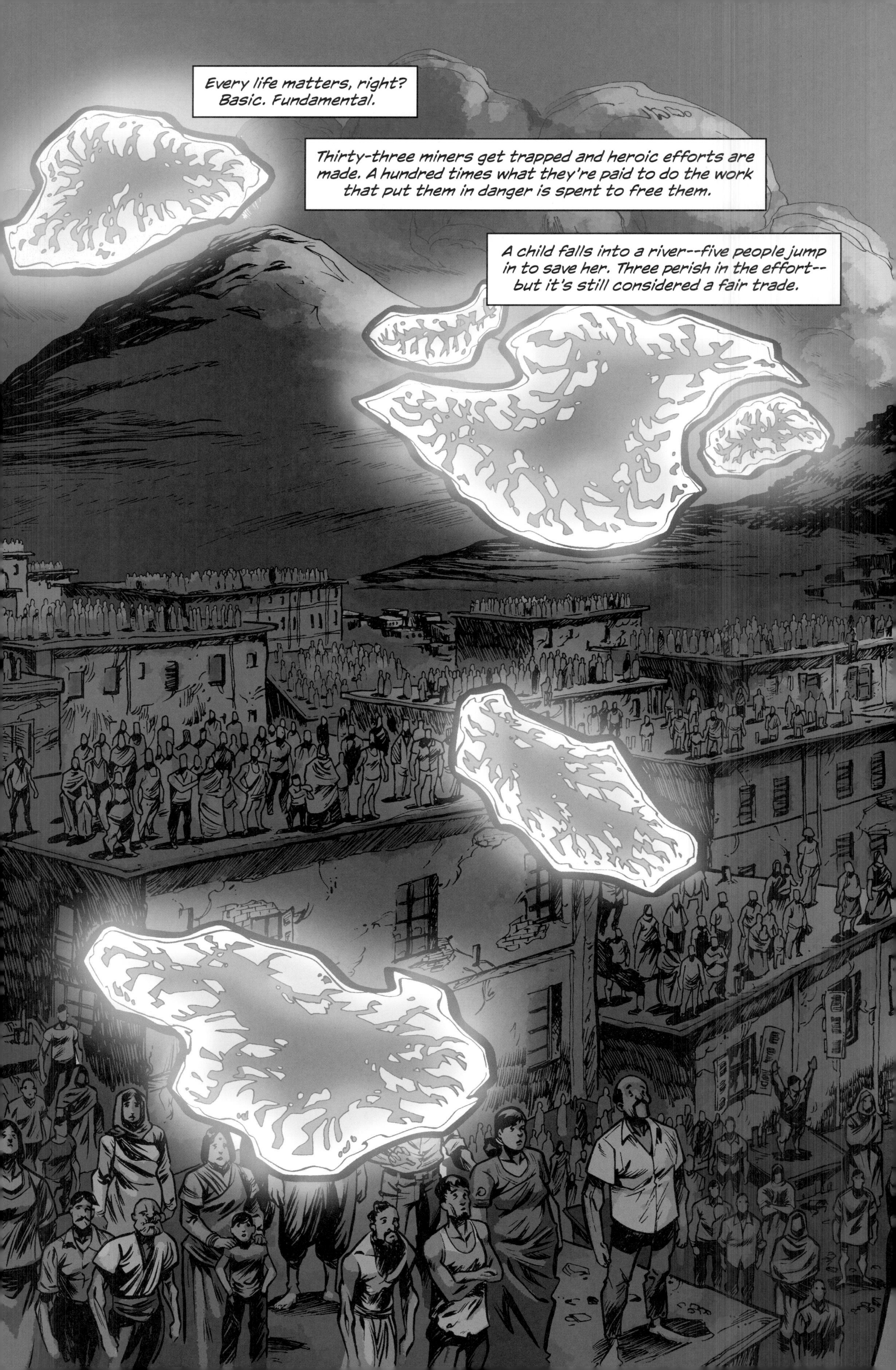
Every life matters, right? Basic. Fundamental.
Thirty-three miners get trapped and heroic efforts are made. A hundred times what they're paid to do the work that put them in danger is spent to free them.
A child falls into a river--five people jump in to save her. Three perish in the effort--but it's still considered a fair trade.

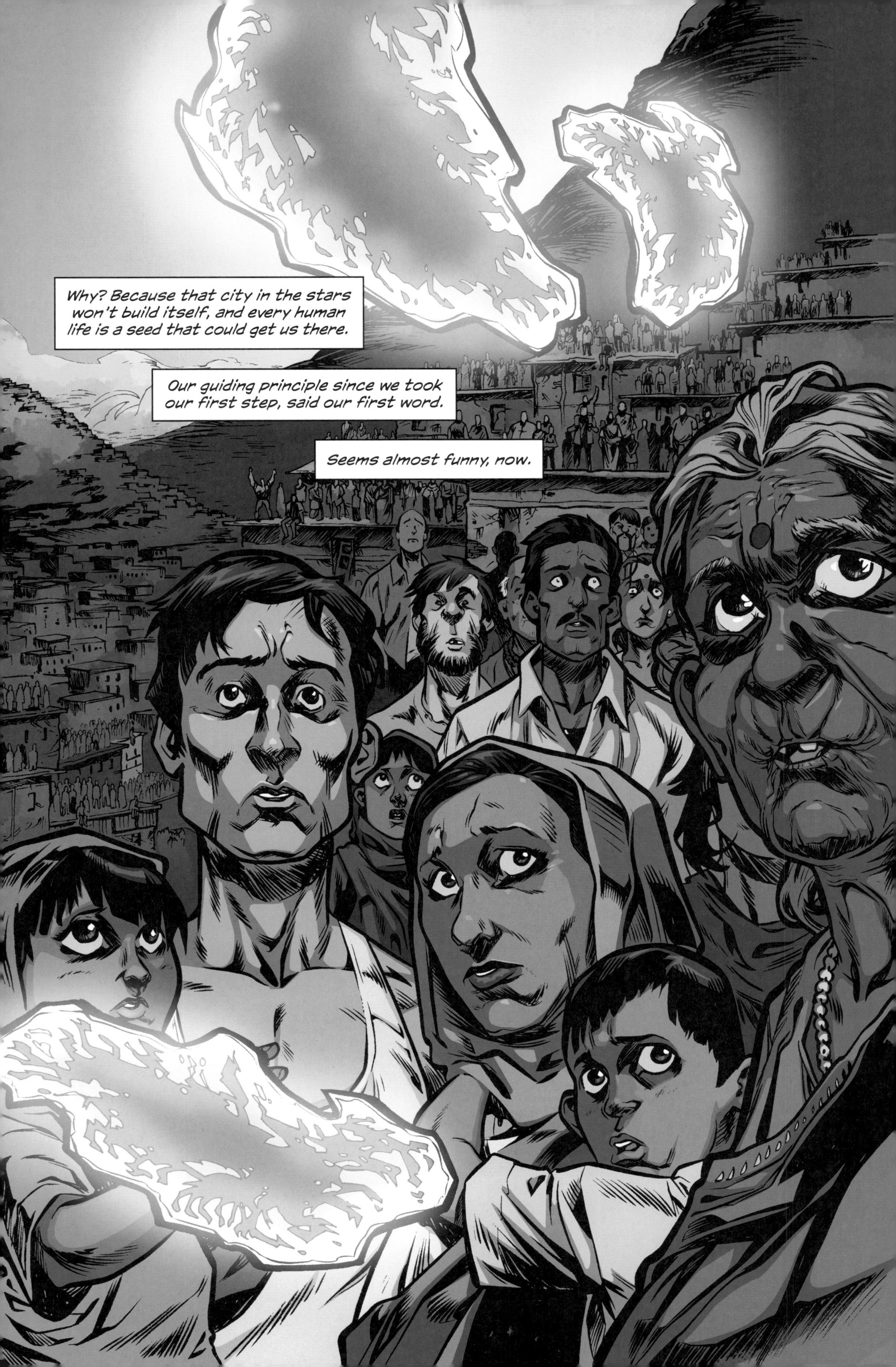
Why? Because that city in the stars won't build itself, and every human life is a seed that could get us there.
Our guiding principle since we took our first step, said our first word.
Seems almost funny, now.

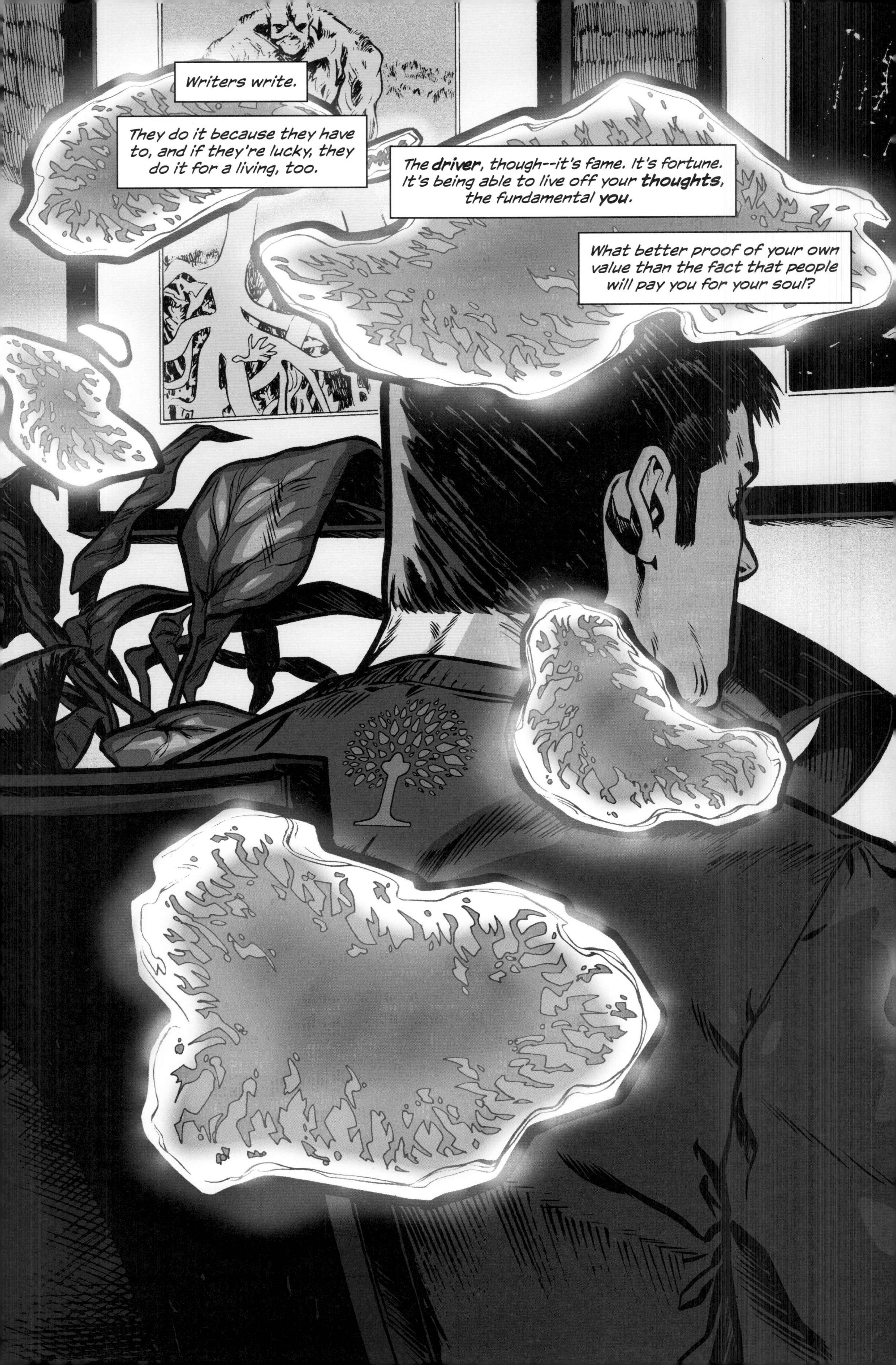
Writers write.
They do it because they have to, and if they're lucky, they do it for a living, too.
The **driver**, though--it's fame. It's fortune. It's being able to live off your **thoughts**, the fundamental **you**.
What better proof of your own value than the fact that people will pay you for your soul?

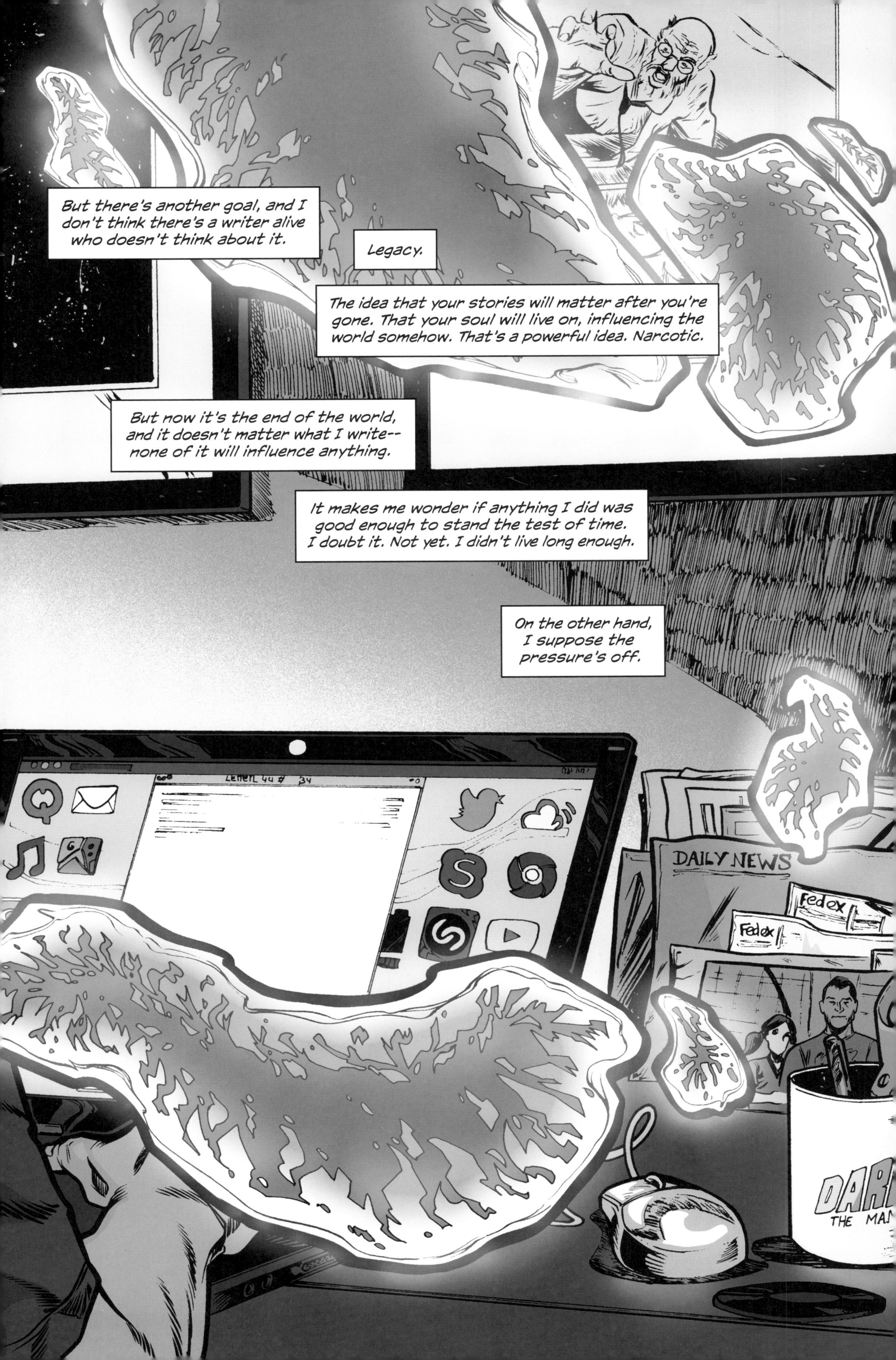

But there's another goal, and I don't think there's a writer alive who doesn't think about it.
Legacy.
The idea that your stories will matter after you're gone. That your soul will live on, influencing the world somehow. That's a powerful idea. Narcotic.
But now it's the end of the world, and it doesn't matter what I write--none of it will influence anything.
It makes me wonder if anything I did was good enough to stand the test of time. I doubt it. Not yet. I didn't live long enough.
On the other hand, I suppose the pressure's off.
DAILY NEWS
Fedex
Fedex

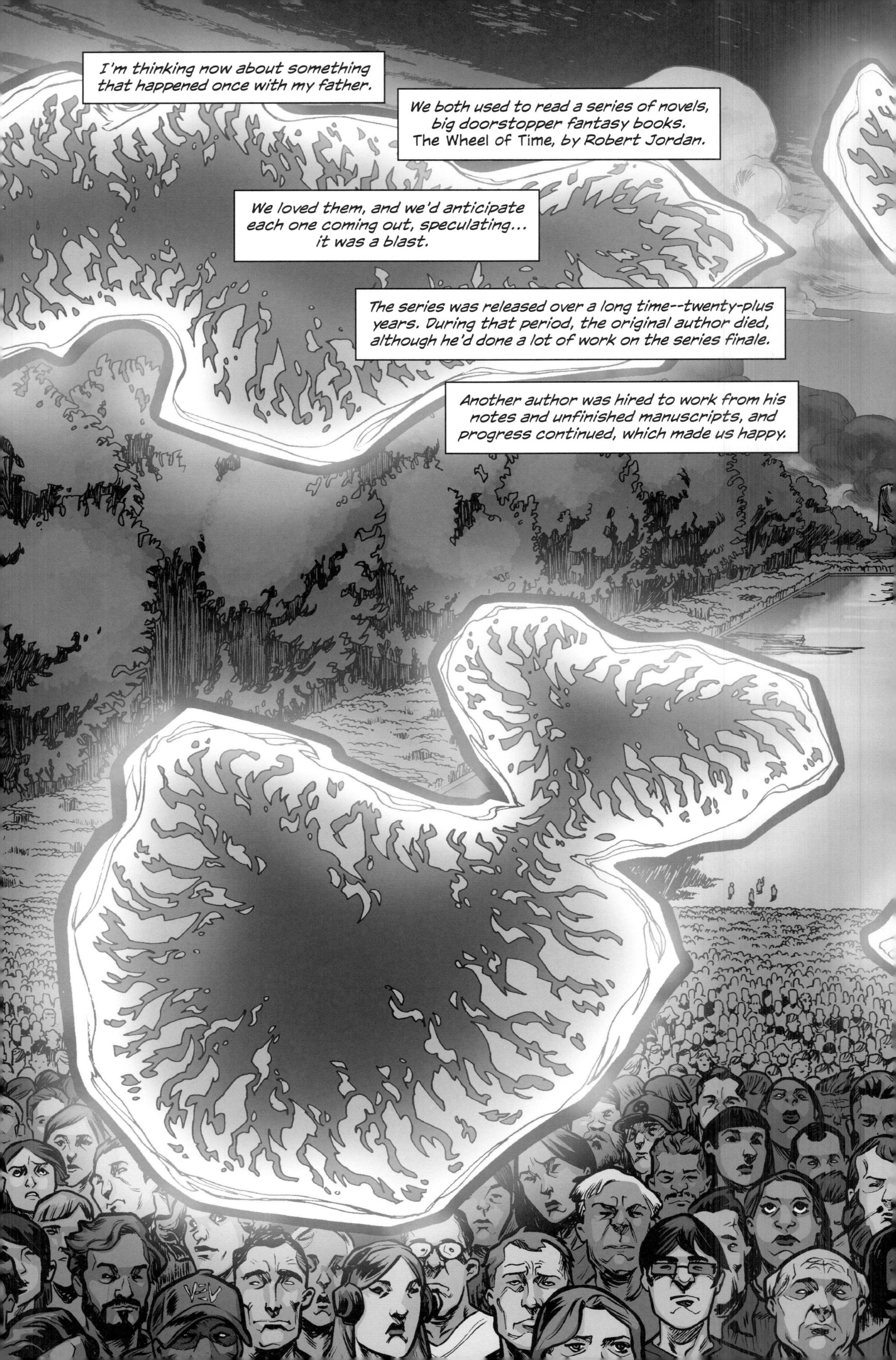
I'm thinking now about something that happened once with my father.
We both used to read a series of novels, big doorstopper fantasy books. The Wheel of Time, by Robert Jordan.
We loved them, and we'd anticipate each one coming out, speculating... it was a blast.
The series was released over a long time--twenty-plus years. During that period, the original author died, although he'd done a lot of work on the series finale.
Another author was hired to work from his notes and unfinished manuscripts, and progress continued, which made us happy.

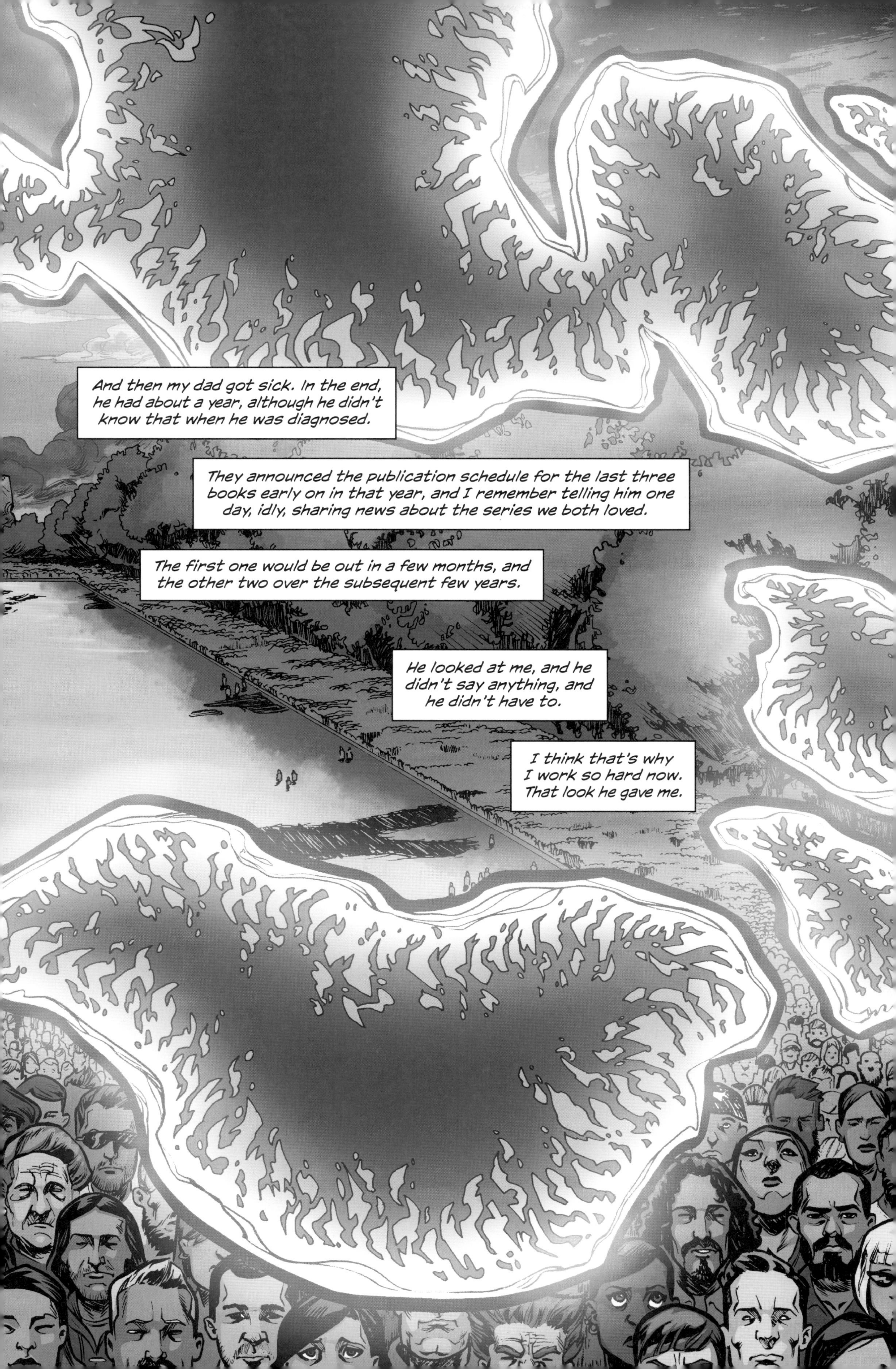
And then my dad got sick. In the end, he had about a year, although he didn't know that when he was diagnosed.
They announced the publication schedule for the last three books early on in that year, and I remember telling him one day, idly, sharing news about the series we both loved.
The first one would be out in a few months, and the other two over the subsequent few years.
He looked at me, and he didn't say anything, and he didn't have to.
I think that's why I work so hard now. That look he gave me.

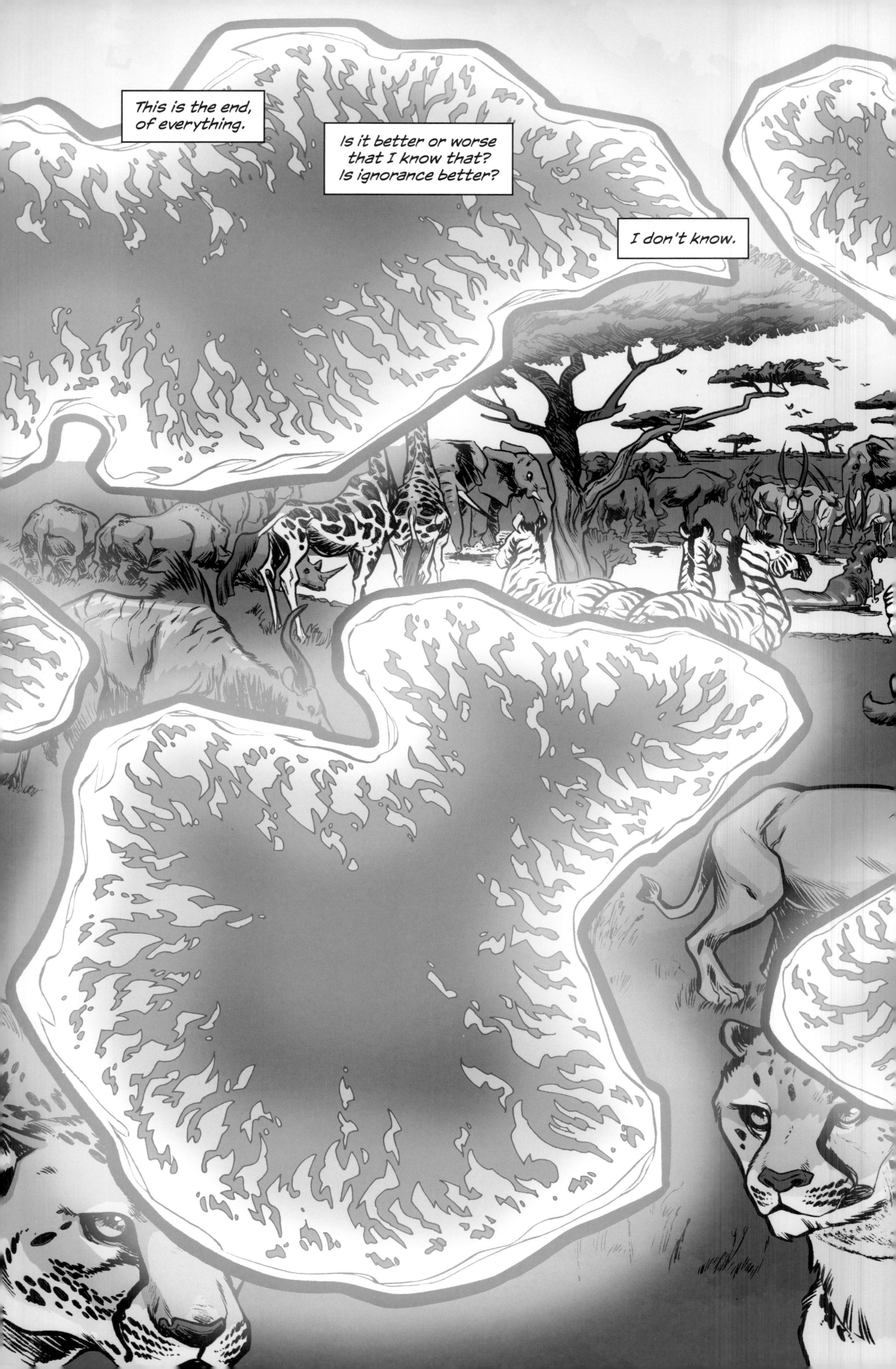
This is the end, of everything.
Is it better or worse that I know that? Is ignorance better?
I don't know.

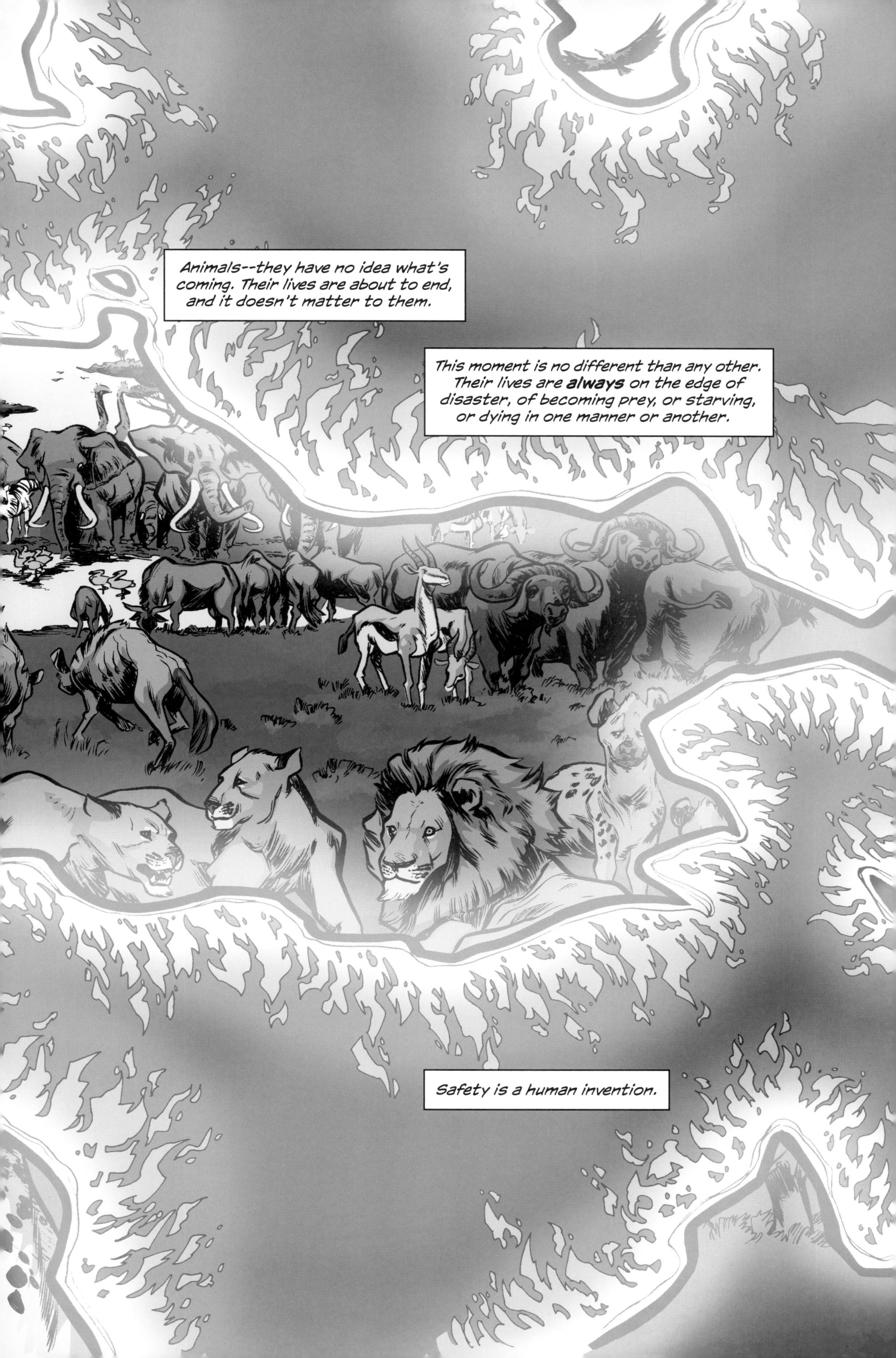
Animals--they have no idea what's coming. Their lives are about to end, and it doesn't matter to them.
This moment is no different than any other. Their lives are **always** on the edge of disaster, of becoming prey, or starving, or dying in one manner or another.
Safety is a human invention.

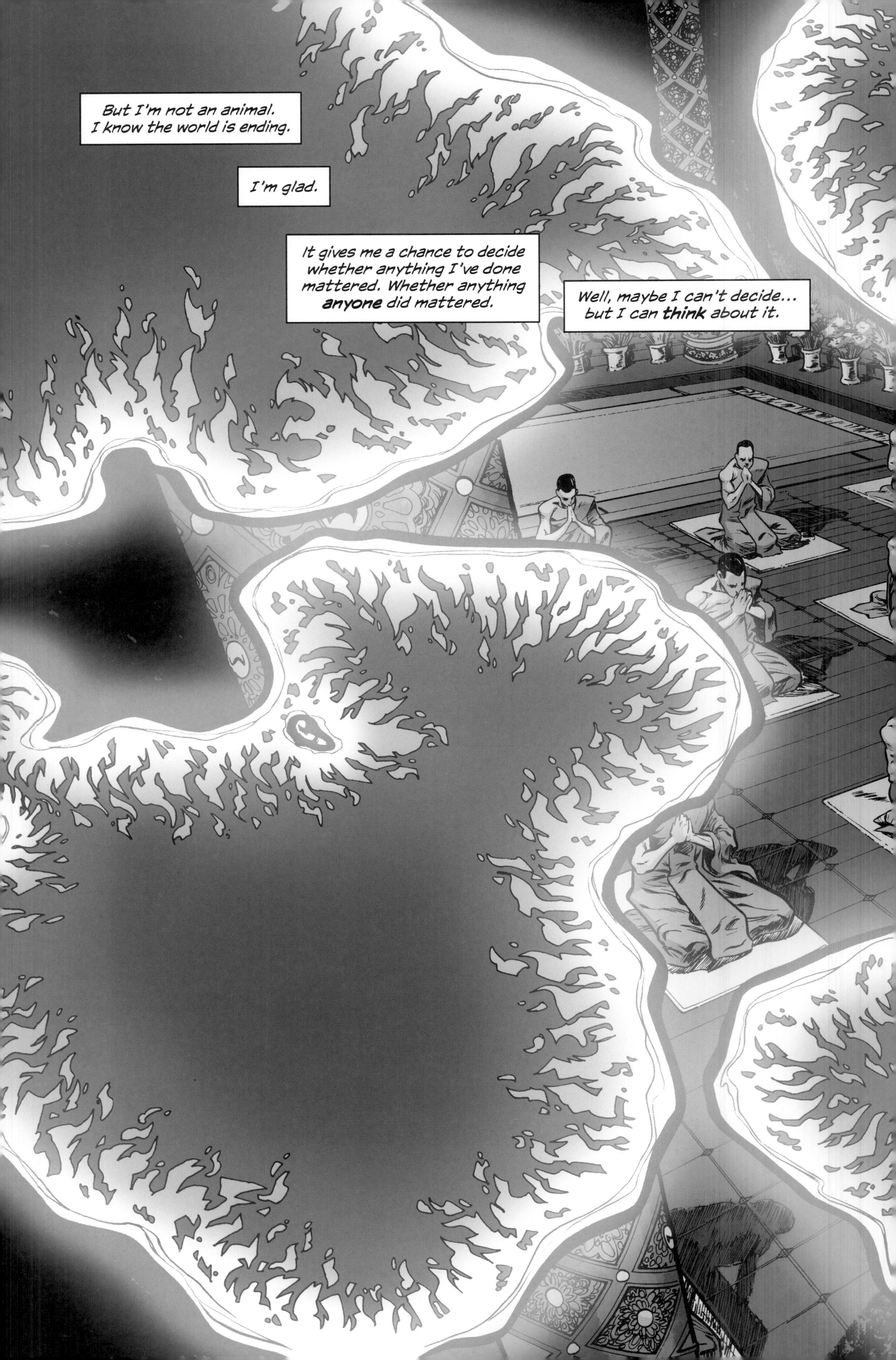
But I'm not an animal. I know the world is ending.
I'm glad.
It gives me a chance to decide whether anything I've done mattered. Whether anything **anyone** did mattered.
Well, maybe I can't decide... but I can **think** about it.

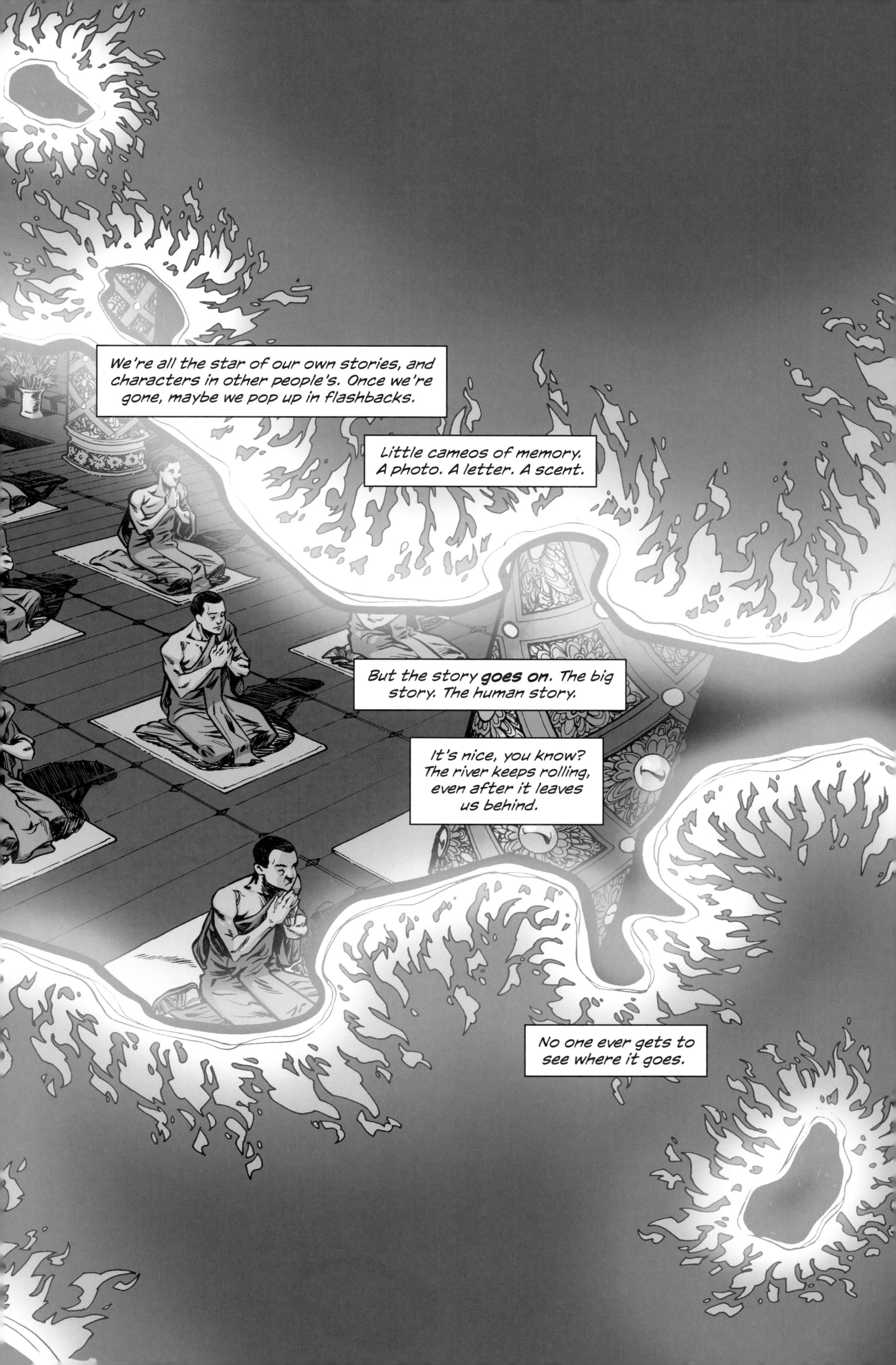
We're all the star of our own stories, and characters in other people's. Once we're gone, maybe we pop up in flashbacks.
Little cameos of memory. A photo. A letter. A scent.
But the story **goes on**. The big story. The human story.
It's nice, you know? The river keeps rolling, even after it leaves us behind.
No one ever gets to see where it goes.

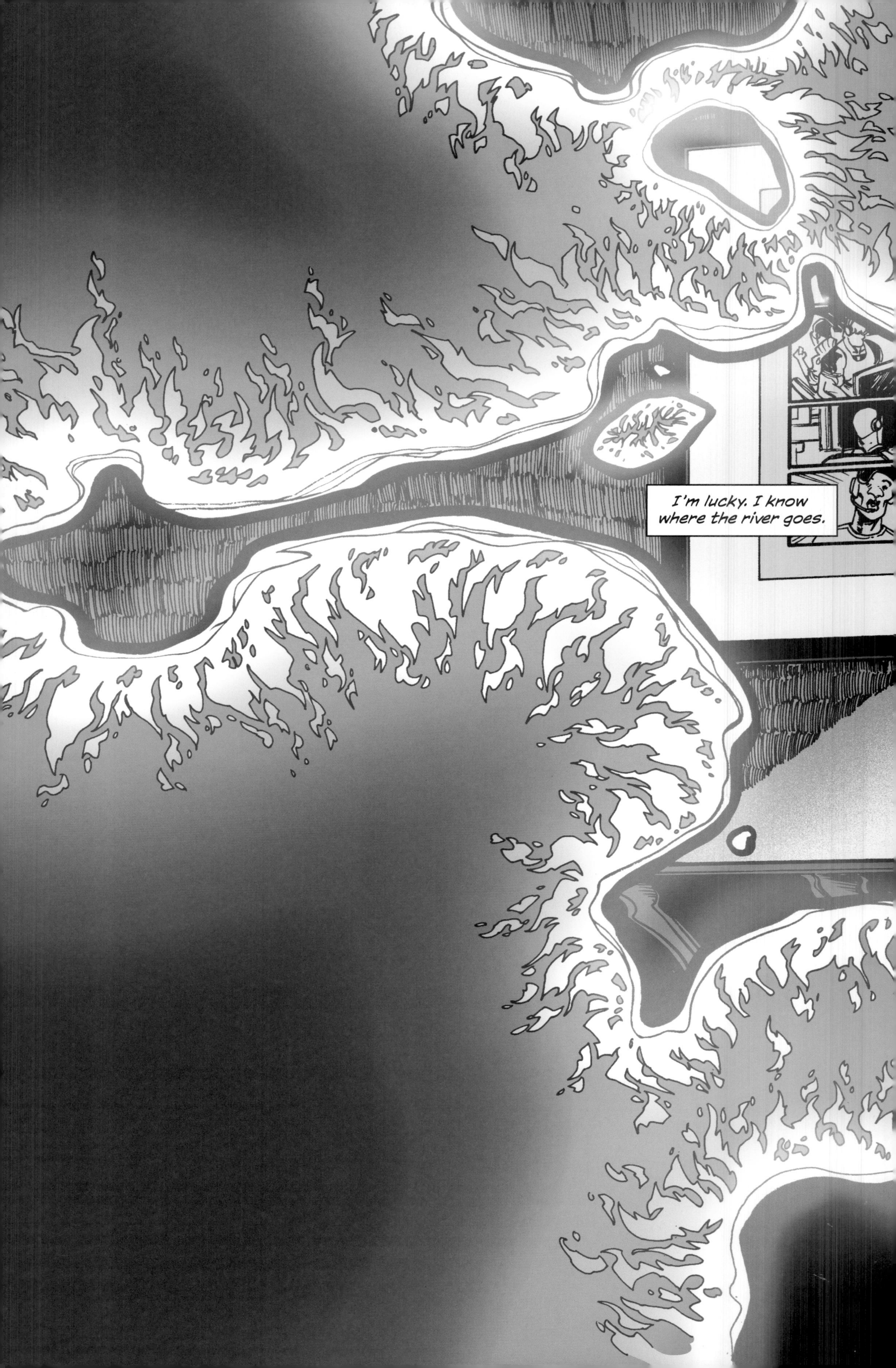
I'm lucky. I know where the river goes.

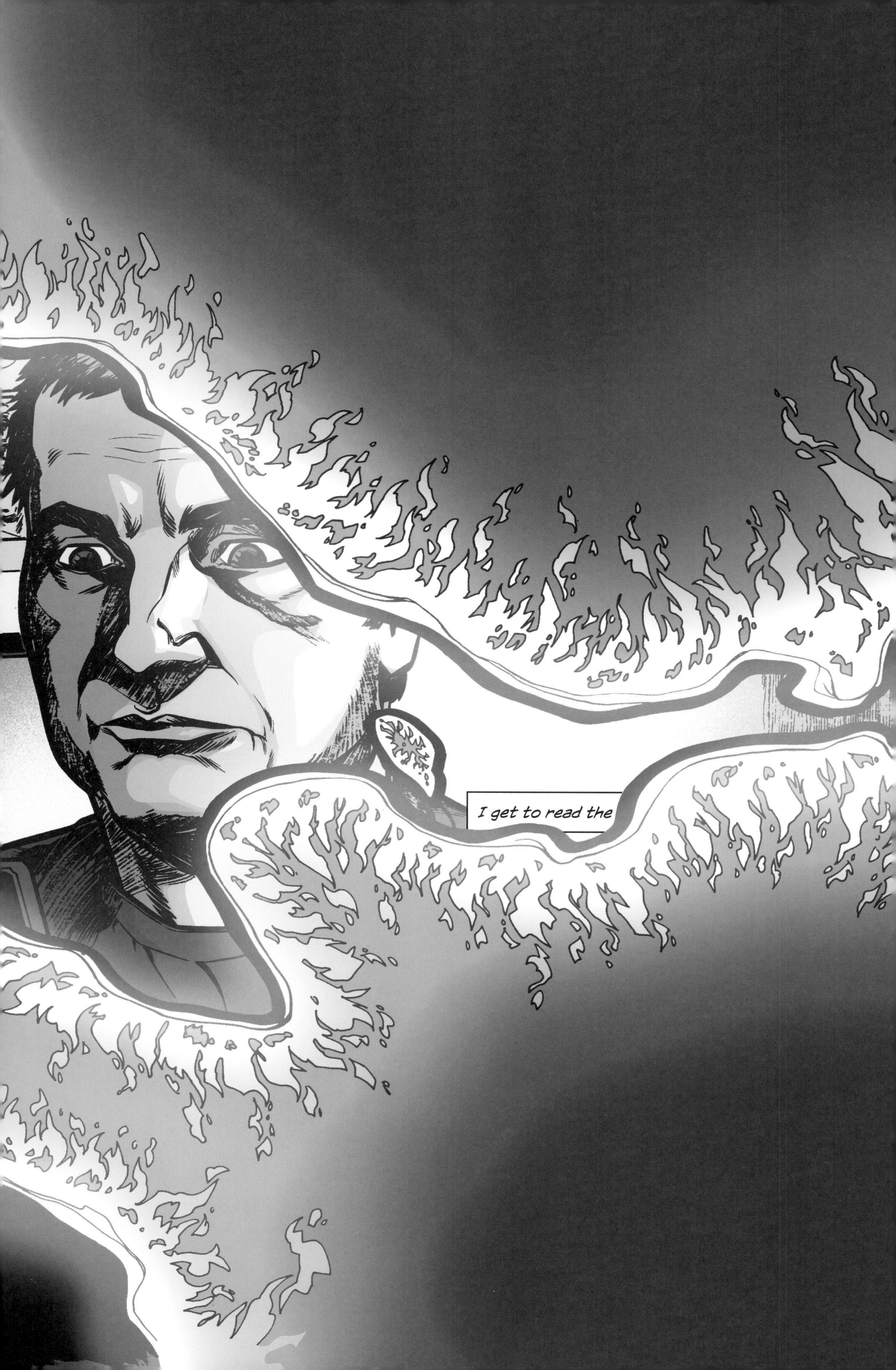
I get to read the

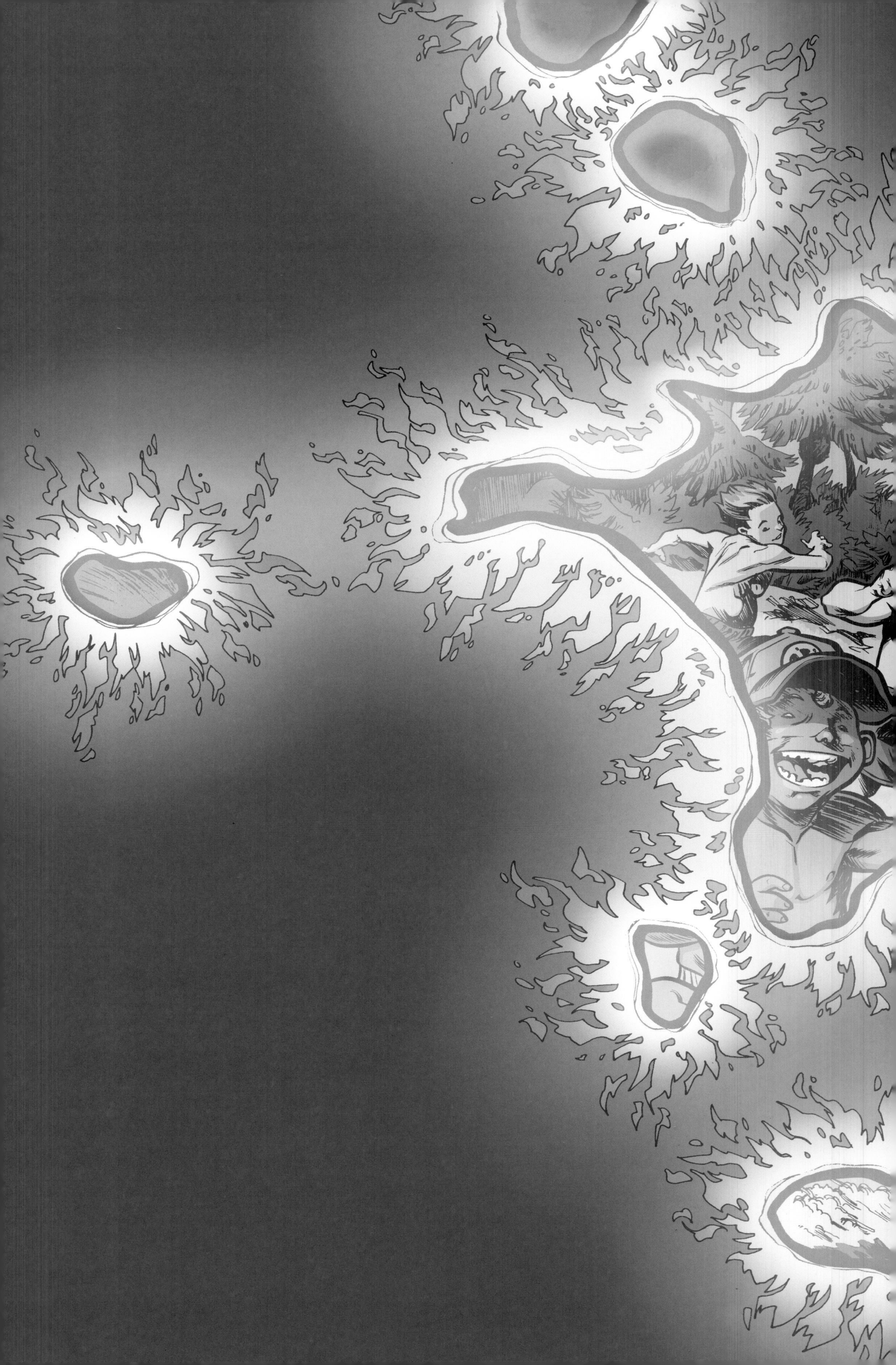

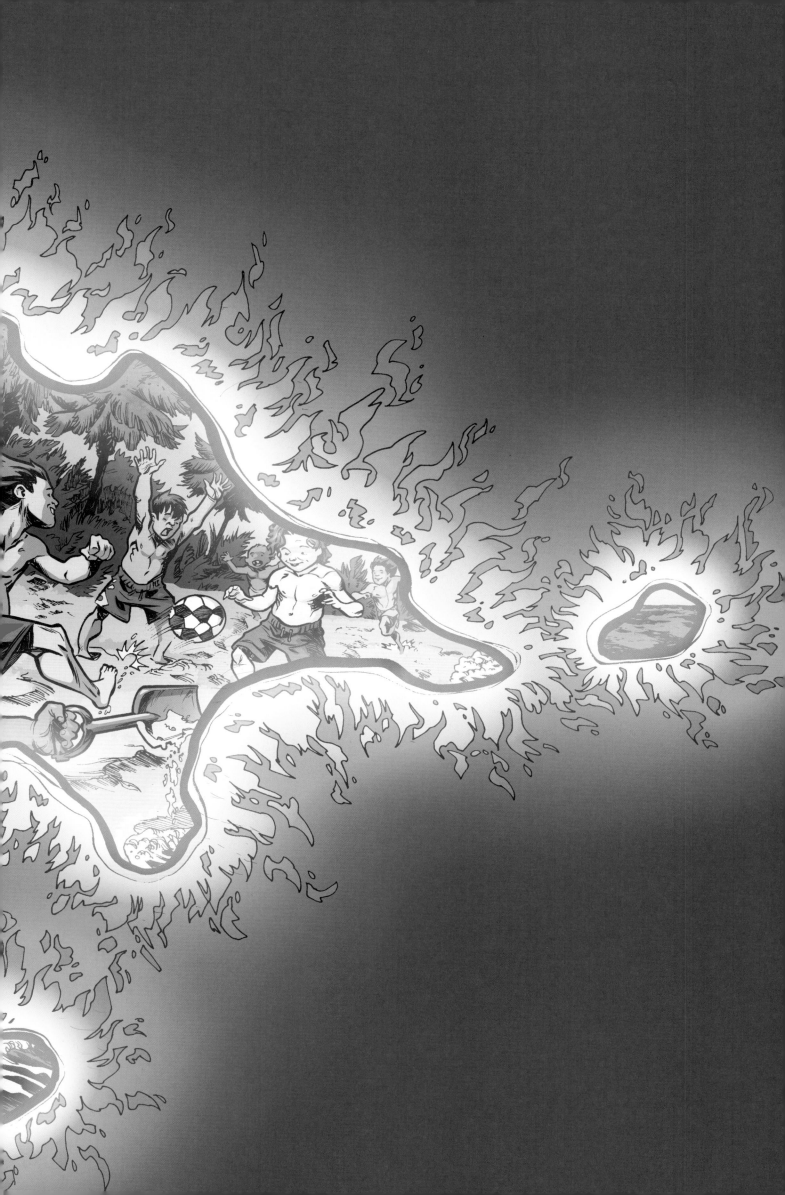

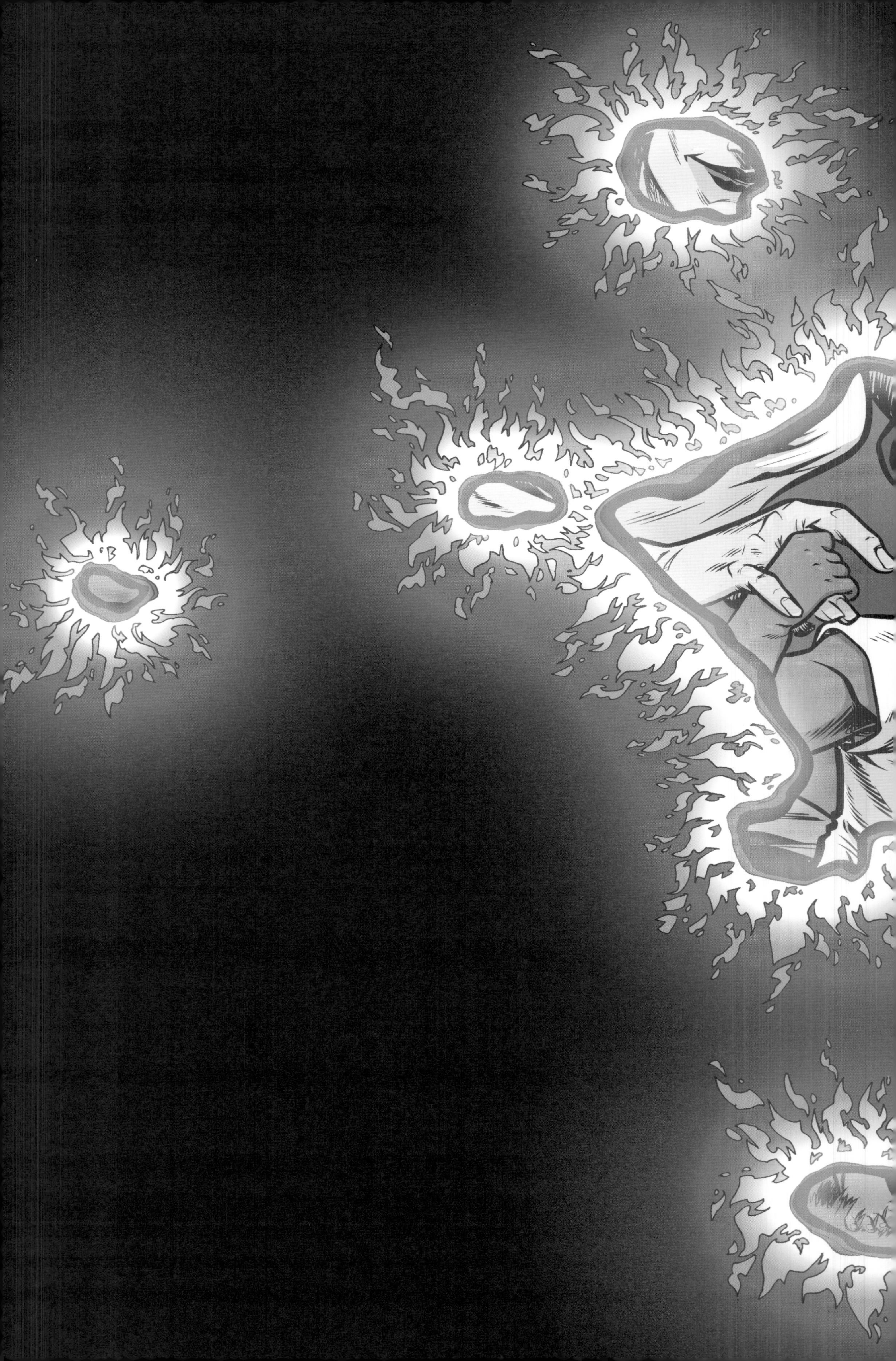

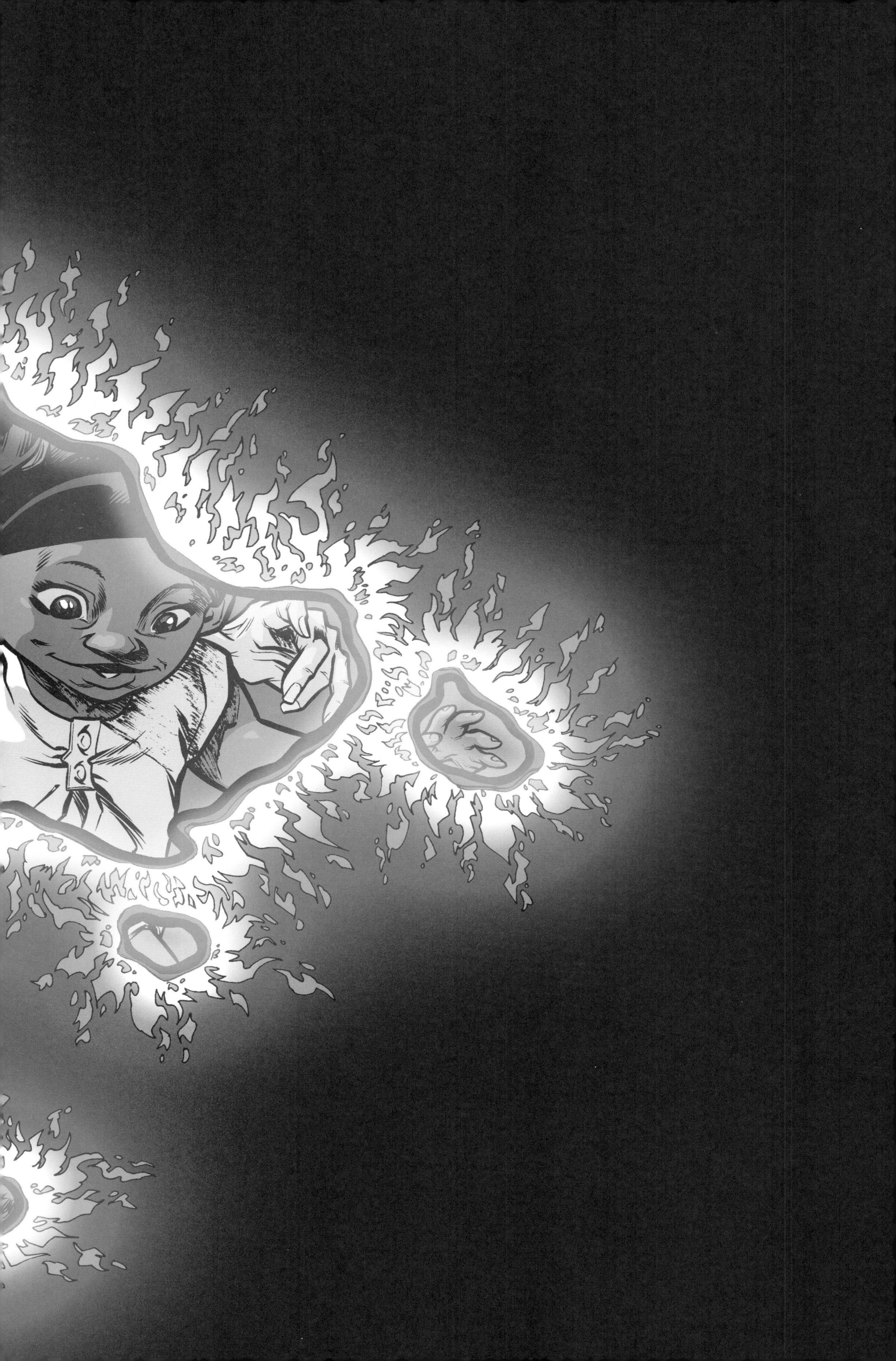

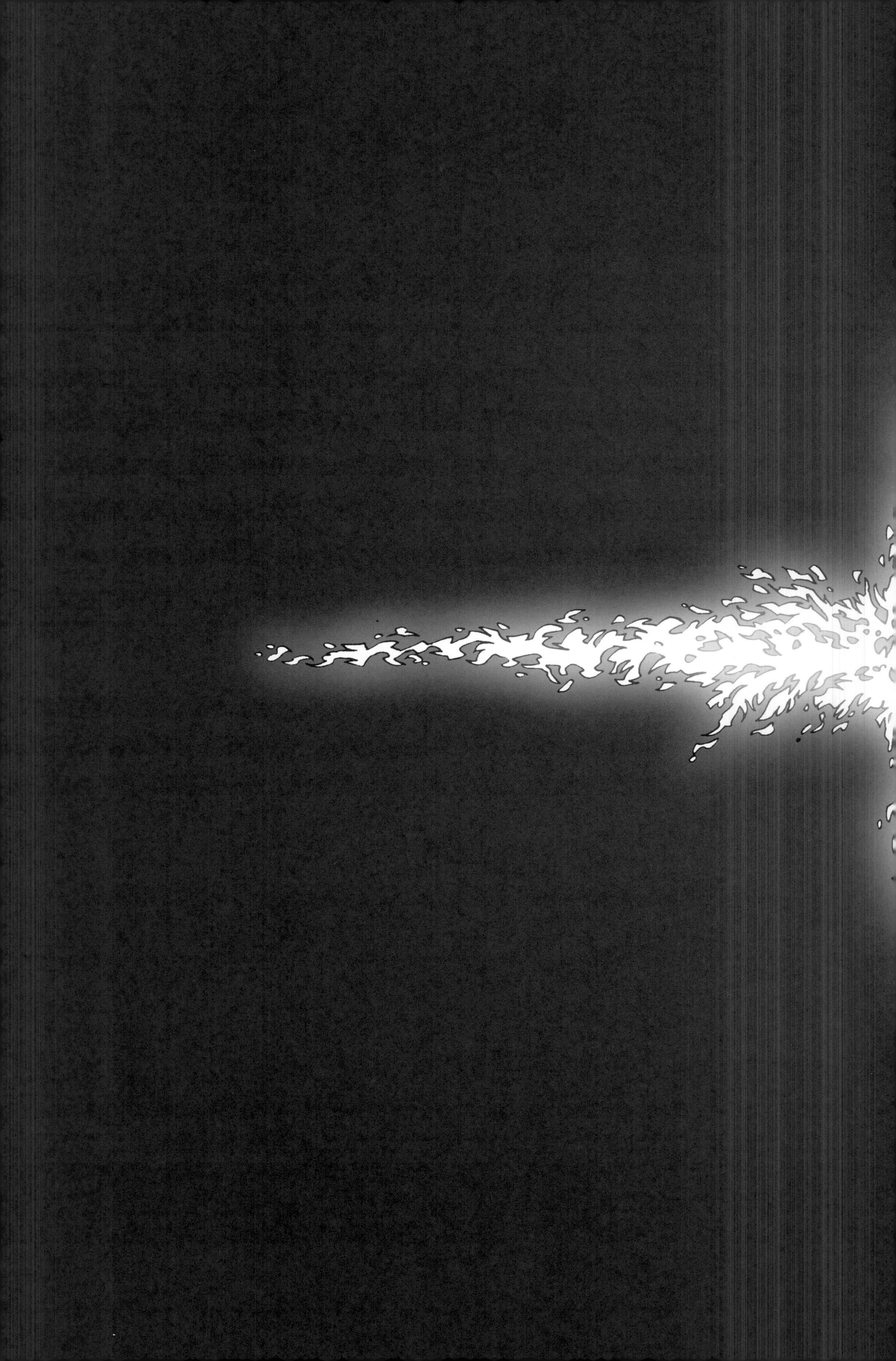

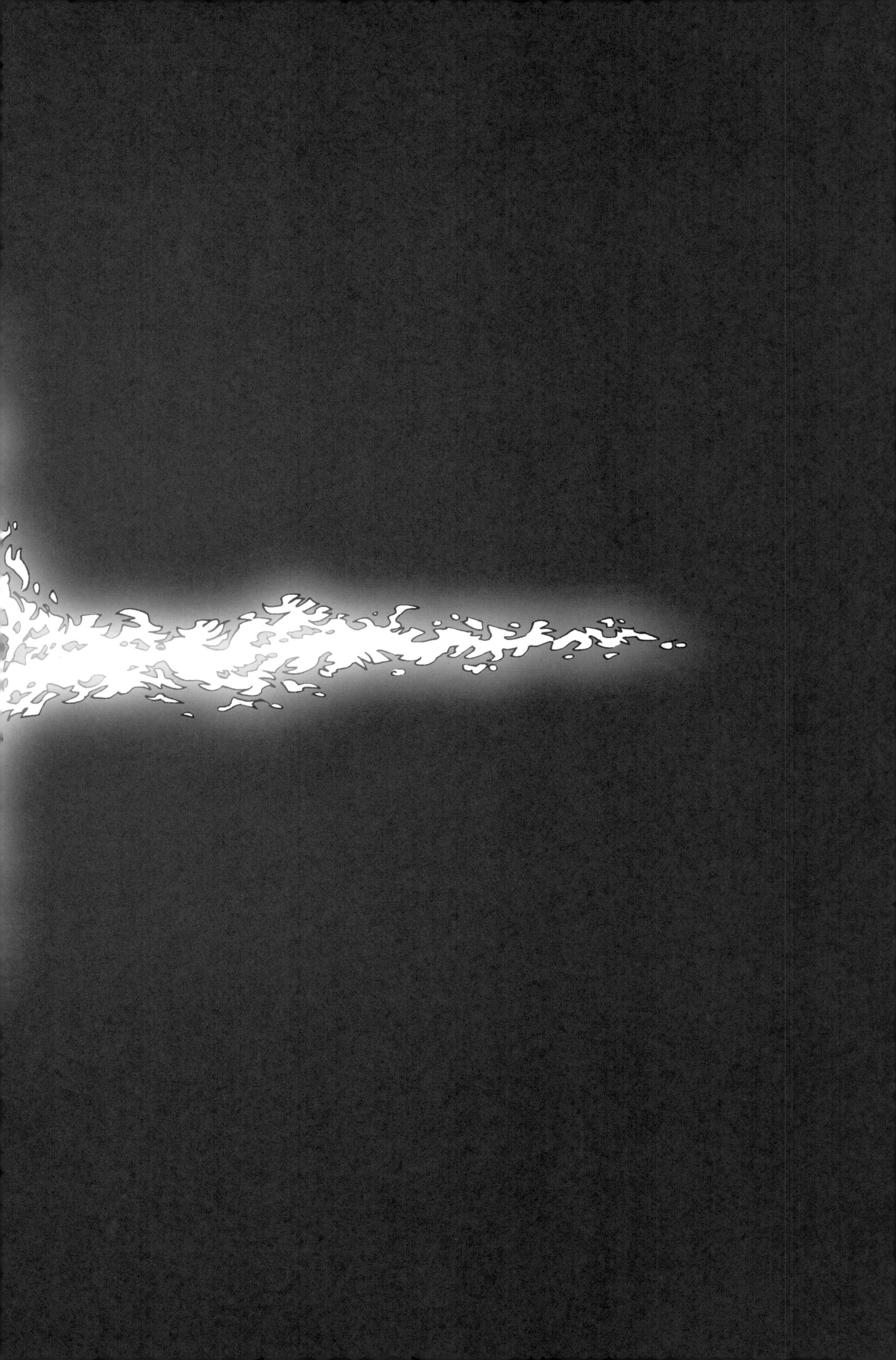

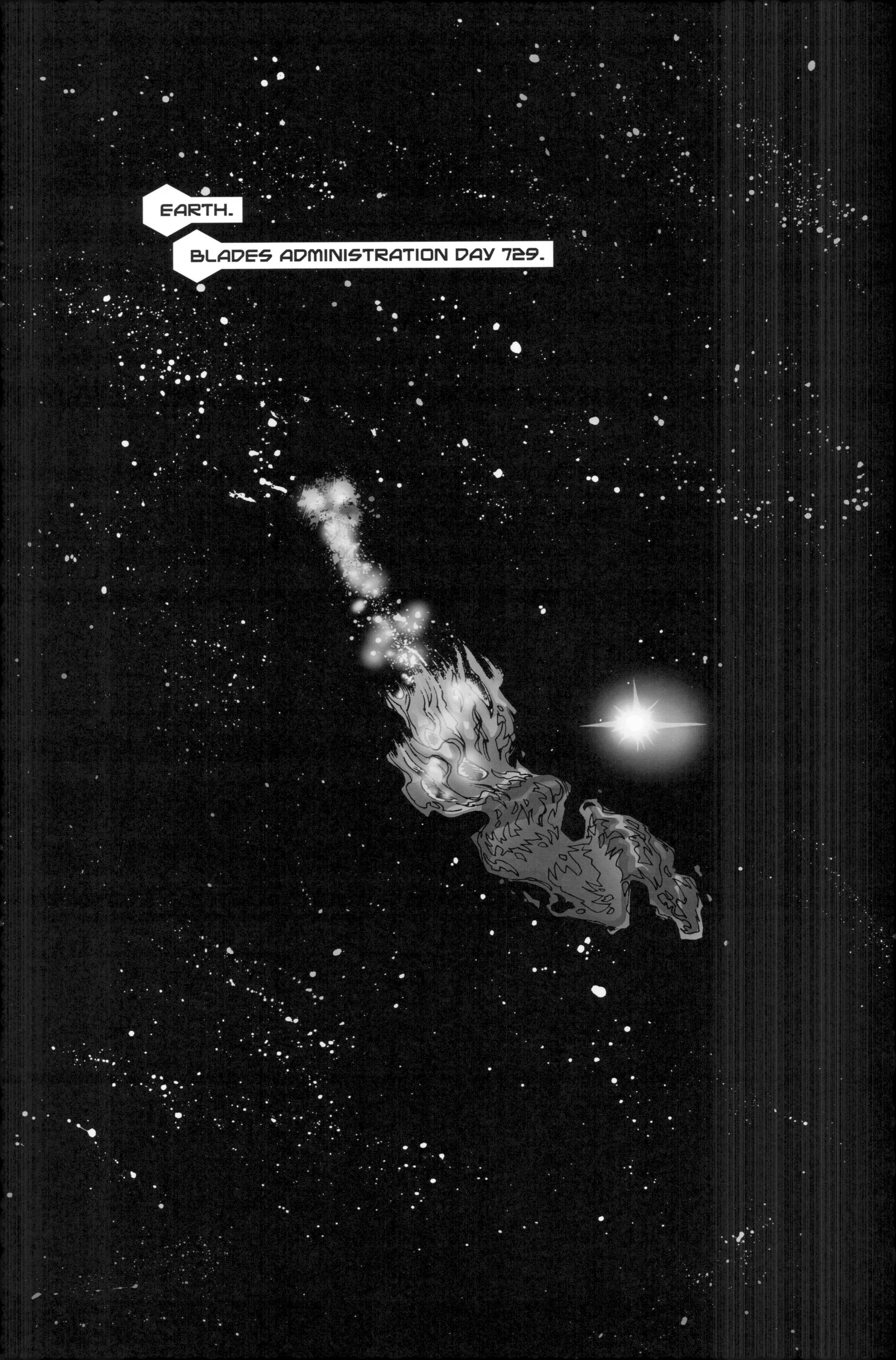
EARTH.
BLADES ADMINISTRATION DAY 729.

LETTER 44

CHAPTER XI

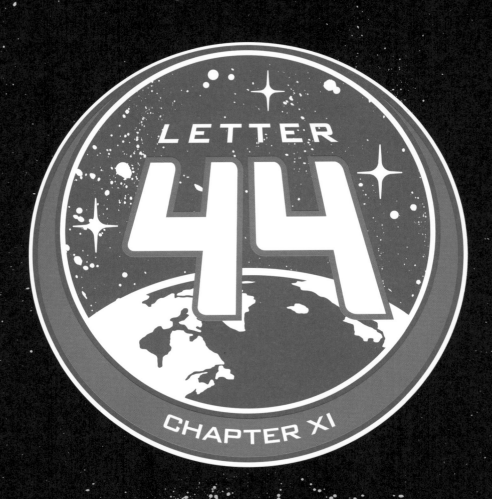

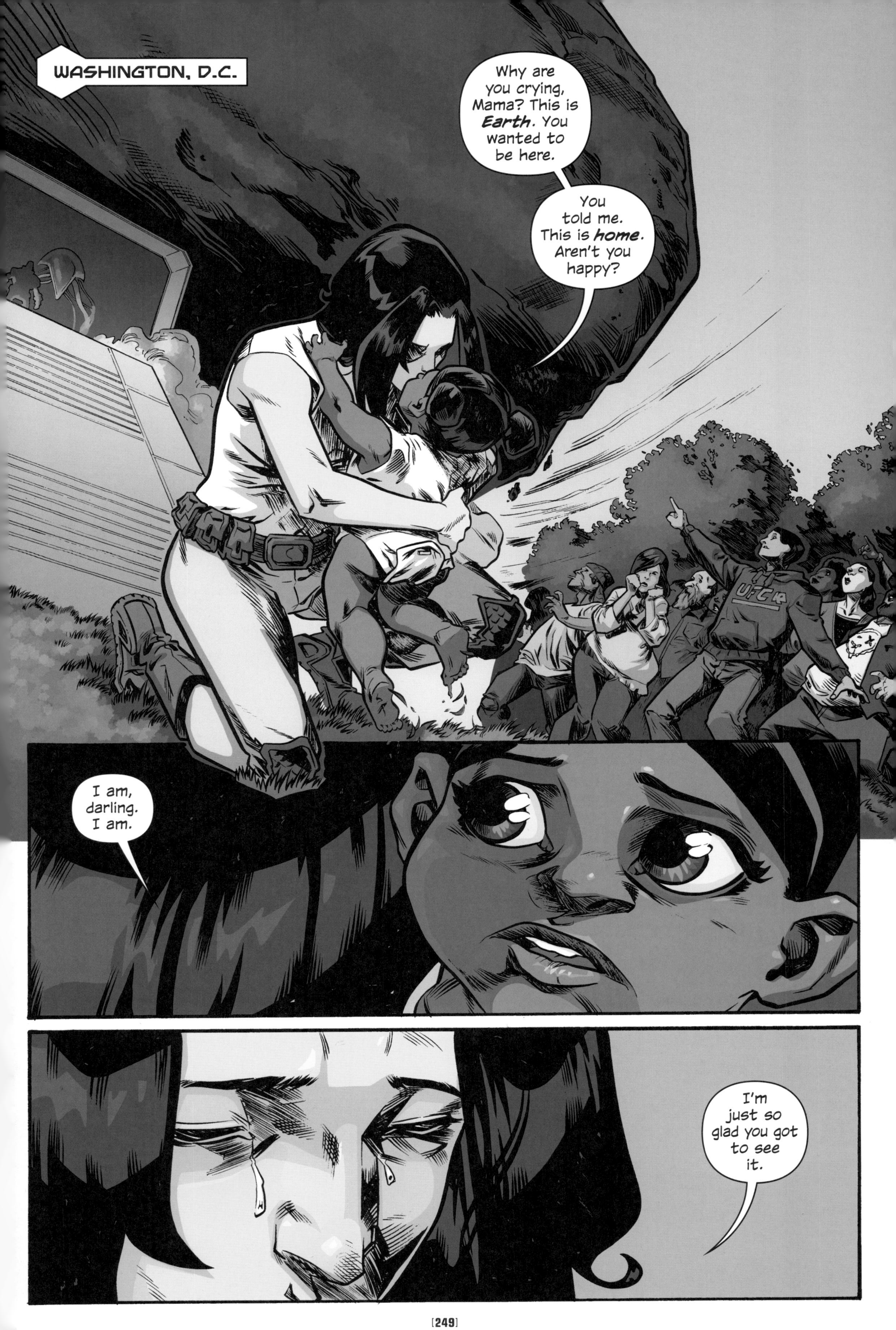
WASHINGTON, D.C.
Why are you crying, Mama? This is *Earth*. You wanted to be here.
You told me. This is *home*. Aren't you happy?
I am, darling. I am.
I'm just so glad you got to see it.

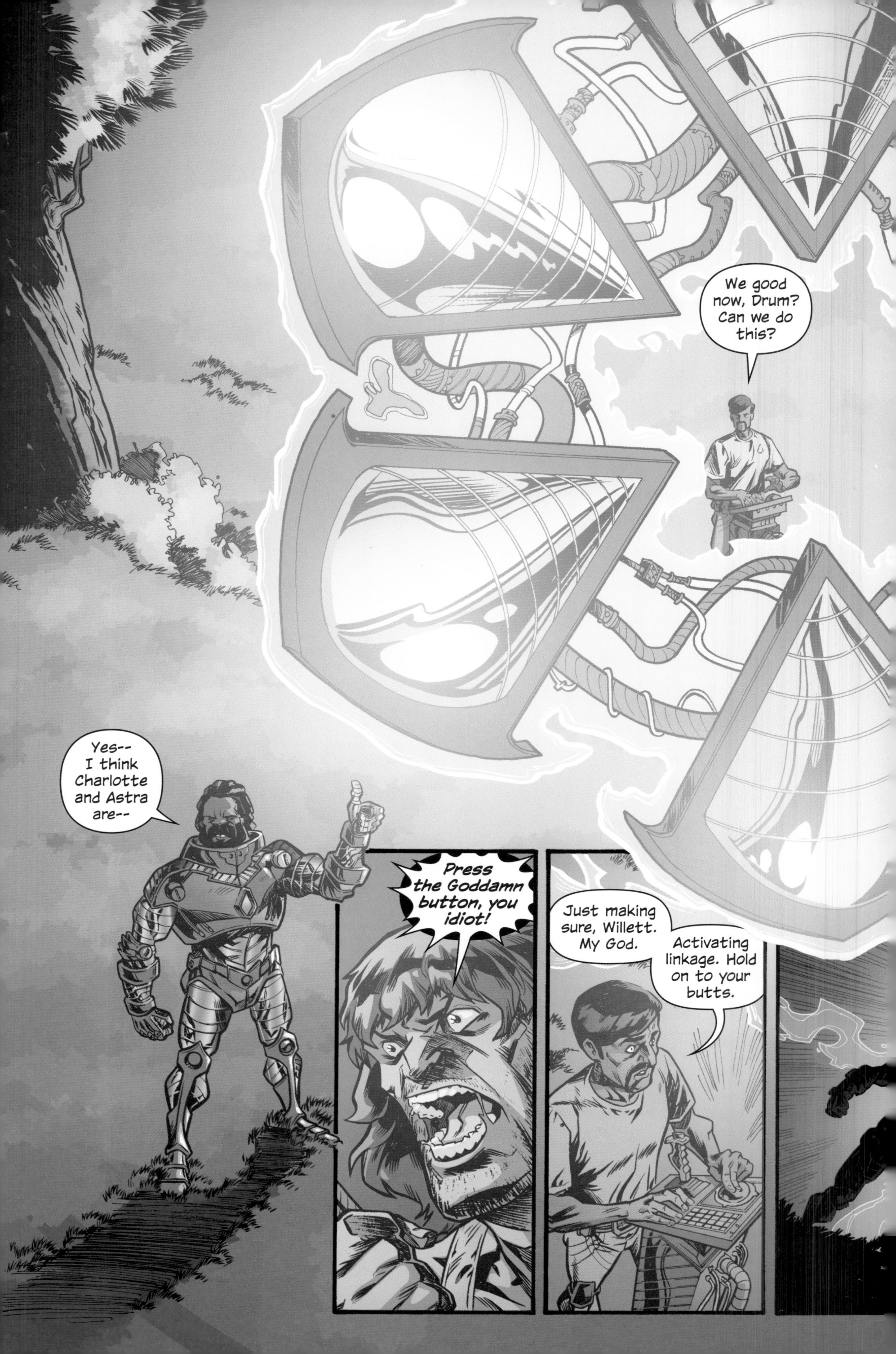
We good now, Drum? Can we do this?
Yes-- I think Charlotte and Astra are--
Press the Goddamn button, you idiot!
Just making sure, Willett. My God.
Activating linkage. Hold on to your butts.

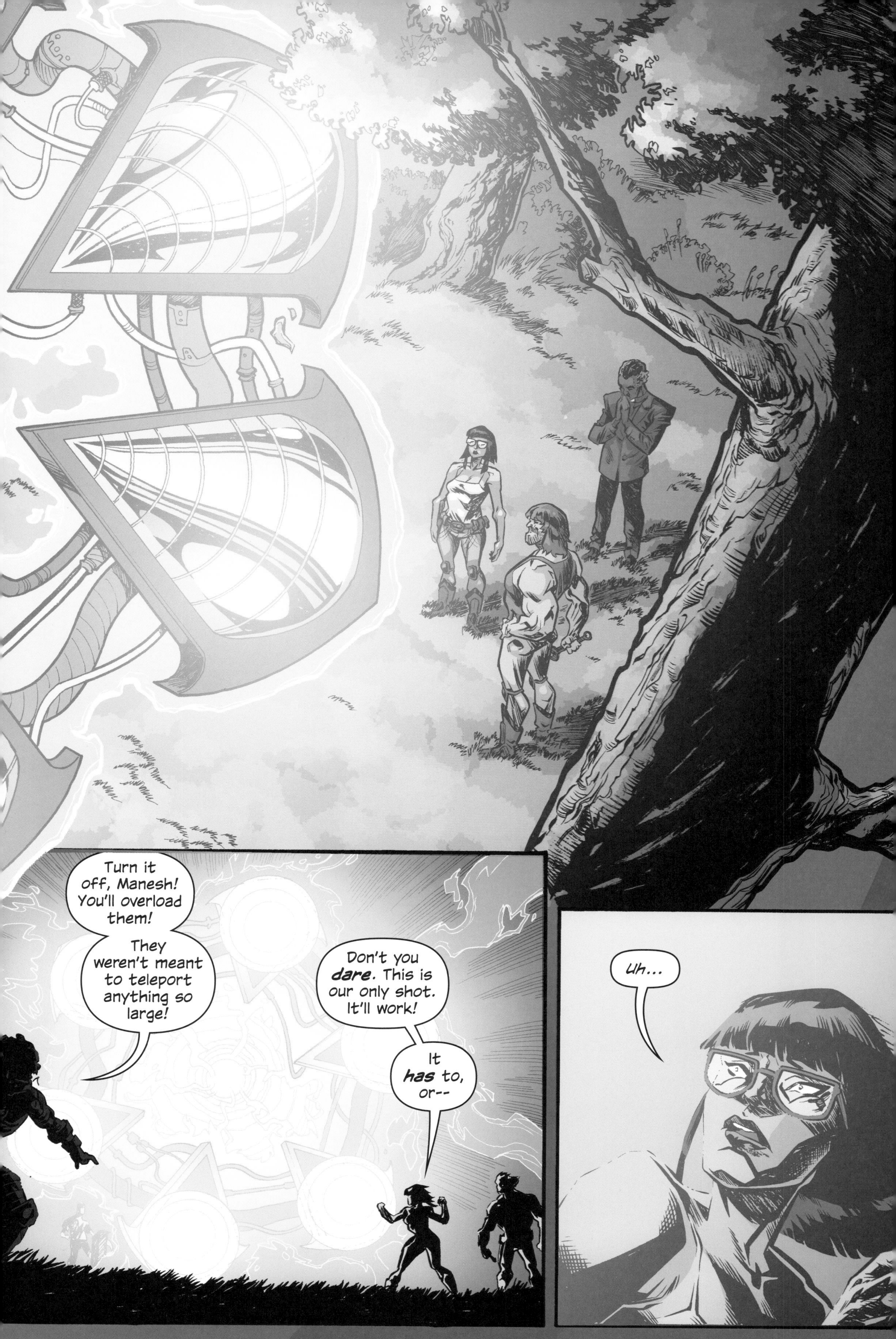
Turn it off, Manesh! You'll overload them!
They weren't meant to teleport anything so large!
Don't you *dare*. This is our only shot. It'll work!
It *has* to, or--
Uh...

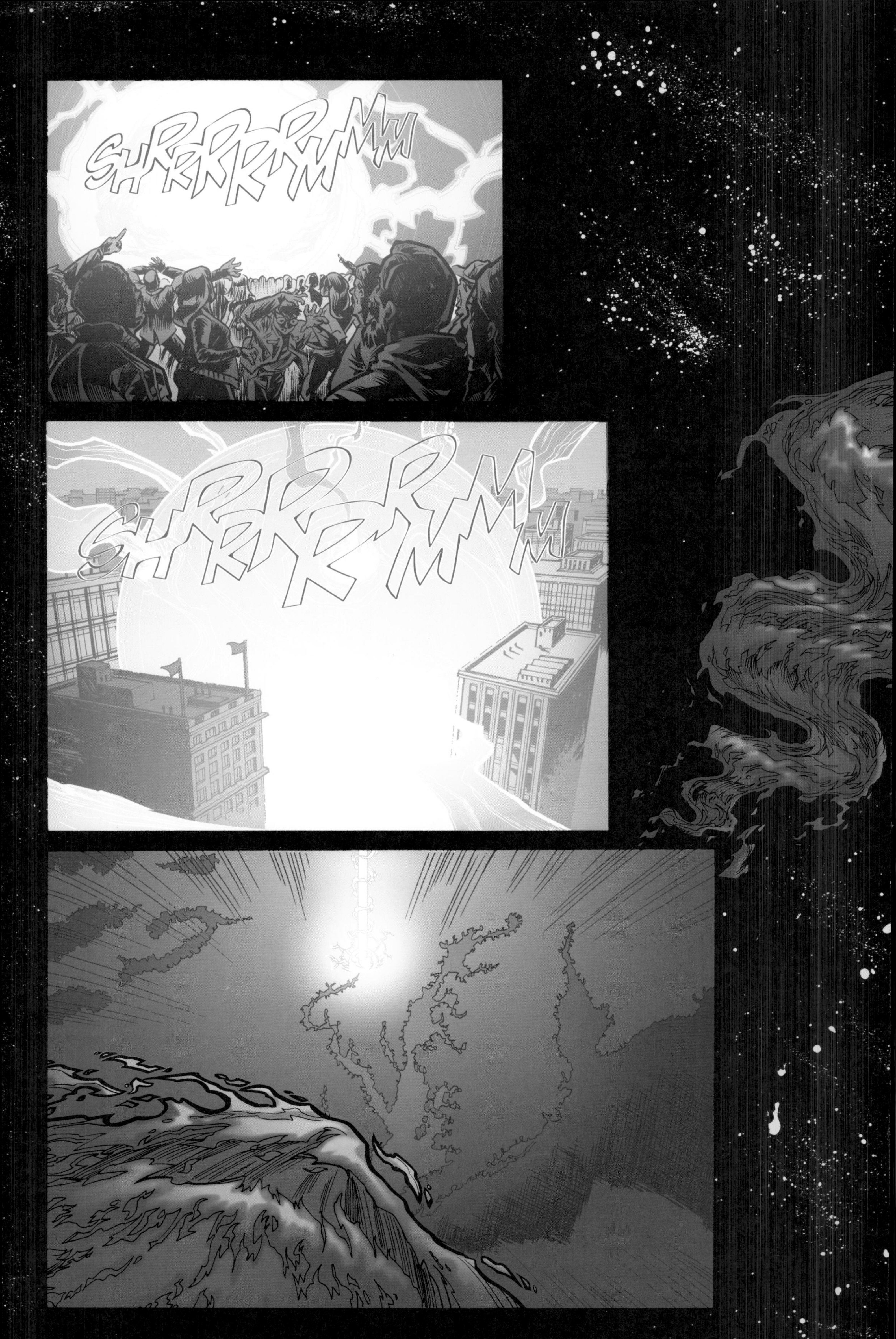
SHRRRRMMM
SHRRRRRMMM

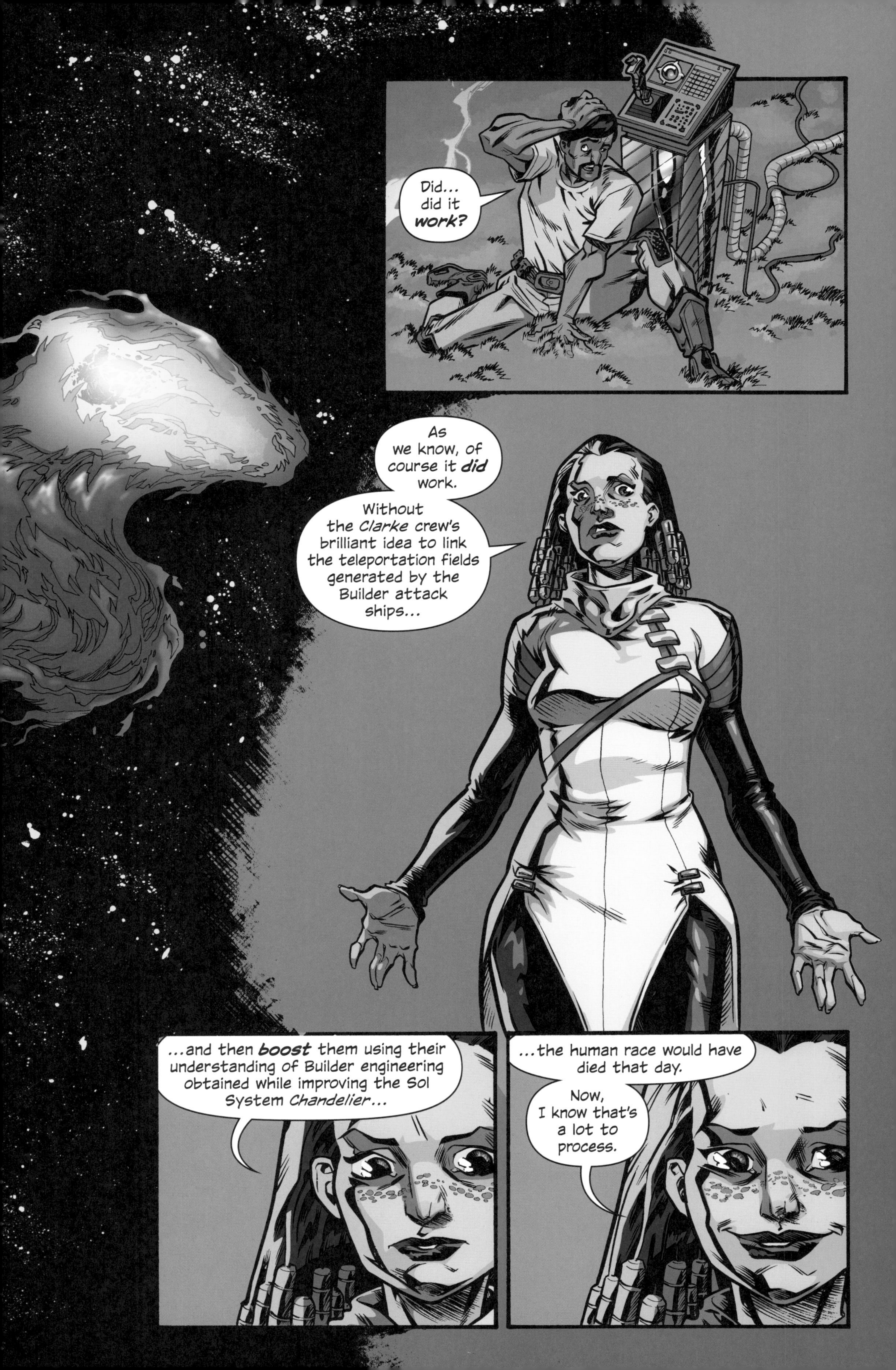

Did... did it **work?**
As we know, of course it ***did*** work.
Without the *Clarke* crew's brilliant idea to link the teleportation fields generated by the Builder attack ships...
...and then ***boost*** them using their understanding of Builder engineering obtained while improving the Sol System *Chandelier*...
...the human race would have died that day.
Now, I know that's a lot to process.

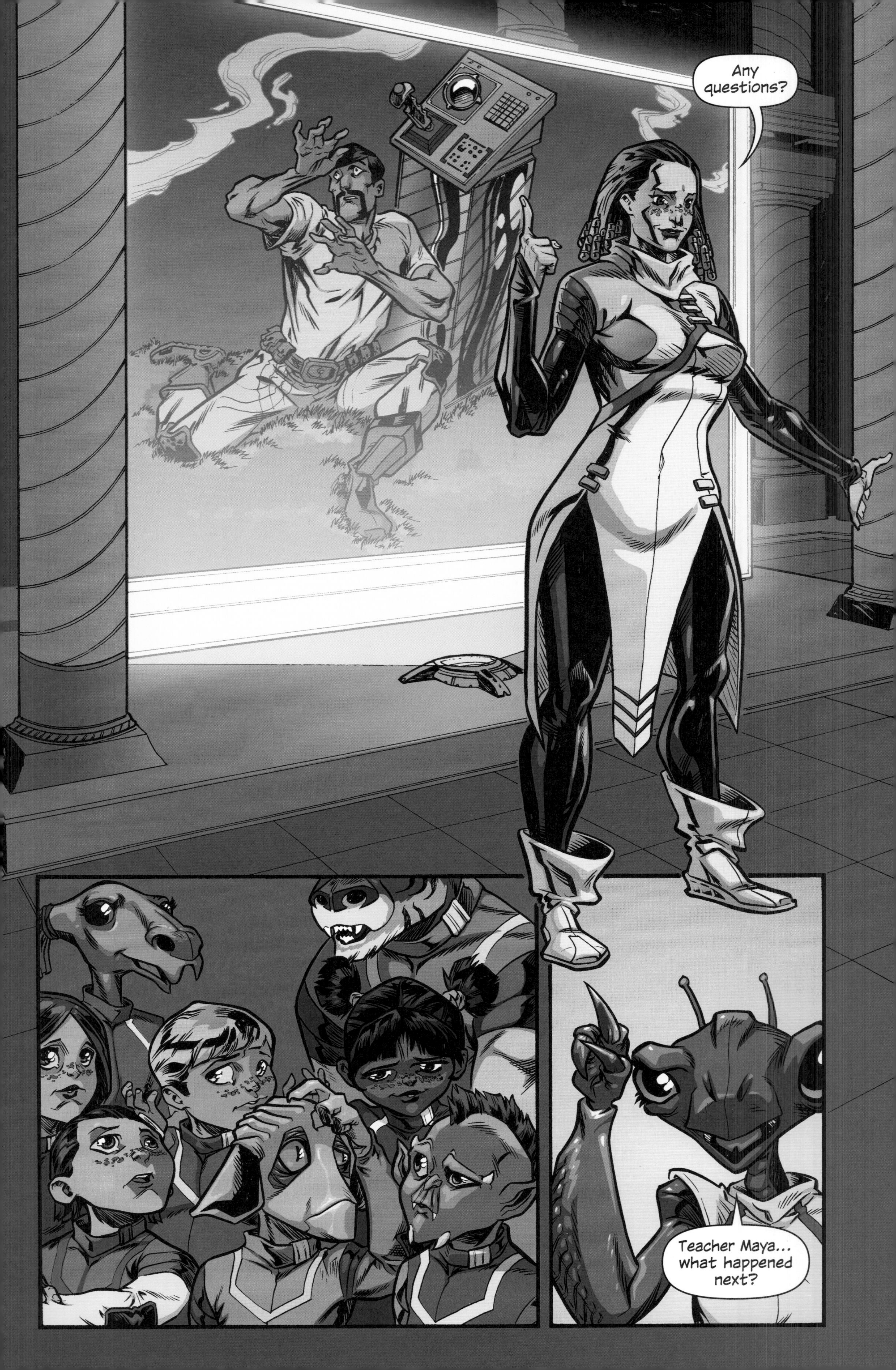
Any questions?
Teacher Maya... what happened next?

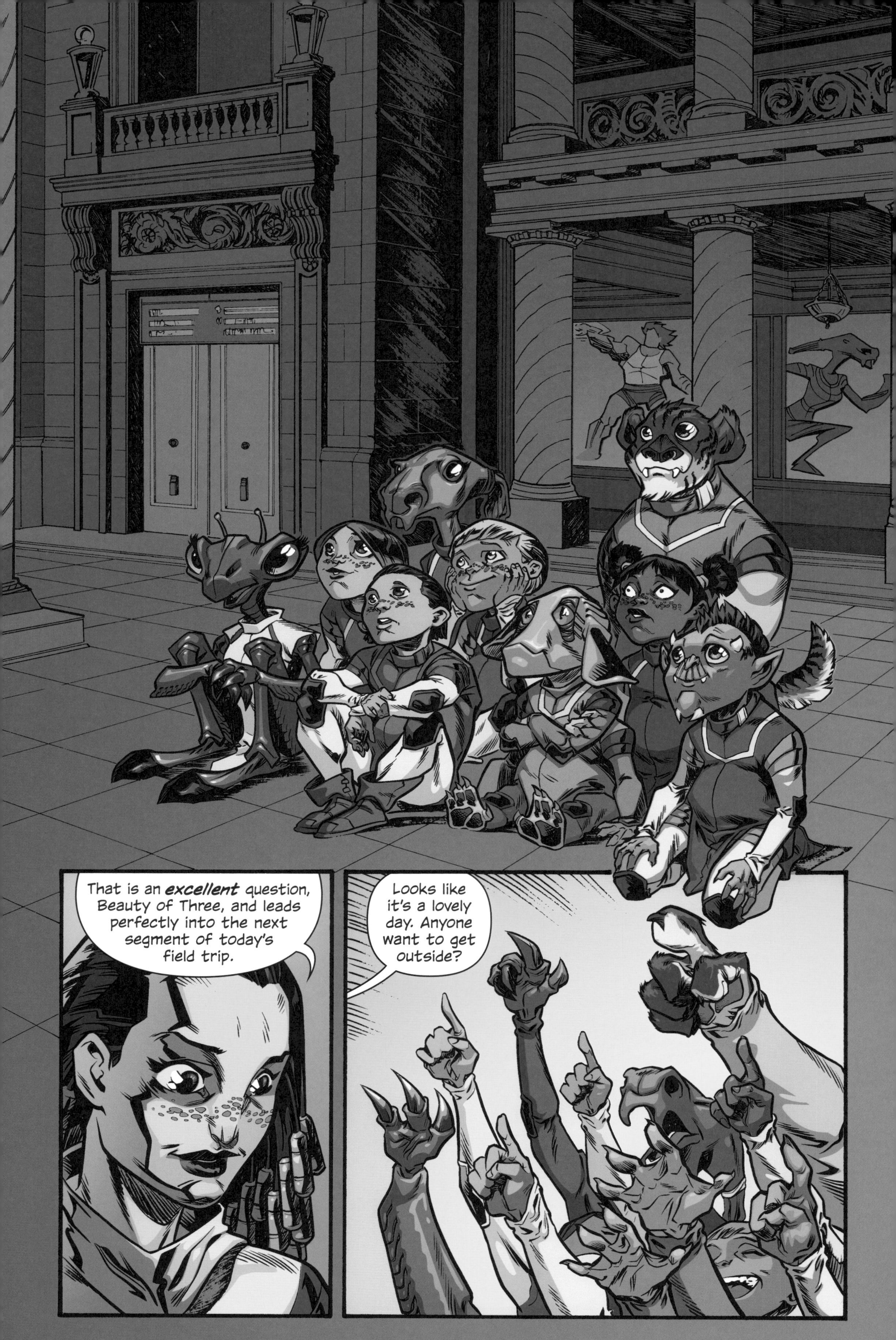
That is an ***excellent*** question, Beauty of Three, and leads perfectly into the next segment of today's field trip.
Looks like it's a lovely day. Anyone want to get outside?

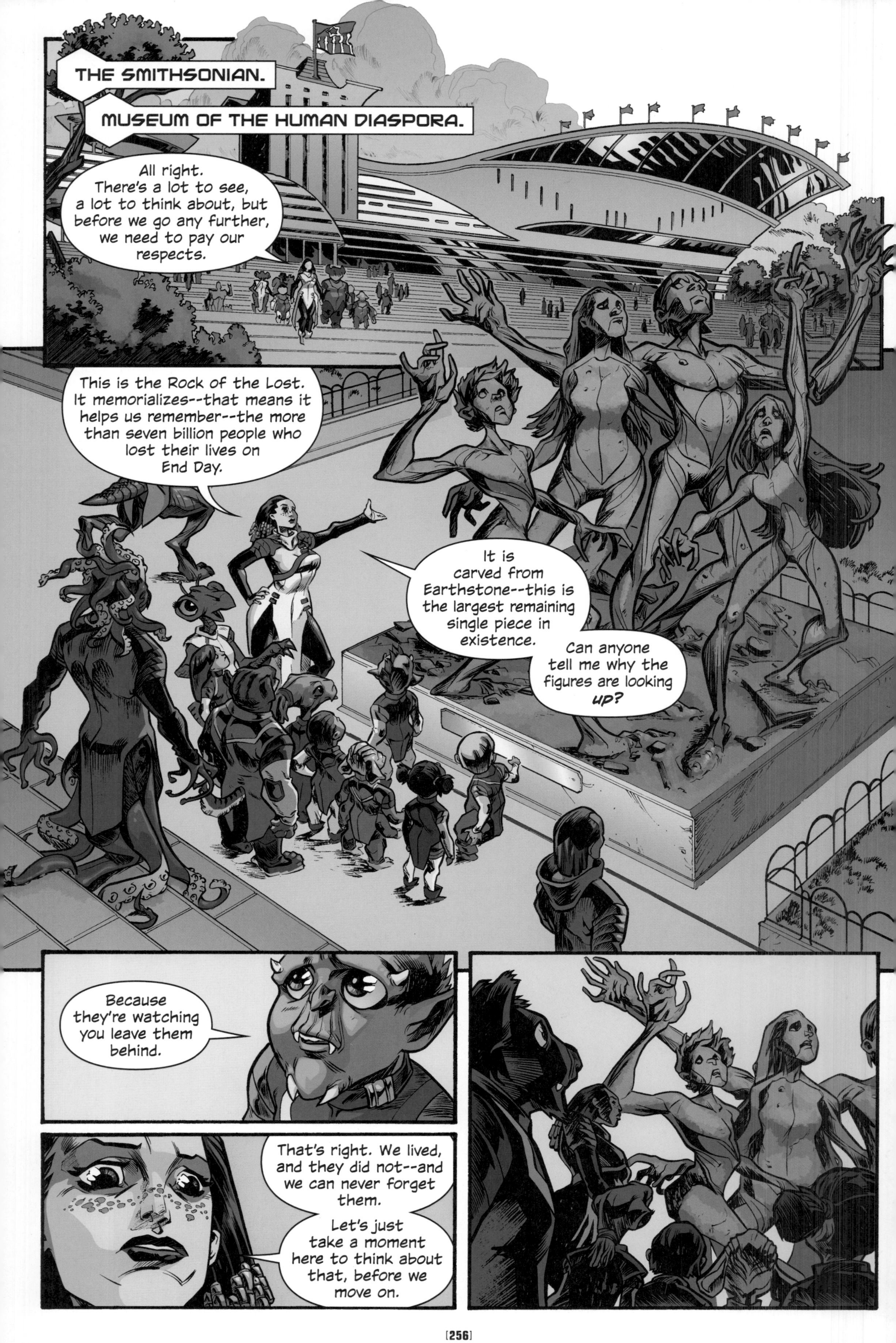
THE SMITHSONIAN.
MUSEUM OF THE HUMAN DIASPORA.
All right. There's a lot to see, a lot to think about, but before we go any further, we need to pay our respects.
This is the Rock of the Lost. It memorializes--that means it helps us remember--the more than seven billion people who lost their lives on End Day.
It is carved from Earthstone--this is the largest remaining single piece in existence.
Can anyone tell me why the figures are looking *up?*
Because they're watching you leave them behind.
That's right. We lived, and they did not--and we can never forget them.
Let's just take a moment here to think about that, before we move on.

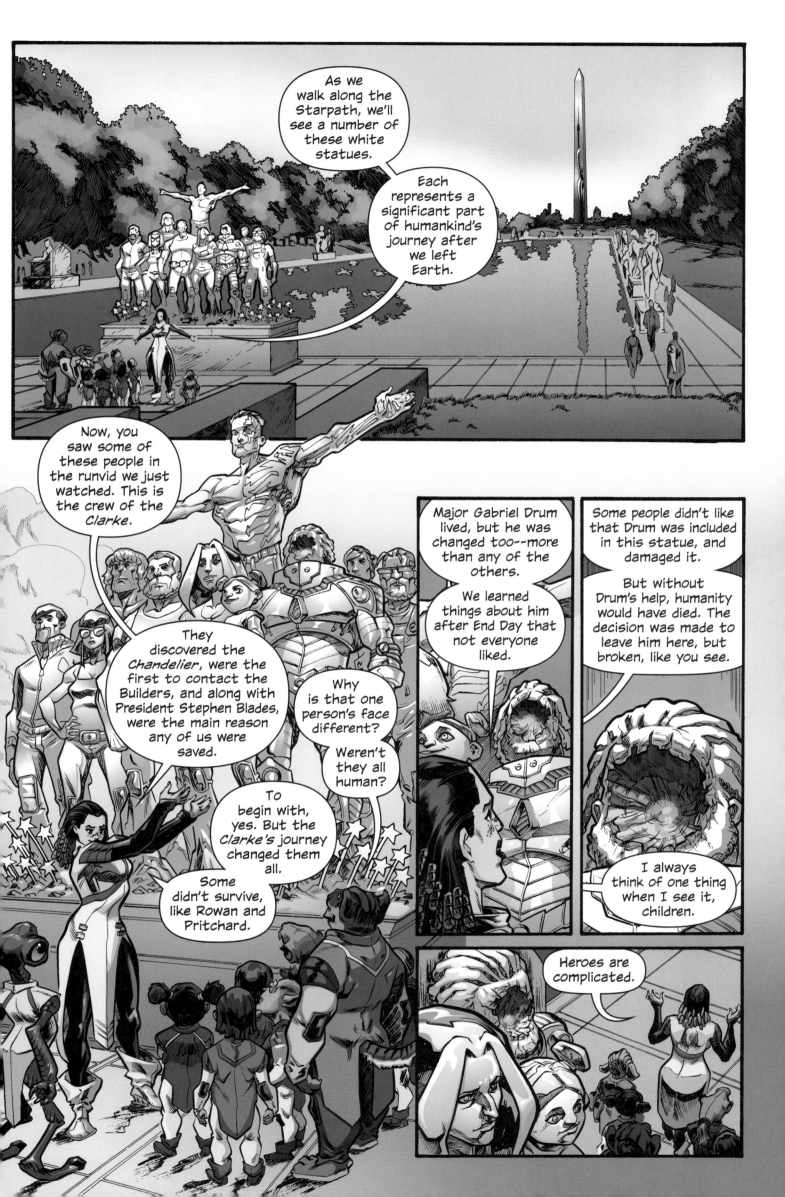

As we walk along the Starpath, we'll see a number of these white statues.

Each represents a significant part of humankind's journey after we left Earth.

Now, you saw some of these people in the runvid we just watched. This is the crew of the Clarke.

They discovered the *Chandelier*, were the first to contact the Builders, and along with President Stephen Blades, were the main reason any of us were saved.

Why is that one person's face different?

Weren't they all human?

To begin with, yes. But the *Clarke's* journey changed them all.

Some didn't survive, like Rowan and Pritchard.

Major Gabriel Drum lived, but he was changed too--more than any of the others.

We learned things about him after End Day that not everyone liked.

Some people didn't like that Drum was included in this statue, and damaged it.

But without Drum's help, humanity would have died. The decision was made to leave him here, but broken, like you see.

I always think of one thing when I see it, children.

Heroes are complicated.

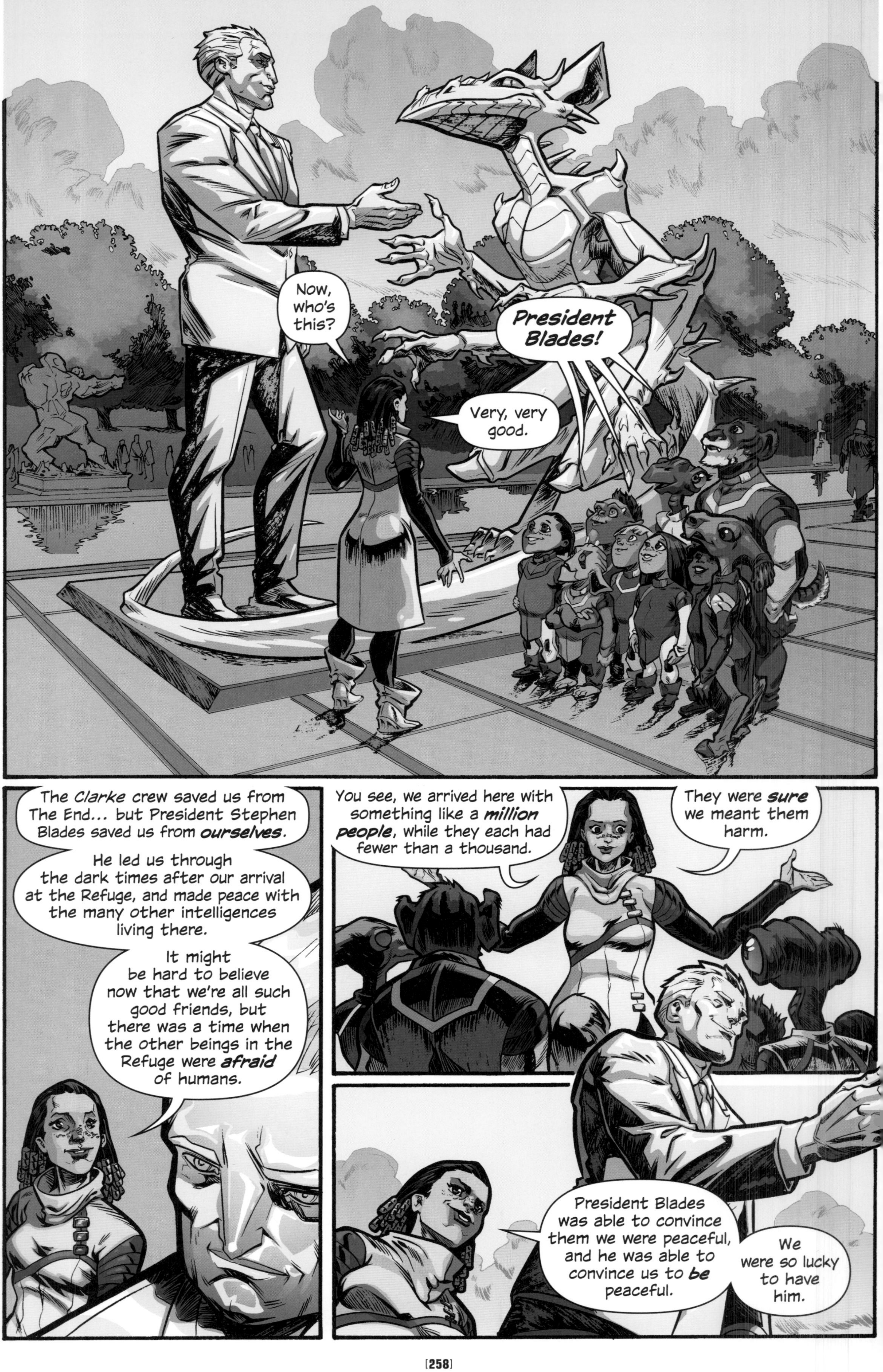
Now, who's this?
President Blades!
Very, very good.
The *Clarke* crew saved us from The End... but President Stephen Blades saved us from ***ourselves***.
He led us through the dark times after our arrival at the Refuge, and made peace with the many other intelligences living there.
It might be hard to believe now that we're all such good friends, but there was a time when the other beings in the Refuge were ***afraid*** of humans.
You see, we arrived here with something like a ***million people***, while they each had fewer than a thousand.
They were ***sure*** we meant them harm.
President Blades was able to convince them we were peaceful, and he was able to convince us to ***be*** peaceful.
We were so lucky to have him.

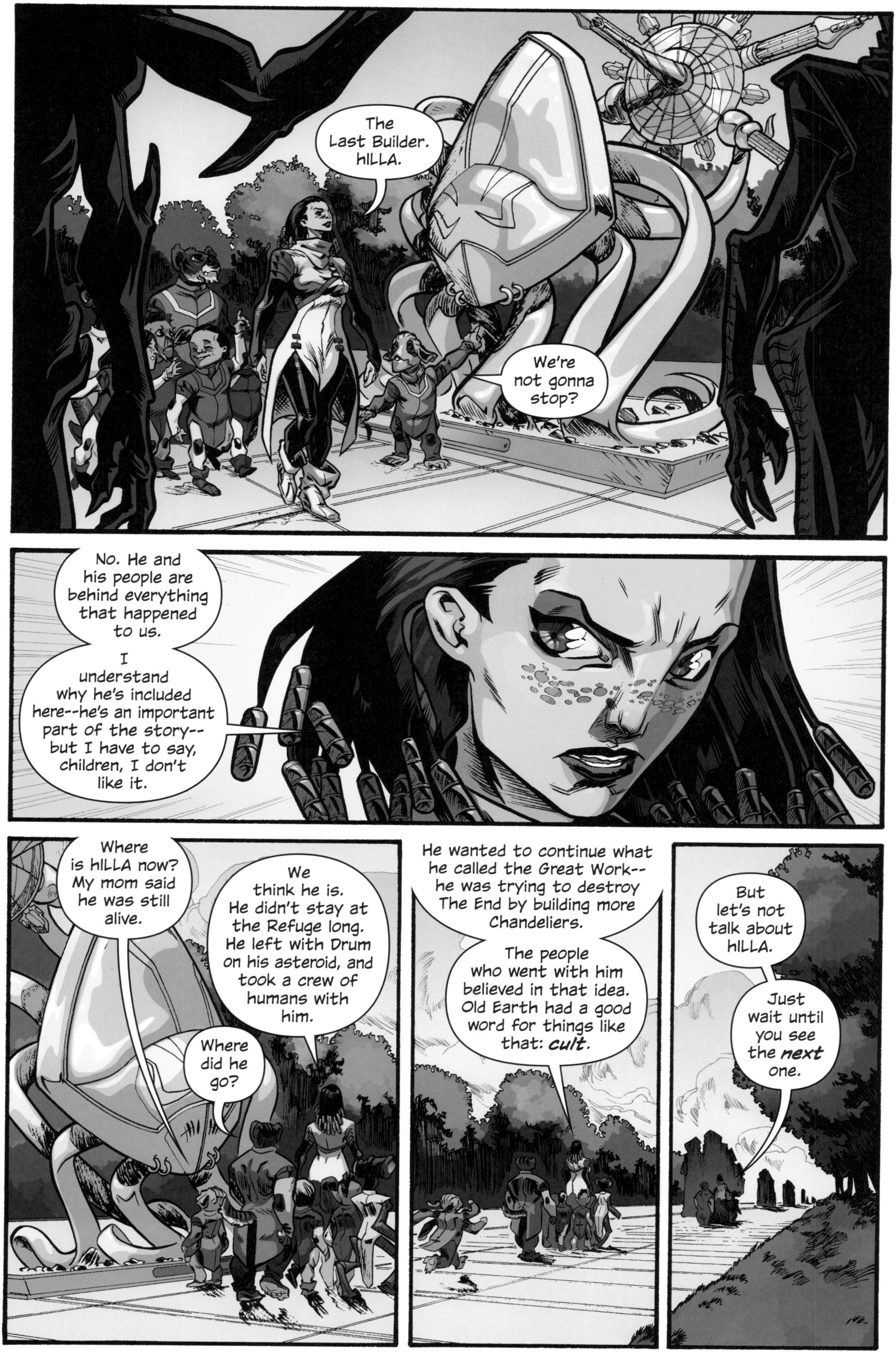

The Last Builder. hILLA.
We're not gonna stop?
No. He and his people are behind everything that happened to us.
I understand why he's included here--he's an important part of the story--but I have to say, children, I don't like it.
Where is hILLA now? My mom said he was still alive.
We think he is. He didn't stay at the Refuge long. He left with Drum on his asteroid, and took a crew of humans with him.
Where did he go?
He wanted to continue what he called the Great Work--he was trying to destroy The End by building more Chandeliers.
The people who went with him believed in that idea. Old Earth had a good word for things like that: *cult*.
But let's not talk about hILLA.
Just wait until you see the *next* one.

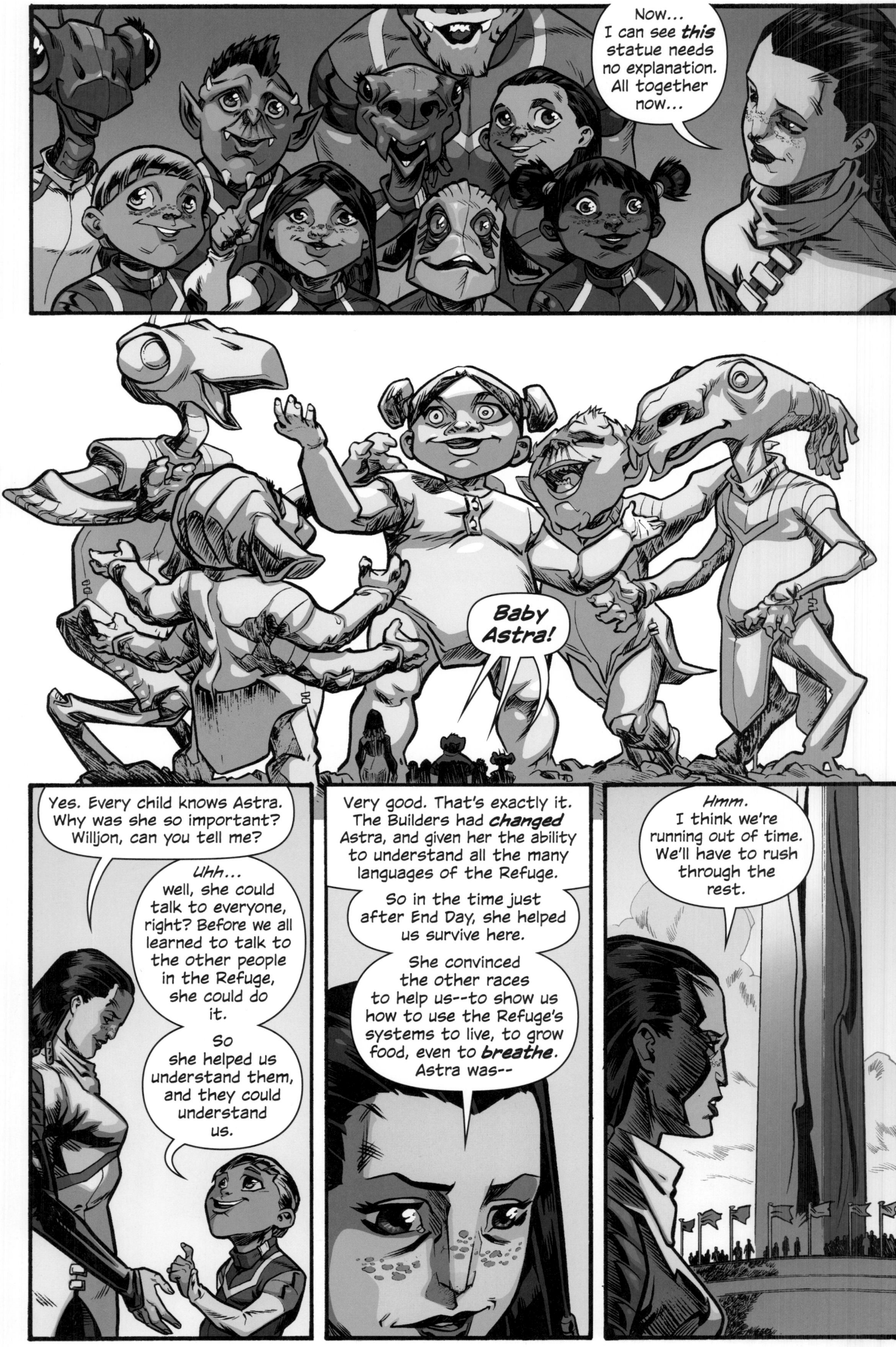

Now... I can see *this* statue needs no explanation. All together now...
Baby Astra!
Yes. Every child knows Astra. Why was she so important? Willjon, can you tell me?
Uhh... well, she could talk to everyone, right? Before we all learned to talk to the other people in the Refuge, she could do it.
So she helped us understand them, and they could understand us.
Very good. That's exactly it. The Builders had ***changed*** Astra, and given her the ability to understand all the many languages of the Refuge.
So in the time just after End Day, she helped us survive here.
She convinced the other races to help us--to show us how to use the Refuge's systems to live, to grow food, even to ***breathe***. Astra was--
Hmm. I think we're running out of time. We'll have to rush through the rest.

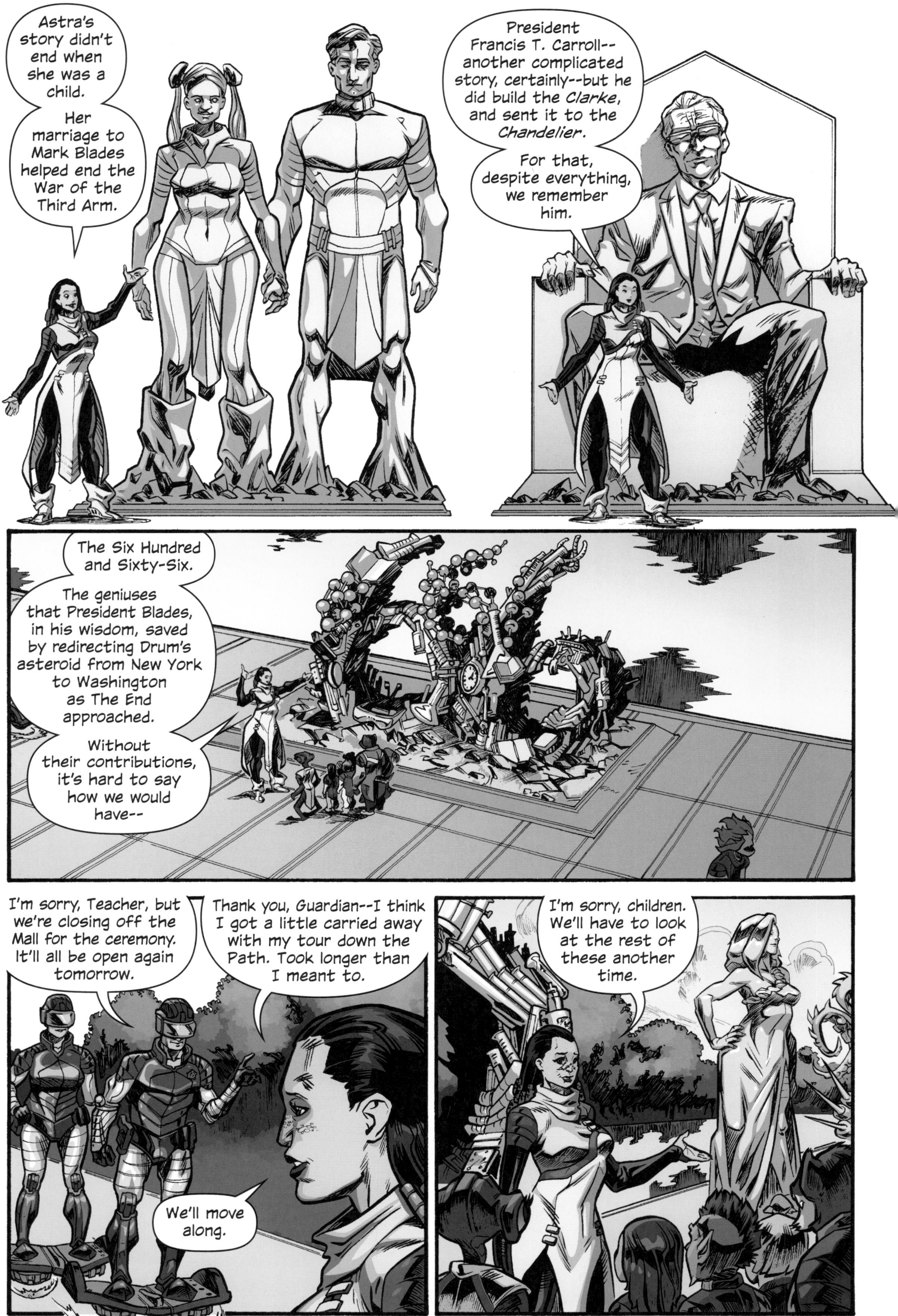
Astra's story didn't end when she was a child.
Her marriage to Mark Blades helped end the War of the Third Arm.
President Francis T. Carroll--another complicated story, certainly--but he did build the *Clarke*, and sent it to the *Chandelier*.
For that, despite everything, we remember him.
The Six Hundred and Sixty-Six.
The geniuses that President Blades, in his wisdom, saved by redirecting Drum's asteroid from New York to Washington as The End approached.
Without their contributions, it's hard to say how we would have--
I'm sorry, Teacher, but we're closing off the Mall for the ceremony. It'll all be open again tomorrow.
Thank you, Guardian--I think I got a little carried away with my tour down the Path. Took longer than I meant to.
We'll move along.
I'm sorry, children. We'll have to look at the rest of these another time.

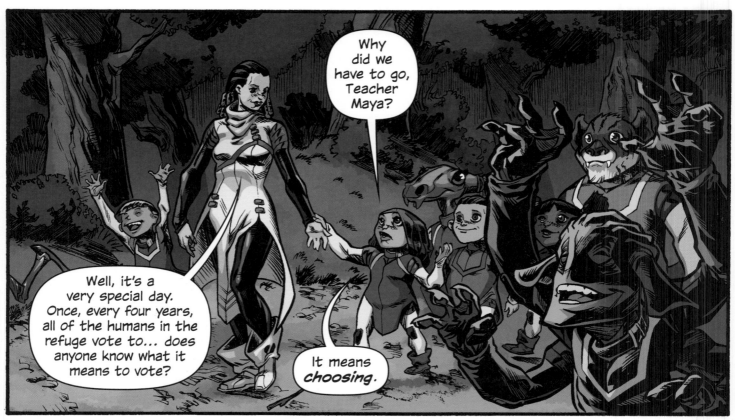

Why did we have to go, Teacher Maya?

It means *choosing.*

Well, it's a very special day. Once, every four years, all of the humans in the refuge vote to... does anyone know what it means to vote?

Yes, but it's bigger than that. To me, voting is *speaking.* Making yourself *heard.* Showing the world you care about what happens in it.

And being in a society that *lets* you vote... it means the world cares about *you,* too. You have a *voice.* It's a good thing.

Every four years we vote to select our next President. It's been that way for a very long time.

After we make our choice, the new President swears an oath to lead us. He makes a promise to do his very best to take care of us.

That is called the *inauguration,* and it's happening today. It's why we had to leave the Mall.

What happens to the old President? Does he die?

Oh, no... he just moves out of the White House, and gets on with his life.

But before he goes, he does do one last thing.

Children, it's the most *wonderful* tradition.

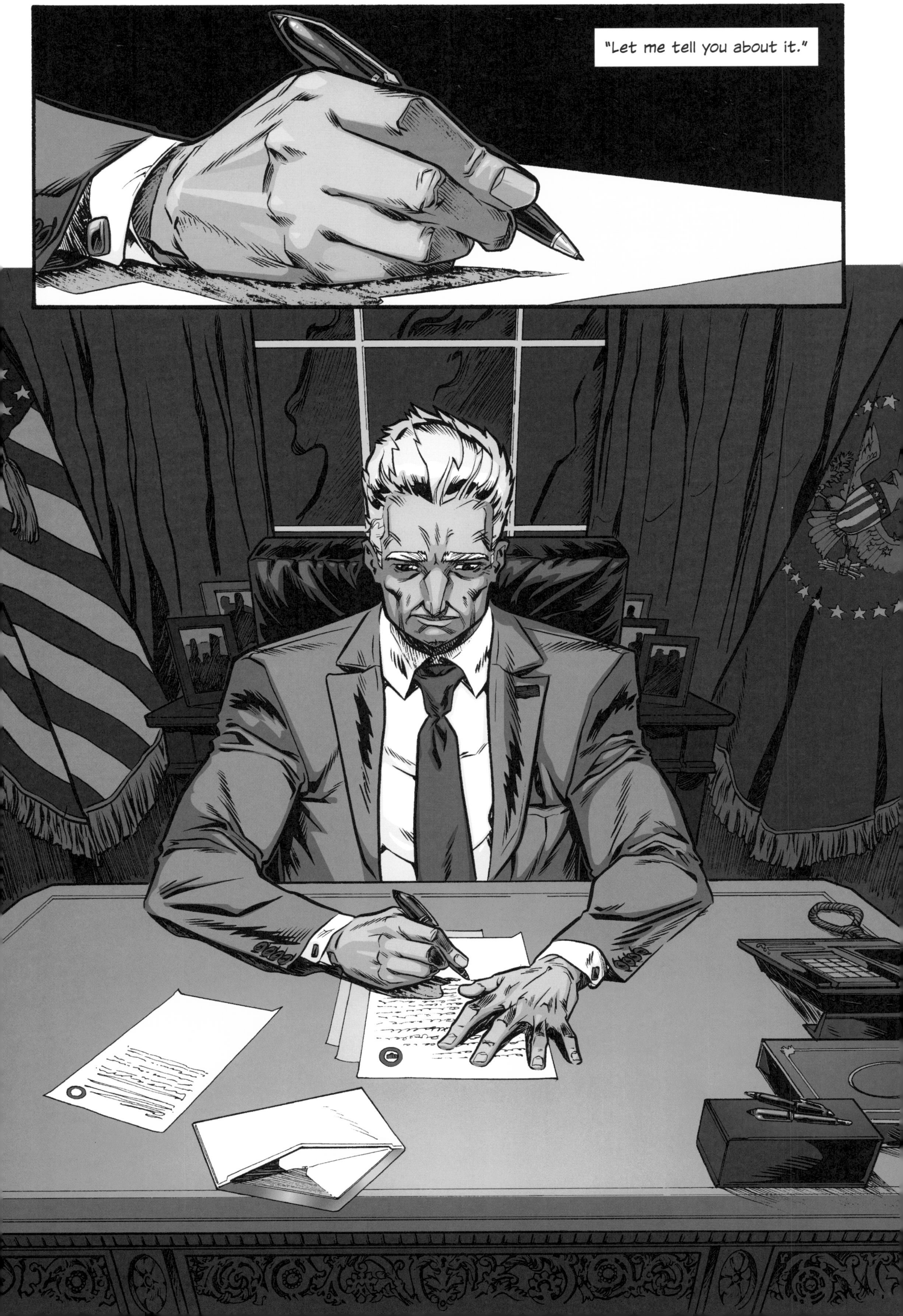
"Let me tell you about it."

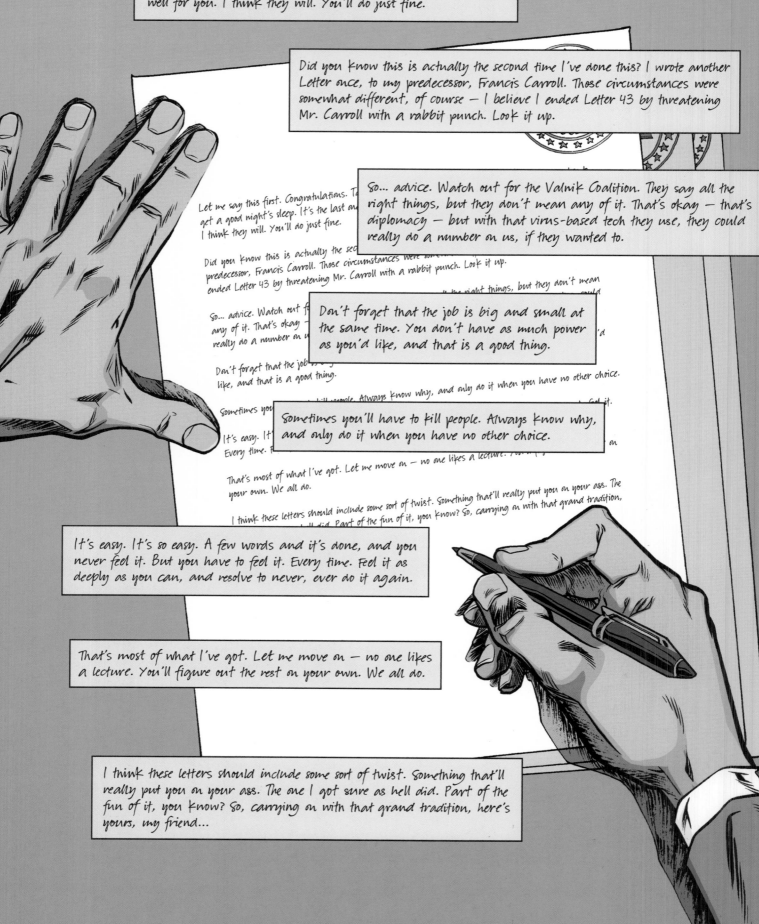

Let me say this first. Congratulations. Take tonight, be happy you won, and for God's sake, try to get a good night's sleep. It's the last one you'll have for four years. Eight, if things go well for you. I think they will. You'll do just fine.

Did you know this is actually the second time I've done this? I wrote another letter once, to my predecessor, Francis Carroll. Those circumstances were somewhat different, of course — I believe I ended Letter 43 by threatening Mr. Carroll with a rabbit punch. Look it up.

So... advice. Watch out for the Valnik Coalition. They say all the right things, but they don't mean any of it. That's okay — that's diplomacy — but with that virus-based tech they use, they could really do a number on us, if they wanted to.

Don't forget that the job is big and small at the same time. You don't have as much power as you'd like, and that is a good thing.

Sometimes you'll have to kill people. Always know why, and only do it when you have no other choice.

It's easy. It's so easy. A few words and it's done, and you never feel it. But you have to feel it. Every time. Feel it as deeply as you can, and resolve to never, ever do it again.

That's most of what I've got. Let me move on — no one likes a lecture. You'll figure out the rest on your own. We all do.

I think these letters should include some sort of twist. Something that'll really put you on your ass. The one I got sure as hell did. Part of the fun of it, you know? So, carrying on with that grand tradition, here's yours, my friend...

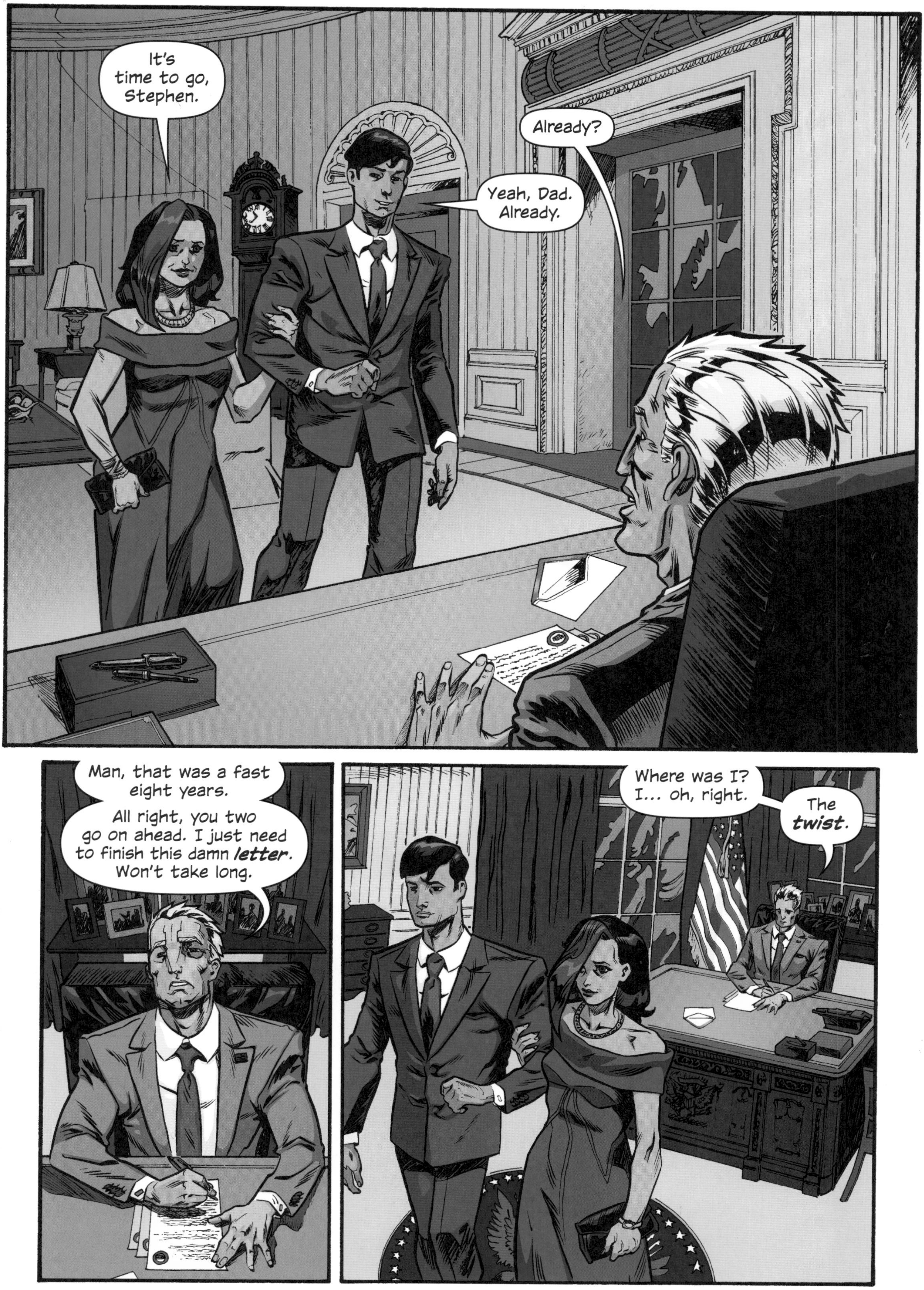
It's time to go, Stephen.
Already?
Yeah, Dad. Already.
Man, that was a fast eight years.
All right, you two go on ahead. I just need to finish this damn *letter*. Won't take long.
Where was I? I... oh, right.
The *twist*.

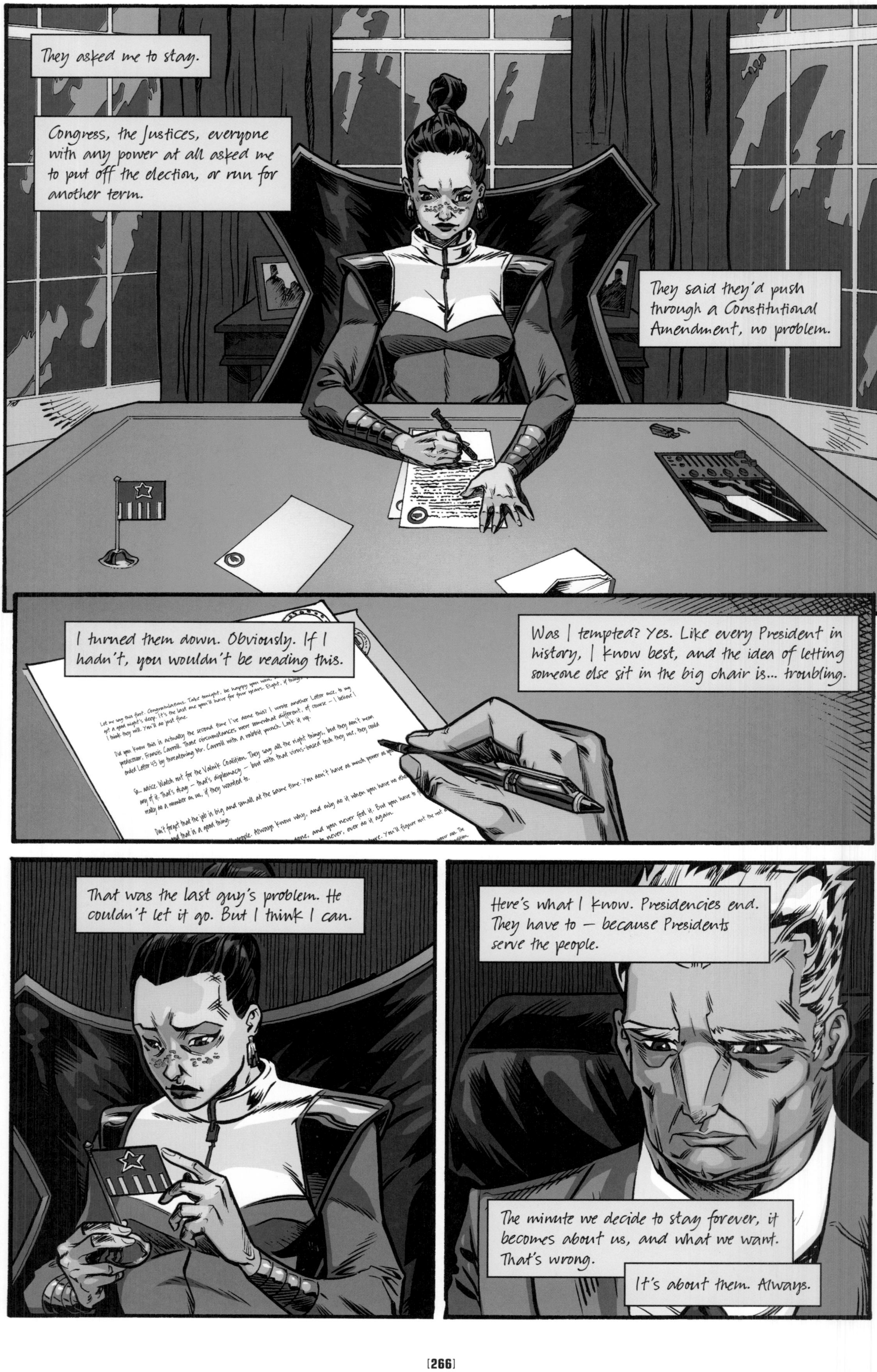

They asked me to stay.
Congress, the Justices, everyone with any power at all asked me to put off the election, or run for another term.
They said they'd push through a Constitutional Amendment, no problem.
I turned them down. Obviously. If I hadn't, you wouldn't be reading this.
Was I tempted? Yes. Like every President in history, I know best, and the idea of letting someone else sit in the big chair is... troubling.
Let me say this first. Congratulations. Take tonight, be happy you won,
get a good night's sleep. It's the last one you'll have for four years. Eight, if things
I think they will. You'll do just fine.
Did you know this is actually the second time I've done this? I wrote another Letter once, to my
predecessor, Francis Carroll. These circumstances were somewhat different, of course — I believe I
ended Letter 43 by threatening Mr. Carroll with a rabbit punch. Look it up.
So... advice. Watch out for the Valnik Coalition. They say all the right things, but they don't mean
any of it. That's okay — that's diplomacy — but with that virus-based tech they use, they could
really do a number on us, if they wanted to.
Don't forget that the job is big and small at the same time. You don't have as much power as you
and that is a good thing.
That was the last guy's problem. He couldn't let it go. But I think I can.
Here's what I know. Presidencies end. They have to — because Presidents serve the people.
The minute we decide to stay forever, it becomes about us, and what we want. That's wrong.
It's about them. Always.

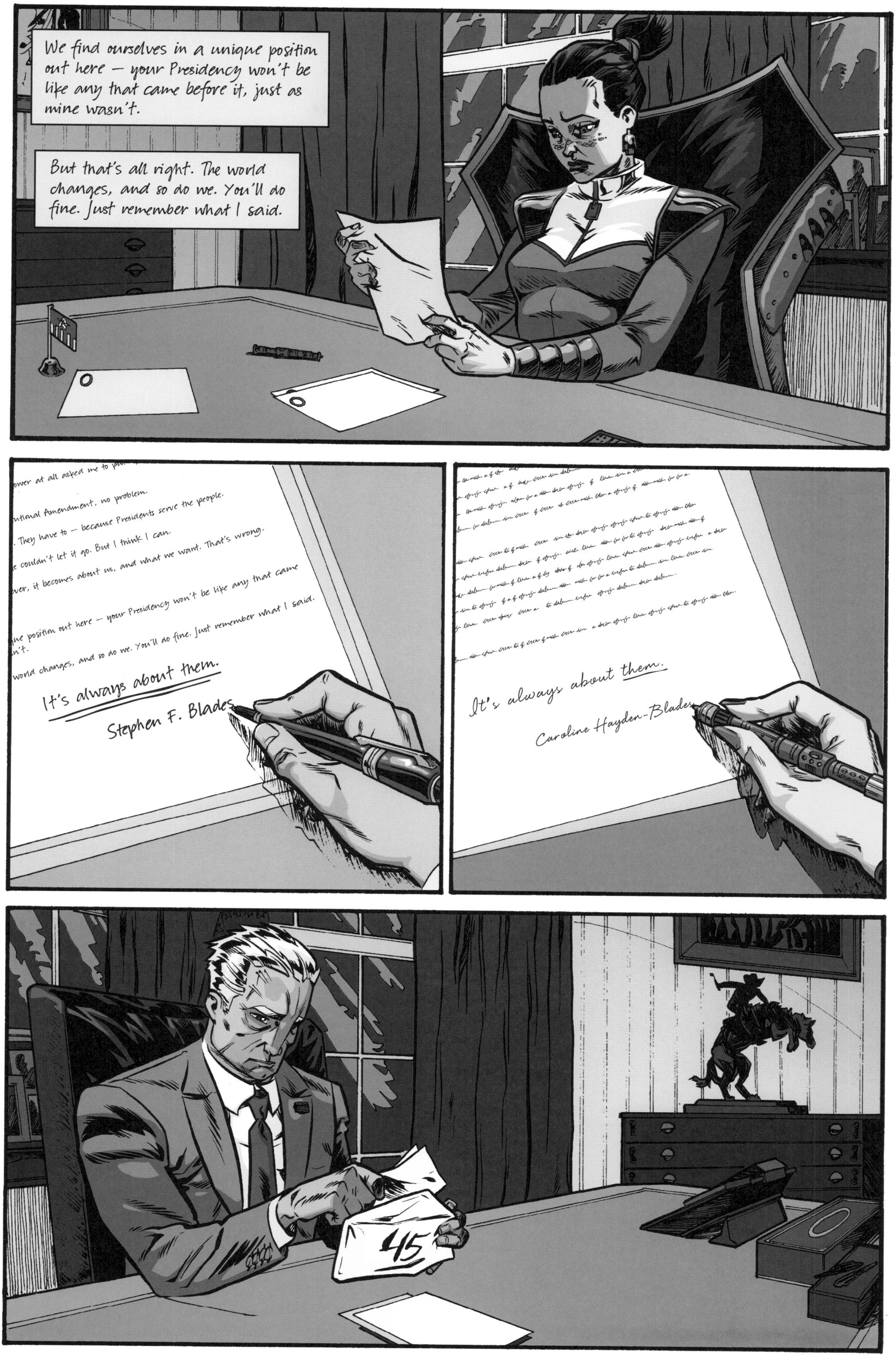
We find ourselves in a unique position out here — your Presidency won't be like any that came before it, just as mine wasn't.
But that's all right. The world changes, and so do we. You'll do fine. Just remember what I said.
ower at all asked me to
utional Amendment, no problem.
. They have to — because Presidents serve the people.
e couldn't let it go. But I think I can.
ver, it becomes about us, and what we want. That's wrong.
ue position out here — your Presidency won't be like any that came
n't.
world changes, and so do we. You'll do fine. Just remember what I said.
It's always about them.
Stephen F. Blades
It's always about them.
Caroline Hayden-Blades
45

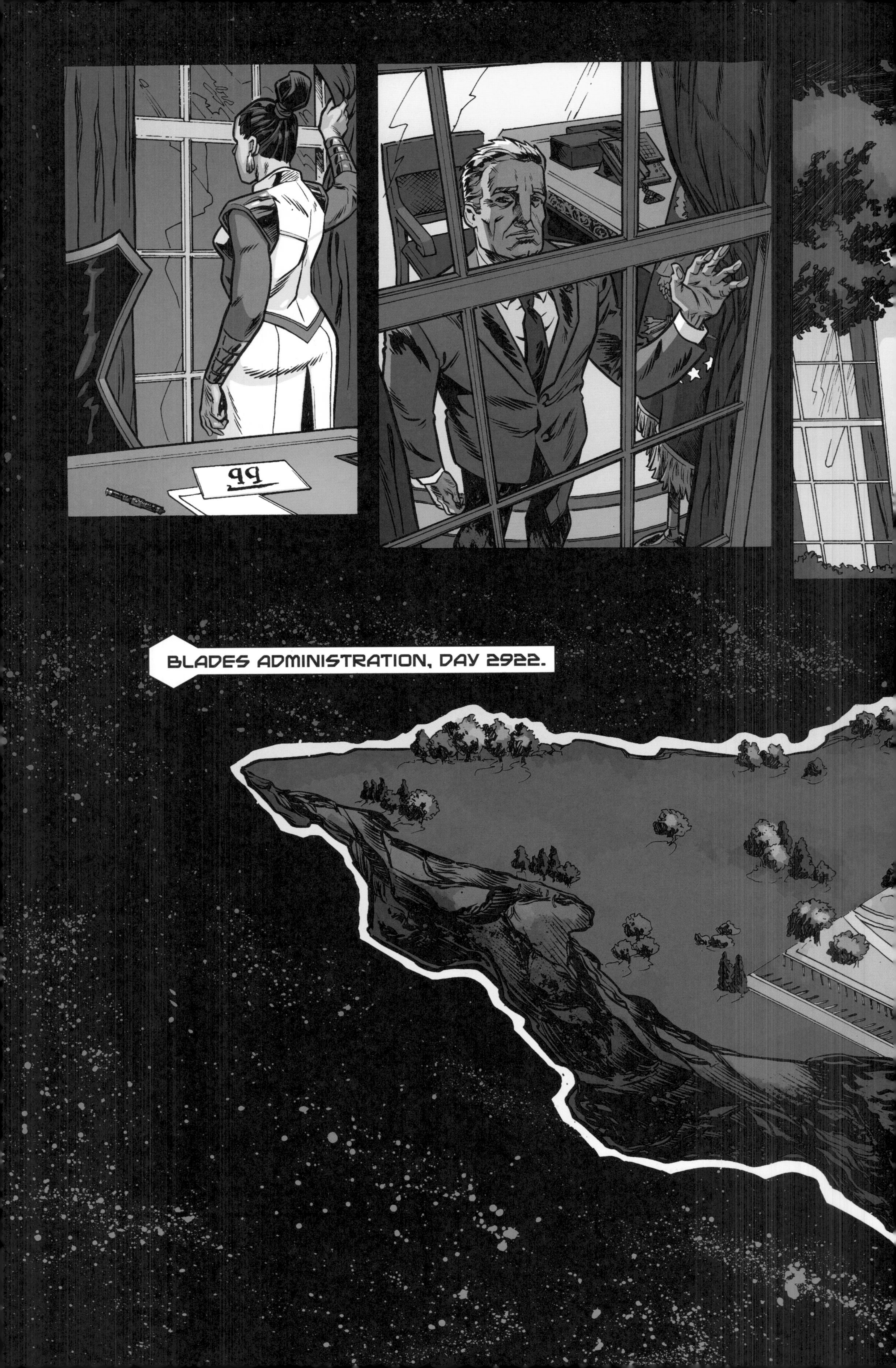
BLADES ADMINISTRATION, DAY 2922.

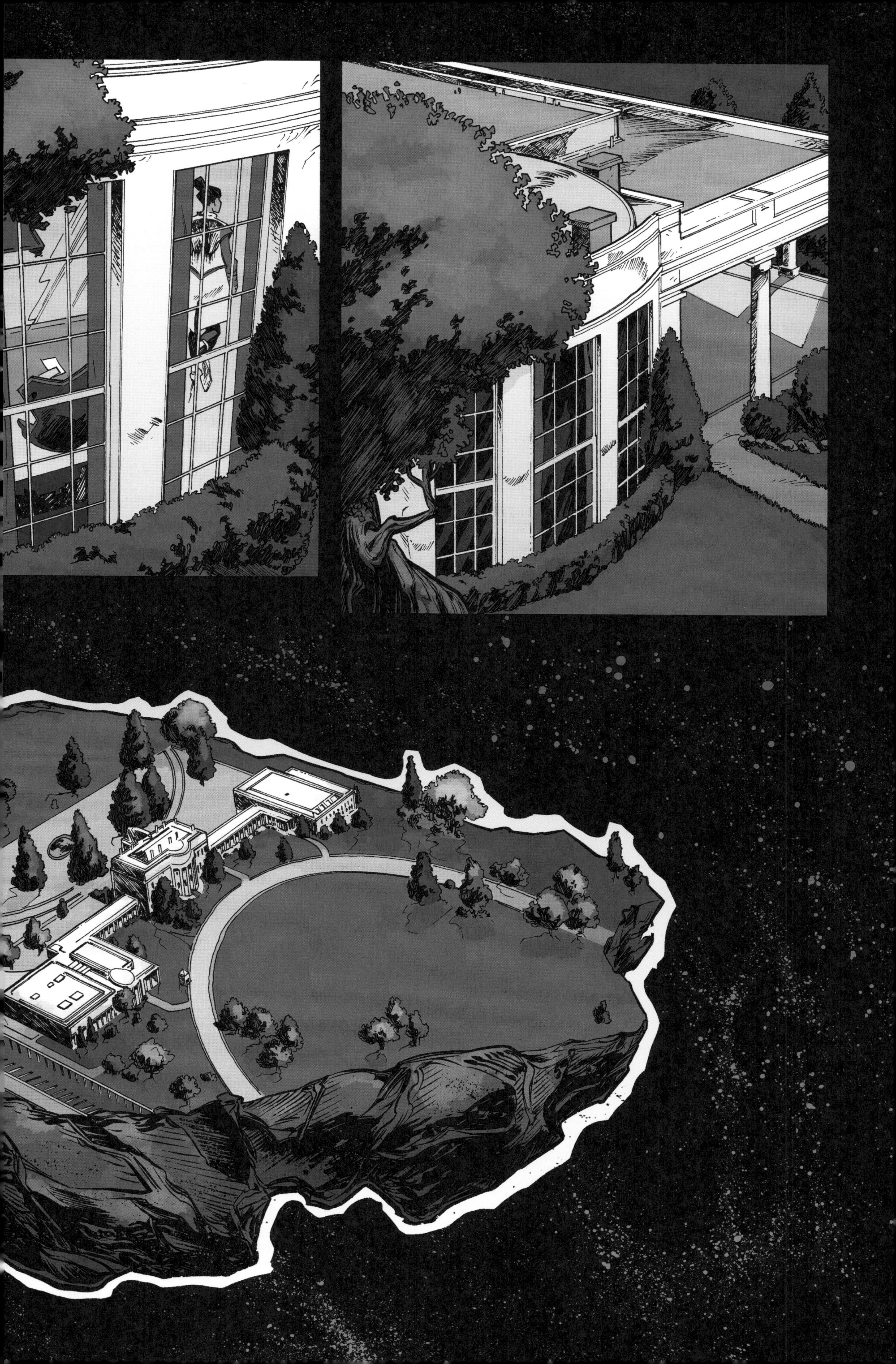

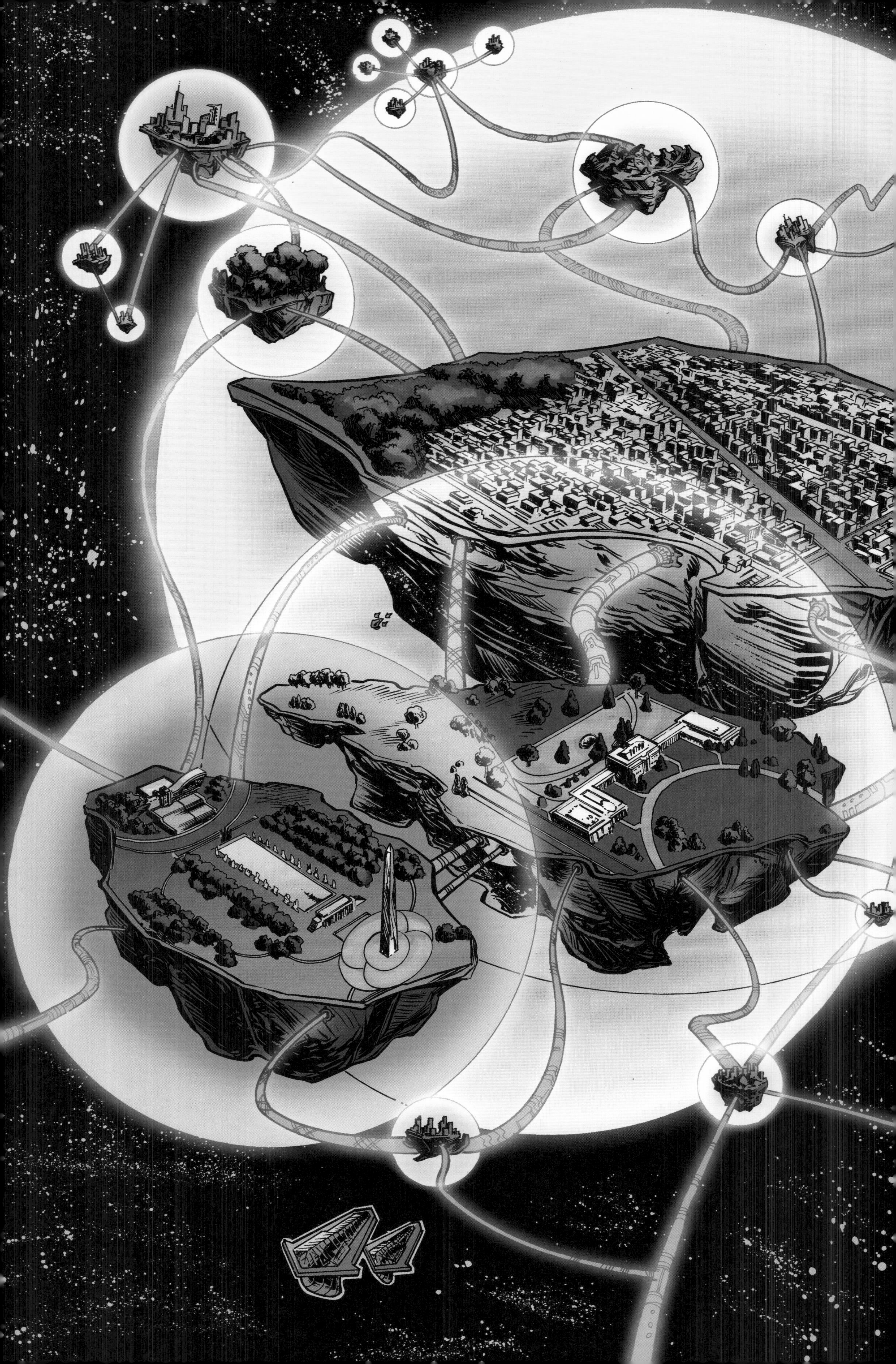

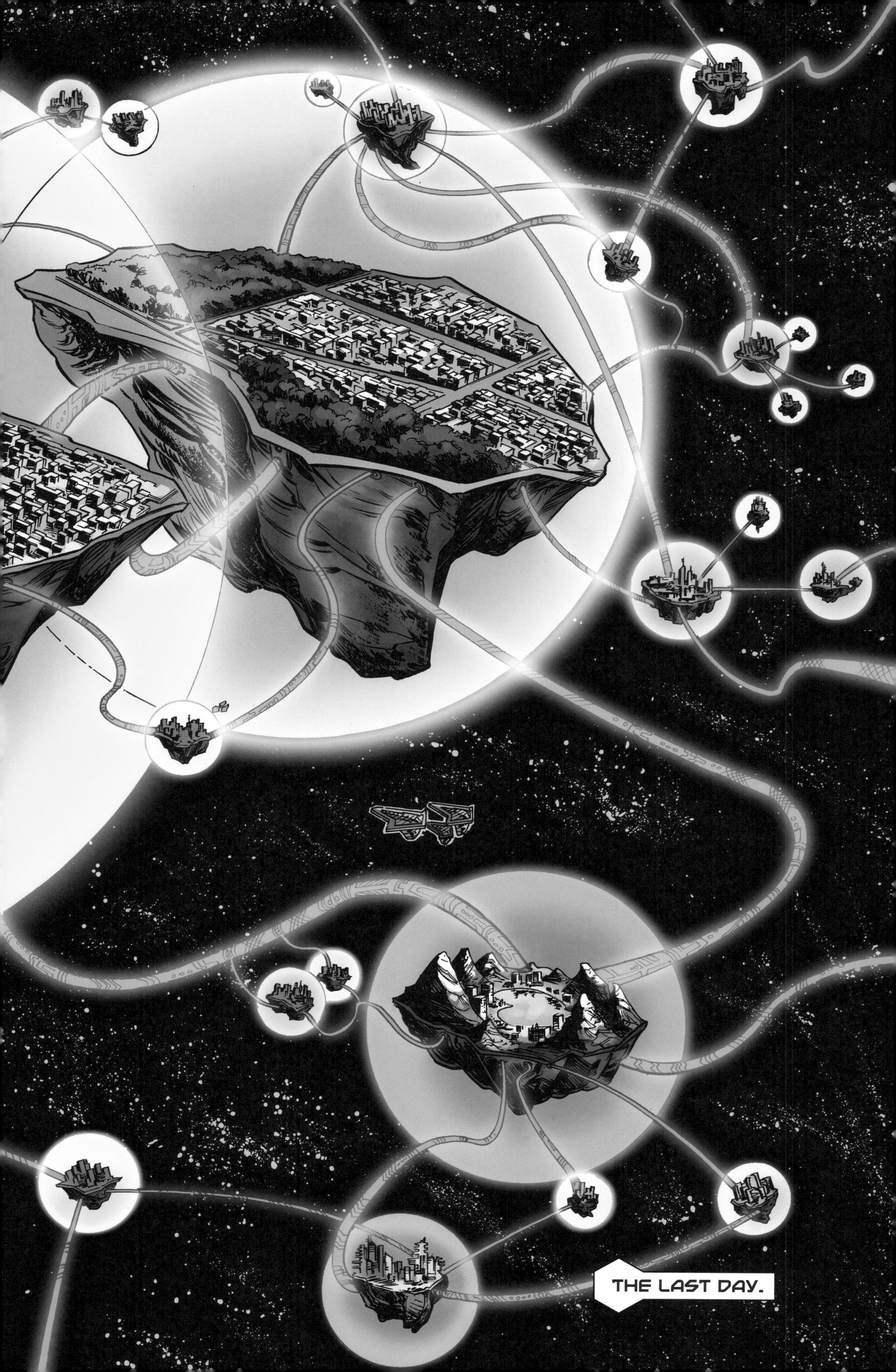
THE LAST DAY.

LETTER
44

COVER GALLERY

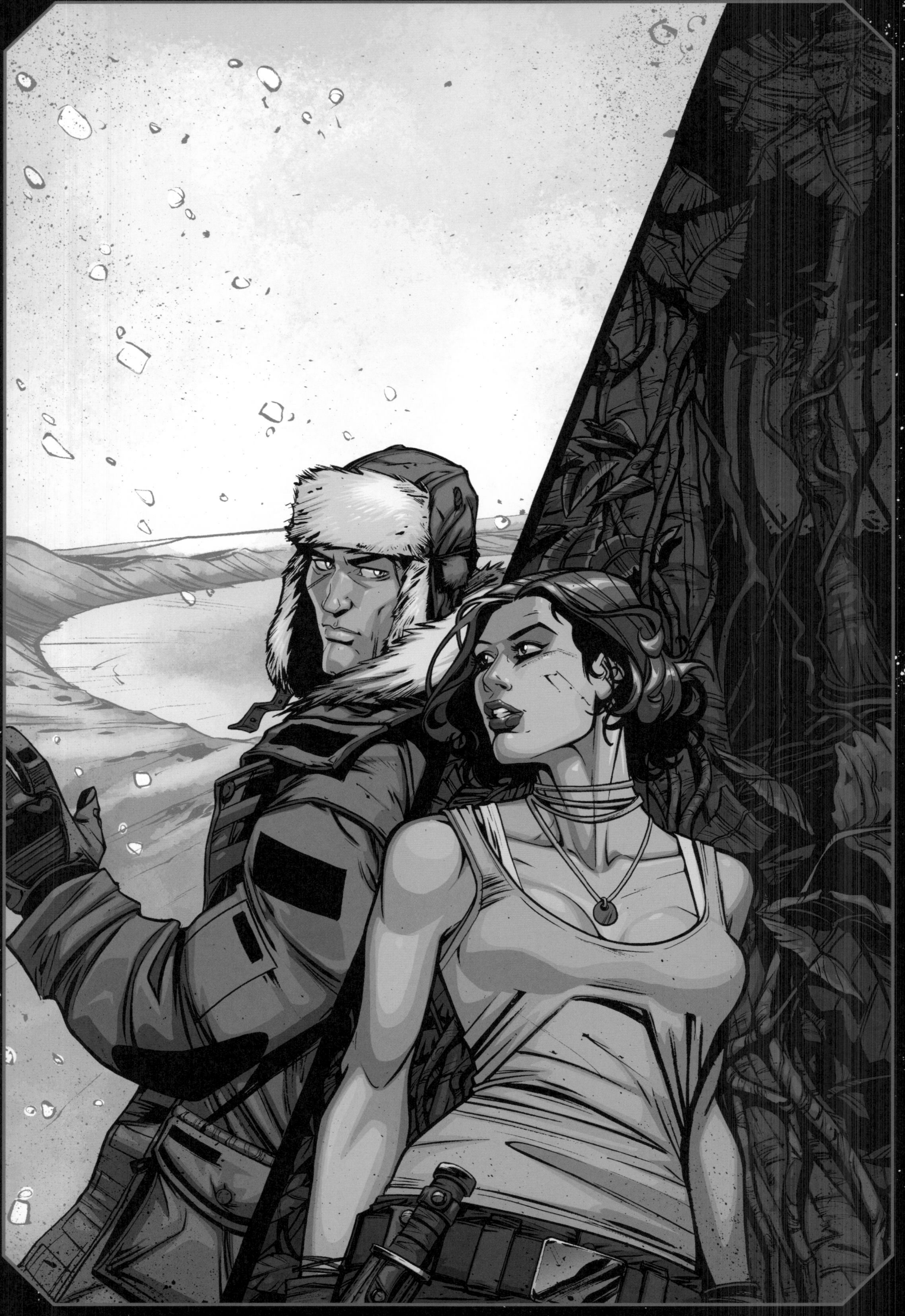

Issue #7 retail cover. Illustrated by Joëlle Jones. Colored by Dan Jackson.

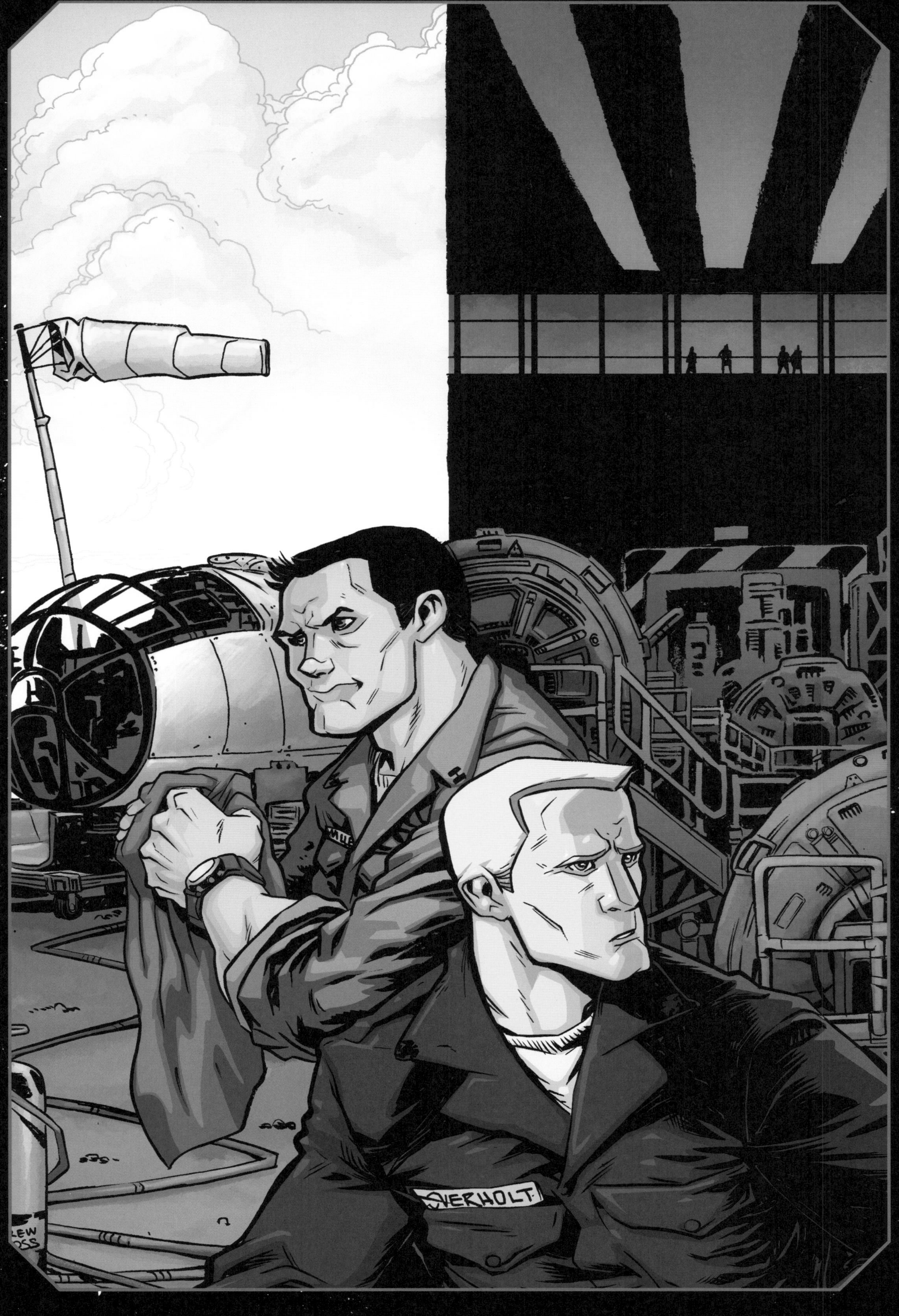
OVERHOLT

Issue #14 retail cover. Illustrated by Drew Moss. Colored by Dan Jackson.

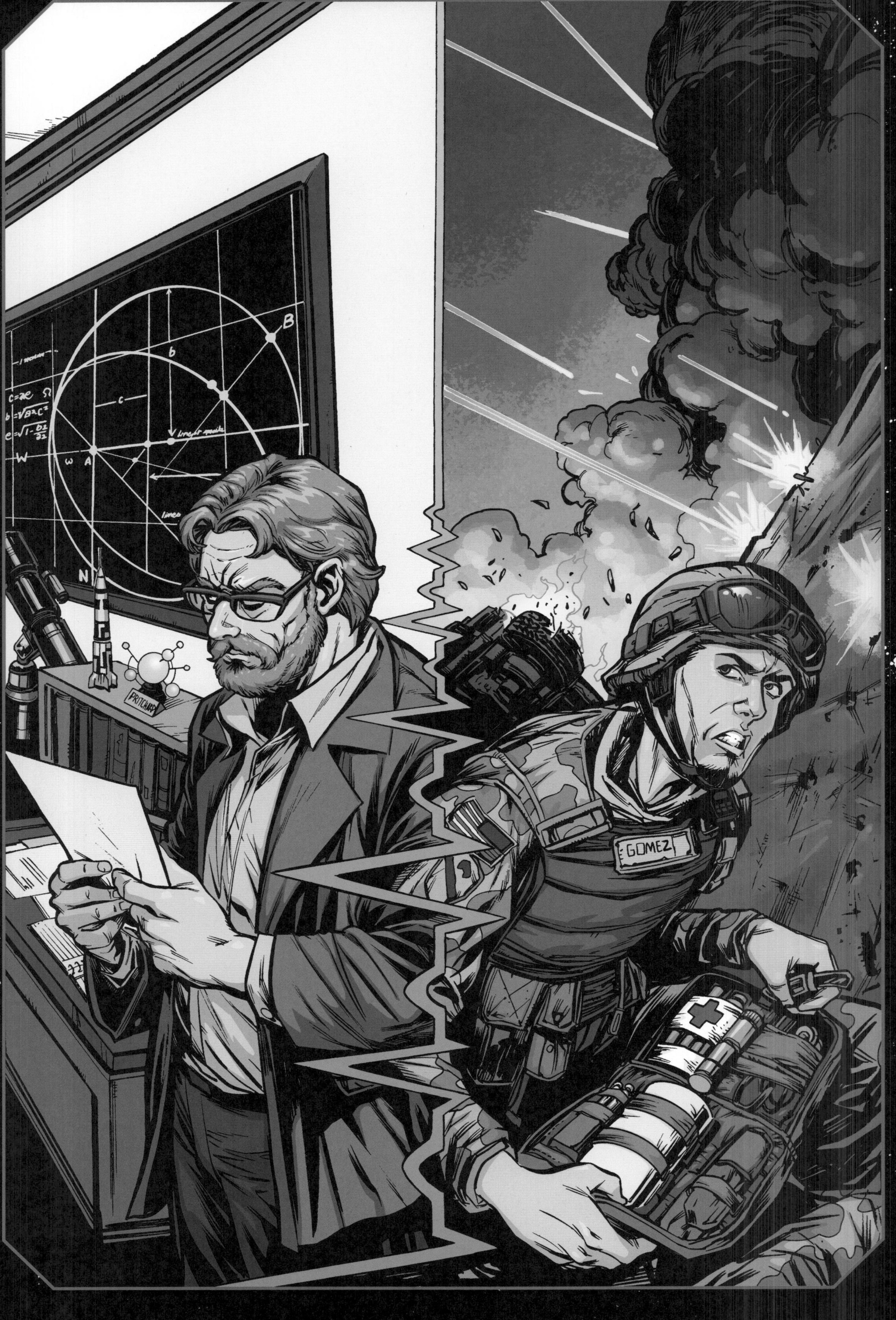

B
b
c
W
A
N
PRITCHARD
GOMEZ

Issue #21 retail cover. Illustrated by Ryan Kelly. Colored by Dan Jackson.

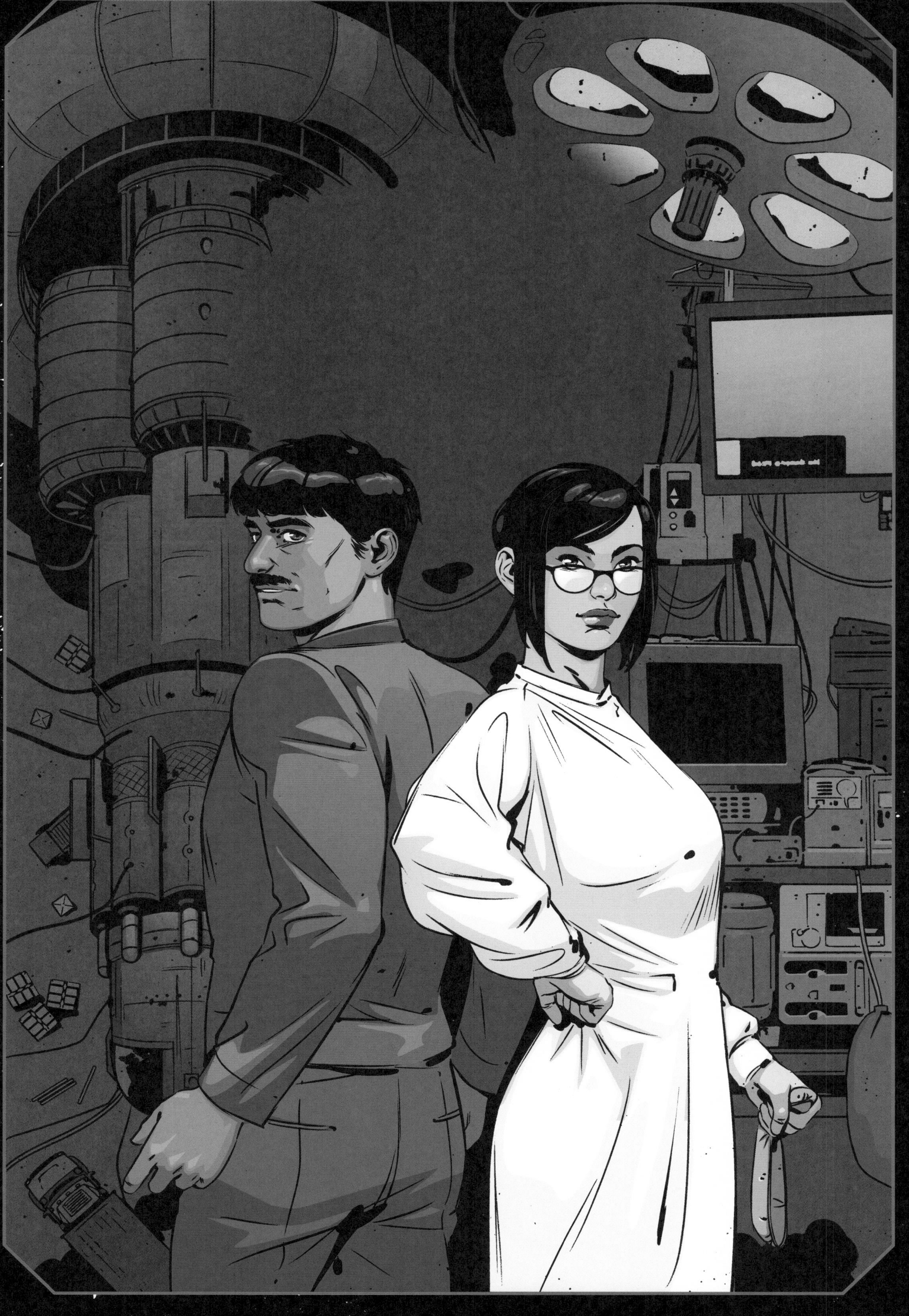

Issue #28 retail cover. Illustrated by Alise Gluškova. Colored by Dan Jackson.

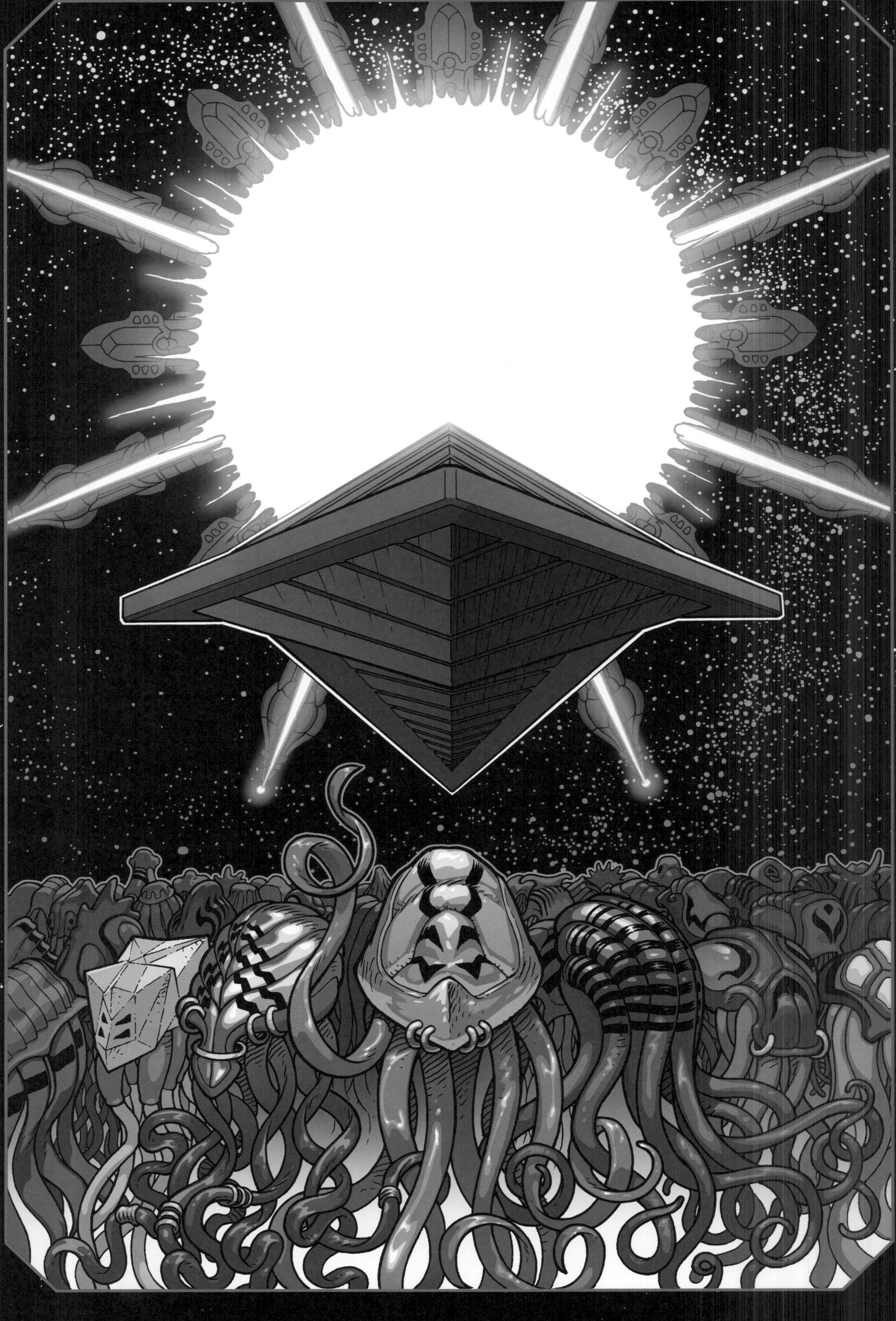

Issue #32 retail cover. Illustrated by Langdon Foss. Colored by Dan Jackson.

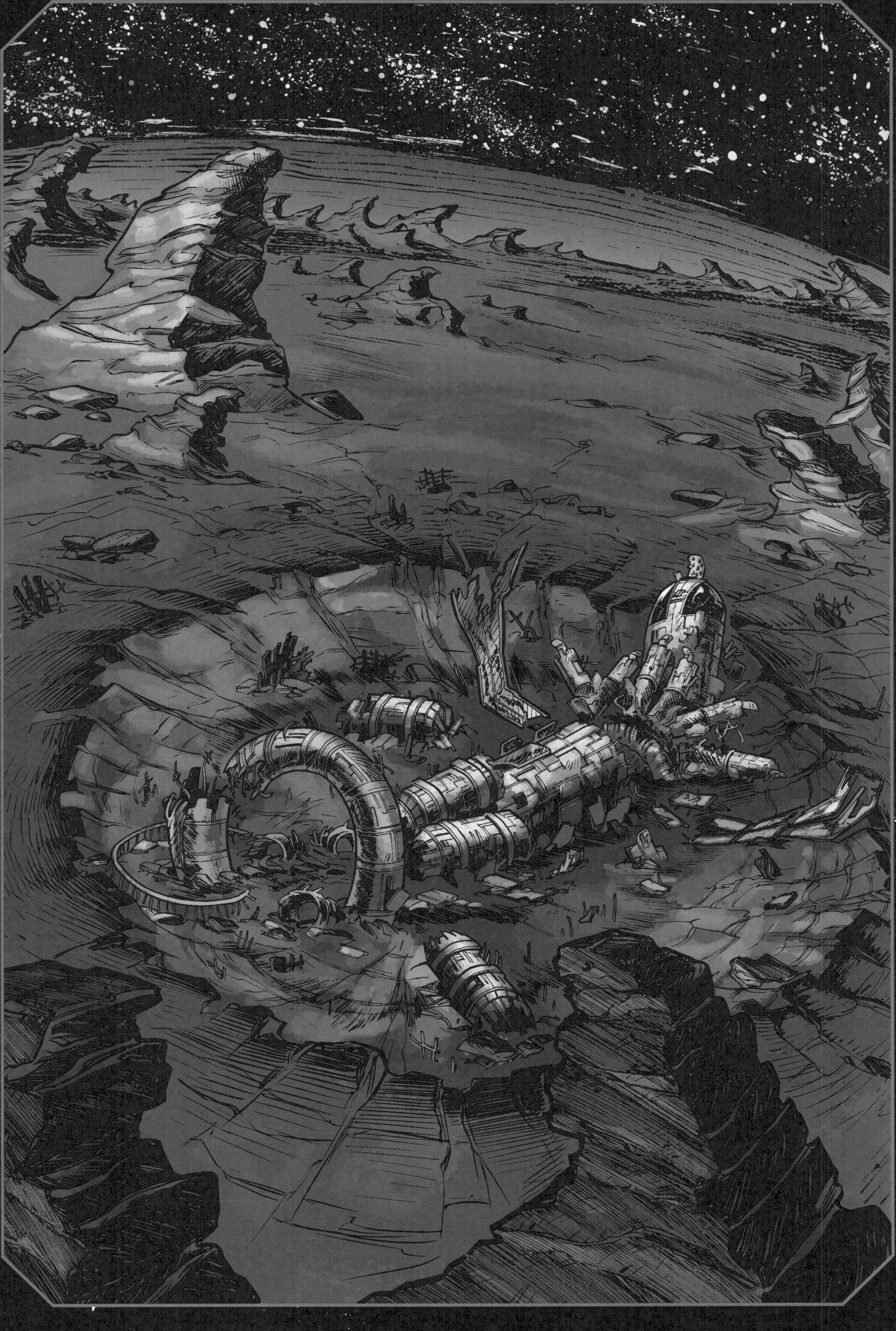

Issue #29 retail cover. Illustrated by Alberto Jiménez Alburquerque. Colored by Dan Jackson.

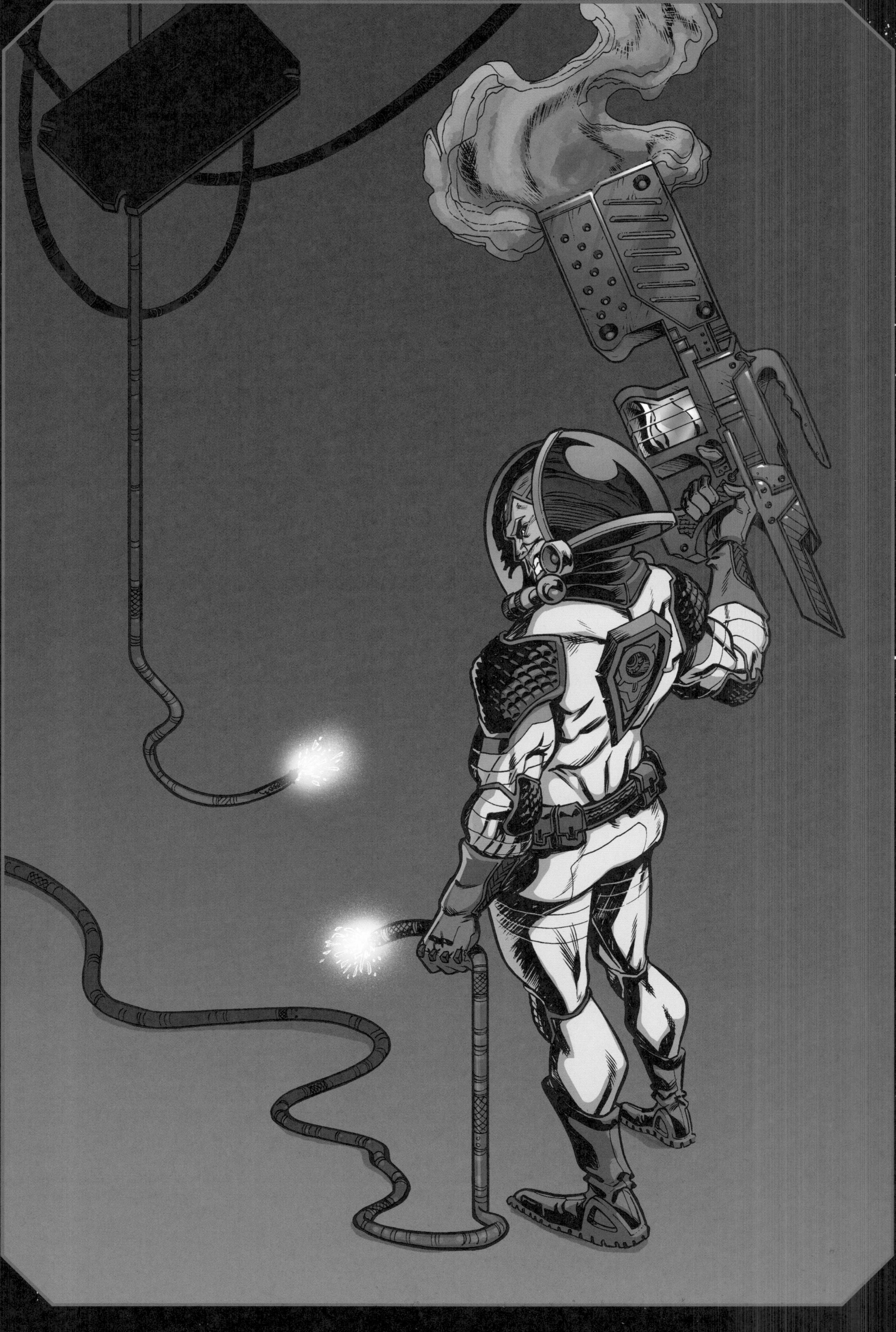

Issue #30 retail cover. Illustrated by Alberto Jiménez Alburquerque. Colored by Dan Jackson.

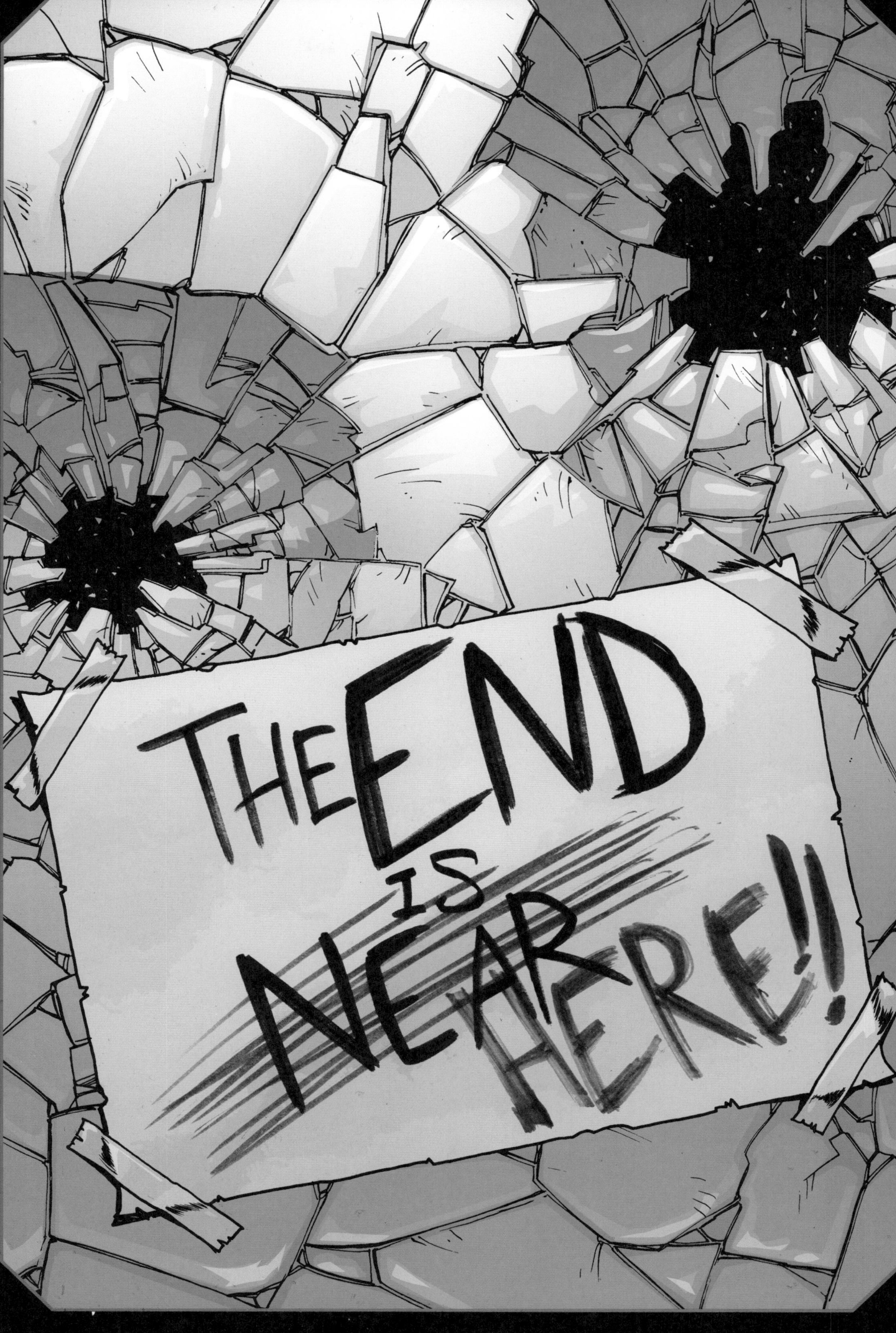
THE END IS NEAR HERE!!

Issue #31 retail cover. Illustrated by Alberto Jiménez Alburquerque. Colored by Dan Jackson.

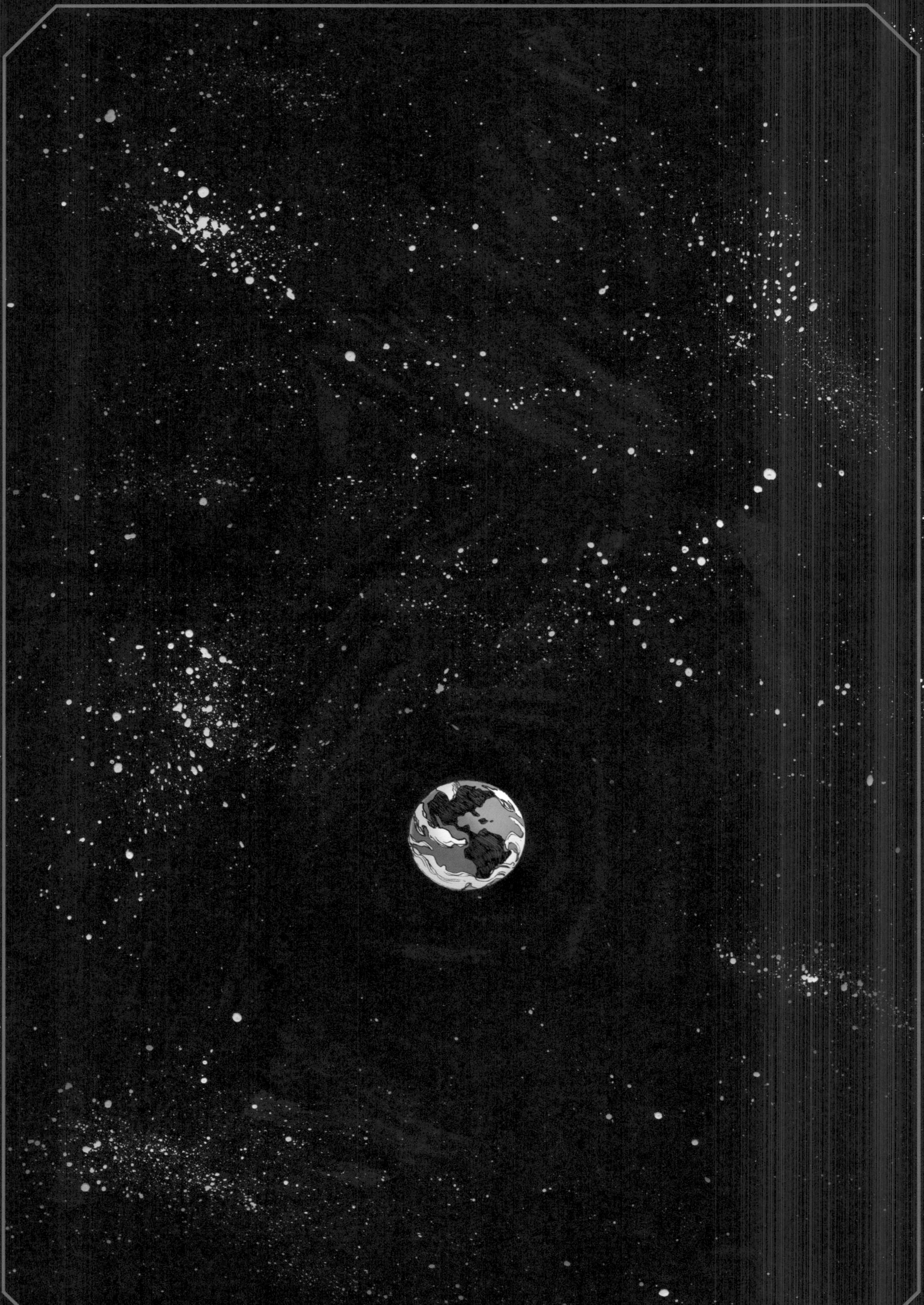

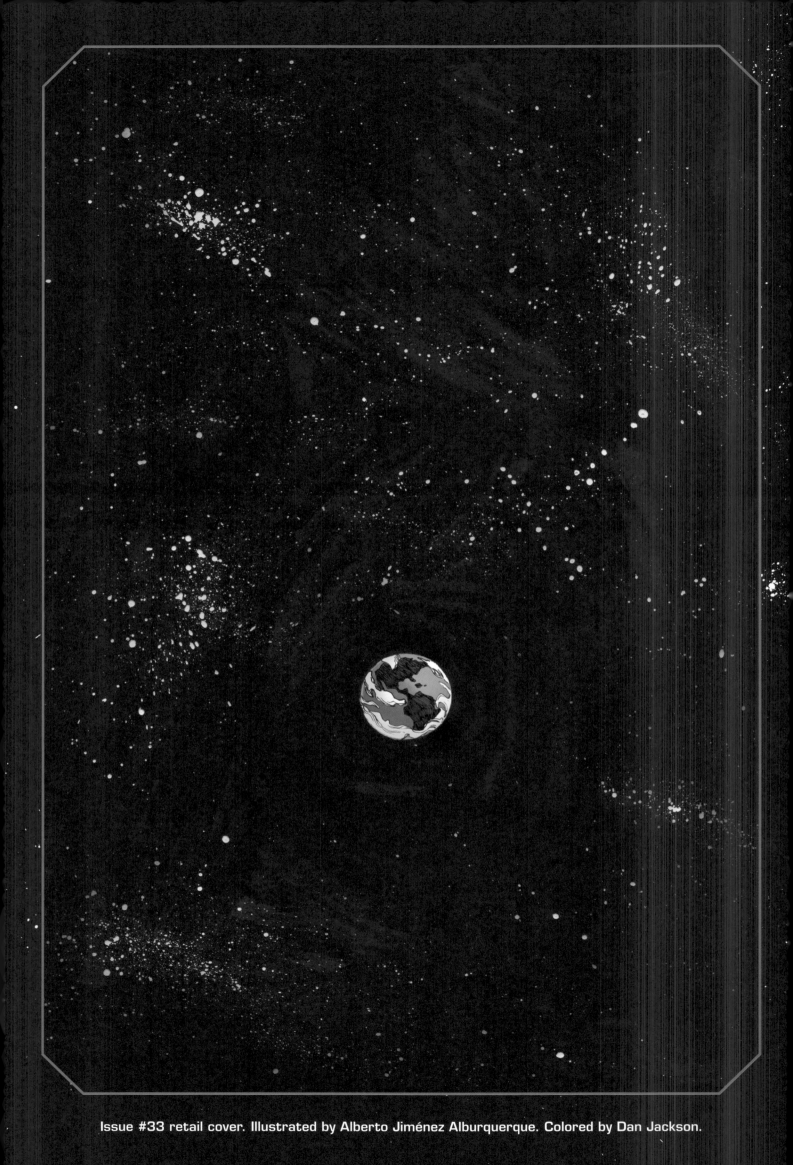

Issue #33 retail cover. Illustrated by Alberto Jiménez Alburquerque. Colored by Dan Jackson.

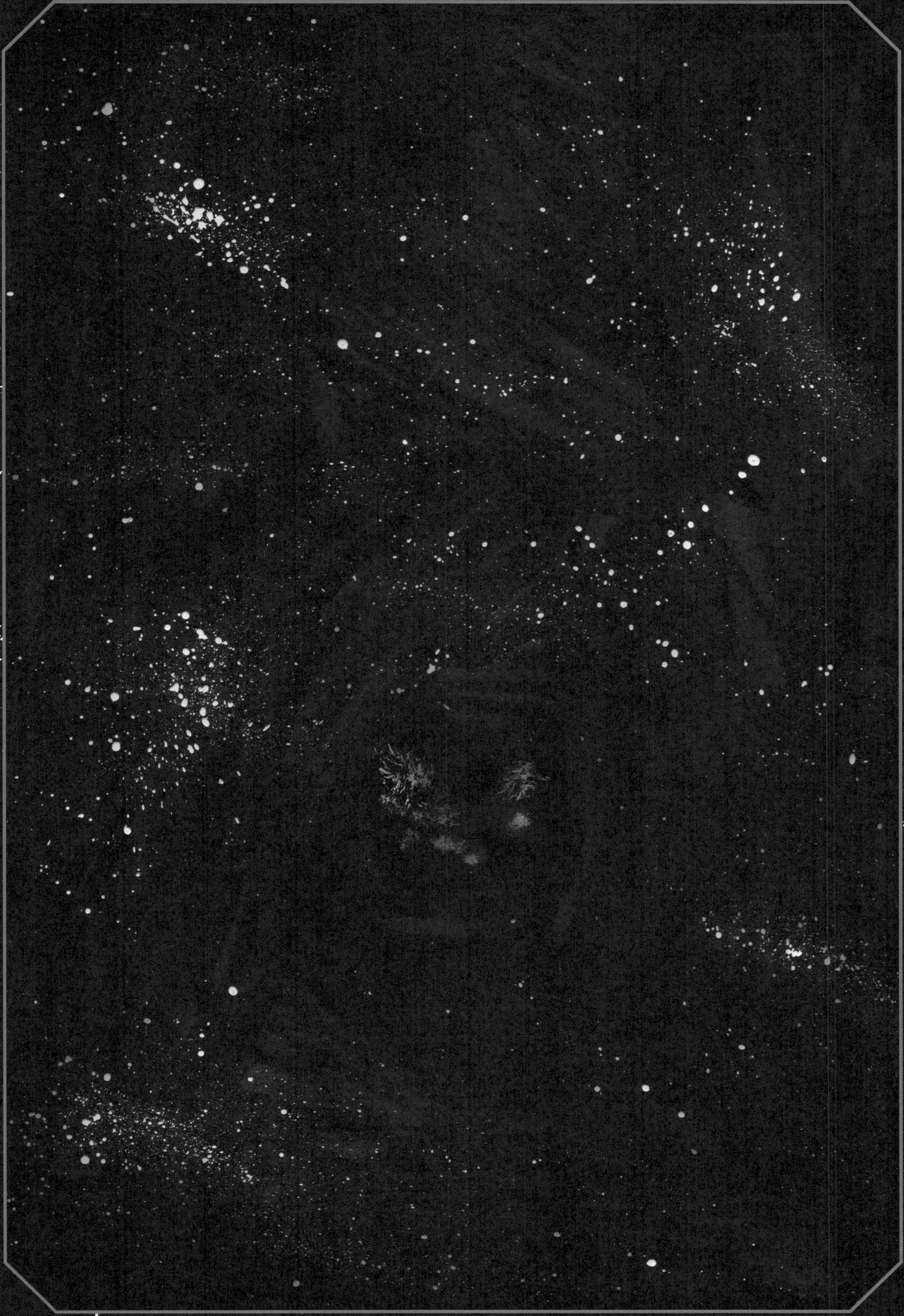

Issue #34 retail cover. Illustrated by Alberto Jiménez Alburquerque. Colored by Dan Jackson.

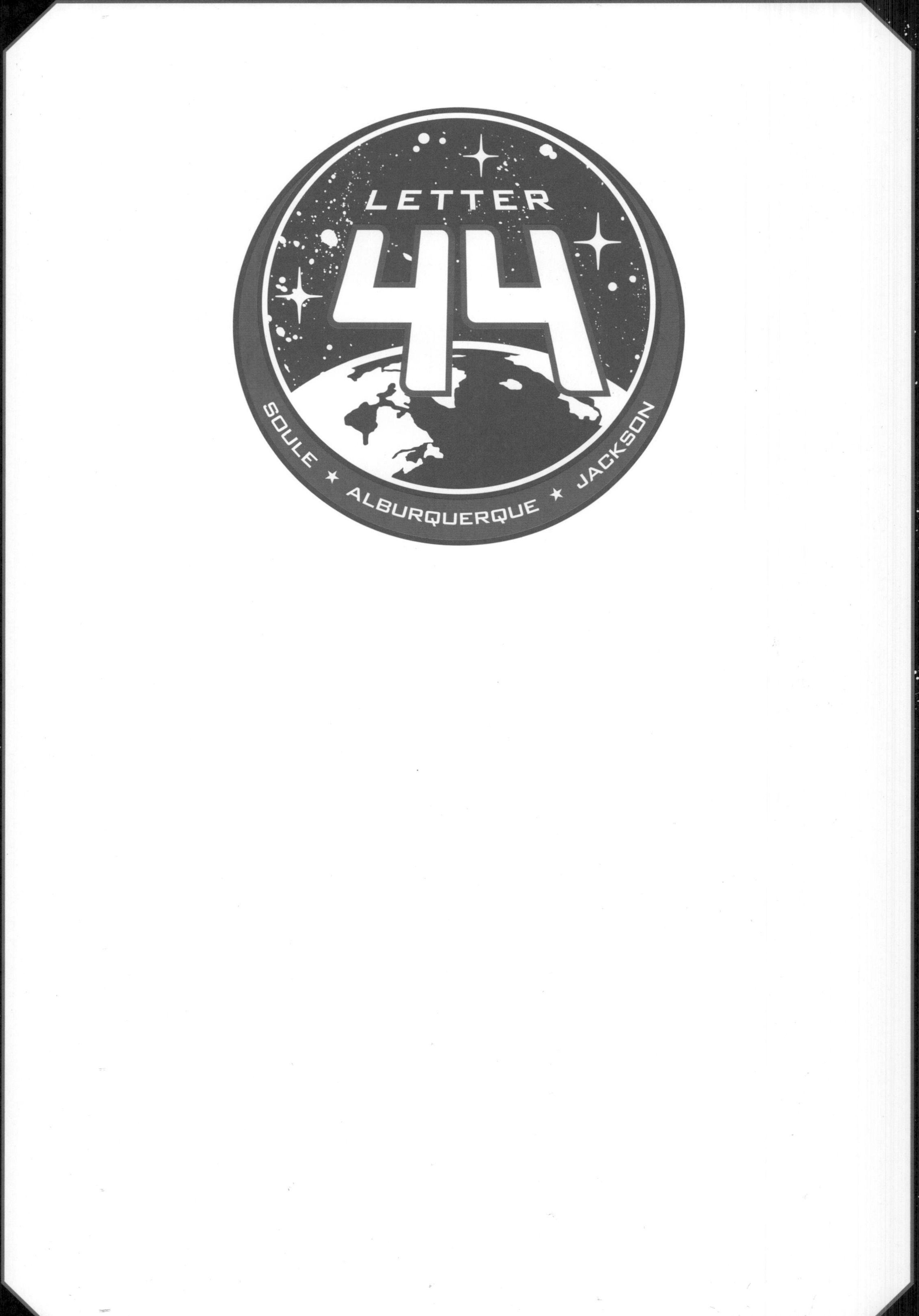
LETTER
44
SOULE ★ ALBURQUERQUE ★ JACKSON

Issue #35 retail cover.

LETTER **44**

JONES ★ MOSS ★ KELLY ★ GLUSKOVA ★ FOSS

INTERVIEWS WITH GUEST ARTISTS

FROM ISSUES
7, 14, 21, 28, AND 32

JOËLLE JONES

ISSUE #7

KNOWN FOR: *HELHEIM, LADY KILLER, CATWOMAN*

You had two major tasks in your issue—it was the first of the "flashback" issues, therefore setting the tone for the rest. Also, it was the first appearance of Cary Rowan, who had been designed but hadn't shown up in the comic yet. How did you face these challenges?

It's been a minute since I did the issue. It's hard to recall everything. Charles' script was really approachable, so it didn't seem like a really big task to do. It actually kind of seemed enjoyable to dive in. The characters were really fleshed out, so it was just up to me to fill in the blanks, really.

Did you feel any pressure doing the first of the flashback issues?

A bit, yeah. I knew that there were a lot of fans of the comic. I loved the art that came before me so I think the pressure was just kind of personal, I wanted to keep up the quality of all the stuff that came before.

Charlotte is a fascinating character. We see through her backstory that she seemingly had everything, then lost it all, pushing her to join Project Monolith. What was it like drawing Charlotte, getting inside her head?

I'm really drawn to stories where there's a huge emotional pull with the characters, and I really enjoyed doing the arc of her backstory—what had happened with her. And it was quite emotional. I think Charles wrote a sequence of her just lying on the sofa and the plants are dying, and she kind of remains static, and I really loved that sequence. I think it sums up the heartache without having to overact or overwrite—it was just really elegantly told. It was just so easy for me to jump in and get where it was going.

Sometimes in order for creators to draw or write a character, they need to be able to find something likable about them. Did you find this was the case? Are there certain things you like or maybe dislike about Charlotte and Cary?

I really like Charlotte. Although I can't relate to winning a Nobel Peace Prize or anything like that. I found her more likable because of the struggles that she's been through. I think that made her a little bit more approachable and interesting to me.

Cary—I don't think I got to delve too much into him in the story. I definitely remember Charlotte way more. Cary's story was mostly action, focused on the things he was doing. I didn't get too much into his interior life.

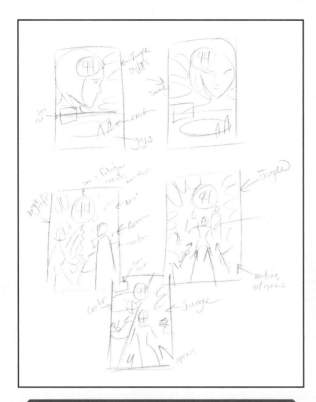

Cover thumbnail sketches ↑
Final cover inks ↓

But you had fun drawing him?

Oh yeah. Everybody loves drawing villains.

What's your favorite stage of the drawing process?

For me, it's finishing. Inking is my absolute favorite. I love inking. All of the heavy lifting has been done and I just get to sit back and relax. I ink with a brush and ink. I just find it really relaxing and enjoyable.

What's your least favorite?

Layouts. I have to really focus, I can't have any music on, or distractions, I've got to dial in... I don't like that. It's too quiet!

What's something that would get you to go on a one-way trip to the asteroid belt?

A lot of money? I'm not really into space exploration. I like my two feet on the ground! I can't even fly overseas. I couldn't do it.

If you could choose five comics or graphic novels to take with you into space, which ones would you choose?

I'm rereading *Maus* right now. I read it years ago, and I get something out of it every time I read it. So, *Maus I* and *II*. I like *The Watchmen* quite a bit—there's something really meaty there that you could pick apart for a really long time. I love *Blacksad*, like a lot. I think just the art alone, I just love poring over it. Oh, and *Monster*, which is like a thousand volumes. I love that.

What would you miss most about Earth if you left?

Let's see... desserts. My dog. Vegging in front of the TV. Just lazy things. Seems like if you go into space you've got a lot of work to do. I think most of all, just feeling safe.

DREW MOSS

ISSUE #14

KNOWN FOR: *BLOOD FEUD, TERRIBLE LIZARD, ROAD OF THE DEAD: HIGHWAY TO HELL*

There are a lot of double-page spreads in your issue, which centers on Col. Overholt and Sgt. Willett. What drew you to those layouts?

Those layouts were tough. I tried to show as much of the environment but had to leave space for the dialogue. So pushing the camera back was essential.

We see Charlotte and Cary very briefly in your issue, when Willett tries to get answers about Project Monolith out of them. Are there any other members of the *Clarke* team you would have liked to draw? Any other characters in the *Letter 44* world?

I was lucky these two were my favorite. I would have loved to draw more scenes in space.

Willett is often seen as the hothead of the *Clarke* crew, and some people may take his brawn and assume he doesn't have brains to match. What was it like to explore this character further?

I found it really interesting to see him go through the rigorous testing and I like to see that there is a reason for his suspicious nature.

What's your favorite stage of the drawing process? What's your least favorite?

My favorite is probably the layouts. It's where the story starts to take shape. I don't know if I have a least. I really enjoy my job. Ha!

What's something that would get you to go on a one-way trip to the asteroid belt?

Space. I would love to be in space and experience no gravity. Flying but not flying.

If you could choose five comics or graphic novels to take with you into space, which ones would you choose?

Hellboy Library Edition, Volume 5. The Waid and Samnee run on *Black Widow*. *Berni Wrightson: A Look Back*. *Rumble*, Volume 1. *Black Science*, Volume 1. And *Joe the Barbarian*.

What would you miss most about Earth if you left?

My friends and family, but if they are coming, probably the ocean. I have lived near the ocean for most of my life so I would miss that a lot.

UNITED STATES
OUTER SPACE CORPS

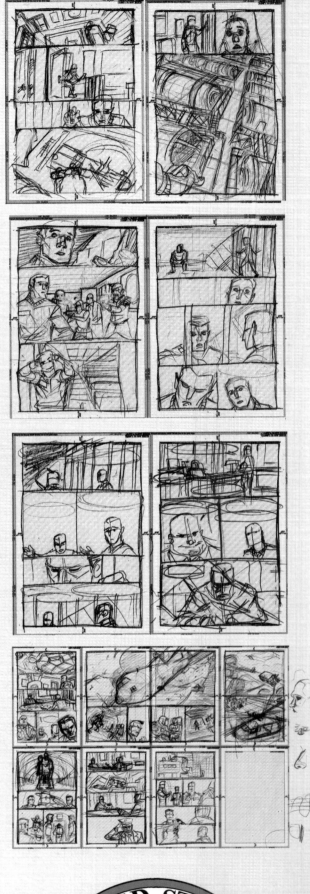

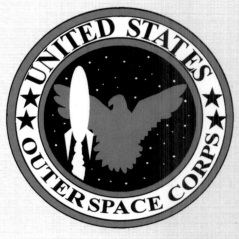

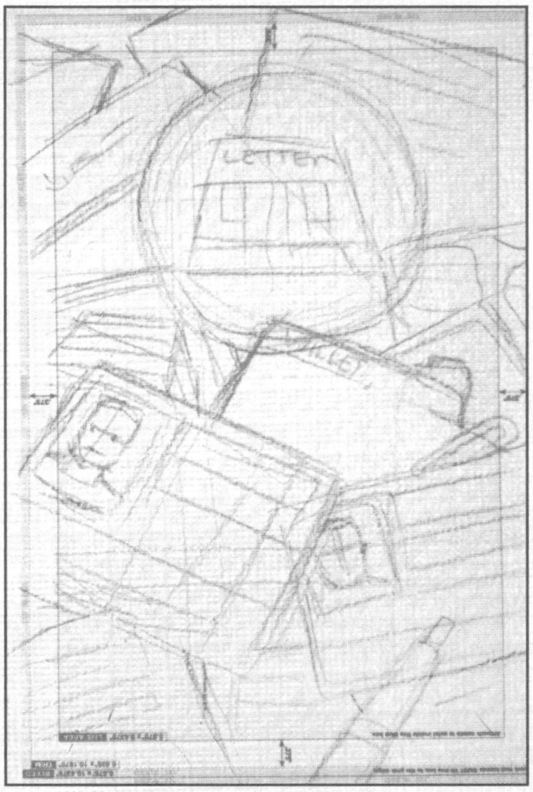
LETTER

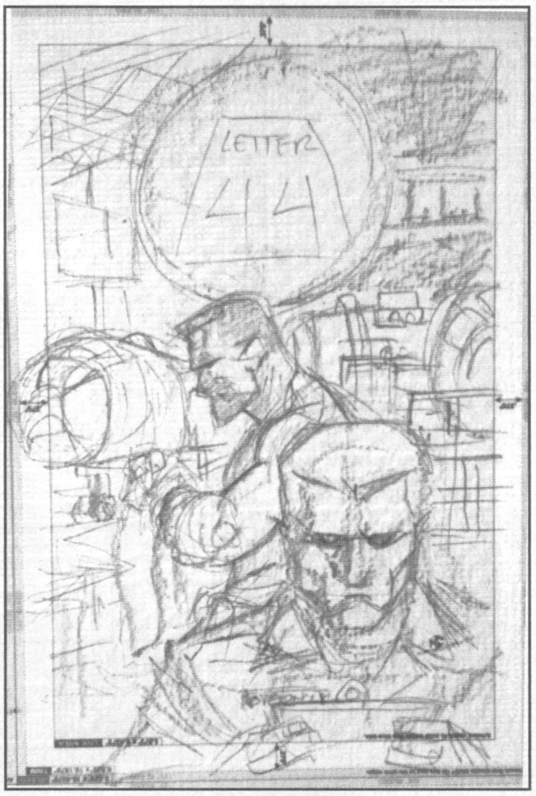
LETTER 44

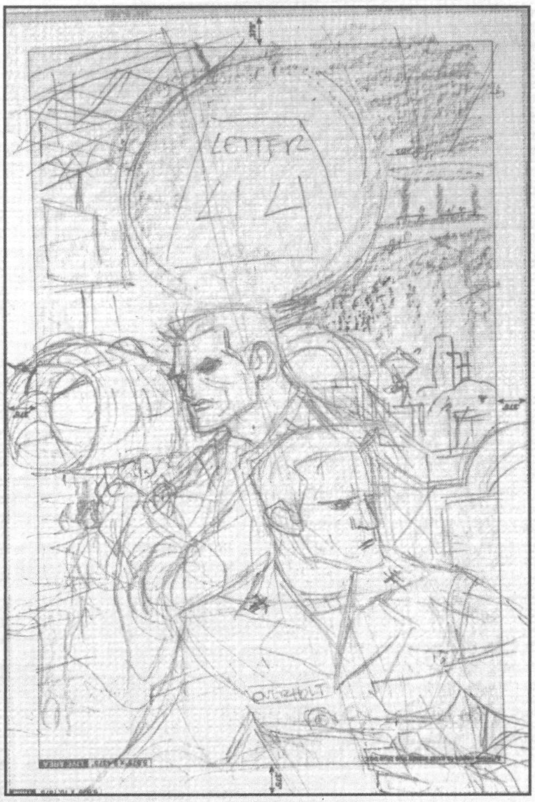
LETTER 44

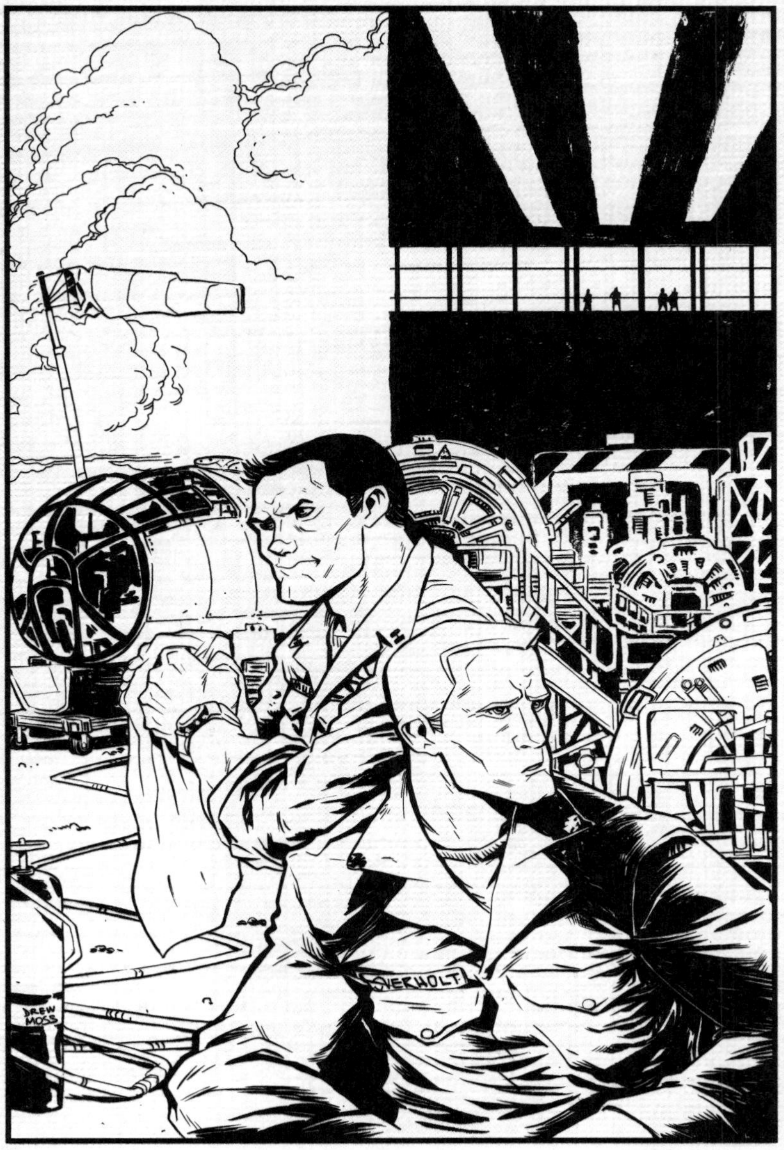
OVERHOLT
DREW MOSS

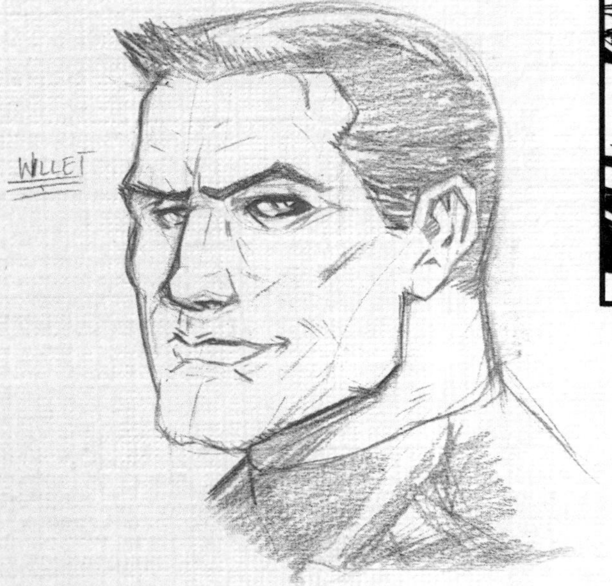
WILLET

RYAN KELLY

ISSUE #21

KNOWN FOR: *LOCAL, SURVIVORS' CLUB, FUNRAMA*

LETTER 44 #21 PG. 22

When this issue came out, it was right after Lt. Gomez's character had died in the main storyline. Due to how scheduling sometimes works in comics, were you aware of his arc (and death), or did you draw the issue without knowing?

I believe Charles—or somebody—mentioned it, off-hand, when I was recruited to draw the book. I didn't think much of it, but I knew I was drawing the origin story of somebody that very recently died and I thought that was unique. I liked that I wasn't drawing a chapter of the main story because it wasn't my book. I was essentially drawing a short story of two people's lives.

This issue gives us two characters we know little about and tells us their motivations to join Project Monolith. Gomez's reasons were more noble—he wanted to help others—while Pritchard's seemed greedier—he abandoned his wife in order to see the stars. Did the contrast between the two affect how you drew them?

I was really taken with Gomez's character and how his life is all sacrifice and service. I like how Charles used his friends to tell his story. It was a nifty way to flesh out Gomez's character and offer some clarity to his motivation to join Project Monolith. I was so absorbed with Gomez, I didn't think much of Pritchard, but I tried to illustrate the painful yearning in Pritchard's facial expressions... to show him wanting to get the heck off Earth at any cost. I understood that he felt like a very small man in the greater universe and wanted to be part of something bigger. It's a little bit selfish and it complimented Gomez's selflessness in the story.

What initially drew you to *Letter 44*, and drawing this issue?

At the time, Charles and I were developing a creator-owned series—a big swashbuckling sci-fi fantasy—but it never got off the ground, so *Letter 44* was a nice opportunity to actually draw one of his stories and I appreciated that. I had actually met Charles years before, in New York, when I was drawing and promoting *Local*. It must have been 2007. So, It was a treat to be offered a creative role in this big *Letter 44* universe he created.

What's your favorite stage of the drawing process? What's your least favorite?

My favorite stage of the drawing process is doing layouts off the script, no doubt. That's it right there, because it's pure comics to me. I actually dislike inking... it feels like a chore—a necessary chore—at that point. Sometimes I wish I could just publish the layouts. I distinctly remember doing the *Letter 44* layouts "en plein air" during my son's little league practices. It was the only time I had to get the work done.

If you could choose five comics or graphic novels to take with you into space, which ones would you choose?

I would choose *Love And Rockets* by the Hernendez Bros... I don't know, all of it please? It's the biggest inspiration for me. I would probably also take Jack Kirby's *Fourth World Omnibus*, Carl Bark's *Uncle Scrooge*, *G.I. Joe: A Real American Hero* #21, and a copy of *Giant Size X-Men* #1. That kinda sums me up right there.

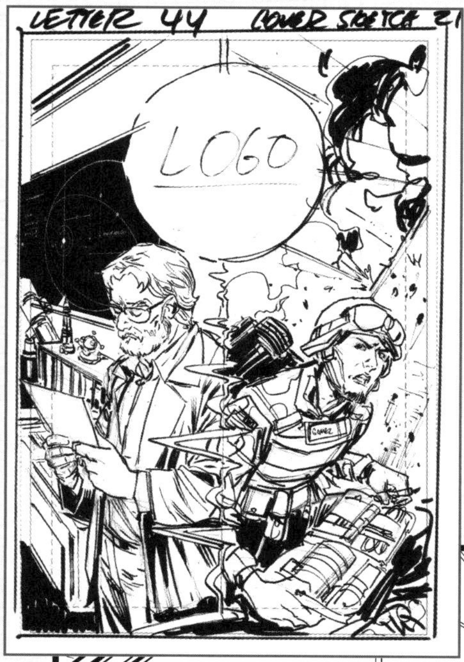
LETTER 44 COVER SKETCH 21
LOGO

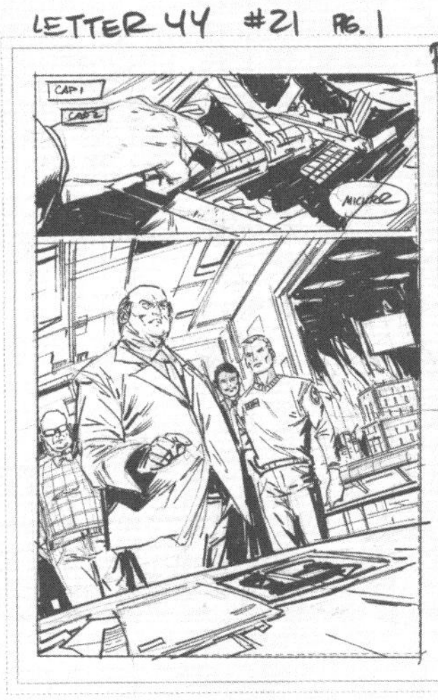
LETTER 44 #21 PG.1

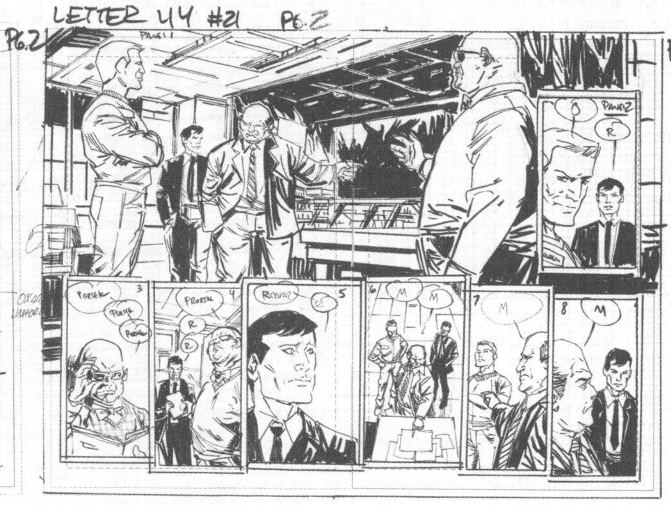
LETTER 44 #21 PG.2
PG.3

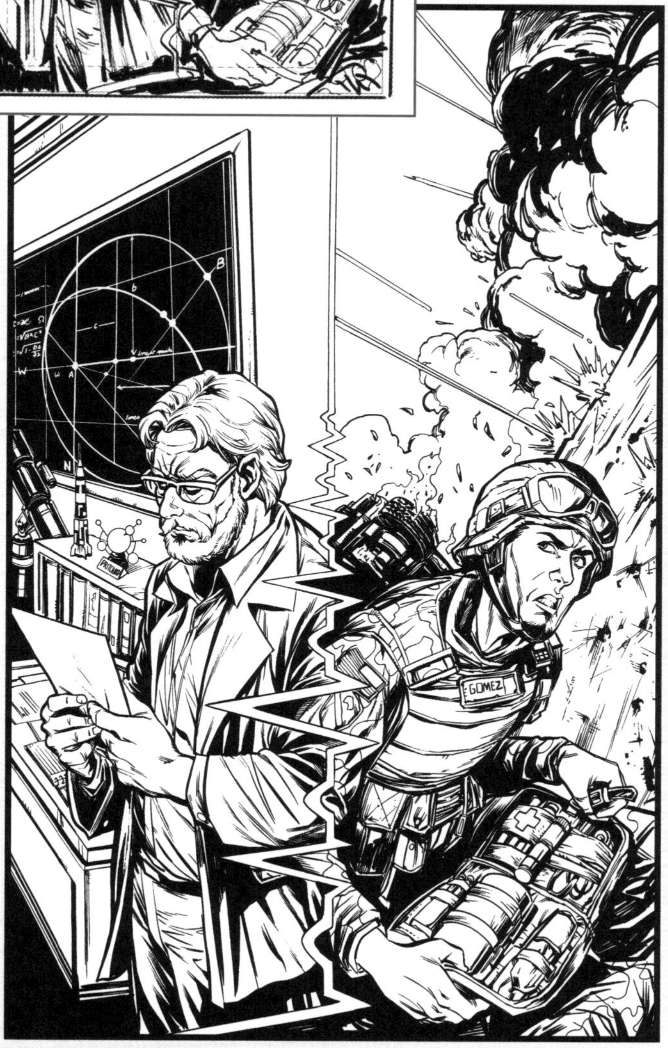
GOMEZ

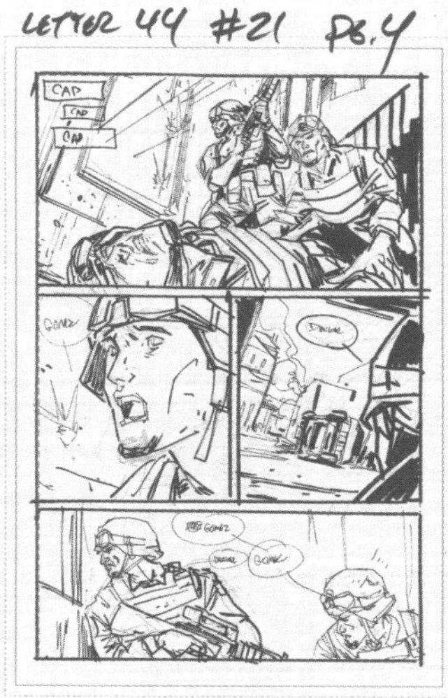
LETTER 44 #21 PG.4

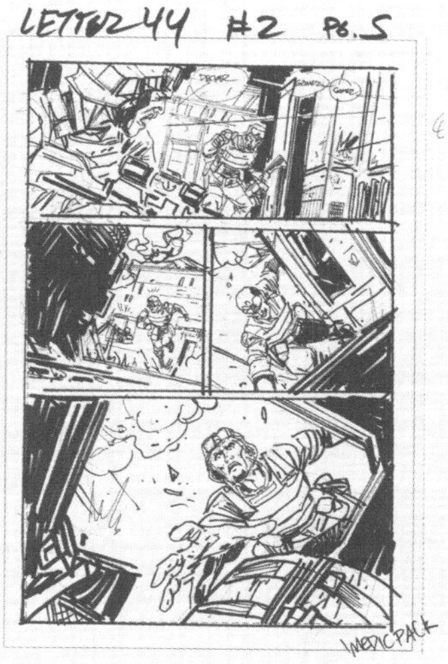
LETTER 44 #2 PG.5

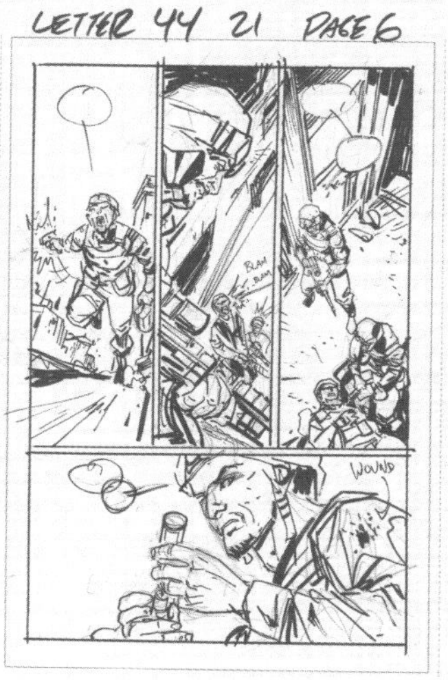
LETTER 44 21 PAGE 6

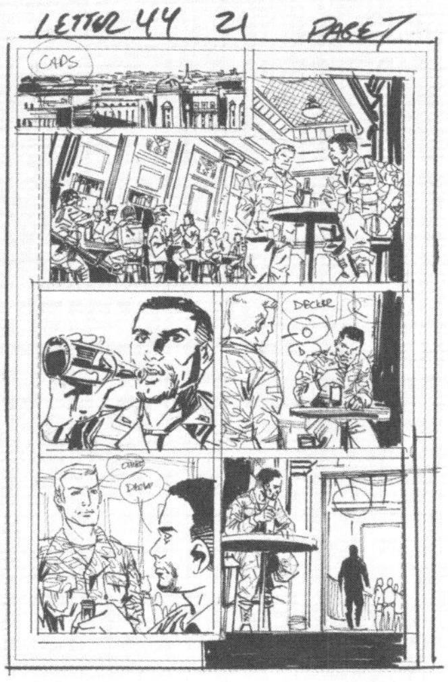
LETTER 44 21 PAGE 7

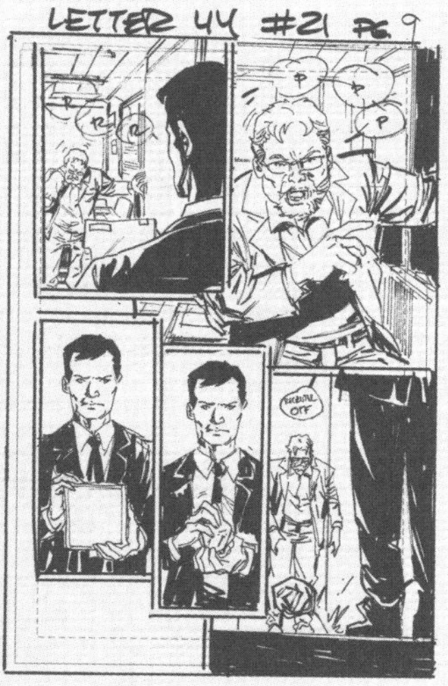
LETTER 44 #21 PG.9

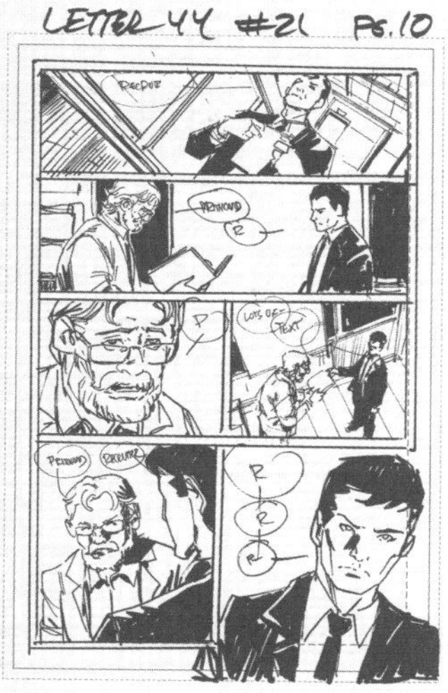
LETTER 44 #21 PG.10

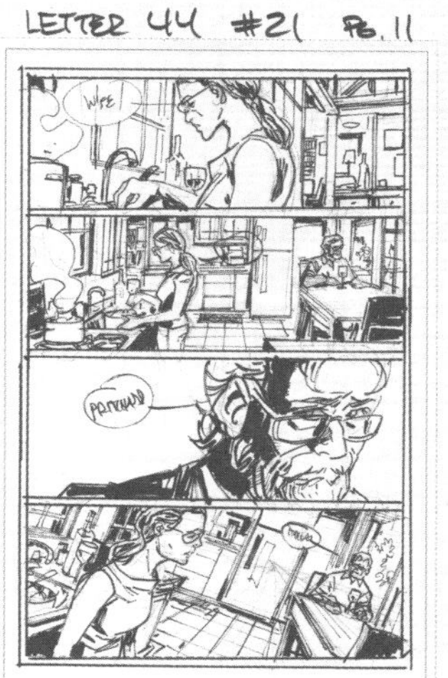
LETTER 44 #21 PG.11

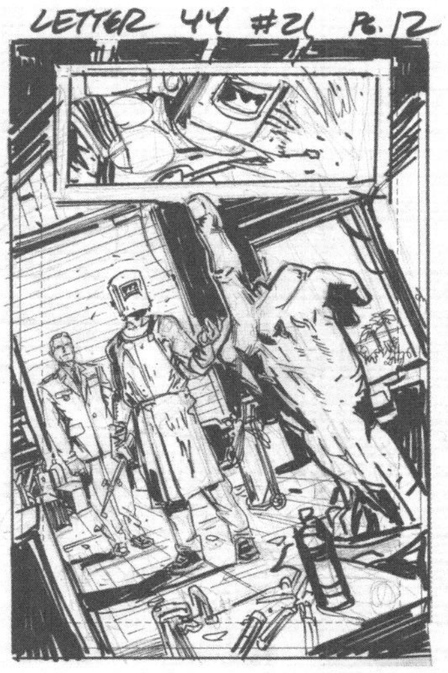
LETTER 44 #21 PG.12

ALISE GLUŠKOVA

ISSUE #28

KNOWN FOR: *ABE SAPIEN, HARROW COUNTY*

All the characters in your issue, which focuses on Manesh and Kyoko, were already established. How did this affect your art? Do you prefer to work with pre-established designs, or do you prefer to create your own?

I don't mind working with other people's designs, as it's fun to figure out how to make the character recognizable while still trying to fit them in my own style.

Manesh and Kyoko are contrasting characters in many different ways. Did you notice these contrasts as you worked? How did you make their worlds seem different, though they were going to the same destination?

Their backgrounds in professions and their way of life are very different, and it's all thanks to Charles' script I could deliver their stories, individuality, and differences in the worlds in which they lived. In the end, Kyoko and Manesh wanted something more and something different—that's what they have in common.

Though this is a science fiction title, this issue had very few science fiction elements in it. How did that affect the way you drew the story? Would you prefer drawing humans on earth to astronauts in space?

Stories set on the ground are much easier to envision, as we are surrounded by and get in contact with day-to-day things constantly. I would think that there is more room to let imagination flow when it comes to space, but then there aren't many resources to know what would be right in that situation. So I do prefer to draw something that is more familiar to me.

What's your favorite stage of the drawing process?

I would say sketching. Doing rough lines and setting everything out is exciting, and while layouts are the hardest part of the process it feels great when they are finished. Also, coloring.

What about least favorite?

My least favorite is doing inking. I tend to overwork on inking, because every line is important and if it's off, it doesn't look good in my eyes, so I tend to redraw lines a lot and it gets frustrating at times.

What's something that would get you to go on a one-way trip to the asteroid belt?

A high chance I will not die early in the trip.

If you could choose five comics or graphic novels to take with you into space, which ones would you choose?

BPRD, Nextwave, Lucky Penny, Boku No Hero Academia, and *Amazing Spider-Man.*

What would you miss most about Earth if you left?

Thunder storms, ever-changing seasons and outdoor open fire.

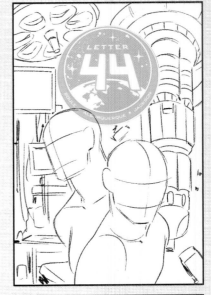

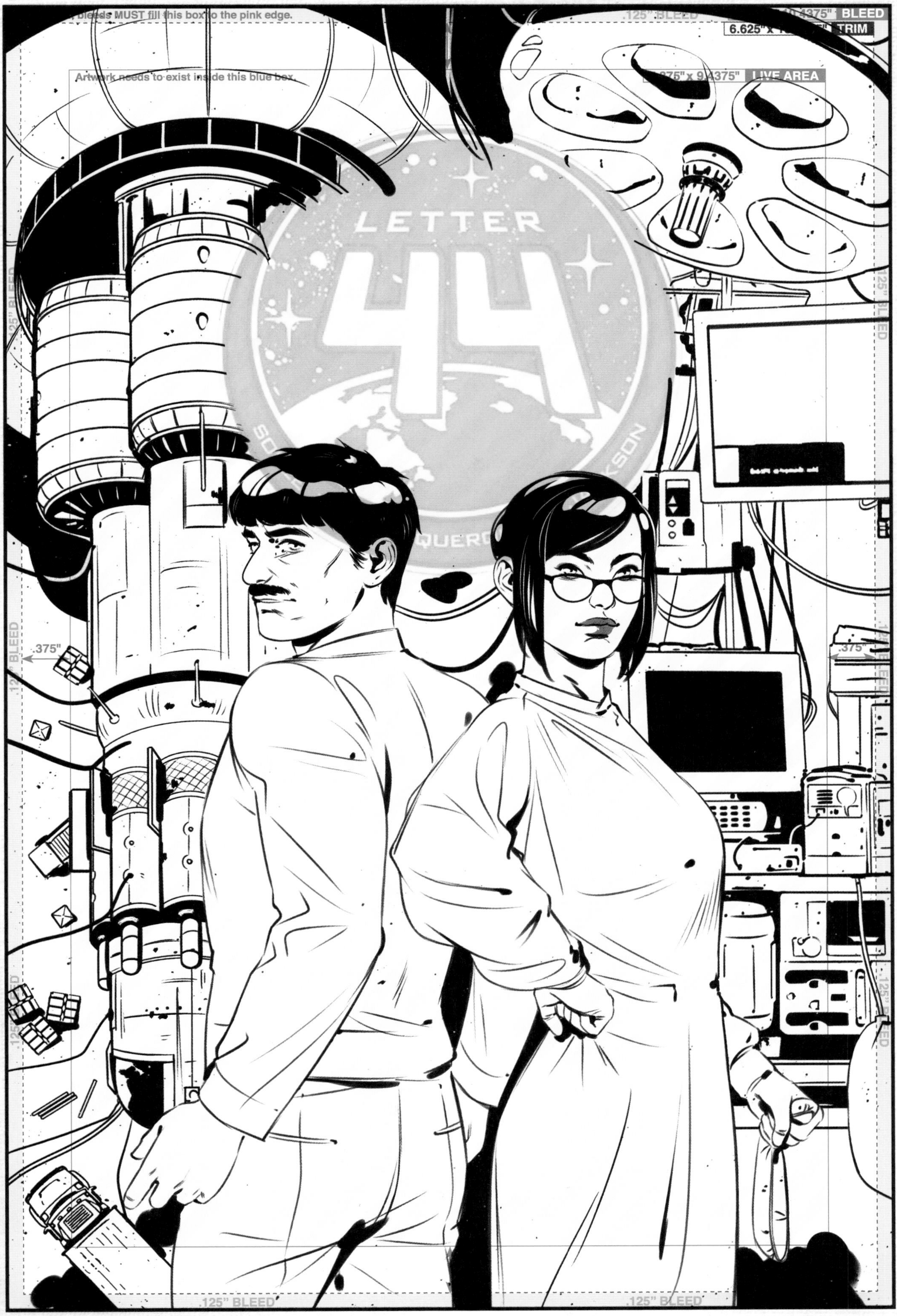

Artwork needs to exist inside this blue box.
BLEED
TRIM
LIVE AREA
LETTER
44
.125" BLEED
.375"

LANGDON FOSS
ISSUE #32

KNOWN FOR: *GET JIRO!*, *BUCKY BARNES: THE WINTER SOLDIER*, *JUDGE DREDD*

You had one of the most difficult issues in the series, because you had to tell an emotionally impactful story with characters who don't have human facial expressions. How did you make sure that the Builders came off as empathetic and relatable? How did you humanize them?

It's probably not a surprise, but I took my lead from lead artist Alberto Alburquerque's take on the Builders. I was immediately impressed with his designs and the life he imbued them with. For my part, I think I approached the expressive qualities of their tentacles the way I draw faces—I know how to construct a face, but I know the emotion is close when I *feel* it when I look at it. Likewise with the Builder's tentacles, some shapes just made me feel different things when I looked at them. I also like to dance, and I've been known to wave my arms around like an (elegant!) octopus, so I think I'd probably mapped a lot of different emotions onto my own kinesthetics!

Because we hadn't seen the Builders' home system at this point in the comics, you had the chance to design a lot of their world. What were some of your favorite things to design?

The sheer scale of the world(s) was what I really wanted to convey, and that was a really intimidating challenge. One of my favorite sequences is when the Quantum Foam is engulfing planets (and the suns!). I loved drawing it break against the worlds, and I was really happy with the tragic scene where bUR is looking out the window and seeing an impossibly large wave approach from beyond the horizon, consuming everything in its path. I thought I conveyed that scale pretty effectively there.

While this is the issue with the least amount of humans, it's also the issue with the most amount of actual space—stars, galaxies, planets, solar systems, ships, moons, and more. Did that present any challenges?

Well, if you've seen my other work, it's probably pretty clear that I have a hard time leaving much empty space on the paper! I decided to let Dan Jackson, the colorist, handle the treatment of the sky. I wanted to convey the Builder's home system as vibrant and alive, not cold and dead, and Dan really did a beautiful job filling the sky with stars and nebulae. It was actually a good exercise for me to play with those huge, empty spaces.

Can I say another thing about Dan? So my wife picked up one of the *Letter 44* trade paperback comps I just received and was looking through it and she told me she almost cried when she saw my story. It had been a couple of crazy months and she hadn't seen any of my finished pages, and she saw that story that she thought was so *beautiful*, she was heartbroken to think that another artist might have drawn it. She was so happy to hear that it was mine, and so much of that was because of Dan's gorgeous colors. I'm so happy with that issue.

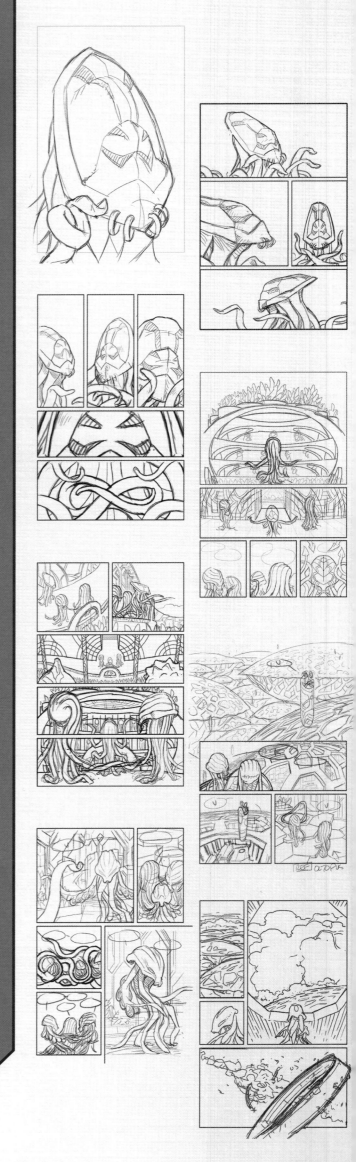

What's your favorite stage of the drawing process? What's your least favorite?

I think my favorite is the penciling stage. I love inviting (or strong-arming) the right image from the paper. It's a process so filled with promise, that laying down inks over pencils feels like I'm murdering all other possible futures the pencils are capable of. But the art is in the inks—with a pen stroke, a decision is made that must collapse that cloud of possibility into a single line. If that makes sense. It's a little terrifying sometimes.

What's something that would get you to go on a one-way trip to the asteroid belt?

If the people I loved most in the world were going, I would without hesitation. I have an explorer's heart, but having kids and loving people is a greater adventure than I ever imagined. A terminal illness would also probably be convincing, or a way to save everything I love by hurling myself into the abyss.... Hey, kinda like a good comic book I know of!

If you could choose five comics or graphic novels to take with you into space, which ones would you choose?

Could I take entire series? That could get really expensive.... Okay, probably because I still have so much to learn from these: Moebius and Jodorowsky's *The Incal*, Otomo's *AKIRA*, something by R. Crumb, Seth Fisher and JH Williams' *Batman: Snow*, and the book I'm currently working on, which I can't tell you about yet! I think it's going to be beautiful, though.

What would you miss most about Earth if you left?

If I had to leave my family and the people I love, them most of all. I'm a big fan of a big, clear sky, though, and being completely alone under it. It would be a challenge to be in a small spacecraft with other people, but I guess I'd have that big, clear sky.

ISSUE #35
REFLECTIONS

FROM CHARLES SOULE
AND ALBERTO ALBURQUERQUE

THE END. IT SUCKS.

When you've been working on a project for more than five years, when the machine is well-oiled and working full-speed, when you love what you're doing, when your partners in crime are awesome and you get to the end... it sucks big time.

Thirty issues leave room for a lot of feelings: excitement, frustration, fear, happiness, etc. But I can't find words to describe how it feels to get to the end of it—maybe that's why I just draw the pictures and leave the harder part to Charles. I was excited that we could finish a complete series the way it deserved to be finished, it was a happy feeling of fulfillment. At the same time, I was having a lot of fun drawing the last issues of the series and I think it was my best work until that moment and, of course, I didn't want it to end. I also felt like I needed to venture into different projects to test myself and get out of my "comfort" zone (drawing *Letter 44* was never "comfortable," but I felt comfortable, if you know what I mean). And of course, the fear... the fear of the unknown, of what's next, of not being able to find any work; that fear is very debilitating and makes you want to stay right where you are.

It was time, though, and I couldn't be happier to have finished the series with issue 35 the way it was. Yes, we saw how Earth was erased completely from the universe in the previous issue, but issue 35... well, it gave us hope! And not in a cheesy, tacky way but in a more palpable, practical approach. I had to draw that issue with a huge mix of emotions but that hope kept me going. I loved drawing that class of multiracial little kids, all different yet together learning how they all got there. It seems like a very concise, close ending, with the storylines well tied up and leaving no room for hesitation. But there were still questions about the future (and some about the past, why not) that are to be answered.

I loved working with Charles (the rest of the team too, of course, Dan, Crank, Robin, Jill, etc., etc.) and I'm sure he has answered those questions in one of his notebooks while he was on a train or a plane... so maybe I'll ask him some day soon and he'll tell me what happened next and, maybe, (why not?) we'll tell you all right after.

See? There's always some hope in the universe.

ALBERTO JIMÉNEZ ALBURQUERQUE
January 2019
Madrid, Spain

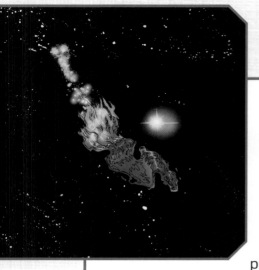

GOOD ENDINGS

are one of the hardest challenges in writing fiction. It's a truism, even a cliché, but that's primarily because it's true. And the bigger the thing is, the longer the thing, the greater the weight of expectations that are layered upon the manner of its conclusion. The reason for that is pure math, to my mind. The longer a story, the more plot points need to be serviced or referenced in the ending, and there are more emotional beats that need to be lived up to or surpassed. The conclusion of a story should serve as a reward for anyone who's stuck with it—almost be an affirmation of the choice to read the thing in the first place.

As with anything when you're writing about writing, especially process, the above is an oversimplification. Sometimes endings can be deeply unsatisfying on purpose, if that's where the author wants to leave their audience. Or perhaps the author is just writing for themselves, and want to find the truth they believe to be true. But generally, and especially when you're working on the ending to a huge, multi-year comic book series like *Letter 44*, you want the thing to land.

I knew from the beginning that the series would conclude with the end of the world, the destruction of Earth. The challenge, then, was to find an ending that would still feel uplifting and hopeful despite so much loss (and especially after issue 34, the second-to-last chapter, which depicted the erasure of humanity in almost excruciating detail, thank you very much Alberto Jiménez Alburquerque and your heartbreaking art). I also wanted to write something that would serve both of the book's themes/plotlines: *Letter 44* is a story about a first-contact situation and all the misunderstandings and tragedy that might result, but it is also about the office of the President of the United States of America.

That particular office was in a weird place as I wrote *Letter 44* #35 back in 2017, and I think it's in an even weirder place now, as I write this in January 2019. I did a lot of research into the Presidency for the series, and I think it's one of the strangest jobs in the world. In order to get it, you have to be absolutely convinced you are a truly extraordinary person, the best human to lead almost three hundred and fifty million people—and affect the entire world with your decisions. The ego, right? But in order to do the job well, you also have to put yourself utterly to the side, and put the needs of the American people (and again, by extension, the world) first. You have to be the most selfish person in the world to become President, and then you have to be the most selfless person in the world to be a good President. What a weird gig.

I felt like that theme had been lost a little in all the crazy, world-ending shenanigans that occupied the last few story arcs of *Letter 44*, and I really wanted to bring it home hard for the finale. So, we get "Letter 45" in issue #35, with President Blades explicitly stating that idea as he writes to his successor. "It's always about them," he says. Being President is not about you. It's about the people you serve.

These days, that feels like an idealistic approach, one not shared by the current occupant of the Oval Office—but it wasn't always, and I believe it will come to be represented again.

Beyond that particular point, the ending of *Letter 44* was designed to give readers

(you, really) a sense of the absolute possibility inherent in the story. That's what good sci-fi does—it expands the borders way beyond what you think is possible. In a single issue, a little over twenty pages, we get about a hundred and seventy-five years of human history—going from a period of great fear, loss and uncertainty to what seems to be something of a golden age as part of an intergalactic colony of intelligent species from all across space. Again, so much of that is down to Alberto Jiménez Alburquerque's artwork, and Dan Jackson's colors, and Chris Crank's letters, as has been the case throughout the majority of the series. Comics can do anything, and I think we definitely did it here.

Letter 44 #35 was supposed to give you a sense that humanity's story didn't end with Earth, that there were volumes and volumes yet to be written, huge possibilities. We didn't have space to tell those stories here, in *Letter 44*, but who knows what the future might bring? We wanted to blow your mind, and I hope we did.

Thank you for coming along on the journey. We'll see you out there... somewhere.

CHARLES SOULE
January 2019
Brooklyn, NY

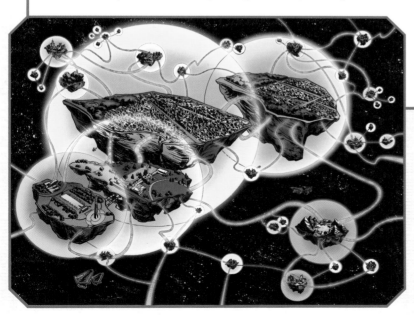

THE WHITE HOUSE

1600 PENNSYLVANIA AVE NW, WASHINGTON, DC 20500

FROM THE DESK OF THE 44TH PRESIDENT, STEPHEN HENRY BLADES

NAME:

Charles Soule

LOCATION:

Brooklyn, NY, United States of America

BIO:

Charles Soule was born in the Midwest but often wishes he had been born in space. He lives in Brooklyn, and has written a wide variety of titles for a variety of publishers, including others' characters (*Swamp Thing, Superman/Wonder Woman, Red Lanterns* (DC); *Thunderbolts, She-Hulk, Inhuman* (Marvel)); and his own: *27* and *Curse Words* (Image); *Strongman* (SLG) and *Strange Attractors* (Archaia). When not writing—which is rare—he runs a law practice and works, writes and performs as a musician. One of his biggest regrets is never personally witnessing a Space Shuttle launch.

SER-471337.C /// DOS. 102-AC-44/13-100 /// AUTH. JMB*JS

CLASSIFIED

N. L-442-0N1.10.A

THE WHITE HOUSE

1600 PENNSYLVANIA AVE NW, WASHINGTON, DC 20500

FROM THE DESK OF THE 44ᵀᴴ PRESIDENT, STEPHEN HENRY BLADES

NAME:

Alberto Jiménez Alburquerque

LOCATION:

Madrid, Spain

BIO:

Alberto Jiménez Alburquerque (AJA) is an artist born, raised and currently living in Madrid, Spain. He has put lines in French comic-books (BD's) for almost a decade now, working for Paquet Ed. and Soleil Ed. Some of his titles are: *Fugitifs de l'Ombre* (Paquet), *Le Dieu des Cendres* (Soleil), and *Elle* (Soleil). He has also drawn some short stories for the American comics *Skull Kickers* (Image) and *Pathfinder's Goblins* (Dynamite), and *Robert E. Howard's Savage Sword* (Dark Horse). He also illustrated *Mystery Girl* from writer Paul Tobin.

NAME:

Joëlle Jones

LOCATION:

L.A., California, United States of America

BIO:

Joëlle Jones is an Eisner-nominated artist currently living and working in Los Angeles, CA. Since attending PNCA in Portland, OR, she has contributed to a wide range of projects and has most recently begun writing and drawing her own series, *Lady Killer*, published by Dark Horse comics. Jones has also provided the art for *Superman: American Alien* (DC), *Helheim*, *Brides of Helheim* (Oni Press) and *Mockingbird* (Marvel). She's also done work for Boom! Studios, *The New York Times*, Vertigo and more! Joëlle will be taking on projects for DC and Marvel this year as well as continuing her series *Lady Killer*.

THE
WHITE HOUSE

1600 PENNSYLVANIA AVE NW, WASHINGTON, DC 20500

FROM THE DESK OF THE 44ᵀᴴ PRESIDENT, STEPHEN HENRY BLADES

NAME:

Drew Moss

LOCATION:

Hampton, Virginia, United States of America

BIO:

Drew Moss is an illustrator based out of southeastern Virginia. Drew has done work for IDW (*The Colonized, The Crow*) Dark Horse (*Creepy*), Oni press (*Terrible Lizard, Blood Feud*) Image Comics (*Copperhead*) and various other publishers. Drew enjoys fine cigars and whiskies and spends too much time writing bios. To see more of Drew's work and upcoming projects you can follow him on twitter @drew_moss or on Instagram @drewerdmoss

NAME:

Ryan Kelly

LOCATION:

St. Paul, Minnesota, United States of America

BIO:

Ryan Kelly has been drawing comics for almost 20 years. After drawing *LOCAL* for Oni Press, he has gone on to co-create a wealth of original books and series; such as *The New York Four, Saucer Country, THREE, Cry Havoc,* and *Survivors Club.* He happily lives and works in St. Paul, Minnesota and is expected to draw even more comics in the future.

THE WHITE HOUSE

1600 PENNSYLVANIA AVE NW, WASHINGTON, DC 20500

FROM THE DESK OF THE 44TH PRESIDENT, STEPHEN HENRY BLADES

NAME:

Alise Gluškova

LOCATION:

Riga, Latvia

BIO:

Alise Gluškova is an artist from Latvia, Riga. Her background work is layout design for print production and motion comics. Her art has been featured in *Aw Yeah Comics*, Dark Horse's *Abe Sapien* and "Bait: Off-Color Stories for You to Color" by Chuck Palahniuk.

NAME:

Langdon Foss

LOCATION:

Colorado Springs, Colorado,
United States of America

BIO:

Langdon Foss makes art and draws comics in Colorado. He's well-known for drawing Anthony Bourdain's graphic novel paean to food and samurai movies, *GET JIRO!*, *The Surface* with Image comics, and most recently his work for Marvel including *Bucky Barnes: Winter Soldier*, the mini-series *VOTE LOKI*, and others. He's currently drawing indie books and developing other projects, and you can keep track of his adventures @LangdonFoss and at www.LangdonFoss.com. He'd love to hear from you.

SER-471337.C /// DOS. 102-AC-44/13-100 /// AUTH. JMB*JS

CLASSIFIED

N. L-442-0N1.10.A

THE
WHITE HOUSE

1600 PENNSYLVANIA AVE NW, WASHINGTON, DC 20500

FROM THE DESK OF THE 44ᵗᴴ PRESIDENT, STEPHEN HENRY BLADES

NAME:

Dan Jackson

LOCATION:

Portland, Oregon, United States of America

BIO:

What is the most unfair thing you can think of? Got it in your head? Okay, forget that because there's a worse one: There's this guy who gets paid money for coloring comic books. Right. Dan Jackson has been gainfully employed to one degree or another with the coloring of comic books for the better part of 17 years. He's done other Great Big Projects with the fine folks at Oni Press, and he's done a bunch of covers and short projects with them as well. He's a pretty versatile guy. Even writes his own bios.

Mr. Jackson lives in the beautiful Pacific Northwest with his scorching hot wife (see? UN-FAIR!), and two hilarious kids.

NAME:

Sarah Stern

LOCATION:

New York, United States of America

BIO:

Sarah Stern is a normal regular human from planet Earth and nowhere else. An artist and colorist from New York, she does Earth activities like riding bicycles and breathing nitrogen-rich air. She uses her normal amount of arms to be the artist of *Cindersong* (Hiveworks), and the colorist for *Goldie Vance* (Boom!), *Mighty Morphin' Power Rangers: Pink* (Boom!), and *Rick and Morty*™ (Oni).